THE NOAH PLAN

LITERATURE CURRICULUM GUIDE

THE PRINCIPLE APPROACH
KINDERGARTEN THROUGH TWELFTH GRADE

Rosalie June Slater

Edited by Carole Goodman Adams

Poetry and hums aren't things which you get,
they're things which get you.
And all you can do is to go where they can find you.
—Winnie the Pooh

FOUNDATION FOR AMERICAN CHRISTIAN EDUCATION
CHESAPEAKE, VIRGINIA

THE NOAH PLAN
LITERATURE CURRICULUM GUIDE
THE PRINCIPLE APPROACH
KINDERGARTEN THROUGH TWELFTH GRADE

Rosalie June Slater
Edited by Carole Goodman Adams

COPYRIGHT © NOVEMBER 1997
FOUNDATION FOR AMERICAN CHRISTIAN EDUCATION

ISBN 0–912498–19–6

PUBLISHED BY
FOUNDATION FOR AMERICAN CHRISTIAN EDUCATION
Free Catalogue and Book Orders:
P.O. BOX 9588, CHESAPEAKE, VIRGINIA 23321
1-800-352-3223 • www.face.net

William Shakespeare
Cover Art from
Wheeler's Graded Studies in Great Authors:
A Complete Speller, 1899

Layout/Design
David C. Reisch, Desktop Direct

Editorial Assistant
Aileen J. S. Collins

ACKNOWLEDGMENT

The substance of the *Literature Curriculum Guide*
is the vast work done by Rosalie J. Slater over three decades,
out of her love for Christian History and for great literature.

A Tribute to Rosalie June Slater
An American Treasure

Those of us who are colleagues, friends, and recipients of Miss Slater's priceless contributions to American Christian education know her to be a cherished American treasure! True to the nature of the word, a treasure must be known about and found and its value appraised to be fully appreciated.

As the co-founder of the Foundation for American Christian Education and the architect of The Principle Approach, Rosalie Slater partnered with Verna Hall in 1960 to teach conservative Americans the "answer program" for the restoration of America. She gleaned from Miss Hall's rich compilations of early American history, the historic method of Biblical education that produced Gospel liberty and Christian civil government. Miss Slater restored that method, which she named "The Principle Approach," to American Christian education.

I will go before thee, and make the crooked places straight:
I will break in pieces the gates of brass,
and cut in sunder the bars of iron:
and I will give thee the treasures of darkness,
and hidden riches of secret places,
that thou mayest know that I, the Lord,
which call thee by thy name,
am the God of Israel.

Isaiah 45:2–3

God called Rosalie out of a secular doctoral program at Stanford University and imparted to her the hidden treasures of America's greatness. From a nation founded on Biblical principles of education and government, America fell into degeneracy from years of progressive and secular influences. As a result, the founding generations' record was hidden from twentieth-century educators. Miss Slater and Miss Hall discovered that the Biblical and historical documentation of America's Christian history had been removed from American textbooks and, to their dismay, that America's historic method of Biblical reasoning and writing had been replaced by workbooks and collective programs of study, such as language arts and social studies.

Miss Slater restored the integrity of classic literature, composition, English grammar, history, government, and geography as individual subjects to the curriculum. Through her courses of study and syllabi, which introduced to teachers and students key individuals whom God had used throughout history in all fields of learning, Miss Slater applied The Principle Approach to teaching and learning in American Christian education which characterized America's education during her founding years. Today, through the Foundation for American Christian Education, other ministries have been birthed and endless testimonies proclaimed glorifying God, now reaching to a third generation of families in America and other nations.

Therefore every scribe which is instructed unto the kingdom
of heaven is like unto a man that is an householder, which
bringeth forth out of his treasure things new and old.

Matthew 13:52

Through her lifelong study of literature and her emphasis on American classical education as it relates Biblically and governmentally, Miss Slater is a repository of knowledge. She has set an example for American educators by treasuring our heritage of English and American classics and poetry that teach the values and virtues of Christ. To treasure is to "collect and reposit for future use." Miss Slater's love of literature which is next to her first love—the love of Christ and His Word—led her to collect an extensive library of not only English and American classics, but America's early literature in the form of rare biographies, colonial and artillery sermons, letters, journals, and diaries. She also founded the June Keith Fund, named for her mother, through which she has generously blessed many Christian educators with children's classics and poetry throughout the years. She restored the joy of teaching and learning complete classics and encouraged us to read them aloud to our children. Her book, *The Family Program for Reading Aloud,* is a treasury for parents and classroom teachers.

A good man out of the good treasure of his heart
bringeth forth good things.

Matthew 12:35a

I have always likened Rosalie to Joseph, one of the patriarchs of the Old Testament. Like Joseph, who was providentially directed by God to raise and store grain for distribution in the years of severe famine in Egypt, Miss Slater collected, stored, and distributed literary and historic riches for use in America's classrooms during this era of extreme famine and spiritual dryness.

Joseph is one of the noble characters of the Old Testament and holds a critical place in the preservation of Israel, God's Messianic nation. The story of his life from the book of Genesis is a mighty revelation of the providential nature of God as He continuously directed and provided for the preservation of His Messianic seed through individuals and events. Throughout the history of Israel, the divine Hand of God silently moved on behalf of His plan of salvation and redemption for man. His provisions for the Israelites were always timely, sufficient, and, more often than not, miraculous! Such was the case in Joseph's time.

Joseph was the favored son of his father Jacob, the Patriarch of Israel. As a young shepherd boy, he was a dreamer and carelessly shared his dreams and their prophetic interpretations with his jealous brothers who, when an opportunity arose to get rid of him, sold him into slavery. The teenager found himself in Egypt during the reign of the Hyksos kings, the Shepherd Kings, who were descendants of wandering tribes of Arabia and Syria and greatly despised by the Egyptians. Through the well-known series of events, Joseph found favor with the Pharaoh through his prophetic interpretation of the Pharaoh's dreams and was elevated to the highest position of authority in Egypt. As prime minister, God used him to organize the storage of grain for the ensuing devastating famine. Joseph's wise counsel, under the direction of the Hand of God, was divinely used to preserve and strengthen the Patriarch's family in Egypt in preparation for taking possession of the promised land. Joseph acknowledged the providence of God when he said to his brothers:

> Do not be grieved or angry with yourselves, because you sold me here; for God sent me before you to preserve life . . . to preserve for you a remnant in the earth, and to keep you alive by a great deliverance. Therefore, it was not you that sent me here, but God; and He has made me a father to Pharaoh and lord of all his household and ruler over all the land of Egypt.
>
> . . . Do not be afraid, for am I in God's place? And as for you, you meant evil against me, but God meant it for good in order to bring about this present result, to

preserve many people alive. So therefore, do not be afraid, I will provide for you and your little ones. (Genesis 45:5,7,8 & 50:19–21)

> *For where your treasure is,*
> *there will your heart be also.*
> *Matthew 6:21*

Likewise, God providentially gifted, prepared, and positioned Rosalie June Slater to be the Joseph of modern American education. God's purposes and overruling providence in the life of a nation cannot be thwarted. His eye runs to and fro looking for those whose hearts are turned toward Him to be willing instruments in His providential Hand. The tender and loving heart of Miss Slater responded to God's divine call to preserve for American Christians the educational philosophy and method of the founding generations, as well as America's rich treasury of classic and historic literature. Miss Slater's "Seven Loves of Literature" furnish us with American Christian ideals to endow our "little ones." And like C. S. Lewis who wrote:

> For every one pupil who needs to be guarded from a weak excess of sensibility there are three who need to be awakened from the slumber of cold vulgarity. The task of the modern educator is not to cut down jungles but to irrigate deserts. The right defense against false sentiments is to inculcate just sentiments. By starving the sensibility of our pupils we only make them easier prey to the propagandist when he comes. For famished nature will be avenged and a hard heart is no infallible protection against a soft head. (*The Abolition of Man,* chapter 1),

Rosalie has always taught us that classic literature, with its noble themes and ideals, is like a "soil softener." The way to our hearts is through a good story that employs Christian virtues and values which pave the way for the truth of God's Word! For those of us who have taught literature in the American Christian classroom, we have experienced the joy of breaking open a classic with one of Miss Slater's many syllabi. Quite often, it is through teaching the classics that our students are bonded to us as teachers. And just ask any third grader what his favorite subject is, and I will wager the answer will be "Literature!"

> *For God, who commanded the light to shine out of darkness,*
> *hath shined in our hearts,*
> *to give the light of the knowledge of the glory of God*
> *in the face of Jesus Christ.*
> *But we have this treasure in earthen vessels,*
> *that the excellency of the power may be of God, and not of us.*
> *2 Corinthians 4:6–7*

When one first meets Miss Slater, her love of Christ and her immeasurable knowledge of the Bible shine brightly. She has always treasured her relationship with the Lord, and His Word has been her "first book of instruction" throughout her life. Her writings sing with the imagery and phrases of the Scriptures, which have inspired many American Christian educators for three decades. Like Joseph, she always glorifies the Lord in her work and gives God the credit for all He has done. Miss Slater has abundantly blessed many thousands of Americans through her generosity and that of the Foundation of American Christian Education, which she co-founded with Verna M. Hall in 1964. What God has given her, she has in turn generously given to so many others. Her abiding love of God and her nation, as well as her genuine love and concern for others, place her at the forefront of twentieth-century Americans most certainly to be honored as world changers.

Thank you, Miss Slater, for documenting and preserving our rich heritage of American Christian education, so that we can treasure what God has wrought in America and instruct our little ones. Thank you for teaching us that the history of our nation is truly Christ, His Story. And thank you for graciously giving so much of yourself away and investing in that which has eternal value. You have forever changed our lives. We love you and honor you as a true American Christian patriot—a treasure above price!

Elizabeth L. Youmans
F.A.C.E. Educational Projects Director
October 8, 1997

TABLE OF CONTENTS

TABLE OF CONTENTS

TABLE OF CONTENTS

THE NOAH PLAN © 1997 • FOUNDATION FOR AMERICAN CHRISTIAN EDUCATION

Foreword

In our summer vacations at the beach on North Carolina's Outer Banks, twilight would find four little cousins settling down from a day of sun, surf, and sand. As soon as supper dishes were done, wet things hung to dry, baths drained, and pajamas on, a voice would call for "our book"—which meant the book we were reading aloud together that summer vacation—one summer *Swiss Family Robinson*, another *Treasure Island*. In our memories, each summer held the character and charm of our book, and we remember the vacations by the book we were "living in" together. Whatever the book, we were united in adventure or romance, in inspiration or ideals, feeding our imaginations, expanding our vocabularies, and filling our souls with nobility, beauty, adventure, and aspiration.

Today when the same children, who are now grown, gather with friends who were among the endless guests of those beach vacations, they sometimes reminisce of David Copperfield or the Black Knight as though speaking of old friends. Evidence of life-lessons learned in the reading of great books shows in the lasting effect on each one of our children.

The role of literature in learning is much too often underrated. In Webster's 1828 *American Dictionary of the English Language*, "learning" is the first definition of literature. The study of literature provides a learning experience that satisfies the need to participate in the subject, to investigate diverse interests, and to relate what is learned to a framework of truth. This is the Biblical Principle Approach in the study of literature. It encompasses much more than typical literary analysis. It includes geography, history, science, English or other languages, composition, even math, because literature is a reflection of life itself. The study of a classic is a whole learning experience as a group of children or a family circle "inhabit" a new land, meet new characters, a new culture, bound together in the anticipation of the unfolding of a story.

My love of literature was nurtured by my mother who loved learning and books and who read to us liberally as children. As a young mother and teacher concerned for my own two children, I met Rosalie June Slater and was mentored in developing the subject of literature for teaching. Her work in the Christian History Literature Program included an elementary course of study, a junior high

course for seventh and eighth grades, an English literature course for ninth and tenth grades, and an American literature course for eleventh and twelfth grades, as well as her much loved *Family Program for Reading Aloud*. Each course is based on the reading of whole books and the study of the author and historical background on the Chain of Christianity. This *Literature Curriculum Guide* contains the content of her courses in chapters 2–6. The curriculum charts, model lesson plans, testimony of the literature teacher, and sample student notebook in chapter 1 are the work of teachers at StoneBridge School in Chesapeake, Virginia.

It is no accident that Jesus spoke in stories. The story is a direct avenue to the heart, illumining reason by igniting the soul. The great stories of our literature are potent with Christian principles and ideals.

One of our StoneBridge teachers taught *The Secret Garden*. In it she saw an opportunity to practice the Principle Approach more broadly through literature. She proposed to her class that they create their own secret garden. Their study began by researching the Bible for spiritual principles represented by plants and gardens. Botany sprang to life for the children. Math became essential to them as they calculated perimeter, area, quantities, and costs for their garden. Geography, history, and all the elements of literature became relevant as the children read and produced a notebook study of Burnett's classic. Finally, they and their parents prepared the ground and planted and nurtured a lovely garden that graces the school grounds with an inviting bench, trellis, birdhouse, and many of the plants named in the original English garden. The real flowering is in the hearts and lives of children who will forever carry a secret garden in their hearts.

My own teaching of literature has been diverse, from children's literature and classics to the high school courses. The joy of developing authors for my own teaching is one of the glad blessings of my life. But nothing equals the joy of imparting literature to children, of living in a classic weeks on end, then celebrating it in a special day at school—seeing the standard of great literature become natural to children whose tastes and ideals are elevated and whose speech and writing are gilded with the gold of our rich literary heritage.

The effect of literature on the heart and life of a child can be best illustrated by the story of one of my students, a fourth grade young man who studied *Carry On, Mr. Bowditch* with my class and shortly afterward moved away with his family to another state. He found the move difficult, made so especially by leaving his school and the "something" that his letter tells left him "becalmed" (see below). I did write Brent back and began sending him some "oars" for his ash breeze in the form of geography and Latin. In this fourth grade boy's heart, Bowditch lived in and enlivened his world.

As you use this guide, create your own literature notebook, collecting your research and ideas and organizing your preparation to enjoy the liberty of teaching whole books to eager students. Your love of literature will ignite their passion for books and ideals.

Carole Adams

Carole Adams, Ph.D.
Chesapeake, Virginia, 1997

March 16, 1983, p.m.

Dear Mrs. Adams,

I am very sorry I haven't written you sooner! I was just looking through my notebook. Then I turned to a page with big bold letters saying, "Harder is better." Right then I realized I have not enjoyed school like I used to.

Like the research on the rivers, planets, and animals and things like that. As I was getting up, my leg hit my literature notebook. It fell open to the picture of Nat Bowditch at the desk in "Ships & Hoges."

Like a bullet it hit me. I am becalmed. I want to sail by "ash breeze." I'm not getting much challenging work. If you can give any suggestions at all, please tell me.

Tell Matt and Carey "Hi." Please write back.

In Christ,

Brent

KEY TO ABBREVIATIONS

The Noah Plan Literature Curriculum Guide continually refers to the resources published by the Foundation for American Christian Education (F.A.C.E.). Following are abbreviations used for these publications in citations and references:

Webster's 1828 *Dictionary*   *The American Dictionary of the English Language*, Noah Webster. 1828 facsimile edition. San Francisco: F.A.C.E., 1967.

C & P   *The Christian History of the American Revolution: Consider and Ponder.* Compiled by Verna M. Hall. San Francisco: F.A.C.E., 1976.

CHOC, I   *The Christian History of the Constitution of the United States of America*, Vol. I: *Christian Self-Government*. Compiled by Verna M. Hall. San Francisco: F.A.C.E., 1960.

CHOC, II   *The Christian History of the Constitution of the United States of America*, Vol. II: *Christian Self-Government with Union*. Compiled by Verna M. Hall. San Francisco: F.A.C.E., 1962.

T & L   *Teaching and Learning America's Christian History: The Principle Approach*, Rosalie J. Slater. San Francisco: F.A.C.E., 1965.

CHAPTER ONE

THE LITERATURE CURRICULUM CHARTS AND METHODS

The Goals for Teaching Literature Should Include:

1. Inspiring a high Christian standard of language by building a diverse and excellent vocabulary

2. Cultivating abilities of expression in speaking and writing

3. Developing literary tastes and sensitivities of the highest quality

4. Instilling a love of the Bible, of classics, and of all types of literature

5. Building a knowledge of elementary facts about literature (figures, terms, elements, types)

6. Connecting the student to the greatest and best minds of the past and the beauty and wisdom of their imaginations

THE NOAH PLAN © 1997 • FOUNDATION FOR AMERICAN CHRISTIAN EDUCATION

Defining Literature

Literature is "the expression of life in words of truth and beauty; it is the written record of man's spirit, of his thoughts, emotions, aspirations; it is the history and the only history, of the human soul. It is characterized by its artistic, its suggestive, its permanent qualities. Its two tests are its universal interest and its personal style. Its object, aside from the delight it gives us, is to know man, that is, the soul of man rather than his actions; and since it preserves to the race the ideals upon which all our civilization is founded, it is one of the most important and delightful subjects that can occupy the human mind." (*English Literature*, William J. Long, 1945, pp. 8–9)

Literature is the highest quality of language for any nation. The Bible is the model for all literature, the most excellent standard. The Bible contains every type of literature.

Long explains the artistic quality of literature:

"A hundred men may pass a hayfield and see only the sweaty toil and the windrows of dried grass; but here is one who pauses by a Roumanian meadow. . . . He looks deeper, sees truth and beauty where we see only dead grass, and he reflects what he sees in a little poem in which the hay tells its own story.

> Yesterday's flowers am I,
> And I have drunk my last sweet draught of dew. . . .
> My breath is sweet as children's prattle is;
> I drank in all the whole earth's fruitfulness,
> To make of it the fragrance of my soul
> That shall outlive my death.
>
> *(The Bard of the Dimbovitza)*

"One who reads only that first exquisite line, 'yesterday's flowers am I,' can never again see hay without recalling the beauty that was hidden from his eyes until the poet found it.

"In the same pleasing, surprising way, all artistic work must be a kind of revelation." (pp. 2–3)

Long describes the suggestive quality of literature:

"The . . . quality of . . . suggestiveness . . . appeals to our emotions and imagination rather than to our intellect. It is not so much what it says as what it awakens in us that constitutes its charm. When Faustus in the presence of Helen asks, 'Was this the face that launched a thousand ships?' he does not state a fact or expect an answer. He opens a door through which our imagination enters a new world, a world of music, love, beauty, heroism. . . . When Shakespeare describes the young Biron as speaking

> In such apt and gracious words
> That aged ears play truant at his tales,

he has unconsciously given not only an excellent description of himself, but the measure of all literature, which makes us play truant with the present world and run away to live awhile in the pleasant realm of fancy. The province of all art is not to instruct but to delight." (p. 4)

Key Words

Literature, n. Learning; acquaintance with letters or books. Literature comprehends a knowledge of the ancient languages, denominated classical, history, grammar, rhetoric, logic, geography, as well as the sciences. A knowledge of the world and good breeding give luster to literature. *To these four young men God gave knowledge and understanding of all kinds of literature and learning.* (Daniel 1:17)

Learning, n. The knowledge of principles or facts received by instruction or study; acquired knowledge or ideas in any branch of science or literature; erudition; literature; science. *Instruct a wise man and he will be wiser still; teach a righteous man and he will add to his learning.* (Proverbs 9:9)

Letters Learning; erudition.

Erudition, n. Learning; knowledge gained by study, or from books and instruction; particularly, learning in literature, as distinct from the sciences, as in history, antiquity and languages.

Webster's 1828 *Dictionary*

The Whole
Principle Approach Curriculum

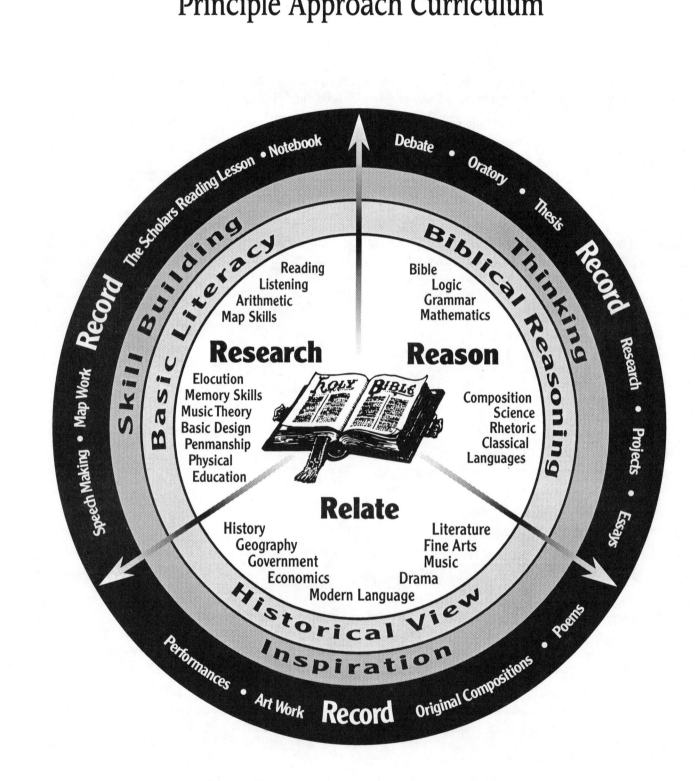

Cultivating Reasoning through the Grades

Grade Level	Metaphor	Research	Reason	Relate	Record
Kindergarten	Planting the seeds of all knowledge	Identifying the subjects by their principles	Understanding symbols (Examples: flag; snowflakes; fingerprints)	Oral language; Mimicry; Narrative; Showing	Recognizing the notebook as a tool of learning
Primary School	Tending the seedlings— (sunning; weeding; watering; regulating; fertilizing; guarding; cultivating)	Mastering the basic skills and vocabulary of each subject	Understanding internal to external; Concrete thinking; Using manipulatives; Skill building	Recitation; Rote; Expository (writing); Drama; Guided Projects	The notebook as a tool of scholarship— notebook skills practiced and guided by teacher
Middle School	Growing the plant— (pruning; guiding; correcting; transplanting; maturing; seasoning; "hardying")	Defining the principles of the subjects	Understanding cause to effect; Questioning; Logic; Critical Thinking; Scientific Method	Independent Projects; Essays; Original Speech (8th)	Notebook mastery— a tool for lifelong independent learning
High School	Reaping the fruit! (cycling growth and harvesting the fruit)	Expressing the principles in life and learning	Original thinking and actual reasoning from a Biblical worldview	Apprenticeship; Service; Debate; Rhetoric; Creative Writing and Speech; Independent Primary Source Research; Original Science Project; Portfolio Project; High School Thesis and Defense	Habit and spirit of organized learning and Biblical scholarship inculcated

LITERATURE

CURRICULUM CHARTS

Kindergarten Literature Curriculum
Four Thirty-five-minute Periods/Week

PURPOSE

1. Inspire the highest standard of the English language.
2. Exercise the God-given gift of communication.
3. Cultivate and refine language skills.
4. Establish the Bible as the greatest literary masterpiece.
5. Plumb the riches of great and noble classics and poems.
6. Restore literature to its chronology in the history of liberty and the character of nations.
7. Instill a lifetime love and enjoyment of classic literature.

TEACHER OBJECTIVES

1. Inspire an appreciation of language towards its mastery through building listening skills through the highest models of literature.
2. Develop the imagination of mental imagery through classics that produce a love for Christian ideals and learning.
3. Impress literary tastes and aesthetic sensibilities.
4. Establish a knowledge about literature:
   a) Types of literature
   b) Qualities of literature
   c) Elements of a classic
   d) R. J. Slater's "Seven loves of literature"
5. Build an enriched, Biblical vocabulary.
6. Begin thinking and reasoning from leading ideas and principles.
7. Form the character of the American Christian Republic in each student.

TEACHER RESOURCES

1. Holy Bible
2. *A Family Program for Reading Aloud*, Slater, 1991.
3. *Bequest of Wings*, Duff, 1954.
4. *Enjoyment of Literature*, Boas and Smith, 1934.
5. *Doorways to Poetry*, Untermeyer, 1938.
6. *American Literature and English Literature*, Long.
7. *Home Book of Verse*, Stevenson, 1967.
8. *American History in Verse*, Stevenson, 1975.
9. *The Book of Life*, Hall and Wood, (1923–1953 editions).
10. *Christ in the Fine Arts*, Maus, 1938.
11. *Divine Songs*, Watts, first printed in 1715.
12. *Stories from Shakespeare*, Chute, 1956.
    See resource list after chapter 6 for full citations.

DEFINITION OF LITERATURE

1. "Learning; acquaintance with letters or books; comprehends a knowledge of language, classics, history, rhetoric, logic, geography, etc." (Webster's 1828 *Dictionary*)
2. "The expression of life in words of truth and beauty; the written record of man's spirit—his thoughts, emotions, and aspirations."
3. "The handmaid of history, unveiling the human soul, revealing man as a doer of deeds and a dreamer of dreams."

METHODS

1. Students recognize the notebook as their tool of learning. Picture pages and illustrations are colored and filed in the notebook, as well as copies of poems studied and memorized.
2. The teacher reads the classic aloud to the students.
3. Students sing, clap, and hop to rhyme schemes and rhythms.
4. The teacher lectures and holds classroom discussions including Reason and Relate Questions for verbal responses.
5. Memory work is assigned from selected poems.

ENRICHMENT

1. Timelines, map work, art masterpieces, displays, and bulletin boards highlight the classics and poems studied.
2. Classroom projects and crafts
3. Music, drama, and art related to the literature curriculum enrich and celebrate.
4. Christian field study tours
5. Special Day celebrations:
   Quarter 2: Winnie the Pooh Day with a Teddy Bear Parade
   Quarter 3: Bambi Day
   Quarter 4: Little House on the Prairie Day

KEY DEFINITIONS

1. literature
2. poetry
3. classic
4. setting
5. characterization
6. plot
7. theme
8. style
9. rhyme
10. rhythm
11. drama
12. comedy
13. tragedy
14. alliteration

STUDENT PERFORMANCE

1. **Research**: Become familiar with the basic vocabulary of literature.
2. **Reason**: Begin to identify internal and external characteristics. Learn the literary elements of characterization and setting.
3. **Relate**: Participate in classroom discussions with verbal responses to Reason and Relate Questions.
4. **Record**: Picture pages, illustrations, map work, projects, and copies of poems studied and memorized filed in the notebook; recitation of poetry and Scripture passages.

LITERATURE SELECTIONS STUDIED

1. Psalm 100 from the Bible
2. Lullabies from a variety of nations
3. Poetry of Christina Rossetti
4. A selection of fairy tales by Hans Christian Andersen
5. Mother Goose and other nursery rhymes
6. *Winnie the Pooh*, Milne
7. Poetry of Henry Wadsworth Longfellow
8. Poetry of Isaac Watts
9. *Aesop's Fables*
10. *Bambi*, Salten
11. *Peter Rabbit*, Potter
12. *Little House in the Big Woods*, Wilder
13. Poetry of Robert Louis Stevenson
14. *As You Like It*, Shakespeare

Kindergarten Literature Curriculum

QUARTER ONE

INTRODUCTION TO LITERATURE
1. Define literature.
2. Identify the qualities of literature.

THE LITERATURE OF THE BIBLE: PSALMS
1. The Bible holds the highest standard of literary excellence; it is the source and seedbed of literature and liberty.
2. The Bible is the textbook from which emanates the heart of all knowledge.
3. Identify types of Biblical literature.
4. The Book of Psalms:
   a) Define psalm.
   b) Read a selection of psalms.
   c) Read and memorize Psalm 100 (KJV).
      (1) Author: King David; inspired by God
      (2) Theme: Offering praise and thanksgiving; define.

LULLABIES FROM AROUND THE WORLD
1. Dutch, Norse, Corsican, American, Jewish, Cornish, Orkney
2. "Away in the Manger" (German)
3. "All through the Night" (Welsh)
4. "Indian Lullaby"
5. "Bye, Baby, Night Is Come" by Mary Mapes Dodge
6. "Sleep, Baby, Sleep" (German)
7. "Hush, Little Baby" (English)
8. "Twinkle, Twinkle, Little Star"
9. "Rock-a-Bye-Baby"

THE CHILDREN'S POETS AND POETRY
1. Define poetry.
2. Identify the qualities of poetry, rhyme, and rhythm.
3. The poetry of Christina Rossetti:
   a) Her life and contributions on the Chain of Christianity
   b) Read selections of her poetry.
   c) Memorize "Holy Innocents."

FAIRY TALES
1. Fairy tales as a type of literature; describe the qualities of a fairy tale.
2. The conflict between good and evil helps teach discernment.
3. Read and discuss:
   a) "The Princess and the Pea"
   b) "Jack and the Beanstalk"
   c) "Brave Little Tailor"
   d) "Bremen Town Musicians"
   e) "Red Riding Hood"
   f) "Emperor's New Clothes"
   g) "The Frog Prince"

QUARTER TWO

MOTHER GOOSE AND OTHER NURSERY RHYMES:
1. Rhymes and rhythms of Mother Goose; our English heritage
   a) Their humor, wit, and nonsense
   b) Portraits of historic personages
2. Read a variety and select one for memorization.
3. Clap, hop, skip, trot, and gallop to the rhythms.

CHILDREN'S CLASSICS: WINNIE THE POOH
1. The study of an animal tale
2. The individuality of the author, A. A. Milne
3. Introduce and summarize the elements of the classic.
4. Read the story aloud.

THE CHILDREN'S POETS AND POETRY
1. Henry Wadsworth Longfellow: his life and place on the Chain of Christianity
   a) Poet of the American home and hearth
   b) Sweet singer of America
   c) Longfellow's poetic style
   d) Read several of his poems.
   e) Include his Christmas poetry.
2. Read the Christmas Story from the Scriptures and a variety of Christmas poetry.
3. The poetry of Isaac Watts:
   a) The life and contributions of Watts on the Chain of Christianity
   b) Identify and discuss the literary qualities of rhyme and rhythm.
   c) Read selections of *Divine Songs in Easy Language for the Use of Children* (1715).

CHILDREN'S CLASSICS: PETER RABBIT AND OTHER OF HER ANIMAL TALES
1. The individuality and contributions of the author Beatrix Potter:
   a) Author
   b) Artist
   c) Naturalist
2. The study of an animal tale; define moral.
3. Read *Peter Rabbit* and other of Potter's animal tales:
   a) Discuss the moral of each tale.
   b) Identify the character qualities of key animals.

QUARTER THREE

FABLES AND MYTHS
1. Fables and myths as a type of literature; define terms.
2. Read *Aesop's Fables*:
   a) "The Ant and the Grasshopper"
   b) "The Dog and His Reflection"
   c) "The Monkey and the Dolphin"
   d) "The Dog in the Manger"
   e) "The Lion and the Mouse"
3. Read *Uncle Remus* by Joel Chandler Harris.

CHILDREN'S CLASSICS: BAMBI
1. The study of an animal tale
2. The individuality of the author: Felix Salten
3. Begin the Notebook Approach: learn the literary elements of the classic using the Notebook Approach (one page for each element). Students record simple phrases using the words of the author:
   a) Setting
   b) Plot
   c) Characters

BIOGRAPHY: ABRAHAM LINCOLN
1. The authors: Ingri and Edgar Parin d'Aulaire
2. Biography as a type of literature: character is causative; plot and setting are secondary; definitions.
3. Geographic Setting
4. Historic Setting:
   a) America's frontier, early 1800s
   b) Civil War
   c) The Hand of Providence in America
5. The life and influences in young Abraham's childhood:
   a) A loving mother
   b) The Bible as a reader
6. Contributions of Lincoln to liberty:
   a) Gettysburg Address
   b) Emancipation Proclamation
7. A study of Christian character:
   a) The character of Jesus Christ
   b) The Pilgrim character qualities
   c) The character of Abraham Lincoln

THE CHILDREN'S POETS AND POETRY
1. Robert Louis Stevenson: his life and place on the Chain of Christianity
2. Read selections from *A Child's Garden of Verse.*

QUARTER FOUR

INDIVIDUALITY OF NATIONS IN LITERATURE: LITTLE HOUSE IN THE BIG WOODS
1. Autobiography as a type of literature: character is causative; plot and setting are secondary.
2. God's Principle of Individuality in literature:
   a) The author—Laura Ingalls Wilder
      (1) Her life and individuality as "inimitably the pioneer girl"
      (2) Her purpose in writing the book
   b) America's individuality on the frontier:
      (1) Map of America and Wisconsin
      (2) Transportation and houses
      (3) Character of the people
      (4) Clothes, music, and cuisine
3. Elements of the classic emphasized:
   a) Setting: Big woods of Wisconsin, 1870s
   b) Characters: Pa, Ma, Mary, Laura, and Baby Carrie Ingalls
   c) Theme: Christian character forged in loving homes helps build frontier towns.
4. Build vocabulary.
5. Leading ideas:
   a) Christianity goes westward in America.
   b) America was built upon the three spheres of government, their Christian character qualities, and their influence in town growth:
      (1) The home—the foundational building block
      (2) The Christian church—an anchor in town growth
      (3) Civil government—the product of American Christianity moving westward
   c) Family love and affection are the building blocks of America.
   d) A pioneer requires a courageous, self-reliant, frugal, and self-governing spirit.
6. Special Day Celebration: Little House Day
   a) Costumes
   b) Crafts
   c) American folk songs
   d) Pioneer snacks and foods

WILLIAM SHAKESPEARE: AS YOU LIKE IT
1. William Shakespeare—Bard of the Bible
2. Drama as a type of literature:
   a) Drama on the Chain of Christianity
   b) Definitions: comedy and tragedy
3. Read *As You Like It* from Chute's *Stories of Shakespeare*—"All the world's a stage and all the men and women merely players."

First Grade Literature Curriculum

Three Thirty-five-minute Periods/Week

PURPOSE

1. Inspire the highest standard of the English language.
2. Exercise the God-given gift of communication.
3. Cultivate and refine language skills.
4. Establish the Bible as the greatest literary masterpiece.
5. Plumb the riches of great and noble classics and poems.
6. Restore literature to its chronology in the history of liberty and the character of nations.
7. Instill a lifetime love and enjoyment of classic literature.

TEACHER OBJECTIVES

1. Inspire an appreciation of language towards its mastery for speech and composition through the highest models of literature.
2. Develop the imagination of mental imagery through classics that produce a love for Christian ideals and learning.
3. Impress literary tastes and aesthetic sensibilities.
4. Establish a knowledge about literature:
   a) Types of literature
   b) Qualities of literature
   c) Elements of a classic
   d) R. J. Slater's seven loves of literature
5. Build an enriched, Biblical vocabulary.
6. Develop skills of Biblical reasoning and critical thinking from leading ideas, principles, and literary themes.
7. Form the character of the American Christian Republic in each student.

TEACHER RESOURCES

1. Holy Bible
2. *A Family Program for Reading Aloud*, Slater, 1991.
3. *Bequest of Wings*, Duff, 1954.
4. *Enjoyment of Literature*, Boas and Smith, 1934.
5. *Doorways to Poetry*, Untermeyer, 1938.
6. *American Literature and English Literature*, Long.
7. *Home Book of Verse*, Stevenson, 1967.
8. *American History in Verse*, Stevenson, 1975.
9. *The Book of Life*, Hall and Wood, (1923–1953 editions).
10. *Christ in the Fine Arts*, Maus, 1938.
11. *Divine Songs*, Isaac Watts, first printed in 1715.
12. *Tales from Shakespeare*, Lamb, 1990.

See resource list after chapter 6 for full citations.

DEFINITION OF LITERATURE

1. "Learning: acquaintance with letters or books; comprehends a knowledge of language, classics, history, rhetoric, logic, geography, etc." (*Webster's 1828 Dictionary*)
2. "The expression of life in words of truth and beauty; the written record of man's spirit—his thoughts, emotions, and aspirations."
3. "The handmaid of history, unveiling the human soul, revealing man as a doer of deeds and a dreamer of dreams."

METHODS

1. Students recognize the value of the notebook as their tool of learning. A limited amount of notes is copied from the chalkboard, using the words of the author, for the five elements of the classic. Notebook pages are illustrated, corrected, and filed.
2. The teacher reads the classic aloud to the students while they read silently from their own copies.
3. Students practice the art of writing using the words of the author for compositions.
4. Memory work is assigned from selected poems.
5. The teacher lectures; places simple notes on the chalk board; reads aloud; holds classroom discussions including Reason and Relate Questions for verbal responses.

ENRICHMENT

1. Timelines, map work, art masterpieces, displays, and bulletin boards highlight the classics and poems studied.
2. Classroom projects and crafts
3. Music, drama, and art related to the literature curriculum enrich and celebrate.
4. Christian history field study tours
5. Special Day celebrations:
   Quarter 2: Italy Day
   Quarter 3: Shakespeare Day
   Quarter 4: Liberty Day

KEY DEFINITIONS

1. literature	8. style
2. poetry	9. rhyme
3. classic	10. rhythm
4. setting	11. drama
5. characterization	12. comedy
6. plot	13. tragedy
7. theme	14. alliteration

STUDENT PERFORMANCE

1. **Research:** Master basic vocabulary of literature.
2. **Reason:** Verbal responses to Reason Questions and classroom discussions; identify internal and external characteristics.
3. **Relate:** Guided projects, Shakespearean drama, compositions.
4. **Record:** Complete notes; memorize poems.

LITERATURE SELECTIONS STUDIED

1. The Book of Genesis in the Bible: the stories of Noah, Isaac, Jacob, and Joseph
2. *Divine Songs*, Watts; memorize "Song II."
3. Poetry of William Blake
4. *Pinocchio*, Collodi
5. Poetry of Robert Louis Stevenson; memorize "The Swing."
6. *Cinnabar*, Henry
7. *Romeo and Juliet*, Shakespeare, as told by Charles and Mary Lamb
8. Poetry of Henry Wadsworth Longfellow including "The Children's Hour."
9. *Abigail Adams*, Witter

First Grade Literature Curriculum

Quarter One	Quarter Two	Quarter Three	Quarter Four

Quarter One

Introduction to Literature

1. Define literature.
2. Identify the qualities of literature.
3. Characterize literary types in elementary curriculum:
   a) Prose
   b) Poetry
   c) Fiction
   d) Non-fiction
   e) Letters
   f) Drama
4. Define the literary elements of a classic.
5. Describe seven loves inspired by literature.

The Literature of the Bible: Genesis

1. Bible holds the highest standard of literary excellence; source and seedbed of literature and liberty.
2. Bible is the textbook from which emanates the heart of all knowledge.
3. Identify types of Biblical literature.
4. Book of Genesis with a focus on basic literary elements through these stories:
   a) Noah: Providential plot
   b) Isaac: Theme
   c) Joseph: Historical setting and character study

The Children's Poets and Poetry

1. Define poetry.
2. The poetry of Isaac Watts:
   a) The life and contributions of Watts on the Chain of Christianity
   b) Identify and discuss the literary qualities of rhyme and rhythm.
   c) Read selections of *Divine Songs in Easy Language for the Use of Children* (1715).
   d) Memorize Song II: "Praise for Creation."
3. The poetry of Robert Louis Stevenson:
   a) His life and place on the Chain of Christianity
   b) Stevenson's poetic style
   c) Read several of his poems.
   d) Study and memorize "The Swing."

Quarter Two

Individuality of Nations in Literature: *Pinocchio*

1. The study of fiction
2. God's Principle of Individuality in literature:
   a) The author—Carlo Collodi:
      (1) His life and individuality
      (2) His purpose in writing the book
   b) Italy's individuality:
      (1) Geographic: complete map of Italy.
      (2) Contributions on the Chain of Christianity:
         (a) Latin
         (b) Vulgate Bible
         (c) Art and architecture
         (d) Use of marionettes ("Little Marys") in the Middle Ages to teach Bible stories and moral lessons
         (e) Explorers: Polos, Cabot, Columbus, Vespucci
      (3) Character of the people
      (4) Customs, music, and cuisine
3. Summarize the elements of the classic using the Notebook Approach (one page for each element using the words of the author):
   a) Setting
   b) Plot
   c) Characters (one page each)
   d) Theme
   e) Style
4. Vocabulary studies
5. Biblical principle derived from *Pinocchio*: "Conscience is my most sacred property."
6. Special Day Celebration: Italy Day
   a) Costumes
   b) Art class: Michelangelo and Sistine Chapel (See *StoneBridge Art Guide* for details.)
   c) Crafts
   d) Italian folk songs and dance
   e) A "visit" to Italy
   f) Italian snacks and foods
7. Complete a composition.

The Children's Poets and Poetry

1. The children's poetry of William Blake
2. Memorize "The Lamb."

Quarter Three

Children's Classics: *Cinnabar*

1. The study of an animal tale; define moral; discuss how animals assume the personalities and characters of humans.
2. The individuality and literary contributions of the author, Marguerite Henry
3. Summarize the elements of the classic using the Notebook Approach (one page for each element using the words of the author):
   a) Setting
   b) Plot
   c) Characters

William Shakespeare—Bard of the Bible: *Romeo and Juliet*

1. The life and contributions of Shakespeare
2. Elizabethan England and customs
3. Drama:
   a) History of drama
   b) Drama on the Chain of Christianity
   c) Elements of a play
   d) Definitions: comedy, tragedy, soliloquy, dramatis personae, playwright, aside
4. Brief study and notebook record of *Romeo and Juliet*:
   a) Dramatis personae: identify the key characters.
   b) Complete simple summaries for setting, plot, and characters by acts using the most important scenes.
5. Read aloud from Lamb's *Tales* or Marchette Chute.
6. Perform the drama of *Romeo and Juliet* (adaptation for first grade available from F.A.C.E.).

The Children's Poets and Poetry

1. Henry Wadsworth Longfellow: his life and place on the Chain of Christianity
   a) Poet of the American home and hearth
   b) Sweet singer of America
2. Longfellow's poetic style
3. Read several of his poems.
4. Study "The Children's Hour."

Quarter Four

Biography: *Abigail Adams*

1. The Christian literature of the American Republic—Ladies in Literature (See "A Teacher's Testimony," p. 42.)
2. Biography as a type of literature: character is causative; plot and setting are secondary; definitions.
3. America's heritage of Christian character:
   a) Pilgrim character qualities
   b) American Christian womanhood and motherhood (*CHOC*, I, pp. 407–10; *C & P*, pp. 71–86).
      (1) Study Proverbs 31 woman.
      (2) Have each student write a poem of gratitude about his or her mother; copy in calligraphy and frame for a Mother's Day gift.
4. Summarize the elements of the classic using the Notebook Approach in the words of the author.
5. Massachusetts on the Chain of Christianity:
   a) Map work
   b) Contributions
   c) Character
6. A study of colonial American life:
   a) Colonial education (*C & P*, pp. 602–16)
   b) American Christian home and family life
   c) New England local self-government
   d) Colonial crafts and food
   e) Music of the *Bay Psalm Book*, early American folk and Revolutionary War songs
7. Introduction to the Presidency of the United States of America
8. Letters as a type of literature:
   a) Read the letters of Abigail, John, and John Quincy Adams.
   b) Have each child write a letter with a quill pen and homemade ink to his or her "Honored Papa" for Father's Day.
9. Celebrate Liberty Day.

Resources for Teaching *Abigail Adams*

1. *T & L*, *CHOC*, and *C & P*
2. F.A.C.E. Syllabus—*Abigail Adams: First Lady of Faith and Courage*
3. *Those Who Love*, Stone, 1965.
4. *The Book of Abigail and John*, 1975.
5. *American History in Verse*, Stevenson, 1975.
6. *Seventeen Seventy-Six*, Musical, F.A.C.E.

Second Grade Literature Curriculum

Three Thirty-five-minute Periods/Week

PURPOSE

1. Inspire the highest standard of the English language.
2. Exercise the God-given gift of communication.
3. Cultivate and refine language skills.
4. Establish the Bible as the greatest literary masterpiece.
5. Plumb the riches of great and noble classics and poems.
6. Restore literature to its chronology in the history of liberty and the character of nations.
7. Instill a lifetime love and enjoyment of classic literature.

TEACHER OBJECTIVES

1. Inspire an appreciation of language towards its mastery for speech and composition through the highest models of literature.
2. Develop the imagination of mental imagery through classics that produce a love for Christian ideals and learning.
3. Impress literary tastes and aesthetic sensibilities.
4. Establish a knowledge about literature:
   a) Types of literature
   b) Qualities of literature
   c) Elements of a classic
   d) R. J. Slater's seven loves of literature
5. Build an enriched, Biblical vocabulary.
6. Develop skills of Biblical reasoning and critical thinking from leading ideas, principles, and literary themes.
7. Form the character of the American Christian Republic in each student.

TEACHER RESOURCES

1. Holy Bible
2. A Family Program for Reading Aloud, Slater, 1991.
3. Bequest of Wings, Duff, 1954.
4. Enjoyment of Literature, Boas and Smith, 1934.
5. Doorways to Poetry, Untermeyer, 1938.
6. American Literature and English Literature, Long.
7. Home Book of Verse, Stevenson, 1967.
8. American History in Verse, Stevenson, 1975.
9. The Book of Life, Hall and Wood, (1923–1953 editions).
10. Christ in the Fine Arts, Maus, 1938.
11. Tales from Shakespeare, Lamb, 1990.
12. Stories from Shakespeare, Chute, 1956.
See resource list after chapter 6 for full citations.

DEFINITION OF LITERATURE

1. "Learning; acquaintance with letters or books; comprehends a knowledge of language, classics, history, rhetoric, logic, geography, etc." (Webster's 1828 Dictionary)
2. "The expression of life in words of truth and beauty; the written record of man's spirit—his thoughts, emotions, and aspirations."
3. "The handmaid of history, unveiling the human soul, revealing man as a doer of deeds and a dreamer of dreams."

METHODS

1. Students recognize the notebook as their tool of learning and practice daily stewardship of it. They are taught the four steps of learning through the Notebook Approach. They develop notebook skills by recording notes, completing maps, drawing and coloring illustrations, and correcting and filing papers. Research skills are begun. Reason and Relate Questions are discussed in class, and students are occasionally assigned simple Reason and Relate Questions for homework.
2. The teacher reads the classic aloud while students read silently from their own copies.
3. The teacher lectures, places notes on the chalkboard, and holds classroom discussions including Reason and Relate Questions for verbal and occasional written responses.
4. Students practice the art of writing using the words of the author for writing compositions and poetry.
5. Memory work is assigned from selected poems, oratory, and dramas.

ENRICHMENT

1. Timelines, map work, art masterpieces, displays, and bulletin boards highlight the classics and poems studied.
2. Classroom projects and crafts
3. Music, drama, and art related to the literature enrich and celebrate the curriculum.
4. Christian history field study tours
5. Special Day celebrations:
   Quarter 2: Jamestown Day
   Quarter 3: Heidi Day
   Quarter 4: Liberty Day

KEY DEFINITIONS

1. literature
2. prose
3. poetry
4. characterization
5. plot
6. theme
7. setting
8. rhyme
9. rhythm
10. meter
11. imagery
12. drama
13. dramatis personae
14. comedy
15. tragedy
16. playwright
17. soliloquy
18. analogy
19. fantasy
20. symbolism

STUDENT PERFORMANCE

1. **Research:** Master basic vocabulary of literature; introduce research skills, particularly with the Bible and Webster's 1828 Dictionary.
2. **Reason:** Identify internal and external characteristics; learn to reason; learn how to articulate verbal and written responses to Reason Questions and classroom discussions.
3. **Relate:** Begin identifying leading ideas and principles through questions, essays, poems, compositions, guided projects, and drama to personal life and circumstances. Learn how to answer Relate Questions.
4. **Record:** Notebook filed with notes, vocabulary studies, maps, illustrations, compositions, poems, essays, homework assignments, and tests; poetry and oratory recitations; dramatic performances.

LITERATURE SELECTIONS STUDIED

1. The Book of Psalms in the Bible
2. Poetry of Emily Dickinson
3. Poetry of Lewis Carroll
4. Heidi, Spyri
5. Pocahontas, d'Aulaire
6. Poetry of Henry Wadsworth Longfellow
7. The Comedy of Errors, Shakespeare
8. Poetry of Eugene Field
9. Benjamin West and His Cat, Grimalkin, Henry
10. Benjamin Franklin, d'Aulaire

Second Grade Literature Curriculum

QUARTER ONE	QUARTER TWO	QUARTER THREE	QUARTER FOUR
INTRODUCTION TO LITERATURE	**INDIVIDUALITY OF NATIONS IN LITERATURE: *HEIDI***	**COMPLETE THE STUDY OF *HEIDI***	**CHILDREN'S CLASSICS:**
1. Define literature.	1. Learning our European heritage of liberty:	**THE CHILDREN'S POETS AND POETRY**	***BENJAMIN WEST AND HIS CAT, GRIMALKIN***
2. Identify the qualities of literature.	*a)* The author, Johanna Spyri.	1. The poetry of Eugene Field:	1. The authors: Marguerite Henry and Wesley Dennis
3. Define and characterize literary types in elementary curriculum:	(1) Her individuality and literary contributions	*a)* His life and contributions to literature	2. Biography as a type of literature: character is causative; plot and setting are secondary; definitions.
a) Prose	(2) Her purpose in writing the book	*b)* "Wynken, Blynken, and Nod"	3. Christian character:
b) Poetry	*b)* Switzerland's individuality:	2. The poetry of Lewis Carroll:	*a)* Jesus Christ is our model.
c) Fiction	(1) Geographic: complete map.	*a)* His life and contributions to literature	*b)* The Pilgrims are American Christian model.
d) Non-fiction	(2) Historic	*b)* Carroll's nonsensical poetic style	4. Historic setting, Pennsylvania, parent colony of religious toleration:
e) Biography	(3) Switzerland's contributions on the Chain of Christianity	*c)* Read "The Walrus and the Carpenter," "The Whiting and the Snail," and "He Thought He Saw."	*a)* Geographic individuality: map work
f) Letters	(4) Switzerland's contributions to liberty	3. The poetry of Emily Dickinson:	*b)* William Penn, founder
g) Drama	(5) Character of the people	*a)* Her life and place on the Chain of Christianity	(1) His Christian character
4. Define the literary elements of a classic.	(6) Customs	*b)* Read varied selections of her poetry.	(2) Contributions to liberty in America
5. Describe Slater's seven loves inspired by literature.	(7) The arts		*c)* Pennsylvania's place on the Chain of Christianity:
	2. Study and summarize each element of the classic using the Notebook Method developed for literature.	**WILLIAM SHAKESPEARE—BARD OF THE BIBLE:**	(1) Self-governing Middle Colony
LITERATURE OF THE BIBLE: THE PSALMS	3. Vocabulary studies	***THE COMEDY OF ERRORS***	(2) Influence of the Quakers
1. Bible holds the highest standard of literary excellence; source and seedbed of literature and liberty.	4. Principles derived from *Heidi*:	1. The life and contributions of Shakespeare, master playwright; Christ in Shakespeare's works.	(3) Founding fathers and patriots
2. Bible is the textbook from which emanates the heart of all knowledge.	*a)* "God's Principle of Individuality"	2. Elizabethan England and customs	(4) Philadelphia: "city of brotherly love"
3. Identify types of Biblical literature: Poetry.	*b)* The principle of sowing and reaping	3. Drama:	(5) Contributions to the arts
4. The Book of Psalms: read a sampling of various types of psalms.	*c)* Principle of Christian Character; the Prodigal Son	*a)* History and timeline of drama	5. Using the words of the author, summarize the elements of the classic using the Notebook Approach.
5. David, "a man after God's own heart"	5. Special Day Celebration: Heidi Day	*b)* Drama on the Chain of Christianity	6. Benjamin West:
6. Study, memorize, and sign the Twenty-third Psalm:	*a)* Costumes	*c)* Elements of a play	*a)* Family life
a) Sheep and their characteristics	*b)* "Language of the Swiss Alps"	*d)* Definitions: comedy, tragedy, farce, dramatis personae, playwright, aside	*b)* Childhood influences and his education
b) The life of a shepherd	*c)* Swiss folk songs, dance, and a craft	*e)* The Globe Theater	*c)* West, the portraitist
c) Jesus Christ, the Great Shepherd	*d)* A "Visit to Geneva"	4. Brief study and notebook record of *The Comedy of Errors*:	*d)* West, the painter
d) Read the Twenty-third Psalm from the *Bay Psalm Book*.	*e)* Swiss breakfast and vocabulary	*a)* Dramatis personae: identify the key characters.	*e)* Contributions to fine art
	f) Complete a composition.	*b)* Complete simple summaries for setting, plot, and characters by acts.	7. In art class, have students make a paintbrush from animal fur and practice painting with it. (See *StoneBridge Art Guide*, p. xiii.)
THE CHILDREN'S POETS AND POETRY		*c)* Biblical theme: "All things work together for good."	8. Visit art museum (if fortunate to be near one with original West paintings) or show slides of West's paintings to students.
1. Define poetry; literary qualities of rhyme and rhythm.	**THE CHILDREN'S POETS AND POETRY**	5. Read aloud from Lamb's *Tales* or Chute's *Stories*.	9. Complete the study with a composition.
2. Henry Wadsworth Longfellow: his life and place on the Chain of Christianity	Read a variety of Christmas poetry.		
a) Poet of the American home and hearth		**THE CHILDREN'S POETS AND POETRY**	**BIOGRAPHY: *BENJAMIN FRANKLIN***
b) Sweet singer of America		The poetry of Emily Dickinson:	1. Read Ingri and Edgar Parin d'Aulaire's biography of Founding Father, Benjamin Franklin.
c) Longfellow's poetic style		*a)* Her life and contributions to literature	2. Record the principles by which Franklin lived:
d) Read "Hiawatha" and memorize a portion of the Prologue.		*b)* Read a varied selection of her poetry.	*a)* Wisdom
		c) Memorize: "The Bee" and "To Make a Prairie."	*b)* Wit
BIOGRAPHY: *POCAHONTAS*			3. Record simple facts about his childhood, education, and contributions to America as a statesman, diplomat, inventor, civic planner, writer, and his contributions toward writing the Declaration of Independence and the U.S. Constitution.
1. Read Ingri and Edgar Parin d'Aulaire's children's biography for the Christian history curriculum.			
2. Celebrate Jamestown Thanksgiving Day.			

Third Grade Literature Curriculum

Three Forty-minute Periods/Week

PURPOSE

1. Inspire the highest standard of the English language.
2. Exercise the God-given gift of communication.
3. Cultivate and refine language skills.
4. Establish the Bible as the greatest literary masterpiece.
5. Plumb the riches of great and noble classics and poems.
6. Restore literature to its chronology in the history of liberty and the character of nations.
7. Instill a lifetime love and enjoyment of classic literature.

TEACHER OBJECTIVES

1. Inspire an appreciation of language towards its mastery for speech and composition through the highest models of literature.
2. Develop the imagination of mental imagery through classics that produce a love for Christian ideals and learning.
3. Impress literary tastes and aesthetic sensibilities.
4. Establish a knowledge about literature:
   a) Types of literature
   b) Qualities of literature
   c) Elements of a classic
   d) R. J. Slater's seven loves of literature
5. Build an enriched, Biblical vocabulary.
6. Develop skills of Biblical reasoning and critical thinking from leading ideas, principles, and literary themes.
7. Form the character of the American Christian Republic in each student.

TEACHER RESOURCES

1. Holy Bible
2. *A Family Program for Reading Aloud*, Slater, 1991.
3. *Bequest of Wings*, Duff, 1954.
4. *Enjoyment of Literature*, Boas and Smith, 1934.
5. *Doorways to Poetry*, Untermeyer, 1938.
6. *American Literature and English Literature*, Long.
7. *Home Book of Verse*, Stevenson, 1967.
8. *American History in Verse*, Stevenson, 1975.
9. *The Book of Life*, Hall and Wood, (1923–1953 editions).
10. *Christ in the Fine Arts*, Maus, 1938.
11. *Tales from Shakespeare*, Lamb, 1990.
12. *Stories from Shakespeare*, Chute, 1956.
13. *The Merchant of Venice*, adapt. by Mulhern, 1988.

See resource list after chapter 6 for full citations.

DEFINITION OF LITERATURE

1. "Learning; acquaintance with letters or books; comprehends a knowledge of language, classics, history, rhetoric, logic, geography, etc." (Webster's 1828 *Dictionary*)
2. "The expression of life in words of truth and beauty; the written record of man's spirit—his thoughts, emotions, and aspirations."
3. "The handmaid of history, unveiling the human soul, revealing man as a doer of deeds and a dreamer of dreams."

METHODS

1. Students are taught the four steps of learning through the Notebook Approach. They know the notebook as their tool of learning and practice daily stewardship of it. They continue developing notebook skills by recording notes, completing maps, drawing and coloring illustrations, and correcting and filing papers. Research skills are taught. Reason and Relate Questions are assigned in class, and students are taught how to write out their answers. Learning is assessed through compositions, quizzes, essay tests, and the notebook.
2. The teacher reads the classic aloud while students read silently from personal copies.
3. The teacher lectures, places notes on the chalkboard, and holds classroom discussions including Reason and Relate Questions for verbal and written responses.
4. Students practice the art of writing using the words of the author for writing poetry, compositions, and essays.
5. Memory work is assigned from selected poems, oratory, and dramas.
6. The students are taught how to articulate and write out answers to Reason and Relate Questions and how to take essay tests.

ENRICHMENT

1. Timelines, map work, art masterpieces, displays, and bulletin boards highlight the classics and poems studied.
2. Classroom projects and crafts
3. Music, drama, and art related to the literature enrich and celebrate the curriculum.
4. Christian history field study tours
5. Special Day celebrations:
   Quarter 2: Dutch Day
   Quarter 3: Bach Tea
   Quarter 4: Liberty Day

KEY DEFINITIONS

1. literature	11. imagery
2. prose	12. drama
3. poetry	13. dramatis personae
4. characterization	14. comedy
5. plot	15. tragedy
6. theme	16. playwright
7. style	17. soliloquy
8. rhyme	18. analogy
9. rhythm	19. fantasy
10. meter	20. symbolism

STUDENT PERFORMANCE

1. **Research**: Master basic vocabulary of literature; introduce research skills, particularly with the Bible and Webster's 1828 *Dictionary*.
2. **Reason**: Identify internal and external characteristics; learn to reason independently; learn how to articulate verbal and written responses to Reason Questions and classroom discussions.
3. **Relate**: Begin identifying leading ideas and principles through questions, essays, poems, compositions, guided projects, and drama to personal life and circumstances. Learn how to answer Relate Questions.
4. **Record**: Notebook filed with notes, vocabulary studies, maps, illustrations, compositions, poems, essays, homework assignments, and tests; poetry and oratory recitations; dramatic performances.

LITERATURE SELECTIONS STUDIED

1. The Book of Jonah in the Bible
2. Poetry of Emily Dickinson
3. Poetry of Charles Dickens
4. Poetry of Robert Louis Stevenson
5. *Hans Brinker, or The Silver Skates*, Dodge
6. *Johann Sebastian Bach, the Boy from Thuringia*, Wheeler and Deucher
7. Poetry of Henry Wadsworth Longfellow
8. *The Lion, the Witch, and the Wardrobe*, Lewis
9. *The Merchant of Venice*, Shakespeare

THE NOAH PLAN © 1997 • FOUNDATION FOR AMERICAN CHRISTIAN EDUCATION

Third Grade Literature Curriculum

QUARTER ONE	QUARTER TWO	QUARTER THREE	QUARTER FOUR

QUARTER ONE

INTRODUCTION TO LITERATURE

1. Define literature.
2. Identify the qualities of literature.
3. Define and characterize literary types in elementary curriculum:
   a) Prose
   b) Poetry
   c) Fiction
   d) Non-fiction
   e) Biography
   f) Letters
   g) Drama
4. Define the literary elements of a classic.
5. Describe Slater's seven loves inspired by literature.

THE LITERATURE OF THE BIBLE: JONAH

1. Bible holds the highest standard of literary excellence; source and seedbed of literature and liberty.
2. Bible is the textbook from which emanates the heart of all knowledge.
3. Identify types of Biblical literature: Allegory.
4. Book of Jonah, minor prophet of Israel:
   a) Setting: Ninevah, capital of Assyria, and its wickedness
   b) Plot
   c) Theme
   d) Characterization of Jonah
   e) Jonah's preservation in the great fish is a type of Christ's burial and resurrection.

THE CHILDREN'S POETS AND POETRY

1. Define poetry.
2. The poetry of Emily Dickinson:
   a) Her life and place on the Chain of Christianity
   b) Identify and discuss the literary qualities of her poetry.
   c) Read varied selections of her poetry.
   d) Memorize: "#1, A Book"; "#2, A Book"; "I'm Nobody, Who Are You?"
3. The poetry of Charles Dickens:
   a) His life and place on the Chain of Christianity
   b) Dickens's poetic style
   c) Study "A Child's Hymn."
4. The poetry of Robert Louis Stevenson:
   a) His life and place on the Chain of Christianity
   b) Memorize "The Land of Counterpane."

QUARTER TWO

INDIVIDUALITY OF NATIONS IN LITERATURE: HANS BRINKER, OR THE SILVER SKATES

1. God's Principle of Individuality in literature:
   a) The author—Mary Mapes Dodge—the singing spirit:
      (1) Her individuality and literary contributions, St. Nicholas
      (2) Her purpose in writing the book
   b) Holland's individuality:
      (1) Geographic: Complete map of the Netherlands to include cities mentioned in the book.
      (2) Holland's contributions on the Chain of Christianity:
         (a) Asylum for all refugees
         (b) Second home of the Pilgrims
         (c) Home of Rembrandt—Biblical artist
      (3) Holland's contributions to America:
         (a) Dutch settlement in New York
         (b) Supported the colonies during the American Revolution: "In love of liberty and in the defense of it, Holland has been our example."—Benjamin Franklin
         (4) Character of the people
         (5) Customs and cuisine
         (6) Flemish art; Dutch architecture
2. Study and summarize each element of the classic using the Notebook Method for literature.
3. Vocabulary studies
4. Principles derived from Hans Brinker:
   a) "God's Principle of Individuality"
   b) Christian character
5. Special Day Celebration: Dutch Day
   a) Costumes, hats, and klompen
   b) Art class: "A Visit to the Rijksmuseum in Amsterdam" (See StoneBridge Art Guide.)
   c) "Language of the Mills"
   d) Dutch folk songs, dance, and a craft
   e) A "Visit to Leiden"
   f) Dutch breakfast and vocabulary
   g) Complete a composition.
6. Test
7. Play available: Hans Brinker, or The Silver Skates: A Play of Old Holland in Three Acts, adapted by Tom Taggart, 1937, 1964. Samuel French, Inc. 25 West 45th St., NY, NY 10036

QUARTER THREE

BIOGRAPHY: JOHANN SEBASTIAN BACH, THE BOY FROM THURINGIA

1. The authors: Opal Wheeler and Sybil Deucher
2. Biography as a type of literature: character is causative; plot and setting are secondary; definitions.
3. Christian character:
   a) King David, the musician
   b) Jesus Christ is our model.
4. Using the words of the author, summarize the elements of the classic using the Notebook Approach.
5. Germany and liberty: home of Christian music
   a) Germany's place on the Chain of Christianity
   b) Map work
   c) Contributions:
      (1) Martin Luther and the Reformation
      (2) First printing press; Gutenberg Bible
      (3) Hymns and Christmas carols
      (4) Contributions to the arts
      d) The German character
6. Historical setting: Baroque Period in Western Civilization (1600–1750)
7. Johann Sebastian Bach:
   a) Family life
   b) Childhood influences; his education and role of the church
   c) Bach the musician and his instruments
   d) Bach: "the composer for all seasons"
      (1) All his music was written to worship God and to glorify Him.
      (2) Unity with diversity: individuality of style
      (3) Preludes and Fugues; Cantatas; Masses
      (4) Influence on other composers: Mozart, Beethoven, Mendelssohn, and Brahms
8. Listen to the music of Bach and be able to identify types and also receive his message.
9. Celebrate with a Bach Tea:
   a) Formal tea with German baked goods.
   b) Attend Bach piano or organ concert.
10. Complete the study with a composition.

THE CHILDREN'S POETS AND POETRY

1. Henry Wadsworth Longfellow: his life and place on the Chain of Christianity
   a) Poet of the American home and hearth
   b) Sweet singer of America
2. Longfellow's poetic style
3. Read "The Children's Hour."
4. Memorize "The Arrow and the Song."

QUARTER FOUR

CHILDREN'S CLASSICS: THE LION, THE WITCH, AND THE WARDROBE

1. The study and delight of a fairy tale:
   a) Fantasy and the imagination
   b) Action carried out by mythical creatures, animals, and humans
2. Analogy and Biblical symbolism
3. The individuality of the author: C. S. Lewis and his contributions on the Chain of Christianity
4. Summarize the elements of the classic using the Notebook Approach (one page for each element using the words of the author):
   a) Setting
   b) Plot
   c) Characters
   d) Theme
   e) Style
5. Christian themes:
   a) Good triumphs over evil.
   b) Insight into truth and man's basic nature

WILLIAM SHAKESPEARE—BARD OF THE BIBLE: THE MERCHANT OF VENICE

1. The life and contributions of Shakespeare, master playwright; the Christ in Shakespeare's works
2. Elizabethan England and customs
3. Drama:
   a) History and timeline of drama
   b) Drama on the Chain of Christianity
   c) Elements of a play
   d) Definitions: comedy, tragedy, soliloquy, dramatis personae, playwright, aside
   e) The Globe Theater
4. Brief study and notebook record of The Merchant of Venice:
   a) Dramatis personae: identify the key characters.
   b) Complete simple summaries for setting, plot, and characters by acts using the most important scenes.
   c) Study negative and positive conflicts between characters.
5. Study Portia's soliloquy on "mercy"; complete a Key Word Study on "mercy"; "Mercy seasons justice!"—theme of drama.
6. Read aloud from Lamb's Tales or Chute's Stories and read excerpts from Shakespeare.
7. Memorize Portia's soliloquy on "mercy."
8. Perform The Merchant of Venice (3rd grade adaptation available from F.A.C.E.).
9. Test

Fourth Grade Literature Curriculum

Three Forty-five-minute Periods/Week

PURPOSE

1. Inspire the highest standard of the English language.
2. Exercise the God-given gift of communication.
3. Cultivate and refine language skills.
4. Establish the Bible as the greatest literary masterpiece.
5. Plumb the riches of great and noble classics and poems.
6. Restore literature to its chronology in the history of liberty and the character of nations.
7. Instill a lifetime love and enjoyment of classic literature.

TEACHER OBJECTIVES

1. Inspire an appreciation of language towards its mastery for speech and composition through the highest models of literature.
2. Develop the imagination of mental imagery through classics that produce a love for Christian ideals and learning.
3. Impress literary tastes and aesthetic sensibilities.
4. Establish a knowledge about literature:
   a) Types of literature
   b) Qualities of literature
   c) Elements of a classic
   d) R. J. Slater's seven loves of literature
5. Build an enriched, Biblical vocabulary.
6. Develop skills of Biblical reasoning and critical thinking from leading ideas, principles, and literary themes.
7. Form the character of the American Christian Republic in each student.

TEACHER RESOURCES

1. Holy Bible
2. *A Family Program for Reading Aloud*, Slater, 1991.
3. *Bequest of Wings*, Duff, 1954.
4. *Enjoyment of Literature*, Boas and Smith, 1934.
5. *Doorways to Poetry*, Untermeyer, 1938.
6. *American Literature and English Literature*, Long.
7. *Home Book of Verse*, Stevenson, 1967.
8. *American History in Verse*, Stevenson, 1975.
9. *The Book of Life*, Hall and Wood, (1923–1953 editions).
10. *Christ in the Fine Arts*, Maus, 1938.
11. *Stories from Shakespeare*, Chute, 1956.
12. *The Story of Phyllis Wheatley*, Graham, 1949.
    See resource list after chapter 6 for full citations.

DEFINITION OF LITERATURE

1. "Learning; acquaintance with letters or books; comprehends a knowledge of language, classics, history, rhetoric, logic, geography, etc." (Noah Webster's 1828 *Dictionary*)
2. "The expression of life in words of truth and beauty; the written record of man's spirit—his thoughts, emotions, and aspirations."
3. "The handmaid of history, unveiling the human soul, revealing man as a doer of deeds and a dreamer of dreams."

METHODS

1. Students are taught the four steps of learning through the Notebook Approach. They know the notebook as their tool of learning and practice daily stewardship of it. They continue developing notebook skills by recording notes, completing maps, drawing and coloring illustrations, and correcting and filing papers. Research skills are taught. Reason and Relate Questions are assigned in class, and students are taught how to write out their answers. Learning is assessed through compositions, poetry, quizzes, essay tests, and the notebook.
2. The teacher reads the classic aloud while students read silently from personal copies.
3. The teacher lectures, places notes on the chalkboard, and holds classroom discussions including Reason and Relate Questions for verbal and written responses.
4. Students practice the art of writing using the words of the author for writing poetry, compositions, and essays.
5. Memory work is assigned from selected poems, oratory, and dramas.
6. The students are taught how to articulate and write out answers to Reason and Relate Questions and how to take essay tests.

ENRICHMENT

1. Timelines, map work, art masterpieces, displays, and bulletin boards highlight the classics and poems studied.
2. Classroom projects and crafts
3. Music, drama, and art related to the literature enrich and celebrate the curriculum.
4. Christian history field study tours
5. Special Day celebrations:
   Quarter 2: Colonial Day (in conjunction with the study of colonial America in history)
   Quarter 3: Treasure Island Day
   Quarter 4: Liberty Day

KEY DEFINITIONS

1. prose
2. poetry
3. setting
4. characterization
5. plot
6. theme
7. style
8. rhyme
9. rhythm
10. metaphor
11. simile
12. alliteration
13. drama
14. playwright
15. dramatis personae
16. couplets
17. protagonist
18. antagonist
19. soliloquy
20. contrast

STUDENT PERFORMANCE

1. **Research**: Master elementary vocabulary of literature and poetry; build research skills, particularly with the Bible and Webster's 1828 *Dictionary*.
2. **Reason**: Identify internal and external characteristics; practice independent reasoning; learn how to articulate verbal and written responses to Reason Questions and classroom discussions.
3. **Relate**: Begin applying leading ideas and principles through questions, essays, poems, compositions, guided projects, and drama to personal life and circumstances. Learn how to answer Relate Questions.
4. **Record**: Notebook filed with notes, vocabulary studies, maps, illustrations, compositions, poems, essays, homework assignments, and tests; poetry and oratory recitations; dramatic performances.

LITERATURE SELECTIONS STUDIED

1. The Book of Proverbs in the Bible
2. Poetry of Alfred Noyes
3. Poetry of Henry Wadsworth Longfellow
4. *Carry On, Mr. Bowditch*, Latham
5. Poetry of Phyllis Wheatley
6. *Treasure Island*, Stevenson
7. *The Secret Garden*, Burnett
8. Poetry of William Wordsworth
9. *Julius Caesar*, Shakespeare

Fourth Grade Literature Curriculum

QUARTER ONE

INTRODUCTION TO LITERATURE
1. Define literature.
2. Identify the qualities of literature.
3. Characterize and define literary types in elementary curriculum:
   - a) Prose
   - b) Poetry
   - c) Fiction
   - d) Non-fiction
   - e) Biography
   - f) Letters
   - g) Essay
   - h) Drama
4. Define the literary elements of a classic.
5. Describe Slater's seven loves inspired by literature.

THE LITERATURE OF THE BIBLE: PROVERBS
1. Bible holds the highest standard of literary excellence; source and seedbed of literature and liberty.
2. Bible is the textbook from which emanates the heart of all knowledge.
3. Identify types of Biblical literature: Didactic Poetry ("Words of the wise").
   - a) Define:
     - (1) Proverb: concise moral truth
     - (2) Acrostic
   - b) Contrast wisdom and foolishness.
   - c) Personification of wisdom: Proverbs 8
   - d) Memorize Proverbs 8:5–23.
   - e) Choral readings
4. Selections from the book of Proverbs:
   - a) Praise of wisdom, chapters 1–9
   - b) Principles of prudence, chapters 10–24

THE CHILDREN'S POETS AND POETRY
1. Define rhythm, rhyme scheme, meter, alliteration.
2. Identify types of poetry:
   - a) Lyrical poetry of the Bible
   - b) Rhymes of childhood
   - c) Historical poetry
   - d) Nonsense verse
   - e) Inspirational verse
3. The poetry of Alfred Noyes:
   - a) His life and place on the Chain of Christianity
   - b) Identify and discuss the literary qualities of rhyme and rhythm.
   - c) Read and memorize a portion of "The Highwayman."
4. America's "sweet singer" Henry Wadsworth Longfellow:
   - a) His place on the Chain of Christianity
   - b) Read "The Village Blacksmith."

QUARTER TWO

BIOGRAPHY: CARRY ON, MR. BOWDITCH FATHER OF AMERICAN MATHEMATICS
1. The author: Jean Lee Latham
2. Biography as a type of literature: character is causative; plot and setting are secondary; definitions.
3. America's Christian character:
   - a) Jesus Christ is our model.
   - b) American Christian character model: the Pilgrim dynamic
   - c) Complete study of Bowditch's character
4. The setting: Colonial America and Salem
   - a) History of Salem, Derby's Wharf
   - b) Life in a seaport
   - c) Character of the people
   - d) Salem's contributions to the Gospel and the Revolutionary War
   - e) Complete a map of the world with Salem trade routes.
5. A study of colonial navigation:
   - a) Terms and vocabulary
   - b) Instruments
   - c) Chandlery
   - d) Ships, schooners, and privateers
   - e) "Sailing by ash breeze"
   - f) Celestial navigation
   - g) Seafaring life
6. Life as an apprentice and the role of self-education
7. Nathaniel Bowditch's place and contributions on the Chain of Christianity:
   - a) Father of American mathematics
   - b) Navigator who wrote the U.S. Navy's "Seaman's Bible"
   - c) Astronomer
8. Using the words of the author, summarize the elements of the classic using the Notebook Approach.
9. Field study tour to colonial seaport
10. Test

THE CHILDREN'S POETS AND POETRY
1. The life and poetry of Phyllis Wheatley, African slave:
   - a) Setting: Colonial Boston
   - b) Read and study her poem: "To His Excellency General Washington."
2. Read "Paul Revere's Ride" by Henry Wadsworth Longfellow.

QUARTER THREE

INDIVIDUALITY OF NATIONS IN LITERATURE: TREASURE ISLAND
1. God's Principle of Individuality in literature:
   - a) The author—Robert Louis Stevenson—Tusitala, "Teller of Tales," and his life, character, and contributions to literature as an author and a poet; purpose in writing the book.
   - b) Key Nations and Classics—Great Britain:
     - (1) Geographic individuality; map work
     - (2) Character and disposition
     - (3) Contributions on the Chain of Christianity:
       - (a) English language
       - (b) The Bible in English (KJV)
     - (4) Contributions to America:
       - (a) English Bible
       - (b) Strong character: love of liberty; respect for laws; initiative; enterprise
       - (c) Great works of literature
2. Read and summarize each element of the classic in the words of the author using the Notebook Method for literature.
3. Vocabulary studies; glossary of terms
4. Pirates and piracy in history
5. Principles derived from Treasure Island:
   - a) "Conscience is my most sacred property."
   - b) America's Christian character
   - c) Principle of Christian Self-Government
6. Celebration: Treasure Island Day
   - a) Costumes
   - b) Keep a "Pirate's Log":
     - (1) Identifying ships and their parts
     - (2) Navigational instruments
     - (3) Life on board an 18th-century ship; watches
   - c) Knot tying, sail making, and crafts
   - d) Eat victuals.
   - e) Sing sea chanteys.
   - f) Listen to "A Pirate's Yarn."
   - g) A treasure hunt
7. Test

QUARTER FOUR

CHILDREN'S CLASSICS: THE SECRET GARDEN
1. The study of fiction
2. The individuality of the author: Frances Hodgson Burnett
3. Develop an appreciation of language and the art of description.
4. Record the elements of the classic using the words of the author:
   - a) Setting:
     - (1) Life in England
     - (2) The secret garden
   - b) Plot
   - c) Characters
   - d) Theme
   - e) Style
5. Design and plant a garden.
6. Test

THE CHILDREN'S POETS AND POETRY
1. William Wordsworth: his life and contributions on the Chain of Christianity
2. Read and discuss several poems:
   - a) Read "The Happy Warrior."
   - b) Study and memorize "The Rainbow."

WILLIAM SHAKESPEARE—BARD OF THE BIBLE: JULIUS CAESAR
1. The life and contributions of Shakespeare, master playwright and poet; the Christ in Shakespeare's works
2. Elizabethan England and customs
3. Drama:
   - a) History and timeline of drama
   - b) Drama on the Chain of Christianity
   - c) Elements of a play
   - d) Definitions: tragedy, soliloquy, aside, iambic pentameter, blank verse, pun, conceit, conspiracy, tyranny, coward
   - e) The Globe Theater
4. Brief study and notebook record of Julius Caesar:
   - a) Dramatis personae: identify the key characters.
   - b) Historical setting and background on Roman life
   - c) Complete simple summaries for setting, plot, and characters by acts using the most important scenes.
   - d) Study negative and positive conflicts between characters.
5. Read aloud from Stories from Shakespeare by Marchette Chute and Shakespeare's play.
6. Test

Fifth Grade Literature Curriculum

Three Forty-five-minute Periods/Week

PURPOSE

1. Inspire the highest standard of the English language.
2. Exercise the God-given gift of communication.
3. Cultivate and refine language skills.
4. Establish the Bible as the greatest literary masterpiece.
5. Plumb the riches of great and noble classics and poems.
6. Restore literature to its chronology in the history of liberty and the character of nations.
7. Instill a lifetime love and enjoyment of classic literature.

DEFINITION OF LITERATURE

1. "Learning: acquaintance with letters or books; comprehends a knowledge of language, classics, history, rhetoric, logic, geography, etc." (Webster's 1828 Dictionary)
2. "The expression of life in words of truth and beauty; the written record of man's spirit—his thoughts, emotions, and aspirations."
3. "The handmaid of history, unveiling the human soul, revealing man as a doer of deeds and a dreamer of dreams."

KEY DEFINITIONS

1. prose	11. simile
2. poetry	12. foreshadow
3. setting	13. drama
4. characterization	14. playwright
5. plot	15. dramatis personae
6. theme	16. couplets
7. style	17. protagonist
8. rhyme	18. antagonist
9. rhythm	19. soliloquy
10. metaphor	20. contrast

TEACHER OBJECTIVES

1. Inspire an appreciation of language towards its mastery for speech and composition through the highest models of literature.
2. Develop the imagination of mental imagery through classics that produce a love for Christian ideals and learning.
3. Impress literary tastes and aesthetic sensibilities.
4. Establish a knowledge about literature:
   a) Types of literature
   b) Qualities of literature
   c) Elements of a classic
   d) R. J. Slater's seven loves of literature
5. Build an enriched, Biblical vocabulary.
6. Develop skills of Biblical reasoning and critical thinking from leading ideas, principles, and literary themes.
7. Form the character of the American Christian Republic in each student.

METHODS

1. Students are taught the four steps of learning through the Notebook Approach. They know the notebook as their tool of learning and practice daily stewardship of it. They continue developing notebook skills by recording notes, completing maps, drawing and coloring illustrations, and correcting and filing papers. Research skills are taught. Reason and Relate Questions are assigned in class, and students are taught how to write out their answers. Learning is assessed through compositions, poems, quizzes, essay tests, and the notebook.
2. The teacher reads the classic aloud while students read silently from personal copies. Portions of Little Women are assigned to be read at home.
3. The teacher lectures, places notes on the chalkboard, and holds classroom discussions including Reason and Relate Questions for verbal and written responses.
4. Students practice the art of writing using the words of the author for writing poetry, compositions, and essays.
5. Memory work is assigned for recitation from selected poems, oratory, and dramas.
6. The students are taught how to articulate and write out answers to Reason and Relate Questions and how to take essay tests.

STUDENT PERFORMANCE

1. **Research:** Master elementary vocabulary of literature and poetry; build research skills, particularly with the Bible and Webster's 1828 Dictionary.
2. **Reason:** Identify internal and external characteristics; practice independent reasoning; learn how to articulate verbal and written responses to Reason Questions and classroom discussions.
3. **Relate:** Begin applying leading ideas and principles through questions, essays, poems, compositions, guided projects, and drama to personal life and circumstances. Learn how to answer Relate Questions through the application of lessons learned through studying classic literature.
4. **Record:** Notebook filed with notes, vocabulary studies, maps, illustrations, compositions, poems, essays, homework assignments, and tests; poetry and oratory recitations; dramatic performances.

TEACHER RESOURCES

1. Holy Bible
2. A Family Program for Reading Aloud, Slater, 1991.
3. Bequest of Wings, Duff, 1954.
4. Enjoyment of Literature, Boas and Smith, 1934.
5. Doorways to Poetry, Untermeyer, 1938.
6. American Literature and English Literature, Long.
7. Home Book of Verse, Stevenson, 1967.
8. American History in Verse, Stevenson, 1975.
9. The Book of Life, Hall and Wood, (1923–1953 editions).
10. Christ in the Fine Arts, Maus, 1938.
11. Stories from Shakespeare, Chute, 1956.
12. Invincible Louisa, Meigs, 1968.
13. F.A.C.E. Little Women Teacher's Syllabus, Slater.
    See resource list after chapter 6 for full citations.

ENRICHMENT

1. Timelines, map work, art masterpieces, displays, and bulletin boards highlight the classics and poems studied.
2. Classroom projects and crafts
3. Music, drama, and art related to the literature enrich and celebrate the curriculum.
4. Christian history field study tours
5. Special Day celebrations:
   Quarter 2: Drama based upon "Sketches of Christmas" from classic literature
   Quarter 3: Pioneers and Trailblazers Day
   Quarter 4: Liberty Day

LITERATURE SELECTIONS STUDIED

1. The Book of Ruth in the Bible
2. Poetry of Robert Frost
3. Little Women, Alcott
4. Poetry of Henry Wadsworth Longfellow
5. Trailblazer of the Sea, Latham
6. Macbeth, Shakespeare
7. Poetry of Edgar Allan Poe
8. The Wind in the Willows, Grahame

Fifth Grade Literature Curriculum

QUARTER ONE

INTRODUCTION TO LITERATURE

1. Define literature.
2. Identify the qualities of literature.
3. Characterize and define literary types in elementary curriculum:
   - a) Prose
   - b) Poetry
   - c) Fiction
   - d) Non-fiction
   - e) Biography
   - f) Letters
   - g) Essay
   - h) Drama
4. Define the literary elements of a classic.
5. Describe Slater's seven loves inspired by literature.

THE LITERATURE OF THE BIBLE: RUTH

1. Bible holds the highest standard of literary excellence; the source and seedbed of literature and liberty.
2. Bible is the textbook from which emanates the heart of all knowledge.
3. Identify literary elements of Biblical literature:
   - a) Historical settings
   - b) Providential plots
   - c) Themes or leading ideas
   - d) Individuality of writers
   - e) Character studies
4. Literary type from the Bible—Short Story:
   - a) Creates a central unity of impression.
   - b) Must be capable of being read in one sitting.
   - c) Deals with a single situation or purpose.
   - d) Demands artistry of the author.
5. Read the Book of Ruth and study:
   - a) Setting
   - b) Complete character studies:
     - (1) Naomi (wise mother-in-law who returned to Bethlehem).
     - (2) Ruth (faithful Moabitess daughter-in-law who became part of the lineage of David and Jesus; "a woman of excellence," Ruth 3:11).
     - (3) Boaz (foreshadowed the role of Jesus Christ as Kinsman-Redeemer).
   - c) Themes:
     - (1) "Blessed be the Lord which hath not left thee this day without a kinsman." (Ruth 4:14)
     - (2) "Whither thou goest, I will go . . . thy people shall be my people, and thy God my God." (Ruth 1:16)

THE CHILDREN'S POETS AND POETRY

1. The poetry of Robert Frost.
   His life and place on the Chain of Christianity
2. Memorize: "The Road Not Taken."

QUARTER TWO

INDIVIDUALITY OF NATIONS IN LITERATURE: *LITTLE WOMEN*

1. God's Principle of Individuality in literature:
   - a) The author: Louisa May Alcott and her life, character, and contributions to literature as an American authoress; purpose in writing the book (autobiographical of her childhood); her literary style.
   - b) Key Nations and Classics—The United States of America, New England:
     - (1) Geographic individuality; map work
     - (2) Historic individuality
     - (3) *Little Women* setting: Concord, Massachusetts during Civil War
     - (4) The New England mind and character
     - (5) Contributions on the Chain of Christianity
2. Read and summarize each element of the classic in the words of the author using the Notebook Method for literature.
3. Vocabulary and Key Word Studies centered about virtuous and honorable character
4. Principles derived from *Little Women*:
   - a) God's Principle of Individuality
   - b) America's Christian character; qualities of a godly and virtuous woman/mother and man/father
   - c) The Christian family, first sphere of government ordained by God, is the building block of nations.
   - d) Christian Principle of American Political Union
5. Celebrate "Christian Womanhood and Manhood" with a formal lunch at a restaurant.
   - a) An etiquette and manners course is taught the students.
   - b) Biblical principles of Christian womanhood and manhood are taught at Breakfast Club each Friday morning.
6. Test

THE CHILDREN'S POETS AND POETRY

1. The life and poetry of Henry Wadsworth Longfellow:
   - a) American poet of home and hearth
   - b) Contributions on the Chain of Christianity
2. Read "Christmas Bells" and "The Three Kings."

QUARTER THREE

COMPLETE *LITTLE WOMEN*

BIOGRAPHY: *TRAILBLAZER OF THE SEA,* MATTHEW MAURY, FATHER OF OCEANOGRAPHY

1. The author: Jean Lee Latham
2. Biography as a type of literature: character is causative; plot and setting are secondary; definitions.
3. America's Christian character:
   - a) Jesus Christ is our model.
   - b) American Christian character model: the Pilgrim dynamic
   - c) Complete study of Maury's Christian character as:
     - (1) Scientist: astronomer, geographer, and oceanographer
     - (2) Naval officer and navigator
     - (3) Virginian
     - (4) Husband
     - (5) Father
     - (6) Educator and author
4. The setting: era of invention and enterprise
5. A study of oceanography:
   - a) Maury's inspiration for charting the pathways of the seas: Psalms 8 & 107; Ecclesiastes 1:8
   - b) Terms and vocabulary
   - c) Map work of the ocean floor, currents, and winds
6. Using the words of the author, summarize the elements of the biography using the Notebook Approach.
7. Matthew Maury's contributions to America and the world
8. Field study tour
9. Test

QUARTER FOUR

THE CHILDREN'S POETS AND POETRY

1. Edgar Allan Poe: his life and contributions on the Chain of Christianity
2. Read and memorize "The Bells."

WILLIAM SHAKESPEARE— BARD OF THE BIBLE: *MACBETH*

1. The life and contributions of Shakespeare, master playwright and poet; the Christ in Shakespeare's works
2. Elizabethan England and customs
3. Drama:
   - a) History and timeline of drama
   - b) Drama on the Chain of Christianity
   - c) Elements of a play
   - d) Definitions: tragedy, comedy, soliloquy, aside, iambic pentameter, blank verse, pun, conceit, ambition
   - e) The Globe Theater
4. Brief study and notebook record of *Macbeth*— an epic struggle between good and evil:
   - a) Dramatis personae: identify the key characters.
   - b) Geographic setting and historic background of medieval Scotland:
     - (1) Map work
     - (2) Scotland's place on the Chain of Christianity
   - c) Complete simple summaries for setting, plot, and characters by acts using the most important scenes; characterization of Lady Macbeth.
   - d) Theme: "What shall it profit a man if he gain the whole world and lose his soul?" Matthew 16:26
5. Read aloud from *Stories from Shakespeare* by Marchette Chute and Shakespeare's play.
6. Test

CHILDREN'S CLASSICS: *THE WIND IN THE WILLOWS*

1. The study of an animal tale: "Every animal, by instinct, lives according to his nature. Thereby, he lives wisely, and betters the traditions of mankind." —K. Grahame
2. The individuality of the author: Kenneth Grahame; his purpose for writing the book
3. Record the elements of the classic using the words of the author:
   - a) Setting
   - b) Plot
   - c) Characters
   - d) Theme
   - e) Style

Sixth Grade Literature Curriculum

Three Forty-minute Periods/Week

PURPOSE

1. Inspire the highest standard of the English language.
2. Exercise the God-given gift of communication.
3. Cultivate and refine language skills.
4. Establish the Bible as the greatest literary masterpiece.
5. Plumb the riches of great and noble classics and poems.
6. Restore literature to its chronology in the history of liberty and the character of nations.
7. Instill a lifetime love and enjoyment of classic literature.

TEACHER OBJECTIVES

1. Inspire an appreciation of language towards its mastery for speech and composition through the highest models of literature.
2. Develop the imagination of mental imagery through classics that produce a love for Christian ideals and learning.
3. Impress literary tastes and aesthetic sensibilities.
4. Establish a knowledge about literature:
   a) Types of literature
   b) Qualities of literature
   c) Elements of a classic
   d) R. J. Slater's seven loves of literature
5. Build an enriched, Biblical vocabulary.
6. Develop skills of Biblical reasoning and critical thinking from leading ideas, principles, and literary themes.
7. Form the character of the American Christian Republic in each student.

TEACHER RESOURCES

1. Holy Bible
2. *A Family Program for Reading Aloud*, Slater, 1991.
3. *Bequest of Wings*, Duff, 1954.
4. *Enjoyment of Literature*, Boas and Smith, 1934.
5. *Doorways to Poetry*, Untermeyer, 1938.
6. *American Literature and English Literature*, Long.
7. *Home Book of Verse*, Stevenson, 1967.
8. *American History in Verse*, Stevenson, 1975.
9. *The Book of Life*, Hall and Wood, (1923–1953 editions).
10. *Christ in the Fine Arts*, Maus, 1938.
11. *English Literature—Sir Walter Scott Teacher's Syllabus*, Slater, F.A.C.E.

See resource list after chapter 6 for full citations.

DEFINITION OF LITERATURE

1. "Learning; acquaintance with letters or books; comprehends a knowledge of language, classics, history, rhetoric, logic, geography, etc." (*Webster's 1828 Dictionary*)
2. "The expression of life in words of truth and beauty; the written record of man's spirit—his thoughts, emotions, and aspirations."
3. "The handmaid of history, unveiling the human soul, revealing man as a doer of deeds and a dreamer of dreams."

METHODS

1. Students are taught the four steps of learning through the Notebook Approach. They know the notebook as their tool of learning and practice daily stewardship of it. They continue developing notebook skills by recording notes, completing maps, drawing and coloring illustrations, and correcting and filing papers. Research skills are taught. Reason and Relate Questions are assigned in class, and students are taught how to write out their answers. Learning is assessed through compositions, poems, quizzes, essay tests, and the notebook.
2. The teacher reads the classic aloud while students read silently from personal copies. Portions of the classics are assigned to be read at home.
3. The teacher lectures, places notes on the chalkboard, and holds classroom discussions including Reason and Relate Questions for verbal and written responses.
4. Students practice the art of writing using the words of the author for writing poetry, compositions, and essays.
5. Memory work is assigned for recitation from selected poems, oratory, and dramas.
6. The students are taught how to articulate and answer Reason and Relate Questions and how to take essay tests.

ENRICHMENT

1. Timelines, map work, art masterpieces, displays, and bulletin boards highlight the classics and poems studied.
2. Classroom projects and crafts
3. Music, drama, and art related to the literature enrich and celebrate the curriculum.
4. Christian history field study tours
5. Special Day celebrations:
   Quarter 2: Christmas Cameos from the Classics
   Quarter 3: Ivanhoe Day
   Quarter 4: Liberty Day

KEY DEFINITIONS

1. prose
2. poetry
3. setting
4. characterization
5. plot
6. theme
7. style
8. rhyme
9. rhythm
10. metaphor
11. simile
12. foreshadow
13. drama
14. playwright
15. dramatis personae
16. couplets
17. protagonist
18. antagonist
19. soliloquy
20. contrast

STUDENT PERFORMANCE

1. **Research:** Master elementary vocabulary of literature and poetry; build research skills, particularly with the Bible and Webster's 1828 *Dictionary*.
2. **Reason:** Identify internal and external characteristics; practice independent reasoning; learn how to articulate verbal and written responses to Reason Questions and classroom discussions.
3. **Relate:** Begin applying leading ideas and principles through questions, essays, poems, compositions, guided projects, and drama to personal life and circumstances. Learn how to answer Relate Questions through the application of lessons learned through studying classic literature.
4. **Record:** Notebook filed with notes, vocabulary studies, maps, illustrations, compositions, poems, essays, homework assignments, and tests; poetry and oratory recitations; dramatic performances.

LITERATURE SELECTIONS STUDIED

1. The Epistles
2. *Sir Walter Scott: Wizard of the North*, Schultz
3. Poetry of John Greenleaf Whittier
4. *Ivanhoe*, Scott
5. *A Christmas Carol*, Dickens
6. Poetry of Henry Wadsworth Longfellow
7. *Twelfth Night*, Shakespeare
8. Poetry of Julia Ward Howe
9. Poetry of James Russell Lowell

Sixth Grade Literature Curriculum

QUARTER ONE	QUARTER TWO	QUARTER THREE	QUARTER FOUR

INTRODUCTION TO LITERATURE
1. Define literature.
2. Identify the qualities of literature.
3. Characterize and define literary types in elementary curriculum:
  a) Prose *d)* Non-fiction *g)* Essay
  b) Poetry *e)* Biography *h)* Drama
  c) Fiction *f)* Letters
4. Define the literary elements of a classic.
5. Describe Slater's seven loves inspired by literature.
 	
THE LITERATURE OF THE BIBLE: EPISTLES
1. Bible holds the highest standard of literary excellence; the source and seedbed of literature and liberty.
2. Bible is the textbook from which emanates the heart of all knowledge.
3. Identify literary elements of Biblical literature:
  a) Historical settings
  b) Providential plots
  c) Themes or leading ideas
  d) Individuality of writers
  e) Character studies
4. Literary type from the Bible—Letters
5. Read Philippians and study.
 	
BIOGRAPHY: *SIR WALTER SCOTT: WIZARD OF THE NORTH*
1. The author: Pearle Henriksen Schultz
2. Biography as a type of literature: character is causative; plot and setting are secondary; definitions.
3. Scotland's individuality and place on the Chain of Christianity:
  a) Map work; study the flora of the heath.
  b) Brief historical overview of Scotland
  c) Contributions that advanced the Gospel
4. Study the biography: record influences and qualities of Scott's Christian character: "He was a patient, dutiful, reverent son; a generous, compassionate, tender husband; and honest, careful, and most affectionate father." (Long's *English Literature*)
5. Scott's home: Abbotsford; read his descriptive poetry about Scotland.
6. Scott's contributions:
  a) Created the historical novel; revitalized history as a source for dramatic fiction.
  b) Identified Christianity as a main force in history, character, and government.
  c) Set a standard for a vitality and quality of historical novels.
	***A CHRISTMAS CAROL*: CHARLES DICKENS**
	1. The individuality and contribution of Charles Dickens
	2. The setting of Victorian England
	3. The purpose, effect, and spirit of this "carol"
	4. The five "staves" of the book
	5. Identification of setting, plot, characterization, theme, and style in the Notebook Approach
	6. Writing characterizations and essays on theme
	
	INDIVIDUALITY OF NATIONS IN LITERATURE: *IVANHOE*
	1. God's Principle of Individuality in literature:
	  a) The author: Sir Walter Scott and his literary style:
	    (1) Most of his novels have Christian themes and Biblical principles.
	    (2) Scott was a moralist, concerned with the nobility of character.
	    (3) His friendship and character helped many other authors.
	  b) Key Nations and Classics—England:
	    (1) Geographic individuality; map work
	    (2) Contributions of England on the Chain of Christianity
	2. The setting of *Ivanhoe*: medieval England during the Anglo-Norman period of history, during the reign of Richard the Lion-Hearted
	3. Historic background:
	  a) Feudalism and the need for written law to identify the limits of government and the rights of the individual
	  b) The Crusades and Jerusalem
	  c) Richard Coeur de Lion and Prince John
	  d) Contrast the Saxon, Norman, and Jewish character of twelfth-century England.
		INDIVIDUALITY OF NATIONS IN LITERATURE: *IVANHOE*
		1. This classic requires two nine-week quarters to teach and read aloud.
		2. Study chivalry and its pagan and Christian elements. Contrast Biblical qualities of conduct with those of chivalry.
		3. A study of knighthood, castles, coats of arms, and medieval armament
		4. Read and summarize each element of the classic in the words of the author using the Notebook Method for literature.
		5. Complete vocabulary and Key Word Studies.
		6. Test
		7. Celebrate the curriculum with an *Ivanhoe* Day:
		  a) Costumes
		  b) Games of medieval England:
		    (1) Archery
		    (2) Jousting
		  c) Create marionettes using the *Ivanhoe* characters and have students write a play from their study or perform a passion play from the period.
		  d) Medieval feast
		  e) Music and dance of medieval England
			POETS AND POETRY
			1. The life and poetry of Henry Wadsworth Longfellow:
			  a) American poet of home and hearth
			  b) Contributions on the Chain of Christianity
			2. Read and memorize "A Psalm of Life."
			
			WILLIAM SHAKESPEARE— BARD OF THE BIBLE: *TWELFTH NIGHT*
			1. The life and contributions of Shakespeare, master playwright and poet; the Christ in Shakespeare's works
			2. Elizabethan England and customs
			3. Drama:
			  a) History and timeline of drama
			  b) Drama on the Chain of Christianity
			  c) Elements of a play
			  d) Definitions: tragedy, comedy, soliloquy, aside, iambic pentameter, blank verse, pun, conceit, ambition
			  e) The Globe Theater
			4. Brief study and notebook record of *Twelfth Night*:
			  a) Dramatis personae: identify the key characters.
			  b) Historic background of Twelfth Night merrymaking
			  c) Setting: Yugoslavia
			  d) Complete simple summaries for setting, plot, and characters by acts using the most important scenes.
			5. Read aloud from Shakespeare's play.
			6. Test
			
			CHILDREN'S POETS AND POETRY
			1. The study of patriotic poetry
			2. Study and memorize the "Battle-Hymn of the Republic," by Julia Ward Howe.
			3. Read the "Flower of Liberty," by Oliver Wendell Holmes.
			4. Read "The Ship of State," by Henry Wadsworth Longfellow.

Seventh Grade Literature Curriculum

God's Principle of Individuality in Author and Literary Type

PURPOSE

1. To present literature as a subject influenced by Christianity's westward move to the New World; America traced from pagan times to the Christian era.
2. The subjects of literature, the types of literature, and the authors of literature all were affected by the Gospel of Grace and redemption through Christ.
3. To study the types of literature through selected examples from classics.

DEFINITION OF LITERATURE

1. "Learning; acquaintance with letters or books; comprehends a knowledge of language, classics, history, rhetoric, logic, geography, etc." (Webster's 1828 Dictionary)
2. "The expression of life in words of truth and beauty; the written record of man's spirit—his thoughts, emotions, and aspirations."
3. "The handmaid of history, unveiling the human soul, revealing man as a doer of deeds and a dreamer of dreams."

KEY DEFINITIONS

1. type	13. narrative
2. poetry	14. fiction
3. essay	15. dialogue
4. short story	16. genre
5. novel	17. epic
6. drama	18. fable
7. biography	19. allusion
8. autobiography	20. myth
9. prose	21. individuality
10. character	22. unity
11. epistle	23. realism
12. romance	24. tragedy

TEACHER OBJECTIVES

1. To cultivate and refine language skills towards the goal of developing masterful communication.
2. To evaluate and comprehend the distinctives of all types of literature: poetry, short story, essay, novel, drama, and biography.
3. To develop the method of Biblical reasoning, reflecting from Biblical principles and primary sources.
4. To create a record of the study in the notebook by the standards of order, neatness, completeness, and accuracy.
5. To cultivate literary appreciation and analysis skills.
6. To lead students to relate and apply Biblical principles to their lives.
7. To develop composition style and competence.
8. To build the vocabulary, discussion skill, oral presentation, debate, and oratory.
9. To grasp God's Principle of Individuality in author and literary style.

METHODS

1. The Notebook Approach is the tool of mastery of literary types. The words of the author are excerpted and recorded to illustrate literary analysis. Literary elements are identified and documented. Composition and essay methods of learning and testing are used.
2. The classic selections are read aloud by the teacher and discussed.
3. Research is done on the author, the background of the selection, and the nation, language, and geographic setting.
4. The Shakespeare study culminates in the production of the selected play.
5. The poetry project includes the study of one poet, his whole body of work, and the writing of original poetry.
6. Five forty-minute periods/week

STUDENT PERFORMANCE

1. **Research:** Master the vocabulary of the types of literature. Identify the individuality of the setting—nations whose literary works are studied, geographically, historically, governmentally.
2. **Reason:** Evaluate styles of various authors and compare styles and their effects. Identify the principles underlying various themes in the works studied. Cause to effect reasoning in analysis of characterization, plot, theme, and style.
3. **Relate:** Written character analysis and literary analysis. Discussion, debate, oral reading and presentation, oratory, and interpretation.
4. **Record:** The notebook completed as a record of the study, illustrated and well-documented.

TEACHER RESOURCES

1. *Literature Curriculum Guide*, Slater, 1997.
2. *A Family Program for Reading Aloud*, Slater, 1991.
3. *CHOC*, I, Hall, 1960.
4. *Enjoyment of Literature*, Boas and Smith, 1934.
5. *Handbook to Literature*, Thrall and Hibbard, 1936.
6. *Doorways to Poetry*, Untermeyer, 1938.
7. *The Abolition of Man*, Lewis, 1947.

See resource list after chapter 6 for full citations.

ENRICHMENT

1. Weave the art and music masterpieces of the nation and period into the study of the literature selections.
2. Attend a performance of a drama; a poetry reading; a short story reading.
3. Produce the Shakespeare drama.

STUDENT RESOURCES

1. *Short Stories*, Schweikert
2. *Essays Old and New*, Jameson
3. *David Copperfield*, Dickens
4. Shakespeare selection
5. *Webster's 1828 Dictionary*
6. The Bible
7. *Home Book of Verse*, Stevenson
8. *American History in Verse*, Stevenson

Seventh Grade Literature Curriculum

QUARTER ONE	QUARTER TWO	QUARTER THREE	QUARTER FOUR

QUARTER ONE

INTRODUCING LITERARY TYPES

The Biblical models of literary types:
1. Definition of literature
2. Qualities of literature

POETRY

The literary type that best expresses the beauty, joy, nobility, heroism, and the knowledge of God, His Creation, and His hand in history. "The poetry of the Bible is found in the lyric poetry of the Psalms which are poems of religious feelings.... Parallelism identifies this Hebrew poetry."—Ryken
1. Poetry of the Bible
2. Enjoying poetry
3. Poetry vs. prose
4. The music of poetry
5. Patterns of poetry
6. Terms of poetry
7. Memory work and poetry
8. The study of selected poets: their character and contribution
9. Writing original poetry

THE ESSAY

A literary type for the development of ideas as a means of identifying the liberty of the individual and Biblical principles of government.
1. Paul's epistles—selected portions, e.g., 1 Cor. 13, "Love"; Heb. 11, "Faith."
2. The history of the essay and its masters: Montaigne, Bacon, Locke, Holmes, Emerson, Dickinson. Study selections including *Farmer's Letters*.
3. Principles of essay writing
4. Writing essays

SPEECHES
1. Discussion of the elements of rhetoric: elocution, the voice, articulation, inflection, emphasis and accent, modulation, gesture, and practical direction.
2. Examples of famous orations and orators:
   a) Lincoln's Gettysburg Address.
   b) Patrick Henry's Address to the House of Burgesses
   c) Daniel Webster's Address on the completion of Bunker Hill Monument, *CHOC*, I, p. 416.
3. Memorize portions.

QUARTER TWO

THE SHORT STORY

A highly specialized type of prose fiction that reflects the character and conscience of nations on the Chain of Christianity moving westward to America.
1. Examples of the short story in Scripture: parables, Ruth
2. Defining and evaluating the short story: selections from Hawthorne, Irving, Poe, Stockton, Hart, O. Henry

THE NOVEL *DAVID COPPERFIELD*

A fictionalized narrative exemplifying a unity of setting, characterization, plot elements, theme, and style. The novel illustrates the character of men and nations on the Chain of Christianity moving westward to America.
1. The novel as developed by Charles Dickens:
   a) Fiction
   b) The art of storybuilding
   c) Character development
2. Dickens: his individuality, contribution, and literary legacy
3. "A Child's Journey with Dickens," Kate Douglas Wiggin, pp. 141–45
4. Review of literary elements
5. Setting up the notebook for the study of a classic novel
6. The study of *David Copperfield*, by Charles Dickens
   a) Victorian England as setting
   b) The geography of England—map work
   c) Characterization; identifying the major and minor characters by internal and external qualities
   d) Style: the qualities of Dickens's style
      (1) Comic effects
      (2) Inflated diction
      (3) Play on curiosity of the reader
      (4) Flat characterization
      (5) Hyperbole
   (e) Theme: identifying the themes that are woven by Dickens into the story of David Copperfield:
      (1) The cruelty of the strong towards the weak
      (2) David's search for a father
      (3) The tender heart in the rough exterior
      (4) The nostalgic yearning for the past
      (5) The triumph of love over hate
      (6) The naiveté of youth
      (7) The correct basis of marriage

QUARTER THREE

CONTINUING *DAVID COPPERFIELD*

   (8) Plot: elements of plot identified as the novel is read aloud and discussed
   (9) Literary devices used by Dickens: foreshadowing, point of view, and irony
   (10) Word studies; vocabulary project
   (11) The notebook is the record of the study of *David Copperfield*—recording the excerpts exemplifying literary elements in the words of the author, theme exposition, and reasoning from Biblical principles.

DRAMA

"A picture or representation of human life in that succession and change of events that we call story, told by means of dialogue and presenting in action the successive emotions involved." —Thrall and Hibbard
1. Review the life and contributions of William Shakespeare, Bard of the Bible.
2. Drama on the Chain of Christianity
3. Select one of Shakespeare's plays for study and dramatic production.
4. Notebook record
5. Read the play aloud to the class.
6. "A Taste of Shakespeare": See pp. 170–71 for suggestions for writing and producing your own play:
   a) Script
   b) Costumes
   c) Scenery
   d) Props
   e) Producing and directing

QUARTER FOUR

BIOGRAPHY

The literary type reflects both the pagan and the Christian idea of man and government and the value of the individual as protected by law on the Chain of Christianity.
1. Principles of biography
2. Biography in the Scripture: David
3. *Abe Lincoln Grows Up*: reading a biography for analysis and instruction

AUTOBIOGRAPHY
1. Definition of autobiography
2. The great autobiographies reveal the character of the author as causative to the events of his life.
3. The autobiography reveals the philosophy of government which prevailed and its impact upon the fruition of the individual life.
4. The American Christian constitution was established to encourage the initiative, the individual enterprise, and the effort of anyone who caught a vision or glimpsed a goal of accomplishment.
5. Reading *The Autobiography of Benjamin Franklin*
6. Chart the development of Benjamin Franklin's education and the unfolding of his character. What is the relation between the two?

Eighth Grade Literature Curriculum

Contrasts between Pagan and Christian Idea of Man and Government in Literature

PURPOSE

1. The purpose of the literature course is to define and illumine the role of literature in history and in God's purpose for us today in comparing the pagan idea of man and government, the Roman idea of man and government, and the Christian idea of man and government.
2. To study the selected works of literature whole and through related primary source research.
3. To show the relationship of the individual to the state. *Among the numberless lessons which we may derive from the study of Grecian history, there is one which cannot be too often inculcated . . . the error of ascribing to the arts, to literature, and to politeness, that power of softening and correcting the human heart, which is, in truth, the exclusive prerogative of religion. Really to mend the heart, and purify the principle, is a deeper work than the most finished cultivation of the taste has ever been able to effect.*
—Hannah More (T & L, pp.160–62)

DEFINITION OF LITERATURE

1. "Learning; acquaintance with letters or books; comprehends a knowledge of language, classics, history, rhetoric, logic, geography, etc." (Webster's 1828 *Dictionary*)
2. "The expression of life in words of truth and beauty; the written record of man's spirit—his thoughts, emotions, and aspirations."
3. "The handmaid of history, unveiling the human soul, revealing man as a doer of deeds and a dreamer of dreams."

KEY DEFINITIONS

1. character
2. setting
3. plot
4. theme
5. style
6. allusion
7. epic
8. fable
9. novel
10. myth
11. personification
12. soliloquy
13. iambic
14. pentameter
15. narrative
16. blank verse
17. versification
18. genre
19. chivalry
20. feudalism
21. metaphor
22. mythology
23. simile
24. symbolism

TEACHER OBJECTIVES

1. To cultivate and refine language skills towards the goal of developing masterful communication.
2. To identify and comprehend the distinctive presuppositions of literature through themes and underlying principles.
3. To develop the method of Biblical reasoning, reflecting from Biblical principles and primary sources.
4. To create a record of the study in the notebook by the standards of order, neatness, completeness, and accuracy.
5. To cultivate literary appreciation and analysis skills.
6. To lead students to relate and apply Biblical principles to their lives.
7. To develop composition style and competence.
8. To build the vocabulary, discussion skill, oral presentation, debate, and oratory.
9. To grasp the Christian idea of man and government as it appears in literature.

METHODS

1. The Notebook Approach is the tool of mastery of literary types. The words of the author are excerpted and recorded to illustrate literary analysis. Literary elements are identified and documented. Composition and essay methods of learning and testing are used.
2. The classic selections are read aloud by the teacher and discussed.
3. Research is done on the author, the background of the selection, and the nation, language, or geography.
4. The geography of the general settings—the Greek, Roman, Hebrew, British, and American—are studied in depth and in relation to geography as the theater of history.
5. Five forty-minute periods/week

STUDENT PERFORMANCE

1. **Research**: Master the vocabulary of the types of literature. Identify the individuality of the setting—nations whose literary works are studied, geographically, historically, governmentally.
2. **Reason**: Evaluate styles of various authors and compare styles and their effects. Identify the principles underlying various themes in the works studied. Cause to effect reasoning in analysis of characterization, plot, theme, style.
3. **Relate**: Written character analysis and literary analysis. Discussion, debate, oral reading and presentation, oratory, interpretation.
4. **Record**: The notebook completed as a record of the study, illustrated and well-documented.

TEACHER RESOURCES

1. *Literature Curriculum Guide*, Slater, 1997.
2. *CHOC*, I & II, Hall, 1960, 1962.
3. *Teaching & Learning*, Slater, 1965.
4. *A Family Program for Reading Aloud*, Slater, 1991.
5. *Consider and Ponder*, Hall, 1976.
6. *Enjoyment of Literature*, Boas and Smith, 1934.
7. *Handbook to Literature*, Thrall and Hibbard, 1936.
8. *Doorways to Poetry*, Untermeyer, 1938.
9. *The Abolition of Man*, Lewis, 1947.
10. *A Wonder Book*, Hawthorne, 1966.

See resource list after chapter 6 for full citations.

ENRICHMENT

1. Weave the art and music masterpieces of the nation and period into the study of the literature selections.
2. Attend a performance of a drama; a poetry reading; a short story reading.
3. Dramatic monologues of selections from readings
4. Produce a melodrama.

STUDENT RESOURCES

1. *The Walls of Windy Troy: A Biography of Heinrich Schliemann*, Brayer
2. *The Odyssey*, Homer
3. *Ben Hur: A Tale of the Christ*, Wallace
4. *The Story of King Arthur and His Knights*, Pyle
5. *Men of Iron*, Pyle
6. *The Idylls of the King*, Tennyson
7. *The Courtship of Miles Standish*, Longfellow
8. *Hamlet*, Shakespeare
9. *Webster's 1828 Dictionary*
10. The Bible

Eighth Grade Literature Curriculum

QUARTER ONE

CONTRAST OF PAGAN AND CHRISTIAN ELEMENTS IN LITERATURE

1. Review of literary elements, definitions, devices, and types of literature exemplified by Scripture
2. Pagan history and literature

CLASSICAL MYTHS

A Christian view of Greek and Roman gods and goddesses. Readings: Nathaniel Hawthorne's *A Wonder Book*—selections for discussion.

PAGAN EPICS AND THE AUTHORS

The gold of Troy—Readings: *The Walls of Windy Troy: A Biography of Heinrich Schliemann* by Marjorie Brayer. Biblical archeology.

HOMER AND THE GREEKS
THE ODYSSEY, THE FITZGERALD TRANSLATION

1. Background and setting: geography and history of Greece; the contribution of Greece; the religion, athletics, background.
2. Epic poem, poetic qualities—meter, epithets, similes.
3. Contrast Jews, Greeks, and Romans in light of religion, language, and law.
4. Homer and his contribution
5. The pagan idea of man: the relationship of the individual to the state
6. Characterization: Penelope, elemakhos, Odysseus, etc.
7. Homer's style: use of flashback; cliffhanging: honoring moral attributes such as courage and skill in war.
8. Greek language and alphabet; study of John 1:1 in Greek. Roman philosophers: pagan thinkers on statesmanship and life contrasted with Gospel—Seneca, *Epistles* excerpt; Cicero, *Essays, Letters* excerpts.

QUARTER TWO

CHRISTIAN HISTORY AND LITERATURE

Background reading: Neander, *T & L*, pp. 210–15; *Consider and Ponder*, pp. 7–18; Mosheim, *CHOC*, II, pp. 92–138.

MAJOR NOVEL STUDY: *BEN HUR: A TALE OF THE CHRIST* BY LEW WALLACE

1. The author, Lew Wallace: individual character, style, contribution
2. The setting of the novel: Jerusalem, Antioch, Rome
3. The background of the period—chariot racing, galley slavery
4. The genre—historical novel
5. Plot elements
6. Character elements: Balthazar, Gaspar, Melchior, Massala, Judah, Iras, Tirzah, Simonides
7. Contrast Rome, Jerusalem, and the Christian future in terms of source of government, type of religion, effect on the individual.
8. Notebook study emphasizing character and Biblical principles
9. Identifying elements of setting, theme, style, plot, characterization in the words of the author
10. Vocabulary study from *Ben Hur*: geographic identities in English vocabulary—wady, absinthe, jasmine, etc.

Read aloud the entire unabridged classic enjoying the language, the story line, the drama, and culture. Students discuss and identify the various themes and principles.

QUARTER THREE

CHRISTIANITY AND ENGLISH CHIVALRY

1. Howard Pyle's *The Story of King Arthur and His Knights*; the Arthur legend in England; geography and setting.
2. Ideals of chivalry
3. "For when, in pursuing this history, I have come to consider the high nobility of spirit that moved these excellent men to act as they did, I have felt that they have afforded such a perfect example of courage and humility that anyone might do exceedingly well to follow after their manner of behavior. . . . For I believe that King Arthur was the most honorable, gentle knight who ever lived in all the world. And those who were his fellows of the Round Table—taking him as their looking-glass of chivalry—made, altogether, such a company of noble knights that it is hardly to be supposed that their like will ever be seen again in this world."

—Howard Pyle's Foreword.

4. *Men of Iron*: Howard Pyle—Outside reading and book review

ALFRED LORD TENNYSON'S *IDYLLS OF THE KING*.

1. Tennyson's style, character, contribution
2. Idyll—a long descriptive narrative poem
3. Symbolism and allegory in *Idylls*
4. Review of Victorian literature and poetry
5. Poetic form: iambic pentameter, blank verse
6. The ideals of knighthood and chivalry—Bulfinch
7. Characterization of Arthur, Guinevere, Lancelot, Merlin
8. Memorization and dramatic interpretation of portions of *Idylls*

WILLIAM SHAKESPEARE: *HAMLET*

1. The life and contributions of William Shakespeare: "He was not of an age but for all time."—Ben Jonson (First Folio)
   a) Master playwright and poet
   b) Bard of the Bible
   c) The Christ in Shakespeare's works

QUARTER FOUR

DRAMA: *HAMLET*
WILLIAM SHAKESPEARE CONTINUED

2. Elizabethan England and customs
3. Study of drama:
   a) History and timeline
   b) Drama on the Chain of Christianity
   c) Elements of a play
   d) Vocabulary
   e) The Globe Theater
4. Notebook Study of *Hamlet*:
   a) Dramatis personae: identify key characters.
   b) Historical setting and background: Denmark
   c) Complete simple summaries for setting, plot, and characters by acts.
   d) Identify pagan and Christian themes.
   e) Study negative and positive conflicts between characters.

POETRY: *THE COURTSHIP OF MILES STANDISH*
HENRY WADSWORTH LONGFELLOW

1. Introduction to Poetry
2. The Author: Henry Wadsworth Longfellow
   a) Short biographical sketch
      (1) "Poet of the American Home and Hearth"
      (2) Foremost of the Fireside Poets
   b) Love of the Pilgrims and their customs
   c) Contributions on the Chain of Christianity
3. History of *The Courtship of Miles Standish*:
   a) The influence of the Bible and Scripture references in the poem
   b) Longfellow's poetic style
4. The Pilgrim Dynamic—Seed of our Christian Republic:
   a) The Pilgrim account
   b) Model of American Christian character
   c) Providential timeline of liberty
5. Biographical sketches:
   a) Miles Standish
   b) John Alden
   c) Priscilla Alden
6. The notebook study and the five literary elements
7. Writing themes from the poem
8. Memorization and dramatization of sections of the poem

Ninth Grade English Literature Curriculum

Tracing the Nobler Stream of Liberty

PURPOSE OF THE COURSE

1. Literature is taught as the handmaid of history.
2. The study of literature enables us to enjoy God's gift of communication and exercise and refine our language skills.
3. The purpose of the English Literature IIA course is to define and illuminate the role of English language and literature in history and in God's purpose for our lives.
4. This course will examine the rich heritage of English literature and the contributions of the Anglo-Saxons in Christ, His Story of liberty.
5. Six periods of literature are studied: Anglo-Saxon, Anglo-Norman, Wycliffe/Chaucer, English Reformation, Elizabethan, and Puritan.

PRINCIPLES TAUGHT

1. English literature's contribution to the Chain of Christianity in the Anglo-Saxon, the Anglo-Norman, Wycliffe/Chaucer, English Reformation, Elizabethan, and Puritan Ages of literature
2. Tracing the thread of liberty for the individual through the Anglo-Saxon character and the planting of the Gospel in English laws and civil government
3. The influence of the Bible and the vitality of Biblical Christianity in English writers

LEADING IDEAS

1. Our Anglo-Saxon heritage of the English Bible; local self-government; language; character of King Alfred
2. The Norman Conquest brings feudalism, French, and centralized government. Magna Charta—the first protection of individual rights in law. Character: William the Conqueror
3. Wycliffe's translation of a Bible "for the government of the people, by the people, for the people." Chaucer writes about the individual in Middle English.
4. An age of wars; Reformation and spiritual freedom; Renaissance; study of Greek and Roman classics; opening of the New World
5. Age of nationalism, patriotism, peace. 1560 Geneva Bible, 1588 Spanish Armada. Exploration and colonization. 1611 King James Bible begins spread of individual liberty.
6. Puritan struggle for righteousness and liberty. Monarchy overthrown, commonwealth established. Reform of national church. Pilgrims separate, flee to Holland, then to America.

COURSE GOALS

1. That each student continue mastering effective, lucid expression in both writing and speaking for the propagation of the Gospel and successful enterprise in his life.
2. That each student's scholarship be further developed through required primary source readings and research through the Portfolio Project.
3. That each student's aesthetic tastes and sensibilities be cultivated and nourished through the interdisciplinary study of the fine arts as they are woven throughout the curricula.
4. The student will participate in a reading and cultural analysis program, *Reading with Reason*, complete a research paper, write an original short story, produce original poetry.

REQUIREMENTS

1. The course consists of five classes each week that include the teaching of literature and instruction in English grammar, vocabulary, and composition.
2. The student notebook is the primary student text, organized as directed by the teacher, kept according to the standard, and graded three times during the year.
3. The *Reading with Reason* program is part of the English literature course during three quarters (see *Reading Curriculum Guide*); the Portfolio Project is due the remaining quarter.
4. The grade is derived from literature, English composition, and grammar: 40% from all quizzes and daily assignments; 35% from all major tests and projects; 15% for class participation; and 10% for notebook grade.
5. Five forty-five-minute periods/week

STUDENT PERFORMANCE

1. Students establish the habits of study and Biblical scholarship through the 4 R-ring method: cultivate the method of Biblical research; reflect and reason from the revelation of the Scripture and primary source materials; personally relate and apply Biblical principles to one's life; maintain a record for future reference.
2. Students effectively articulate ideas and concepts through essay writing, research papers, portfolio project, class discussions, and speeches.
3. Students deal with their own character and capacity for self-government through: thinking governmentally (cause to effect, choices to consequences); effective study habits; time management skills; productivity in quality and quantity which proceeds from Christian character.

TEACHER RESOURCES

1. *English Literature*, Long, 1945.
2. *Handbook to Literature*, Thrall and Hibbard, 1936.
3. *The Oxford Companion to English Literature*, 1985.
4. *Everyday Life in Roman and Anglo-Saxon Times*, Quennell
5. *Men of Iron*, Pyle, 1965.
6. *When Knights Were Bold*, Tappan, 1939.
7. *Geoffrey Chaucer of England*, Chute, 1936.
8. *Readings in T & L*, Slater, 1965; *CHOC*, I, 1960; II, 1962.
9. *A Reader's Guide to Religious Literature*, Batson, 1968.
10. *Short History of the English People*, Green, 1894.
11. *Enjoyment of Literature*, Boas and Smith, 1934.
12. *Doorways to Poetry*, Untermeyer, 1938.
13. Holy Bible
14. *The Noah Plan Reading Curriculum Guide* (for "Reading with Reason"), F.A.C.E., 1997.

See resource list after chapter 6 for full citations.

ENRICHMENT

1. In addition to the vital life of the classroom in studying whole classic works, discussing, and presenting research and study, the English literature course offers opportunities for further enrichment. Some suggestions follow:
2. Student publications: literary magazine, newspaper, and other creative writing as an outgrowth of the study of the styles of the major writers studied.
3. A poetry reading night in a local coffee shop (with permission of the owner); invite parents and friends to hear students recite and read dramatically from works studied and from students' original poetry.
4. Art exhibits, opera, and concerts featuring works from the periods studied or related to the literary works. Discussion afterwards to make the experience more personal and real.

STUDENT RESOURCES

1. *Beowulf*, trans. by Raffel
2. "The Seafarer" and selections from Anglo-Saxon literature
3. Caedmon, Cynewulf
4. Selection from *Asser's Life of King Alfred*
5. Selection from Malory's *Morte d'Arthur; The Pearl*
6. *Ivanhoe*, Scott (if not studied previously)
7. Wycliffe's Bible, selections
8. Chaucer: Prologue to *Canterbury Tales*
9. *Foxe's Book of Martyrs*
10. *Faerie Queene*, Spenser
11. *Voyages of the English Nation*, Hakluyt
12. Essays; Bacon; Poetry of Donne, Herbert
13. *Henry VIII*, Shakespeare
14. *Portable Milton*, Poetry, Essays, Epic
15. *The Pilgrim's Progress*, Bunyan

Ninth Grade English Literature Curriculum

QUARTER ONE

ANGLO-SAXON LITERATURE 450–1066

1. Introduction to English literature; timeline; qualities

2. Introduction to Anglo-Saxon period: the coming of the Angles and Saxons to Britain. Anglo-Saxon life and language; the Saxon Scop; love of the sea; scholarship in the monasteries

3. *Beowulf*—notebook study of characterization, plot, style, themes, setting. The epic and its meanings. What qualities of Anglo-Saxon character become identified with the English character? with American character? Memorization of lines from *Beowulf*

4. Map work: England and the invasions

5. Caedmon: What enabled Caedmon to produce such marvelous poems?

6. Alfred the Great, "Father of English Literature." Describe the contribution of Alfred to the Chain of Christianity.

7. Bede, "Father of English learning"

8. Boethius's *Consolation*; *The Anglo-Saxon Chronicle*; "The Seafarer"

9. *Reading with Reason:* "The Reach of Rome"

ANGLO-NORMAN LITERATURE 1066–1350

1. The background of the Anglo-Norman period. The Norman Invasion and its consequences. William, "the greatest general and statesman of his time." The Bayeux Tapestry. Describe how the Norman invasion affected literature.

2. Readings in chivalry: Malory's *Morte d'Arthur*; *When Knights were Bold*. Geoffrey's *History*; Layamon's *Brut*

3. The French language and its influence upon English giving feminine qualities and embellishment to the Anglo-Saxon

4. Magna Charta: King John is forced to yield certain "rights" to his barons—the beginning of rights for every freeman, *T & L*, pp. 347–48. (Continuing the study of Anglo-Norman literature)

5. "The Pearl"—with loss of liberty there is little imaginative literature written.

ESSAYS AND QUARTER EXAM

QUARTER TWO

WYCLIFFE AND CHAUCER 1350–1400

1. Introduction to the age of Wycliffe and Chaucer. The emerging of the individual and the nation, and England's mission: the Bible in English.

2. The age of three pilgrimages: the pilgrimage to truth—*Piers Plowman* and Christian revival; the pilgrimage to Canterbury—Chaucer and the individual in literature; the pilgrimage to Christ—Wycliffe, "the morning star of the Reformation" begins the Reformation with the common man for whom he translates the Gospel. The beginning of individual evangelism.

3. John Wycliffe. A powerful preacher whose followers were called "Lollards," a scholar, "Father of English prose," translated the gospels for use in his preaching. *T & L*, p. 166. What are the contributions of Wycliffe on the Chain of Christianity?

4. Geoffrey Chaucer: For the first time the individual of any occupation becomes a subject of writing. *The Canterbury Tales*, Chaucer's masterpiece. Study of the Prologue and the individuality of the various pilgrims. Memorization of passages. What principle did Chaucer restore to literature?

5. The English language reaches a peak in its preparation for bringing the Bible to the language of the people.

6. *Reading with Reason*, "The Hebrew Question"

ENGLISH REFORMATION 1400–1550

1. God prepares England for the Reformation. William Caxton learns printing and brings first press in 1475.

2. Erasmus, Dutch scholar, arrives at Cambridge in 1506, edits the New Testament in Greek with Latin translation resulting in the conversion of "Little Bilney" beginning the Reformation in England. Tyndale translates the Bible.

3. *Foxe's Book of Martyrs*, Bilney, Tyndale, Cranmer, Ridley, and Latimer

4. Preparation for the Pilgrims—invention, exploration, Columbus

QUARTER EXAM

QUARTER THREE

ELIZABETHAN LITERATURE 1550–1620

1. What preparations were taking place which would advance the Chain of Christianity?

2. From the Geneva Bible to the Pilgrims: Elizabeth's long reign enables literature to flower in order to produce the English Bible, first the Geneva then the King James Version. The defeat of the Spanish Armada, 1588.

3. Edmund Spenser, selections from *The Faerie Queene Book I*, The Poet's Poet. The setting is medieval chivalry, but Spenser envisions life as a challenge to individual Christian character. Memorization of lines. Explain Spenser's use of allegory as a means of introducing Christian idealism. What is the literary contribution of the Spenserian stanza?

4. Michael Drayton, poetry, "To the Virginia Voyage"

5. William Shakespeare, Bard of the Bible. His plays reference both the historical facts and the characters of the Bible and derive their religious principles and sentiments, as well as poetry, from God's written Word. *Henry VIII*: A thorough study of Shakespeare and the play using the notebook approach to record elements and to write expositions of the themes and style identified.

6. Portfolio Project—selected topic, preparation and presentations in quarter 3. (Continuing Elizabethan Period)

7. Francis Bacon *Essays*, "Of Riches," "Of Friendship," "Of Studies"

8. Hakluyt; Raleigh. Why was the Puritan Age and not the Elizabethan Age the age of religious freedom and individual liberty?

9. *Reading with Reason*: "Origins"

QUARTER EXAM

QUARTER FOUR

PURITAN AGE 1620–1660

1. Puritan struggle for righteousness and liberty. Monarchy overthrown, Commonwealth established. Reform of national church. Pilgrims separate, flee to Holland, then to America.

2. John Milton's *Paradise Lost*. Notebook study of the narrative poem. Identification of literary elements, style, and themes.

3. Study of Dore's paintings that depict *Paradise Lost*

4. George Herbert, poetry; John Donne, poetry

5. John Bunyan's *Pilgrim's Progress*. Notebook study of the allegory. Why was England called "a people of the Book?" How did America profit from the Puritan Age in England? Why has Bunyan appealed to Americans in every century? Is he still relevant today? John Milton had the greatest single influence of any author upon Americans. Identify his influence in the following areas: upon the clergy; upon the statesman of the American Revolution; upon educators in the new republic; in defense of Christianity. What ages does Herbert encompass in his poem, "The Church Militant"?

FINAL ESSAYS AND EXAM

Tenth Grade English Literature Curriculum

England Relinquishes Her Christian Heritage

PURPOSE OF THE COURSE

1. Literature is taught as the handmaid of history.
2. The study of literature enables us to enjoy God's gift of communication and exercise and refine our language skills.
3. The purpose of the English Literature IIB course is to define and illuminate the role of English language and literature in history and in God's purpose for our lives.
4. This course will examine the rich heritage of English literature and its contributions to America.
5. Five periods of literature are studied: Restoration, Eighteenth Century, Romanticism, Victorian, and Twentieth Century.

PRINCIPLES TAUGHT

1. England relinquishes her Christian heritage.
2. England's Christian heritage is seriously eroded by evolution, Marxism, and atheism.
3. In every generation, Christian writers restore the vitality of Biblical Christianity to literature:

   Milton! thou shouldst be living at this hour:
   England hath need of thee: she is a fen
   Of stagnant waters: altar, sword and pen,
   Fireside, the heroic wealth of hall and bower,
   Have forfeited their ancient English dower
   Of inward happiness. We are selfish men;
   —Wordsworth

LEADING IDEAS

1. Internal influences of Puritanism on the life and character of the nation and on literature. External reaction to Puritanism. Restoration of the monarchy.
2. Last of Stuart kings: 1689—William and Mary, Bill of Rights, toleration. Age of prose, newspapers, magazines, coffeehouses. Age of social progress. Liberty and property, taxation without representation. Loss of the American colonies.
3. Age of individualism and revolution. God or man the source of liberty? Adam Smith's capitalism in conflict with European mercantilism. Reform of society internal or external? Decline of individual Christian character.
4. England established as a constitutional monarchy. Industrial revolution and social injustice. Retreat of Christianity from marketplace. Rise of evolution, social Darwinism, socialism.
5. Influences of Fabian socialism in literature. Rise of the Irish school of writers. Decline of colonialism. Return of influence of the reformed faith.

COURSE GOALS

1. That each student continue mastering effective, lucid expression in both writing and speaking for the propagation of the Gospel and successful enterprise in his life.
2. That each student's scholarship be further developed through required primary source readings and research.
3. That each student's aesthetic tastes and sensibilities be cultivated and nourished through the interdisciplinary study of the fine arts as they are woven throughout the curricula.
4. The student will participate in a reading and cultural analysis program, *Reading with Reason*, complete a research paper, write an original short story, produce original poetry.

REQUIREMENTS

1. The course consists of five classes each week that include the teaching of literature and instruction in English grammar, vocabulary, and composition.
2. The student notebook is the primary student text, organized as directed by the teacher, kept according to the standard, and graded three times during the year.
3. The *Reading with Reason* program is part of the English literature course during three quarters; a research paper is due the remaining quarter.
4. The grade is derived from literature, English composition, and grammar: 40% from all quizzes and daily assignments; 35% from all major tests and projects; 15% for class participation; and 10% for notebook grade.
5. Five forty-five-minute periods/week

STUDENT PERFORMANCE

1. Students establish the habits of study and Biblical scholarship through the 4 R-ing method: cultivate the method of Biblical research; reflect and reason from the revelation of the Scripture and primary source materials; personally relate and apply Biblical principles to one's life; maintain a record for future reference.
2. Students effectively articulate ideas and concepts through essay writing, research papers, portfolio project, and class discussions and speeches.
3. Students deal with their own character and capacity for self-government through: thinking governmentally (cause to effect, choices to consequences); effective study habits; time management skills; productivity in quality and quantity which proceeds from Christian character.

TEACHER RESOURCES

1. *English Literature*, Long, 1945.
2. *Handbook to Literature*, Thrall and Hibbard, 1936.
3. *The Oxford Companion to English Literature*, 1985.
4. *The Story of English*, McCrum, Cran, MacNeil, 1986.
5. Readings in *T & L*, Slater; *CHOC*, I, II, Hall.
6. *A Reader's Guide to Religious Literature*, Batson, 1968.
7. *Short History of the English People*, Green 1894.
8. *Enjoyment of Literature*, Boas and Smith, 1934.
9. *Doorways to Poetry*, Untermeyer, 1938.
10. Holy Bible
11. *All God's Children and Blue Suede Shoes*, Myers, 1989.
12. *Norton's Anthology of English Literature*, Abrams, 1987.
13. *Painting in Britain*, Sunderland, 1976.
14. *The Noah Plan Reading Curriculum Guide* (for "Reading with Reason"), F.A.C.E., 1997.

See resource list after chapter 6 for full citations.

ENRICHMENT

1. The historical study of literature will be reinforced by parallel studies in the music and art of each age, establishing the causative seed of an artist's understanding of God, man, and government, and how that philosophical foundation affects his ideas of excellence and beauty in any art medium. The Baroque, Neoclassical, Romantic, Victorian, Impressionist, Expressionist, Cubist, and Pop art ideals will be discussed, using representative music and art in the classroom.
2. Student publications: literary magazine, newspaper, and other creative writing
3. Participation in Poetry Coffeehouse (see Grade 9)
4. Art exhibits, opera, and concerts featuring works from the periods studied or related to the literary works

STUDENT RESOURCES

1. Holy Bible
2. *Teaching and Learning*, Slater
3. *Songs of Innocence and Songs of Experience*, Blake
4. *The Lady of the Lake*, Scott
5. Poetry of William Wordsworth
6. *The Rime of the Ancient Mariner*, Coleridge
7. Poetry of John Keats
8. *Pride and Prejudice*, Austen
9. Poetry of Tennyson, Brownings
10. *Great Expectations*, Dickens
11. Poetry of A. E. Housman
12. *The Screwtape Letters*, Lewis
13. *Elements of Style*, Strunk and White

Tenth Grade English Literature Curriculum

QUARTER ONE

RESTORATION LITERATURE 1660–1700

1. The history and literature of the Restoration: external reaction to Puritanism. Charles II returns the evils of monarchy to the throne.
2. Internal influence of Puritanism: Puritan ideals embedded in English hearts gradually reassert themselves in the national life.
3. Influence of Puritan writers Milton and Bunyan. Biblical themes in literature—man's struggles with sin and his need of a Savior. Relationship between righteousness and liberty.
4. John Dryden's *Rules for Literature*. Prose, Poetry
5. Puritan writers on Government. Locke and Sidney search the Scriptures for the principles of government and the basis of civil liberty. *CHOC*, I, pp. 37, 50A, 51–60.
6. Algernon Sidney: Discourses concerning Government
7. John Locke: readings on his life: *CHOC*, I, pp. 51–56; *T & L*, pp. 353–54. Locke develops Biblically the idea that life, liberty, and property are from God. Locke defines man's obligations to God and how civil government protects God-given rights.
8. Samuel Pepys, *The Diary*
9. Newton's *Principia* identifies God as the basis of all scientific law. Modern science born through a Christian.
10. Revolution of 1688 steps towards a constitutional monarchy.

EIGHTEENTH CENTURY 1700–1800

1. Rise of parliamentary system, England's constitutional monarchy. Continuing struggle to identify principles of liberty with a Biblical source of law—internal restraint. Contrast of America's war of independence based upon Christian principles of liberty, and the anti-Christian conspiracy of the French Revolution.
2. The Age of Prose: political and historical writings; literary interest in society

QUARTER EXAM

QUARTER TWO

EIGHTEENTH CENTURY, CONTINUED

1. Alexander Pope Classicism: artificial elegance and formalism; poetry, essay
2. Jonathan Swift's satire, *Gulliver's Travels*
3. Joseph Addison, Richard Steele; the beginning of the modern essay: *The Tatler, The Spectator*
4. Samuel Johnson, the dictionary
5. James Boswell, *Life of Johnson*
6. Edmund Burke, selections from his speech on Conciliation with the Colonies
7. Poetry: selections from Thomas Gray, Cowper, Burns, Blake
8. Blackstone codifies the common or Christian law of the land—bestseller in America.
9. First novels have Christian concerns: *Robinson Crusoe*, Daniel Defoe.
10. Gibbon—the writing of history

AGE OF ROMANTICISM 1700–1850

1. Liberty of the individual: In contrast to the restraints of classicism, romantic individualism soars free in literature. It is an upward flight at first viewing only the beauties of nature and the finest ideals of man as he contemplates truth and beauty.
2. God or man the source of liberty: This age reflects the age-old struggle to identify man's source of liberty—either God-given or man-evolved and ultimately government-granted.
3. The Romantic Age produces many literary forms of idealism particularly the historical, romantic novel with its roots of character in the Anglo-Saxon, its manners in the age of chivalry, and its idealism in Christianity.
4. Poetry: Wordsworth, selections; Coleridge, *The Rime of the Ancient Mariner*; Byron, Shelley, Keats, Lamb
5. Scottish patriotism, *The Lady of the Lake*, Walter Scott; narrative poem
6. The Romantic novel: *Pride and Prejudice*, Jane Austen

QUARTER EXAM

QUARTER THREE

VICTORIAN AGE

1. In a period of Christianity's "falling away," some authors still express Christian, Biblical standards of life and character. What evidence is there of the inroads of evolution, Marxism, and socialism? Which writers are the "torch bearers" in this period? What answer does Dickens give to the problems of an industrial society? How can the change of emphasis be seen in the Christian socialist Ruskin?
2. Historical background and literary characteristics
3. Victorian poets: Tennyson, *Idylls of the King*; Robert and Elizabeth Browning, selected poetry; Francis Thompson
4. The Victorian novel: *Great Expectations*, Charles Dickens. Thorough notebook study of the novel identifying themes, style, and literary elements.
5. Survey of other novelists: George Eliot, *Silas Marner, Adam Bede*; Bronte sisters, Robert Louis Stevenson, Lytton
6. Macaulay, Carlyle, historians
7. Ruskin, prose

THE TWENTIETH CENTURY 1900–PRESENT

1. Influences of Fabian socialism in literature
2. Rise of the Irish school of writers. Decline of colonialism. Return of influence of the reformed faith.
   a) Rudyard Kipling, poetry
   b) H. G. Wells, prose
   c) John Galsworthy, novelist, plays
   d) J. M. Barrie, *Peter Pan*, plays
   e) Joseph Conrad, novelist
   f) John Masefield, poetry
   g) Alfred Noyes, poetry
   h) A. E. Housman, poetry
   i) George Bernard Shaw, plays, prose

QUARTER EXAM

QUARTER FOUR

THE TWENTIETH CENTURY, CONTINUED

   j) W. B. Yeats, poetry, plays
   k) John Synge, plays
   l) Lytton Strachey, biography
   m) C. S. Lewis, Christian fantasy
   n) *Perelandra, Screwtape Letters*
   o) T. S. Eliot, poetry
   p) W. H. Auden, poetry
   q) Dylan Thomas, poetry
   r) George Orwell, novelist
   s) Virginia Woolf, prose
   t) K. Mansfield, short story
   u) E. M. Forster, novelist
   v) Graham Greene, novelist, plays
   w) Aldous Huxley, prose
   x) C. P. Snow, prose
   y) J. R. R. Tolkien, fantasy

3. Describe the vitality and appeal of Kipling today. Identify Barrie's appeal in today's world of realism and cynicism.
4. Describe how Shaw took the conflict of Christianity versus socialism into the ideological rather than the religious area.
5. Which writers continued to debate Christianity as an intellectual experience?
6. Why do we owe so much to the Irish in the 20th century?
7. What must Christian writers do to restore the vitality of Biblical Christianity to literature?

FINAL EXAM

Eleventh Grade American Literature Curriculum

Planting the Seed of the American Christian Republic

PURPOSE OF THE COURSE

1. Literature is taught as the handmaid of history.
2. The study of literature enables us to enjoy God's gift of communication and exercise and refine our language skills.
3. American Literature IIIA inspires the highest standard of language through the greatest American literary masterpieces. The course examines the rich heritage of American literature that is our legacy as American Christians today.
4. Three periods of literature will be studied in depth: the Colonial Period, 1607–1765; the American Revolution Period, 1765–1787; and the Federal Period, 1787–1840.

COURSE GOALS

1. That each student continue mastering effective, lucid expression in both writing and speaking for the propagation of the Gospel and successful enterprise in his life.
2. That each student's scholarship be further developed through required primary source readings and research.
3. That each student's aesthetic tastes and sensibilities be cultivated and nourished through the interdisciplinary study of the fine arts as they are woven throughout the curricula.
4. The student will participate in a reading and cultural analysis program, *Reading with Reason*, complete a research paper, write an original short story, produce original poetry.

TEACHER RESOURCES

1. *American Literature*, Long, 1964.
2. *Webster's 1828 Dictionary*
3. *CHOC*, I, II, Hall, 1960, 1962.
4. *T & L*, Slater, 1965.
5. *Consider and Ponder*, Hall, 1976.
6. *Handbook to Literature*, Thrall and Hibbard, 1936.

See resource list after chapter 6 for full citations.

PRINCIPLES TAUGHT

1. Early American literature's contribution to the Chain of Christianity from the Colonial through the Federal periods
2. The principles of Christian character and self-government revealed through the writings of men and women who had a call from God to found a new nation and to plant their Puritan ideals of freedom and righteousness in the New World
3. The literature is their diaries, letters, historical records, and documents of liberty "written in a plain style, with singular regard unto the simple truth in all things." It reveals the Hand of God directing the course of human history for Christ and His Story.
4. "Religion stands on tiptoe in our land,
   Ready to pass to the American strand . . . .
   Then shall Religion to America flee:
   They have their times of Gospel,
      e'en as we." —George Herbert

REQUIREMENTS

1. The course consists of five classes each week that include the teaching of literature and instruction in English grammar, vocabulary, and composition.
2. The student notebook is the primary student text, organized as directed by the teacher, kept according to the standard, and graded three times during the year.
3. The *Reading with Reason* program is part of the English literature course during three quarters; a research paper is due the remaining quarter.
4. The grade is derived from literature, English composition, and grammar: 40% from all quizzes and daily assignments; 35% from all major tests and projects; 15% for class participation; and 10% for notebook grade.
5. Five forty-five-minute English and literature periods/week.

ENRICHMENT

1. The historical study of literature will be reinforced by parallel studies in the music and art of each age, establishing the causative seed of an artist's understanding of God, man and government, and how that philosophical foundation affects his ideas of excellence and beauty in any art medium. The Baroque, Neoclassical, Romantic, Victorian, Impressionist, Expressionist, Cubist, and Pop art ideals will be discussed, using representative music and art in the classroom.
2. Student publications: literary magazine, newspaper, and other creative writing
3. Participation in Poetry Coffeehouse (see Grade 9)
4. Art exhibits, opera, and concerts featuring works from the periods studied or related to the literary works

LEADING IDEAS

1. The Chain of Christianity
2. Colonial Period: Christian individualism in the parent colonies; *Captain John Smith's America: Of Plimoth Plantation*, William Bradford; William Penn; John Winthrop. Missionary Writers: Alexander Whitaker, John Eliot. Colonial Clergy: Thomas Hooker, Jonathan Edwards, Cotton Mather, Samuel Sewall.
3. Anne Bradstreet; colonial bestsellers
4. The American Revolution: influence of the clergy on a Biblical philosophy of government; literature in statesmanship; poetry, drama; satire
5. The Federal Period: first fruits of a Republic, liberty of the individual flowers in literature. Washington Irving, James Fenimore Cooper

STUDENT PERFORMANCE

1. Students establish the habits of study and Biblical scholarship through the 4 R-ring method: cultivate the method of Biblical research; reflect and reason from the revelation of the Scripture and primary source materials; personally relate and apply Biblical principles to one's life; maintain a record for future reference.
2. Students effectively articulate ideas and concepts through essay writing, research papers, portfolio project, and class discussions and speeches.
3. Students deal with their own character and capacity for self-government through: thinking governmentally (cause to effect, choices to consequences); effective study habits; time management skills; productivity in quality and quantity which proceeds from Christian character.

STUDENT RESOURCES

1. *Captain John Smith's America*, Lankford, ed.
2. *CHOC*, I, Hall
3. *Consider and Ponder*, Hall
4. *CHOC*, II, Hall
5. Selected poems of Anne Bradstreet
6. *Magnalia Christi Americana*, Cotton Mather
7. *Come Over and Help Us*, Slater
8. *The Journal of Major George Washington*
9. *The Autobiography of Benjamin Franklin*
10. Selected poems of Phillis Wheatley, Philip Freneau, and Francis Hopkinson
11. Selections from state papers
12. *The Deerslayer*, Cooper
13. *The Sketch Book*, Irving
14. Selected poems of William Cullen Bryant, and Edgar Allan Poe

THE NOAH PLAN © 1997 • FOUNDATION FOR AMERICAN CHRISTIAN EDUCATION

Eleventh Grade American Literature Curriculum

QUARTER ONE	QUARTER TWO	QUARTER THREE	QUARTER FOUR

COLONIAL PERIOD 1607–1765
1. The Chain of Christianity: summary of events in Old World preparation for America; America's heritage of Christian character
2. Identify each of the following writers as to (a) character of the man, (b) relationship to his colony, (c) individuality of his writings, (d) contribution to the Chain of Christianity:
3. Captain John Smith (1580–1631) of Virginia, earliest book in American literature. Study of selections from Smith
4. William Bradford (1590–1657), Governor of Plymouth Plantation, first American citizen, first American writer, historian of America's first Christian history. Study of entire excerpt from Bradford's history given in *Teaching and Learning America's Christian History: The Principle Approach*
5. William Penn (1644–1718), Proprietor, Quaker
6. John Winthrop (1588–1649), first governor of Massachusetts Bay Colony. Memorize "Little Speech on Liberty."
 	
Missionary Writers
1. Alexander Whitaker, Apostle to Virginia. Selections, "Good News from Virginia"
2. John Eliot, Apostle to the Indians. First Christian scholar in America. John Eliot's Indian Bible, 1663, the first Bible printed in America
3. Daniel Gookin, Magistrate; commander of colonial military forces; superintendent of Indians; co-worker with John Eliot in labor for Indians; originator of "taxation without representation"
 	
Colonial Clergy
1. Thomas Hooker, sermon preached in 1638, led to framing the "Fundamental Orders of Connecticut," first American constitution—the first constitution in the world based upon Biblical principles of government.
2. Jonathan Edwards, famous sermon, "Sinners in the Hands of an Angry God," begins the Great Awakening.
3. Cotton Mather, theologian and America's first biographer
4. Samuel Sewall, wrote first famous American diary of colonial life.
 	
QUARTER EXAM
	COLONIAL PERIOD 1607–1765 (CONTINUED)
	Poetry and Colonial Best Sellers
	1. Anne Bradstreet, selected poetry
	2. The *Bay Psalm Book*—1640. The first book printed in English America, compiled by Richard Mather, John Eliot, Thomas Welde.
	3. *New England Primer*—America's first textbook in education, issued before 1690
	
	The Influence of the Clergy
	Principles of Christianity and Government. An American Christian pastor, *T & L*, pp. 248–49; *C & P*, pp. 191–210; *CHOC*, I, pp. 372–90.
	
	REVOLUTIONARY PERIOD 1765–1787
	The pew and the pulpit have been educated to self-government. Election sermons from *CHOC* and *T & L*; Mayhew, Payson, Davies, Clark, Witherspoon, Stillman, and Muhlenberg
	
	Literature in Statesmanship. Selections read:
	1. James Otis: "The Rights of the British Colonies" (*CHOC*, II, pp. 368–96)
	2. John Dickinson: "Farmer's Letter" (*CHOC*, II, pp. 443–47)
	3. Samuel Adams: "The Rights of the Colonists" (*CHOC*, I, pp. 350–70)
	4. John Adams: "Timidity" (*CHOC*, II, p. 397)
	5. Thomas Jefferson, "Declaration of Independence"
	
	Famous Speeches
	1. Patrick Henry: "Give Me Liberty" (*CHOC*, II, p. 397)
	2. George Washington: "Farewell Address"
	
	QUARTER EXAM
		REVOLUTIONARY PERIOD 1765–1787 (CONT'D)
		America's Greatest Statesmen
		1. Benjamin Franklin, *Autobiography*
		2. *The Journal of Major George Washington*, an account of his first official mission for the governor of Virginia at age twenty-one. God's providential preparation of Washington.
		
		Letters
		1. Mercy Warren, America's first woman historian
		2. Correspondence of John and Abigail Adams
		
		Poetry of the Revolution
		1. Phillis Wheatley was brought on a slave ship in 1761. This remarkable girl learned the English language without any help from schools. She read and relished poetry and wrote some of her own, "To His Excellency General Washington." Philip Freneau, the poet of the American Revolution.
		2. Francis Hopkinson, political satirist and writer, "The Battle of the Kegs"
		3. Joel Barlow, "Hasty Pudding"
		
		QUARTER EXAM
			THE FEDERAL PERIOD 1787–1840
			First Fruits of a Republic
			1. Washington Irving—first man of letters; biographer of Columbus, Washington, Goldsmith
			2. Essayist, *The Sketch Book*. Historian, *Knickerbocker's History of New York*. Travels, *Tales of Alhambra*. Study selections.
			3. William Cullen Bryant, first poet of the Republic. Study selections.
			4. Edgar Allan Poe, study selected poetry.
			5. James Fenimore Cooper, *The Deerslayer*. Thorough study of the novel by the Notebook Approach.
			  a) Identify the style of Cooper and excerpt examples.
			  b) Characterize the major and minor characters according to internal and external qualities.
			  c) Study the geography of the setting and excerpt in the author's phrases his references to setting.
			  d) Identify the major themes of the novel and excerpt phrases that express the themes.
			  e) Identify the plot elements.
			
			FINAL EXAM

Twelfth Grade American Literature Curriculum

America Falls Away from Her Christian Founding and Character

PURPOSE OF THE COURSE

1. Literature is taught as the handmaid of history.
2. The study of literature enables us to enjoy God's gift of communication and exercise and refine our language skills.
3. American literature IIIB, studied in relation to the Chain of Christianity, defines and illumines the role of the subject in His Story and in our individual lives.
4. Three periods of literature will be studied in depth: the Civil War Period, 1840–1876; the National Expansion Period, 1876–1925; and the Twentieth-Century, 1925–Present.
5. The study of complex ideas and arguments expressed by others leads to discernment and the full exercise of personal, Biblical liberty.

COURSE GOALS

1. That each student continue mastering effective, lucid expression in both writing and speaking for the propagation of the Gospel and successful enterprise in his life.
2. That each student's scholarship be further developed through required primary source readings and research.
3. That each student's aesthetic tastes and sensibilities be cultivated and nourished through the interdisciplinary study of the fine arts as they are woven throughout the curricula.
4. The student will participate in a reading and cultural analysis program, *Reading with Reason*, complete a research paper, write an original short story, produce original poetry.
5. Studies in grammar, usage, rhetoric, and research are tailored to specific areas of discerned need each week.

TEACHER RESOURCES

1. *American Literature*, Long, 1964.
2. *Teaching & Learning*, Slater, 1965.
3. *CHOC*, I, II, Hall, 1960, 1962.
4. *Handbook to Literature*, Thrall and Hibbard, 1936.
5. *Enjoyment of Literature*, Boas and Smith, 1934.
6. *Idols for Destruction*, Schlossberg, 1983.
7. *How Should We Then Live*, Schaeffer, 1976.

See resource list after chapter 6 for full citations.

PRINCIPLES TAUGHT

1. America falls away from her Christian founding as Romanticism, Transcendentalism, Utopianism, individualism, factionalism, and atheism erode our Christian foundations: "If the foundation be destroyed, what can the righteous do?" Psalm 11:3
2. "Whenever the pillars of Christianity shall be overthrown, our present forms of republican government, and all the blessings which flow from them, must fall with them."

—Jedediah Morse

REQUIREMENTS

1. The course consists of five classes each week that include the teaching of literature and instruction in English grammar, vocabulary, and composition.
2. The student notebook is the primary student text, organized as directed by the teacher and kept according to the standard.
3. *Reading with Reason* is part of the English literature course during two quarters; the Senior Thesis is done second semester.
4. The grade is derived from literature, English composition, and grammar: 40% from all quizzes and daily assignments; 35% from all major tests and projects; 15% for class participation; and 10% for notebook grade.
5. Five forty-five-minute English and literature periods/week.

ENRICHMENT

1. The historical study of literature will be reinforced by parallel studies in the music and art of each age, establishing the causative seed of an artist's understanding of God, man and government, and how that philosophical foundation affects his ideas of excellence and beauty in any art medium. The Baroque, Neoclassical, Romantic, Victorian, Impressionist, Expressionist, Cubist, and Pop art ideals will be discussed, using representative music and art in the classroom.
2. Student publications: literary magazine, newspaper, and other creative writing
3. Participation in Poetry Coffeehouse (see Grade 9)
4. Art exhibits, opera, and concerts featuring works from the periods studied or related to the literary works

LEADING IDEAS

1. The American Christian character in the life of the Republic's Civil War Period: One nation under God endures; character of Lincoln and Lee; oratory, essayists, poets, novelists, historians
2. National Expansion Period: the diversity of America reflected in literature; first seeds of breakdown of Christian principles; the Chain of Christianity reaches California.
3. Christian literature of the regions and states
4. Twentieth Century: decline of Biblical standards of life and literature; the debunkers; the "lost" generation; the persistence of the American spirit; revival and restoration

STUDENT PERFORMANCE

1. Students establish the habits of study and Biblical scholarship through the 4 R-ring method: cultivate the method of Biblical research; reflect and reason from the revelation of the Scripture and primary source materials; personally relate and apply Biblical principles to one's life; maintain a record for future reference.
2. Students effectively articulate ideas and concepts through essay writing, research papers, portfolio project, and class discussions and speeches.
3. Students deal with their own character and capacity for self-government through: thinking governmentally (cause to effect, choices to consequences); effective study habits; time management skills; productivity in quality and quantity which proceeds from Christian character.

STUDENT RESOURCES

1. The Clay-Calhoun Debate; the Hayne-Webster debate; Lincoln
2. *The Glory and the Dream*, Musmanno
3. Selected poetry of Whittier and Holmes
4. *Evangeline*, Longfellow
5. Selected essays, Emerson
6. *Christian History of the Constitution*, Vols. I and II; *The Oregon Trail*, Parkman; selections from Prescott
7. "The Gentle Boy," Hawthorne
8. *The Country of the Pointed Firs*, Jewett; *The Notorious Jumping Frog of Calaveras County*, Twain; *The Outcasts of Poker Flat*, Harte; *The Thread That Runs So True*, Stuart; *My Antonia*, Cather.
9. Thoreau and Audubon: Contrasting philosophies of two naturalists; O. Henry
10. Poetry of Whitman, Poe, Sandburg, Lanier, Riley, Field, Dickinson, Masters, Robinson, Frost, Eliot, and Millay
11. Selected readings from Faulkner, Fitzgerald, and Hemingway

Twelfth Grade American Literature Curriculum

QUARTER ONE

THE CIVIL WAR PERIOD 1840–1876

Political Orators: Debating the balance between state and nation

1. Henry Clay (1777–1852), the "great compromiser"; Biography: "The Consequences of Secession"
2. John C. Calhoun (1782–1850), defender of states' rights; biography
3. Daniel Webster (1782–1852), "Liberty and Union, now and forever, one and inseparable." Biography: "Reply to Hayne"
4. Abraham Lincoln (1809–1865), 16th President of the United States, one nation under God; biography by Carl Sandburg; Second Inaugural Address; Gettysburg Address; *The Glory and the Dream: Abraham Lincoln before and after Gettysburg*, Michael A. Musmanno; "A Heart That Yearned for God," Frederick Owen
5. Robert E. Lee—biography and letters

Poets

1. Henry Wadsworth Longfellow (1807–1892), "Sweet Singer of America," *Evangeline*, and selections of poetry
2. John Greenleaf Whittier (1807–1892), Quaker poet of the Republic; biography, selected poetry
3. Oliver Wendell Holmes (1809–1894), the beginnings of American humor, selected poetry
4. James Russell Lowell (1819–1891), representative of American life and letters: selected poetry—"June" from "The Vision of Sir Launfal," "Once to Every Man and Nation," "Lincoln" from ode recited at Harvard Commemoration
5. Sidney Lanier (1842–1881), music in poetry: "Song of the Chattahoochee," "The Marshes of Glynn," "A Ballad of Trees and the Master"
6. Walt Whitman (1819–1892), poet of democracy, glorification of self. "Song of the Open Road," "A Ballad of Trees and the Master," America Singing," "For You O Democracy," "When I Heard the Learn'd Astronomer," "Song of Myself," "A Noiseless Spider" all from *Leaves of Grass*.
7. Ralph Waldo Emerson (1803–1882), nature lyrics, meditative verse. "The Humble Bee," "The Rhodora," "The Snow-Storm," "Concord Hymn," "So Nigh Is Grandeur"

QUARTER EXAM

QUARTER TWO

THE CIVIL WAR PERIOD 1840–1876 (CONT'D)

Prose Writers of the Republic

1. Ralph Waldo Emerson, the cult of individualism: "Self-reliance"; from "The American Scholar," from "Man the Reformer"
2. Oliver Wendell Holmes, American essays and conversation: from "The Autocrat of the Breakfast Table"
3. James Russell Lowell, literary essays: from "Among My Books"
4. Henry David Thoreau (1817–1862), individualist naturalist: selections from *Walden* and *Civil Disobedience*
5. John James Audubon (1785–1851), creationist naturalist: selections from *Delineations of American Scenery and Character* and his *Journals*
6. Nathaniel Hawthorne (1804–1864), American Puritan: biography; "The Gentle Boy"

Review the Civil War Period.

1. How could a civil war occur in a Christian nation?
2. Why is the Gettysburg Address the most famous oration ever given?
3. What was George Bancroft's major theme concerning America?
4. Why was Longfellow the most loved American poet?
5. What were the subjects of Hawthorne's writings?
6. What qualities in Emerson's writings enabled him to inspire other great men?
7. What does Emerson's success tell us about Christianity in America at that period?
8. Discuss and research the two great elements of testing the Christian principle of American Political Union:
   a) Local self-government and national union acting in harmony. See *CHOC*, I, pp. 148–50 and *CHOC*, II, pp. 3–15.
   b) Discuss " . . . whether that nation, or any nation so conceived and so dedicated can long endure."

QUARTER EXAM

QUARTER THREE

NATIONAL EXPANSION PERIOD 1876–1925

Diversity of American character: Regional Literature

1. Maine: Sarah Orne Jewett, *The Country of the Pointed Firs*
2. New York City: *Best Short Stories*, O. Henry
3. The South: *Uncle Remus Stories*, Joel Chandler Harris
4. Mississippi: *The Notorious Jumping Frog of Calaveras County*, Mark Twain
5. Westward movement: *The Oregon Trail*, Francis Parkman
6. California: *Best Stories of Bret Harte*, "The Outcasts of Poker Flat"
7. Midwest: *My Antonia*, Willa Cather; *Death Comes for the Archbishop*

Poetry

1. James Whitcomb Riley, Eugene Field, Emily Dickinson, Sidney Lanier, Edgar Lee Masters, Carl Sandburg, Robert Frost
2. Review of National Expansion Period: contrast two American writers of this period in terms of their ability to make their local scene appealing or interesting.
   a) What unique contribution to the short story did O. Henry make?
   b) . . . did Bret Harte make?
   c) Why was this age called an age of "realism" in literature?
   d) What was Christianity's relationship to it?

QUARTER EXAM

QUARTER FOUR

THE TWENTIETH CENTURY 1925–

1. Decline of Biblical standards of life and literature; the "lost" generation; the persistence of the American Spirit; revival and restoration
2. Historical background; World War I and the "lost" generation
3. Novelists: F. Scott Fitzgerald, Ernest Hemingway, William Faulkner, John Steinbeck, Jack London, Upton Sinclair, Pearl Buck
4. Biography and Autobiography: *Up from Slavery*, Booker T. Washington; *Biography*, George Washington Carver; *Story of My Life*, Helen Keller; *The Thread That Runs So True*, Jesse Stuart; *Alone*, *Discovery*, Richard E. Byrd; *The Spirit of St. Louis*, Charles A. Lindbergh; *Reminiscences*, Douglas MacArthur
5. Poets: Edna St. Vincent Millay; Edgar Lee Masters, Edwin Arlington Robinson, T. S. Eliot, Robert Frost, Carl Sandburg; other modern poets and the philosophies they reflect
6. American Drama: Tennessee Williams, Thornton Wilder, Arthur Miller, Maxwell Anderson, Robert Sherwood
7. Will the American Christian of the twentieth century return to the Gospel purpose of America and to the support of those unique Biblical principles which established our Christian constitutional form of government allowing us individual liberty and opportunity?

FINAL EXAM

A Teaching Plan for Literature
in the Principle Approach

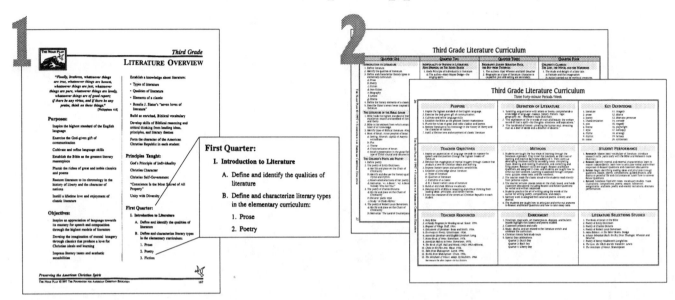

- Review the grade-level guideline in *The Noah Plan Program Notebook*.
- Select the unit to be developed and define Poetry and Prose (ex. Third Grade, First Quarter)

- Examine the Literature Curriculum Chart for the grade level chosen (ex. Third Grade pp. 14–15).
- Highlight the details of each component to be taught in this unit.

Review this curriculum guide for direction in teaching components.

Use the teacher's Plan Sheet (p. 35) for the components of preparing to teach literature.

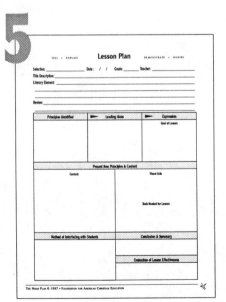

Write the lesson plan using the format (pp. 38–39). See sample lesson plans following.

Quarterly Plan Sheet for Teaching Literature

Quarter _____ Week _____ Teacher _____ Grade _____

WEEK	CLASSIC OR LITERARY SELECTION	LITERARY ELEMENTS IDENTIFIED	BACKGROUND OF AUTHOR OR LITERARY WORK	PRINCIPLES AND LEADING IDEAS	COMPOSITION AND NOTEBOOK WORK	ENRICHMENT
1						
2						
3						
4						
5						
6						
7						
8						
9						

Unit Study

TELL • EXPLAIN   DEMONSTRATE • INSPIRE

Subject: _Literature_   Grade: _K_   Teacher: _Mrs. Beale_

Title Description: _The Tale of Peter Rabbit, Beatrix Potter_

Literary Element: _Setting, characters, theme, and vocabulary are identified (through reading and discussion)._

Review: _Definitions of setting, characters (internal and external aspects) are reviewed. These literary elements have been a component of kindergarten literature lessons throughout the year._

PRINCIPLES IDENTIFIED ➤	LEADING IDEAS ➤	EXPRESSION
The individuality of a character can be seen through his/her actions or choices. Our actions/choices result in consequences (good or bad).	Peter's disobedience placed him in danger and caused him to become ill.	**GOAL OF LESSON:** To identify several basic literary elements of a classic (setting, characters, leading ideas) To enlarge the students' vocabulary and teach an appreciation for literature and language To help the students apply the lessons learned in the story to their own lives

PRESENT NEW PRINCIPLES & CONTENT

CONTENT:

1. Read The Tale of Peter Rabbit.
2. Identify the setting of the story. (A rabbit hole under the fir tree, Mr. MacGregor's garden)
3. Identify and discuss the internal and external aspects of the characters. (Peter Rabbit, Mrs. Rabbit, Flopsey, Mopsey, Cotton Tail, Mr. MacGregor)
4. Identify and discuss new vocabulary: mischief p. 13, unfortunately p. 30, currant p. 14, gooseberry p.33, naughty p. 18, implored p. 33, dreadfully p. 29, exert p. 33.
5. Discuss each word and have a student use it in a sentence.
6. Discuss the theme through questions about leading ideas:
   What were Mrs. Rabbit's instructions to her children before she went out?; What had happened to Peter's father?; Did the rabbit children obey Mrs. Rabbit?
   Where did Peter go?; What happened to Peter in Mr. MacGregor's garden? What happened when Peter got home?

VISUAL AIDS

The watercolor illustrations in The Tale of Peter Rabbit by Beatrix Potter

Individual color pictures of characters in the story

Pictures of a garden (to represent the setting)

TOOLS NEEDED FOR LESSON:

A pocket chart for the display of the items mentioned above would be helpful.

The above mentioned visual aids and a copy of The Tale of Peter Rabbit

METHOD OF INTERACTING WITH STUDENTS

1. Reading and discussing the story and its elements (using suggestions above)
2. Create a character chart corporately (list Peter's internal and external character qualities).
3. Chose a related activity to enrich and broaden the student's understanding.
   Suggestions: Discuss gardening; examine the seeds of plants discussed in the story (lettuce, carrots, parsley, French beans, etc.); Plant some of the seeds mentioned in the story and watch them grow; Sample some of the foods mentioned in the story (carrots, beans, lettuce, parsley, chamomile tea, blackberries, etc.); Sketch pictures of a rabbit or a garden.

CONCLUSION & SUMMARY

Students enjoy and celebrate the creativity and language of Beatrix Potter as well as learning literary elements and characters.

EVALUATION OF UNIT STUDY

Children were attentive during the lessons. They demonstrated a love for literature and for stories and showed evidence of learning the language of the story.

THE NOAH PLAN © 1997 • FOUNDATION FOR AMERICAN CHRISTIAN EDUCATION

Distinctives of the Principle Approach Lesson
The Principle Approach lesson creates a specific *effect* in the student.

Lesson Distinctives:

1. **The lesson appears in a subject taught in the context of America's Christian history and government.**
   RESULT: *a)* Students learn the chronology of God's Story and can identify every subject by it;
   b) They understand God's purpose for each subject as it is used to further the Gospel and liberty for the individual.

2. **The philosophy affirms the full value of each student which:**
   RESULT: *a)* Satisfies his intellectual needs;
   b) Appeals to his heart and conscience for a self-governed-under-God response;
   c) Presents appropriate challenges to build character.

3. **The lesson is governed by a Christian teacher who has himself mastered the subject and the Biblical philosophy of education.**
   RESULT: Students are engaged in producing a product, their own education, therefore, they are able to:
   a) Research Biblically;
   b) Think reflectively;
   c) Develop and write curriculum, leaving a record of scholarship;
   d) Use the tools and practice the habits of Christian scholarship;
   e) Develop a love of lifetime learning.

4. **Each lesson is guided by Biblical principles which:**
   RESULT: *a)* Maintain the integrity of the subject, consecrating it;
   b) Provide truths in the lesson which fit into the whole revelation of God's purposes in history;
   c) Enliven the subject, giving inspiration.

5. **The teacher guides the student's thinking with leading questions, calling upon reflective learning. The student:**
   RESULT: *a)* Observes;
   b) Identifies;
   c) Discovers;
   d) Articulates for himself.

6. **The vocabulary of the subject is defined and taught.**
   RESULT: *a)* Preciseness of language is mastered;
   b) Ideas and thoughts are masterfully articulated—perspicuity inculcated;
   c) Logic and rhetoric are studied.

7. **Notes are recorded in an organized way in the student's notebook which:**
   RESULT: *a)* Makes the lesson productive and reflective rather than just another reading or writing assignment;
   b) Provides the student a permanent record of his learning.

8. **The textbook is a living person—the teacher.**
   RESULT: Every classroom is a reflection of a unique individual responding to the high calling of American Christian education.

9. **Principle Approach education produces a gentle, inquiring, dignified spirit within the school.**
   RESULT: *a)* Readiness for learning;
   b) An honoring, godly, wholesome character;
   c) A dynamic that envelops and warms the student, cultivating, inspiring, and consecrating him for God's call and purposes for his life.

10. **The end product of the American Christian Principle Approach is a self-governing, Christ-reflecting character, one who is enterprising and productive, the future leaders we as parents and educators pray for daily—the kind that will change the world for the glory of God.**

11. **What is the fruit?**
    a) Independent Christian scholar
    b) Lifetime love for learning and reflection
    c) Biblical worldview
    d) Christian character
    e) Heart to serve Christ and community

Lesson Plan

Subject: _____ Date: _____ Grade: _____ Teacher: _____

Title Description: _____

Literary Element: _____

_____

Review: _____

_____

PRINCIPLES IDENTIFIED ➤	LEADING IDEAS ➤	EXPRESSION
		GOAL OF LESSON:

PRESENT NEW PRINCIPLES & CONTENT

CONTENT:	VISUAL AIDS
	TOOLS NEEDED FOR LESSON:

METHOD OF INTERACTING WITH STUDENTS	CONCLUSION & SUMMARY
	EVALUATION OF LESSON EFFECTIVENESS

Guide to Writing Lesson Plans

INSPIRITING THE LESSON: To infuse or excite spirit in; to enliven; to animate; to give new life to; to encourage; to invigorate. (Webster's 1828 *Dictionary*)

CONNECTING WITH EACH STUDENT	CULTIVATING THE SPIRIT OF THE CLASSROOM	CREATING A LOVE OF LEARNING
Greeting: shaking hands; showing interest; rapport; being accessible; cheerful; consistent; dependable; accepting.	Maintaining discipline and standards fairly; providing respect for each individual and his work; listening; establishing the productivity of each student; encouraging the class spirit and image; establishing an attractive and functional classroom environment.	Enthusiasm; animation; appreciation; enrichment; interest for independent inquiry and study with scholarship. (Webster's 1828 *Dictionary*)

TEACHING THE LESSON

TEACH: (v.t. Saxon—to teach)
1. To instruct; to inform; to communicate to another the knowledge of that which he was before ignorant.
2. To deliver any doctrine, art, principles or words for instruction.
3. To tell.
4. To show; to exhibit so as to impress on the mind.
5. To admonish; to counsel and direct.

(Webster's 1828 *Dictionary*)

LEARNING THE LESSON

LEARN: (v.t. Saxon—to teach and learn)
1. To gain knowledge of; to acquire knowledge or ideas of something before unknown.
2. To acquire skill in anything; to gain by a practice; faculty of performance.
3. To teach; to communicate the knowledge of something before unknown.

(Webster's 1828 *Dictionary*)

PRESENTATION OF INFORMATION	VISUAL AIDS AND TOOLS	STUDENT INTERACTION WITH LESSON	REINFORCEMENT FOR MASTERY
Outlining	Books: Text, Resource, Library, Reference	Practice	Further Homework
Chalkboard Notes	Posters, Pictures, Art Masterpieces	Note Taking	Unit/Cumulative Test
T-Chart	Charts	Guided Discussion	Long Term Project
Hand Drawn Illustration	Timeline	Directed Research	Book Review
Experiment	Maps	Field Investigation/Study Tours	Speech/Oratory/Dramatic Role
Demonstration	Subject Equipment	Experiments	Character Study
Guided Discussion	Manipulatives	Homework Assignment	Essay, Research Paper
Charting of Information	Computer	Completion of Maps, Charts	Common-place Book/Journal Writing
Diagramming Abstract Concepts	Tapes, Records	Quiz/Test	High School Portfolio Project
Observation and Classification	Videos, Films	Illustrations	High School Senior Thesis
Practice Problems	Transparencies, Slides	Essay Questions	Spelling Bee
Scripture Search	Music/Musical Instrument	Memory Work	Science/Math Fair
Key Word Study	Costumes	Manipulatives	Orchestral/Choral Competition
Scholars Reading Lesson (See *Reading Guide*)	Guest Speaker	Student Presentation	Fine Arts Festival
Taped Readings (Poetry, Oratory, etc.)	Participatory Activity/Craft	Student Conferences	Speech Meet
Choral Reading	Special Days	Peer Tutoring	Athletic Competition
Field Study Tour	Learning Center	Student Conferences	Peer Tutoring
	Bulletin Board	Song	Student Teaching
		Orchestra/Chorus	High School Apprenticeship/Missions
		Art Project, Craft	Student Conferences
		Drama, Puppet Show	

CRITIQUING THE LESSON: A critical examination of the merit of a performance. (Webster's 1828 *Dictionary*)

EVIDENCE OF TEACHING SUCCESS	EVIDENCE OF LEARNING SUCCESS
1. Each student engaged in lesson.	1. Ability to articulate the subject at the grade level effectively.
2. Lesson satisfies individual learning styles.	2. Continued independent inquiry.
3. Student work reflects understanding and scholarship.	

Lesson Plan

Subject: _Literature_   Date: _2 / 4 / 97_ Grade: _3_   Teacher: _Mrs. Youmans_

Title Description: _Hans Brinker, or The Silver Skates, Mary Mapes Dodge; "Hans and Gretel"_

Literary Element: _Matthew 6: 22-23: "The eye is the lamp of the body. If your eyes are good, your whole body will be full of light. But if your eyes are bad, your whole body will be full of darkness." NIV_

Review: _Mary Mapes Dodge's purpose in writing the book. Why it's a classic. Five literary elements of a classic._

PRINCIPLES IDENTIFIED ➤	LEADING IDEAS ➤	EXPRESSION
The window of the soul is the eye.	The internal character of an individual is revealed in his eyes.	GOAL OF LESSON: To identify Hans Brinker's internal character and relate to each student

PRESENT NEW PRINCIPLES & CONTENT

CONTENT:	VISUAL AIDS
Define character and goodness on vocabulary page. Record notes on character as a literary element. Discuss unfamiliar vocabulary: canal, peasant, grimace, Klompen, zomerhuis, lithe. Read chapter 1 aloud. Set up Hans Brinker's Character notebook page—internal and external. Record notes on Hans's character: "He was a solid hearty boy, with honest eyes and a brow that seemed to say 'goodness within.'"	Colorful bulletin board on Holland Picture (from book) of Hans for notebook page on Hans's character. TOOLS NEEDED FOR LESSON: Copy of Hans Brinker, or The Silver Skates, by Mary Mapes Dodge Rulers and colored pencils Glue or stapler

METHOD OF INTERACTING WITH STUDENTS	CONCLUSION & SUMMARY
Copying notes from chalkboard Character study discussion Relating the study of character to self Reading aloud	Our character is a result of choices and decisions we make. The condition of our heart shines through our eyes for all to see.
	EVALUATION OF LESSON EFFECTIVENESS
	Students were fully engaged. This lesson would make a great theme for a composition.

Lesson Plan

TELL • EXPLAIN   DEMONSTRATE • INSPIRE

Subject: _American Literature_   Date: _3 / 10 / 97_ Grade: _11_   Teacher: _Miss Slater_

Title Description: _The First American Poetess: Anne Bradstreet_

Literary Element: _Biblical References: Genesis 2:18, 21-24, and Matthew Henry's Commentary on these verses_

Review: _The setting of colonial Puritan literature; Christian History of the Constitution: Christian Self-Government, p. 182; pp. 48-50._

PRINCIPLES IDENTIFIED ➡	LEADING IDEAS ➡	EXPRESSION
The balance of male and female in creation—understanding the complementary roles of man and woman through the writings of Anne Bradstreet.	Pilgrims and Puritans in America The challenge of being an American Christian writer Biblical womanhood Poetry as a genre and its influence	GOAL OF LESSON: Learn the poetry of Anne Bradstreet and her contribution of character and ideals to American thought. Write a paper reflecting this thinking.

PRESENT NEW PRINCIPLES & CONTENT

CONTENT:	VISUAL AIDS
Read text from Bible and CHOC. Discuss. Introduce Anne Bradstreet. How did she handle her life as a Biblical woman? Define: complement, feminist, scripturist, male, female, deviate, humor, choler, melancholy, phlegm. Read foreword and introduction of The Works of Anne Bradstreet. Read three poems from each section of the book. Read six selections from "Meditations Divine and Moral." After discussion, students write a paper on a theme of her poetry.	Map of colonial New England Chalkboard analysis of one poem TOOLS NEEDED FOR LESSON: The Christian History of the Constitution: Christian Self-Government, Verna Hall The Works of Anne Bradstreet Webster's 1828 Dictionary Notebook; Bible

METHOD OF INTERACTING WITH STUDENTS	CONCLUSION & SUMMARY
Discuss: What did Anne Bradstreet contribute to American literature? How did her view of God, man, and woman affect her writing? Did her role as a faithful daughter, affectionate wife, devoted mother, enhance her writing? How? What is your assessment of our own times and the role of women? How can men and women complement each other? Student presentations of completed papers.	Students appreciate, discuss, and reflect upon the principles and leading ideas of the topic.
	EVALUATION OF LESSON EFFECTIVENESS
	Each student demonstrated engagement with the topic and produced an individual expression of it.

Teacher Preparation for Teaching a Classic: A Personal Testimony

by Elizabeth Youmans

I joined the faculty of StoneBridge School in the spring of its first year, replacing the music teacher who was hospitalized and faced with a long term recovery period. As a parent of a third grade student, I had been keenly interested in the rich curriculum of my son. A dietitian by profession, I had a B.S. degree with a near void in liberal arts. My education in hospital dietetics was comprised of science courses and an internship with varied experiences and highly specialized courses all pertaining to foods and nutrition.

When I was asked to teach the biography, *Abigail Adams*, by Evelyn Witter, to a class of first through third graders, I felt that I wasn't qualified and said so. The administrator, a woman of great vision, handed me the F.A.C.E. syllabus on this children's biography, written by Rosalie J. Slater, copies of the Christian History books, and reassured me that I could do it.

I had six weeks to prepare myself to teach a book whose setting lies in the period of great historic value in America—one that encompasses the Great Awakening, the Revolutionary War, the founding of the republic, the writing of the U. S. Constitution, and John Adams's term in the Presidency!! My knowledge of this period was sketchy at best, filled with large blocks of hazy names and dates, and certainly was not ennobled with a Christian perspective. The assurances kept coming that I was at an advantage not having to "unlearn" any humanistic teaching of the period, nor was I bound by previous teaching experiences in a public school.

I pursued an intensive home study course in American Christian history that not only prepared me to teach the period with a basic understanding of God's purpose for America, but that also dramatically changed my life and deepened my love and commitment to Christ.

How did I accomplish this task and what did I read? I took Miss Slater's syllabus and did *everything* it recommended a teacher do in order to prepare to teach *Abigail Adams*. (You must remember this was my first experience in teaching literature and history.) I began by reading the Mott Media children's biography of Abigail Adams to be used in the classroom. Notes were made concerning historical events and characters I needed to research. I began Irving Stone's biography of the Adamses called *Those Who Love* and reread the children's biography, this time using colored pencils to highlight the various elements of the book. (For example, blue was used to highlight setting passages, red was used for plot elements, green highlighted the various characters, and yellow highlighted Abigail's character.) This later proved to be invaluable as I began teaching in the classroom.

A notebook was set up with dividers for setting, plot elements, characters, theme, and style and a section was devoted to colonial American life, one to the Revolutionary War period, and a section to the Pilgrims.

I read every reference in the F.A.C.E. syllabus entitled "Teacher Preparation and Presentation" making notes as I proceeded and writing out questions I needed answered. (When I got to Bradford's *History* in CHOC, I must confess I wondered if a *year* would provide enough preparatory time, but plodded onward and also purchased a much larger notebook!)

Heading for the library, I found several books of John and Abigail Adams's correspondence that were invaluable in creating a love for Abigail's character:

1. *Abigail Adams: An American Woman*, by Charles W. Akers

2. *The Book of Abigail and John: Selected Letters of the Adams Family, 1762–1784*. Edited by Butterfield, Friedlaender, and Kline.

3. *The Adams Chronicles, Four Generations of Greatness*, by Jack Shepherd

4. *Dearest Friend*, by Lynne Withey. (Various letters were duplicated and filed in my notebook and pictures were copied to be used as I taught the children.)

I also located several children's books on colonial life that had great illustrations:

1. *Diary of an Early American Boy*, by Eric Sloane

2. *Colonial Living*, by Edwin Tunis

3. *Colonial Craftsmen*, by Edwin Tunis, which provided a rich pictorial history of everyday life in the colonies.

Because I was also teaching primary and elementary music in the school, I researched the music of the period including the *Bay Psalm Book*, early American folk songs, and Revolutionary War ditties. Many songs were sung by these same children during music class and were truly enjoyed by them. Music is an excellent enrichment vehicle that can be used during a literature or history period to recreate a particular spirit in time and to reinforce the learning of materials presented in class.

For the skeptic who is thinking this seems like a great deal of preparation to teach one small biography to a group of six- to eight-year-olds, I can only respond that because the "teacher is the textbook" in this method of instruction, the children will only receive what you have ingested—teaching always draws from within the individual. Learning is an internal process—the mind and spirit of the teacher communicating with the mind and spirit of the learner. That's why a great teacher is always an avid learner. Children rapidly discern between the average and the great teacher. Like sponges they soak in your enthusiasm for a favorite poem or passage in a book; they cry with you as you are moved to tears while reading a tragic portion of literature; their favorite poets and authors are your favorites. They listen as you relate your excitement at finding a great classic published eighty years ago in an old book store. They ask to see your notebook, secretly setting a goal to someday have an Abigail Adams notebook like their teacher. You are their model and inspiration for learning and wield great influence in developing their choices of reading material.

Your standard of enthusiasm as the classroom teacher is unconsciously reproduced in your students. Create an atmosphere of excellence and produce that standard for literary enjoyment that equals God's standard in Christ. Set about the task of educating yourself! Procure a copy of *Abigail Adams*, a large notebook, and a copy of the F.A.C.E. syllabus on Abigail Adams. Enter the world of self-education and bask in the light of the philosophy of the Principle Approach. Enjoy being a learner with the expectation of seeing a personal liberty develop within yourself.

*Elizabeth Youmans,
1985*

How to Use a F.A.C.E. Syllabus

The following instructions for teaching literature are written in a practical style. The value of great literature in the curriculum and its purposes, goals, and fruit are found in this guide. The purpose of this instruction is to launch the prospective teacher out on the sea of the literature classroom, equipped with the navigational tools to prevent abandoning ship mid-course, and enable him to sail smoothly to the targeted destination.

Assuming that you have thoroughly prepared yourself and constructed your own notebook, the joy of sharing your excitement and knowledge is about to begin!

As a way of creating interest in the students, introduce your book and Abigail with great enthusiasm. Project some of her character qualities or exciting events in her life, or reveal some of her friends with whom the children can identify. Share her as one of your great friends and a model of outstanding Christian womanhood.

Help the students make a title page to go in their literature notebook labelled with a divider tab marked "Abigail Adams." Provide a picture of Abigail for the children to staple and color on their title page. An example of first through third grade notebook work is provided in the following pages and includes the introductory teaching and the labor of the first chapter as a sample of student work.

The Literary Elements Recorded

The next step in teaching a classic is to present the life and character of the author with a page in the student's notebook devoted to him and his place on the Chain of Christianity. Because Evelyn Witter is not among the great classical writers, no information is available to impart to the children. With a novel like *David Copperfield* or *Little*

Women, it would be important to spend several class periods studying the lives of Charles Dickens or Louisa May Alcott. Always provide a list of other books by the same author for the children to record in their notebook to help guide their future reading selections.

Abigail Adams is a biography. Generally the value of its language will not be as greatly emphasized as the study of the character portrayed. Introduce the children to biography as a type of literature. In a great biography, the plot and setting are secondary to the development of the character. A great biography will reveal the character of the individual as causative rather than the circumstances or environment in his life. A character study will reveal the philosophy of government of that individual. Define biography and character for the children and discuss the character qualities of Jesus Christ and the Pilgrim model, referring to them often throughout the study. Contrasting or comparing a character in history to Christ or the Pilgrims is a wonderful method of encouraging reflective thinking and writing. Please turn to the example in the student notebook section (p. 50).

Background to the Biography

The next step in preparing the young learners to appreciate the first chapter and its great emphasis on setting is to establish an appreciation for the history of Massachusetts, its individuality, and place on the Chain of Christianity. Then when you have the opportunity to sit and read the opening paragraphs of chapter 1 aloud with the children, you have provided an introduction to the character, the setting, and the geographical location. The children will know where the colony of Massachusetts is, what was important in America during the 1740s, and who Abigail Smith was.

> *A great biography will reveal the character of the individual as causative rather than the circumstances or environment in his life.*

Setting up the Notebook

Prior to reading chapter 1 and beginning your notebook work, take the time to have the students set up notebook pages entitled:

Setting
Plot Elements
Characters
Theme
Style
Vocabulary

In this study, the characters of Abigail and John are emphasized. For each one, use a sheet of notebook paper and prepare as follows:

On one side entitle "Abigail's Internal Character" and on the reverse side of the sheet, entitle "Abigail's External Character."

Repeat the same process for John Adams. Then as you're reading aloud with the children and you come across a passage that describes Abby's physical appearance, you can stop and have the students record on the side entitled "Abigail's External Character." This same procedure would apply for any descriptions of Abby's internal character such as her love of Scripture, her desire to know more about the world around her, her personality and temperament. The same method would be applied to John Adams's character when he is introduced to the reader in a later chapter. At the end of the book the children have recorded in the author's words a detailed description of Abigail and John Adams and are able to write several paragraphs about their characters. These great Christian patriots will forever be their friends and they will always be able to articulate why. Please review the sample in the children's notebook section on Abigail's character (pp. 62–63).

The first chapter in Witter's book is filled with various references to life in a New England colonial town. In teaching chapter one, it is important to go slowly and recreate the spirit and character of colonial family life as this is the foundation of the rich Christian character of the patriots who were used mightily by God to birth a new nation. In essence, the character and spirit of this generation of individuals became the character of our country as they imparted their spirit and forged a new form of government. The author has painted this picture in a few short paragraphs, and so it becomes the teacher's joyous responsibility to enhance and expand the painting with additional material.

The Notebook Approach

The notebook method provides an excellent tool as the student can record notes, staple pictures provided by the teacher, draw illustrations, color and label maps, and reason and relate through composition work. The teacher can also creatively display colonial life in her classroom, have re-creations, dress up in colonial garb, serve a colonial meal, or visit a local historic colonial site. This chapter requires several class periods to draw primary-aged children into the spirit of colonial life. Soon they are secretly wishing they could go back in history and spend some time with Abby. It's one of the most exciting periods of history to teach and the time spent in developing chapter 1 is valuable towards establishing the cornerstone of America's birth in their minds.

Begin your study of chapter 1 with the setting, Abigail's New England childhood home. Have the students turn to their notebook page entitled "Setting" and review what the literary element of setting reveals in a book.

Generally each chapter will have a time frame, a geographical location, and a season; sometimes a chapter will have multiple settings. Choose those that are most important to the plot elements and write the author's passages that best describe the setting in quotations referring to the page number in the book on the chalkboard. Later, as you and the children are reading along and they have grown more familiar with the literary elements of a classic, you might want to pause and ask them to identify the element about which the author has just written; or, in an upper elementary class, you could assign the task of recording various descriptive passages of a certain literary element in a chapter after you have read the chapter together. As you read the descriptive passages, you may wish to write them on the chalkboard at that moment. Sometimes the spirit of the story is destroyed by frequent interruptions, and postponing the notebook work until after you have completed a chapter might be more appropriate.

Composition

After several days' work with setting notes, it is important to encourage the children to write sentences or a paragraph describing the setting of chapter 1 using as many of the author's words as they can incorporate. In the primary classroom this provides an excellent composition theme that can be assigned during an English period, and the writing can be done in the literature notebook on the setting page and labelled "Summary." Older students are able to write more quickly and can write an assignment such as this for homework or as an assignment to culminate a class period. Help them get started, if needed, by writing the topic sentence on the board. Restate some of the descriptive phrases. Move through the classroom encouraging your less language-oriented children. Get them writing! This step in the learning of a classic is the most frustrating step and if abandoned will not encourage the development of writing skills and the use of new words in their vocabulary. It is said that Nathaniel Hawthorne was once asked the secret of his style. The writer replied with a smile—"It is the result of a great deal of practice!"

This crucial step of practicing with the author's words is likened to the novice painter sitting in front of a Rembrandt painting copying the master's technique. What better way to learn to write well than to employ the master writer's style and use of words? Beethoven studied Bach and confessed a great love for practicing and playing his music more than any other composer. Would his own style have been so ingenious if he had neglected Bach?

In order to restore composition and nurture an ennobled vocabulary in communication, teachers must provide students with an excellent standard and a method of teaching composition that inspire them to develop their own style.

In the colonial era, composition was taught by having students emulate great writers. Individuals, educated in this manner, were selected by God to compose and write such documents as the Declaration of Independence, the Bill of Rights, and the greatest Christian document, the U.S. Constitution. Interestingly, all the writers of these documents were educated in the colonies, not in mother England—Thomas Jefferson, Sam Adams, James Madison, John Adams, Benjamin Franklin, George Washington, Noah Webster, and Abigail Adams. They have produced a great portion of our richest American literature.

Colonial Education

The colonial parents' dedication to the task of educating their children has never again been equalled in America's history, and it produced the highest literacy rate our nation has ever had. Fathers and mothers assumed the responsibility of their children's education, and this is one of the themes of chapter 1. A class period spent on the education of the New England child is needed to develop Abigail's character. The history of Massachusetts colony reveals the founding of the first public school system supported at the local level. Boys attended a school receiving a more classical education while girls often went to a dame's school. Abby was schooled at home and her first books provide a key to her character development. Please refer to the student notebook section.

Colonial Crafts

A craft class was spent during the week of this lesson to construct a hornbook cut from poster board. The children printed their alphabet and a Scripture on a piece of paper and glued this on to the hornbook. Wax paper was stapled over the Scripture to represent the "horn." A hole was punched in the handle and threaded with string enabling the children to wear their hornbooks home as the colonial school children might have done.

For primary-aged children, illustrations and pictures should be provided. Some of the inclusions I used for chapter 1 are as follows: A picture of a painting of Abigail's childhood home was duplicated for each child to staple in his setting notes. A fireplace scene was provided emphasizing the importance of the fireplace for heat and light, a place where the New England family would read the Scriptures aloud, Mom would sew, and the children could complete their studies for the day. A map of Massachusetts was completed with colored pencils using the map standard, and the students marked and labelled each town mentioned in the book as they were studied.

Because of the importance of the American colonial period in God's purpose for man, and because Abby's birthday gifts vividly reflect the life of the colonial girl, I wanted each child to have a real appreciation for the standard of living and the values of this period in U.S. history. For Abby's birthday party, an old small trunk was brought in filled with old books and a blue dress. Each one of the gifts—the fur muff, maple sugar confections, aprons, the metal ink well, and two bayberry candles—was passed around and discussed, smelled, or tasted. At the end of the period, the children were asked to answer these questions: What were the differences between a birthday party in the 1740s and now? Would you be grateful to receive a candle, an apron, or an ink well? Is the quality of life better or worse now? Tell why.

Activities

One of the goals of teaching literature is to create or encourage in every student an enjoyment of the best books. It is very important, particularly at the primary level, not to overkill with notebook work, and so the written work must be balanced with other methods of teaching.

As the book progressed, I wove a number of various high-interest activities into my notebook work. For example, in chapter 3, Abigail visits her Grandmother Quincy's home. Grandmother has a goal to teach Abby the social graces of the period. She teaches Abby by having a practice tea party. I dressed up in my "finest colonial garb" (a lace mobcap is a necessity for teaching this book), brought in my silver tea service with some sugar cookies, and the class and I had a tea party while I read the story. (I was never able to teach another literature classic without having tea and cookies at least once.) Several of the children volunteered to do a colonial craft, and one student dipped candles and presented an oral report with a demonstration. Another made a simple piece of crewel work. I had a sampler displayed the day we read chapter 3, which inspired this project.

Later in the study of the book when the Adams family letters were read and emphasized, I provided quill pens and homemade ink and the children wrote letters to "Honored Papa" thanking him for sending them to StoneBridge School. They addressed their letters in fine colonial fashion and we sealed them with wax and sent them home to "Papa." They soon had developed an enormous appreciation for the difficulty in handling a quill pen with ink and the vast amount of time spent by the Adams family in correspondence.

As you can now envision, a literature book is like a treasure chest waiting for the teacher to unlock it with the key of creativity. You have probably thought of other imaginative ways to enhance the teaching of *Abigail Adams*. Set your goals and begin—as the only obstacle to accomplishing the task is your telling yourself that you can't do it because it's too hard or too time consuming. Begin building your Abby notebook and venture into the treasure chest. Thomas Carlyle, the great Victorian essayist and biographer, wrote, "Great men are profitable company. We cannot look, however imperfectly, upon a great man without gaining something by him. He is the living, light-fountain, which it is good and pleasant to be near." Abigail and John Adams are good and pleasant to be near!

The Effect on the Student

If we as parents and teachers are to call the current generation of American Christian students to leadership, then we must assume the responsibility to provide them with the tools to lead! We must set aside easy methods and humanistic philosophies of education and generate an atmosphere that will produce reflective thinkers and imaginative and skilled writers.

Noah Webster, father of American Christian education and author of the Webster's 1828 *Dictionary* and Blue-Backed Spellers, believed that children should learn to acquire knowledge by severe effort. He believed that to make everything easy for learners was wrong! Consequently, Noah Webster felt that the object of early training was to form the mind into a capacity of surmounting intellectual difficulties of any and every kind! He said the young have much to learn in early life, the use of which they cannot then comprehend. He believed that all those systems which lead children forward no faster than they can understand and apply every word they spell, were radically erroneous. As the product of this "easy method," I know he is correct.

This method of teaching literature requires more from the teacher and from the student; however, the fruit that has developed in our students through the teaching of *Abigail Adams* to a class of twelve six- to eight-year-

olds and the enhancement in our curriculum have been abundant.

After completing the study of Abigail's character, the children were asked to write a short essay on the qualities of a virtuous mother. With Mother's Day only a few weeks away, this assignment led to an essay about their own mothers' virtuous characters which were copied and framed for a very special Mother's Day gift.

From the teaching of *Abigail Adams* and the music of the period evolved the writing of a Revolutionary War Musical for our Spring Open House. The letters of John and Abigail became the narration for a recreation of the events leading up to the War to the selection of George Washington as our first president. Beautiful costumes were made for the children and props fashioned, as they presented a patriotic festival and established fond memories to which they still refer.

One of our first-grade girls was so in love with Abby, that when her grandmother offered to take her anywhere in the eastern United States for a week's vacation (thinking, of course, she would desire a trip to Disney World), she was taken aback at the immediate and delightful cry of, "Let's go to Boston and visit Abigail's home." Her grandmother did take her to Boston and Plymouth (what a wonderful grandmother) and the student made a scrapbook of her adventure which she still enjoys showing. This young girl at the end of her fourth-grade year opened a summer school in her home and taught neighborhood children using her notebooks and curriculum.

The following year during Workshop Week, we provided an opportunity for the students to make marionettes. What characters did they request to design? Abigail and John Adams, little John Quincy Adams, George and Martha Washington, and Revolutionary War soldiers! Their love for the colonial characters studied in history and literature was reflected in the creation of their puppets and the writing of a puppet show.

Great men are profitable company. We cannot look, however imperfectly, upon a great man without gaining something by him. He is the living, light-fountain, which it is good and pleasant to be near.
—Thomas Carlyle

The children assisted in designing the settings, composing the music, and producing the puppet show for their parents.

Special Days for Celebrating Literature

Wonderful "Special Days" have evolved from our first year of dressing up and displaying period memorabilia at StoneBridge School. We routinely have three or four special days on our school calendar, and the children eagerly await these cherishable moments every year. We've had "Great Characters of Literature Day" when the children dressed up as their favorite character in literature and the remaining students had to guess who they were; "Colonial Day," complete with a colonial meal; "George Washington Day"; "Columbus Day"; "Sailing Day"; a "Shakespeare Festival"; and "Plimoth Plantation Day" (an annual celebration at Thanksgiving reflecting our great love for the Pilgrims).

As wonderful as this has been, the most inspirational harvest from the years of cultivating the Principle Approach came at the close of the current school year at our Spring Open House for parents. To highlight a study of the Civil War with these same students (who are now fifth and sixth graders), the class was assigned the task of memorizing and reciting the Gettysburg Address. They entered into the assignment with great fervor and it became such an enjoyable challenge for them, we decided to present a recitation to our parents at Open House. The competition was so keen among the students that the two runners-up were asked to write biographical sketches— one about Abraham Lincoln, the other about Robert E. Lee. Using their notes from history class, they both returned the following day with the most anointed tributes to these godly men of the Civil War period. Two days later, the three ten-year-olds presented their biographical sketches and the recitation of the Gettysburg Address. When they sat down, there were very few dry eyes in the audience. The work of geniuses? No, we believe it's the tribute and proof that the Principle Approach, combined with the inspired Christian teacher, produces a genuine love of learning in the student and forges within him the quality of character that enables the diligent pursuit of truth, the capacity to rightly divide knowledge, and the ability to communicate it effectively, both in his speech and in his writing.

Daniel Webster said in regard to educating young children: "Make them intelligent, and they will be vigilant; give them the means of detecting the wrong, and they will apply the remedy." How does a teacher make a child intelligent? I believe it is possible to build literacy through the consistent application of the Principle Approach using the Notebook Method in a curriculum that lavishes the learner with great language, Christian ideals and characters, and enables him to perceive history from God's eye view. He learns how to govern himself with the knowledge that God has a high calling and purpose for him on His Chain of Christianity. There is no shortcut to excellence in our children. Allow yourself the joy and beauty of inspiration and refreshment. Drink at the well of the masters and be prepared to see an aspiring literature teacher spring forth!

Make them intelligent, and they will be vigilant; give them the means of detecting the wrong, and they will apply the remedy.
—Daniel Webster

ADDITIONAL RESOURCES:

1. Abigail Adams Society, Weymouth, MA 02188

2. Adams National Historic Site, Quincy, MA 02170

Sample Student Notebook Work
for the Study of *Abigail Adams*

The following pages present sample student notebook work recorded during the teaching and learning of the Evelyn Witter biography, *Abigail Adams*, to first through third graders. This sample is given to show the teacher how a student notebook could be organized to make the study of the biography a whole unit of work. This section is one part of the literature notebook which also contains the record of the entire year's literature curriculum. The illustrations were drawn by StoneBridge High School student, Melody González.

Abigail Adams
1744-1818

by

Evelyn Witter

Abigail Adams - A Biography

I. Abigail Adams is a form of literature called biography.

    A. A biography is non-fiction and is the history of the life and character of a real person.

    B. Character is defined as those peculiar qualities of a person that make him different from others.

II. A biography is a study of external events and internal character qualities of a person who is living or dead.

III. The Pilgrim character qualities are a model to us of great American Christian character.

    A. Christian care
    B. Liberty of Conscience
    C. Faith
    D. Denied self
    E. Persevered in times of trouble
    F. Steadfastness
    G. Industry

THE NOAH PLAN © 1997 • FOUNDATION FOR AMERICAN CHRISTIAN EDUCATION

Massachusetts on the Chain of Christianity

I. It was the second permanent colony and home of the Pilgrims.
  A. The Pilgrims landed in Plymouth in 1620.
  B. They planted the seeds of Christian self government.

II. It was the birthplace of three U.S. presidents:
  A. John Adams
  B. John Quincy Adams
  C. John F. Kennedy

Setting

The setting tells us where and when the story takes place.

Chapter One:

I. The time is 1749.
  A. 1749 was during a period in American history called Colonial America.
  B. It was also a time known as the Great Awakening. (God's Spirit turned many hearts toward the Lord.)

II. The place is Abigail's New England home in Weymouth, Massachusetts.

  A. It was a two-story home.
     "she came down eight steps in her special way" p. 3
  B. The house had glass window panes.
     "snowflakes hit the window panes" p. 2

 The Noah Plan © 1997 • Foundation for American Christian Education

C. It was heated by a great open fireplace. p. 2

A typical colonial fireplace

D. It was lit by candlelight.
   "candles burned in every room" p. 8

E. The home was beautifully furnished.
   "lemon colored satin curtains" p. 3

   "thick Brussels carpet" p. 3

   "Father's study shelves were full of books." p. 6

F. Homes in New England were built close together around the meeting house.

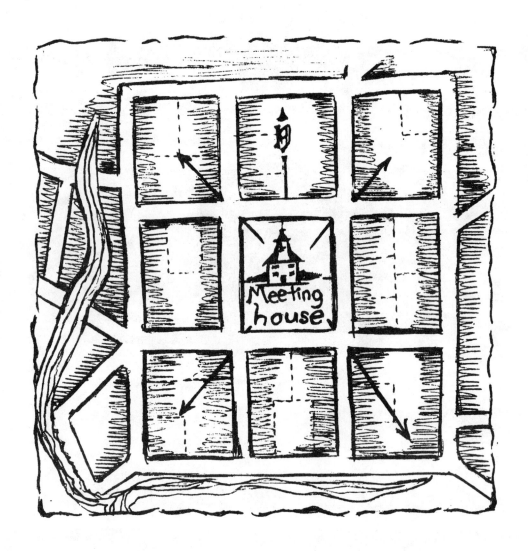

III. The season is winter.

A. "In Weymouth, storms were often big, keeping people in their homes for days." p. 2

B. "I heard the crunch of the sleigh runners on the snow." p. 2

C. "The icy wind grabbed our breaths right out of our bodies." p. 12

Foot Warmer

IV. Abby's gifts describe colonial life.

A. "two bayberry candles for her room"
   There was no electricity.
B. "two maple sugar confections"
   Candy was a rare treat!
C. "three aprons"
   Young girls helped in the kitchen
D. "a white fur muff"
   There was no heat in the meeting house.
E. "a silver ink well"
   Writing was done with a quill and ink.
F. "a blue dress with crewel work trim"
   Clothes were made by hand.
G. "books, books, and more books"
   Children spent many hours reading.

V. The food served on Abby's birthday shares another part of Colonial life with us:

A. "Quince tarts" (quince is a small, yellow tart fruit) p. 2

B. "Corn pudding with maple sugar" p. 7 (better known as hasty pudding)

C. "Baked chicken" p. 7

D. "Biscuits and milk" served by Phoebe the black servant p. 7

E. "Roast turkey, geese, beef and ham"

F. "Pantry shelves filled with custards, puddings, pies and cakes" p. 13

G "Pans of corn bread" p. 13

Colonial Education

I. Colonial children were taught to read by their parents from the Bible.

II. The Bible taught them wisdom and truth and ways to govern themselves.

III. In some colonies schools were built to teach the boys, but many children were taught at home.

Abby's Education

I. Abby's education was different than most other girls in her colony.

II. She was "too delicate" to attend Dames School and was taught at home.

III. Her first books helped form her character:
   A. The Bible
   B. The New England Primer
   C. The Bay Psalm Book

IV. Grandmother Quincy made library available and taught Abby many social graces.

V. She was later greatly influenced by Greek and Roman classics.

VI. She read sermons.

VII. The conversation in her home gave her an interest in colonial events.

THE NOAH PLAN © 1997 • FOUNDATION FOR AMERICAN CHRISTIAN EDUCATION

Characters

1. Abigail Smith Adams was a colonial woman whose many letters have inspired us. She was the wife of our second U.S. president and mother of our sixth U.S. president.

2. Mary Smith was Abby's older sister.

3. Grandmother Quincy was Abby's grandmother who influenced her character and taught her many social graces.

4. Colonel John Quincy was Abby's grandfather who was interested in government.

5. Reverend William Smith was Abigail's father and a preacher in Weymouth.

6. Will Smith was Abby's brother.

7. Elizabeth Quincy Smith was Abigail's lovely mother who taught her at home.

8. Paul Revere was a Boston silversmith and good friend of Abby's father.

9. Betsy Smith was Abby's younger sister.

Abigail's External Characteristics

"I was thought to be too delicate to go to school." p. 6

"I was slight of build and only five foot and two inches tall." p. 31

"Her health has never been good." p.31

" grown to be a pretty young lady" p. 47

" moves with such grace and dignity"p.55

Abigail's Internal Characteristics

"the friendliest girl in Massachusetts" p.17

"Abigail learns easily" p.6

"always looking out for other people" p.17

"I felt ashamed. Father had told me before not to gossip." p.27

"Abigail never complains... she helps most willingly" p.30

"Grandmother and I were kindred souls ... taken Christ as Savior, loved God, admired common sense and liked to laugh." p.52

"I trusted that the Lord knew best." p.64

"I prayed God would bless our marriage." p.69

"I knew God directed our steps." p.76

"She's a heroine. She's the only one who didn't run away." p.92

"The large collection of books were all mine to enjoy." p.53

Theme

The theme is the message or ideas the author is sharing with us.

I. The rich colonial family life gave young children a Christian foundation for governing themselves.

II. Character is built by the choices one makes, not by external events.

III. God's word helps build faith and courage to help us overcome difficulties.

A Colonial Family

Plot Elements

The plot elements are a series of events which lead to a conclusion.

Chapter One:

I. "The men talked of the Molasses Act." p. 7
The first of many ways Mother England found to get money from the colonies to support their British soldiers in America.

II. "a French expedition on the Ohio" p. 7
This refers to the building of French forts along the frontier land of the Ohio River, which led to a war between the French and the British in just five years.

Style

The style is the individuality of the author in his writing.

Chapter One:

I. Evelyn Witter has used the gifts of Abby's birthday to describe colonial life.

II. The party reveals the loving Christian values of this special colonial family.

Vocabulary

1. <u>Hornbook</u> - the first book of Colonial children made of wood with a page of lessons covered with horn.

2. <u>Confection</u> - a candy or sweet treat

3. <u>Internal</u> - something found on the inside

4. <u>External</u> - something found on the outside

5. <u>Colony</u> - a group of people who have left their native country to form a new land but are still under the rule of the native country

Glossary

Teachers of literature should refer to a good literature handbook.

Elements of the Classic

1. **Setting:**
   the background of the story—place, time, society, environment, climate.

2. **Characterization:**
   the internal and external qualities of the individual characters.

3. **Plot:**
   the sequence of events leading up to a conclusion.

4. **Theme:**
   the message or lesson that the author presents.

5. **Style:**
   the individuality of the author expressed in his writing.

Allegory:
A form of extended metaphor in which objects or persons are equated with meaning that lies outside the narrative.

Alliteration:
The repetition of initial identical consonant sounds or any vowel sounds in successive syllables.

Allusion:
A figure of speech making casual reference to a famous historical or literary figure or event.

Climax:
The point of highest interest in the plot where the reader makes his greatest emotional response.

Dialogue:
Conversation of two or more people as reproduced in writing; most common in fiction.

Epic:
A long narrative poem in elevated style presenting characters of high position in a series of adventures.

Essays:
A moderately brief prose discussion of a restricted topic.

Fable:
A fictitious narration intended to instruct or amuse; usually presents some useful truth or precept; animals are often the central characters.

Foreshadowing:
A feeling for what is going to happen; a presage; an indication beforehand.

Fantasy:
A conscious breaking away from reality; a work which takes place in a non-existent world.

Genre:
A term used in literary criticism to designate the distinct types or categories into which literary works are grouped according to form, technique, or subject matter.

Imagery:
The collection of images within a literary work; sometimes taken to be keys to deeper meaning in the literature.

Irony:
A figure of speech in which the actual intent is expressed in words which carry the opposite meaning.

Legend:
A collection or body of unverified popular stories handed down from earlier times.

Metaphor:
An implied analogy which imaginatively identifies one object with another.

Myth:
A fictitious or fanciful narrative, having an analogy more or less remote to some real event.

Mythology:
A system of fables or fabulous opinions and doctrines, respecting the deities which heathen nations have supposed to preside over the world.

Personification:
A figure of speech which endows animals, ideas, and inanimate objects with human characteristics.

Simile:
A figure of speech in which a similarity between two objects is directly expressed; usually introduced by like or as.

Soliloquy:
A speech of a character in a play delivered when the speaker is alone—usually to inform the audience.

Sonnet:
A lyric poem of fourteen lines following one or another of several set rhyme schemes.

Symbolism:
The use of one object to represent or suggest another; the use of symbols in writing.

Chapter Two

Learning the Literature of the Bible

The Bible as Literature
The Source and Seedbed of Literature and Liberty
The Highest Model of Literature

The Holy Bible is the acknowledged greatest book in the world!
The Holy Bible is the most influential book in the world!
The Holy Bible is the literary masterpiece of the world!
This is not surprising for the Bible is God's Book!

With any subject, it is natural to go to God's Word for direction. Thus the study of the teaching and learning of literature will begin with the Bible itself and what the Word teaches us in this cherished field of character and feeling.

Man and woman, as unique from all else in creation, require a relationship with their Creator. In fact, the central concern of Holy Scripture is Christ's work of redemption and the relationship of man to his Savior. From this major theme of Scripture flows all of the emotions which God put within man—his or her hopes and fears, aspirations, joys, and sorrows.

The Bible was not written as literature, yet, it is not surprising to find it filled with literary forms of expression. Since all the major emotions of man are called forth in this Book of books, the Bible represents almost all the important forms of literature.

An overview of the literary forms found in the Bible, best exemplified in English in the Authorized King James Version of 1611, might include the following:

The Language, Style, and Expression of the Bible
Language of the Bible for a God-centered Life

Righteousness, justice, purity, honesty, obedience, sincerity, reverence, worship, hope, faith, love, etc.

Expression of the Bible

"No single book has so profoundly affected universal expression as has the English Bible." (*The Bible in English Literature*, Edgar Whitaker Work, 1917, p. 27)

Style of the Bible

The style of highly gifted individuals. A.B. Simpson observes: "Each man's message was colored by the complexion of his own mind . . . each has its unique colors, forms, fragrance and individuality." (*Teaching and Learning America's Christian History: The Principle Approach*, Rosalie J. Slater, 1965, p. 154)

Literary Types Found in the Bible
Poetry

"O taste and see that the Lord is good: Blessed is the man that trusteth in him." Psalms 34:8

Letters

The Epistles of the New Testament

Essay

"Train up a child in the way he should go, and when he is old, he will not depart from it." Proverbs 22:6

Drama

The Story of Joseph, Genesis, chapters 37–48.

Short Narrative or Short Story

The Parable of the Good Samaritan, Luke 10:25–37.

Epic or Long Narrative

The Life of David, 1 Samuel, chapter 16–
1 Kings, chapter 2.

Biography, Autobiography

Jonah, The Acts of the Apostles

Literary Types Unique to the Bible

Parallelism

The form of Hebrew poetry

Proverbs

Concise moral truths

Pastorals

Shepherd literature

Parables

Brief narratives of our Lord

Literary Elements from the Bible

Historical Settings

The Garden of Eden, The Home of Potiphar the Egyptian, Solomon's Temple, The House of Peter, Lydia's Home in Philippi

Character Studies

Ruth, Esther, Stephen, Aquilla and Priscilla, The Apostles, Paul, Peter, Timothy

Providential Plots

Abraham and Isaac, Daniel in Babylon, Saul on the Damascus Road, John on Patmos

Themes or Leading Ideas

Preparation, Protection, Direction, Deliverance

Individuality of Writers

Prophets, Kings, Herdsmen, Soldiers, Fishermen, Scholars, Evangelists

The chart on the following page suggests an approach to studying the Bible as literature that can be adapted to any selection from the Bible.

Researching the Literary Elements of the Bible

Subject	Settings	Characterizations	Plot Elements	Themes	Style/Writings
Moses	The most famous home in history Palace in Egypt The "backside" of the desert At Sinai and in the desert	Egypt: 40 years home and palace Desert: 40 years God's preparation of Moses Wilderness: 40 years service to God and nation Israel	Life providentially spared Instructed by God to deliver Israel from bondage Talked to God "face to face" Instrument of God's Law to Israel	Providential preparation Deliverance Teacher of God's Law	The Pentateuch The Song of Moses Historian and instructor in government of the individual and nation
Samuel	Home of Elkanah and Hannah The Temple Israel	The Child Prophet The Character of a prophet, priest, and judge	Providential birth Temple ministry under Eli Work of revival in Israel Founding the Schools of the Prophets Monarchy established	Holiness in God's Temple A people to love the Lord The Council of the Prophets The character of kings	His recorded words in 1st and 2nd Samuel
David	Birthplace in Bethlehem Hillsides of Judea In flight in the wilderness King in Hebron and Jerusalem	Shepherd, player of the harp Military man Friend King Man after God's heart	Relationship to first king, Saul Friend of Prince Jonathan Three times anointed to serve God A prototype of Christ	The character of a ruler, "must rule in the fear of the Lord." Fallibility of man	The Psalms of David His recorded words in 1st and 2nd Samuel, 1st and 2nd Kings, 1st Chronicles
John the Baptist	Home: "hill country of Judea" Preaching: deserts of Judea, countryside about Jordan Death: Machaerus castle, Dead Sea	Old Testament prophet in New Testament era The forerunner of the Savior	400 years of prophetic silence Linked Old and New Testaments A witness to the Truth Martyred by Herod	Revival and Repentance. "The voice crying in the wilderness" announcing the coming of the "Lamb of God which taketh away the sins of the world."	Prophetic words of Isaiah fulfilled Words recorded in the four Gospels
Jesus Christ	Home in Nazareth Galilean area The Synagogue The Temple at Jerusalem On the banks of Jordan In the wilderness with wild beasts Palestine Jerusalem: The Sanhedrin Antonia Fortress Golgotha	Some of the names for Jesus Christ in Scripture: Alpha and Omega Ancient of Days Anointed of the Lord Beloved of God Branch of Righteousness Bread of Life Bridegroom Bright and Morning Star Captain of Salvation Carpenter's Son Chief Cornerstone Day Star Dayspring Door of Sheepfold Emmanuel First Fruits The God-man Holy One of God I Am Jesus of Nazareth Lamb of God Lily of the Valley Lion of the tribe of Judah Living Bread Rock Sun of Righteousness True Vine	Biblical childhood Education in the Scriptures Appearances at the Temple On the banks of the Jordan In the wilderness with "wild beasts" Preaching, teaching, healing, redeeming, in Palestine Arrests and trials Crucifixion Resurrection Ascension	The Life of Blessedness The Message of Repentance and Salvation The Lamb of God offered as a sacrifice for sin	His Gospel words reflect the Old Testament teachings of Moses and the Prophets concerning Him. His teachings reflect his upbringing in Galilee—the love and knowledge of nature and the rural countryside.

A Biblical Approach to Poetry

The Bible was not written as literature, yet, it is not surprising to find it filled with literary forms of expression. Since all the major emotions of man are called forth in this Book of books, the Bible represents almost all the important forms of literature. And poetry is one of its most beautiful forms.

The lyric poetry of the Bible is found in the Psalms. While it is God speaking, the individuality and the diversity of the writer is not lost. As A. B. Simpson writes of the Biblical authors:

> We know that they acted with perfect individuality, and that each man's message was colored by the complexion of his own mind . . . . The Book of God is like a beautiful garden, where all the flowers grow upon the same soil and are watered from the same heaven, but each has its own unique colors, forms, fragrance, and individuality. (*Teaching and Learning*, Slater, 1965, p. 154)

The Psalms were almost all written by David and they reflect his unique experience and distinctions of character. But, since this is God's Book, the Psalms reveal aspects of His nature and character. It is this unity with diversity which identifies God's Principle of Individuality.

To begin the study of poetry with the Psalms, the Twenty-third Psalm best identifies both the Creator and the Author of the Psalms. As David began to reflect on God—when he became aware of God in his own life and in the life of the universe—he was a humble shepherd. It is natural then that "the sweet singer of Israel" should characterize God as Shepherd. Thus, the Twenty-third Psalm, above all the songs, hymns, or psalms which David wrote, best exemplifies the relationship of the Shepherd to His sheep—both spiritually and in actuality. This aspect of the nature of God is, of course, a major theme of Scripture, bringing to the fore "the Lamb of God, which taketh away the sin of the world." (John 1:29)

To study the Twenty-third Psalm, to appreciate both its internal and external message, is to have started with a major purpose of literature, namely: to know God better, to love Him more, and to walk in His ways. So as we walk the hills and valleys of Judea with David the Shepherd Boy, we can come to know also the tender relationship of our Shepherd to His flock and of His tireless watchfulness over those who claim His Salvation.

Begin then with the reading of this Psalm; first the teacher, then the class. As you read it together, you will discover why the King James Version has become the most memorized and the most quoted of all translations. It reads musically, and it is a literary masterpiece. As your class reads this Psalm, let them identify their feelings.

Begin your own Biblical and historical research about David, about sheep and shepherds. Then consider the educational implications for your class including those principles which will make this study important to their own hearts and lives.

Twenty-third Psalm—The Shepherd's Psalm

External	Internal

The Lord is my shepherd; I shall not want.

Sheep require more care than many animals. Some shepherds give good care and attention to the needs of their sheep. Others, like the hireling, flee their duties. Even the sheep reflect confidence in a good shepherd. (John 10:13)	Individually we are secure when we know we belong to the Lord. He is our Shepherd. We come to a blessed assurance of our every need being met in Him. "Behold he that keepeth Israel shall neither slumber nor sleep." (Psalm 121)

He maketh me to lie down in green pastures:

Sheep will not lie down in fear. They must be free from enemies, free from hunger, assured of a sense of peace and contentment in their shepherd. If they see him in the field—they rest assured.	The Lord alone gives rest and refreshment and assurance. The green pastures nourish the soul-sense. "It is by a constancy of the means of grace that the soul is fed." —Matthew Henry

He leadeth me beside the still waters.

Sheep cannot drink from agitated waters. Waters must be pure, not polluted. Stillness and purity are reassuring to the sheep.	Stillness is a spiritual quality which the Lord alone can impart to hearts totally yielded to Him. "The joys of the Holy Ghost are these still waters, by which the saints are led." —Matthew Henry

He restoreth my soul:

One writer indicates that sheep can be "cast down" or turned over on their backs. It is critical to restore them to their feet.	He restores me when I go astray like a lost sheep. God restores us to His Truth and brings us back to the right path and fold. (Matthew 18:11–14, Parable of the Lost Sheep)

He leadeth me in the paths of righteousness for his name's sake.

Sheep require new pasture lands else they will overgraze and pollute. To keep them on the move, leading them into fresh pasture is good management and good care.	The Lord leads us to the paths into which he would have us go. "He instructs me by His word and directs me by conscience and providence." —Matthew Henry

Yea, though I walk through the valley of the shadow of death, I will fear no evil: For thou art with me;

A shepherd's life, as revealed by David's writings, is full of moments of danger, especially in conducting the sheep to the high country of summer pasturelands. It is in the valleys where lurks the foe. "The Lord delivered me out of the paw of the lion, and out of the paw of the bear." (1 Samuel 17:37)	The "shadow" or fear of death is where the presence of God in one's life becomes a victory over the power of evil. The sense of the abiding presence of God brings confidence and assurance of our deliverance from every danger, internal or external.

External	Internal

Thy rod and thy staff they comfort me.

The shepherd's rod is used as a weapon against marauders. The staff, symbol of the shepherd, is a useful tool—to lift up sheep or to place lambs gently with their own mothers.

Rod is a Biblical symbol of authority. It is also a disciplinary means of accounting for the sheep as they come into the fold. "The gospel is called the rod of Christ's strength."
—Matthew Henry

The staff or old-style crook fits the sheep's neck and can be a source of helpfulness. So do we lean upon the Lord and depend upon His principles as proper means of guidance and defense.

Thou preparest a table before me in the presence of mine enemies:

One writer identifies the high country as having plateaus or veritable tablelands of pasture.

David was sustained even in the presence of his enemies. Even so are we blessed by our trials.

Thou anointest my head with oil; My cup runneth over.

Olive oil from the region was often poured on the sheep to heal and soothe scratches and bites. A sheep drinks best from an overflowing vessel—a typical "two-handled cup into which a fevered sheep might sink its nose."
—Leland Ryken

Oil reflects the act of consecration—either actual, as when Samuel anointed David king, or as spiritual dedication. Joy is full and running over when we can freely and fully rejoice in our state and estate.

Surely goodness and mercy shall follow me all the days of my life:

The sheep hear the voice of the shepherd— "And a stranger will they not follow. The sheep hear his voice: and he calleth his own sheep by name and leadeth them out . . . and the sheep follow him: for they know His voice." (John 10)

God's goodness and mercy shall follow me as long as I follow Him. "It shall come new every morning like the manna."
—Matthew Henry

And I will dwell in the house of the Lord for ever.

Home for the sheep is their sheepfold—that place where they will be cared for and cared about.

"The thoughts and feelings expressed by the poet are those which people most long for. The psalm speaks of peace, comfort, security, provision, freedom, hope. These are the things for which the human heart longs. . . as understandable to a child as to an adult."
—Leland Ryken

Singing a Psalm

After the study and discussion of Psalm Twenty-three, you will want to introduce the idea that poetry can have a meter—a rhythm—like music which carries us along. And here our own history is at hand to help us.

When our forefathers and mothers came to America, one of the most distinct practices of their Separatist church service was singing. For a long time singing had no instrumental accompaniment, so determined were they to break away from any form of ceremonial observance as had characterized the established hierarchical churches. When the Pilgrims traveled from England to Holland, in Amsterdam they met Henry Ainsworth (1571?–1623), whose name is ever remembered in connection with *The Ainsworth Psalter*. This metric version of the Psalms had been published in Amsterdam in 1612 for the group of Separatists who had fled from England to Holland early in the seventeenth century. William Bradford's group of Pilgrims had their first singing with this version and it was brought into New England by the Puritans. Finally, in 1640, a new version was published in Massachusetts. In fact the *Bay Psalm Book* was the first book published in America—a singing book of the poetry of the Bible.

How did these Pilgrim and Puritan groups sing the psalms without musical accompaniment? The quaint custom of "lining-out the psalm" to be sung implied that each line of the psalm was sung first by a deacon or preceptor, then by the assembled congregation. This is a good way to introduce the singing of this psalm to your class.

Here is the *Bay Psalm Book's* rendering of the Twenty-third Psalm into meter, and with its original spelling. The comparative ease into which these lines fall into verse form again bear witness to the lyric quality of these psalms.

A Psalme of David

1   The Lord to mee a shepheard is,
     want therefore shall not I,
2   Hee in the folds of tender-grasse,
     doth cause mee down to lie.
    To waters calme hee gently leads
3   Restore my soule doth hee:
    he doth in paths of righteousness:
     for his names sake leade mee.
4   Yea though in valley of deaths shade
     I walk, none ill I'le feare:
    because thou art with mee, thy rod,
     and staffe my comfort are.

5   For mee a table thou hast spread,
     in presence of my foes:
    thou does annoynt my head with oyle,
     my cup it over-flowes,
6   Goodness & mercy surely shall
     all my dayes follow mee:
    and in the Lords house I shall dwell
     so long as dayes shall bee.

—*Bay Psalm Book*

A Literary Study of a Book of the Bible

Amos: Prophet and Statesman

This study of Amos is an example of how a book of the Bible can be presented by the teacher as a literary study.

Prophet

Amos (Name means "burden" or "burden-bearer.")

Training

A shepherd and dresser of sycamore trees, a gatherer of wild figs. A native of Tekoa, a town in Judah, some miles south of Bethlehem.

Date of Prophecy

Eighth century before Christ (760 B.C.)

Historic Period

Amos prophesied during the reigns of Jeroboam II in Israel and Uzziah in Judah at a time of unusual prosperity when a prophet of doom would not be believed nor welcomed. Yet within fifty years of Amos's prophecy the doom of Israel which he announced was fulfilled.

Theme of Amos's Message

The righteousness of God as the only basis of social justice. "But let judgment ["justice" in *Amplified Old Testament*] run down as waters, and righteousness as a mighty stream." (Amos 5:24, KJV)

Significance of Amos's Message

"He believed religion involved justice toward one's fellowman, and conferred great responsibility as well as blessing. Because Israel had been given an unusual opportunity to know the will of God, she would be expected to live by this higher standard of righteousness. (Open Bible)

Acceptance of Amos's Message

Amos came into conflict with "the established custodians of the religious institutions. It was so with Jesus, who met the hostility of the Jewish priests and Sadducees; and it was the entrenched bitterness of the religious leaders which brought about His death on the cross." (Open Bible)

Amos Rejected by the Establishment

"Then Amaziah the priest of Bethal sent to Jeroboam king of Israel, saying, Amos hath conspired against thee in the midst of the house of Israel: the land is not able to bear all his words. For thus Amos saith, Jeroboam shall die by the sword, and Israel shall surely be led away captive out of their own land. Also Amaziah said unto Amos, O thou seer, flee thee away into the land of Judah, and there eat bread and prophesy there: But prophesy not again any more at Bethel: for it is the king's chapel, and it is the king's court." (Amos 7:10–13)

In *Matthew Henry's Commentary on the Whole Bible,* Vol. IV, p. 1257, we read: "One would have expected" that the people would awaken to repentance. God never sent a message of warning without "a way to escape"—a reprieve if the people would repent and reform. This should have "endeared" the prophet Amos to them. But, Amos ran up against the establishment of his day. Henry continues:

"The informer was Amaziah the priest of Bethel, the chief of the priests that ministered to the golden calf there, the president of Bethel (so some read it), that had the principal hand in civil affairs there. . . .

"Amaziah brings information to Jeroboam against Amos. . . . The crime he is charged with is no less than treason. . . . Note, it is no new thing for the accusers of the brethren to misrepresent them as enemies to the king and kingdom, as traitors to their prince and troublers of the land, when really they are the best friends to both.

"See the malice of Amaziah; he does not tell the king how Amos had interceded for Israel, and by his intercession had turned away first one judgment and then another, and did not let fall his intercession till he saw the decree had gone forth; he does not tell him that these threatenings were conditional, and that he had often assured them that if they would repent and reform the ruin should be prevented. . . .

"Amaziah tried to persuade Amos to leave the country. Bethel was not the place for him to exercise his ministry for it was the place where the royal family resided and where were set the thrones of judgment. . . because it was not fit that the king and his house should be affronted in their own court and chapel by the reproofs and threatenings of which Amos was continually teasing them in the name of the Lord. . . . He persuades him that the land of Judah was the fittest place for him to set up in."

Amos's Response to Opposition

Amos produces his divine commission. "Then answered Amos, and said to Amaziah, 'I was no prophet, neither was I a prophet's son; but I was a herdsman, and a gatherer of sycamore fruit. And the Lord took me as I followed the flock, and the Lord said unto me, Go prophesy unto my people Israel.'" (Amos 7:14–15)

A Famine of God's Word Prophesied— the Loss of Israel's Spiritual Heritage

Of all the judgments which God gave to Amos to prophesy to Israel, one was most serious for it threatened to remove the source of their unique identity as the children of God—to remove their unique history and responsibility, to remove the reason for their unique individuality and purpose.

"Behold, the days come, saith the Lord God, that I will send a famine in the land, not a famine of bread, nor a thirst for water, but of hearing the words of the Lord:

"And they shall wander from sea to sea, and from the north even to the east, they shall run to and fro to seek the word of the Lord, and shall not find it." (Amos 8:11–12)

Judgment Tempered with Mercy; Future Restoration

"And I will bring again the captivity of my people Israel, and they shall build the waste cities, and inhabit them; and they shall plant vineyards, and drink the wine thereof; they shall also make gardens, and eat the fruit of the land. And I will plant them upon their land, and they shall no more be pulled up out of their land which I have given them, saith the Lord thy God." (Amos 9:14–15)

Religious Sins

Idolatry of Israel. "Have ye offered unto me sacrifices and offerings in the wilderness forty years, O house of Israel? But ye have borne the tabernacle of your Moloch and Chiun your images, the star of your God, which ye made to yourselves." (Amos 5:25–26) God condemns their "pocket-idols for your private superstition."

Sins of Character for Israel

Women of Israel—idle and heartless—"Cows of Basham."

"Hear this word, ye kine of Basham, that are in the mountain of Samaria, which oppress the poor, which crush the needy, which say to their masters, bring, and let us drink." (Amos 4:1)

"The virgin of Israel is fallen: she shall no more rise: she is forsaken upon her land; there is none to raise her up." (Amos 5:1)

The Men of Israel—no longer mindful of their heritage and responsibility. "Woe to them that are at ease in Zion, and trust in the mountain of Samaria, which are named chief of the nations, to whom the house of Israel came!" (Amos 6:1)

Those that dwelt in the holy city, where the temple was, were "quiet from all fear of evil. . . . It is hard to be great and not to be proud. Great nations and great men are apt to overvalue themselves, and to overlook their neighbours, because they think they a little overtop them. But, for a check to their pride and security, the prophet bids them take notice of those cities that were within the compass of their knowledge, that had been as illustrious in their time as ever Zion or Samaria was, and yet were destroyed." (*Matthew Henry's Commentary*, Vol. IV, p.1250)

Nature of the Judgment upon Israel

Blight, death, destruction, and captivity were prophesied upon this special nation by the prophet Amos.

Amos saw Israel "ripe" for destruction, though it would be almost fifty years until this all came to pass. "Thus hath the Lord God shewed unto me: and behold a basket of summer fruit. And he said, Amos, what seest thou? And I said, A basket of summer fruit. Then said the Lord unto me, The end is come upon my people of Israel; I will not again pass by them any more. And the songs of the temple shall be howlings in that day, saith the Lord God: there shall be many dead bodies in every place; they shall cast them forth with silence." (Amos 8:1–2)

The Prophecy of Amos

1. Amos gave warning to all the states of Palestine, to Damascus, Gaza, Tyre, Edom, Ammon, Moab, and Judah.

2. Amos prophesied that there would be judgments on Israel herself.

Unique Relationship and Responsibility of Israel to God

1. God destroyed "the Amorite before them, whose height was like the height of cedars, and he was strong as the oaks." (Amos 2:9)

2. God delivered them from their Egyptian bondage. "Also I brought you up from the land of Egypt, and led you forty years through the wilderness, to possess the land of the Amorite." (Amos 2:10)

3. The distinguishing favor God has shown to the family of Jacob. "Hear this word that the Lord hath spoken against you, O children of Israel, against the whole family which I brought up from the land of Egypt, saying, You only have I known of all the families of the earth: therefore I will punish you for all your iniquities." (Amos 3:1–2)

4. Israel is admonished to make her peace with God by obedience and repentance. "Can two walk together, except they be agreed." (Amos 3:3)

The Sins of Israel Which Will Bring About God's Judgment upon Her

External Sins—luxury and exploitation, violence and robbery: "It was a time of political success, for Jeroboam had won back all that the Syrians had taken from the kingdom before his time. With this came material prosperity and its attendant luxury and indulgence. It is against this background of wealth and splendor—'houses of ivory,' 'great houses,' palaces of 'hewn stone,' 'beds of ivory,' 'that drink wine in bowls,' 'that chant to the sound of the viol'—that Amos sees in sharp contrast the condition of the poor, set aside and trampled upon by corrupt judges, priests and nobles who make the measure small and the price great—'making the ephah small, and the shekel great,' 'and falsifying the balances by deceit' so as to sell the innocent for silver and the needy for a pair of sandals. (Amos 2:6) Men who are so absorbed in business that they can hardly wait for feast days and Sabbaths to pass, so that they can resume their trade in wheat, though it is only the poorest of it that they will sell to the common people of the land." (Amos 8:5) (*The Story of the Old Testament*, Edgar J. Goodspeed, 1936)

Religious Sins

The hypocrisy of worship—offensive to God. "I hate, I despise your feast days. . . . Though ye offer me burnt offerings and your meat offering, I will not accept them." (Amos 6:21–23)

Israel Urged to Repentance

1. Seek the Lord. "For thus saith the Lord unto the house of Israel, Seek ye me, and ye shall live. Seek good, and not evil, that ye may live: and so the Lord, the God of

hosts, shall be with you, as ye have spoken. Hate the evil, and love the good, and establish judgment in the gate; it may be that the Lord God of hosts will be gracious unto the remnant of Joseph." (Amos 5:4, 14–15)

2. The character of Israel's God. "Seek him that maketh the seven stars and Orion, and turneth the shadow of death into the morning, and maketh the day dark with night: that calleth for the waters of the sea, and poureth them out upon the face of the earth: the Lord is his name. That strengtheneth the spoiled against the strong, so that the spoiled shall come against the fortress." (Amos 5:8–9)

"What a God he is whom we are to seek. He is a God of almighty power himself. The idols were impotent things, could do neither good nor evil, and therefore it was folly either to fear or trust them; but the God of Israel does everything, and can do any thing, and therefore we ought to seek to him; he challenges our homage who has all power in his hand, and it is our interest to have him on our side. Divers proofs and instances are here given of God's power, as Creator, in the kingdom of nature, as both founding and governing that kingdom. . . . The stars are the work of his hands. . . . He makes the seven stars and Orion, two very remarkable constellations, which Amos, a herdsman, while he kept his cattle by night, had particularly observed the motions of. . . . The constant succession of day and night is under his direction, and is kept by his power and providence. . . . The rain rises and falls as he appoints. . . . It is God that has made these things; Jehovah is his name, the name by which the God of nature, the God of the whole earth, has made himself known to his people Israel and covenanted with them.

"As he is a God of almighty power himself, so he gives strength and power unto his people that seek him, and renews strength to those that had lost it, if they wait upon him for it; for he strengthens the spoiled against the strong to such a degree that the spoiled come against the fortress and make bold and brave attacks upon those that had spoiled them. This is an encouragement to the people to seek the Lord, that, if they do so, they shall find him able to retrieve their affairs, when they are brought to the lowest ebb; though they are the spoiled, and their enemies are the strong, if they can but engage God for them, they shall soon recruit so as the next time to be not only the aggressors, but the conquerors; they come against the fortress, to make reprisals and become masters of it." (*Matthew Henry's Commentary*, Vol. IV, p. 1246)

3. Theme of Amos: plea from God to Israel. "But let judgment run down as waters, and righteousness as a mighty stream." (Amos 5:24)

Style of Amos the Herdsman

Reverend A. B. Simpson spoke of the individuality of the prophets in their writings. "We know that they acted with perfect individuality, and that each man's message was colored by the complexion of his own mind. . . . The Book of God is like a beautiful garden, where all the flowers grow upon the same soil and are watered from the same heaven, but each has its own unique colors, forms, fragrance and individuality." (*Teaching and Learning*, Slater, p.154)

The Individuality of Amos's Writings

Amos was no prophet, trained in a school of the prophets; God called him "as I followed the flock," "I was a herdsman, and a gatherer of sycamore fruit."

Just as David's psalms reflect his life as a shepherd in the hills of Judea or fleeing from his enemies in the wilderness of Engedi, so Amos's style of writing exemplifies his life as a plain country man.

Vivid Imagery

1. "Behold I am pressed under you, as a cart is pressed that is full of sheaves." (Amos 2:13)

   "I am loaded and burdened by you, and can no longer bear it. . . . The great God complains of sin, especially the sins of his professing people, as a burden to him." (*Matthew Henry's Commentary*, Vol. IV, p. 1232)

2. "Therefore thus saith the Lord God; an adversary there shall be even round about the land; and he shall bring down thy strength from thee, and thy palaces shall be spoiled. Thus saith the Lord; As the shepherd taketh out of the mouth of the lion two legs, or a piece of an ear; so shall the children of Israel be taken out that dwell in Samaria in the corner of a bed, and in Damascus in a couch." (Amos 3:11–12)

   "Their countrymen shall not escape. They shall be in the hands of the enemy, as a lamb in the mouth of a lion, all devoured and eaten up, and they shall be utterly unable to make any resistance. . . . And those that do escape shall do so with the utmost difficulty and hazard by hiding themselves in the corner of a bed or under the bed's foot." (*Matthew Henry's Commentary*, Vol. IV, pp. 1236–37)

3. "Woe unto you that desire the day of the Lord! To what end is it for you? The day of the Lord is darkness, and not light. As if a man did flee from a lion, and a bear met him; or went into the house, and leaned his hand on the wall, and a serpent bit him." (Amos 5:18–19)

   "He shows the folly of those who impatiently wished for a change of God's judgments, in the hopes that the next would be better and more tolerable. They desire the day of the Lord, in hopes to better themselves (though their hearts and lives be not amended). . . . But the prophet tells them that they know not what they ask. . . . It is as if a man did flee from a lion and a bear met him, a beast of prey more cruel and ravenous than a lion, or as if a man, to escape all dangers abroad, went into the house for security, and leaned his hand on the wall to rest himself, and there a serpent bit him. Note, those who are not reformed by the judgments of God will be pursued by them; and, if they escape one, another stands ready to seize them." (*Matthew Henry's Commentary*, Vol. IV, p.1248)

4. "Thus he shewed me: and, behold, the Lord stood upon a wall made by a plumb line, with a plumb line in his hand. And the Lord said unto me, Amos, what seest thou? And I said, a plumb line. Then said the Lord, Behold, I will set a plumb line in the midst of my people Israel: I will not again pass by them any more." (Amos 7:7–8)

   "The vision is of a plumb line, a line with a plummet at the end of it, such as masons and bricklayers use to run up a wall by, that they make work it straight and true, and by rule. Israel was a wall, a strong wall, which God himself had reared, as a bulwark, or wall of defence, to his sanctuary, which he set up among them. . . This wall was made by a plumb line, very exact and firm. . . . But, God now stands upon this wall, not to hold it up, but to tread it down, or, rather, to consider what he should do with it. . . . Thus God would bring the people of Israel to the trial, would discover their wickedness, and show wherein they erred; and he would likewise bring his judgments upon them. . . . " (*Matthew Henry's Commentary*, Vol. IV, p.1256)

Amos's Intercession for Israel

Upon two occasions Amos's intercession for Israel had caused God to repent and call off a plague of grasshoppers, and a drought. (Amos 7:16)

Words from the Prophet Amos

"Behold, the days come that I will send a famine in the land, not a famine of bread, not a

NOTES

thirst for water, but of hearing the words of the Lord. And they shall wander from sea to sea, and from the north even to the east, they shall run to and fro to seek the word of the Lord, and shall not find it." (Amos 8:11–12)

"God in his mercy spare our own land from such a famine as that! Better were it for us to endure war, or pestilence, or any other variety of famine, than a famine of the Word of the Lord." (The Jubilee of the American Bible Society, New York, May 10, 1866, as quoted in *Consider and Ponder*, Hall, 1975, p. 20–21)

Note:

Any book of the Bible can be taught as a literary study identifying author and literary elements. It is a joy to look into the Bible for its literary qualities and academic application.

CHAPTER THREE

THE ELEMENTARY LITERATURE PROGRAM

The Christian History Literature Program for Elementary School

Literature, like history, if studied chronologically, tells us *who* we are as a people, *where* our principles and ideals come from, and *why* we are here—our purpose as a nation. The Christian History Literature Program identifies the study of literature with the westward movement of Christianity and the appearing of greater liberty for the individual in every sphere—the civil or political, the religious or ecclesiastical, and the economic. It includes all the individual links that have been forged by men and nations promoting the Christian idea of man and government which was to appear as America:

> All the past has contributed to the excellence of her foundation, and modern Europe has supplied her with the most desirable building material both of ideas and of men. Without Asia, Greece, and Rome, there would have been a very imperfect modern Europe; and without modern Europe, America must have begun at the beginning, with all the lessons, discoveries and discipline of thousands of years to learn. *(Christian History* of the *Constitution of the United States of America,* [CHOC] Vol. I, by Verna M. Hall, 1960, p. 9)

Just as America has a purpose to fulfill in propagating the Gospel, which includes extending Biblical principles into the civil sphere so that a Christian Constitution can preserve individual liberty, so do American Christian schools have an obligation to extend their Gospel ministry into every subject of the curriculum. The field of literature is an excellent example of a subject area which must be identified with a philosophy of education and government. Without this identification of philosophy, literature becomes organized around the socialistic ideals of the day and vulnerable to humanistic feelings and goals. If literature does not include both its American and its Christian aspects, it will fall into the camp of progressive education and, despite the best intentions, actually promote social goals rather than Christian principles. Thus we find Christian schools which theologically reject the social gospel from the pulpit, but promote the social gospel educationally (and thus governmentally) in literature—a field which plays a large part in shaping ideals and emotions. This is particularly evident in the "thematic" approach to literature which robs both authors and their works of proper identification and signification by appropriating them to illustrate categories selected by compilers.

Literature Collectivized

The architecture of socialism, through the medium of progressive education, has housed the sorry remnants of our heritage of literature in conglomerate collections. Known as "anthologies," these unwieldy volumes have been responsible for watering down our treasury of great literature and diverting the attention of students from the distinctive talents of great authors. Literature has been replaced by a concern for the environment—be that environment social, political, or economic.

In 1963, when Drs. James J. Lynch and Bertrand Evans of the University of California did a critical study of "High School English Textbooks," they found the study of literature completely surrendered to the programming of the anthologies. Furthermore, their minute examination of seventy-two of the leading conglomerates in literature led them to some of the following conclusions:

1. Most of the "literature" selected for the anthologies was either non-literature or second-rate literature.

2. Much of the content of the selections was either drastically abridged or completely re-written and "adapted" for vocabulary relaxation.

3. Chronology was simplified to selections from the past of no earlier than 1900—preferably since 1930; thus the past was relegated to the dim past.

4. The organization of the anthologies was structured around social themes denoting a life-adjustment philosophy and all selections were fitted into these categories.

5. Editorial apparatus—teaching suggestions and student projects—was over-burdened.

While these criticisms apply to high school anthologies, much the same specific evaluation can be made of those reading series for elementary schools which are classified as "literary" in content. Without a clear identification of a philosophy of education and government that is American Christian, these readers flow into the same stream as that of progressive education with humanistic ideals and socialistic goals. Even those series published by Christian publishers, because they do not identify the distinctions between a Christian philosophy and a progressive philosophy of education, consciously or unconsciously, find their series including that which would undermine and subvert their Christian intent and purpose. It has been said: "If you don't know what you stand for, you will fall for anything." The failure to extend Christian principles of education into the field of literature has made Christian educators vulnerable. The desire to improve the field of literature for students in Christian schools must include the identification of the gulf between the Christian and the pagan or secular conception of life in all areas, and the Christian idea of man and thus of his government—or that which influences and controls him. It is evident that the failure of Christians to teach the Chain of Christianity's westward movement and God's hand in the affairs of men and nations affects all subjects in the curriculum. Thus, Christianity actually strengthens the

progressive curriculum by Christianizing it—by adapting to it in an evolutionary manner, rather than shaping and determining it from the standpoint of a distinctive Christian philosophy of education.

The study of literature in a Christian school should turn the eyes of students away from man and his many inventions towards the Lord. It should only be an instrument to glorify the Creator and His "handiwork." The study of literature, as of every subject in the curriculum of an American Christian school, should produce the following attitudes and convictions:

1. **A Love for God**. A heart and mind trained to see His Hand in all things great and small.

2. **A Love for God's Written Word—The Holy Bible**. Learning the Bible as the textbook of education, of literature and the study of character—as the Handbook of life.

3. **A Love for Home and Family**. An appreciation for each one in the home—father and mother, sister and brother, grandfather and grandmother, and the aunts, uncles, and cousins, too. What home means in our American Christian republic and its special contribution as a Christian institution must be taught to every generation.

4. **A Love for Individual Christian Character**. The understanding and appreciation of the talents which God has given each one of us to be shaped and fashioned for His use are part of this product which the study of literature, history, and all subjects makes visible.

5. **A Love for the Chain of Christianity** as it moves westward and the contributions which individual links have made.

6. **A Love of Country—America**. To learn America's relationship to Christianity and what unique contribution she has made by extending Christian principles into the establishment of institutions of government is key to this understanding. One writer defined her role as "destined to furnish the

most complete expression of the Christian civilization; and to become the fountain of a new and higher life for all the races of men." Another stated, speaking of America:

"There the Englishman, the German, the Frenchman, the Italian, the Scandinavian, the Asiatic, and the African all meet as equals. There they are free to speak, to think, and to act. They bring the common contributions of character, energy, and activity to the support and enlargement of a common country, through all the lands of their origin." (*CHOC*, I, p. 8)

7. A Love of Learning. This is important for the future raising up of Christian scholarship and a return to the quality of thinkers and writers equal to our Pilgrim and Constitutional periods when men, theologically educated, were our leaders in every field.

The Christian History Literature Program for the elementary school includes the following emphasis—to present the Christian History principles in literature. It is particularly applicable to relate God's principle of individuality to the distinctiveness of authors and to the uniqueness of style, subject, and ability. This principle must also be extended to the identification of the contributions of nations to the field of literature. The Christian principle of self-government made a difference to writers in America—free for the first time to write under a Christian republic which was based upon the importance of individual liberty and responsibility. How was this American writing identified to the world and by whom? Christian character and the property of conscience have been discussed and they are a major emphasis of this study of literature. Finally, the Christian History Literature Program seeks to present to young American Christians:

1. **A Treasury of Ideals of Our Nation**

2. **A Record of Christian Character**—or the lack of it

3. **An Instrument for the Cultivation of the Imagination**—"that inward eye which is the bliss of solitude"

4. **An Instrument to Glorify God and His Handiwork**, rather than to exalt man and "his many inventions"

One final word must be stated here about restoring the *wholistic* study of authors and their works—of books not diluted nor changed by editors who seek to make them more palatable to youth. The following statements were made by Horace Scudder (1838–1902), editor of *The Riverside Magazine for Young People* (1867–70), of *Atlantic Monthly* (1890–1898), and author of a number of books, in an article published in *Atlantic Monthly* in 1887:

American Classics in School

The real point of practical reform, however, is not in the preference of American authors to English, but in the careful concentration of the minds of boys and girls upon standard American literature, in opposition to the dissipation over a desultory and mechanical acquaintance with scraps from a variety of sources, good, bad and indifferent. . . . There is plenty of *vagrancy* in reading; the public libraries and cheap papers are abundantly able to satisfy the truant; but it ought to be recognized once for all that the schools are to train the mind into appreciation of literature, not to *amuse* it with idle diversion; to this end, the simplest and most direct method is to place before the boys and girls for their regular task in reading, not *scraps* from this and that author, duly paragraphed and numbered, but a wisely selected series of works by men whom their country honors, and who have made their country worth living in. . . .

The *continuous reading* of a classic is in itself a liberal education; the fragmentary reading of commonplace lessons in minor morals, such as make up much of our reading-books, is a pitiful waste of the growing mental powers. Even were our reading-books composed of choice selections from the highest literature, they would still miss the very great advantage which follows upon the steady growth of acquaintance with a sustained piece of literary art. . . .

There is a great deal of mischief in teaching young people *about* literature and perhaps giving them occasional specimens, but all the while keeping them at a distance from the real thing.

Let us then restore the study of literature to its rightful place in the curriculum of an American Christian school and make it distinctive as we pray that our lives may be distinctive to the honor and glory of Jesus Christ.

Reading "Whole Books" Instead of "Fragments"

Horace Scudder of Connecticut, the Constitution State, was responsible for making available to young Americans hundreds of classics in inexpensive bindings. Associated for many years with Houghton Mifflin Co., he was responsible for *The Riverside Series for Young People*, for he was convinced that "whole works were superior to the fragments in the old-fashioned readers."

In order to combat the fragmentation of literature through the use of "Readers" and "Anthologies," F.A.C.E. agreed that we should teach whole books, not fragments. So we began to develop "Key Classics on the Chain of Christianity" for classroom study. For each of these classics, F.A.C.E. also produced a syllabus, so that the teacher would have a background of historical and Biblical reasons as to why each particular book is important to both literature and liberty. These classics are listed in the F.A.C.E. catalogue, with syllabi, for all levels of learning.

Restoring Key Authors in the Literature of Liberty

A serious change has come about in American education with the decline of reading ability. Early classics in English and American literature were not "written down" for young people's consumption. There was no "dividing line" between the young and old. Consequently several generations could enjoy together the writings of Sir Walter Scott, Charles Dickens, Jane Austen, Robert Louis Stevenson, Rudyard Kipling, and many other English writers. F.A.C.E. has made a particular effort to restore to the curriculum these English authors, as well as American authors like Washington Irving, James Fenimore Cooper, Nathaniel Hawthorne, Henry Wadsworth Longfellow, and many more.

appeal to his heart and mind and later the words wrap around this wonder of being loved. The word "nestle" from Noah Webster's 1828 *Dictionary* is defined: "(1) To settle; to harbor; to lie close and snug, as a bird in her nest; (2) To cherish, as a bird her young."

How comforting is this bedtime—this going to sleep, this nestling of the newborn. "I will both lay me down in peace, and sleep: for thou, Lord, only makest me dwell in safety." The Psalmist echoed the tender sentiment deep in the heart of each one of us. To cultivate this conviction we lose not a day when we make slumber time a time of conscious trust and security. How better can we convey it than through the gentle words of a lullaby.

Literature in Lullabies

For a Christian, one of the most precious lullabies is that written by Martin Luther (1483–1546), and usually sung at Christmas time. The music is found in most hymnals:

Away in a Manger

Away in a manger,
No crib for a bed,
The little Lord Jesus
Laid down His sweet head;
The stars in the heavens
Looked down where He lay,
The Little Lord Jesus
Asleep in the hay.

The cattle are lowing,
The poor baby wakes,
But little Lord Jesus,
No crying He makes;
I love Thee, Lord Jesus!
Look down from the sky,
And stay by my cradle
'Til morning is nigh.

Famous throughout the English-speaking world is this Welsh lullaby whose harmonies have lulled many a wee one to slumberland:

All through the Night

Sleep, my child, and peace attend thee
All through the night;
Guardian angels God will send thee,
All through the night.

Soft the drowsy hours are creeping,
Hill and vale in slumber steeping,
I my loving vigil keeping,
All through the night.

While the moon her watch is keeping,
All through the night,
While the weary world is sleeping,
All through the night.

O'er thy spirit gently stealing,
Visions of delight revealing,
Breathes a pure and holy feeling,
All through the night.

Surely, one of the most delightful to sing is this lullaby by England's Poet Laureate, Alfred Lord Tennyson:

Lullaby

Sweet and low, sweet and low,
Wind of the western sea,
Low, low, breathe and blow,
Wind of the western sea!
Over the rolling waters go,
Come from the dying moon, and blow,
Blow him again to me;
While my little one, while my pretty one,
    sleeps.

Sleep and rest, sleep and rest,
Father will come to thee soon;
Rest, rest, on mother's breast,
Father will come to thee soon;
Father will come to his babe in the nest,
Silver sails all out of the west
Under the silver moon;
Sleep, my little one, sleep, my pretty one,
    sleep.   —Alfred Tennyson

Lullaby of an Infant Chief

O hush thee, my babie, thy sire was a knight,
Thy mother a lady, both lovely and bright;
The woods and the glens, from the towers
    which we see,
They all are belonging, dear babie, to thee.
O ho ro, i ri ri, cadul gu lo,
O ho ro, i ri ri, and
O fear not the bugle, though loudly it blows,
It calls but the warders that guard thy re-
    pose;
Their bows would be bended, their blades
    would be red,
Ere the step of a foeman drew near to thy
    bed.
O ho ro, i ri ri, cadul gu lo,
O ho ro, i ri, ri, and
O hush thee, my babie, the time soon will
    come
When thy sleep shall be broken by trum-
    pet and drum;
Then hush thee, my darling, take rest, while
    you may,
For strife comes with manhood, and wak-
    ing with day.
O ho ro, i ri ri, and . . . .
                    —Sir Walter Scott (1815)

The clock struck one,
The mouse ran down,
Hickory, dickory, dock.

Here is action for the imagination. Here is food for further discussion and conversation, to say nothing of providing opportunities for memorization.

The second reason Dr. Barnes advances for children's interest in Mother Goose is because they are rhythmical—there is a regularity of metrical accent.

A diller, a dollar, a ten o'clock scholar,
What makes you come so soon?
You used to come at ten o'clock,
But now you come at noon.

To stress the strongly marked accents, Dr. Barnes indicates the use of alliteration—the repetition of initial consonant sounds—and the use of rhyme. A popular example of alliteration is this song:

Sing a song of sixpence,
A pocket full of rye;
Four-and-twenty blackbirds
Baked in a pie;

And a good example of the reinforcement of accent by rhyme is the famous:

Jack and Jill went up the hill,
To fetch a pail of water;
Jack fell down and broke his crown
And Jill came tumbling after.

Undoubtedly, then, one of the most decided characteristics of the Mother Goose jingles is the unbroken regularity of strongly marked accents. Children like that. The feeling for time seems to be the fundamental musical feeling; it seems to have developed first in the early races and to develop first in children. And the primary demand is for absolutely regular time. Later, if the sense of rhythm is developed, the ear takes pleasure in ritards and accelerandos, in holds and rests, in the various devices in music and poetry to vary the meter to conform to the particular idea or emotion expressed. But children care most for that verse which is marked by the uninterrupted, never varying recurrence of strongly stressed syllables.

The third reason for Mother Goose success is children's love of *non*-sense humor. But even a ridiculous rhyme about a ridiculous situation or character can begin to teach distinctives of character. While we will forever see Jack and Jill tumbling down that steep hill it does suggest carelessness. While Jack Horner's thumb always brings up a plum, we wonder at his manners and question his appetite. Miss Muffet has our sympathy as we too have jumped away from insects and spiders—but, also, she suggests our appraisal of individuals who allow the unexpected occurrences of daily life to upset them needlessly. And Simple Simon could be anyone who shops well but not too wisely—and here a question of value and good sense comes up for consideration.

And children love putting together delightful sound combinations that don't have to make sense like:

Hickety, pickety, my black hen
She lays eggs for gentlemen;
Gentlemen come every day
To see what my black hen doth lay.
or,
Dickery, dickery dare,
The pig flew up in the air;
The man in brown
Soon brought him down,
Dickery, dickery, dare.

Progressive education emphasizes the experience of laughter and fun. American Christian education considers that laughter and enjoyment has to be a "reflective" skill—it must have discernment. It must begin to measure by God's Word what is *true*—and what is untrue and therefore ridiculous. While we laugh at the obvious impossibility of a cow jumping over the moon, we consider in its proper time and place what a wise and wonderful Creator we have Who made all things perfectly in keeping with their designed functions. Thus *non*-sense provides a contrast for what does make good sense. Only a Christian teacher can make the reality of God's microcosms—the little worlds of a seed, a drop of water, a feather—as full of wonder as any marvel of man's invention.

The History of Mother Goose

Obviously we want to know where our Mother Goose with her jingles came from. There are many interesting histories of how we came by this literature. It seems to have originated in France with the publication of some fanciful tales of *La Mére l'Oye* in 1650. France had popularized a number of animal characters, so it was not surprising for Charles Perrault to publish a collection of Mother Goose in 1697. England's contribution to Mother Goose was to render her into verse; and when John Newberry (1713–1767), one of the eighteenth century's most distinguished publishers, put out an edition in 1767, it was prefaced by Oliver Goldsmith.

Crossing the ocean, Mother Goose was reprinted by Isaiah Thomas in Worcester, Massachusetts in 1785. A later edition published in 1824–1825 began to make changes from the English edition. The famous Boston edition of 1833 nurtured many of America's famous authors and was referred to familiarly as "the Boston Mother Goose." A 1905 facsimile of this edition includes an introduction by the Reverend Edward Everett Hale, author of *The Man without a Country.*

It makes a good story when we learn that one Thomas Fleet in Boston did marry an Elizabeth Goose and that he published a book in 1719 entitled *Mother Goose's Melody.* No one will ever know if "Mother Goose" was the wife or the mother-in-law of Thomas Fleet. But whether or not there was a real flesh and blood individuality for Mother Goose, she was claimed by the Americans. Today on the continent, and especially in England, these traditional verses are identified as "nursery rhymes," whereas we in America call them "Mother Goose Rhymes." Americans have kept the comfortable, motherly old Goose alive in picture and verse, and she waddles through the heads of countless children century after century. Let us hope that millions more will learn the rudiments of rhyming and reasoning as they recite their Mother Goose rhymes to attentive parents and teachers.

The Real Personages of Mother Goose

The Real Personages of Mother Goose by Katherine Elwes Thomas, 1930.

This delightful book of research in Mother Goose folklore provides us with a vivid backdrop to English history and, in fact, makes an excellent accompaniment for high school students. For students in Christian schools studying America's Christian history, the historical personages of Mother Goose fit into the study of history from the standpoint of the Chain of Christianity moving westward.

The period of Henry the Eighth is a period which seems dark for evangelical Christianity. Yet while His Majesty was waging a theological battle to permit him to divorce Catherine of Aragon and marry Anne Boleyn, he was actually separating England from the Pope. The hand of God, as some historians have pointed out, was preparing the seed and the soil for the Pilgrims who were to carry Christianity westward to America. Many of the popular nursery rhymes with which we are familiar are purported to have been written about personages and events which were fomenting at the political level of English history. Meanwhile, under the surface of great events, a purifying stream of evangelism was preparing the country for the publication of a Bible in English so that every individual might read the Word. Henry the Eighth authorized the sale and reading of The Great Bible in England in 1539 in order to help jar his people away from the spiritual domination of the Pope. What he did not count upon was that the power of the Word began to transform the hearts and minds of Englishmen so that such a people as the Separatists would have the courage to become Pilgrims for the sake of the Gospel.

"Little Jack Horner" eating his "Christmas pie" and pulling out a "plum" illustrates the wicked policies of Henry the Eighth. The pie, which a real Mr. Horner was supposed to be carrying to the king, contained twelve title deeds to certain church estates which Henry was repossessing from the church now separated from Rome. Jack's plum was one of these deeds which he claimed to have been given him from the king. The descendants of Jack Horner do indeed possess the original deed bearing the king's signature though they deny it was ever a plum in a pie but rather came to them direct from the king.

Little Jack Horner is also supposed to be the Jack who built his house in the popular "This is the house that Jack built." Mrs. Thomas had the pleasure of inspecting the present-day Horner estate and of identifying the location of places and personages which the poem mentions.

> Sing a song of sixpence,
> A pocket full of rye,
> Four-and-twenty blackbirds
> Baked in a pie;
> When the pie was opened,
> The birds began to sing;
> Wasn't that a dainty dish
> To set before a King?

This song and its next verse indeed make a great case for Henry's wicked ways. Once again the pie is full of deeds to church properties which Henry is fast appropriating to the Crown. Henry is supposed to be rejoicing over his new income. At the same time Catherine of Aragon is eating the bread of England coated with the honey of Spain's assurances that she will not be divorced by Henry. But the maid in the garden "hanging out the clothes" is Anne Boleyn whose new wardrobe from France will clothe her for a thousand fateful days as Henry's legal wife before her fate is sealed by the executioner's axe. The "blackbird" who will have her head "snipped off" is Cardinal Wolsey.

But the fate of Cardinal Wolsey is also predicted in a famous nursery rhyme so familiar to us all:

> Little Boy Blue, come blow your horn,
> The sheep's in the meadow, the cow's in
>   the corn.
> Where is the boy that looks after the sheep?
> He's under the haycock fast asleep!

Cardinal Wolsey, known as Little Boy Blue, allowed material riches, pomp, and power to put him to sleep while he lived lavishly at Hampton Court. When the day of his downfall came, Wolsey might have echoed these words which Shakespeare puts into his mouth in *Henry VIII*:

> Cromwell, I charge thee, fling away ambition:
> By that sin, fell the angels; how can man then,
> The Image of his Maker, hope to win by it?
> . . . .
> O Cromwell, Cromwell!
> Had I but serv'd my God with half the zeal
> I serv'd my king, he would not in mine age
> Have left me naked to mine enemies.

The history of the Mother Goose personages neither adds nor subtracts from their purpose in introducing children to their heritage of oral literature. For the adult student they provide an interesting backdrop of historical probability. For the child who learns the rippling rhymes of Mother Goose, the knowledge that they might have been provoked by political rhymesters to point out the evil deeds of men and women in "high places" would tarnish their luster.

Mother Goose in Our Literature

Most of the nursery jingles that we call Mother Goose melodies came from England. They were not the product of any one person. The Mother Goose rhymes are popular poetry, that is, poetry of the people. They originated with the people and were handed down by them. Many of the jingles are very old and were popular as far back as we have any knowledge of them. There is a strong probability that not a few nursery rhymes were built up by accretion. Someone improvised a jingle on a certain subject; someone else added a stanza, and someone else added another, and so on, until it became a fairly long poem. Examples of this kind of a creation: "Mother Hubbard," "London Bridge," "Gay Go Up and Gay Go Down."

Some of the ditties seem to have originated in little scenes and incidents of child life and so we have, "Diddle, diddle, dumpling, my son

John." The Mother Goose jingles were composed by the people—not written down, not studied, not elaborated. They were spontaneous utterances of such excellence that they remained in the memory of the people and were transmitted from generation to generation by "word of *mother*."

Does any one doubt that oral tradition was able to preserve and transmit the Mother Goose verses through the long period of two or three hundred years? Let him but remember that folk tales and fairy stories lived orally for centuries before the Grimms and Jacobs and Langs gathered them into books. Let him but remember that the popular ballads of England and Scotland were transmitted orally from the fifteenth and sixteenth centuries to the time of Percy in the eighteenth century. Or let him but study the history of such singing games as "King William was King James's Son" or "London Bridge is Falling Down," or observe how the boys of today use in their games certain terms and phrases that are hundreds of years old—terms that have never found their way into books, not even into any but the most recent dictionaries. Oral tradition has been the amber in which nearly all of the folklore, folk games, and folk literature we now possess has been preserved." (*The Children's Poets* by Dr. Walter Barnes, from his chapter on "Mother Goose." World Book Company, 1932.)

Teaching Our Heritage of Mother Goose

Remove not the ancient landmark,
which thy fathers have set.
—Proverbs 22:28

Home is the place to begin the teaching of children's literature. But the schoolroom also can be a place to establish many of the good things associated with home. Our early memories of home should include the lullabies, the nursery rhymes, and the Mother Goose rhymes as well as our prayers, our hymns, and our first study of the Bible.

An American Christian school has a responsibility to teach students, and if possible their parents, that part of their heritage which will become an introduction to English and American poetry—indeed to the whole field of literature.

One author-illustrator, Marguerite de Angeli, had this to say in the Foreword of her *Book of Nursery and Mother Goose Rhymes*, about the connection of this area of literature to home, history, and the satisfying memories of childhood:

When I think of the nursery rhymes and my first memory of them, I remember my mother, sitting in a low rocker, singing during a thunderstorm. What she was singing is not clear. It could have been "Sing a Song of Sixpence," "Rock-a-bye Baby" or any one of the familiar rhymes, or all of them, for there were many rockings and many comfortings. Later, when my younger brothers came along, I often sat in my mother's place and sang to them, choosing my own favorites and making up the tunes as I went. In those days we sang and rocked the children to sleep, and felt their dear heaviness when they finally gave up the fight to keep awake.

Still later, when I had been married and we had children of our own, the habit of singing the nursery rhymes was continued, and now that we have grandchildren, it goes on. They still listen as long as the words continue, and at the pause for breath say, "Do it again."

Sometimes, instead of my mother's voice, it is my English grandfather's voice that I hear when I think of "Please to remember the fifth of November" and "Guy Fawkes' Day," or it is my father's voice saying, "Theophilus Thistle, the successful thistle sifter."

When my husband and I went to England a few years ago, those early mental images came alive. And now the flowery fields and blossoming hedgerows, the stone walls and castles, the cobblestone streets have all crept into the pictures for the nursery rhymes. A twelfth-century bridge I sketched turned up in the painting for "Hark, Hark, the Dogs Do Bark"; the oven in the kitchen at Hampton Court I remembered when I drew the "Queen of Hearts." In my mind "Wee Willie Winkie" has always run down a narrow cobbled street and around a corner as I pictured him, and I saw many streets where he belonged. The chalky cliffs with the cap of green that are in "I Saw Three Ships A-Sailing" were the cliffs of Dover that we saw when we crossed the Channel.

In the pictures of children, our own children are represented, of course, but new types have come forth that resemble our grandchildren. I was surprised to find, after it was finished, that in "Bless the Master of This House" I had pictured my own brothers and sister, my mother and father, in our right age relation, sitting around the table. Though it was unconscious, perhaps it was natural, because all the time I was so happily painting I had been thinking how much we used to enjoy the "current" baby in his high chair and how we all loved Christmas. No doubt Bob Crachitt's family came into my mind, too, and that accounts for the period of the costume.

Saying or singing the rhymes seems always to open a long corridor in my mind through which I see generations of mothers going about their needful work, the children at their heels or in their laps enchanted by the rhythmic sound of words; words that are sometimes pure nonsense, sometimes full of age-old wisdom, or seeming to have lost their meaning because of time and custom past. One of the favorites in our family has been "One misty, moisty morning," partly because we often have that kind of morning in Philadelphia, but mostly because it was our daughter Nina's favorite when she could barely say it, and her way of saying it lent it charm. Not long ago, when I came upon an article in the *National Geographic* about the Jutland man so well preserved in the peatland since the seventh century, still wearing his leather cap with a strap beneath his

chin, I had the uncanny feeling that he was to be one of the most ancient, going back hundreds and hundreds of years, long before there were books of rhymes and pictures.

I have loved doing the book.

—Marguerite de Angeli, 1953

Choosing Mother Goose Rhymes to Teach

Literature notebooks should contain a selection of the Mother Goose rhymes chosen for each grade. Older students would be interested in the historical background of some of the verses.

Select some rhymes for their musical quality; after the children know them by heart, they can skip, gallop, run, walk, swing, trot, and hop to the sound of them. Other rhymes are for imagining comic action: the Cow jumping over the moon, Miss Muffet running away from the spider; Jack and Jill tumbling down, etc. Some Mother Goose rhymes have story interest, e.g., "The Queen of Hearts" and "Old Mother Hubbard and her dog." Of course, humor plays a big part in the enjoyment of reciting Mother Goose: "Simple Simon," "Humpty Dumpty," and "Peter Peter" who keeps his wife in a pumpkin shell. Mother Goose helps memory, imagination, and speech, for clear, crisp enunciation in rhythm brings joy to the listener as well as the performer. (*Children and Books*, May Hill Arbuthnot, 3d ed.,1964)

May Hill Arbuthnot suggests that "it is a rewarding task to make a list of the different kinds of verses in Mother Goose." How many categories can you identify?

> Twice five years
> Or less I might have seen, when first my mind
> With conscious pleasure opened to the charm
> Of words in tuneful order, found them sweet
> For their own *sakes*, a passion, and a power;
> And phrases pleased me chosen for delight,
> For pomp, or love.
>
> —Wordsworth,
> *The Prelude*, Bk. v.

Categories of Mother Goose Rhymes

People (a rich gallery of characters):

"Mistress Mary, quite contrary"
"Peter, Peter, pumpkin eater"
"The old woman who lived in the shoe"
"Little Miss Muffet"
"Little Boy Blue"
"Little Tommy Tucker"
"Jack Sprat," etc.

Animals:

"Pussy-cat, pussy-cat"
"Mary's Little Lamb"
"Little Birdie"
"The City Mouse and the Garden Mouse"
"Cock Robin," etc.

Finger Plays and Baby Games:

"The Five Little Fairies"
"Baby at Play"
"Pat-a-cake," etc.
"Pease-porridge hot"
"Mix a pancake," etc.

Riddles:

"Humpty Dumpty"
"As I was going to St. Ives"
"Little Nanny Netticoat," etc.

Counting Rhymes:

"One, two, buckle my shoe," etc.

Alphabets:

"A was an apple pie," etc.

Superstitions:

"See a pin and pick it up," etc.

Time Verses:

"Thirty days hath September," etc.

Dialogue:

"Who killed Cock Robin?"

Songs:

"A frog he would a-wooing go"

Street Cries:

"Hot-cross buns," etc.

Weather:

"Rain, rain, go away"

Tongue Twisters:

"Peter Piper picked a peck of pickled peppers," etc.

Accumulative Stories:

"This is the house that Jack built," etc.

Nonsense:

"Three wise men of Gotham"

Resources for Teaching Lullabies, Mother Goose, and Nursery Rhymes

References for the Teacher

The Annotated Mother Goose with an Introduction and Notes by William S. Baring-Gould and Ceil Baring-Gould, illustrated by Caldecott, Crane, Greenaway, Rackham, Parrish, and historical background of our literary heritage from Mother Goose. The black and white illustrations include the most famous illustrators of these jingles and rhymes. [HB & PB, out-of-print]

The Oxford Dictionary of Nursery Rhymes. Edited by Iona and Peter Opie. Oxford University Press, 1951. This is a scholarly [HB] edition classifying and identifying more than 500 rhymes of our traditional literature of the nursery. Included are some illustrations and copious notes in fine print of the history and information concerning this initial area of children's literature.

Picture Books of Mother Goose

Marguerite de Angeli's Book of Nursery and Mother Goose Rhymes, Doubleday & Company, PB, 1979 [out-of stock]. This author-illustrator production complements itself in that the illustrations keep the traditional flavor of earlier famous illustrators of Mother Goose. There is a softness and tenderness in the drawings which allow the child to enter into the spirit of the lively rhymes without being distracted. The large pages permit breathing spaces so that the subjects under consideration may be savored and enjoyed without the feeling of pressure or confinement. A lovely book for home or schoolroom.

Lavender's Blue: A Book of English Nursery Rhymes. Compiled by Kathleen Lines, and pictured by Harold Jones. New York: Oxford University Press, 1990. PB [only the HB is out-of-print]. This collection represents the old favorites and some lesser known verses. The illustrations have a nice sense of detail and the black and white illustrations provide the occasion for lots of quiet satisfying study. This is a comfortable size for little hands and colors are muted and soft. A very complete English book of nursery rhymes.

Books for Young Children—to Buy or Look For

The Oxford Nursery Rhyme Book. Assembled by Iona and Peter Opie, with additional illustrations by Joan Hassal. Oxford University Press, 1967. A classic collection of well-known rhymes, accompanied by charming woodcuts and engravings which appeared with early children's books. The value of this collection is that it progresses in a natural sequence from baby games and lullabies to the first songs and games which a mother or teacher might employ in teaching baby his heritage of oral language. 800 jingles, riddles, catches, tongue trippers, counting rhymes, baby games, toe games, alphabets, prayers, songs, and lullabies.

The Oxford Book of Children's Verse. Chosen and edited by Iona and Peter Opie. Oxford University Press, 1971. Arranged chronologically, these 332 entries represent some of the finest cherished poetry of all times. Iona and Peter Opie live in Hampshire, England, where their library of children's literature is one of the most extensive of its kind. Following in the tradition of *The Oxford Book of English Verse*, edited in 1900 by Sir Arthur Quiller-Couch, English man of letters, we are treated to a classic heritage of children's verse with obvious emphasis upon Biblical values.

The Kate Greenaway Book: A Collection of Illustration, Verse, and Text. Viking, Penguin, 1976. Meet Kate Greenaway—In the late nineteenth century, Kate Greenaway, an English painter and illustrator especially of children's books, launched her charming volumes. She regarded children as "worthy of the best draftsmanship, imagination, and publishing integrity." If you can find any of Kate Greenaway's original books in your searches for early books, consider that you have found a treasure for your family.

The Study of Fairy Tales
Is the Study of Nations

God's Principle of Individuality indicates to us that as we look to the history—the national testimony—of a nation, we begin to see the character, interests, and inclinations of its people, and can begin to determine whether that nation has been used of God, or can be used of God. Also, as American Christians, we can decide what qualities of folk tales and fairy tales we wish to appropriate to our literature for children and what we will teach that identifies nations. Literature can be as individual as the history of a nation.

Definition of Fairy Tales

A story relating mysterious pranks and adventures of supernatural spirits who manifested themselves in the form of diminutive human beings. These spirits possessed certain qualities which are constantly drawn upon for tales of their adventures: supernatural wisdom and foresight, a mischievous temperament, the power to regulate the affairs of man for good or evil, the capacity to change themselves into any shape at any time. Fairy tales as such—though they had existed in varying forms before—became popular toward the close of the seventeenth century. Almost every nation has its own fairy literature, though the folklore element embodied in fairy tales prompts the growth of related tales among different nations. Some of the great source-collections are the *Pentamerone* of Basilio (Italian), the *Contes de ma Mère l'Oye* of Perrault (French), the *Cabinet des Fées* (French), and those of the Grimm brothers in German and of Keightley and Croker in English. Hans Christian Andersen, of Denmark, is probably the most famous writer of original fairy tales. (*A Handbook to Literature* by Thrall and Hibbard, 1936, pp. 175–76)

Definition of Folk Tales

We have another past besides the past that history tells us about, a past which is in us, in individuals, more livingly than the recorded past. It is a past in which men slowly arrived at self-consciousness while building up the community, the arts, and the laws. ("Introduction," *Grimm's Fairy Tales*, 1944)

As old as language, folk tales have encircled the world. They are the most gifted travelers, adapting themselves to culture after culture, yet keeping a hard core of individuality. Wherever people gathered—in market places, about the hearths of homes, at tasks of weaving or sowing or planting—the stories told were not only the entertainment, but the philosophy and the living tradition of masses of unlettered people.

They were preserved, altered, adapted by the devices of story-tellers, and they have outlived succeeding generations of man through the simple mediums of the human voice and memory. The vast reservoir of folk tales lies within the great oral tradition that makes up the body of folklore, one of the major divisions, the other categories being Myth and Legend, Fable, Ballads and Romances, Epics and Sagas. (*Anthology of Children's Literature*, Johnson, Sayers, and Sickels, 1970)

The reader of folk tales soon discovers certain types of stories which occur over and over, for example:

1. The Accumulative Tale—a tale of simple repetition, addition, and variation.

   "The House That Jack Built," "The Old Woman and Her Pig," "Titty Mouse and Tatty Mouse," "Johnny Cake," "The Gingerbread Man," "The Three Bears," "Three Billy Goats."

2. The Animal Tale—animals as the protagonists:

a) *Fables of Aesop,* "Reynard the Fox," *Just So Stories.*

b) Among the most pleasing and popular: "Henny Penny," or "Chicken Licken," "The Foolish Timid Rabbit," "Brother Rabbit Takes Some Exercise," "Wolf and Seven Kids," "The Story of the Three Pigs."

3. The Humorous Tale—stories of numbskulls and simpletons, full of exaggerated nonsense: "The Bremen Town Musicians," "Hop-o'-My-Thumb," "How Six Traveled through the World," "Drakesbill."

4. The Realistic Tale—stories of the real and practical world: "Hans in Luck," "Three Sillies," "Lazy Jack," "The Story of the Little Red Hen," "The Tin Soldier," "What the Goodman Does Is Sure to Be Right."

5. The Romantic Tale—it arouses emotion, pity, or the sense of the heroic; it contains adventure: "Cinderella," "Sleeping Beauty," "Red Riding Hood."

6. The Modern Tale (beginning with Andersen's Fairy Tales): *Andersen's Fairy Tales, Alice in Wonderland, Happy Prince, Little Lame Prince, Peter Pan, Water Babies, King of the Golden River, Pinocchio, Blue-Bird, Just So Stories, Jungle Book, Wonderful Adventures of Nils, Uncle Remus Tales, Peter Rabbit.*

What Fairy Tales Can Contribute

A modern psychologist was astounded at the quality of literature which he found in the readers which we use to teach our children.

The pre-primers and primers from which a child is taught to read in school are designed to teach the necessary skills, irrespective of meaning. The overwhelming bulk of the rest of the so-called "children's literature" attempts to entertain or to inform, or both. But most of these books are so shallow in substance that little of significance can be gained from them. The acquisition of skills, including the ability to read, becomes devalued when what one has learned to read adds nothing of importance to one's life.

There is a widespread refusal to let children know that the source of much that goes wrong in life is due to our very own natures—the propensity of all men for acting aggressively, asocially, selfishly, and out of anger and anxiety. Instead we want our children to believe that inherently, all men are good. But little children know that they are not always good. (*The Uses of Enchantment: The Meaning and Importance of Fairy Tales,* Bettleheim, 1976, pp. 6–7)

Dr. Bettleheim's concern that children find meaning in their books led him to discover the role that folk and fairy tales can play in the development of the child's understanding of life. Jeanne S. Chall, in her book *Learning to Read: The Great Debate,* is quoted in Bettleheim's book:

My own personal content preference for first and second graders is folk and fairy tales. They have universal appeal. . . . These tales contain struggle and triumph, right and wrong, laughter and tears—themes that have disappeared from modern stories based upon familiar experiences. (Bettleheim, p. 26)

A study of European primers led Dr. Bettleheim to conclude:

How to live a good life right now and in the future—that is the greatest concern of all children. They know very well the merits of having fun, they don't need to be taught that in school. But they also know that much more is needed for leading a good life than having fun. To learn about this—of what it consists, what it entails, how it may be achieved—is what school from its very beginning should be all about. (Bettleheim, p. 264)

As Christians, with the Bible as a reader, we have the inside advantage of teaching children how to overcome evil and practice being good. Children learning to discern the core of their spiritual being and of their new-born character in Christianity, can even better appropriate the enjoyment of seeing good and evil challenged in imaginative tales.

Fairy Tales Identify the Character of Nations

We are interested in the character of nations. As Americans who have received into our nation all other nations, it is of special interest to observe the distinctive folk and fairy tales of different countries.

English Fairy Tales

Remembering that one of three crosses in the British flag is the cross of Saint George, it is not surprising that the first fairy tale in a collection of *English Fairy Tales* is entitled "St. George of Merrie England." The character of a knight is to seek redress of grievances, as Alfred Lord Tennyson wrote in *Idylls of the King*:

> For now I see the true old times are dead.
> When every morning brought a noble chance,
> And every chance brought out a noble knight.

From the arrival of the first of the Anglo-Saxons in England, the challenge to injustice and tyranny was evident. Thus "Jack the Giant Killer" is another characteristic English fairy tale. We are amused at the clever feats of Jack as he destroys the giants one by one.

King Arthur and his Knights of the Round Table are mentioned in "The True History of Sir Thomas Thumb," the diminutive baby rewarded to an English ploughman and his wife, christened by the Fairy Queen as Tom Thumb. Tom's diminutive size provided him with many adventures in this monstrously big world, but in the end he triumphs.

Another typical English fairy tale is "Dick Whitington and His Cat." With the help of his cat Dick achieves success. There are a number of excellent collections of English fairy tales, identifying English traits.

French Fairy Tales

Charles Perrault (1628–1703), is the fairy tale master of France. So often these tales emerged from a father and son telling and retelling stories to each other. These tales became classic as the "master-academician's touch . . . added a bit of court manners, or a satirical hit at the vanity and failings of man. (*Study of Fairy Tales*, Kready, 1916, p. 68)

The 1969 Dover Edition of Perrault's *Fairy Tales* contains some of the earliest versions of "Cinderella," "Sleeping Beauty," "Little Red Riding Hood," and "Puss in Boots."

German Fairy Tales

Two brothers, Jakob Grimm (1785–1803) and William Grimm (1786–1859), became famous for their collections of folk and fairy tales, taken from the lips of ordinary people.

> Our first care was faithfulness to the truth. We strove to penetrate into the wild forests of our ancestors, listening to their noble language, watching their pure customs, recognizing their ancient freedom and hearty faith. (Kready, p. 67)

Unlike Perrault who enjoyed classical embellishment of his tales, the Grimm brothers kept close to the original, "rendering the stories in a style and language and development of detail which was their own literary German." (Ibid., p. 68)

Of the long list of their stories some memorable ones come to mind, namely "The Elves and the Shoemaker," "Snow White and Rose Red," The Bremen Town Musicians," "The Wonderful Porridge Pot," and many more.

Spanish Fairy Tales

Our own Washington Irving, whose greatest inspiration for literature came during his years in Spain, began his biography of Columbus while he had access to primary sources. But Irving also recorded for readers in English several volumes of Spanish history. Most importantly Irving's finest work on Spain was his *Tales of the Alhambra*, the great

Moorish palace built during the seven-hundred-year occupation by the Moslems of the Iberian peninsula. Irving spent many months living by himself in this ancient palace and here he composed a series of Arabian Legends, in essence, folk tales which emphasized the influence of the Arabian beliefs. A few of these titles are: "Legend of the Arabian Astrologer," "Legend of the Three Beautiful Princesses," Legend of Prince Ahmed Al Kamel, or The Pilgrim of Love," "Legend of the Moor's Legacy," and "Legend of the Rose of the Alhambra."

Scandinavian Folk and Fairy Tales—Denmark

One of the most delightful writers of folk and fairy tales is Hans Christian Andersen. Brought to America by Horace Scudder, who was responsible for *The Riverside Magazine for Young People* and *The Riverside Literature Series* of nearly three hundred titles, Andersen was beloved by many generations.

Born in 1805 of impoverished parents in Odense, a little Danish town steeped in the tradition of the Middle Ages, Hans Christian Andersen was required to combat the combined forces of ignorance and his own sensitive nature during his childhood. He died an intimate friend of European royalty and of the distinguished figures of his day, acclaimed by the world for his contributions to literature. Between the beginning and the end of his life stretches an amazing tale of a struggle against odds, overcome by sheer talent. ("Introduction" by Jean Hersholt, *The Andersen-Scudder Letters*, 1949, p. xi)

The following titles may remind you of some of your own favorite tales: "The Fir Tree," "The Princess and the Pea," "The Emperor's New Clothes," "The Ugly Duckling," "The Little Match-Seller," "Thumbelina."

American Folk Tales

It is interesting to note that we have no fairy tales in this land of reality and high adventure in our history. We do have, however, some legendary folk heroes—like John Bunyan the huge, legendary lumberman of the northwest. Probably our most charming folk tale character is Uncle Remus, the benign Negro storyteller of the South, created by Joel Chandler Harris. His *Tales of Uncle Remus* created such unforgettable characters as Brer Rabbit and Brer Fox.

Arabian Fairy Tales

Once again, we are indebted to two American writers and editors who have brought *The Arabian Nights: Their Best-Known Tales* to our American readers. Kate Douglas Wiggin and her sister, Nora A. Smith, are part of that glorious collection, the *Scribner Illustrated Classics*. Published in 1909 and reset in 1956, this particular edition was illustrated by Maxfield Parrish.

Perhaps you remember the legend which brought these stories forth was that a prisoner was held and his life granted as long as each night he had a new tale to tell his captor. *Tales of a Thousand and One Nights* resulted. The most famous of these tales are "Aladdin and His Wonderful Lamp," "Ali Baba and the Forty Thieves," and "Sinbad the Sailor."

Your Further Research

As you research other nations on the Chain of Christianity moving westward towards America, you will make some new discoveries of folk or fairy tales which will give insight on the ideas and ideals of many nations who are a part of our world.

Types of Children's Tales

Fairy Tales

Andersen, Hans Christian
Fairy Tales

Arabian Nights
Edited by Kate Douglas Wiggin and Nora A. Smith

Asbjörnsen, Peter Christian
East o' the Sun and West o' the Moon

Barrie, James M.
Peter Pan

Carroll, Lewis M.
Alice's Adventures in Wonderland
Through the Looking Glass

Enchanted Book, The
Stories from Many Lands
Selected by Alice Dalgliesh

Grimm's Fairy Tales
Selected and Illustrated by Eleanore Abbot

Jacobs, Joseph
English Fairy Tales

Kingsley, Charles
The Water Babies

Lagerlof, Selma
The Wonderful Adventures of Nils

Lang, Andrew
The Blue Fairy Book

Lewis, C. S.
The Lion, the Witch, and the Wardrobe

MacDonald, George
At the Back of the North Wind
The Princess and Curdie

Opie, Iona and Peter
The Classic Fairy Tales

Perrault, Charles
French Fairy Tales

Pyle, Howard
Merry Adventures of Robin Hood
The Wonder Clock

Ruskin, John
The King of the Golden River

Scottish Fairy Tales
Leodhas, Sorche Nic
"Heather and Broom"
"Thistle and Thyme"

Fables and Myths

Aesop's Fables
Franklin Watts Edition, 1969
Introduction by G. K. Chesterton
Illustrated by Arthur Rackham

Colum, Padraic
The Children's Homer
The Golden Fleece

Coolidge, Olivia
Greek Myths and Legends of the North

Fables de la Fontaine

Graves, Robert
The Siege and Fall of Troy

Harris, Joel Chandler
Uncle Remus

Hawthorne, Nathaniel
A Wonder Book
Tanglewood Tales

Kingsley, Charles
The Heroes

Lanier, Sidney
The Boy's King Arthur

Sutcliff, Rosemary
Beowulf

Animal Tales

Grahame, Kenneth
The Wind in the Willows

Kipling, Rudyard
Just So Stories

Milne, A. A.
Winnie the Pooh
The House at Pooh Corner

Potter, Beatrix
The Tale of Peter Rabbit

Animal Stories That Teach

When God created the "beasts" in the first chapter of Genesis, He made each of them "after its own kind" and with certain characteristics. Of all the animals that God created, one in particular seems to have a special devotion to man—namely the dog. A number of authors have captured the relationship of the dog to man. In fact, we have some very special classics in this genre. Let us look at a few.

English Sheep Dog

The first dog story with a dog true to its real dog qualities appeared in 1898. *Bob, Son of Battle*, by Alfred Ollivant is an exciting story about an English sheep dog. These intelligent animals, when trained to shepherd sheep, are a marvel to watch as they work with their flock. In fact, at one time, and perhaps still, Madison Square Garden in New York City hosted an annual exhibition and contest between such dogs. Of course, in the country where Bob, Son of Battle lived, this was a very important event.

This book is a contrast between two dogs and their masters. The crisis comes when a sheep killer begins to attack the flocks and Bob is suspected and hunted. The climax reflects the character of these two dogs and their masters.

Scottish Highland Terrier

Greyfriars Bobbie by Eleanor Atkinson, 1912—a true story of a Highland Terrier characterized by his fidelity to his dead master as shown by his slipping into the cemetery of Greyfriars Church and sleeping nightly on the grave. Eventually, the whole city of Edinburgh becomes involved in the fate of this tiny terrier, including the magistrates and students of Edinburgh University, the soldiers of Edinburgh Castle, and especially the children of the tenements which overlooked Greyfriars cemetery where for fourteen years Bobbie slept on his master's grave.

American Dog Stories

The Call of the Wild by Jack London—Jack London was an acknowledged socialist. Perhaps that is why his *Call of the Wild* is one of the greatest of dog stories reflecting the harshness and conflict of the Yukon territory in Canada and the role a great-hearted dog plays for his master. Despite his political leanings, Jack London was a student of literature and his writing reflects a brilliant, carefully chosen vocabulary. This is an unforgettable man and dog story.

Lad: A Dog by Albert Payson Terhune, first published in 1919. Sunnybrook, at Pompton Lakes, New Jersey, was the name of the Terhune home where beautiful Lad, an eighty-pound thoroughbred collie, grew up. We learn from his master that he was a thoroughbred in spirit as well as in blood. This is quite a different kind of dog from Jack London's Buck. Lad loves the place and he guards his Master and his Mistress; and when the Baby comes Lad offers his full devotion. One of the most interesting accounts is when Lad, muzzled in the back seat of the family car, falls out in the middle of New York City and must find his way back to Sunnybrook in New Jersey. Once we meet this courageous, gentle, dignified dog we know that we have truly met a thoroughbred.

Old Yeller by Fred Gibson, 1956, is set in Texas in the pioneer days of the 1870s. It is the moving story of a boy and his dog.

Where the Red Fern Grows by Wilson Rawls is set in the Oklahoma and Cherokee country, the Ozarks. Here coon dog hunting reigns supreme. Old Dan and Little Ann become a remarkable team with Billy Colman. There is tragedy, however, in the ultimate death of the two dogs.

Big Red by Jim Kjelgaard, 1943, is the story of a champion Irish Setter and a trapper's son who grew up together, roaming the wilderness.

Horses

My Friend Flicka, Thunderhead, **and** *Green Grass of Wyoming*—This trilogy by Mary O'Hara is about the McLaughlin family, especially about Ken whose first horse of his very own was Flicka. In the second book, Flicka's white colt, Thunderhead, becomes a race horse, king of the wild horses. In the final volume, the author brings a beautiful culmination to Ken's life and love of horses and his own love.

The Black Stallion Books—In 1941, Walter Farley began his twelve *Black Stallion* books. Made into a marvelous film, the first book deals with Alexander Ramsay and The Black, shipwrecked off the coast of Arabia. Here the boy and the horse begin a friendship which, when they are rescued and arrive in America, enables Alex to train The Black for some of the big races in America. The film *Black Stallion* is for me the finest horse story I have enjoyed, complete with musical sequences on the island where Alex and The Black first come to know each other. Francis Ford Coppola is the producer with Kelly Reno as Alex, Teri Garr as his mother, and Mickey Rooney as the retired horse trainer who teaches Alex and The Black how to become successful in the big race.

Horse Stories by Marguerite Henry

Misty of Chincoteague begins the true account of the Pony Penning Day to catch the wild horses on the island of Chincoteague off the tidewater country of Maryland and Virginia. These wild ponies are descendants of ponies from the mines of Peru, shipwrecked on our Atlantic coast. This event becomes the subject of several delightful books by Mrs. Henry, illustrated by Wesley Dennis.

Mustang: Wild Spirit of the West by Marguerite Henry, illustrated by Robert Lougheed—This is the true story of Wild Horse Annie, who almost single-handedly saved the wild western mustangs who once roamed the American west proud and free. Annie, stricken with polio as a child, grew up to marry and to save the wild mustangs who were being captured and converted into pet food. In 1962, after Annie's impassioned pleas before Congress, the Department of the Interior created the first American wild horse refuge in Nevada. More followed. Annie was able to preserve a wonderful American horse who had played a part in our history.

An American Burro

Brighty of the Grand Canyon by Marguerite Henry, illustrated Wesley Dennis—One of God's sacred beasts is the burro. Did you know that God has given special markings to this stalwart, sometimes stubborn little animal who has contributed to the life of the west? In this story we have a modern recognition of God's special marking of this sturdy little animal. A bridge has been built over the Colorado River, between the North Rim and the South. Until then the land of Arizona had been cut off by the River. For the occasion the Governor of Arizona had invited Theodore Roosevelt to be present. Uncle Jim and Brighty were to have the honor of being the first to cross the bridge.

Just as Uncle Jim and Brighty were about to step on the swaying bridge, someone made a remark about the little burro calling him "low-life." Uncle Jim exploded:

"'Low-life is it. Who was it Jesus chose to carry Him into Jerusalem? Who?' . . . 'Why, t'was a li'l long-eared feller, the spit image o' Brighty. . . . Ever since that day burros has been marked with the cross. Look-a-here!' Uncle Jim traced the black stripe down Brighty's back and the crossbar over his shoulder. 'See them lines? Where'd ye find a stouter-marked cross than this 'un?'"

And so, as Jim carefully eased Brighty's tiny hooves onto the swaying bridge, to the trumpeting notes of "Onward Christian Soldiers," the old prospector and the burro "with the cross of Jesus going on before" were the first to celebrate the completion of the new bridge over the Colorado River.

A Bright Red Fox Outfoxes George Washington

Cinnabar, the One O'Clock Fox by Marguerite Henry, illustrated by Wesley Dennis. When Marguerite Henry began her book about George Washington and the "One O'Clock Fox," her research began by acquiring "three red puppy foxes" whom she kept by her to study and observe. In an introductory article entitled, "No Cage Shall Hold Them," she writes:

> For months now I have studied them by day as they sleep curled up like kittens; and by night as they race pell-mell from one end of the cage to the other, lashing their tails to and fro, and talking some mystic kind of gibberish. . . .
>
> These little foxes gingerly take delicacies of chicken livers and beetles right out of my hand, but always their amber eyes gaze at me with an ancient wisdom and dignity, as much as to say: "For now, while we are still cubs, we shall be your pets. But remember, we are creatures of the wildwood, and some night when the moon spills its gold, no cage will hold us." And no cage shall!
>
> I am quick to admit that the fox Cinnabar towers in capabilities above my foxes. But Cinnabar, you see, was never captive. He lived in the time of George Washington, and often—so legend says—he challenged the General to a chase.

Cinnabar represented the spirit of the times, the spirit of a people who fought for freedom and lived for freedom's sake. He eluded all who would catch or trap him, and he finished out his days as a free wild thing. (*Cinnabar*, Marguerite Henry, Introduction, pp. 8–9)

A Boy's Love for a Fawn

The Yearling by Marjorie Kinnan Rawlings, 1938. In 1939, N.C. Wyeth, premier illustrator of American classics, traveled to Florida to study the setting of Marjorie Kinnan Rawling's novel, which Charles Scribner's Sons were going to publish. Jody Baxter lived with his father and mother in a primitive section of Florida where the living was hard and the land beautiful. Here Jody found a fawn who had lost its mother; he brought it home and the boy and the fawn began a precious companionship. The climax of the book comes when the family's survival depends upon Jody's being willing to sacrifice his fawn. The death of the fawn and Jody's flight from home and his return, marks his coming into young manhood. As his father remarks, "You've done come back different. You've taken punishment. You ain't a yearlin' no longer Jody."

The Yearling is a major novel of the twentieth century. It is true to Scriptural principles. It is a special "Read Aloud" book.

Teaching and Learning Poetry in the Elementary Grades

American Christians have a rich heritage of poetry which many of the modern collections are ignoring. Try to find collections that help us to teach and learn those poets who contributed to the purpose of literature—to teach us who we are, our principles and ideals, and to strengthen our purpose as a nation. These poems also are true to the Scriptural admonition of Paul to the Philippians: "Finally, brethren, whatsoever things are true, whatsoever things are honest, whatsoever things are just . . . pure . . . lovely . . . of good report; if there be any virtue . . . think on these things."

Successful teaching of the poetry of the Bible develops the *inner* ear which responds to the music and sound of words. And teaching of the Nursery Rhymes and Mother Goose begins to reinforce the ability to put words together in a measured meter. Poetry, like music, commences the listening literary life of a child. It should be started, as was indicated, when the babe is in Mother's and Father's arms. It should be continued without a break by parents at home and teachers at school. Every aspect of life and living can include poetry so that it becomes as much a part of every day as work and play, food and rest, sunshine and rain.

Reading the definitions of "Music," "Poesy," and "Rime," in Noah Webster's 1828 *American Dictionary of the English Language*, the following ideas are expressed:

Music: The art of combining sounds in a manner to please the ear. Order; harmony in revolutions; as the *music* of the spheres.

Poesy: The art or skill of composing poems; as the heavenly gift of *poesy*. Poetry; metrical composition.

Rime: In poetry the correspondence of sounds in the terminating words of syllables of two verses, one of which suc-

ceeds the other immediately, or at no great distance.

Poetry and music have always been intertwined for good or for evil and thus it is natural to see them brought together in arriving at a definition of poetry. Many of our English and American poets have identified the relationship of God to poetry as the following verse from "The Singers" by Henry Wadsworth Longfellow:

God sent his Singers upon earth
With songs of sadness and of mirth,
That they might touch the hearts of men,
And bring them back to heaven again.

John Keats echoed the same conviction when he stated in his "Ode":

Bards of Passion and of Mirth,
Ye have left your souls on earth!
Ye have souls in heaven too,
Double-lived in regions new.

There are as many definitions of poetry as there are individual poets. We tend to choose what represents our own conviction. Thus the following indicate three aspects important for American Christian teachers:

Poetry is simply the most beautiful, impressive, and widely effective mode of saying things, and hence its importance.   —Matthew Arnold

God Himself is the best Poet,
And the Real is His song.
                    —Robert Browning

I would define, in brief, the Poetry of words as the Rhythmical Creation of Beauty. Its sole arbiter is Taste.
                    —Edgar Allan Poe

The effective expression of the beautiful and the true is governed by the Word of God. Is the poem a violation of God's commands—of the letter or the spirit of the Word? Does it encourage the love of God? Is it in good taste? Taste is, according to Noah Webster, "the faculty of discerning beauty, order, congruity, proportion, symmetry, or whatever constitutes excellence, particularly in the fine arts and belles lettres." And finally, is it rhythmical? Does it convey the "music of the spheres," or the order of God's universe, governed by unchanging laws which have a rhythm to them though multifarious in expression?

Teaching Poetry

Whether we look, or whether we listen, We hear life murmur, or see it glisten. . . .
—James Russell Lowell

The Rhythmical Sounds of God's Creation

Noah Webster indicates that "rhythmical" means "having proportion of sound, or one sound proportioned to another: harmonical." Man introduces many dissonant sounds which often compete with one another. But the sounds of God's creating are rhythmical and blend together in one vast symphony to make a large refrain. We have to learn to listen to the rhythmical sounds of God's Creation.

We know that the universe is filled with sound. Job reminds us that there is music in the heavens for when God laid the foundations of our earth "the morning stars sang together, and all the sons of God shouted for joy." (Job 38:6–7)

Here again individual teachers may become ingenious in order to provide or help with opportunities to listen to the sounds of God's world. These sounds are often drowned out by our man-made sounds. What sounds can you find for your class to record? What sounds can they distinguish as to individuality of pattern or rhythm? We know there are bird songs, and sounds, there are wind sounds—and these differ from breezes in the trees or over the ocean. There are many insect sounds that have a definite rhythm. From God's great book of nature what can we look at and listen to and come to recognize?

Poets, like artists, have the gift of helping us see and hear what we might pass by. Have you ever thought of the grass as having a voice? Look in a collection for "The Voice of the Grass."

James Russell Lowell, in a beautiful passage from the longer poem, *The Vision of Sir Launfal*, records the month of June and the distinctions of the father bird and the mother bird: "And what is so rare as a day in June? Then, if ever, come perfect days. . . ."

Bird Songs

How many bird songs can your children or students identify? God's principle of individuality indicates a full book. Each bird has a separate repertoire: love calls, fighting calls, scolding sounds. The robin, chosen state bird for several states, has his rain song, his evening song, and his morning song. Paying attention to birdsong may help us to listen to our own voice sounds—and to learn to modulate them. Poets help us listen to birdsong. In the older collections such as the *Home Book of Verse for Young Folks,* there are some poems about birds and their sounds.

The unity and diversity of birds and their individuality can be identified in song and feeding and nest building. Poetry can help us open our eyes and wake up our ears. And our feelings about God the Creator and His Infinite Individuality which we see everywhere can increase in expression.

Seasons

Californians do not witness the drastic changes of weather and season as do other parts of the country. But God's Rhythmic Round of Creation goes on. What sights and signs can we teach students to observe in Autumn (or Fall)? Which leaves change? What colors do we see in the West? What has happened to plant life to make leaves dry up, drop off, or change color? How does a tree's individuality express itself? What are God's principles of renewal and of the continuance of Creation?

Helen Hunt Jackson, author of "Ramona," a California story, provides us with a fine individuality for this season entitled "October's Bright Blue Weather." There are a number of elements of this poem which would be true for that geographical area. And James Whitcomb Riley's "When the Frost Is on the Punkun" is another seasonal poem. Have your students begin their poetry notebook and help them copy these poems into their books and memorize the words and feelings into their minds and hearts.

> To every thing there is a season, and a time to every purpose under heaven. (Ecclesiastes 3:1)

There are many seasons in the cycle of weather. There are also seasons of the heart. Seek to develop an awareness of godly seasons and times and help them discern heaven's purposes for changes. Man's changes are for the sake of change.

The Duty of Children—Christian Graces

Children in America under the regime of progressive education have not only grown up graceless—but without manners—which proceed from the same source. So, Christian homes and schools provide us with many opportunities to teach our students what it means to be "gracious."

Do you have in your room a reminder of the two "very, very little keys"—"I Thank You," and "If You Please"?

Robert Louis Stevenson defined the "Whole Duty of Children" in four lines. John Wesley (1703–1791), English evangelist, defined what children should do in "John Wesley's Rule."

There are many grace notes of living to the Lord in a manner pleasing to Him and to His children and to others. Some poems are humorous like "Greedy Jane." Some of the poems remind us of the animals who by instinct act out qualities which we can emulate. But whether it is how we treat each other or God's creatures, there are many opportunities in verse for reflective thinking and many gems for one's notebook of life.

Rhymes of Childhood

There are a number of children's poets whose works have lasted through the years and have appealed to children. Robert Louis Stevenson, William Blake, Eleanor Farjeon, Walter de la Mare, Eugene Field, Henry Wadsworth Longfellow, and others who are worthy of an author study. Some background on each author can be given and a study of the style or individuality of the poet. What makes Stevenson unique? Is it what he writes about or how you feel about what he writes? Could you recognize a poem by William Blake or Walter de la Mare if it were read to you without giving the author's name?

"Rhymes of Childhood" introduces us to a number of children's poets describing aspects of childhood precious to them. Both Robert Louis Stevenson and James Whitcomb Riley have a number of poems and offer contrasting styles. People play a big part in some—"A Boy's Mother," "Mr. Nobody," "Little Orphan Annie," and "The Barefoot Boy." These poems can help students to be more observant of individuals they know—people in their own lives. Could they describe in words unique aspects of individuals they see and meet?

Just Nonsense

Comical verse helps us all see "the funny side of life." Edward Lear becomes a new delightful poet and Lewis Carroll introduces us to the delights of *Alice in Wonderland*, or *Through the Looking Glass*. To appreciate nonsense, you have to have some sense. So, enjoy this section, find more poems by these same authors, and learn some limericks. What pieces of nonsense can your students memorize?

Fairyland

The land of fairies is the land of imagination. A nation can be studied by the kind of "wee folk" it has brought to life in its literature and culture. Children can be told that fairies don't exist but they should enjoy some of the delightful poems in which the poets celebrate fairies, elves, and such like. Read "The Little Elf," "The Fairies," and others.

Stories in Rhyme

When literature first began it consisted of a "vast collection of dear familiar stories told around the cottage fires in humble houses or in the great poetic narratives recited or sung in the halls of palace and castle. These last were recounted to the harp music of those gifted wanderers called variously scops or bards or gleemen or minstrels. . . . Among those listening to the cottage tales there was always a goodly proportion of children, young persons who hearkened and remembered and told the same stories to their children in their own time. (*A Critical History of Children's Literature*, Meigs, 1953)

Some of these famous old tales, told in verse, can be found in collections, usually done by one of our outstanding English or Scottish poets. See "Lord Ullin's Daughter," "The Pied Piper of Hamelin" by Robert Browning; Scott's rollicking "Young Lochinvar" from his longer poem *Marmion*. Macaulay's "Horatius at the Bridge" celebrates an earlier day of the Roman republic when courage and determination were high. Longfellow's "The Skeleton in Armor" is another of the Viking exploits of love and the heroic spirit on the seas. Perhaps the most famous and most often committed to memory is "The Highwayman" by Alfred Noyes, which has the feel of "riding, riding" as "a highwayman comes riding, up to the old inn-door."

The Happy Warrior

John Quincy Adams relates in his *Memoirs* that he ever thanked his mother for greeting him every morning, after his prayers, with William Collins's ode to the patriot warriors of Scotland who fell in battle:

How sleep the brave, who sink to rest
By all their country's wishes blest!

John Quincy Adams never had to bear military arms for his nation, but in his more than fifty years service to America, he was heroic in his efforts to maintain the Biblical constitutional principles which his own parents had helped establish in the world's only Christian republic. A poem like Collins's ode is sometimes excerpted from Sir Walter Scott's longer *The Lady of the Lake*, and entitled "Soldier, Rest! Thy Warfare O'er."

A number of the poems in the early collections relate to history. They will complement *My Country* and also *American History in Verse,* another book edited by Mr. Stevenson which follows American history chronologically. In them you might find "Sir Humphrey Gilbert"; "Drake's Run"; and "Columbus" by Joaquin Miller, a California poet, included in Stevenson's *American History in Verse*; "Incident of the French Camp" by Browning; and, of course, the famous "Charge of the Light Brigade" by Tennyson, which also has a rhythmic pattern of horse's hooves and cavalry advancing through thick and thin, based on a real event of history.

Life's Lessons

Each section of this book brings us deeper into the themes of our greatest English and American poets. They are themes of Biblical origin and leave the valleys of the common for the heights and peaks of the idealistic. Teenagers need to have their idealism fed and love to hear this kind of music. It should be compatible with all that they are learning in other courses of the Christian history program. Feelings are high and often found in subjects which seem humble but hide a star. Some favorites are "Abou Ben Adhem" by Leigh Hunt, "The House by the Side of the Road," and Robert Burns's "For A' That and A' That," which may interest you and your students in doing more poems by Burns. Kipling's "Recessional" is the last of England's far flung empire being recalled to God.

Continue to expand your horizons of poetry and increase your acquaintance with many of the great poets. There are many to commit to notebook and to memory.

Teaching the Individuality of Poetic Form

The lyric poem is the most broadly inclusive of all the various types of verse and the most frequently used.

What is lyric poetry and how can it be identified?

Webster's 1828 *Dictionary*:

Lyrical: Pertaining to a lyre or harp. Lyric Poetry is such as is sung to the harp or lyre (a stringed instrument).

A Handbook to Literature, Thrall and Hibbard:

Lyric is a brief subjective poem strongly marked by imagination, melody, and emotion, and creating for the reader a single, unified impression. The early Greeks distinguished between Lyric and Choric poetry by terming that poetry lyric which was the expression of the emotion of a single singer accompanied by a lyre, and choric, those verses which were the expression of a group and were sung by a chorus.

Lyric—the individual and personal emotion of the poet for the listener; a single, unified impression.

Kinds of Lyric Poetry

1. Simple Emotional Lyric

2. Pictorial Lyric

3. Meditative Lyric

4. Dramatic Lyric

Identifying the Lyric Poem

The lyric is that form of verse which is nearest to music. The first rule of the lyric is that it must sing—swiftly and personally. (*The Singing World*, Untermeyer) Since it is more "personal" than any other kind of poetry, it is limited in length.

A poem you may find in some older collections which has the qualities of the lyric poem and sings is "The Wonderful World" by William Brighty Rands.

Have your class read this poem silently. Then read it together and perhaps have individuals read it through again. Then discuss what feelings are conveyed by the poem.

Simple Emotional Lyrics

Poems in this group are purely personal. Perhaps that is why they are so popular. We all respond to feelings of courage, sorrow, of dreams or of images of delight to our imagination. There are many lyric poems in the section of the *Home Book* entitled "This Wonderful World."

Examples of Simple Emotional Lyrics:

"The Sea Gypsy" by Hovey
"Sea Fever" by Masefield
"She Walks in Beauty" by Byron
"To Helen" by Poe
"Hills" by Guiterman

Read these poems as a class, discuss the unified effect of them and in each case identify the images and words which the poet uses for achieving his effects. Find other examples.

The Pictorial Lyric

The pictorial lyric paints a scene or picture. Wordsworth's famous poem, "I Wandered Lonely as a Cloud," about the "host of golden daffodils," provides us with a beautiful image with which to furnish our minds and hearts and to be recalled or reflected upon in tranquillity.

Tennyson's "The Brook's Song" has pictorial elements, as has Stevenson's famous poem on "The Wind," as well as Christina Georgina Rossetti's charming "Who Has Seen the Wind?" Find other examples of the pictorial lyric.

The Meditative Lyric

The meditative lyric presents philosophy and melody in a closely packed condensation of verse. You will be able to find many examples of the meditative lyric:

See "Ozymandias of Egypt" by Shelley. This poem always provokes discussion. A sonnet by Milton, "On His Blindness," contains an entirely different mood. This is a rewarding sonnet to learn. Look for one of Horatius Bonar's terse poems, "Honesty."

The Dramatic Lyric

The dramatic lyric almost tells a story—a dramatic moment. Many historical and patriotic poems will contain examples of dramatic lyrics: "The Ship Constitution"; "Aye, Tear Her Tattered Ensign Down—Old Ironsides"; "The Ship of State"; "Concord Hymn" by Emerson; and others.

Poetry Notebook

Have students copy into their own notebooks poems which they will memorize. Give some background on the author where he is representative of the best of English and American poetry.

The Ballad as a Form of Lyric Poetry

Telling a Story in Verse

Many collections will feature a section of "stories in rhyme" with many examples of ballads. These are representative of the oldest form of literature and provide us with a variety of stories in verse to be sung or told to audiences small or large, old and young.

Classic Collections of Poetry

by Rosalie June Slater

Fortunate to have been brought up in both American and European schools, I enjoyed the wealth of classical learning. Especially in collections of poetry in both English and French, I acquired some "portables" which I might carry with me wherever our family traveled.

My father always had our American private school assemble many of the books we needed to keep up with our American grade levels. But when we arrived at our Swiss school there was such a wealth and variety of subjects taught in French, that we considered the loss of keeping up an actual gain.

As I glance back at my wondrous time at Le Grand Verger (The Great Shepherd School) in Switzerland where I was saved, I also rejoice that I went to school with girls of eighteen different nations. Of twins we had two sets: the restrained English, and the hearty, horse-riding German twins, Mia and Nasi; there was a blonde Swede, Poppy; a dear brunette Italian, Marcella; three weird old princesses from Communist Albania who sought refuge in our walls; and a number of cocky Americans and some other quiet girls, with European teachers to match and a large Swiss-German headmistress who presided but did not teach. One boy visited briefly, a heel-clicking, arm-saluting Nazi, forever my image of Hitler Youth.

But what really inspired my days was looking out from my room upon the Swiss Alps across Lake Geneva, anticipating the coming of Christ into my life, and feeding on the lines of William Wordsworth's long, long poem, "The Prelude."

Today, we seek to convey to our children the inspiration of the Holy Spirit and the cultivation of an inner reflective mind and heart. Even among our most lively students, this is a desired goal.

What we might say as we cultivate taste in our children:

Just as you make a few friends, and cultivate and cherish them, let us cultivate the "greats"; then we can enlarge our horizons and come to know many people.

Here are some of the classic collections that you still may find in public libraries, buy in antiquarian book stores, or find elsewhere where the Lord leads.

Classic Collections of Poetry for Teachers

Palgrave's *The Golden Treasury of the Best Songs and Lyrical Poems in the English Language*—Selected and arranged by Francis Turner Palgrave, first published 1861, Oxford University Press. This edition has been published many times and upgraded. It is also in paperback, considered to be the most popular selection of English poems. It included some fourteen pages of notes by Francis Turner Palgrave.

The Oxford Book of English Verse, 1250–1918. Chosen and edited by Sir Arthur Quiller-Couch. Oxford: Clarendon Press, 1939.

The Oxford Shakespeare: The Complete Works of William Shakespeare. Edited with a Glossary by W. J. Craig. Dublin: Trinity College, 1905.

The Golden Treasury. American Edition, The Macmillan Company, 1928, 1956, 1967. This improved edition includes many more poems and a number of useful features to help you locate what you need to find more quickly:

Index of First Lines

Index of Poems

Index of Writers with Dates of Birth and Death

The Cambridge Editions of *The Complete Poetical Works* of:

Elizabeth Barrett Browning
Robert Browning
Burns
Byron
Dryden
Oliver Wendell Holmes
Keats
Longfellow
Amy Lowell
James Russell Lowell
Pope
Shelley
Spenser
Tennyson
The Selected Works of Thoreau
Whittier
Wordsworth

This fine series of the complete works of some of our major English and American poets has had two lives. The first Cambridge Editions under the editorship of Horace E. Scudder were source books for four generations of readers, a "living monument" in the field of English and American Literature.

The New Cambridge Editions are based upon the original text and plates, with some additions and new introductions. It is important to see the whole body of work of a poet.

A few of these Cambridge Editions are still being sold by the publisher, Houghton Mifflin Company, Boston. Earlier volumes can be found.

Classic Collections for Children

The Home Book of Verse for Young Folks. Selected and arranged by Burton Egbert Stevenson, decorations by Willy Pogay, Holt, Rinehart and Winston, 1915; Revised and enlarged edition, 1929, 1967.

When Verna Hall and I began to work together to produce the Christian History program in 1961, this last edition of *Home Book of Verse* was available for teachers and many, many schools bought the volume. But it gradually disappeared.

In 1995, a new volume was published, entitled: *The Home Book of Great Poetry, a Treasury of over One Thousand Favorite Poems*, compiled by Burton E. Stevenson, published by Galahad Books.

Having rediscovered the work of Mr. Stevenson I rejoiced, until I read in the "Introduction" that the present volume is an extension of Stevenson's *Home Book of Modern Verse*. This explained the changes in the Table of Contents. But one statement really saddened me:

> Of religious poetry, in the old sense, there is very little, but if the poets have, for the most part, turned definitely away from the fundamentalist conception of God and the universe, it is evident that they have come closer to Him as the source of being, and that they still tread confidently among the stars.

I miss some of the wonderful sections of the very first collection of *The Home Book of Verse for Young Folks*:

In the Nursery
The Duty of Children
The Glad Evangel
This Wonderful World
My Country
The Happy Warrior
Life's Lessons, etc.

The Home Book of Great Poetry has had a short existence. It is already being "remaindered," which means it is out-of-print and being sent to discount houses. It is still a useful collection, but we miss some of the earlier sections.

A Child's Garden of Verse by Robert Louis Stevenson, first printed in England in 1885, is the most published book of verse for children, and the most loved. Many of these poems can be memorized and should make up a large part of the repertoire of our primary grades. The life of Stevenson should be included, and also, as you discover one, a beautiful illustrated edition of this childhood masterpiece.

Introducing Children to Their Heritage of English and American Poets

America's Unique Heritage of "the Best Gift of God to Man"

It is always wonderful to discover that our children's minds and hearts can encompass much more than we thought possible if we introduce them to the writers and poets who can "enlarge the borders of their tents."

If you have not yet discovered a love for poetry, just open your mind to realizing how much a part of our colonial education was spent enjoying English poetry. Then as soon as our ancestors had achieved the setting of liberty with law, and as soon as they became aware of the wondrous land which the Lord had given them, they began to express their own literary character and individuality.

Noah Webster was particularly aware of our English heritage of literature during the years when he was preparing his *American Dictionary of the English Language*. But because Noah Webster was brought up in Connecticut, the Constitution State, he was well aware of the relationship of a philosophy of government to every area of life—beginning in the home and church, and coming to its expression of political liberty in local, state, and national government.

Indeed, Noah Webster was one of the first American scholars to express the idea that some of our best American writers were as excellent as the best of English writers. In fact, Noah Webster believed that in some areas of writing, our American authors were "equaled only by that of the best British authors, and surpassed by that of no English compositions of a similar kind." (See *Teaching and Learning*, p. 300.)

And yet Webster did not believe that American superiority in writing was a matter of national pride. He attributed it to our Biblical heritage.

The United States commenced their existence under circumstances wholly novel and unexampled in the history of nations. They commenced with civilization, with learning, with science, with constitutions of free government, and with that best gift of God to man, the Christian religion. Their population is now equal to that of England; in arts, and sciences, our citizens are very little behind the most enlightened people on earth: in some respects they have no superiors. (Ibid., p. 301)

Thus it is natural that we should look to our English heritage of liberty and learning before we seek out our own unique heritage of American Christian literature. Actually, with the Mother Goose and the Nursery Rhymes, some derived, as we noted, from English history, we already have had introduction.

Can We Also "Gladly Learn and Gladly Teach"?

To encourage us as teachers, we find a special envoy to us in one of our great English poems, not to be studied until mid-grades. In Chaucer's *Canterbury Tales*, we have a review of English society before the Industrial Revolution begins to break up old enclaves. One of the meekest and poorest of the pilgrims traveling to Canterbury, in Chaucer's inimitable style, has some characteristics of the kind of teacher which we admire (from "The Prologue," in modern English):

There was also a Clerk of Oxford,
who had long since devoted himself to
    the course of logic.
His horse was as lean as a rake,
and he himself was not exactly fat, I
    assure you,
but looked hollow and serious.
His outer cloak was very threadbare,
for as yet he had not got himself a
    benefice,
nor was he worldly enough to hold a
    secular office.
He would rather have twenty volumes
of Aristotle and his philosophy, bound in
black or red, at the head of his bed than

rich robes, or a fiddle or lively harp.
But although he was a philosopher,
he still had little gold in his coffers; . . .
he spent all that he could get from his
    friends on books and learning,
and diligently prayed for the souls
of those who gave him money to carry on
    his studies with.
He gave most of his attention to studying.
He never spoke a word more than was
    necessary,
and what he did say was in due form, and
    reverent,
and short and to the point, and full of lofty
    thought:
his talk tended toward moral qualities,
**and gladly would he learn, and gladly
teach.**

When the opportunity to visit England comes, and spending a delightful day at Canterbury is a goal, you will enjoy reviewing *The Canterbury Tales*. For that study you will need the help of *Geoffrey Chaucer of England* by Marchette Chute. Look for the treasury of her volumes on English literature. She will encourage you to become, if you are not already, a lover of books and one who imparts this love to students. Chute observes:

Chaucer was very fond, however, of the Clerk. The Clerk spent all his money on books and Chaucer's heart went out to him. With his shabby coat and thin horse he was the kind of man who gets on in the world and enrages more successful people by not minding. The Clerk's own idea of success was to have twenty books at the head of his bed where he could reach them easily.

Chaucer said of him, "Gladly would he learn and gladly teach," which is the handsomest compliment that one lover of books could give to another. (*Geoffrey Chaucer of England*, Marchette Chute, 1936, p. 252)

The Individuality of Our English Heritage

England became the "people of the Book" in the seventeenth century—the century of Shakespeare, Bard of the Bible. Not only did Shakespeare include Biblical themes, ideals, and characters in his plays, but he spread the language and imagery of seventeenth-century Biblical English. This was the time when many people had the Word of God in English. Never had the Word of God been preached so vigorously. This was a time when Biblical morality was learned through many of the Bard's plays.

William Shakespeare (1564–1616) Bard of the Bible

Shakespeare's Knowledge and Use of the Bible by Charles Wordsworth, Bishop of St. Andrews, in 1864, provides us with many examples of the Bard's Biblical application of God's Word. Like the majority of Englishmen, he loved his country. Thus in one of his most moving passages, he puts these words into the mouth of one of his main characters:

The Tragedy of King Richard II

Act II, Scene I:

John of Gaunt, Duke of Lancaster

. . . This royal throne of kings, this scepter'd
    isle,
This earth of majesty, this seat of Mars,
This other Eden, demi-paradise,
This fortress built by Nature for herself
Against infection and the hand of war,
This happy breed of men, this little world,
This precious stone set in the silver sea,
Which serves it in the office of a wall,
Or as a moat defensive to a house,
Against the envy of less happier lands,
This blessed plot, this earth, this realm, this
    England,
This nurse, this teeming womb of royal
    kings,
Fear'd by their breed and famous by their
    birth,
Renowned for their deeds as far from
    home,
For Christian service and true chivalry,
As is the sepulchre in stubborn Jewry
Of the world's ransom, blessed Mary's Son:
This land of such dear souls, this dear,
    dear land. . . .

Researching Major Poets

William Blake (1757–1827)

It is a pure joy to know this self-educated mystic who taught himself Milton, the Bible, and Shakespeare. Horace Scudder wrote of him:

> When he was a little boy, he came home one day and told his mother that he had seen a tree filled with angels. . . . We sometimes say, especially in hymns, that with the eye of faith we may see the heavenly country. . . . Now Blake had this eye of faith.
>
> . . . There were few who cared for him and his work, but he said, "I see the face of my Heavenly Father: He lays His hand upon my head, and gives a blessing to all my work." (Horace Scudder, *The Riverside Magazine for Young People*, Vol. I, Feb. 1867, p. 91)

William Blake was a painter as well as a poet, and it is a treat to find some small volume of his poetry with his accompanying illustrations.

Robert Browning (1813–1889)

One of England's most productive poets, Robert inherited from his father a "voracious" love of books and from his mother, "a Scottish gentlewoman, . . . a gentle, and affectionate nature and a simple, earnest religious belief."

The contrast of the immense energy of Robert Browning with the quiet invalid, Elizabeth Barrett, reminds us of the love story which freed Elizabeth from her stern, possessive father, gave her health, a husband and son, and enabled her to live in the warmer climate of Italy and write her *Sonnets of the Portuguese*.

The most charming of all Browning's verse is found in these lines from "Pippa Passes," about the twelve-hour day off of the little silk weaver, Pippa—the one day of the year she spends away from the mills. She passes by many of the more fortunate or indolent individuals in her city, unaware that they are affected by her innocent song. It is a spring morning in an Italian town:

> The year's at the spring
> And day's at the morn;
> Morning's at seven;
> The hillside's dew-pearled;
> The lark's on the wing;
> The snail's on the thorn;
> God's in his heaven—
> All's right with the world;
> ("Pippa Passes")

On his gravestone Robert Browning had these two lines placed from one of his poems,

> Open my heart and you will see
> Graved inside of it,"Italy."

However, one of the liveliest of Browning's poems, "Home Thoughts from Abroad," somewhat betrays those lines:

> Oh to be in England,
> Now that April's there. . . .

Look up this poem and you will love it.

Robert Burns (1759–1796)

Born in Scotland, Robert Burns came from a poor-but-proud farming family. Because of his desire to help his younger brothers and sisters to get an education, Robert read and studied as he could. He grew in his ability to write poetry and learned how to run the farm successfully. Married to his true love, he gradually became the successful Bobbie Burns and the author of some of Scotland's most beloved poetry.

Sir Walter Scott (1771–1832)

> O Caledonia! stern and wild,
> Meet nurse for a poetic child!
> Land of brown heath and shaggy wood,
> Land of the mountain and the flood,
> Land of my sires! what mortal hand
> Can e'er untie the filial band,
> That knits me to thy rugged strand.

Walter Scott was born the son of a lawyer in Edinburgh. A childhood illness left him lame, but always with a game and hearty spirit. At the request of his father he took up the law, but his heart was in the Highlands exploring and learning the stories and legends of Scotland's past. God allowed Scott to bring back Scotland's heritage in his narrative poems like *The Lady of the Lake* and *Marmion*. These writings brought thousands of visitors into the land of "heath and heather." After restoring Scotland's heritage of liberty, Scott composed a series of historical novels called *The Waverley Novels*, and began to build his estate which he named *Abbotsford*. Scott's character was reflected in his determination when his printing firm failed, for he spent the rest of his life endeavoring to repay the debt.

Sir Walter Scott: Wizard of the North by Pearle Henricksen Schultz has been our inspired biography of Scott, which we have permission to reprint. *The Lady of the Lake* is Scott's compelling poem which drew so many visitors to Scotland to visit Loch Katrine:

The Lady of the Lake

Canto the First—The Chase

Harp of the North! that mouldering long
　　hast hung
On the witch-elm that shades Saint Fillan's
　　spring,
And down the fitful breeze thy numbers
　　fling,
　Till envious ivy did around thee cling,
　Muffling with verdant ringlets every string,
O Minstrel Harp, still must thine accents
　　sleep?
Midst rustling leaves and fountains mur-
　　muring,
Still must thy sweet sounds their silence
　　keep,
Nor bid a warrior smile, nor teach a maid
　　to weep?

I

The stag at eve had drunk his fill,
Where danced the moon on Mona's rill,
And deep his midnight lair had made
In lone Glenartney's hazel shade;
But when the sun his beacon red
Had kindled on Benvoirlich's head,
The deep-mouth'd bloodhound's heavy
　　bay
Resounded up the rocky way,
And Faint, from farther distance bourne,
　Were heard the clanging hoof and horn.

Alfred Lord Tennyson (1809–1892)

The age of chivalry and King Arthur and his Knights of the Round Table have inspired writers and poets on both sides of the Atlantic. It reflects the Christian idea of man and Christian self-government. On a recent trip to England, we found new research confirming Arthur as a real historical personage.

And slowly answer'd Arthur from the
　　barge;
The old order changeth, yielding place to
　　new,
And God fulfils himself in many ways,
Lest on good custom should corrupt the
　　world.
Comfort thyself; what comfort is in me?
I have lived my life, and that which I have
　　done
May He himself make pure! but thou,
If thou shouldst never see my face again,
　　Pray for my soul. More things are
　　wrought by prayer
Than this world dreams of. Wherefore, let
　　thy voice
Rise like a fountain for me night and day.
For what are men better than sheep or
　　goats
That nourish a blind life within the brain,
If, knowing God, they lift not hands of
　　prayer
Both for themselves and those who call
　　them friend?
For so the whole round earth is every way
Bound by gold chains about the feet of God.
But now farewell. I am going a long way....
(*Idylls of the King*: "The Passing of Arthur")

Young Alfred Tennyson, due to the strictness of his father, hated school. However, due to the influence of his mother, "who as a woman of simplicity and charm, innocent and tender-hearted," he came to love and be influenced by the style of some of England's greatest poets. Before he reached his teens he was writing poetry. He was influenced in his writing by Scott, by Milton, and the romantic poet, Byron. Tennyson's friendship with Arthur Hallam, also a poet and soon engaged to Tennyson's sister, aided him to gain a name in literature. Later a happy marriage for Tennyson and the Poet Laureateship in 1850 established him as a "British Institution." In 1884, he was elevated to the peerage and took his seat in the House of Lords.

It is wonderful to explore the great body of poetry produced by Alfred Lord Tennyson, to discover his many works, and to read aloud and memorize what most appeals to you.

William Wordsworth (1770–1850)

Orphaned early in life, William Wordsworth schooled himself to become a great poet by keeping before himself as examples Chaucer, Shakespeare, Spenser, and Milton. This study, in addition to the large portions of the great English poets which he learned by heart, prepared him to become one of England's most prolific writers. The beautiful Lake Country where William, his sister Dorothy, and eventually his wife Mary, lived was a constant source of renewal and inspiration.

Wordsworth seemed to have two great concerns—his love of what God's universe communicated to him of reflective ideals, and England's great need to return to her heritage of character and "plain living and high thinking." One of his greatest contributions to us is his Christian history of England reflected in his Ecclesiastical Sonnets. Perhaps his lovely poem of the daffodils by the lake is his most inspiring:

I wandered lonely as a cloud
That floats on high o'er vales and hills.
When all at once I saw a crowd,
A host of golden daffodils—
Along the lake, beneath the trees.
Ten thousand dancing in the breeze.

The waves beside them danced, but they
Outdid the sparkling waves in glee—
A poet could not be but gay
In such a laughing company.
I gazed and gazed, but little thought
What wealth the show to me had brought.

For oft when on my couch I lie,
In vacant or in pensive mood,
They flash upon that inward eye
Which is the bliss of solitude,
And then my heart with pleasure fills
And dances with the daffodils.

Restoring America's Poet Laureate
Henry Wadsworth Longfellow (1807–1882)

In the last one hundred years as Americans have forgotten the providence of God in America, they have gradually eliminated teaching and enjoying America's "poet of hearth, home, and history." Henry Wadsworth Longfellow is the only American poet whose monument you will find in Westminster Abbey among England's great. Yet this New Englander of the nineteenth century was beloved on both sides of the Atlantic.

Building a notebook study of Longfellow will be one of your most satisfying tasks as a teacher, for this dear man is well worthy of restoring to our own and future generations.

The closing lines of Longfellow's "Psalm of Life" set the tone for our understanding of this poet's spirit:

Let us, then, be up and doing,
    With a heart for any fate:
Still achieving, still pursuing,
    Learn to labor and to wait.

(*The Poetical Works of Longfellow*, Cambridge Edition, Houghton Mifflin Company, 1975.)

English Poets

Blake, William 1757–1827
"Three Things to Remember"
"Reeds of Innocence"
"Little Lamb"
"The Tiger"

Brooke, Rupert 1887–1915
"The Soldier"

Browning, Robert 1812–1889
"Home-Thoughts from Abroad"
"Incident of the French Camp
(April 23, 1809)"
"Prospice"
"Song"
"The Pied Piper of Hamelin"
"How They Brought the Good News
from Ghent to Aix"

Burns, Robert 1759–1796
"A Red, Red Rose"
"Ye Banks and Braes o' Bonnie Doon"
"A Child's Grace"
"My Heart's in the Highlands"
"For a'That and a'That"
"To a Mouse"

Byron, George Gordon 1788–1824
"She Walks in Beauty"
"Roll On, Thou Dark Blue Ocean"
"The Destruction of Sennacherib"
"The Glory that Was Greece"

Campbell, Thomas 1777–1844
"Ye Marriners of England"
"Lord Ullin's Daughter"

Carroll, Lewis 1832–1898
"The Walrus and the Carpenter"
"Jabberwocky"
"You Are Old Father William"

Clough, Arthur Hugh 1819–1861
"Say Not the Struggle Naught Availeth"

Coleridge, Samuel Taylor 1772–1834
"Kubla Khan"
"The Rime of the Ancient Mariner"

De la Mare, Walter 1873–1956
"The Listeners"
"Silver"

Gray, Thomas 1716–1771
"Elegy Written in a Country Churchyard"
"The Epitaph"

Hogg, James 1770–1835
"A Boy's Song"
"Where the Pools Are Bright and Deep"

Hovey, Richard 1864–1900
"The Sea Gypsy"

Hunt, (James Henry) Leigh 1784–1859
"Abou Ben Adhem"

Keats, John 1795–1821
"To Autumn"
"Ode on a Grecian Urn"
"Ode to a Nightingale"
"On First Looking into Chapman's Homer"
"La Belle Dame Sans Merci"

Kipling, Rudyard 1865–1936
"If"
"Recessional"

Lear, Edward 1812–1888
"The Owl and the Pussycat"

Masefield, John 1878–1967
"Sea Fever"

Milton, John 1608–1674
"On His Blindness"
"On May Morning"

Noyes, Alfred 1880–1958
"The Young Highwayman"

Rossetti, Christina 1830–1894
"Who Has Seen the Wind"
"The Pancake"
"The City Mouse and the Garden Mouse"
"Before the Paling of the Stars"

Shelley, Percy Bysshe 1792–1822
"To a Skylark"
"Ozymandias of Egypt"
"To Night"
"Ode to the West Wind"

Scott, Sir Walter 1771–1832
"Soldier, Rest! Thy Warfare O'er"
"Young Lochinvar"
"Alice Brand"
"Hunting Song"
"Waken, Lords and Ladies Gay"
"Innominatus"
"Breathes there a man with soul so dread"

Shakespeare, William 1564–1616
"Fairy Songs"
"Sonnets"
"Under the Greenwood Tree"

Stevenson, Robert Louis 1850–1894
"The Land of Storybooks"
"The Wind"
"Escape at Bedtime"
"My Shadow"
"The Land of Counterpane"
"Whole Duty of Children"
"Windy Nights"

Taylor, Ann 1782–1866
"My Mother"

Taylor, Jane 1783–1824
"The Star"

Tennyson, Alfred 1809–1892
"The Brook"
"Lullaby (Sweet and Low)"
"The Charge of the Light Brigade"
"What Does Little Birdie Say?"
"The Lady of Shalott"
"Blow Bugle Blow"
"Ring Out, Wild Bells"
"Flower in the Crannied Wall"
"The Eagle"

Watts, Isaac 1674–1748
"How Doth the Little Busy Bee"

"A Morning Song"
"A Cradle Hymn"

Wordsworth, William 1770–1850
"I Wandered Lonely as a Cloud"
"Written in March"
"Stern Daughter of the Voice of God"
"Three Years She Grew"
"To a Child"
"To a Skylark"
"To the Daisy"
"The World is Too Much with Us"
"Character of the Happy Warrior"
"It Is a Beauteous Evening"
"The Kitten and Falling Leaves"
"The Rainbow"
"She Dwelt among the Untrodden Ways"
"The Solitary Reaper"

American Poets

Bryant, William Cullen 1794–1878
"Oh Mother of a Mighty Race"
"To a Waterfowl"
"The Planting of the Apple-Tree"
"Song of Marion's Men"
"Thanatopsis"
"To the Fringed Gentian"

Dickinson, Emily 1830–1886
"The Grass"
"The Robin"
"The Train"
"Autumn"
"Pedigree"

Emerson, Ralph Waldo 1803–1882
"Concord Hymn"
"Fable"
"Forbearance"
"The Rhodora"
"So Nigh Is Grandeur"

Field, Eugene 1850–1895
"Wynken, Blynken, and Nod"
"Little Boy Blue"
"The Duel"

Frost, Robert 1875–1963
"Tuft of Flowers"
"Stopping by Woods on a Snowy Evening"
"The Pasture"
"Mending Wall"
"Birches"
"The Road Not Taken"

Holmes, Oliver Wendell 1809–1894
"The Chambered Nautilus"
"The Deacon's Masterpiece"
"Old Ironsides"

Longfellow, Henry Wadsworth 1807–1882
"The Children's Hour"

"The Village Blacksmith"
"A Psalm of Life"
"The Wreck of the Hesperus"
"The Skeleton in Armor"
"The Arrow and the Song"
"Christmas Bells"
"Paul Revere's Ride"
"Evangeline"
"Courtship of Miles Standish"
"Hiawatha"
"The Building of the Ship"

Lowell, James Russell 1819–1891
"The Vision of Sir Launfal"

Miller, Joaquin 1841–1913
"Columbus"

Poe, Edgar Allan 1809–1849
"Anabel Lee"
"To Helen"
"The Raven"
"The Bells"

Riley, James Whitcomb 1849–1916
"A Boy's Mother"
"Little Orphan Annie"
"Our Hired Girl"
"The Raggedy Man"
"When the Frost Is on the Punkin"

Sandburg, Carl 1878–1967
"The Fog"
"Washington Monument by Night"

Whitman, Walt 1819–1892
"O Captain! My Captain!"

Whittier, John Greenleaf 1807–1892
"Barbara Frietchie"
"The Barefoot Boy"
"Pipes at Lucknow"
"Snow-Bound"

Teaching Poetry through God's Principle of Individuality

by Carole Goodman Adams

Poetry is an essential ingredient in any elementary classroom. To teach poetry is to unleash boundless inspiration and to elevate the student's language. We teach poetry to our children because it is sheer joy, but joy that also imparts a transcending richness of language and ideals.

Every poem is the expression of an individual—of his life and his gifts and, often, of his faith. Poetry must be taught through the individuality of the poet so that the student meets the poet personally and learns to appreciate his style along with the best-loved poems. If the poet is not taught with the poem, the work becomes a blur, buried in a modern anthology, and we miss an opportunity to inspire students with models of individual achievement and greatness.

Developing a poet for elementary students is an enriching experience for the teacher. Preparation to teach poetry should include:

1. The selection of the poets that the teacher loves. The teacher's enthusiasm for the poet and his poetry will inspire the same love in the children. Each teacher should have a repertoire of poets and their poetry for the teaching of literature in a grade level—at least three to teach in depth per year of literature.

2. The reading and relishing of the poet through study and the compiling of a personal notebook. Read a biography or two. Read all the poetry of your poets. Prepare a brief biography for students by the Notebook Approach to give them a whole sense of this person who so delights and enriches them.

3. The collection of portraits of the poet, pictures of his home, family, and nation. *National Geographic* is a good source. Search old book stores for the wonderful sets like *Great Men and Famous Women*, ten volumes edited by Charles F. Horne, published in New York, 1894, and filled with biographies and portraits.

4. The presentation of the poet to the children:

   a) Begin with an appealing poem and teach it lovingly with many repetitions, inspiring students with its beauty, craftsmanship, worth, and charm.

   b) Once they love the poem, introduce them to the person behind the poem giving them as much personal information as appropriate. Put up a bulletin board with pictures of the poet's life and nation and with space for the poems your students will write.

   c) Read many of the poems of this poet, leading the class in memorizing at least one.

   d) Lead the children in writing their own poetry, patterned after the poet's style. Allow time for sharing their own poetry and display it.

   e) Watch for opportunities throughout the year to recall the poet, relish the favorite poems, and do further study.

America's Christian History in Verse

Burton E. Stevenson has been the guardian of our literary heritage of verse for more than a century. Now Bob Jones University has re-published and made available his *American History in Verse.* What a wonderful teaching resource we have as we follow the chronology of God in America's unfolding history. While the facts of His Story move constantly like an escalator, literature, and especially poetry, capture the deep feelings of every period of the events recorded.

"America," by Samuel Francis Smith, presents the overview theme. Written at the Park Street Church in Boston, July 4, 1832, it presents God as the "Author of Liberty."

The opening poem by Katherine Lee Bates, "America the Beautiful," is a constant reminder to us as, in crowded planes, we cross our nation and glimpse its "purple mountain majesties" and its "fruited plain," "its thoroughfare for freedom beat across the wilderness." This is one of many beautiful hymns about our country which we should all know by heart (memorize).

The sections which follow celebrate the Hand of God in our discovery and establishment, beginning with "The Greatest Voyage in History"—great poems about Columbus.

In "The Virginia Colony" and "The Pilgrims and the Puritans," we have the opportunity to review God's Hand in these first colonies. (We rejoice that F.A.C.E. and StoneBridge School in Virginia have prepared educational materials to help you research and plan special celebrations of both "Jamestown, Virginia, the first permanent English colony," and the "Pilgrims' Thanksgiving.")

Verna Hall's *The Christian History of the American Revolution: Consider and Ponder*, contains many contributions from the years of constitutional debate before we cut our mother country's apron strings and declared that we were no longer colonists but "one nation under God." *American History in Verse* has a number of sections about our efforts for independence. It includes stirring poems, some by famous poets, and it takes us on the path of liberty, reminding us again and again of God's providence for us to be the world's first Christian constitutional republic.

Through the war years in poetry and prose, we learn and remember our heroes and heroines, and yes, our traitors, too. Verse seems to help us relive those moving scenes. A whole section is devoted to George Washington, "first in war, first in peace, first in the hearts of his countrymen." The Christian History Program is unique in its presentation of the man God providentially prepared and preserved to lead us into nationhood.

How better to learn some stirring events in both the American Revolution, and in the Civil War, than in poetry form. The move "westward across the wide Missouri," the inclusion of the large states, Texas and California, introduce us to a new kind of character in America—of pioneering to establish our Christian constitutional republic from "sea to shining sea." Dorothy Dimmick's Christian history of California, entitled *The Making of American California: A Providential Approach*, is distinct from any other account of how God prepared this state to become part of our constitutional republic.

American History in Verse takes us historically to the end of World War II and leaves room for the next poets to celebrate the rebirth of Christian self-government in our land.

Longfellow's poem, "The Republic," written in the nineteenth century, echoes the mighty refrain, ". . . sail on, O Ship of State!":

> Sail on, nor fear, to breast the sea!
> Our hearts, our hopes are all with thee,
> Our hearts, our hopes, our prayers, our tears.
> Our faith triumphant o'er our fears,
> Are all with thee—are all with thee!

Teachers should plan their notebooks to include those pearls of prose and verse which we wish to pass on to succeeding generations.

Teaching Historical Poetry in the Elementary Christian School

from *American History in Verse*. Edited by Burton Stevenson.
A Suggested Sequence for Teaching Historical Poetry

Part I. The New World:

"America" by Samuel Francis Smith, Frontispiece
"America the Beautiful" by Katharine Lee Bates
The Greatest Voyage in History:
    Poems about Christopher Columbus
The Virginia Colony:
    John Smith, Pocahontas
The Pilgrims and the Puritans:
    "Landing of the Pilgrim Fathers" by Felicia Dorothea Hemans
    "Five Kernels of Corn" by Hezekiah Butterworth

Part II. The New Nation:

The Bursting of the Storm:
    "Paul Revere's Ride" by Henry Wadsworth Longfellow
    "Concord Hymn" by Ralph Waldo Emerson
The War Begins:
    "The Green Mountain Boys" by William Cullen Bryant
    "The Surprise at Ticonderoga" by Mary A. P. Stansbury
    "The Ballad of Bunker Hill" by Edward Everett Hale
    "The Death of Warren" by Epes Sargent
Independence:
The First Campaign:
    "Across the Delaware" by Will Carleton
    "The Battle of Trenton"
    "Assunpink and Princeton" by Thomas Dunn English
Victory:
    "Valley Forge" by Thomas Buchanan Read
First in the Hearts of His Countrymen:
    Poems about George Washington

Part IV. The Struggle for the Union:

"Battle Hymn of the Republic" by Julia Ward Howe
"Lincoln, the Man of the People" by Edwin Markham
"O Captain! My Captain!" by Walt Whitman

Part V. America Goes Crusading:

The Making of a Giant

History as Literature

William Bradford, Governor of Plymouth Plantation, writing our first American Christian classic in the seventeenth century, set for us a standard of history as literature when he penned the purpose of his work: ". . . that their children may see with what difficulties their fathers wrestled in going through these things in their first beginnings, and how God brought them along notwithstanding all their weaknesses and infirmities." (*Christian History*, Vol. I, p. 197)

Writers who have been conscious of God as Author and Disposer of the events of history have upon occasion written some work especially with posterity in mind in order to direct their hearts and minds to "think on these things."

In 1828, **Sir Walter Scott** dedicated his *Tales of a Grandfather: Being Stories from the History of Scotland*, to Hugh LittleJohn, Esq., as follows:

My Dear Child,

I now address to you two volumes of Scottish Stories, which brings down the History of that Country, from the period when England and Scotland became subject to the same King, until that of the Union when they were finally united into one Kingdom. That you, and children of your age, may read these little books with pleasure and improvement, is the desire and hope of

My dearest Child,
Your very affectionate Grandfather,
Walter Scott

Abbotsford, 15th October, 1828

Tales of a Grandfather

In the first chapter of Scott's work, entitled "Progress of Civilization in Society," he goes back to the Genesis account of Creation and differentiates man from the beasts by their means of permanent communication. After

tracing many of the means by which God has enabled man to progress—the gift of speech, the knowledge of right and wrong, "the capacity of amending our condition by increase of knowledge," and other arts of civilized life, he deals with the importance of writing. Finally, he comes to the climax in the means of progress:

Another discovery, however, almost as important as that of writing, was made during the fifteenth century. I mean the invention of printing. . . . The Bible itself, in which we find the rules of eternal life, as well as a thousand lessons for our conduct in this world, was, before the invention of printing, totally inaccessible to all, save the priests of Rome, who found it their interest to discourage the perusal of the Scriptures. . . . But when, by means of printing, the copies of the Bible became so numerous, that every one, above the most wretched poverty, could, at a cheap price, possess himself of a copy of the blessed rule of life, there was a general appeal from the errors and encroachments of the Church of Rome, to the Divine Word on which they professed to be founded; a treasure formerly concealed from the public, but now placed within the reach of every man, whether of the clergy or laity. The consequence of these inquiries, which printing alone could have rendered practicable, was the rise of the happy Reformation of the Christian church.

Scott drew an important conclusion from this invention of printing:

In a word, the printing-press is a contrivance which enables any one individual to address his whole fellow-subjects on any topic which he thinks important, and which enables a whole nation to listen to the voice of such individual, however obscure, with the same ease and greater certainty of understanding what he says, than if a chief of Indians were haranguing the tribe at his council-fire. Nor is the important difference to be forgotten, that the orator can only speak to the person present, while the author of a book addresses himself, not to the race now in existence, but to all succeeding generations, while his work shall be held in estimation.

Charles Dickens first mentioned his intention in 1843 of "writing a little history of England for my boy." His eldest son, Charles, was then six. But it was not until some time later, in 1850, when he began to edit a new weekly journal, *Household Words*, that Dickens commenced his *A Child's History of England* (1880), which appeared in serial form. Just as he did in his novels, Dickens maintained his forthright approach and his Christian base to justice. He wrote history as he did fiction—with feeling and with concern for character. The following excerpt from his chapter 3 on "England under the good Saxon, Alfred" indicates his style and stance:

Alfred the Great was a young man, three-and-twenty years of age, when he became king. . . . Learning, however, was so little cared for, then, that at twelve years old he had not been taught to read. . . . But he had—as most men who grow up to be great and good are generally found to have had—an excellent mother; and, one day, this lady, whose name was Osburga, happened, as she was sitting among her sons, to read a book of Saxon poetry. The art of printing was not known until long and long after that period, and the book, which was written, was what is called "illuminated," with beautiful bright letters, richly painted. The brothers admiring it very much, their mother said, "I will give it to that one of you four princes who first learns to read." Alfred sought out a tutor that very day, applied himself to learn with great diligence and soon won the book. He was proud of it, all his life. . . .

As great and good in peace, as he was great and good in war, King Alfred never rested from his labours to improve his people. He loved to talk with clever men, and with travellers from foreign countries, and to write down

what they told him, for his people to read. He had studied Latin after learning to read English, and now another of his labours was, to translate Latin books into the English-Saxon tongue, that his people might be interested, and improved by their contents. He made just laws, that they might live more happily and freely; he turned away all partial judges, that no wrong might be done them; he was so careful of their property, and punished robbers so severely, that it was a common thing to say that under the great King Alfred, garlands of golden chains and jewels might have hung across the streets, and no man would have touched one. He founded schools; he patiently heard causes himself in his Court of Justice; the great desires of his heart were, to do right to all his subjects, and to leave England better, wiser, happier in all ways than he found it. . . .

I have more to tell of the Saxons yet, but I stop to say this now, because under the Great Alfred, all the best points of the English-Saxon character were first encouraged, and in him first shown. It has been the greatest character among the nations of the earth. Wherever the descendants of the Saxon race have gone, have sailed, or otherwise made their way, even to the remotest regions of the world, they have been patient, persevering, never to be broken in spirit, never to be turned aside from enterprises on which they have resolved. In Europe, Asia, Africa, America, the whole world over; in the desert, in the forest, on the sea; scorched by a burning sun, or frozen by ice that never melts; the Saxon blood remains unchanged. Wheresoever that race goes, there, law and industry, and safety for life and property, and all the great results of steady perseverance, are certain to arise.

I pause to think with admiration, of the noble king who, in his single person, possessed all the Saxon virtues. Whom misfortune could not subdue, whom prosperity could not spoil, whose perseverance nothing could shake. Who was hopeful in defeat, and generous in success. Who loved justice, freedom, truth, and knowledge. Who, in his care to instruct his people, probably did more to preserve the beautiful old Saxon language, than I can imagine. Without whom, the English tongue in which I tell this story might have wanted half its meaning. As it is said that his spirit still inspires some of our best English laws, so, let you and I pray that it may animate our English hearts, at least to this—to resolve, when we see any of our fellow-creatures left in ignorance, that we will do our best, while life is in us, to have them taught; and to tell those rulers whose duty it is to teach them, and who neglect their duty, that they have profited very little by all the years that have rolled away since the year nine hundred and one, and that they are far behind the bright example of King Alfred the Great.

Nathaniel Hawthorne's *Grandfather's Chair*

It was our own American Puritan, Nathaniel Hawthorne, who carried on the idea initiated by Scott, and later carried out by Dickens. Hawthorne had very high standards for writing for children and of the three authors, Scott, Dickens, and Hawthorne, the last seemed to have carried it off with the best balance of history and imagination.

Hawthorne spent six months writing for a family periodical only to give it up as "scribbling," a kind of writing that did not dignify either the writer or the reader. Besides Hawthorne had a deep sense of responsibility in writing for children:

> The author regards children as sacred, and would not for the world, cast anything into the fountain of a young heart, that might embitter and pollute its waters.

In 1841 Hawthorne began publishing his *True Stories from History and Biography*, entitled *Grandfather's Chair*. The Chair was the connecting link that carried his youthful audience through the history of New England. He used a conversational approach and made emphasis upon the Hand of God—Providence—and the Christian character of the men and women of history.

Biography and Autobiography as Character Study

Noah Webster's definition of "character" in the 1828 *American Dictionary of the English Language* includes its derivation from the Greek verb meaning "to scrape, cut, engrave." He follows with these facets:

1. A mark made by cutting or engraving, as on stone, metal or other hard material. . . .

2. The peculiar qualities, impressed by nature or habit on a person, which distinguish him from others; these constitute real character, and the qualities which he is supposed to possess, constitute his estimated character, or reputation. Hence we say, a character is not formed, when the person has not acquired stable and distinctive qualities.

Unstable character might be illustrated in Scripture by the following words of our Lord to Peter, when he said: "Simon, Simon, behold, Satan hath desired to have you, that he may sift you as wheat: But I have prayed for thee, that thy faith fail not: and when thou are converted, strengthen thy brethren." (Luke 22:31–32) As Peter was impressed more and more in his life by the character of Christ, the unstable qualities within him became transformed—and he stood like a rock.

In the same manner the real character of Stephen was in evidence when his enemies, "cut to the heart" by his testimony, stoned him to death: "And they stoned Stephen, calling upon God, and saying Lord Jesus, receive my spirit. And he kneeled down, and cried with a loud voice, Lord, lay not this sin to their charge. And when he had said this, he fell asleep." (Acts 7:59–60)

The study of internal character should be the subject of biography, rather than a mere rehearsal of the external events of an individual's human experience. Unfortu-nately, few biographies today portray their subjects internally struggling and dealing with life's temptations in their development of character. That is why the Bible must be our keynote for the identification and illustration of character before other biographies and autobiographies are studied. The following sentence from the *Life of David Livingstone, the Heroic Christian Missionary and African Explorer* by Annie Maria Barnes, published in 1888, Nashville, Tennessee, illustrates the development of character:

> While not despising his humble surroundings, nor yet rebellious against the hardness of his lot, there was nevertheless born within him from the moment his hands knew daily toil the pure purpose to raise himself step by step to higher and broader levels, and to make of his life in the end that which would be an honor to God, a satisfaction to himself, and a blessing to his fellowmen.

In the study of the great literature of the world outside of the Bible there are many opportunities to furnish models for character study. These examples should be dealt with from their relationship to the character standards set forth by the whole Bible. Both good and evil characters emerge from the pages of literature. However, we must not fall into the snare of Satan and feel any false obligation to detail the study of evil and degraded character so that we are actually committing original sin by tasting and eating of the tree of knowledge of evil. Our obligation is to detail the study of what constitutes worthwhile character and to identify evil, but not to study it under the microscope and so to magnify it to the attention and interest of our young people. We must not feed our young people with erroneous models, but rather lift their vision to the Christian traditions, ideals, and standards of character which formerly flowed throughout study of literature. The Apostle Paul set the standard for our study of character when he said:

> Finally, brethren, whatsoever things are true, whatsoever things are honest, whatsoever things are just; whatsoever things are pure, whatsoever things are lovely, whatsoever things are of good report; if there be any virtue, and if there be any praise, think on these things. (Philippians. 4:8)

Biographical Series

A number of publishers have endeavored to provide patriotic and historical biographies for the elementary school. Two of these are the Childhood of Famous Americans series and Piper Books.

Childhood of Famous Americans

This series has been in existence for some years and new titles are constantly being added. It follows a chronological sequence of American history having titles in colonial days, struggle for independence, early national growth, westward movement, the nation divided, reconstruction and expansion, turn of the century, in recent years. The series is helpful in that it presents many outstanding Americans to the young student. But these postage-stamp biographies do not contribute much to the understanding of the qualities which contribute to or identify character—this must be supplied by the Christian teacher. It is therefore urged that a teacher present only one or two biographies a semester. If these books are used, much greater background should be presented into what qualities of character are being developed by the individual American under scrutiny. This is a major purpose in the study of biography.

The Pilgrim character always provides us with the "touchstone" for our study of character. Teachers can identify those qualities which promote American Christian character and those that do not contribute to our nation. Furthermore, expansion of these character qualities into every field of our national life can be a vital part of the history program.

Piper Books

Almost all of the titles in this series would be acceptable in an American Christian educational setting. Historically they seem to be more accurate than other series and depend less upon imaginative recreations of how it might have happened. Once again, however, they reflect the current trend in biographical writing for the young—internal struggles of character are left out. Teachers must provide the "in-depth" biographical background so that the real man or woman stands forth for contemplation. Only as we restore the Biblical standards of character prerequisites will we be able to measure and discuss with students the details of what is required to be an American Christian man or woman worthy and ready to be a useful instrument for the Lord.

Character study, like portraiture, is a neglected art today. Let us in American Christian schools create a real interest and taste for this study in our youth, so that they may begin to look, not only on "the outward appearance" but also "on the heart"—the character of a man or woman.

Teacher Preparation and Presentation

1. Biography as the Study of Character

Does the individual being studied exemplify Biblical principles of character? To what extent does the biographer identify these qualities of character? Is character seen as causative rather than the circumstances of the individual's life, the environment, being the causative principle? Is plot secondary to character? Is setting secondary to character?

2. Biography in a Setting or Philosophy of Government

Fine Christians live out their lives all over the world in many countries. But the degree to which the individual's God-given talents can be brought to their fruition and outreach depends upon the philosophy of government which prevails. Despite the current interpretations of government-granted opportunity, Americans of every kind of background, color, and character have achieved a greater degree of success than that achieved by individuals in any other nation. The American Christian constitution was established to encourage the initiative, the individual enterprise, and effort of anyone who caught a vision or glimpsed a goal of accomplishment. Our original philosophy of government did not insure the individual of success. Rather, it gave the individual the liberty to exercise to the fullest his or her God-given talents. So long as one individual did not interfere with or infringe upon the life, liberty, and property of another, the only limitations were those of individual character, determination, and energy.

The blessings of liberty in America have brought about all kinds of improvements in the life of the nation. But the external benefits such as financial independence, high standard of living, and freedom of choice in products competitively produced, are not all. This is only the fruit of an attitude toward the individual never seen elsewhere. Its blessings have been unselfishly shared and have been of inestimable benefit to the en-tire world. The Gospel outreach glimpsed by the Pilgrims has been made possible through the American Christian constitutional form of government.

3. Historical Setting—Relation to the Chain of Christianity

Each biography can reveal the contribution of the historical background or setting, to the advancement or the retardation of the Gospel outreach. Does the individual studied represent the area he or she comes from? Is he or is she a good or bad example of those qualities of character which identify that country or section?

4. Literary Achievement of the Biographer

To what degree can the author or biographer be considered as making a contribution to literature? How well is character portrayed in its qualities? How well does the author indicate that character is the result of overcoming obstacles—of yielding to the Hand of God in one's life? How well does the biographer combine the events to bring character to the foreground? What distinguishes the writer as a biographer? Can the biography be considered a classic?

Biography as Character Study

Abe Lincoln Grows Up by Carl Sandburg. Harcourt, Brace & World, 1954.

Abraham Lincoln: Friend of the People by Clara Ingram Judson. Follett Publishing Co., 1950.

Benjamin Franklin by Clara Ingram Judson. Follett Publishing Co., 1957.

Benjamin Franklin by Ingri and Edgar Parin d'Aulaire. Doubleday & Co., 1950.

Captain Paul by Commander Edward Ellsberg. Dodd, Mead & Co., 1941.

Carry On, Mr. Bowditch by Jean Lee Latham. Houghton Mifflin Co., 1955.

Famous Men of the American Revolution (Two hundred and forty-three of the sages and heroes are presented) by L. Carroll Judson, 1889.

George Washington: Leader of the People by Clara Ingram Judson. Follett Co., 1951.

The Glory and the Dream: Abraham Lincoln, before and after Gettysburg by Michael A. Musmanno. The Long House, 1967.

Heroic Colonial Christians, Edited by Russell T. Hitt. Biographies of Jonathan Edwards, Gilbert Tennent, David Brainerd, and John Witherspoon. J. B. Lippincott Co., 1966.

John Eliot "Apostle to the Indians" by Ola Elizabeth Winslow. Houghton Mifflin Co., 1968.

Life of David Livingstone by Annie M. Barnes. Nashville, Tenn.: 1888.

Life of Rear-Admiral John Paul Jones. Compiled from his original journals and correspondence. St. Nicholas Series for Boys and Girls [before 1900].

Lindbergh: Lone Eagle by Adele deLeeuw. Westminister Press, 1949.

Lives of Bradford and Winthrop, Cotton Mather. Old South Leaflet No. 77, The Old South Association, Boston, Massachusetts.

Noah Webster: Father of the Dictionary by Isabel Proudfit. Julian Messner, 1942.

People of Destiny: Helen Keller by Norman Richards. Children's Press, 1968.

Trailblazers of the Sea by Jean Lee Latham

Washington by Lucy Foster Madison. Hampton Publishing Co., 1925.

Women of Colonial and Revolutionary Times Series:

1. *Margaret Winthrop* by Alice Morse Earle. Charles Scribner's Sons, 1895.

2. *Martha Washington* by Anne Hollingsworth Wharton. Charles Scribner's Sons, 1897.

3. *Mercy Warren* by Alice Brown. Charles Scribner's Sons, 1896.

Autobiography as Character Study

Alone by Richard E. Byrd

The Autobiography of Benjamin Franklin. Houghton Mifflin Co., 1966.

John of the Mountains: Journals of John Muir

The Journal of John Wesley

Mover of Men and Mountains by R.G. LeTourneau. Moody Press, 1967.

Seven Came Through: Rickenbacker's Full Story by Captain Edward V. Rickenbacker. Doubleday & Co., 1943.

The Spirit of St. Louis by Charles A. Lindbergh

The Story of My Life by Helen Keller

Up from Slavery by Booker T. Washington

We by Charles A. Lindbergh

Witness by Whittaker Chambers. Random House, 1952.

Studying Elementary Literature on the Chain of Christianity

Switzerland

Heroes of the Reformation; Home of the Geneva Bible; Calvin's City of Biblical Law

Heidi by Johanna Spyri

The Netherlands: Holland

The Second Home of the Pilgrims

Hans Brinker, or The Silver Skates by Mary Mapes Dodge

England, Our Mother Country

English Bible, English Common Law, English Character, English Literature

William Shakespeare

John Milton

George Herbert

John Locke

John Bunyan

Sir Walter Scott

Charles Dickens

Italy: Home of Columbus (Born in the Republic of Genoa)

The birthplace of Christian art

Pinocchio by Carlo Lorenzini Collodi

Spain: Queen Isabella and Columbus

Life of Columbus by Washington Irving

Tales of the Alhambra by Washington Irving

Don Quixote by Miguel de Cervantes

El Cid

France

Home of the Huguenots whose refugees filled our American history

Marquis de Lafayette

Joan of Arc by M. Bouter de Monvel

The Story of Roland

French Fairy Tales by Charles Perrault

Jules Verne—Literature of the scientific imagination

Germany: European Reformation

Grimm Brothers' *Fairy Tales*

The Story of Siegfried by James Baldwin

Johann Sebastian Bach, the Boy from Thuringia by Opal Wheeler and Sybil Deucher

Denmark: Viking Explorers

Hans Christian Andersen's *Fairy Tales*

Note: The interest in other nations stems from their contribution of Christian character and their own historical effort for civil and religious liberty.

Key Classics Available with a F.A.C.E. Syllabus
for the Notebook Approach
Written by Rosalie June Slater

America's Establishment of Liberty

Classic: *Of Plimoth Plantation* by William Bradford
Syllabus: Teaching Providential History: Bradford and the Pilgrims
Syllabus and Poem: *The Courtship of Miles Standish* by Henry Wadsworth Longfellow

Classic: *To Have and to Hold* by Mary Johnston
Syllabus: Virginia Colony—Love for England and English Institutions (available 1998)

Classic: *Benjamin West and His Cat, Grimalkin* by Marguerite Henry
Syllabus: William Penn and the Colony of Religious Toleration

Classic: *Abigail Adams: First Lady of Faith and Courage* by Evelyn Witter
Syllabus: Patriotic Women in the American Revolution

Classic: *The Deerslayer* by James Fenimore Cooper
Syllabus: James Fenimore Cooper, First Novelist of the Republic

Classic: *Carry On, Mr. Bowditch* by Jean Lee Latham
Syllabus: American Men of Science and Invention

Classic: *Little Women* by Louisa May Alcott
Syllabus: The New England Mind and Character

Classic: *Little House in the Big Woods* by Laura Ingalls Wilder
Syllabus: Extending Pilgrim-Pioneer Character Westward

Classic: *Spirit of St. Louis* by Charles Lindbergh
Syllabus: We Three: God Had a Plan, God Had a Man, God Had a Machine

Syllabus: Noah Webster: American Character in Education

Our European Heritage of Liberty

Classic: *Heidi* by Johanna Spyri
Syllabus: Switzerland and Liberty

Classic: *Hans Brinker, or The Silver Skates* by Mary Mapes Dodge
Syllabus: Holland and Liberty

Classic: *Ivanhoe* by Sir Walter Scott
Syllabus: Anglo-Saxon, Anglo-Norman Periods and Sir Walter Scott
Biography: *Sir Walter Scott: Wizard of the North* by Pearle Henricksen Schultz (reprint anticipated)

Classic: *Lady of the Lake and Other Poems* by Sir Walter Scott
Syllabus: Harp of the North (available 1998)

Classic: *Men of Iron* by Howard Pyle
Syllabus: English Chivalry and Seeds of Constitutional Liberty

Classic: *Robinson Crusoe* by Daniel Defoe
Syllabus: English Literature—Liberty of the Individual

Syllabus: Christopher Columbus: Christ Bearer to the New World

June Keith Literature Progam

A syllabus for these books is available from the June Keith Literature Program for schools teaching America's Christian history and teaching the Principle Approach with notebooks for some key classics. The syllabus identifies the Principle Approach and guides teachers in developing literary skills in writing with their students.

Teaching and Learning a Classic
Teacher Presentation

Reading Aloud

The Literature Program for Elementary Christian Schools is presented through the technique of *reading aloud*—the teacher to the class. The Literature Program is not the "Learning to Read Program." Teaching literature is teaching character and teaching life. It should help students read books of depth—to learn how to plumb the riches and to gain greater satisfaction from books of significance.

Learning to Listen

Listening is a skill of concentration. It is learning how to "turn off" external sounds, how to control the "internal" sounds—one's own distracting thoughts and feelings. It is a *reflective skill* which is at the heart of the Principle Approach to American Christian education—the opposite of the *stimulus-response* of progressive education.

Seeing Things Whole

As the teacher *reads a classic aloud* to the class, there are many good opportunities to enjoy a *mental review of plot, character, setting*. This enables the students to keep in their minds the whole book—and to anticipate its unfolding. Much reading done by students today is *impressionistic*—they have little recall which deals with an understanding of character, which can describe setting, and which can discuss aspects of the plot. This is a major purpose of the literature program.

Imagination—Mental Imagery

We have a dependent mentality today—educated as we are by the audio-visual world of mechanical devices. This does not help constitute the free and independent man— the quality for a Christian republic. We need to educate students to *ask questions*—not just *answer* questions. We need to help them through literature develop the *inner eye* and the *inner ear*—the *imagination* which does not require external images. This requires the patient and loving guidance of a teacher helping students "see" and even "hear" what the writer is conveying through words. If the teacher is excited about literature and loves to rekindle his or her own enjoyment of a book or a subject in others, then students, too, will catch on fire with enthusiasm and interest.

The House You Live In

What do you have in your mental house? Do you, like Louisa May Alcott, "enjoy your mind"; do you like the thoughts that fill it and the feelings which furnish it? Literature helps to furnish our mental houses with either Scriptural beauty or with transitory thoughts ever on the move—waiting for the next event to happen. What do you have to offer the students whose lives you wish to enrich and deepen? The field of literature can be your own avenue of enrichment while you are teaching. Teaching is learning; and researching, reasoning, relating, and recording—writing down your own responses—will begin to give you your own thoughts. As you increase your own vision you will find that you are able to help open the eyes of your students to see more of the wondrous works of the Lord all about them—in Creation and in people, places, and things. Appreciation is part of Christian joy in living.

Author and Chain of Christianity

Identify the author in the light of the Chain of Christianity moving westward. Did this author contribute to Christian principles of literature? If the classic is a *biography* or *historical* work, give the students a background in terms of the individual or period to be studied.

Individuality of Style

This program emphasizes major authors—so we can really come to know and appreciate them. What makes them unique in literature? Begin to point this out before reading the book. As the book is read to the class the teacher can help students anticipate particular literary techniques. It should be possible to recognize an author by his or her writing. We begin simply in the elementary years, but it helps both teacher and student to become discerning of detail and emphasis.

Character and Philosophy of Government

The study of character is the real purpose of literature. Each nation has some outstanding characteristics—many of these contributed to our American republic. The philosophy of government of a nation is the setting for the character of an individual. This is why the people in Europe were so eager to read the first American books. They wanted to see how those Americans who had that precious *individual liberty* would like and how they would use this *God-given* privilege. If our founding fathers had not extended *Christian liberty* into the form of a constitutional republic, we today would not enjoy the blessings of liberty which we do enjoy.

Types of Literature Studied

Here we begin to distinguish between the individuality which is characteristic of different *types* of literature. In elementary school we begin simply—lay the foundations, so that later grades can go on in the expanding and deepening.

Attitudes Emphasized

On pages 85 and 86 can be found a list of seven attitudes or "loves" which literature should produce in students. Which of these does a particular piece of literature emphasize?

Christian History Principles

Which of the Christian history principles can be seen in this work? Sometimes we can see why they are absent from the literature of other countries, or from some form of pagan literature like folk tales.

God's Word Our Standard

One has only to read the purposes for literature in most major programs to determine that God's Word is not a major consideration. Books which teach morality are shunned today. It is "social approval," not pleasing God which counts. Our purpose is to do just the opposite. We pray that boys and girls will have their eyes opened to the Lord through the study of literature and the guidance of their teachers.

Purposes for the Notebook Method in Literature

Literature Identifies the Character of Our Nation

As stated in the purposes for the study of literature in American Christian education, we are first of all concerned with identifying the *character*, the *principles*, and the *purposes* of our nation on the Chain of Christianity: Who we are as a people, Where our principles and ideals come from, Why we are here—our purpose as a nation as was identified by our founders.

Thus as we study the character of nations, reading some Key Classics, we seek to identify their contribution to the westward movement of Christianity, especially as they blessed our nation.

Literature and the Art of Writing

The study of literature, as distinct from merely reading through a good book and writing a book report, provides us with wonderful opportunities to study the art of writing and to practice these skills. So we study the literary skills of authors already accomplished in conveying the *setting*, *characterization*, *plot elements*, and *themes* in a style that is pleasing to read.

Once we have learned how to identify the literary elements in a particular book and to record them in our notebook so that we have a picture of that book in words, then we are ready to do some of our own writing. If we use what we have learned from the master writers—studying them as an apprentice—then we can utilize what we have learned from them to expand our own writing abilities.

The Notebook Method in the study of literature gives us opportunities to identify *Setting, Characterization, Plot Elements, Themes,* and to record these from each chapter in our own notebooks. As we select something from each area we can then go through our notebook and see a *Summary* in words of the five literary elements.

Practice with the Author's Words First

Just as a student of painting practices the techniques of his teacher of art, so the student of writing practices the techniques of the author using the words chosen for painting that the author has used until the student has learned what characterizes the author.

Finally, having learned from the author how words paint pictures, describe feelings, and identify character, the student can write some individual pieces in his or her own words.

Progressive education plunges students into "creative writing" long before they have developed any writing or literary skills. It is our purpose to allow the student to grow in writing talent by first being willing to follow in the path of the artist-writer and practicing what is learned before launching out on his own.

Identifying Literary Elements in Key Classics

How Is Setting Defined?

Setting is "the physical, and sometimes spiritual, background against which the action of a narrative (novel, drama, short story, etc.) takes place. The elements which make up a setting are:

1. The actual geographical location, its topography, scenery, and such physical arrangements as the locations of windows and doors in a room, e.g., Hawthorne's *House of the Seven Gables.*

2. The occupations and daily manner of living of the characters.

3. The time or period in which the action takes place, e.g., epoch in history, season of the year, etc.

4. General environment of the characters, e.g., religious, mental, moral, social, and emotional conditions through which the people in the narrative move." (*A Handbook to Literature,* Thrall and Hibbard)

How Is Characterization Defined?

Characterization: "The depicting, in writing, of clear images of a person, his actions and manners of thought and life." (Thrall, p. 75)

1. Biblical Standards: The Holy Bible should be the standard of character and morality. Characters should clearly identify right and wrong and the consequences of action.

2. Depravity and Vice in Characters: Models of depravity should be avoided if the descriptions are too realistic as they may become avenues to destroy the innocence and purity of youth.

How Is Plot Defined?

Plot: A series of actions moving in a related sequence to a logical and natural outcome. The action of the plot has two directions:

1. *Rising Action*—events build towards a climax.

2. *Falling Action*—events resolve themselves from the climax.

3. *Denouement*—the solution or unravelling of all elements.

Plot which focuses upon *character* as the internal cause of events is most effective.

How Is Theme Defined?

The attitudes or convictions of the author on basic principles, ideas, and character are the *themes.*

Style Is Defined: "A combination of two elements: the idea to be expressed and the individuality of the author. It is the arrangement of words in a manner which at once best expresses the individuality of the author and the idea intent in his or her mind." (*Handbook to Literature*, Thrall and Hibbard)

Setting, Character, and Plot all are used by the author to convey themes or leading ideas and convictions.

Charles Dickens (1812–1870)
His Literary Legacy

In his thirty-five years of productive writing, Charles Dickens composed fifteen novels, several plays, innumerable short stories, and a host of miscellaneous articles in the pages of his two weeklies, *Household Words* and *All the Year Around*. A list of his masterpieces includes the following works with descriptive phrases from the April 1974 *National Geographic* feature article, "The England of Charles Dickens" by Richard W. Long, and Adam Woolfitt, photographer, (p. 452):

The Posthumous Papers of the Pickwick Club (1837). A well-stuffed Christmas stocking of colorful characters, the record of Samuel Pickwick's wanderings made Dickens famous overnight.

The Adventures of Oliver Twist (1838). In an angry protest against England's social system, young Oliver Twist runs off to London, where he falls into—and, happily, out of—the clutches of larcenous Fagin and murderous Bill Sikes.

The Life and Adventures of Nicholas Nickleby (1839). In Dickens's exposé of the often cruel Yorkshire school system, Nicholas becomes a teacher at Dotheboys Hall, the boarding school of boy-beating Mr. Wackford Squeers—and administers a beating of his own.

The Old Curiosity Shop (1841). In a tragic tale of love, Little Nell dies just as Kit Nubbles arrives to save her.

Barnaby Rudge (1841). Against the grim background of Newgate Prison, Barnaby Rudge tries to regain his wits while those about him are losing theirs.

The Life and Adventures of Martin Chuzzlewit (1844). "Ah! what a wale of grief!" cries Mrs. Gamp as she and her imaginary companion, Mrs. Harris, observe tribulations that work the moral regeneration of the senior and junior Martin Chuzzlewit.

Dombey and Son (1848). In a parable of pride and its fall, Paul Dombey heaps his hopes and expectations on the future of his son, only to see him die in childhood.

The Personal History of David Copperfield (1850). "Whether I shall turn out to be the hero of my own life, or whether that station will be held by anybody else, these pages must show," wrote Dickens in the autobiographical story of young David's rise from factory boy to writer.

Christmas Books (1852). A collection of stories, the volume opens with Ebenezer Scrooge's rejuvenation in "A Christmas Carol."

Bleak House (1853). Its pervasive element the dreary, muffling London fog, this novel centers on absurdities of the legal system and the plight of the uneducated and poor.

Hard Times (1854). In a brutally materialistic world, hard-bitten Thomas Gradgrind learns to make his account books "subservient to Faith, Hope, and Charity."

Little Dorrit (1857). A child of the Marshalsea—the same jail in which Dickens's father was once held for debt—Little Dorrit grows up to wed Arthur Clennam in the shadow of the prison walls they both have known.

A Tale of Two Cities (1859). Amid the historical drama of the French Revolution, Dickens weaves a web of righteous murder and sacrifice that allows Sidney Carton his chance to make good—and ruins Mme. Defarge's knitting in the bargain.

Great Expectations (1861). "Be grateful, boy, to them which brought you up by hand," Uncle Pumblechook advises young Philip Pirrip (Pip), whose backside shows a curious inability to be grateful for its treatment. Pip grows from orphan boy to wealthy gentleman—only to lose his happiness.

Our Mutual Friend (1865). In a satire of the nouveau riche and those who would become so, John Harmon throws off his assumed identity to claim his bride and inheritance.

The Mystery of Edwin Drood (1870). Heavily influenced by newly fashionable mystery novels, Edwin Drood and its secret lay unfinished at Dickens's death in 1870.

Biographical References

Charles Dickens, His Tragedy and Triumph, a biography by Edgar Johnson, in two volumes. New York: Simon and Schuster, 1952. A complete study of the life and literature of Charles Dickens.

Introducing Charles Dickens by May Lamberton Becker. New York: Dodd, Mead and Company, 1940. A biography for young students—but with an adult treatment which makes it useful to any age.

A Child's Hymn

This poem appeared in the 1856 Christmas issue of *Household Words*, a periodical which Charles Dickens edited weekly. Its name was taken from this quotation from Shakespeare: "Familiar in their mouths as *household words*."

A Child's Hymn

Hear my prayer, O! Heavenly Father,
　　Ere I lay me down to sleep;
Bid Thy Angels, pure and holy,
　　Round my bed their vigil keep.

My sins are heavy, but Thy mercy
　　Far outweighs them every one;
Down before Thy Cross I cast them,
　　Trusting in Thy help alone.

Keep me through this night of peril
　　Underneath its boundless shade;
Take me to Thy rest, I pray Thee,
　　When my pilgrimage is made.

None shall measure out Thy patience
　　By the span of human thought;
None shall bound the tender mercies
　　Which Thy Holy Son has bought.

Pardon all my past transgressions,
　　Give me strength for days to come;
Guide and guard me with Thy blessing
　　Till Thy Angels bid me home.

(*Charles Dickens, Complete Works:
　　Miscellaneous Papers II*, pp. 487–88)

The weekly edited by Dickens became an instrument for education, and especially a means by which his Christian concern for the social evils of his times might be dramatically exposed. In his novels he revealed the problems of a class-structured society where the practice of Christian principles seemed slow in filtering down to the least common denominator—the individual. We are indebted to him for his vast canvass of human character—enhanced by his skill in making them bigger than life so that we might see into the human heart.

When Dickens was praised by a clergyman for the publication of this poem, he made the following statement about it, after indicating that he himself was the author: "There cannot be many men, I believe, who have a more humble veneration for the New Testament, or a more profound conviction of its all-sufficiency, than I have. If ever I am (as you tell me I am) mistaken on this subject, it is because I discountenance all obtrusive professions of and tradings in religion, as one of the main causes why real Christianity has been retarded in this world; and because my observation of life induces me to hold in unspeakable dread and horror those unseemly squabbles about the letter which drive the spirit out of hundreds of thousands." (*The Life of Charles Dickens*, John Forster, vol. 3, 1874, p. 447)

"With *Pickwick Papers*, at the age of twenty-four, he stepped into instant fame, and from then on he marched from triumph to triumph. His readers in England probably numbered more than one out of every ten inhabitants. He was read all over the continent of Europe, from Italy to Russia, and cheerfully pirated by the hundreds of thousands in the United States. From the leading intellectual reviews to the popular press there was no significant disputation of his literary eminence. It would be difficult to name any novelist of our own time who has so commanded the respect of serious criticism and at the same time reached anything like so widespread an audience. In the end, this writer who was the son of a perennially improvident father became the most celebrated literary figure of his time and left an estate equivalent to more than a million dollars today." (*Charles Dickens, His Tragedy and Triumph*, vol. 1, Edgar Johnson, 1952, pp. 3–4)

In 1870, when Charles Dickens died, he had left a literary legacy to England and to the world which can never be forgotten as long as England, and especially the city of London, remains. The characters which his pen brought forth have become immortalized in the memories of millions and many of the evils of Dickens's day still speak to our hearts crying out for the ultimate Christian solution.

"A Child's Journey with Dickens"

by Kate Douglas Wiggin

"When I was a little girl (I always think that these words, in precisely this juxtaposition, are six of the most charming in the language)—when I was a little girl, I lived, between the ages of six and sixteen, in a small village in Maine. My sister and I had few playmates, but I cannot remember that we were ever dull, for dullness in a child, as in a grown person, means lack of dreams and visions, and those we had a-plenty. We were fortunate, too, in that our house was on the brink of one of the loveliest rivers in the world. When we clambered down the steep bank to the little cove that was just beneath our bedroom windows, we found ourselves facing a sheet of crystal water as quiet as a lake, a lake from the shores of which we could set any sort of adventure afloat; yet scarcely three hundred feet away was a roaring waterfall—a baby Niagara—which, after dashing over the dam in a magnificent tawny torrent, spent itself in a wild stream that made a path between rocky cliffs until it reached the sea, eight miles away. No child could be lonely who lived on the brink of such a river; and then we had, beside our studies and our country sports, our books, which were the dearest of all our friends. It is a long time ago, but I can see very clearly a certain set of black walnut book-shelves, hanging on the wall of the family sitting room. There were other cases here and there through the house, but I read and re-read the particular volumes in this one from year to year, and a strange, motley collection they were, to be sure! On the top shelf were George Sand's 'Teverino,' 'Typee,' 'Undine,' Longfellow's and Byron's 'Poems,' 'The Arabian Nights,' Bailey's 'Festus,' 'The Lamplighter,' 'Scottish Chiefs,' Thackeray's 'Book of Snobs,' 'Ivanhoe,' and the 'Life of P. T. Barnum.' This last volume, I may say, did not represent the literary inclinations of my parents, but had been given me on my birthday by a grateful neighbor for saving the life of a valuable Jersey calf tethered on the too steep slopes of our river bank. The *Life of Barnum* was the last book on the heterogenous top shelf, and on the one next below were most of the novels of Charles Dickens, more eagerly devoured than all the rest, although no book in the case had escaped a second reading save Bailey's *Festus*, a little of which went a very long way with us.

"It seems to me that no child nowadays has time to love an author as the children and young people of that generation loved Dickens; nor do I think that any living author of to-day provokes love in exactly the same fashion. From our yellow dog, Pip, to the cat, the canary, the lamb, the cow, down to all the hens and cocks, almost every living thing was named, sooner or later, after one of Dickens's characters; while my favorite sled, painted in brown, with the title in brilliant red letters, was 'The Artful Dodger.' Why did we do it? We little creatures couldn't have suspected that 'the democratic movement in literature had come to town,' as Richard Whiteing says, nevertheless we responded to it vigorously, ardently, and swelled the hero's public.

"For periodical literature we had in our household 'Harper's Magazine' and 'Littell's Living Age,' but we never read newspapers, so that there was a moment of thrilling excitement when my mother, looking up from the 'Portland Press,' told us that Mr. Dickens was coming to America, and that he was even then sailing from England. I remember distinctly that I prayed for him fervently several times during the next week, that the voyage might be a safe one, and that even the pangs of seasickness might be spared so precious a personage. In due time we heard that he had arrived in New York, and had begun the series of readings from his books; then he came to Boston, which was still nearer, and then—day of unspeakable excitement!—we learned that he had been prevailed upon to give one reading in Portland, which was only sixteen miles away from our village.

"It chanced that my mother was taking me to Charlestown, Massachusetts, to pay a visit to an uncle on the very day after the one appointed for the great event in Portland. She, therefore, planned to take me into town the night before, and to invite the cousin, at whose house we were to sleep, to attend the reading with her. I cannot throw a more brilliant light on the discipline of that period than to say that the subject of my attending the reading was never once mentioned. The price of tickets was supposed to be almost prohibitory. I cannot remember the exact sum; I only know that it was mentioned with bated breath in the village of Hollis, and that there was a general feeling in the community that any one who paid it would have to live down a reputation for riotous extravagance forever afterward. I neither wailed nor wept, nor made any attempt to set aside the parental decrees (which were anything but severe in our family), but if any martyr in Fox's 'Book' ever suffered more poignant anguish than I, I am heartily sorry for him; yet my common sense assured me that a child could hardly hope to be taken on a week's junketing to Charlestown, and expect any other entertainment to be added to it for years to come. The definition of a 'pleasure' in the State of Maine, county of York, village of Hollis, year of our Lord 1868, was something that could not reasonably occur too often without being cheapened.

"The days, charged with suppressed excitement, flew by. I bade good-bye to my little sister, who was not to share my metropolitan experiences, and my mother and I embarked for Portland on the daily train that dashed hither and thither at the rate of about twelve miles an hour. When the august night and moment arrived, my mother and her cousin set out for the Place, and the moment they were out of sight I slipped out of the door and followed them, traversing quickly the three or four blocks that separated me from the old City Hall and the Preble House, where Dickens was stopping. I gazed at all the windows and all the entrances of both buildings without beholding any trace of my hero. I watched the throng of happy, excited, lucky people crowding their way into the hall, and went home in a chastened mood to bed—a bed, which as soon as I got into it, was crowded with Little Nell and the Marchioness, Florence Dombey, Bella Wilfer, Susan Nipper, and little Em'ly. There were other dreams, too. Not only had my idol provided me with human friends, to love and laugh and weep over, but he had wrought his genius into things; so that, waking or sleeping, every bunch of holly or mistletoe, every plum pudding was alive; every crutch breathed of Tiny Tim; every cricket and every singing, steaming kettle had a soul.

"The next morning we started on our railroad journey, which I remember as being full of excitement from the beginning, for both men and women were discussing the newspapers with extraordinary interest, the day before having been the one on which the President of the United States had been formally impeached. When the train stopped for two or three minutes at North Berwick, the people on the side of the car next the station suddenly arose and looked eagerly out at some object of apparent interest. I was not, at any age, a person to sit still in her seat when others were looking out of windows, and my small nose was quickly flattened against one of the panes. There on the platform stood the Adored One! His hands were plunged deep in his pockets (a favorite gesture), but presently one was removed to wave away laughingly a piece of the famous Berwick sponge cake, offered him by Mr. Osgood, of Boston, his traveling companion and friend.

"I knew him at once!—the smiling, genial, mobile face, rather highly colored, the brilliant eyes, the watch chain, the red carnation in the button-hole, and the expressive hands, much given to gesture. It was only a momentary view, for the train started, and Dickens vanished, to resume his place in the car next to ours, where he had been, had I known it, ever since we left Portland.

"When my mother was again occupied with her book, I slipped away and entered the next car. I took a humble, unoccupied seat near the end, close by the much patronized tank of (unsterilized) drinking-water, and the train-boy's basket of popcorn balls and molasses candy, and gazed steadily at the famous man, who was chatting busily with Mr. Osgood. I remembered gratefully that my mother had taken the old ribbons off my gray velvet hat and tied me down with blue under the chin, and I thought, if Dickens should happen to rest his eye upon me, that he could hardly fail to be pleased with the effect of the blue ribbon that went under my collar and held a very small squirrel muff in place. Unfortunately, however, his eye never did meet mine, but some family friends espied me, and sent me to ask my mother to come in and sit with them. I brought her back, and fortunately there was not room enough for me with the party, so I gladly resumed my modest seat by the popcorn boy, where I could watch Dickens, quite unnoticed. There is an Indian myth which relates that when the gaze of the Siva rested for the first time on Tellatonea, the most beautiful of women, his desire to see her was so great that his body became all eyes. Such a transformation, I fear, was perilously near to being my fate! Half an hour passed, perhaps, and one gentleman after another came from here or there to exchange a word of greeting with the famous novelist, so that he was never for a moment alone, thereby inciting in my breast my first, and about my last, experience of the passion of jealousy. Suddenly, however, Mr. Osgood arose, and with an apology went into the smoking-car. I never knew how it happened; I had no plan, no preparation, no intention, no provocation; but invisible ropes pulled me out of my seat, and, speeding up the aisle, I planted myself timorously down, an unbidden guest, in the seat of honor. I had a moment to recover my equanimity, for Dickens was looking out of the window, but he turned in a moment, and said with justifiable surprise:

"'God bless my soul, where did you come from?'

"'I came from Hollis, Maine,' I stammered, 'and I'm going to Charlestown to visit my uncle. My mother and her cousin went to your reading last night, but, of course, three couldn't go from the same family, so I stayed home. Nora, that's my little sister, stayed at home, too. She's too small to go on a journey, but she wanted to go to the reading dreadfully. There was a lady there who had never heard of Betsy Trotwood, and had only read two of your books!'

"'Well, upon my word!' he said; 'you do not mean to say that you have read them!'

"'Of course I have,' I replied; 'every one of them but the two that we are going to buy in Boston, and some of them six times.'

"'Bless my soul!' he ejaculated again. 'Those long thick books, and you such a slip of a thing.'

"'Of course,' I explained conscientiously, 'I do skip some of the very dull parts once in a while; not the short dull parts, but the long ones.'

"He laughed heartily. 'Now, that is something that I hear very little about,' he said. 'I distinctly want to learn more about those very dull parts.' And whether to amuse himself, or to amuse me, I do not know, he took out a notebook and pencil from his pocket and proceeded to give me an exhausting and exhaustive examination on this subject; the books in which the dull parts predominated; and the characters and subjects which principally produced them. He chuckled so constantly during this operation that I could hardly help believing myself extraordinarily agreeable, so I continued dealing these infant blows, under the delusion that I was flinging him bouquets.

"It was not long before one of my hands was in his, and his arm around my waist, while we talked of many things. They say, I believe, that his hands were 'undistinguished' in shape, and that he wore too many rings. Well, those criticisms must come from persons who never felt the warmth of his handclasp! For my part, I am glad that Pullman chair cars had not come into fashion, else I should never have experienced the delicious joy of snuggling up to Genius, and of being distinctly encouraged in the attitude.

"I wish I could recall still more of his conversation, but I was too happy, too exhilarated, and too inexperienced to take conscious notes of the interview. I remember feeling that I had never known anybody so well and so intimately, and that I talked with him as one talks under cover of darkness or before the flickering light of a fire. It seems to me, as I look back now, and remember how the little soul of me came out and sat in the sunshine of his presence, that I must have had some premonition that the child, who would come to be one of the least of writers, was then talking with one of the greatest; – talking, too, of the author's profession and high calling. All the little details of the meeting stand out as clearly as though it had happened yesterday. I can see every article of his clothing and of my own; the other passengers in the car; the landscape through the window, and above all the face of Dickens, deeply lined, with sparkling eyes and an amused, waggish smile that curled the corners of his mouth under his grizzled mustache. A part of our conversation was given to a Boston newspaper next day, by the author himself, or by Mr. Osgood, and a little

more was added a few years after by an old lady who sat in the next seat to us. (The pronoun 'us' seems ridiculously intimate, but I have no doubt I used it, quite unabashed, at that date.)

"'What book of mine do you like best?' Dickens asked, I remember; and I answered, 'Oh I like "David Copperfield" much the best. That is the one I have read six times.'

"'Six times—good, good!' he replied; 'I am glad that you like Davy, so do I;—I like it best, too!' clapping his hands; and that was the only remark he made which attracted the attention of the other passengers, who looked in our direction now and then, I have been told, smiling at the interview, but preserving its privacy with the utmost friendliness.

"'Of course,' I added, ' I almost said "Great Expectations," because that comes next. We named our little yellow dog Mr. Pip. They told father he was part rat terrier, and we were all so pleased. Then one day father showed him a trap with a mouse in it. The mouse wiggled its tail just a little, and Pip was so frightened that he ran under the barn and stayed the rest of the day. Then all the neighbors made fun of him, and you can think how Nora and I love him when he's had such a hard time, just like Pip in "Great Expectations"!'

"Here again my new friend's mirth was delightful to behold, so much so that my embarrassed mother, who had been watching me for half an hour, almost made up her mind to drag me away before the very eyes of our fellow passengers. I had never been thought an amusing child in the family circle; what then, could I be saying to the most distinguished and popular author in the universe?

"'We have another dog,' I went on, 'and his name is Mr. Pocket. We were playing with Pip, who is a smooth dog, one day, when a shaggy dog came along that didn't belong to anybody, and hadn't any home. He liked Pip and Pip liked him, so we kept him, and named him Pocket after Pip's friend. The real Mr.

Pip and Mr. Pocket met first in Miss Havisham's garden, and they had such a funny fight it always makes father laugh till he can't read! Then they became great friends. Perhaps you remember Mr. Pip and Mr. Pocket?' And Dickens thought he did, which, perhaps, is not strange, considering that he was the author of their respective beings. Mr. Harry Furniss declares that 'Great Expectations' was Dickens's favorite novel, but I can only say that to me he avowed his special fondness for 'David Copperfield.'

"'Did you want to go to my reading very much?' was another question. Here was a subject that had never once been touched upon in all the past days—a topic that stirred the very depths of my disappointment and sorrow, fairly choking me, and making my lip tremble by its unexpectedness, as I faltered, 'Yes; more than tongue can tell.'

"I looked up a second later, when I was sure that the tears in my eyes were not going to fall, and to my astonishment saw that Dickens's were in precisely the same state of moisture. That was a never-to-be-forgotten moment, although I was too young to appreciate the full significance of it.

"'Do you cry when you read out loud?' I asked curiously. 'We all do in our family. And we never read about Tiny Tim, or about Steerforth when his body is washed up on the beach, on Saturday nights, or our eyes are too swollen to go to Sunday School.'

"'Yes, I cry when I read about Steerforth,' he answered quietly, and I felt no astonishment.

"'We cry the worst when it says, "All the men who carried him had known him and gone sailing with him, and seen him merry and bold",' I said, growing very tearful in reminiscence.

"We were now fast approaching our destination—the station in Boston—and the passengers began to collect their wraps and bundles. Mr. Osgood had two or three times made his appearance, but had been waved away with a smile by Dickens—a smile that seemed to say—'You will excuse me, I know, but this child has the right of way.'

"'You are not traveling alone?' he asked, as he arose to put on his overcoat.

"'Oh, no,' I answered, coming down to earth for the first time since I had taken my seat beside him—'oh, no, I had a mother, but I forgot all about her.' Whereupon he said, 'You are a passed-mistress of the art of flattery!' But this remark was told me years afterwards by the old lady who was sitting in the next seat, and who overheard as much of the conversation as she possibly could, so she informed me.

"Dickens took me back to the forgotten mother, and introduced himself, and I, still clinging to his hand, left the car and walked with him down the platform until he disappeared in the carriage with Mr. Osgood, leaving me with the feeling that I must continue my existence somehow in a dull and dreary world.

"That was my last glimpse of him, but pictures made in childhood are painted in bright hues, and this one has never faded. The child of to-day would hardly be able to establish so instantaneous a friendship. She would have heard of celebrity hunters and autograph collectors and be self-conscious, while I followed the dictates of my countrified little heart, and scraped acquaintance confidently with the magician who had glorified my childhood by his art.

"He had his literary weaknesses, Charles Dickens, but they were all dear, big, attractive ones, virtues grown a bit wild and rank. Somehow when you put him—with his elemental humor, his inexhaustible vitality, his humanity, sympathy, and pity—beside the Impeccables, he always looms large! Just for a moment, when the heart overpowers the reason, he even makes the flawless ones look a little faded and colorless!" ("A Child's Journey with Dickens," from *The Writings of Kate Douglas Wiggin*, Vol. I, 1917, pp. 293–307).

CHAPTER FOUR

TEACHING SHAKESPEARE

Contributors to this chapter were Erich D. Schwartz, teacher at Dayspring
Christian Academy in Lancaster, Pennsylvania; Diana González, teacher at
StoneBridge School in Chesapeake, Virginia; and Elizabeth L. Youmans, editor
of *The Noah Plan*.

Introduction to Teaching Shakespeare

1564   1616

W. William Shakespeare

Next to the Bible, Shakespeare offers our children the richest and most lasting experience with language and literature. Shakespeare's comedies, tragedies, histories, and sonnets create a threshold from which our children pass into a new realm of language mastery. The great joy of Shakespeare is that his works were meant to be heard and·seen, not just read. Even the youngest children delight in acting out famous scenes from the plays and can develop a love of the Bard that de-mystifies his work and cultivates a taste for the great classic tradition in literature and in theater.

The best reasons for studying Shakespeare appear in the following article, written by C. T. Cook, and reprinted with permission from *The Christian Reader,* Aug.–Sept., 1964:

William Shakespeare—
Bard of the Bible

"The fourth centenary of the birth of William Shakespeare has been celebrated throughout the English-speaking world, and in many other countries, on a scale accorded to no other literary figure in history. The reason for this is plain. Outside the Bible, no collection of literary masterpieces offers so many valid answers to human problems, nor has any poet approached Shakespeare's genius as an interpreter of human emotions.

"Along with the Authorized Version of the Bible, Shakespeare's poetic and dramatic works are a fount of noble Elizabethan English, with an even more extensive vocabulary. It is not surprising, therefore, that the creations of his unrivaled genius form an essential item in the curriculum of schools and colleges. In view of this it is understandable that Christian parents, anxious that their young people's education should be directed 'to all that is true, all that is noble, all that is just and pure, all that is lovable and gracious, whatever is excellent and admirable' (Phil. 4:8, NEB), should inquire concerning Shakespeare's attitude to the Bible and the great truths of the Christian faith.

"The answer to this is both definite and reassuring. Shakespeare does not set out to be a preacher, in the usual meaning of that word, nor are his plays religious plays. On the other hand unlike some modern stage and film productions, and not a few novels, he nowhere calls in question the doctrines of the Gospel nor does he sneer at religious morals and customs; and God, with His attributes, is mentioned about 700 times.

"But his attitude to the things we believe is not simply negative. The late Archbishop R. C. Trench spoke of Shakespeare's 'intimate, nay, in one sense, profound acquaintance with the Scriptures,' revealed in a 'strong grasp which he had of their central truths. He knew the deep corruption of our fallen nature, the desperate wickedness of the heart of man.' Further, Trench says: 'He set forth the scheme of our redemption in words as lovely as have ever proceeded from any inspired pen.'

"Touching Shakespeare's knowledge of the Bible, a few years ago, in a broadcast on 'The Bible and English Poetry,' the speaker said of him: 'The Bible is never his subject, yet there are hundreds of passages, prose and verse, which have some relation to the Bible, fused and transmuted by the furnace-heat of his genius. All that Bible poets can do or have done, with Bible texts and themes, he also does.'

"The lecturer went on: 'He alludes to every part, to at least 42 Books, 18 of the Old Testament, 18 of the New, and six of the Apocrypha.' He names no fewer than 23 Bible characters, 'and he knows he can rely on a public ready with an intimate knowledge of the Bible, whether in the Geneva or Bishops' versions, or the Prayer Book Psalter, all of which he uses. . . . He employs every possible mechanism—direct reference, hidden allusions, musical echo, verbal echo, reminiscence, coalescence of parallels, mixed metaphor, and even parody.'

"Some people have suggested that Shakespeare was a Roman Catholic, but that claim has been effectively disposed of by the 'Roman' Catholic Encyclopedia, which points out that Shakespeare was baptized, as later were his daughters, in the Parish Church at Stratford-on-Avon, where the poet and his wife are buried. The article refers to the poet's familiarity with 'the Protestant versions of the Bible,' to his living for six years in the house of a French Huguenot refugee in London (the fight with the Spanish Armada occurred during this period), and states that his daughters 'were undoubtedly brought up as Protestants,' and that one, Mrs. Hall, 'had Puritan sympathies.'

"The preface to his will indicates that Shakespeare's attachment to the Reformed faith was more than nominal: 'I commend my soul,' he writes, 'into the hands of God, my Creator, hoping and assuredly believing through the only merits of Jesus Christ my Savior, to be made partaker of life everlasting; and my body to the earth whereof it is made.'

"One cannot read his works without gaining an impression that he was a great moral teacher. It is in his tragedies that we perceive his deeps thoughts. In them man's soul is the raging battleground between heaven and hell. Answers to such questions as whether there is an overruling Providence, whether righteousness will triumph, whether it is worthwhile to strive for the best, it is important to note, are not always settled by what the characters say. Shakespeare does not make them speak; rather, he listens to them speaking. They speak and act as he imagines they will. They are men, not marionettes. They do not necessarily say or do what the author believes.

"It is just here that we observe a vital difference between Greek tragedy and Shakespeare. In Greek tragedies, men are helpless victims of fate, of the caprice of deities destitute of dignity or morality, incapable of love or care, who commission men to unnatural crimes. Men move to doom without volition of their own. Shakespeare's men and women, on the other hand, are moral and responsible beings.

"Nowhere in literature is the face of conscience more superbly pictured than in his writings. No external necessity drives Macbeth, Iago, and Goneril to do evil. No man saw more clearly than Shakespeare that as a man sows, so shall he reap. Macbeth makes his bed in hell. Shakespeare, moreover, was a realist also in not ensuring a happy ending for every story. The romance of Romeo and Juliet does not end in wedding bells, but in their deaths, unless we add that the tragedy ends the feud between their respective families. A pure and beautiful soul like Desdemona dies because Iago is a villain.

"Shakespeare makes the reader feel that vice never looks so odious, nor crime so execrable as when placed under the burning light of his indignation. A fierce disgust of sexuality, for instance, runs through the plays of Hamlet, Macbeth, Othello, Lear, and Timon. On the other side, the simplest virtue, the humblest effort to do good, is never more compelling when depicted in his matchless words.

"This brings us to another aspect of Shakespeare's characterization which must not be overlooked. He introduces us to a gallery of noble women. John Ruskin has pointed out that there is hardly a play that has not a perfect woman in it—'steadfast in grave hope and errorless purpose.' The poet does not hesitate to probe the deeps of the human heart, yet there emerges a faith in womanhood to which literature affords no parallel.

"Would that some of our modern novelists had a tithe of the chivalric ideal of a good woman which Shakespeare upheld through his entire book! Cordelia, Hermione, Imogen, Perdita, Sylvia, Viola, Rosalind, Desdemona, Helene, Virgilia—what maidenly sweetness, gracious simplicity, purity,

THE BIRTHPLACE

Nowhere in literature is the face of conscience more superbly pictured than in his writings.

One cannot read his works without gaining an impression that he was a great moral teacher.

wifely perfection they reveal. How brave, clear-eyed, resourceful, sacrificial! Of course, not all his women are good. There is Cleopatra, who subordinated everything to the sensuous; there is Lady Macbeth, just as there is a Jezebel in the Old Testament, yet it is certain Shakespeare felt deeply the baleful influence of a bad woman. But whence did he get his exalted thought of women? Surely, it was from the faithful women who ministered to our Lord.

"One could give many illustrations from his writings of his belief in the sovereignty of God in providence and grace, in judgment and mercy. No writer outside the Bible surpasses him in his profound and penetrating story of temptation.

"It has been truly said that no one leaves a tragedy of Shakespeare a prey to atheism or despair. He leaves it awed and pitiful and reverent. That is true, yet it draws attention to a defect in his picture of human need. One misses a clear and definite recognition of conversion. Conscience may torment the wicked, but it does not lead to repentance. He drives home the lesson: 'What shall it profit a man if he gain the whole world and lose his own soul?' What he failed to sound is the note of assurance that the Redeemer who died, can save to the uttermost all who call upon Him."

Most scholars acknowledge that the Bible of Shakespeare was the scholarly 1560 Geneva translation with its marginal notes from reformers Calvin, Knox, and Whittingham, the Bible of our Pilgrim forefathers.

Shakespeare and the Bible

The writings of William Shakespeare reflect the philosophy and quality of education during Elizabethan England, the period of the Protestant Reformation. Lord Macaulay in his "Essay on Bacon" referred to the eloquence of Elizabethan statesmen as "the eloquence of men who had lived with the first translators of the Bible and with the authors of the Book of Common Prayer." The Bible had come into the hands of the individual Englishman in his own tongue, and Shakespeare wrote plays and sonnets for a people whose knowledge was deeply familiar with God's Word. Shakespeare's mind, like that of Governor William Bradford of Plymouth Planta-

tion, was saturated with the Scriptures, and the very language of the Book came readily to his pen. Observing with what ease and ingenuity he makes use of the Bible, it is obvious that he was intimate with the Scriptures and fully appreciated the value of its literary material. Most scholars acknowledge that the Bible of Shakespeare was the scholarly 1560 Geneva translation with its marginal notes from reformers Calvin, Knox, and Whittingham, the Bible of our Pilgrim forefathers.

The Bible's events, scenes, characters, and expressions had lodged themselves in Shakespeare's memory, and he alluded to nearly every part of the Bible. He cited dozens of Bible characters and many historic events, and when he referred to the Bible it was done naturally and without effort. He was at home with the Scriptures and wrote with recurrent Biblical illustrations, imagery, and lyrical rhythms, such as when Hamlet says:

> There's a divinity that shapes our ends, Rough-hew them how we will;
>
> There is a special providence in the fall of a sparrow.

or when Portia says in *The Merchant of Venice:*

> The quality of mercy is not strain'd.
> It droppeth as the gentle rain from heaven
> Upon the place beneath: it is twice bless'd;
> It blesseth him that gives, and him that takes.
> T'is mightiest in the mightiest, it becomes
> The throned monarch better than his crown;
> His sceptre shows the force of temporal power,
> The attribute to awe and majesty,
> Wherein doth sit the dread and fear of kings;
> But mercy is above this sceptred sway,
> It is enthroned in the hearts of kings,
> It is an attribute to God himself,
> And earthly power doth then show likest God's,
> When mercy seasons justice.
>
> — Act IV, Scene I

"When we come to consider Shakespeare's relation to the Bible, the evidence is very pronounced. Not merely is it the spirit of the Scripture that haunts his mind, but it is the very wording of Scripture as well. If only we could know the story of his early life, and his home environment! Imagination is tempted to reconstruct it. One sees a home where the small household Bible, the Genevan version, had found a welcome. The discipline of such a home perhaps required attention to the Book, but we should suppose that such discipline would not be necessary. It was practically a new book, and the curiosity of active minds, unaccustomed to such rich and varied material, would be motive enough to inspire interest. The alert mind of a growing boy in such a home, already, as we suppose, alive with interest in the dramatic presentations of Scripture at Coventry, would require no whip to create interest in such a book as the Bible.

"It is interesting to contemplate the opportunities afforded him to acquaint himself with the Scripture. The home and the school may be thought of as cooperating in this. We may think of him as growing up in the companionship of the Bible, becoming familiar with its persons, scenes and incidents, learning its language and style, imbibing its spirit of dramatic life and action and, most of all, drinking in its air of largeness, of inspiration, of creativeness, and of imaginative power. . . . His contact with the Bible must rather have been marked by eager and spirited imagination, and by those awakened and constructive powers which lie at the command of genius." (Excerpted from *The Bible in English Literature*, "Shakespeare and the Bible," Edgar Whitaker Work, 1917.)

Resources That Document Shakespeare's Use of the Bible

There are two books of great interest to us today that document Shakespeare's knowledge and use of the Bible and its themes, values, and characters: *The Christ in Shakespeare*, by Charles Ellis, 1902; and *Shakespeare's Knowledge and Use of the Bible*, by Charles Wordsworth, 1864.

1. *The Christ in Shakespeare*

Following are excerpts from Charles Ellis's book, in which he lays the Geneva Translation of the Bible side by side with Shakespeare's writings to show, not only the influence of the Scriptures in the writing of Shakespeare, but that the Bible of Shakespeare was the Genevan Translation, the same Bible of the Pilgrims:

"The name of Shakespeare is the greatest in our Literature." (Hallam) He was the glory of his Age, and is the glory of the present Age. "The noblest literary man of all time," writes Henry Irving, the finest and yet most prolific writer—the greatest master of man's highest gifts,—of language—surely it is treason to humanity to speak of such a one as in any sense a common place being.

Imagine him rather as he must have been, the most notable courtier of the court, the most perfect gentleman who stood in the Elizabethan throng. The man in whose presence divines would falter and hesitate, lest their knowledge of "THE BOOK" should seem poor by the side of his, and at whom even queenly royalty would look askance with an oppressive sense that there was one to whose . . . true imagination the hearts of kings and queens and peoples had always been an open page!

"His genius," says a recent writer, "was colossal, raising him far above all other men that ever lived, yet he is nearer to us . . . than any other. . . . Truly he was titled 'the gentle,' for while he instructs, he does not lecture; though he reproves, he never jibes. We believe, that the home education of William Shakespeare was grounded upon the Bible, and that if this Book had not been sealed to his childhood, he might have been the Poet of nature—of passion—his humour might have been as rich as we find it, and his wit as pointed, but he would not have been the Poet of the most profound as well as the most tolerant philosophy; his insight into the nature of man (his

Over whole acres walked those blessed feet, Which fourteen hundred years ago were nail'd For our advantage on the bitter cross.
—Shakespeare's *Henry IV*

The home education of William Shakespeare was grounded upon the Bible.

The spiritual mind of Shakespeare is brought to light by the light of the Bible.

The two loves Shakespeare had—of comfort and despair—were Christ, His comfort, and himself, despair; but his choicest figures . . . are one unbroken allegory of truth.

He avoids quoting the text of Scripture, lest he should incur the reproof of or offend the clergy, and thus defeat his happy purpose of pointing to the Word of life.

meanness and his grandeur, his weakness and his strength) would not have been what it is." (*Shakespeare's True Life,* Major James Walter, 1890)

It is no fancy, but an admitted truth, that the spiritual mind of Shakespeare is brought to light by the light of the Bible (Psalm 119:105), and his deep musings therein found their delightful embodiment in a poetic correspondence with one or more earthly friends. (footnote: "We scarcely open (the pages) of Shakespeare," says Mr. Selkirk of Selkirk, "as if by accident, without encountering one or other of the great truths (of the Bible) which his genius has assimilated and reproduced in words that seem to renew its authority and strengthen its claims upon men's attention."

Although the Poet's primary aim was not to display his spirituality to a general reader, if he ever pondered such a thing, he had never the wish to hide from his friend or from anyone the exalted views which he had derived from the study of the Scriptures. On the contrary, it is evident that he wrote at all times as prompted by the warmth of his heart, with the manly dignity so conspicuous in all his writings. (Preface, pp. 23–30)

In the chapter entitled "A Selection of Shakespeare's Sonnets Illustrated by the Sacred Word," the author begins:

That the mind of our Poet was permeated with the Word of God, has, for many years, been clearly apparent to the author. . . . The text is that of the Bible of Shakespeare's own day—the Genevan Edition—which, Dr. Smyth tells, "followed the Great Bible (virtually Tyndale's) of 1539, and was the favourite of the people." (p. 165)

In the Memorandum, the author writes:

The two loves Shakespeare had—of comfort and despair—were Christ, His comfort, and himself, despair; but his choicest figures in his purest embodiments, as well as in his saddest and most repulsive, are one unbroken allegory of truth.

Shakespeare's references to the Scriptures occur in his Dramas, with very few exceptions . . .; but with peculiar care and delicacy, he avoids quoting the text of Scripture, lest he should incur the reproof of or offend the clergy, and thus defeat his happy purpose of pointing to the Word of life. He therefore ingeniously endeavours to awaken the curiosity of the ignorant, and enliven the devout intelligence of Scripture readers, and all church members, by his method of application.

In his Poems he pursues an entirely different course; abstaining from an open reference to Bible figures incident to its teaching, he breathes out spiritual truth in figurative language full of devout aspirations, presenting, out of his own secret experience, the corruption of the natural heart, and the discovered remedy in the new man, Christ Jesus; faith in whom is the wellspring of a new life to every willing soul. (p. 167)

2. *Shakespeare's Knowledge and Use of the Bible*

Charles Wordsworth, Bishop of St. Andrews, wrote this book in 1864. It documents Shakespeare's use of the Bible throughout his writings and provides insights for the contemporary literature teacher. Charles Wordsworth, nephew of the poet William Wordsworth, wrote the 300-page book to ascertain just "how far Shakespeare was conversant with Holy Scripture, and whether or not he made use of his knowledge of the Bible to guide and assist him in the production of his immortal works." (p.1) Following are excerpts from his introduction and his conclusion.

From the Introduction:

Shakespeare has not yet received the credit, which I think I shall be able to prove that he deserves, of having been in a more than ordinary degree, a diligent and a devout reader of the Word of God; . . . His marvelous knowledge of the Book of Nature is admitted on all hands: his knowledge of the Book of Grace, though far less noticed, will be found, I believe, to have been scarcely less remarkable. His works have been called "a secular Bible": my object is to show that while they are this, they are also *something more*, being saturated with Divine Wisdom, such as could have been derived only from the very Bible itself.

And I enter upon my task with keener interest and heartier zeal upon two accounts; first, because I trust I shall be paying a duteous service to the memory of this great man, whom every Briton should delight to honour, by removing an imputation which has been (I am persuaded) hastily and inconsiderately cast upon him, as though he had, in some instances, designed to treat the Inspired Word with profaneness; and secondly, because, if it shall appear (as I doubt not it will) that a genius so incomparable was content to study, and not unfrequently to draw his inspiration from the pages of Holy Scripture, submitting his reason to the mysterious doctrines which it reveals, and his conscience to the moral lessons which it prescribes; it may be hoped that no one of my readers will consider it beneath him to follow an example, set by an authority so highly, so justly, and so universally esteemed.

"He was indeed *honest*," says his friend Ben Jonson, "and of an open and free nature." Upon such unquestionable testimony, it is pleasant to be permitted to think of our greatest poet, as one "who is an *honest* and good heart, having heard the Word, kept it, and brought forth fruit with patience." That he brought forth fruit—immortal fruit—to the glory of God and the benefit of mankind, no one can deny.

Whatever blemishes there may have been in the character of the first Scottish sovereign who sat upon the throne of England, it is only just to bear in mind that we owe to him, under the good Providence of God, that inestimable work, the translation of the Bible which we all use; and moreover that to him we owe also the satisfaction which we must all feel when we learn that the best of uninspired writers was not without royal encouragement. Detract what we may from the merit of King James, on the score of pedantry, or of disingenuousness, the facts will remain, which, considering the subject I have now in hand, I rejoice to mention in his praise, and to interweave, as among the brightest ornaments of his crown—that he wrote to William Shakespeare a letter of commendation with his own hand, and that he gave "special command" for the publication of the Scriptures in the revised and improved form, which Shakespeare and his contemporaries were the first to read.

. . . It is probable that our translators of 1611 owed as much, or more, to Shakespeare than he owed to them. According to the chronological order of our poet's plays, as determined by Mr. Mallone, only two of them were written after 1611; all the rest having been composed in the interval between that year and 1591. And the Bibles most commonly used during that period were either Parker's, called also the Bishops' Bible, of 1568, required to be read in churches; or various reprints of the Genevan Bible of 1560, with short marginal notes, and much used in private families (a translation which was due in part to John Knox, while resident abroad); or the version by the Roman Catholics of the New Testament, published at Rheims in 1582, and of the whole Bible at Douay in 1609. (pp. 2–6)

From the Conclusion:

I have now gone through the interesting and instructive task which I proposed to myself; and the conclusion at which I have arrived is this: — Take the entire range of English literature; put together our best authors, who have written upon subjects not professedly religious or theological, and we shall not find, I believe, in them *all united,* so much evidence of the Bible having been read and used, as we have found in Shakespeare *alone.* . . .

His works have been called "a secular Bible."

That he brought forth fruit—immortal fruit—to the glory of God and the benefit of mankind, no one can deny.

It is probable that our translators of 1611 owed as much, or more, to Shakespeare than he owed to them.

He is certainly one of the greatest moral philosophers that ever lived.

According to the testimony of Charles Lamb, a most competent judge in regard to all the literary elements of the question, our poet, "in his divine mind and manners, surpassed not only the great men his contemporaries, but all mankind." (*Specimens of Dramatic Poets,* Preface, vol. I, p. 7) And looking at this superiority from my own point of view, I cannot but remark that, while most of the great laymen of that great Elizabethan age—Lord Bacon, Sir Walter Raleigh, the poet Spenser, Sir Philip Sidney, Lord Burleigh, Ben Jonson—have paid homage to Christianity, if not always in their practice, yet in the convictions of their understanding, and in the profession of their faith, none of them has done this so fully or so effectually as Shakespeare.

Not a little remarkable is it that those only have disputed the superior merit and excellency of our poet who have also denied the value and authority of Holy Scripture.

"We are apt," says Mrs. Montagu, in her celebrated essay, "to consider Shakespeare only as a poet; but he is certainly one of the greatest moral philosophers that ever lived." And whence did he become such? I answer without hesitation, because, while he possessed the keenest natural powers of observations, together with an unfailing spirit of gentleness and love and universal sympathy, he drew his philosophy from the highest and purest source of moral truth.

Others, I trust, will not hesitate for the future to declare in his behalf, that God's own "infinite Book" of Grace and Truth had not been revealed to him in vain. . . . there is nothing—nothing of a literary kind—for which we have greater reason to thank the *Giver of all good,* than for a large proportion of those works—excepting only the *Book of Common Prayer,* and *that,* which has imparted alike to it and to them no small share of the surpassing excellence, which, though in very different ways, they both possess—*His own incomparable, most holy, everlasting Word.* (pp. 291–301)

Bard of the Bible

William Shakespeare has been called the "Bard of the Bible." As Bard, he penned the truths of Scripture, mirrored its stories, and proclaimed its doctrines in the lives of his characters. He is credited with over twelve hundred Biblical references in his plays and sonnets.

> Not till God makes men of some other metal than earth. . . . Adam's sons are my brethren.
> —*Much Ado about Nothing*, II–1:54ff.

> O, when the last account 'twixt heaven and earth is to be made, then shall this hand and seal witness against us to damnation!
> —*King John*, IV–3:216–19

> Therefore, friends,
> As far as to the sepulchre of Christ,
> Whose soldier now, under whose blessed cross
> We are impressed and engaged to fight. . . .
> Holy fields
> Over whose acres walked those blessed feet,
> Which fourteen hundred years ago were nail'd
> For our advantage on the bitter cross.
> —*Henry IV,* Part I, I–1:18–27

> Wisdom cries out in the streets,
> And no man regards it.
> —*Henry IV,* Part I, I–2:86f.

> O, if men were to be saved by merit, what hole in hell were hot enough for him?
> —*Henry IV,* Part I, I–2:104f.

Shakespeare made specific references to many Biblical characters, such as Jesus, Adam, Eve, Cain, Abel, Noah, Job and his wife, Egyptians under the plagues, Jephthah, Samson, Goliath, Jezebel, Herod, Lazarus, the Prodigal Son, Judas, Legion, and Lucifer.

Many of his Biblical references were penned as allusions, or figurative or dramatic parallels. These include Bertram and Helena of *All's Well That Ends Well*, as types of Judah and Tamar in Genesis 38; Henry V as King David; Hamlet as David feigning insanity in Gath (1 Samuel 21); King Lear as the insane Nebuchadnezzar; Macbeth and Lady Macbeth as Ahab and Jezebel; also Macbeth, Banquo, and the witches as Saul, Samuel, and the witch of Endor.

Shakespeare affirmed solid Biblical principles in his writing. All of the basic truths of Scripture surface in Shakespeare's plays. Following are a few examples of Biblical themes:

. . . on the sovereignty and providence of God—

There's a divinity that shapes our ends,
Rough-hew them how we will.
                            —*Hamlet*, V–2:10f.

. . . on the justice and judgment of God—

Put we our quarrel to the will of heaven;
Who, when they see the hours ripe on earth,
Will rain hot vengeance on offenders' heads.
                            —*Richard II*, I–2:6ff.

. . . on sin—

I have been, madam, a wicked creature, as you and all flesh and blood are.
                            —*All's Well That Ends Well*, I–3:34f.

. . . on repentance—

Who by repentance is not satisfied
Is nor of heaven, nor earth, for these are
    pleased.
By penitence the Eternal's wrath's appeased.
                            —*The Two Gentlemen of Verona*, V 4:79ff.

. . . on honesty—

Three knights upon our party slain to-day,
A noble earl and many a creature else
Had been alive this hour,
If like a Christian thou hadst truly borne
Betwixt our armies true intelligence.
                            —*Henry IV*, Part I, V–5:6ff.

. . . on faith—

And, to add greater honours to his age
Than man could give him, he died fearing God.
                            —*Henry VIII*, IV–2:67f.

Shakespeare contrasted pagan and Christian elements in his writings. He used pagan elements in his plays for dramatic effect. The many references to mythology serve as literary illustrations, but do not have that dramatic force which shapes character and history. Biblical references reveal the true dynamic at work in a characterization or plot. Witches appear in *Macbeth,* and the devil and his demons are often mentioned, but there is no glory given Satan. In Shakespeare's "world," God rules supremely as surely as He does in the real world.

Biographical Sketch of William Shakespeare

William Shakespeare was the third of eight children born to Mary Arden and John Shakespeare, a glove maker in Stratford-on-Avon. William was born on April 23, 1564 and was baptized three days later in the Stratford parish church.

Shakespeare withdrew early from school due to a family misfortune. He had been educated to the point where he was an independent learner, and the precocious student pressed on. The second greatest literary work on which the playwright relied, Holinshed's *Chronicles*, was published after Shakespeare withdrew from school. One unchanging influence through childhood and adulthood, however, was the Bible, whose words in quotation and allusion delight us in the plays of this genius.

At eighteen, Shakespeare married Anne Hathaway and the following year, she bore Susanna. In February of 1585, the twins Hamnet and Judith were born. Hamnet died as a young teen in 1596. Shakespeare's daughter Susanna married a physician named John Hall and gave him his first grandchild, Elizabeth. Shakespeare's daughter Judith married Thomas Quiney.

Shortly after the birth of the twins, Shakespeare moved to London—the center for theater. There, Henry Chettle was moved to say of the young Shakespeare, "I have seen his demeanour no less civil than he was excellent in the quality he professes. Besides, divers of worship have reported his uprightness of dealing, which argues his honesty, and his . . . grace in writing, that approves his art."

Shakespeare was one of eight shareholders in The Chamberlain's Men, which began engagements at The Theater in 1594. In 1599, Shakespeare and six others invested in the Globe Theater. The King's Men assumed the Blackfriar's Theater as their playhouse in 1608, and Shakespeare was one of seven stockholders.

ANNE
HATHAWAY'S
COTTAGE

Through his art, Shakespeare testified before kings. He may have belonged to The Queen's Men, the company commissioned by Elizabeth, and certainly performed before Elizabeth many times, often in roles he had written as a member of The Chamberlain's Men. The plays presented to James I in his first Revel season included Shakespeare's *Othello, The Merry Wives of Windsor, Measure for Measure, The Comedy of Errors, Henry V, Love's Labour's Lost,* and *The Merchant of Venice.*

Though Shakespeare retired from acting in 1605 and no longer toured with The King's Men, he continued to write. In 1610 his semi-retirement found him back in Stratford. Six years later in January of 1616, Shakespeare employed the solicitor, Francis Collins, to prepare his will, which he signed on March 25. In this last statement of his earthly wishes, the Bard prefaced his desires by these words:

> I commend my soul into the hands of God, my Creator, hoping and assuredly believing, through the only merits of Jesus Christ my Saviour, to be made partaker of life everlasting; and my body to the earth whereof it is made.

He died on his birthday, April 23, 1616, and was buried two days later in Holy Trinity Church.

Tributes to the Bard throughout the Centuries

HOLY TRINITY CHURCH

Sweet Swan of Avon! What a sight it were
To see thee in our waters yet appear
   Soul of the age!
The applause! delight! the wonder of
   our stage.
My Shakespeare, rise. I will not lodge
   thee by Chaucer or Spencer or bid
   Beaumont lie
A little further to make thee room;
Thou are alive still, while thy book dothe
   live
And we have wits to read and praise to
   give,
Triumph my Britain, thou hast one to
   show
To whom all scenes of Europe homage
   owe.
He was not of an age, but for all time.
—Ben Jonson, *To the Memory of My Beloved, the Author, Mr. William Shakespeare,* 1623

He was the man who of all modern, and perhaps ancient poets, had the largest and most comprehensive soul.
—John Dryden,
Essay of Dramatic Poesy, 1668

When learning's triumph o'er her
   barb'rous foes
First reared the stage, immortal
   Shakespeare rose;
Each change of many-colored life he
   drew,
Exhausted worlds, and then imagined
   new:
Existence saw him spurn her bounded
   reign,
And panting Time toiled after him in
   vain.
—*Prologue at the Opening of Drury Lane Theater,* 1747

We must be free or die, who speak the
   tongue
That Shakespeare spake; the faith and
   morals hold
Which Milton held.
—William Wordsworth,
It Is Not to Be Thought Of, 1807

Shakespeare becomes all things, yet ever remaining himself.
—Samuel Taylor Coleridge,
Biographia Literaria, 1817

Shakespeare is not our poet, but the world's....
—Walter Savage Landor,
To Robert Browning, 1846

Truly he was titled 'the gentle,' for while he instructs, he does not lecture; though he reproves, he never jibes....We believe that the home education of William Shakespeare was grounded upon the Bible, and that if this Book had been sealed to his childhood, he might have been the Poet of nature—of passion—his humour might have been as rich as we find it, and his wit as pointed, but that he would not have been the Poet of the most profound as well as the most tolerant philosophy; his insight into the nature of man (his meanness and his grandeur, his weakness and his strength) would not have been what it is.
—Major James Walter,
Shakespeare's True Life, 1890

When we come to examine his writings, we find abundant evidence on every hand of his familiarity with the Bible. We find that his knowledge is not casual and accidental, like that of one who has touched it lightly, and with indifference. Rather we are compelled to believe that his acquaintance with Scripture was that of easy familiarity and of sympathetic interest. The thoughts of Scripture appear to be running through his mind, and the very language of the Book comes readily to his pen. Observing with what ease and aptness he makes use of the Bible, one cannot resist the impression that he had read the Good Book with an open mind, and had fully appreciated the value of its literary material.

Its incidents, persons, scenes, and idioms had lodged themselves in his memory. When he refers to the Bible, it is done naturally and without effort...he does not strain his point, he does not drag his references in by force. We mean, in other words, that Shakespeare seems to be at home in the Bible, like one in modern days, who having read the Bible from childhood, thinks naturally in terms of the Bible, and speaks and writes with recurrent biblical tropes and illustrations... From the abundance of Shakespeare's references to the Bible there is warrant for saying that his mind was fairly saturated with the Scripture.

—Edgar Whitaker Work,
The Bible in English Literature, 1917

Elizabethan England

And who knows yet
But from this lady may proceed a gem
To lighten all this isle?
—*Henry VIII*, II–3: 77ff.
(re Anne Boleyn, mother of Elizabeth)

In order to fully appreciate the genius and literary contributions of Shakespeare, one

Timeline of Elizabeth I of England

Year	Event
1533	Birth to Henry VIII and Anne Boleyn
1536	Act of Parliament declaring Anne Boleyn's marriage to Henry VIII null, thus casting Elizabeth as illegitimate
1536	Execution of Anne Boleyn
1544	Act of Parliament affirming Elizabeth's right of royal succession after Edward and Mary
1547	Edward VI, Elizabeth's half-brother, ascends to the throne.
1553	"Bloody" Mary I, Elizabeth's half-sister, ascends to the throne.
1554	Elizabeth's imprisonment in the Tower to await execution in the wake of Wyatt's Rebellion
1558	Elizabeth ascends to the throne.
1559	Coronation of Elizabeth I as Queen of England, France, and Ireland, Defender of the Faith
1559	*The Book of Common Prayer* adopted
1560	Geneva Translation of the Bible, the Bible of Shakespeare
1566	Thirty-nine Articles adopted in the Anglican Church
1570	Pius V's Papal Bull excommunicating Elizabeth I
1571	Rise of the Puritans
1577	Drake's voyage around the world
1584	Elizabeth's expulsion of Spanish ambassador after Philip II of Spain participates in a plot to assassinate her
1587	Execution of Mary, Queen of Scots, Elizabeth's cousin
1587	Sir Walter Raleigh explored New World, named Virginia after the virgin Queen.
1588	Defeat of the Spanish Armada
1590	Protestantism for all English churches
1603	Death of Queen Elizabeth I; James I ascends to the throne.

must place him in his geographic setting and comprehend the mindset and the times. Shakespeare lived during the English Reformation and the reigns of Henry VIII, Elizabeth I, and James I. As an actor, he was one of Elizabeth's and James's courtiers and performed many times in their courts.

Queen Elizabeth I was the daughter of Henry VIII and his second wife, Anne Boleyn. Elizabeth was the virgin queen for whom Virginia was named. She commissioned and encouraged international exploration and highly enjoyed the fine and performing arts. Elizabeth attended the theater and wrote plays for special performances. Shakespeare gave thirty-two performances at her court during her reign as queen of England.

By God's grace, Elizabeth I sat peaceably on her throne while God providentially moved on behalf of England. Spain was England's great enemy, and in their rivalry God set the stage for the spread of the Christian idea of man in government to America. The Spanish Armada was a political tool of the Roman church used by Philip II of Spain as a weapon against Protestant Elizabeth. In 1587 Sir Francis Drake destroyed and seized Armada ships and provisions. He returned to England with a Spanish galleon in tow and no loss to his own fleet.

The following year, a rebuilt Armada of 120 vessels sailed toward England, who prepared a defense with eighty-two ships. God's mighty Hand of Providence is evident as the Armada was seriously damaged by storms before it ever reached the English Channel. The Spanish losses were thousands of men (four thousand in one day) and many ships. The English lost sixty men and no ships. The Spanish retreated and God's winds drove them into the North Sea, where many shipwrecked on the Irish Coast, thousands drowned, and others were slaughtered by the Irish natives. In all, the Spanish lost seventy-six ships and seventeen thousand men. Over a matter of days, the Lord turned the tide of Spanish Catholic expansion and opened the westward pathway through the Atlantic Ocean to the North American continent for the doctrine of England's Reformation.

God awakened a spirit of creativity through the Reformation in Elizabethan England. The Queen received a classic education through Roger Ascham. She spoke fluent French and Italian and could also translate and speak Latin and Greek. She translated a play by Euripides and studied theology every day, particularly Protestant doctrine, as well as history. In the area of arts, Elizabeth was a playwright, a poet, and a composer of music. She played the lute and the virginal. More importantly, she sponsored and inspired the scholars and artists of the age towards excellence in the arts.

The Great Bible of 1539, authorized for use in Anglican churches, marked the beginning of the flowering period of the English language. It established a beautiful and elevated standard of English, particularly in its New Testament, which was translated by William Tyndale. In mid-century, Cranmer's *Book of Common Prayer* was also officially adopted. These two books spread the imagery and richness of Biblical English into the common language.

During Elizabeth I's reign, and largely at her instigation, there was also a reformation of official English doctrine. In 1566 Parliament passed the *Thirty-nine Articles* and outlined an official creed for the Anglican Church, including a description of predestination, salvation by faith, and a spiritual Eucharist.

John Foxe's *Book of Martyrs* was published in 1559. It detailed the Catholic persecution of Protestants under Elizabeth's half-sister, Bloody Mary, and through it God quickened the spirit of the Protestant Reformation in England.

The Geneva Bible was published in 1560. This was the Bible of Shakespeare and the Pilgrims translated by Calvin, Knox, and Whittingham. Twenty years later, English Separatist Robert Browne traveled to Holland where he published tracts "outlining a democratic constitution for Christianity" in the midst of the persecution of Puritans and Separatists in England. These last two publications are examples of work written in resistance to England's state religion under Elizabeth. In His manifold grace, the Lord used the shortcomings of Queen Elizabeth and King James I to inspire our Pilgrims toward a deeper faith and the North American continent.

English Education at the Time of Shakespeare

Shakespeare was born in a pastoral setting, that of the prosperous medieval farming village, Stratford-on-Avon. Its most famous native sons were John of Stratford, who had become Archbishop of Canterbury and Sir Hugh Clopton, who had become Lord Mayor of London. The great stone bridge that Clopton had built over the river opened a year-round highway to and from London. This well-traveled road brought prosperity to Stratford's marketplace and community by opening trades for the local men. Stratford was famous for its fairs and regular stage productions from touring companies of actors. Shakespeare's father was a profitable glove maker and a local constable, chamberlain, and eventually Justice of the Peace and High Bailiff (mayor), the highest official in town—a man who could read and write.

The Stratford charter stipulated "a free grammar school for the training and education of children" to be "continued forever." It was financed before the Reformation by the Guild of the Holy Cross. The boys in Stratford were expected to attend as soon as they knew how to read and write. It fell to the parish clerk to teach the young boys their letters; however, it was troublesome for the young to learn, and "one weak-minded English uncle . . . spent twenty times as much on sugar plums as on hornbooks before his nephew succeeded in learning his

letters." (*Shakespeare of London*, Marchette Chute, 1949, pp. 13–14)

Education for the young English boy was the way of the hornbook, *The ABC,* and the *Little Catechism.* Generations of children learned to read in this manner, and young William, the son of Stratford's mayor, most certainly was educated in this way. His handwriting indicates that he used the "secretary" style of the medieval ages.

"As soon as he could read and write and knew his Catechism, young William Shakespeare was ready to enter Stratford grammar school. He was the son of one of the most prominent men in Stratford, but he received the same education that was democratically open to every boy in town and there was no charge for the instruction.

"The curriculum of Stratford grammar school, like that of every other grammar school in England, was serious, thorough and dull. There was no attempt whatever to fit the boys for the ordinary life they were going to find when they graduated, for all school theory in England was based on the medieval system. The purpose of schools in the Middle Ages was to turn out learned clerks for church positions, and therefore what the little boys of Renaissance England learned was Latin, more Latin and still more Latin. About a decade after Shakespeare entered the classroom a London teacher urged that English should also be taught in the schools, but no one paid any attention to so radical a suggestion.

"The chief difference between the education given Shakespeare and that given Geoffrey Chaucer two centuries earlier was that Chaucer's comparatively simple instruction book, called the Donat, had been replaced by an authorized Latin grammar written by William Lily. Lily was the first headmaster of the school at St. Paul's Cathedral, and his book must have made him more cordially hated by harassed seven-year-olds than any man before or since. The whole of

From *Shakespeare of London* by Marchette Chute. Copyright 1949, renewed © 1977 by Marchette Chute. Used by permission of Dutton Signet, a division of Penguin Books USA, Inc.

the English educational system united to pound Lily's Latin grammar into the heads of the young, and if a schoolboy was wise he resigned himself to having to memorize the whole book." (Chute, pp. 14–15)

The average grammar school boy attended school both summer and winter for four years. Classes began at seven in the morning and went until five at night, with two hours off at midday to walk home for lunch. Students learned to read and write Latin and to recite Latin. There was no English literature, history, geography, natural sciences, math, nor modern language instruction. The young boys were taught how to make pens and to keep a commonplace book in which to record favorite quotations from the ancients. For Shakespeare, education beyond his Latin grammar school was found in London.

"Writers of the late sixteenth century had a lighthearted sense of freedom where their native tongue was concerned because it had never been laid out in the schoolroom and expounded. Much respect was given to the Latin language, but all the affection, the excited experimentation and the warm sense of personal ownership went into the English. If a writer needed an effective word he could not go to a dictionary for it. There were no English dictionaries. . . . The writer could either reach back into his memory, a practice that forced every writer to be also an alert listener, or else he could invent a new word entirely. . . . Young Shakespeare was free to discover the great reaches of the English language as a freeborn and independent citizen." (Chute, pp. 18–19)

History of English Drama

In order to fully appreciate Shakespeare's Dramas, it is essential to place him in his Elizabethan setting and to understand the place of theater and drama in England.

In Europe, as in Greece, the drama had a distinctly religious origin. The first characters were drawn from the New Testament, and the object of the first plays was to make the church service more impressive or to emphasize moral lessons by showing the reward of the good and the punishment of the evildoer.

The following descriptions of drama types are found in *English Literature*, by J. C. Metcalf, 1914.

"Pre-Elizabethan Drama

Elizabethan drama was not simply an outburst of artistic energy in an age of boundless activity; it was at the same time the outgrowth of centuries of popular interest in plays and spectacles of one sort and another. The Normans were fond of shows and splendid pageantry, secular and religious, and they early stimulated in the people a desire for dramatic spectacle. It was in the Church, however, that this love of dramatic ceremonial found its most effective expression. The priests perceiving the need of a more concrete and pictorial form of religious instruction for the ignorant masses, arranged in the chancel on certain important festivals of the Church a scenic representation of the sacred event celebrated.

"Medieval Drama

Gradually other ceremonies developed which grew into little sacred plays. By the middle of the thirteenth century, this liturgical or church drama was fully developed. During the next hundred years, English was gradually substituted for Latin, as the play lost its strictly ecclesiastical character; the performance passed from the church to the churchyard, and then to the market place or public square. By this time the plays had so developed as to cover a wide range of Biblical subjects.

"Miracle Plays

In England these dramatized Bible stories were called 'miracle plays.' The growing popularity of the miracle plays and the more elaborate staging necessary for the interpretation of newer themes caused the drama to pass from the control of the Church to that of guilds, or trade-unions. Isolated plays were joined together into a dramatic cycle setting forth striking incidents in Biblical history from

In Europe, as in Greece, the drama had a distinctly religious origin.

the creation to judgment day. Each guild undertook to equip and present one play, meeting all expenses and providing the actors, who were now of course from the laity. The proper presentation of a cycle of plays would require an entire day or even several days. Humorous elements are to be found even in the earlier miracle plays, while in the latter the comic element is conspicuous, sometimes degenerating into broad farce. The wide popularity of the miracle play is proved by the fact that they were given in as many as one hundred twenty English towns and villages, most popular during the fourteenth and fifteenth centuries.

"Morality Plays

Along with the miracle plays there grew into popular favor an allegorical species of drama called the Morality. The purpose of the Miracle Play, was concrete religious instruction in Bible story through the presentation in a realistic way of scenes and characters from the Scriptures. The purpose of the Morality Play, on the other hand, was ethical instruction; it undertook to supplement the Miracle Play by applying religious teaching to the conduct of life. The Miracle Play sought to confirm faith, while the Morality Play sought to strengthen virtue. It represented the conflict between good and evil in the soul of man by means of personified abstractions, such as the World, the Flesh, Mercy, Justice, Covetousness, Hypocrisy, Pity, Beauty, Knowledge. The early moralities dealt in a general way with the whole scope of human life and its interests, such as the *Everyman*. Eventually, morality plays introduced historical characters thinly veiled and dealing with matters of contemporary interest in Church and State. Thus the morality grew into a social and political satire, and out of that into a form of chronicle play. Among the characters in the later moralities was the Vice. Dressed as a court fool, or jester, and carrying a wooden sword, the Vice amused the crowd by beating and otherwise worrying the Devil, only to be carried off at last on the Devil's back howling

into hell-mouth. The Vice survives in the fool of Shakespeare's plays.

"Folk Plays

Closely akin to the interlude (a comic relief episode that developed into an independent form), was the strictly native drama which dealt with the near and familiar—Christmas, May Day, and other holiday festivals. Among these popular amusements were the 'Robin Hood Plays' and the 'St. George Plays,' known as 'mummings,'—that is, plays in which masked revellers (mummers) took part. Stock characters were Old Father Christmas, St. George, the Dragon, Old King Cole, and the Morris Men. All these native secular elements tended to make the drama more truly an expression of the national spirit. In the first quarter of the sixteenth century, the term 'Masque' began to be applied to elaborate court shows, becoming later an important spectacular element in the Elizabethan Drama.

"The Classical Influence

The native drama in its development from the miracle and morality plays on through the interludes lacked a definiteness of structure. The widespread interest in the Latin and Greek classics following the Renaissance proved exceedingly helpful to the English drama. It became the fashion at the great public schools of England, such as St. Paul's, Westminster, and Eton, as well as at the universities, to present in Latin the comedies of Plautus and Terence and the tragedies of Seneca, with the students as actors. Indeed, even in the grammar schools, the boys acted these plays either in Latin or in translations. The Elizabethans gained a sense for form and dramatic technique from the imitation and translation of classic plays, and henceforth the classical five-act division with clearly marked scenic subdivisions was to prevail in the English drama.

"The Elizabethan Drama

The fifty or sixty years from 1580 are the most fruitful in the history of dramatic literature. Within these three score years the

It was in the Church that this love of dramatic ceremonial found its most effective expression.

Performance passed from the church to the churchyard, and then to the market place or public square.

Dramatized Bible stories were called "miracle plays."

The Miracle Play sought to confirm faith, while the Morality Play sought to strengthen virtue.

Elizabethans gained a sense for form and dramatic technique from the imitation and translation of classic plays.

The fifty or sixty years from 1580 are the most fruitful in the history of dramatic literature.

Elizabethan Drama rapidly developed from somewhat crude beginnings, flourished for two or three decades with unexampled splendor, and then slowly waned. To properly understand the Elizabethan Drama we must bear in mind first that many of the playwrights had practical experience as actors, and constructed their plays with a definite audience in mind; second, that these writers served a severe apprenticeship by first revising or actually making over old plays; and third, that dramatists frequently worked together in shaping into plays a common fund of old stories. All three kinds of experience Shakespeare himself undoubtedly had. It is highly important, therefore, to remember that from the very first the writers of regular plays shaped their work directly for the stage. Schoolmasters adapted classic plays for boy actors, and young university graduates wrote plays on classic myths for the companies of choir boys who acted before the court in the royal chapels; dramatic trainers called 'Masters of the Revels' prepared spectacular entertainments, or Masques, for the court or worked over Italian comedies and popular English farces. Out of all this dramatic experimenting came definite results when a number of men appeared, each with sufficient constructive genius to develop artistically into a play certain phases of life and thought." (*English Literature,* Metcalf)

Shakespeare fulfilled the desires of his Elizabethan audiences. "He gave them their stories, and his genius was great enough to show in every play not only their own life and passions, but something of the meaning of all life, and of that eternal justice which uses the war of human passions for its own great ends. Thus good and evil mingle freely in his dramas; but the evil is never attractive, and the good triumphs as inevitably as fate. Though his language is sometimes coarse, we are to remember that it was the custom of his age to speak somewhat coarsely, and that in language, as in thought and feeling, Shakespeare is far above most of his contemporaries.

"With his successors all this was changed. The audience itself had gradually changed, and in place of plain people eager for a story and for information, we see a larger and larger proportion of those who went to the play because they had nothing else to do. They wanted amusement only, and since they had blunted by idleness the desire for simple and wholesome amusement, they called for something more sensational. Shakespeare's successors catered to the depraved tastes of this new audience. With the exception of Ben Jonson, they neglected the simple fact that man in his deepest nature is a moral being, and that only a play which satisfies the whole nature of man by showing the triumph of the moral law can ever wholly satisfy an audience or a people. . . . In 1642 twenty-six years after Shakespeare's death, both houses of Parliament voted to close the theaters as breeders of lies and immorality." (*English Literature,* Long, pp. 156–57)

Drama on the Chain of Christianity
The Timeline of Drama
By Diana González

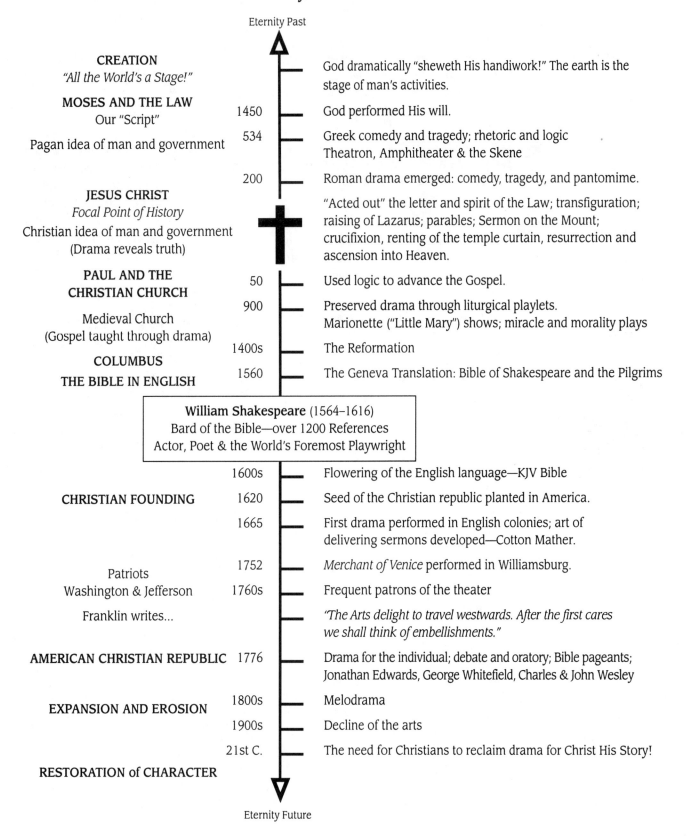

Eternity Past

CREATION
"All the World's a Stage!"

God dramatically "sheweth His handiwork!" The earth is the stage of man's activities.

MOSES AND THE LAW
Our "Script"

1450 — God performed His will.

Pagan idea of man and government

534 — Greek comedy and tragedy; rhetoric and logic
Theatron, Amphitheater & the Skene

200 — Roman drama emerged: comedy, tragedy, and pantomime.

JESUS CHRIST
Focal Point of History
Christian idea of man and government
(Drama reveals truth)

"Acted out" the letter and spirit of the Law; transfiguration; raising of Lazarus; parables; Sermon on the Mount; crucifixion, renting of the temple curtain, resurrection and ascension into Heaven.

PAUL AND THE CHRISTIAN CHURCH

50 — Used logic to advance the Gospel.

900 — Preserved drama through liturgical playlets.
Marionette ("Little Mary") shows; miracle and morality plays

Medieval Church
(Gospel taught through drama)

1400s — The Reformation

COLUMBUS
THE BIBLE IN ENGLISH

1560 — The Geneva Translation: Bible of Shakespeare and the Pilgrims

> **William Shakespeare** (1564–1616)
> Bard of the Bible—over 1200 References
> Actor, Poet & the World's Foremost Playwright

1600s — Flowering of the English language—KJV Bible

CHRISTIAN FOUNDING

1620 — Seed of the Christian republic planted in America.

1665 — First drama performed in English colonies; art of delivering sermons developed—Cotton Mather.

1752 — *Merchant of Venice* performed in Williamsburg.

Patriots
Washington & Jefferson

1760s — Frequent patrons of the theater

Franklin writes...

"The Arts delight to travel westwards. After the first cares we shall think of embellishments."

AMERICAN CHRISTIAN REPUBLIC

1776 — Drama for the individual; debate and oratory; Bible pageants; Jonathan Edwards, George Whitefield, Charles & John Wesley

EXPANSION AND EROSION

1800s — Melodrama

1900s — Decline of the arts

21st C. — The need for Christians to reclaim drama for Christ His Story!

RESTORATION of CHARACTER

Eternity Future

Drama in Shakespeare's Day

People attended Elizabethan dramas not only to be amused, but to be informed. There were no magazines, newspapers, television news shows, or the internet. "Like children, they wanted to see a story acted, and like men, they wanted to know what it meant." (*English Literature,* Long, p. 156) The **gentry** sat on stools in the **galleries** on each side of the stage. Women made up a large part of the audience. Those who could not afford the expense to be seated paid a penny to **stand** in the **penny public** out in the open courtyard.

Shakespeare was first and foremost an actor. In Elizabethan drama, only men were actors. Boys were often used for female roles, and boys and men played the roles of ghosts, witches, and jesters. An Elizabethan actor had to be an expert in the following areas:

Fencing: Audiences loved duels, battles, and contests.

Tumbling: As gods or ghosts, they had to disappear through holes in the stage.

Dancing: Most plays ended with the whole company dancing.

Elocution: Words were often more important than actions.

Acting: Each actor had to double in many different roles.

Music: Actors had to learn to play some instrument adeptly.

Troupes and Companies

In medieval times, actors roamed in troupes including other entertainers (musicians, acrobats, etc.) Some actors, however, were able to settle in one locale as inn courtyard performances increased in Elizabeth's London. Under the great queen, six acting troupes were licensed to perform in London and, in 1583, she commissioned her own company, The Queen's Men. The Lord Chamberlain's Men, Shakespeare's company, was formed around 1594. They gave thirty-two performances at Elizabeth's court, and just ten days into his reign from London, King James assumed sponsorship of The Chamberlain's Men, renaming them The King's Players. These Players gave more than one hundred Court performances in the first ten years of James's reign. Through all of its name-changes, Shakespeare was a regular with this company until about 1605.

Theaters

In 1576 James Burbage built The Theater in London and dedicated it to Leicester's Men in 1577. The Theater was wooden, circular or polygonal, with a diameter of about sixty feet (roughly half the diameter of the largest medieval amphitheaters). It was roofless and had perhaps three galleries which circled the arena. These structures were built to accommodate the audience, one on top of another, and each was about ten feet high and twelve feet deep. The audience was confined to these galleries, permitting the actors a large area for their performance; but most action was upon the stage which projected from one point of the theater's circle into the arena. A throne was placed on a platform at the back of the stage for the monarch. The Theater's "heaven" was probably above the throne, on a level with the upper gallery.

This theater was the prototype for most great theaters of the age. Other famous theaters were: the Curtain (1577?); the Blackfriar's (1576) which was a long hall and the first permanent indoor theater of the era, thus more akin to our modern theaters; the Rose (1587); the Swan (1595?); the Fortune (1599); and the Hope (1614).

As the sixteenth century ended, The Theater failed to draw crowds, and so Richard and Cuthbert Burbage (sons of James) dismantled it, carried the lumber to the Bankside of London, and reformed and reassembled it as the famous Globe Theater. Shakespeare shortly after produced three of his greatest plays: the comedy, *Much Ado about Nothing*; the tragedy, *Julius Caesar*; and the history, *Henry V,* which were performed in the Globe.

The Globe

The Globe's exterior was octagonal, its interior perhaps circular. Audience galleries encircled the stage completely, and these, along with standing room, accommodated around three thousand people. All action was on the stage, and none in the yard. The main stage supported a smaller curtained area, the new inner stage. The throne was no longer on the stage, but could be lowered onto it from "heaven."

On June 29, 1613, the Globe Theater burned down when thatch was set afire upon the discharge of guns at one of the first performances of Shakespeare's last play, *Henry VIII*. By the grace of God, all present escaped. The manuscripts of Shakespeare's plays, half of which had not been published, were also salvaged from the burning theater. An improved Globe was immediately rebuilt and opened the following spring.

The Stage

The stage design of the Elizabethan theater developed from the open courtyards at inns where many plays were produced. The Elizabethan stage gave the playwright great freedom to create action, mood, locality, and characterization. When the **flag** was flying over the roof, it meant that a play was being performed. Performances were usually given in the afternoon to use natural lighting.

The roof of the stage was called the **heavens** or the **shadows** for special effects and provided protection against bad weather. At the rear of the building was an **entrance** used by the actors. An **inner stage** at the rear was used for scenes that needed setting up ahead of time. **Props** were used in front of the corridor. To either side of the corridor were the **actor's room** and the **dressing** or **tiring room**. A **curtained upper stage** over the platform was used for seating the musicians or for special scenes. On either side of the upper stage were stairs for the actors. The **front stage**, which is where most of the action took place, could be viewed from three sides and faced out into the open court. It had no curtain.

An Elizabethan play lasted about two and one-half hours. It had **no program** and also had **no acts**, but it offered **frequent intermissions**. The **prologue** set the scene and the end of scenes was indicated by **rhymed tags** or a change of actors. **No scenery** was used, but elaborate props and costumes were designed to lend the air of reality. Many **devices**, such as trap doors and scaffolds, were used to produce or make trees or gods disappear. The closeness of the stage to the audience led to use of **asides** and **soliloquies**. What the audience wanted (and got!) was lots of **action**—duels, murders, headless horsemen, soldiers, clowns, ghosts, witches, and gods; **wit**—puns, asides, and conceits; **evil overcome; patriotism; earthy humor; and noise**—music, shouting, and sound effects.

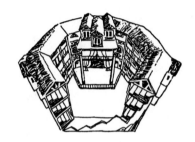

Types of Shakespearean Dramas

The four types of Shakespearean dramas are histories, comedies, tragicomedies, and tragedies. Shakespeare's tragedies are ancient, his comedies are Mediterranean, and his histories are English, in which he recognized God's hand moving in history.

In Shakespeare's tragedies, the burden of man presses upon the characters. Compare the vanity of Ecclesiastes or the sorrow and turmoil of 1 and 2 Kings. All of the tragedies end without hope, with one exception—*Macbeth*. *Macbeth* is the only tragedy that is set in Christian England. Other tragedies employ pagan characters who do not have the spiritual resources to triumph.

The settings for his comedies include France, Bohemia, Italy, and the Mediterranean islands. Indeed, the Bard penned some of his most beautiful Scriptural truths in his comedies, but these nations seem stagnant in Shakespeare's dramas.

The setting for most of Shakespeare's histories is England. In these plays there is action with import—not just struggle as in the tragedies, nor stagnant as in the comedies. Characters act, and the consequences—good and bad—are profound. The hand of God is visible in *Henry V* and *Henry VIII*.

Shakespeare's Dramas
Comedies

Much Ado about Nothing
As You Like It
Comedy of Errors
Love's Labour's Lost
Twelfth Night
Merry Wives of Windsor
The Taming of the Shrew
Two Gentlemen of Verona
A Midsummer Night's Dream
The Merchant of Venice
Troilus and Cressida
All's Well That Ends Well
Measure for Measure

Tragedies

Hamlet
Othello
King Lear
Titus Andronicus
Romeo and Juliet
Macbeth

Tragicomedies

Timon of Athens
Cymbeline
The Winter's Tale
Tempest

Histories

Henry VI
Richard III
King Henry IV
Henry VIII
King Henry V

Julius Caesar
Richard II
Antony and Cleopatra
King John
Richard II
Coriolanus

Shakespeare's Style

He was not of an age, but for all time.

— Ben Jonson (*First Folio*), first poet laureate of England

The English language has never been the same since Shakespeare gave it imagery, poetry, and drama. His phrases and ideas are quoted thousands of times every day in the media and in conversation all around the world. His writing style included:

Puns:

humorous play on words indicating different meanings.

Metaphors:

comparing something in terms of something else, such as "a ship plows the sea."

Blank verse or iambic pentameter:

five feet to a line, each beat consisting of an unaccented syllable followed by an accented syllable —

$$/ \; -\;'\; / \; -\;'\; / \; -\;'\; / \; -\;'\; / \; -\;'\; /$$
$$1 \qquad 2 \qquad 3 \qquad 4 \qquad 5$$

Conceit:

whimsical, extravagant, or fanciful ideas

Soliloquy:

someone talking to himself; a speech made by a character, usually alone on the stage, revealing his or her inner thoughts.

Asides:

saying something to the audience that other players "can't hear."

Teaching Shakespeare in American Christian Education

Religion stands on tiptoe in our land.
Ready to pass to the American strand.

The Puritan poet, George Herbert (1593–1633), wrote these lines in his great poem on the westward course of the Gospel. Our heritage from England began with the English Bible, English law, and English literature. The English became "the people of the Book" in the seventeenth century—the century of Shakespeare, Bard of the Bible, the century when English as a language flowered. Not only did Shakespeare include Biblical themes, ideals, and characters in his plays, but he spread the language and imagery of seventeenth-century Biblical English. Never had so many people had the Word of God in their hands. Never had the language of Scripture been so dramatically presented.

"This was the century of England's preparation for the colonization of America. It was a time when a people would learn Biblical morality through many of the Bard's plays. These Biblical principles would be transferred to the American continent to be transformed into a philosophy of government—the Christian idea of man in government. And Shakespeare helped advance the Gospel of Jesus Christ by his knowledge and use of the Word throughout his plays, sonnets, and letters." (Rosalie Slater)

Teacher Preparation for Teaching Shakespeare

1. Organize a Shakespeare notebook for accumulating your own studies and notes, lesson plans, and modes of inspiration from Shakespeare's writings. Include:

   a) Elizabethan England, Drama, and Maps

   b) The Life of Shakespeare and a Timeline

   c) The Bible in Shakespeare

   d) Drama on the Chain of Christianity and a Timeline

   e) Vocabulary

   f) Literary Elements in Shakespeare's Works

   g) Individual Dramas Studied to Include:

      (1) Resources

      (2) Lesson Plans

      (3) Visuals

2. Choose a drama and make it your own!

   a) Read the play and read about it.

   b) If possible, see it on stage or rent a movie.

   c) Complete the Notebook Approach for the selected drama.

   d) Note quotations that inspire you for student memorization and/or writing.

Student Participation in Learning Shakespeare

1. The Goals for Teaching Shakespeare:

    a) Cultivate a love for language from the foremost English writer.

    b) Teach truth, principle, and appreciation of the Word of God.

    c) Identify Shakespeare's use of Biblical themes, phrases, and imagery.

    d) Overcome the fear of difficult language by familiarity and study.

    e) Develop a knowledge of Shakespeare's masterpieces and the ability to reason and articulate from them.

    f) Elevate the vocabulary and imagination of the student.

2. The Student Notebook Should Contain:

    a) Background of Shakespeare, Elizabethan England, theater, and history

    b) Literary style and elements found in Shakespeare

    c) Elements of the plays: characterization, plot, setting, and theme excerpted in the author's words. (See example on pages 182–83.)

    d) Vocabulary

    e) Nations on the Chain of Christianity from Shakespeare's historic plays to include map work. (Example: Medieval Scotland/*Macbeth*)

    f) Essay work to include reasoning, descriptive writing, characterizations, and Biblical research by the student

    g) Assignments including quizzes, memorization record, essays, projects, tests, lists of famous quotes, vocabulary, etc.

3. The Methodology:

    a) The play should be read aloud, relishing the language and mediating the meanings and imagery for the students' understanding. (With a limited amount of time, select portions from each act and scene to read aloud and summarize the remainder.)

    b) For young children, read from Lamb's *Tales from Shakespeare,* or Marchette Chute's *Stories from Shakespeare.* Design coloring pages to make the story come alive for them.

    c) Shakespeare's dramas were written to be SEEN ON STAGE!

        (1) Write your own script by excerpting passages from important scenes, but keeping the language of Shakespeare intact. (See example on page 184.) Cull the number of characters to match the number of children in the classroom. Have students memorize their lines and present the performance for the whole school. (See pages 170–71 for ideas for producing a drama.)

        (2) Arrange for the students to attend a Shakespearean performance.

        (3) Rent one of the classic film productions and show the students AFTER they have completed their Notebook Study.

The blank form on the following page may be photocopied.

_____

by William Shakespeare

Act _____ Scene _____

Setting: _____

_____

Characterization: _____

_____

_____

_____

_____

_____

_____

_____

_____

Plot: _____

_____

_____

_____

_____

Theme: _____

_____

_____

Scripture: _____

_____

_____

_____

_____

Vocabulary: _____

_____

_____

_____

_____

_____

Using Drama to Enliven the Literature Curriculum

"All the World's a Stage!"

By Elizabeth Youmans

A. Drama Defined

Drama is a portrait of life painted by a storyteller in comic or tragic colors. His brush has the power to impart great life-messages from one soul to another, a shared experience that is permanent and abiding.

The word *drama* originates from the Greek verb meaning "to make." It is defined as "a poem or composition representing a picture of human life, and accommodated to action. The principal species of the drama are tragedy and comedy." (Webster's 1828 *Dictionary*)

B. The History of Drama and Theater

Read the "Drama on the Chain of Christianity Timeline" on page 163.

C. The Role of Drama in the Christian History Curriculum

1. Appeals to the imaginative, dramatic nature in every child and encourages a response, naturally. Every child loves to "dress up" and "make believe."

2. Drama is a moral instructor—it makes truth "come alive."

3. Drama offers opportunities to creatively "act out" spiritual values.

4. As an art form, it affects the human soul, interprets the innermost experiences, and prepares the heart for the truth from the Sword of the Spirit.

D. Purposes for Drama in the Curriculum

1. Enlivens and inspirits the lesson!

2. When a child "lives" a story, assumes the role of a character, and represents the action in his own person, the story becomes his permanent possession.

3. Refines the students' speech and oratorical skills.

E. Drama in the Classroom or Homeschool Setting

"Drama is behaving metaphorically."—Diana González, StoneBridge Drama Teacher

1. Drama should flow out of your curriculum.

2. Maintain simplicity! whether tackling a spontaneous re-enactment, a puppet play, or a schoolwide performance.

3. Enjoy the experience! Don't permit a dramatic performance to become a labor of weariness.

4. Document your effort both on paper and with your video camera!

5. Add a festive meal or simple buffet to precede a dramatic performance or serve dessert or crumpets and tea at intermission. Charge a small entrance fee to cover costs or use as a fund raising adventure.

6. Have students prepare a program listing the dramatis personae and a short synopsis of each act. Adorn the cover with student art work.

7. Use the performance as a ministry to reach out to the community or neighborhood.

F. Suggestions for Writing and Producing Your Own Play

1. **Script:**
   Use Scripture, great plays, classic literature, and primary source documents to "write your own" script.

Maintain the integrity of the author's rich language. Distill to its simplest form, matching the length of the play to the age of the children. Add soliloquies to challenge and enrich capable students.

Keep the setting subordinate to characterizations. Use narration in the author's words to evoke setting and transition for change of scenes. Richness of the language sustains the mood. Narration is an opportunity to refine students' rhetorical skills. Have parents assist you in the classroom and at home to drill lines.

2. Costumes:

Costumes should always serve the character, not obstruct. Hint at authenticity! Old clothes and costume jewelry usually suffice. Thrift stores are a great resource for hats and hard-to-find items.

3. Scenery:

Backdrops can be anything available—simple lines drawn on the chalkboard or bulletin board paper, a room divider draped with fabric. A staple gun will affix any creative hints of scenery easily. A painting or a coloring book line drawing can be projected on the wall from an overhead projector, or use an outdoor gazebo, a garage, or an outbuilding.

4. Props:

Understate! Use simple props to support characters. Children can make hard-to-find items.

G. A Taste of Shakespeare— Teaching the Bard of the Bible

"He was not of an age but for all time." Ben Jonson (*First Folio*)

Teach Shakespeare in the literature curriculum, selecting a different play each year.

Teacher preparation and notebook organization: Include a study of drama on the Chain of Christianity, Elizabethan England, the life of Shakespeare, maps, the Bible in Shakespeare, and the literary elements and definitions related to his work. Read the play and see it on stage, if possible. Collect inspiring quotes and cultivate a love for the language of the world's greatest playwright.

Student Participation: Do a full notebook approach studying the elements of the play. Assignments should include essay work—reasoning, characterization, descriptive writing, and research; art work to include maps, staging, scenes, and characters. Assignments should include quizzes, essays, memorization record, projects, tests, lists of famous quotes, and vocabulary.

The play should be read aloud by the teacher, relishing the language, mediating the meaning and imagery for student understanding. For very young children, *Lamb's Tales from Shakespeare* or Marchette Chute's *Stories from Shakespeare* should be used.

H. Resources

The Book of Life (1923–1953 editions). Edited by Hall & Wood, 8 Vols.

Christ in the Fine Arts by Cynthia Maus

Stories from Shakespeare by Marchette Chute

Tales from Shakespeare by Charles and Mary Lamb

Study Guide for *The Merchant of Venice*

Setting the Stage

Shakespeare, Bard of the Bible, restored to us the Christian idea of woman.

This article, by Rosalie J. Slater, first appeared in the *Prompter*, Vol. III, No. 3., published by F.A.C.E. "The quality of mercy is not strained. . . ."

"Religion stands on tiptoe in our land. Ready to pass to the American strand." George Herbert, Puritan poet (1593–1633), wrote these lines in his great poem of the westward course of the Gospel. Our heritage from England begins with the English Bible, English law, and English literature.

England became the people of the Book in the seventeenth century—the century of Shakespeare, Bard of the Bible. Not only did Shakespeare include Biblical themes, ideals, and characters in his plays, but he spread the language and imagery of seventeenth-century Biblical English. Never had so many people had the Word of God in their hands. Never had the Word of God been preached so vigorously. Never had the language of Scripture been so dramatically presented.

This century of England's preparation for the colonization of America was a time when a people would learn Biblical morality through many of the Bard's plays. These Biblical principles would be transferred to the American continent to be transformed into a philosophy of government—the Christian idea of man in government. And Shakespeare helped advance the Gospel of Jesus Christ by his knowledge and use of the Word throughout his plays, sonnets, and letters.

A basic principle of the Christian idea of man is "the independent value" of each individual (*The Christian History of the Constitution*, Vol. I, Hall, p. 2). It was this Christian idea of man which found its way into government in the American Declaration of Independence, penned by Thomas Jefferson in 1776.

The Merchant of Venice (1596)
Shakespeare's Christian Idea of Woman

Shakespeare: Bard of the Bible, restored to us the Christian idea of woman, she who in the garden of Eden was created to be a *help mate* for man. Portia of *The Merchant of Venice* exemplifies some wonderful Biblical qualities of womanhood. First we admire Portia's faithfulness to her dead father's plan to protect her from an unworthy husband in the *trial of the three caskets* in which her suitors must engage. This indicates the closeness of the father-daughter relationship. It is in fact this relationship which prepared his daughter to have some skill in *jurisprudence*. It is Portia who sees the Biblical solution to the forfeiting of Antonio's debt with Shylock. As we learn of Portia's early life, it was doubtless her father who allowed her to enlarge the talents of her mind and in this way prepare herself to defend her husband Bassanio's best friend, Antonio, from destruction at the hands of his usurer, Shylock.

Lady Martin, Actress of Shakespeare's Female Characters

One of the treasures which we have found in our Shakespearean research is the written Christian record of a well-known Shakespearean actress of the nineteenth century. Helena Faucit, Lady Martin, wrote to a friend of her experiences in playing the parts of several of Shakespeare's well-known female characters. Lady Martin not only learned the roles of these famous individuals in Shakespeare's plays, but she became so much a part of the lives of these women she portrayed on the stage, that she sometimes had her own interesting extension of the lives of her characters after Shakespeare's ending of the drama.

Here are some excerpts from Lady Martin's account to a sick friend of her study and portrayal of Shakespeare's Portia of *The Merchant of Venice*:

> I have always looked upon [Portia] as a perfect piece of Nature's handiwork. Her character combines all the graces of the richest womanhood with the strength of purpose, the wise helpfulness, and sustained power of the noblest manhood. Indeed, in this instance, Shakespeare shows us that it is the woman's keener wit and insight which see into and overcome the difficulty which has perplexed the wisest heads in Venice.

Lady Martin then indicates Portia's wonderful background and education, furnished her by an adoring father:

> I think of her then as the cherished child of a noble father—a father proud of his child's beauty, and of the promise which he sees in her of gifts both of mind and heart. . . . From the first his aim has been to train her to succeed him in his high position. With this view he has surrounded her with all that is beautiful in art, and ennobling in study, and placed her in the society of scholars, poets, soldiers, statesmen, the picked and noblest minds of her own and other lands. (*On Some of Shakespeare's Female Characters*, Helena Faucit Martin, 1904, p. 26)

Among these honored guests to Portia's "princely estate of Belmont," is her father's learned cousin, Dr. Bellario. This man of the law finds in Portia a mind drawn to the subject of jurisprudence. Lady Martin believed that in her youth Portia, in the company of Dr. Bellario, "turned over many books together." She even believed that she might have attended some "famous trials of the day"—and all preparing her so that "when

her own hour of trial comes, when heart and head must alike be strong," she will know the ways of the courts. How could she have had the "power to overcome the Jew" had she not had some assurance of her ability to deal in court with him? (p. 27)

Portia's noble father not only fosters and trains the gifts in his daughter that he sees, but he endeavors to anticipate the dangers which will occur to a wealthy heiress when he is dead.

The Choice of a Worthy Husband

In his introduction to this play, Dr. A. L. Rowse, the world's foremost authority on the Elizabethan Age, makes this comment: "the play [*Merchant of Venice*] was often referred to as 'The Jew of Venice'; Shylock was the dominant character, the one who remains above all the rest in the mind, and the play relates to the theme that has had so terrible a resonance in our time: the Jew in Europe and the veil phenomenon of anti-Semitism. It is necessary to confront it directly and simply, without flinching." (*The Annotated Shakespeare*, Rowse, 1978, p. 279)

We might argue whether or not Shylock is the character that remains above all the rest in our minds. For many of us it is the noble character of Portia, into whose mouth our Bard places many of his greatest lines. We see Portia as a young woman of high morality and virtue, first in her conduct toward her suitor, Bassanio. He has before him the three caskets: gold, silver, lead. He must choose the right casket in order to win Portia's hand. This was the method her dead father had chosen in order to protect his daughter from a husband of the wrong character. On the following pages are excerpts from Act III, Scene 2:

Act III, Scene 2

Portia: . . . I could teach you
How to choose right, but then I am forsworn.
So will I never be; so may you miss me;
But if you do, you'll make me wish a sin—
That I had been forsworn. Beshrew your eyes!
They have o'erlooked me and divided me;

One half of me is yours, the other half yours—
Mine own, I would say, but if mine, then yours,
And so all yours! O, these naughty times
Put bars between the owners and their rights!
And so, though yours, not yours. Prove it so, . . .

Bassanio: Let me choose,
For as I am, I live upon the rack.

Portia: Upon the rack, Bassanio? Then confess
What treason there is mingled with your love.

Bassanio: None, but that ugly treason of mistrust,
Which makes me fear th' enjoying of my love.
There may as well be amity and life
'Tween snow and fire as treason and my love.

Portia: Ay, but I fear you speak upon the rack,
Where man enforced do speak anything.

Bassanio: Promise me life, and I'll confess the truth.

Portia: Well then, confess and live.

Bassanio: "Confess and love"
Had been the very sum of my confession.
O happy torment, when my torturer
Doth teach me answers for deliverance!
But let me to my fortune and the caskets.

Portia: Away then! I am locked in one of them;
If you do love me, you will find me out.

Note: Portia leaves her suitor, Bassanio, to test his character
against the outward appearance of the three caskets.

Bassanio: So may the outward shows be least themselves;
The world is still deceived with ornament.
In law, what plea so tainted and corrupt
But, being seasoned with a gracious voice,
Obscures the show of evil? In religion,
What damned error but some sober brow
Will bless it, and approve it with a text,
Hiding the grossness with fair ornament?
There is no vice so simple but assumes . . .
Thus ornament is but the guiled shore
To a most dangerous sea; the beauteous scarf
Veiling an Indian beauty; in a word,
The seeming truth which cunning times put on
To entrap the wisest. Therefore, thou gaudy gold,
Hard food for Midas, I will none of thee:
Nor none of thee, thou pale and common drudge

'Tween man and man: but thou, thou meagre lead
Which rather threaten'st than dost promise aught,
Thy plainness moves me more than eloquence,
And here choose I. Joy be the consequence!

Bassanio has reasoned from an internal rather than an external position of value. Therefore, since he has not looked at the value of the caskets, but rather the dangers they represent if trusted in—he seeks worth not in the outward show, but in the inward promise. Bassanio opens the lead casket and exclaims:

Bassanio: Fair Portia's counterfeit! What demigod
Hath come so near creation? Move these eyes?
Or whether, riding on the balls of mine,
Seem they in motion? Here are severed lips,
Parted with sugar breath—so sweet a bar
Should sunder such sweet friends . . . .
Here's the scroll,
The continent and summary of my fortune.

[reads]

You that choose not by the view,
Chance as fair and choose as true!
Since this fortune falls to you,
Be content and seek no new.
If you be well pleased with this
And hold your fortune for your bliss,
Turn you where your lady is
And claim her with a loving kiss.

Note: So, Bassanio has won the prize—Portia. He truly discerned that value first lies within. Bassanio was not deceived by the outward appearance of value. We will let our readers of the play seek out Portia's happy response to Bassanio. However, their newfound joy is short-lived. Bassanio indicates that Antonio, his best friend, the man from whom he has borrowed money to pursue his suit to Portia, has lost his merchant venture. His ships have crashed. He is now subject to Shylock and his condition for the loan to Antonio—a pound of his flesh—if he cannot repay the money.

Hatred and Prejudice

Now we are ushered into the main theme of the play—the hatred and contempt between Jew and Gentile in the Elizabethan world. It provides the Master Dramatist with the opportunity to write into his drama some of his greatest lines.

We first meet Shylock the Jew, whose role as a money-lender allows him his only acceptance in the Elizabethan world. He is despised by the Christians; Shylock in turn hates the Christians who consider him only as a source of funds. When asked to dine with a potential borrower, Shylock retorts angrily (Act I, Scene III):

Shylock: I never heard a passion so confused,
So strange, outrageous, and so variable,
As the dog Jew did utter in the streets:
"My daughter! O my ducats! O my daughter!
Fled with a Christian! O my Christian ducats!
Justice! The law! My ducats, and my daughter!
A sealed bag, two sealed bags of ducats,
Of double ducats, stol'n from me by my daughter!
And jewels, two stones, two rich and precious stones,
Stol'n by my daughter! Justice! find the girl!
She hath the stones upon her, and the ducats."

Note: We have already learned that Shylock's daughter, Jessica, since the death of her mother has been unhappy at home. While she admonishes Launcelot Gobbo, her father's servant, for going to a new master, Lorenzo, she indicates the climate of the home in these words (Act II, Scene III):

Jessica: I am sorry thou wilt leave my father so.
            Our house is hell, and thou, a merry devil,
            Didst rob it of some taste of tediousness. . . .

Later, Shylock again bemoans the loss of his daughter and his jewels when he tells his servant Tubal (in Act III, Scene I) that,

"A diamond gone cost me two thousand ducats in Frankford! The curse never fell upon our nation till now; I never felt it till now. Two thousand ducats in that, and other precious, precious jewels. I would my daughter were dead at my foot, and the jewels in her ear: would she were hearsed at my foot, and the ducats in her coffin! No news of them? . . ."

Then Tubal reports Antonio's ill luck. His fleet of ships has been wrecked. Shylock is exuberant:

Shylock: I thank God, I thank God! Is't true, is't true?

Tubal: I spoke with some of the sailors that escaped the wreck.

Shylock: I thank thee, good Tubal. Good news, good news! ha, ha! Heard in Genoa!

Tubal: Your daughter spent in Genoa, as I heard, one night fourscore ducats.

Shylock: Thou stick'st a dagger in me—I shall never see my gold again—fourscore ducats at a sitting! Fourscore ducats!

Note: Now we receive another view of Shylock's character, when Tubal reports that one of the sailors "showed me a ring he had of your daughter for a monkey." Shylock recognized it as his turquoise ring:

Shylock: . . . I had it of Leah when I was a bachelor. I would not have given it for a wilderness of monkeys.

So, now we learn that the bitter money-lender has a sorrow gnawing deeply at his heart, the loss of his beloved wife, Leah, Jessica's mother. He has already given to us his greatest speech in which Shakespeare has him state what is in effect the Christian idea of man. He is speaking to Salanio and Salarino who have just questioned him regarding the debt which Antonio will have to forfeit.

Salarino: Why, I am sure, if he forfeit, thou wilt not take his flesh. What's that good for?

Shylock: To bait fish withal. If it will feed nothing else, it will feed my revenge. He hath disgraced me, and hind'red me half a million; laughed at my losses, mocked at my gains, scorned my nation, thwarted my bargains, cooled my friends, heated mine enemies—and what's his reason? I am a Jew. Hath not a Jew eyes? Hath not a Jew hands, organs, dimensions, senses, affections, passions? Fed with the same food, hurt with the same weapons, subject to the same diseases, healed by the same means, warmed and cooled by the same winter and summer as a Christian is? If you prick us, do we not bleed? If you tickle us, do we not laugh? If you poison us, do we not die? And if you wrong us, shall we not revenge? If we are like you in the rest, we will resemble you in that. If a Jew wrong a Christian, what is his humility? Revenge. If a Christian wrong a Jew, what should his sufferance be by Christian example? Why, revenge. The villainy you teach me I will execute, and it shall go hard but I will better the instruction.

Can Mercy Cancel Hatred and Prejudice?

This plaintive plea out of the mouth of Shylock is to be answered by Portia in her role as an advocate or defender of Antonio. After Portia and Bassanio have been joined in marriage, he hastens to the side of his friend, Antonio, who is to be tried in the court of Venice for his inability to pay his debt to Shylock. Shylock has already announced that he will enjoy taking his due in the flesh of this despised Christian.

But Shakespeare, Bard of the Bible, will show both *God's mercy and His judgment*. Portia sends for legal aid from Dr. Bellario, but alas he is ill. He has a marvelous suggestion. Let Portia go in his place, disguised as a learned doctor of laws.

Act IV: Courtroom Scene

The Duke of Venice represents the executive branch of The Republic of Venice and the Magnificoes of Venice are Officers of the Court of Justice. The scene is set for the trial and the Duke and Antonio confer and indicate that Shylock is set for his revenge. The hated Jew enters and there is an exchange of venom between the Duke and the two legal combatants, Antonio and Shylock. Some memorable passages occur ripe with Biblical implications. The Duke endeavors to appeal to Shylock's pity. (Act IV, Scene 1)

Duke:
> Shylock, the world thinks, and I think so too,
> That thou but leadest this fashion of thy malice
> To the last hour of act, and then 'tis thought
> Thou'lt show thy mercy and remorse more strange
> Than is thy strange apparent cruelty;
> And where thou now exacts the penalty,
> Which is a pound of this poor merchant's flesh,
> Thou wilt not only loose the forfeiture,
> But, touched with humane gentleness and love,
> Forgive a moiety of the principal. . . .
> We all expect a gentle answer, Jew.

Shylock:
> I have possessed your Grace of what I purpose,
> And by our holy Sabbath have I sworn
> To have the due and forfeit of my bond:
> If you deny it, let the danger light
> Upon your charter and your city's freedom.
> You'll ask me why I rather choose to have
> A weight of carrion flesh than to receive
> Three thousand ducats. I'll not answer that!
> But say it is my humour, . . .

Bassanio then endeavors to forestall the carrying out of the dread sentence by offering double the amount that Antonio owes Shylock—not three thousand ducats, but six thousand. This sum Bassanio has received from his new wife, Portia. When Shylock refuses any amount of money but would have his bond, the Duke remarks,

Duke: How shalt thou hope for mercy, rend'ring none?

Shylock:
> What judgment shall I dread, doing no wrong? . . .
> The pound of flesh which I demand of him
> Is dearly bought, 'tis mine, and I will have it.
> If you deny me, fie upon your law!
> There is no force in the decrees of Venice.

Here the play reaches a standstill. The dramatic moment reaches a new height when first Nerissa and then Portia, enter the court, dressed as a lawyer and his clerk. As Portia, now playing the role of Balthasar, the young doctor of laws from Rome, reviews the case, she admits the debt and states to Shylock:

Portia: Then must the Jew be merciful.

Shylock: On what compulsion must I? Tell me that.

This anguished query of Shylock brings forth Shakespeare's great Biblical soliloquy on Mercy which Portia speaks:

Portia: The quality of mercy is not strained,
It droppeth as the gentle rain from heaven
Upon the place beneath. It is twice blest
It blesseth him that gives, and him that takes.
'Tis mightiest in the mightiest. It becomes
The throned monarch better than his crown,
His sceptre shows the force of temporal power,
The attribute to awe and majesty,
Wherein doth sit the dread and fear of kinds;
But mercy is above this sceptred sway,
It is enthroned in the hearts of kings,
It is an attribute of God himself;
And earthly power doth then show likest God's
When mercy seasons justice. Therefore, Jew,
Though justice be thy plea, consider this,
That, in the course of justice, none of us
Should see salvation. We do pray for mercy,
And that same prayer doth teach us all to render
The deeds of mercy. I have spoke thus much
To mitigate the justice of thy plea.
Which if thou follow, this strict court of Venice
Must needs give sentence 'gainst the merchant there.

But Shylock, who has never experienced mercy himself, is incapable of expressing this God-like quality. He craves, demands that the law be fulfilled.

Shylock: My deeds upon my head! I crave the law.
The penalty and forfeit of my bond.

Portia inquires if the money cannot be repaid, and Bassanio indicates that he has offered Shylock twice the amount owed, and if that will not suffice "I will be bound to pay it ten times o'er, or forfeit of my hands, my head, my heart."

Bassanio then begged the doctor of law to *bend the law a little*.

        Wrest once the law to your authority,
To do a great right, do a little wrong,
And curb this cruel devil of his will.

But the Bard of the Bible was not going to compromise the law.

Portia: It must not be, there is no power in Venice
Can alter a decree established.
'Twill be recorded for a precedent,
And many an error by the same example
Will rush into the state. It cannot be.

The conclusion of the whole matter seems to be that pound of flesh will be taken—lawfully claimed by the Jew. Elaborate preparations are made. The knife is sharpened, the surgeon standing by to "stop his wounds, lest he do bleed to death." Antonio shakes his friend's hand. But wait, the young Doctor of Law seems to have been biding his time, for, just as he is called upon by Shylock to pronounce the sentence, Portia cries out:

Portia: Tarry a little; there is something else.
This bond doth give thee here no jot of blood.
The words expressly are "a pound of flesh."
Take then thy bond, take thou thy pound of flesh;
But in the cutting it if thou does shed
One drop of Christian blood, thy lands and goods
Are, by the laws of Venice, confiscate
Unto the state of Venice.

Shylock: Give me my principal, and let me go.

But Portia restrains Bassanio.

Portia: He hath refused it in the open court:
He shall have merely justice and his bond.

Shylock: Shall I not have barely my principal?

Portia: Thou shalt have nothing but the forfeiture,
To be so taken at thy peril, Jew.

Shylock is now ready to go. But the law upon which he hung his case has not done with him. The young lawyer accosts him.

Portia: Tarry, Jew,
The law hath yet another hold on you.
It is enacted in the laws of Venice,
If it be proved against an alien
That by direct or indirect attempts
He seek the life of any citizen,
The party 'gainst the which he doth contrive
Shall seize one half his goods; the other half
Comes to the privy coffer of the state;
And the offender's life lies in the mercy
Of the duke only 'gainst all other voice.
In which predicament, I say thou stand'st;
For it appears, by manifest proceeding,
That indirectly and directly too
Thou has contrived against the very life
Of the defendant; and thou has incurr'd
The danger formerly by me rehearsed.
Down therefore and beg mercy of the duke.

One of Antonio's friends, Gratiano, cannot restrain a remark at the Jew's plight:

Gratiano: Beg that thou mayst have leave to hang thyself;
And yet, thy wealth being forfeit to the state,
Thou hast not left the value of a cord;
Therefore thou must be hanged at the state's charge.

Duke: That thou shalt see the difference of our spirits,
I pardon thee thy life before thou ask it:
For half thy wealth, it is Antonio's;
The other half comes to the general state,
Which humbleness may drive into a fine.

Portia: Ay, for the state, not for Antonio.

Shylock:	Nay, take my life and all; pardon not that: You take my house when you do take the prop That doth sustain my house; you take my life When you do take the means whereby I live.
Portia:	What mercy can you render him, Antonio?
Antonio:	So please my lord the duke and all the court To quit the fine for one half of his goods, I am content; so he will let me have The other half in use, to render it, Upon his death, unto the gentleman That lately stole his daughter: . . . that he do record a gift, Here in this court, of all he dies possessed, Unto his son Lorenzo and his daughter.
Duke:	He shall do this, or else I do recant The pardon that I late pronounced here.
Portia:	Are thou contented, Jew? What does thou say?
Shylock:	I am content.
Portia:	Clerk, draw a deed of gift.
Shylock:	I pray you, give me leave to go from hence; I am not well: send the deed after me, And I will sign it.
Duke:	Get thee gone, but do it. (*Exit Shylock*)

Lady Martin as Portia

I could never part with my characters when the curtain fell and the audience departed. As I had lived them through their early lives, so I also lived with them into their future. . . .

For Portia I have always dreamed of a holier and far more difficult task. I do not believe that such a woman as I conceive her to have been would leave the despised, deserted Jew to his fate. When she finds that even Antonio's "mercy" is not of the kind to satisfy her woman's heart, she vows to herself that, out of her own great happiness, and in abounding gratitude for it, she will devote herself to the all but impossible task of converting this "inexorable Jew." She goes alone to his wretched, lonely home, to which he has been accompanied only by the execrations of the mob. These still ring in his sick ears as he lies there stunned, bewildered, defeated, deserted. But sharper, more harrowing than all, are his self-upbraidings that he should have left a loophole in the bond by which the hated Christian merchant has escaped. In his rage, in his bitter self-accusations, he lashes himself into a state of frenzy. If left alone much longer to these wild, mad moods, he might destroy himself. But before he has time for this, there comes to his door, and will not be denied, this noble lady.

[Shylock] knows her not, and roughly forbids her entrance; but with gentle force, and with the charm of her winning manners and noble and gracious presence, she contrives to gain an entrance. There is little she can do in her first visits. Still she repeats them, bringing wine and oil and nourishment for the sick body, and sacred ointment for the bruised mind. The reviled, despised Jew finds himself for the first time (for, oh, so long!) tended, thought of, cared for. Why should this be? Never has this been since his early days—since his beloved Leah left him. . . . The Jew would find in Portia a likeness to his beautiful Leah. (pp. 39–40)

Lady Martin actually envisioned Portia's ministering spirit as able to comfort the old money-lender, whose sorrow and bitterness had shriveled and drained his life. And above all, the behavior and treatment of the privileged Christians had rendered him hateful and revengeful. She concludes:

> I think that the Jew will not live long. His mind and body have been too sorely bruised and shaken. But Portia's spell will be upon him to the end. His last looks will be upon the eyes which have opened his, and shown him the "light to lighten his darkness"; and he who was despised, reviled, and himself at war with all men, will now have felt the happiness of bestowing forgiveness, and the blessed hope of being himself forgiven. (p. 42)

Lady Martin confesses to her friend that much of what she had written about the extension of Portia's dealing with Shylock might seem fanciful. "But this is how Portia has pictured herself to my thoughts." (p. 43)

Shakespeare wrote in an age of strong antagonism between Christians and Jews. And while he spoke to a particular age, he actually speaks to every age. By making a *comedy* of prejudice and hatred, Shakespeare stirs our own consciences to contrition and brings home to our hearts and minds the tragedy of our Lord and Savior. His testimony of love and forgiveness, even as He hung in suffering on the Cross of Calvary, rises before our eyes as we cringe at the vitriolic exchanges between Shylock and his antagonists. No wonder *The Merchant of Venice* with its great soliloquy—"the quality of mercy" which "is not strained"—is one of Shakespeare's greatest testimonies as Bard of the Bible.

The Bard

A Sample Study for Elementary Children

The Merchant of Venice

by William Shakespeare

Act _IV_ Scene _1_

Setting: _Courtroom of Justice in Venice, Italy_

Characterization:

Portia: Heroine of the Play	_Shylock:_ Tragic figure of the play
Intelligent	Unforgiving
Witty and clever	Hatred in his heart
Beautiful-within and without	Prejudiced
Noble moral character	Vengeful
Generous	Bitter
Eloquent	Sorrowful
Habitually good	
Self-controlled	

Portia is one of Shakespeare's most noble characters in whose mouth he placed many of his greatest lines and Biblical themes.

Plot: At the trial, Shylock refuses to forgo his claim to "a pound of Antonio's flesh." Disguised as a doctor of law, Portia comes to court. Shylock rejects mercy and demands justice—his desire is to have the law fulfilled! After preparation to remove the pound of flesh, Portia reminds Shylock that no blood may be shed. She also declares his life and goods are forfeit. Ultimately, Shylock departs with half his goods for a lifetime and interest on the other half with the condition that he become a Christian and bequeath his possessions to his daughter.

Theme: Mercy seasons justice! Without mercy none would see salvation. (Line 198) Shakespeare portrays God's character of mercy and justice in this scene.

Portia's soliloquy on "Mercy" (Lines 183-96) to be memorized by students.

Scripture:

1. " . . . righteousness and judgment are the habitation of his throne." (Psalm 97:2b)
2. "Justice and judgment are the habitation of thy throne: mercy and truth shall go before thy face." (Psalm 89:14)
3. "For as the heaven is high above the earth, so great is his mercy toward them that fear him." (Psalm 103:11)
4. "O give thanks unto the God of heaven: for his mercy endureth forever." (Psalm 136:26)
5. "And the Word was made flesh, and dwelt among us, (and we beheld his glory, the glory as of the only begotten of the Father, full of grace and truth." (John 1:14)
6. "When the righteous are in authority, the people rejoice: but when the wicked beareth rule, the people mourn." (Proverbs 29:2)

Scripture: 7.   "An angry man stirreth up strife, and a furious man aboundeth in transgression." (Proverbs 29:22)

8.   "An unjust man is an abomination to the just: and he that is upright in the way is an abomination to the wicked." (Proverbs 29:27)

9.   "For God so loved the world that he gave his only begotten Son, that whosoever believeth in him should not perish, but have everlasting life." (John 3:16)

10.   "O Lord, rebuke me not in thine anger, neither chasten me in thy hot displeasure. Have mercy upon me, O Lord: for I am weak. . . ." (Psalm 6:1-2)

11.   "The whole law is fulfilled in one word: you shall love your neighbor as yourself." (Galatians 5:14)

Vocabulary: Mercy:

"That benevolence, mildness or tenderness of heart which disposes a person to overlook injuries or to treat the offender better than he deserves; the disposition that tempers justice, induces the injured to forgive trespasses and forbear punishment or inflict less law. Eternal life is the fruit of mercy." (2 Timothy 1)

Justice:

"The virtue which consists in giving to everyone what is his due; practical conformity to the laws and principles of rectitude in the dealings of men with each other; merited punishment."

Equity:

"Agreeableness to right."

—Webster's 1828 Dictionary

The Merchant of Venice

by William Shakespeare

Student Production

Shortened for Primary School

The story should be read from Lamb's *Tales from Shakespeare* to present the entire plot before children are introduced to the adaptation of the play for production.

Dramatis Personae

Portia	An heiress
Nerissa	Portia's gentlewoman-in-waiting
Shylock	A Jew
Bassanio	Nobleman and worthy hero
Antonio	Merchant of Venice—noble and unselfish
Solanjo	Friend to Antonio and Bassanio
Soleria	Friend to Antonio and Bassanio
Gratiano	Friend to Antonio and Bassanio
Jessica	Shylock's daughter
Lorenzo	In love with Jessica
Duke	Suitor to Portia
Musicians	
Narrator	

Synopsis of the Play

This play is about a Jewish moneylender, a prosperous merchant, and a poor nobleman who wins the hand of a rich lady. In Shakespeare's day, it was against the law to lend money and charge interest on it (usury). Businessmen and many noblemen needed money, however, and were forced to borrow it and pay high rates of interest. Usury was considered a sin, but soon became legal because it was necessary for trade. It was not unusual for young noblemen, like Bassanio, to borrow money to court a lady with a fortune.

Shylock hates Antonio because he sometimes lends out money for nothing, while Shylock earns his living by lending money and charging usury. He hatches a plot to lend 3,000 ducats with the condition that if the debt is not paid, he will demand one pound of Antonio's flesh "cut off and taken in what part of your body pleaseth me." The height of the drama is when Portia disguises herself as a lawyer to defend Antonio. Her warning to Shylock, that in taking the pound of flesh, he must not shed "one drop of Christian blood"—otherwise, all his property will be confiscated—causes Shylock to realize that he cannot win and is, therefore, defeated. This drama contains Portia's beautiful soliloquy on "mercy—the attribute of God himself." It lends itself to a Biblical study of justice and mercy. (See pages 182–83.)

The Merchant of Venice Script

(May be duplicated)

Narrator: *The Merchant of Venice* is one of Shakespeare's most popular dramas. It is a tragicomedy. The setting is the busy commercial city of Venice, Italy. The first scene begins on a street in Venice. A merchant named Antonio is commenting to his friends about his melancholy spirit.

(Enter Antonio, Salerio and Solanio)

Act I Scene 1

Antonio: In sooth, I know not why I am so sad. It wearies me. How I caught it, or came by it, what stuff 'tis made of, I am to learn.

I hold the world but as the world, Solanio;
A stage where every man must play a part,
And mine a sad one.

(Salerio and Solanio speak)

Solanio: Your mind is tossing on the ocean. If I had such a venture, my hopes would be abroad with my ships at sea. You are thinking of your argosies with portly sails. That is the cause of your melancholy, good Antonio.

(Antonio shakes his head)

Solerio: Why sir, you must be in love. Not in love, either? Then let us say you are sad because you are not merry. I would stay to make you merry, sir—but I will leave you now with better company. Here comes Bassanio. Come Solanio. Fare ye well, good lord.

Antonio: Fie! Fie! You both speak an infinite amount of nothing!

(Enter Bassanio)

Bassanio: Good morrow, Antonio. 'Tis not unknown to you, Antonio, how much I have disabled mine estate. To you, Antonio, I owe the most in money, but now my difficulties are multiplied even greater.

(Antonio speaks)

Antonio: I pray you good Bassanio, let me know it. Be sure—my purse, my person, my extremest means lie all unlocked to your occasions. Therefore, speak to me of this pressing need.

Bassanio: In Belmont is a lady richly left; and she is fair, and fairer than that word, of wondrous virtues. Her sunny locks hang on her temples like a golden fleece. If I had but the means to woo her, good Antonio—I should be the most fortunate of all men.

Antonio: Thou know'st that all my fortunes are at sea; neither have I money, nor commodity to raise a sum; however, I'll inquire about obtaining a loan from the Jew, Shylock.

(Exit Antonio and Bassanio)

Act I Scene 2

Narrator: Meanwhile . . . the beautiful rich heiress, Portia, is lamenting the poor selection of suitors who have come to woo her hand.

(Enter Portia)

Portia:	By my troth, Nerissa, my little body is weary of this great world. If to do were as easy as to know what were good to do, chapels had been churches and poor men's cottages, prince's palaces. Oh, me—the word choose! I would neither refuse who I dislike, or choose who I would.
Nerissa:	Your virtuous father left a test to choose your good husband. In these three caskets of gold, silver, and lead—who chooses best of all your suitors, chooses you, fair Portia. But love you any of your suitors?
Portia:	I pray thee, name these suitors and I will describe them according to my affections.
Nerissa:	First there is the Neapolitan prince . . .
Portia:	Aye, that's a colt indeed, for he doth nothing but talk of his horse!
Nerissa:	Then there is the Count Palatine . . .
Portia:	He doth nothing but frown. He hears merry tales and smiles not. I had rather be married to a death's head with a bone in his mouth than to either of these.
Nerissa:	How say you by the French lord, Monsieur le Bon?
Portia:	I say he is vile in the morning and viler in the afternoon after too much drink. He is little better than a beast! Ah, Nerissa. I think only of one man worthy of my praise—Bassanio of Venice.

(Exit Portia and Nerissa)

Act I Scene 3
(Venice)

Narrator:	Back in Venice, Bassanio arranges a meeting with Shylock and Antonio to discuss the terms of the loan so he can travel to Belmont.

(Enter Bassanio and Shylock)

Shylock:	Three thousand ducats—well. For three months? And you say Antonio the Christian, shall be bound? Then so be it! Three thousand ducats for three months, and Antonio bound. May I speak with Antonio?
Bassanio:	Yes, Antonio is coming now.
Shylock:	(Aside) I hate him, for he is a Christian. He lends out money and brings down the rate of usury. Cursed be my tribe if I forgive him.

(Enter Antonio)

Antonio:	Well, Shylock, what rate of usury will you charge us?
Shylock:	Let me see what shall your bond be? Go with me to a notary; seal me there your bond. If you repay me not in three months, I shall take an equal pound of your fair flesh, to be cut and taken off, in what part of your body I pleaseth.
Antonio:	Content, in faith, I'll seal to such a bond.
Bassanio:	Seal not to such a bond for me, good Antonio. I'd rather be in need than harm to you.
Antonio:	Have no fear, good Bassanio. I'll not forfeit the bond. Within two months I expect the return of my ships. In this there can be no dismay My ships come home a month before the day.

(All Exit)

Act II Scene 1
(Belmont)

Narrator: The bond thus being sealed, Bassanio travels to Belmont to win the hand of fair Portia. Upon his arrival, he learns he must take a test to win her hand. Will Bassanio prove to be a worthy suitor?

(Enter Portia, Nerissa, Bassanio and Gratiano)

Portia: I pray you tarry; pause a day or two before you choose. For in choosing wrong, I lose your company. I could teach you how to choose right, but then, I am forsworn.

Bassanio: Let me choose. Lead me to my fortune and the caskets.

Nerissa: This way good Bassanio. Follow your heart in your choice.

Portia: Away then. I am locked in one of them. If you do love me, you will find me out.

(Bassanio examines caskets)

Bassanio: This first, of gold, which this inscription bears:
Who chooseth me shall gain what many men desire.
The second, silver, which this promise carries:
Who chooseth me shall get as much as he deserves.
This third, dull lead, with warning all as blunt:
Who chooseth me must give and hazard all he hath.

Nerissa: (Reads inscription on gold casket)
All that glitters is not gold;
Often have you heard that told:
Many a man his life hath sold
But my outside to behold:
Gilded tombs do worm infold.
Had you been as wise as bold,
Young in limbs, in judgment old,
Your answer had not been inscroll'd,
Fare you well; your suit is cold.

Portia: Tell me where is fancy bred, Or in the heart, or in the head?

Bassanio: (Opens lead casket)
What find I here? Fair Portia's counterfeit! Here's the scroll!
You that choose not by the view
Chance as fair and choose as—
Since this fortune falls to you,
Be content and seek no new.

If you be well pleased with this
And hold your fortune for your bless,
Turn you where your lady is
And claim her with a loving kiss.

(Exit with Portia)

Gratiano: My eyes can look as swift as my lord Bassanio's. He saw the mistress, I beheld the maid. He loved, I loved. O, sweet Nerissa, wilt thou give thyself to be my wife? If yes, we shall be married on the morrow with good Bassanio and fair Portia.

Nerissa: O yes, Gratiano, it would give me great honor to become thy wife.   (Pause)

Someone is at the door.   (Open door)

Jessica:	Please, good Nerissa. I have left the house of my angry father, Shylock. My husband, the Christian Lorenzo, and I have no other shelter. Would the kind mistress Portia allow us to take refuge here? I fear the wrath of my father!
Lorenzo:	Yes, please help us! We have traveled all night from Venice and we are very weary. I am concerned for my beloved Jessica. May we have a place to rest our weary bodies?
Nerissa:	You are welcome to have refuge here as long as you need. Come, I'll show you to your room.

(Exit All)

Narrator:	A double wedding is performed for Portia and Bassanio and Nerissa and Gratiano. The brides give their husbands precious gold rings, and the husbands pledge never to take them off. Their blissful happiness is cut short by sobering news from Venice. Antonio's ships are lost at sea and Shylock demands his pound of flesh. Upon hearing the news, Portia sends Bassanio and Gratiano to aid Antonio. In the meantime, she disguises herself as Dr. Balthasar, a doctor of laws, and travels to Venice with Nerissa to try and save Antonio's life. In a courtroom of Venice, Antonio's fate is decided.

Act III Scene 1
(Courtroom in Venice)

(Enter Duke, Antonio, Shylock, Bassanio and Gratiano)

Duke:	Hear ye! Hear ye! The court of law is now in session. May justice prevail. Is Antonio here?
Antonio:	Ready, so please your grace.
Duke:	I am sorry for thee. Thou art come to answer a stony adversary, an inhuman wretch, uncapable of pity and mercy.

(Enter Portia and Nerissa)

Duke:	Sir, are you the noble doctor of laws to represent Antonio?
Portia:	I am, Dr. Balthasar. I am informed thoroughly of the case.
Shylock:	My deeds upon my head I demand justice!
Portia:	(To Antonio) Do you confess the bond?
Antonio:	I do. . . . I am a tainted wether of the flock, Meetest for death; the weakest kind of fruit Drops earliest to the ground; and so let me; You cannot better be employ'd, Bassanio, Than to live still, and write mine epitaph.
Portia:	Then the Jew must be merciful! The quality of mercy is not strain'd. It droppeth as the gentle rain from heaven Upon the place beneath: it is twice bless'd; It blesseth him that gives, and him that takes: 'Tis mightiest in the mightiest; it becomes The throned monarch better than his crown; His sceptre shows the force of temporal power, The attribute to awe and majesty, Wherein doth sit the force of temporal power,

[Soliloquy on *Mercy*]

But mercy is above this sceptred sway,
It is enthroned in the hearts of kings,
It is an attribute to God himself;
And earthly power doth then show likest God's
When mercy seasons justice.

Shylock: I demand justice!

Portia: If Shylock will not take payment for the bond, then there is no power in Venice that can alter the decree. Justice must be done!

Shylock: A Daniel come to judgment! Yea, a Daniel—a wise judge!

Portia: I pray you, let me look upon the bond. Why, this bond is forfeit, and by the law, the Jew may claim a pound of flesh. Get ready your knife.

Shylock: A noble judge! O excellent young man!

Bassanio: Antonio, I am married to a wife which is as dear to me as life itself. But my wife, and all the world I would lose, aye sacrifice them all to deliver you.

Portia: Your wife would give you little thanks for that!

Bassanio: Dr. Balthasar, if you can deliver dear Antonio, I'll give you my life, or any possession that I have.

Antonio: Good Bassanio, I gladly give my life for your true friendship.

Portia: (Slowly) Tarry a little . . . . there is something else—this bond doth give thee here no jot of blood. The words expressly are "a pound of flesh!" Take then thy bond, take thou thy pound of flesh. But in the cutting of it, if thou dost shed one drop of blood, thy lands and goods must be taken by the state of Venice.

**Gratiano and
Nerissa:** O learned judge! Behold, a Daniel hath come to judge this day!

Shylock: I take this offer then. Pay the bond thrice, and let Antonio go.

Portia: Soft! Shylock shall have all justice. He must give up half of his earthly goods to his good daughter, Jessica.

Nerissa: Justice and mercy done this day! A wise judge!

(Enter Musicians)

Musician: How sweet the moonlight sleeps upon this bank! Here will they sit, and let the sounds of music creep in their ears; soft stillness and the night become the touches of sweet harmony.

Musician: Let us all ring fancy's knell. I'll begin it—Ding, dong, bell.

(The End)

Shakespeare Resources

The Bible in English Literature, Edgar Whitaker Work. New York: Fleming H. Revell Co., 1917.

Bible Truths with Shakespearian Parallels, J. B. Selkirk. 6th ed. London: 1886. Reprint, New York: AMS Press, 1975.

Biblical References in Shakespeare's History Plays, Naseeb Shaheen. Cranbury, N.J.: Associated University Press, 1989.

The Christ in Shakespeare, Charles Ellis. London: 1902.

Complete Works of Shakespeare

The Development of Shakespeare as a Dramatist, George Pierce Baker. London: Macmillan & Co., 1907.

Folger Shakespeare Library: 201 E. Capitol Street, S.E., Washington, DC 20003; (202) 544-4600.

Here's Shakespeare: Study Guides, Activities, Quizzes, Aileen M. Carroll. Portland, Maine: J. Weston Walch, 1985.

The Heroines of Shakespeare, Charles Heath. Boston: Phillips, Sampson & Co., [1850?].

Master Skylark, John Bennett. New York: Airmont Publishing Co., 1965.

On Some of Shakespeare's Female Characters, Helena Faucit Martin. 7th ed. London: William Blackwood and Sons, 1904.

Representative Men, Ralph Waldo Emerson. Edited by Philo Melvyn Buck, Jr. London: Macmillan Co., 1926.

Shakespeare, Martin Fido. 1978. New York: Peter Bedrick Books, 1985.

Shakespeare and His Forerunners, Sidney Lanier. New York: Doubleday, Page & Co., 1902.

Shakespeare Coloring Book, Bellerophon Books, 36 Anacapa St., Santa Barbara, CA 93101.

Shakespeare of London, Marchette Chute. New York: E. P. Dutton & Co., 1949.

Shakespeare's Biblical Knowledge, Richmond Samuel Hose Noble. New York: The Macmillan Company, 1935.

Shakespeare's England, William Winter. New York: Macmillan & Co., 1895.

Shakespeare's Flowers, Jessica Kerr. New York: Crowell, 1969.

Shakespeare's Julius Caesar. Edited by George W. Hufford and Lois G. Hufford. New York: The Macmillan Co., 1905.

Shakespeare's Knowledge and Use of the Bible, Charles Wordsworth. London: Smith, Elder & Co., 1864.

Shakespeare, the Art of the Dramatist, Roland M. Frye. New York: Houghton Mifflin & Co., 1970.

The Shakespearian Dictionary, Thomas Dolby. London: Smith, Elder, & Co., 1832.

Shakespearian Fairy Tales, Fay Adams Britton. Chicago: Reilly & Britton Co., 1907.

Shakespearian Tales in Verse, Laura Valentine. New York: A.C. Armstrong.

Spiritual Values in Shakespeare, Ernest Marshall Howse. New York: Abingdon Press, 1955.

Stories from Shakespeare, Marchette Chute. World Publishing Co., 1956.

Tales from Shakespeare, Charles and Mary Lamb. Everyman, 1990.

Teaching Shakespeare in the High School, Bertrand Evans. New York: Macmillan Co., 1966.

Who's Who in Shakespeare, Peter Quennell and Hamish Johnson. New York: W. Morrow, 1973.

CHAPTER FIVE

THE JUNIOR HIGH LITERATURE PROGRAM

Introduction to the
Christian History Literature Program

for Seventh and Eighth Grades
Developed by Rosalie June Slater

This two-year program presents literature to the seventh and eighth graders as a subject field influenced by Christianity's westward move to the New World—America. The Gospel made a difference. It presented a new view of man—the Christian idea of man and government in contrast to the pagan idea of man and government. The relationship of the individual to the force and power of the state began to change as Christianity presented man in relationship to Jesus Christ, and to His force and power in lives.

"This, in its essence was the assertion of the principle of individuality, or of true spiritual freedom." (*CHOC*, I, p. 1) "Christianity then appeared with its central doctrine, that man was created in the Divine image, and destined for immortality; pronouncing that, in the eye of God, all men are equal. This asserted for the individual an independent value. It occasioned the great inference, that man is superior to the State, which ought to be fashioned for his use." (*CHOC*, I, p. 2)

For centuries the pagan idea of man and government had assumed: "The natural inequality of men. The individual was regarded as of value only as he formed a part of the political fabric, and was able to contribute to its uses, as though it were the end of his being to aggrandize the State." (*CHOC*, I, p. 1)

As Richard Frothingham is quoted in *The Christian History of the Constitution of the United States of America: Christian Self-Government:* "The struggle between the pagan and Christian elements was severe." (p. 2)

It took a long time in the history of the world before the Christian idea of man and government prevailed over the pagan. But as the Chain of Christianity moved westward across Europe to England and then to America, the effect of Christianity upon all areas of human life reflected the results of this struggle for liberty. In America and with the establishment of the American Christian constitution, the liberty of the individual was made the basis of government. For the first time in human history, in 1789, the state became separated from the church. For the first time in history, a document of government set forth the Biblical principles which would gradually allow for the equality of all men under the law so that each one might be secure in his life, liberty, property, and productivity. These privileges had been first stated as God-given, not government-granted, in our Declaration of Independence in 1776.

As literature is traced from pagan time through the Christian era, the relationship of the individual to the state is reflected. The focal point of all history is the appearance of our Savior, Jesus Christ. First internal liberty, evangelical liberty, was forthcoming. Then internal liberty brought forth political or governmental liberty. As the Bible was translated into English and put into the hands of the individual, this too became a moving force in history and literature. The subjects of literature, the types of literature, and the authors of literature all were affected by the gospel of grace and redemption when Christ came to a dying world.

Seventh Grade Literature Program

A study of the influence of the Gospel and individual liberty as expressed in distinct literary types on the Chain of Christianity

The Literary Type

The Biblical Standards

Poetry

A literary type which lends itself to the inspiration of a people Biblically educated to appreciate beauty, joy, nobility, heroism, the love of God, His Creation reflected in man and the universe, His Hand in history.

Enjoyment of poetry
Definition of poetry
Principles of poetry
Examples of poetry
Memorization of poetry
Practice in writing poetry

"The poetry of the Bible is found in the lyric poetry of the Psalms which are poems of religious feelings."   —Ryken

Study of the Psalms: "Parallelism identifies this Hebrew Poetry."   —Ryken

The Essay

A literary type for the development of ideas, this form reflects its westward movement as a means of identifying the liberty of the individual and Biblical principles of government.

Definition of essays
Principles of the essay
History of the essay
Examples of the essay
Practice in writing essays

Old Testament: "Proverbs are concise expressions of moral truth."   —Ryken

New Testament: Paul's Epistles are essays in Christian character and church-building.

The Short Story

This highly specialized type of prose fiction is a reflection of the character and conscience of nations on the Chain of Christianity moving westward to America.

Definitions of the short story
Principles of the short story
Examples of the short story

New Testament: Our Lord's use of the short narrative to illustrate profound Biblical truths

The Literary Type

The Biblical Standards

Drama

"A picture or representation of human life in that succession and change of events that we call story, told by means of dialogue and presenting in action the successive emotions involved."

—Thrall & Hibbard

The individuality of nations is well represented in what each one chooses to dramatize.

Definition of drama
Principles of drama
History of drama
Examples of drama

"Perhaps the distinction between biblical and non-biblical tragedy can be summed up by saying that in non-biblical tragedy the tragic hero is, above all, the sympathetic tragic victim, while in biblical tragedy he is the unsympathetic sinner. The appropriate response in the first case is, 'Isn't it too bad that all this happened to the tragic hero?' The appropriate response to biblical tragedy is, 'Isn't it too bad that he disobeyed God, when it might have been otherwise.'"

—Ryken

The Novel

Fictionalized narrative exemplifying a unity of setting, characterization, plot elements, theme, and style. The novel can illustrate the character of men and nations on the Chain of Christianity moving westward to America.

Definition of the novel
Principles of the novel
Examples of the novel

"A large part of the Bible consists of heroic narrative."

—Ryken

"History rather than fiction is the chief subject of Biblical narrative."

—Ryken

"The narrative mode is uniquely important in Christianity."

—Amos Wilder

Biography

"The history of particular men's lives"

—Dryden, 1683

This literary type reflects both the pagan and the Christian idea of man and government and the value of the individual as protected by law as the Chain of Christianity moved westward to America.

Definition of biography
Principles of biography
History of biography
Examples of biography

"The Bible affirms individualism."

—Ryken

The Bible reveals the life and the testimony of individuals—men and nations.

Autobiography

"History is . . . the autobiography of him 'who worketh all things after the counsel of his own will'(Eph.1:11), and who is graciously timing all events in the interests of his Christ, and of the kingdom of God on earth." (*Consider and Ponder*, Hall, p. 47)

Teacher Preparation and Presentation
Literary Type: Poetry
Suggested Reference and Text:
Enjoyment of Literature, Boas and Smith, 1934.

Emphasis

1. Enjoying Poetry:
Recognition of familiar poems:

a) Select poems which sharpen appreciation of nature.
b) Select poems which intensify common experiences.
c) Select poems which stir the imagination.

Memorize a poem from above selections.

2. Distinguishing between Poetry and Prose:
a) Regularity of metrical pattern
b) Poet's use of words
c) Feeling created through poetic suggestion

Memorize a poem, or poems, from above. Select a poem which shows how the poet conveys his meaning in a few well-chosen words.

3. The Music of Poetry:
Poet's use of *sound* to create feeling or mood

a) Through meter or beat,
b) Through sound of words regardless of meter,
c) Onomatopoeia—sounds of the words indicate their sense.

Memorize an example from *a*), *b*), or *c*).

Readings

Select several poems from a good anthology of poetry such as:

"June," James Russell Lowell

"The Tiger," William Blake

"Abou Ben Adhem," Leigh Hunt

"A Psalm of Life," H. W. Longfellow

Compare poetry and prose by reading aloud some prose passages and a poem which has a definite metrical pattern:

"The Charge of the Light Brigade," A. L. Tennyson

"The Donkey," G. K. Chesterton

"Sea Fever," John Masefield

Identify the sounds in the following:

"The Highwayman," Alfred Noyes

"Home Thoughts from Abroad," R. Browning

"Ozymandias of Egypt," P. B. Shelley

"How They Brought the Good News from Ghent to Aix," R. Browning

"Paul Revere's Ride," Longfellow

"The Brook's Song," Tennyson

4. The Rhythms of Poetry:

  a) Accent Pattern, Beat, or Meter

  (1) Technical names for beats or accent patterns

  (2) Most common beats or accent patterns in English

  b) The Foot or Time interval

  c) Terminology for lines of poetry

  d) Scansion of poetry

Accents or Beats, Names for Meters

- Monometer, a line with one accent

- Dimeter, a line with two accents

- Trimeter, a line with three heavily accented beats

- Tetrameter, a line with four heavily accented beats

- Pentameter, a line with five heavily accented beats

- Hexameter, a line with six heavily accented beats

- Heptameter, a line with seven heavily accented beats

- Octameter, a line with eight heavily accented beats

5. The Patterns of Poetry:

  a) Define and illustrate the following:

stanza and verse	quintet
blank verse	ballad
rhymed couplets	sonnet
quatrain	free verse

  b) Understandings and definitions of the patterns of poetry above

The Foot in Poetry

Line of poetry named for (1) the number of heavily accented syllables and (2) prevailing foot in the line.

- Iambus, a foot of two syllables, accent on the second syllable

- Trochee, a foot of two syllables, accent on the first syllable

- Spondee, a foot of two syllables with accent evenly divided between them

- Dactyl, a foot of three syllables, with accent on the first syllable

- Anapest, a foot of three syllables, with accent on the third syllable

- Amphibrach, a foot of three syllables, with accent on the second syllable

6. Practice in Writing Poetry:

When the poetry study is well underway, students should begin writing their own poetry. This could begin by using well-loved poems as models of rhythm or sound. Poems should be read aloud and shared and collected for a class anthology.

A Poetry Project

The in-depth study of a favored poet including his life and contribution, analysis of his best-loved poems, and the memorization of at least one of them.

Teacher Preparation and Presentation
Literary Type: The Essay
Suggested Reference and Text: *Essays Old and New.*
Edited by Robert U. Jameson, 1957.

Emphasis
Definition of the Essay:
The essay is the free expression in prose of a writer's ideas. The essay is never a complete presentation of its subject matter. The essay permits great variety of subject matter and treatment; the essay reflects its age.

Types of Essays
Personal Essays:
Charles Lamb: "Dissertation upon Roast Pig"
Helen Keller: "Three Days to See"

Descriptive Essays:
Agnes Repplier: "A Kitten"
Lincoln Steffens: "I Get a Colt to Break In"

Character Sketch:
William Allen White: "Mary White"

Reflective Essays:
Francis Bacon: "Of Studies," "Of Friendship"
David Grayson: "I Entertain an Agent Unaware"

Humorous Essays:
Christopher Morley: "On Unanswering Letters"
Heywood Broun: "The Fifty-first Dragon"

Biblical Source of the Essay
"In one form or another, the essay is very old. While we do not know how the first essays came to be written or who wrote them, we do know that the essay is as old as civilization. In capital biblical times the form of the essay was not established; each writer used the form best suited to his purpose. The book of Proverbs is a collection of gnomic essays—that is, essays made up of a series of related maxims or wise sayings. Prophets such as Hosea, Amos, Isaiah, and Nehemiah wrote philosophical essays about man's conduct and his relationship to God.

"In the New Testament we find essays in other forms. St. Paul's Epistles are essays except in name; indeed, some critics speak of them as epistolary essays—essays written as letters.

"Most of the parables of Jesus are essays too, though again the form is different. He told a story, not for the sake of the story, but to give an idea significance, to dramatize it, and to make it understandable to those of little understanding. The story of the Prodigal Son is so movingly told that we are not likely to forget the idea that it dramatizes." *(Essays Old and New*, 1957, p. x)

Solomon introduced "a new way of writing in which divine wisdom is taught us by Proverbs, or short sentences, which contain their whole design within themselves." *(Matthew Henry's Commentary*, Vol. III, p. 790)

Biblical Model: Proverbs
"Happy is the man that findeth wisdom, and the man that getteth understanding. For the merchandise of it is better than the merchandise of silver, and the gain thereof than fine gold. She is more precious than rubies: and all the things thou canst desire are not to be compared unto her. Length of days is in her right hand; and in her left hand riches and honor. Her ways are ways of pleasantness, and all her paths are peace. She is a tree of life to them that lay hold upon her: and happy is everyone that retaineth her." (chapter 3)

The Essay on the Chain of Christianity

The influence of the Gospel on individual liberty
expressed in literary forms as Christianity moved westward

Asia...
Continent of Origins

The Bible:

    Old Testament:
        Proverbs
        Prophets

    New Testament:
        Parables
        Epistles

Europe...
Continent of Development

Greece and Rome:

    Seneca, Lucius Annaeus, "the younger" (philosopher and states-man), "On study and true riches."
    Cicero: Political

France:

    Michel de Montaigne
    Personal or informal essay
    Francis Bacon—Elizabethan classical

England:

    Joseph Addison and Richard Steele, 18th-century writer moralists with great literary skill—to bring about an improvement in ideas and behavior.

    Publicists—political ideas and pamphlets

America...
Christian Civilization

    Founding fathers were students of classical writers and English. Identified Biblical principles in their writings and a concern for individual liberty.

The Essay: Teaching an Essay on the Chain of Christianity
John Dickinson's "Farmer's Letter"

Teacher Preparation
Research:

Individuality of essay form

Webster: Definitions of verb and noun *essay*

The Bible: Form found in Old and New Testaments

Identify types of essays.

Reason:

Read chart 6A, *CHOC*, I, and follow the path of Liberty. Read pp. 5–9, *CHOC*, I.

Relate:

Relate the path of liberty to the understanding of the principle of property. *T & L*, pp. 125–27.

What is America's purpose as a nation? Include both Gospel and government. In *T & L* have students review the source of that fundamental principle "no taxation without representation." *CHOC*, I, pp. 15–16.

Teacher's preparation for "Farmer's Letter" will include:

Record:

Introduce the Farmer, John Dickinson. You might want to read sections of his introduction and add some biographical detail.

Having read *Lessons In Liberty*, and having selected a key essay to study, present the historical situation to your students and ask them what they would write in defense of liberty.

Presentation

Guide students in Webster's 1828 *Dictionary* to reason out and select definitions for the notebook.

Read some examples of essay form from the Bible.

List types of essays for notebooks.

Have students follow in books.

Let students review this principle by paraphrasing in their own words with examples from the history they have already studied.

Review pages 236–38 on "Life, Liberty, and Property."

Help students review the "Stamp Act of 1765" from *CHOC*, I, or *C & P* and its Repeal in 1766.

Now they are ready to see how *essays* on this basic principle played a part in the history of liberty.

Students record in their notebooks this introduction.

First do this in class discussion. Then put on the board their own ideas and sentences. Then begin your study of a selected Letter from the Farmer, so that you can compare. The goal is to have them rewrite their first essay after they have studied John Dickinson's essay to learn from him how to express this principle.

Teacher Preparation and Presentation
Literary Types: The Short Story
Suggested Reference and Text:
Short Stories. Edited by H. C. Schweikert, 1934.

Emphasis
Short Story Exemplified in the Bible

Readings
The books of Esther and Ruth; the parable of "The Prodigal Son" in the New Testament

Definition:
The Short Story is a highly specialized type of prose fiction which must be capable of being read at a single sitting, which must deal with a single situation, create a single impression, and accomplish a single purpose. Plotting, characterization, and atmosphere must be condensed and emphasized to these ends. It therefore demands of the author more craftsmanship but less range of power than the novel.

Reading Short Stories:
Washington Irving: "The Legend of Sleepy Hollow"

Nathaniel Hawthorne: "The Ambitious Guest"

O. Henry: "The Third Ingredient"

Edgar Allan Poe: "The Fall of the House of Usher"

Edison Marshall: "The Elephant Remembers"

Ben Ames Williams: "They Grind Exceeding Small"

Sinclair Lewis: "Young Man Axelrod"

Bret Harte: "The Postmistress of Laurel Run"

Arthur Conan Doyle: "The Speckled Band"

For discussion as the stories are read:
1. What type of story is this? Is the title clear, inviting, short, attractive, and fitting? Do the characters have reality or are they only types?
2. What is the theme? Is it symbolic of a greater truth or an interesting anecdote affecting only the actors?
3. State the plot in not more than two sentences. Is the setting predominant? Does it have any effect upon plot or characters?
4. Write down the series of incidents that create a complication. Explain the complication in one sentence. Is it brought about by direct action, or by some other factor? Is there an element of suspense? If so, where?
5. What is the climax? Is it foreshadowed? Are there any other crises?
6. Who is the main character? Is the main character introduced by description? conversation? action?
7. Is there any humor? If so, where?
8. Is there any dialect? State your opinion of its use.
9. What is the "single effect" obtained from the story? Which character stays longest in your mind? Why? Is he clearly individualized?
10. Does the story end satisfactorily? Explain. Does it persuade you of a truth while you are reading it?

Teacher Preparation and Presentation
Literary Types: Drama
Suggested Reference and Text:
Modern One-Act Plays by Griffith and Mersand, 1950;
Tales from Shakespeare, Charles and Mary Lamb, 1990.

Emphasis

Definition

Drama is a literary composition involving conflict, action, crisis, and atmosphere designed to be acted by players on a stage before an audience. Thus it depends more than any other form on cooperation between literary artist and those who produce, act, and witness the play.

The study of plot construction and the study of characterization, setting, atmosphere

Producing a Shakespearean Play

See seventh grade literature chart and chapter 4: "Shakespeare," for direction.

Readings

Drama Is Meant to Be Acted

Read in parts, four or more of the one-act plays including: *The Stolen Prince, The Bottle Imp, God and Texas, Franklin and the King.*

Plots of the following Shakespearean plays— read in Lamb's *Tales from Shakespeare:*

> *The Taming of the Shrew*
> *A Midsummer Night's Dream*
> *Romeo and Juliet*
> *The Merchant of Venice*
> *As You Like It*
> *Julius Caesar*
> *Macbeth*

Types of Plays

Tragedy

A play written in a serious style, in which the conflict results in disaster for the leading characters. (Example: *Hamlet*)

Comedy

A play in which the difficulties or problems of the leading characters have a successful or happy solution. (Example: *Twelfth Night*)

Musical comedy

Emphasizes the musical setting, as in *Oklahoma!*

Serious drama

Sometimes used to describe a serious play which is not a tragedy. (Example: *The Barretts of Wimpole Street*)

Melodrama

A drama in which the plot and the situations, the emotions, and the language are exaggerated to the point of sensationalism or improbability. (Example: *Angel Street*)

Farce

A comedy in which plot, characters, and situation are also exaggerated to the point of improbability; the emphasis begins on ridiculous types and events to heighten the entertainment value of the play. In both melodrama and farce the characters tend to be types rather than individuals. (Example: *You Can't Take It with You*)

Teacher Preparation and Presentation
Literary Types: The Novel
Suggested Reference:
Enjoyment of Literature, Boas and Smith, 1934.

Emphasis

Prose fiction is the name given to any story in prose about imaginary happenings to imaginary people. It is a popular form of literature because it provides its reader with a story, acquaints him with interesting people and places, reflects life as it is lived by human beings, and presents ideas about life and its problems.

Readings

Review favorite novels read in lower grades. Identify the elements of the novel as to plot, character, setting, moral point of view for the following:

Bambi, Salten
Black Beauty, Sewell
The Yearling, Rawlings
Tom Sawyer, Twain
Peter Pan, Barrie
Swiss Family Robinson, Wyss
Little Women, Alcott
Heidi, Spyri
Pinocchio, Collodi

1. The Study of Story Building

The author's way of telling his story varies according to his purpose. He may use letters, diaries, a straightforward chronological order of events, detached episodes, anticipations, retrogressions, or some scheme of parallel progress involving different sets of characters. Subplots must be combined with the main plot. The story must have unity and coherence. The story develops the action through incidents or episodes progressing from minor crises to a climax and coming to a satisfactory ending.

2. Studying Characterization

Principle characters are those with whom the plot is chiefly concerned. Subordinate characters serve as instruments in the plot, provide humor, fill in the scene, give local color, comment on the action and theme of the story, and act as foils to the main characters. Static characters remain unchanged throughout the story. Kinetic characters are developed as a result of what happens in the story.

The Study of a Novel

David Copperfield by Charles Dickens

A fictionalized narrative exemplifying a unity of setting, characterization, plot elements, theme, and style. The novel illustrates the character of men and nations on the Chain of Christianity moving westward to America.

a) The novel as developed by Charles Dickens
   (1) Fiction
   (2) The art of storybuilding
   (3) Character development
b) Dickens: his individuality, contribution, and literary legacy
c) "A Child's Journey with Dickens," Kate Douglas Wiggin, p. 141
d) Review of literary elements
e) Setting up the notebook for the study of a classic novel
f) The study of *David Copperfield* by Charles Dickens
   (1) Victorian England as setting
   (2) The geography of England—map work

Emphasis

3. Setting

Is the background of the story in time and place. Setting, plot, and characters usually react upon one another to make the pattern of the story.

4. Theme

Is the story's underlying idea.

5. Style

Is the author's way of expressing himself showing the author's power to use language so as to make the story real to us.

Readings

(3) Characterization; identifying the major and minor characters by internal and external qualities

(4) Style: the qualities of Dickens's style
  (a) Comic effects
  (b) Inflated diction
  (c) Play on curiosity of the reader
  (d) Flat characterization
  (e) Hyperbole

(5) Theme: identifying the themes that are woven by Dickens into the story of David Copperfield:
  (a) The cruelty of the strong towards the weak
  (b) David's search for a father
  (c) The tender heart in the rough exterior
  (d) The nostalgic yearning for the past
  (e) The triumph of love over hate
  (f) The naiveté of youth
  (g) The correct basis of marriage

(6) Plot: elements of plot identified as the novel is read aloud and discussed.

(7) Literary devices used by Dickens: foreshadowing, point of view, irony.

(8) Word studies; vocabulary project

(9) The notebook is the record of the study of David Copperfield, recording the excerpts exemplifying literary elements in the words of the author, theme exposition, and reasoning from Biblical principles.

Teacher Preparation and Presentation
Literary Types: Biography and Autobiography

Emphasis

Biography: "The history of particular men's lives." —Dryden

Definition

Principles (See pages 129–32.)

History

Examples:

Abe Lincoln Grows Up by Carl Sandburg

Up from Slavery by Booker T. Washington

The Story of My Life by Helen Keller

The Spirit of St. Louis by Charles Lindbergh

Biography, Autobiography, and Memoirs

Biography, autobiography, and memoirs are related forms. A biography is the true story of a person's life told by another. An autobiography is the true story of a person's life told by himself. Memoirs are collections of facts, anecdotes, and opinions about people, places, and public events of the author's lifetime; they do not necessarily include an account of the author's life.

The biography which is a historical record gives a faithful chronicle of events. The laudatory biography praises its subject. The critical biography presents only those events which support the author's interpretation of the subject. The psychological biography is an analysis of the subject's mind. The novelized biography gives an imaginative picture of the subject's life.

Readings

The biography affirms individuality. This literary type reflects both the pagan and the Christian idea of man and government and the value of the individual as protected by law as the Chain of Christianity moved westward to America.

Eighth Grade Literature Program

A Study of Literary Influences:
The Pagan and the Christian Idea of Man
and Government in Literature

Introductory Readings:

1. *Christian History of the Constitution*, Vol. I: *Christian Self-Government*. Compiled by Verna M. Hall, 1960. See pages 1–2 for the statement of the contrast in pagan and Christian ideas of man and government in literature.

2. *The Christian History of the Constitution of the United States of America*, Vol. II: *Self-Government with Union*, Verna M. Hall, 1962, pp. 92–138.

3. *Teaching and Learning America's Christian History: The Principle Approach*, Rosalie J. Slater, 1965, pp. 210–15.

4. *The Christian History of the American Revolution: Consider & Ponder*, Verna M. Hall, 1976, pp. 7–18.

Pagan View

The Age of Myths: A Christian view of Greek and Roman gods and goddesses.

Readings: Nathaniel Hawthorne's
   A Wonder Book—selections for discussion

Pagan Epic: Homer, Virgil.

Readings: *The Odyssey*, Homer. Robert Fitzgerald translation. *The Children's Homer—The Adventures of Odysseus and the Tale of Troy*, retold by Padraic Colum.

For Background in Greek and Roman History: *Lives of Noble Grecians and Romans* by Plutarch

For Introduction to Archeology: *Homer's Troy*, Heinrich Schliemann; *The Walls of Windy Troy*, biography of Heinrich Schliemann by Marjorie Braymer.

Christian View

Major Novel Study: *Ben Hur: A Tale of the Christ* by Lew Wallace

Background Novel: *The Martyr of the Catacombs: A Tale of Ancient Rome*, 1882

The Age of Chivalry: Christianity and English Chivalry

Background Novel: *Men of Iron* by Howard Pyle

Major Study of Chivalry: *The Story of King Arthur and His Knights* by Howard Pyle

Poet for Study: *Idylls of the King* by Alfred Lord Tennyson

Shakespeare, Bard of the Bible: Study of *Hamlet*

Classic Narrative Poem: "The Courtship of Miles Standish" by Henry Wadsworth Longfellow

---

Then loudly cried the bold Sir Bedivere:
"Ah! my Lord Arthur, whither shall I go
Where shall I hide my forehead and my eyes?
For now I see the true old times are dead,
When every morning brought a noble chance,
And every chance brought out a noble knight.
Such times have been not since the light that led

The holy Elders with the gift of myrrh.
But now the whole Round Table is dissolved
Which was an image of the mighty world,
And I, the last, go forth companionless,
And the days darken round me, and the years,
Among new men, strange faces, other minds."
(Tennyson, *Idylls of the King*, "The Passing of Arthur")

The Pagan Epic

Homer's *Odyssey*

Just as the Greek myths suffered at the hands of immoral poets, so did the epic, fashioned by the poet Homer, lift the standard of pagan literature as high as it could go. John Lord speaks of "the wonderful truthfulness" of *The Iliad* and *The Odyssey*, of "their clear portraiture of character, their absence of all affectation, their serenity and cheerfulness, their good sense and healthful sentiments, withal so original that the germ of almost every character which has since figured in epic poetry can be found in them. We see in Homer a poet of the first class, holding the same place in literature that Plato holds in philosophy or Newton in science, and exercising a mighty influence on all the ages which have succeeded him. . . . His poems form the basis of Greek literature. . . . The unconscious simplicity of the Homeric narrative, its high moral tone, its vivid pictures, its graphic details, and its religious spirit create an enthusiasm such as few works of genius can claim. Moreover it presents a painting of society, with its simplicity and ferocity, its good and evil passions, its tenderness and its fierceness, such as no other poem affords." (*Beacon Lights of History*, John Lord)

Christian View of *The Odyssey*

This is the story of Odysseus's great effort to return to his home and wife after the Trojan War. We liken this to man's continuing search and longing to come home to God, and this pagan epic makes a fine contrast to our later study of John Bunyan's *Pilgrim's Progress*. We recommend the Fitzgerald translation of *The Odyssey*.

The Age of Myths

Reference Books on Greek Mythology

Bulfinch's Mythology by Thomas Bulfinch. This study by Thomas Bulfinch (1796–1867) is a classic in this field and provides a complete study of "The Age of Fable." It also includes "The Age of Chivalry" which will be useful in a later section of the eighth grade program. A modern library giant, it is now available in paperback in two volumes: *The Age of Fable* and *The Age of Chivalry*, from Airmont Classics.

The Classic Myths in English Literature and in Art by Charles Mills Gayley. This book was based originally on Bulfinch's *Age of Fable* (1855). The twenty-eighth printing of this new edition was in 1967. It is a college text and has many useful descriptions for the high school teacher preparing to teach the subject of Mythology.

Classical Myths That Live Today by Frances E. Sabin and Ralph V. D. Magoffin. This is a most useful book as it not only identifies the divinities of ancient Greece and Rome, but makes application of their continuing influence in the arts, science, and business community. It supplies many useful illustrations of the use of mythological symbols in today's world.

A Wonder Book, for Girls and Boys by Nathaniel Hawthorne. One of America's greatest Christian authors has deliberately retold six of the most prominent and instructive of the Greek myths. He maintains the identity of the characters and story yet manages to remove the harsh and immoral elements which are present in so many current books on the subject. This is the most delightful book which Nathaniel Hawthorne ever penned and the style is one of beauty and of Christian morality, which cannot be disregarded even in dealing with a pagan area of study. Highly recommended.

Beacon Lights of History by John Lord.

The Pagan Divinities Identified

"These divinities, moreover, were not manifestations of supreme power and intelligence, but were creations of the fancy, as they came from popular legends, or the brains of poets, or the hands of artists, or the speculations of philosophers." (*Beacon Lights of History*, John Lord)

ZEUS (GREEK) OR JUPITER (ROMAN), also known as Jove

Identity: Jupiter is king of the gods, father of the skies and heavens, supreme ruler and protector of the state, of law and order, and protector of human relations.

Qualities/Symbols: Majesty and dominion are associated with Jupiter. "He was the supreme ruler of the universe. . . controlled the rains, the winds, and the seasons. Hurled the thunderbolt and the lightning.

His special messenger was the eagle. The god was represented as seated on his throne, held in his right hand a scepter." (*The Classic Myths*)

Christian View of Pagan Gods: "In regard to the gods and goddesses of the Grecian Pantheon, we observe that most of them were immoral; at least they had the usual infirmities of men. The Jupiter of the Romans was in his Grecian presentment a rebellious son, a faithless husband, and sometimes an unkind father." (*Beacon Lights of History*)

POSEIDON (GREEK) OR NEPTUNE (ROMAN), the brother of Zeus

Identity: God of the waters, his palace was in the depths of the sea.

Qualities/Symbols: "Usually represented as a dignified elderly man, either standing or seated in his sea-chariot. He bears a trident in his hand as the symbol of his power. Sometimes a dolphin or some other suggestion of the sea accompanies the figure." The bull is also a symbol of Neptune. (*Classical Myths That Live Today*)

Christian View of Pagan God: "The brother of Zeus was represented as the god of the ocean, and was worshipped chiefly in maritime states. His morality was no higher than that of Zeus; moreover, he was rough, boisterous, and vindictive." (*Beacon Lights of History*)

APOLLO (GREEK) OR PHOEBUS OR APOLLO (ROMAN), son of Jupiter

Identity: God of the sun and of poetry and music, patron of athletes. Apollo had a supposed knowledge of the future.

Qualities/Symbols: "Since the sun is necessary for health, it is easy to understand why the Greeks associated healing powers with Apollo. They did not regard him as the god of medicine, however, preferring rather to give this title to his son Aesculapius. . . . Apollo represented for the Greeks the highest type of manly beauty and physical perfection, and in the education of their youth sought to emulate him by putting great emphasis upon the training of the body. . . . Apollo became the patron of athletes and it was to him that the Greek youth prayed for success in his contests in the gymnasium and on the track." His oracle at Delphi was supposed to disclose the future. (*Classical Myths That Live Today*)

Christian View of Pagan God: "A favorite of the poets. He had a form of ideal beauty and grace." (*Beacon Lights of History*)

The Holy Bible on external beauty: 2 Samuel 14:25, "But in all Israel there was none to be so much praised as Absalom for his beauty: from the sole of his foot even to the crown of his head there was no blemish in him." Chapters 15–18 describe the downfall of Absalom.

HEPHAESTUS (GREEK) OR VULCAN (ROMAN), son of Jupiter and Juno

Identity: The god of fire and of volcanic eruption, patron of artisans

Qualities/Symbols: "Vulcan was the blacksmith of the gods, the finest artificer in metals among them." He was unattractive and lame. He is usually portrayed as a blacksmith working at his forge on Mt. Olympus. (*The Classic Myths*)

Christian View of Pagan God: "The god of fire was a sort of jester at the Olympian court, and provoked perpetual laughter from his awkwardness and lameness. He forged the thunderbolts for Zeus, and was the armorer of heaven. It accorded with the grim humor of the poets to make this clumsy blacksmith the husband of Aphrodite, the queen of beauty and love." (*Beacon Lights of History*)

ARES (GREEK) OR MARS (ROMAN)

Identity: The god of war. The name means "Slayer, Avenger, Curse."

Qualities/Symbols: "Mars exults in the noise of battle, revels in the horror of carnage." Mars is usually portrayed in battle array—on his head the gleaming helmet and floating plume, on his arm the leathern shield, in his hand the spear of bronze. (*The Classic Myths*)

Christian View of Pagan God: "Ares, the god of war, was represented as cruel, lawless, and greedy of blood." (*Beacon Lights of History*)

HERMES (GREEK) OR MERCURY (ROMAN)

Identity: Messenger of the gods, the god of thieves, of trade and commerce, the god of gamblers and chance

Qualities/Symbols: "Mercury, swift as the wind, was the servant and herald of Jupiter and the other gods. . . . Mercury is generally represented as a handsome young man, wearing winged sandals and often a winged cap, and carrying the caduceus—a staff with two snakes twined around it." The caduceus is now associated with Medicine. (*Classical Myths That Live Today*)

Christian View of Pagan God: "Hermes was the impersonation of commercial dealings, and of course was full of tricks and thievery—the Olympian man of business, industrious, inventive, untruthful, and dishonest. He was also the god of eloquence." (*Beacon Lights of History*)

HERA (GREEK) OR JUNO (ROMAN), wife of Zeus

Identity: Queen of Heaven "the chosen guardian of women, their aid in seasons of distress." (*The Classic Myths*) "The divinely appointed defender of the dignity of marriage." (*Classical Myths That Live Today*)

Qualities/Symbols: "She is the type of matronly virtues and dignity." (*The Classic Myths*) "Pictured in the poems of Homer as a very human person . . . sometimes irritable, quick to resent a slight, and relentless in her anger toward those who had offended her. Quarrels with her husband were frequent. . . . Juno should not be reproached for her indignation at Jupiter's many love affairs, inasmuch as it was part of her duty as a goddess to watch over the welfare of women and of wives in particular. . . . Juno appears as a dignified matron wearing a long garment. Frequently she carries a scepter as symbolic of her queenly power. The peacock is her favorite bird and is sometimes seen beside her." (*Classical Myths That Live Today*)

Christian View of Pagan Goddess: "Had a character without a flaw. . . . She even expostulated with Zeus himself when he was wrong. But on the other hand she had few attractive feminine qualities." (*Beacon Lights of History*)

ARTEMIS (GREEK) OR DIANA (ROMAN), twin sister of Apollo

Identity: Goddess of the moon, huntress, goddess of unmarried girls

Qualities/Symbols: "A virgin goddess, the ideal of modesty, grace and maidenly vigour. . . . Despising the weakness of love, Diana imposed upon her nymphs vows of perpetual maidenhood, any violation of which she was swift and severe to punish. . . . She was not only huntress, but guardian of wild beasts." (*The Classic Myths*) Diana is usually portrayed in a short tunic, with a quiver of arrows, and a stag at her side. "A crescent above her head identifies her as the goddess of the moon." (*Classical Myths That Live Today*)

Christian View of Pagan Goddess: "A shadowy divinity . . . presided over the pleasures of the chase, in which the Greeks delighted—a masculine female who took but little interest in anything intellectual." (*Beacon Lights of History*)

HESTIA (GREEK) OR VESTA (ROMAN)

Identity: The goddess of the Hearth, who presided over the Home. "The Romans paid special attention to the worship of Vesta. . . . They built for her a very beautiful temple in the Forum . . . in which her attendants, the Vestal Virgins lived, a sisterhood made up of six women . . . who promised not to marry and to serve the goddess faithfully for thirty years." (*Classical Myths That Live Today*)

Qualities/Symbols: "As goddess of the burning hearth, Vesta is the divinity of the home: she is worshipped first of the gods at every feast. Before her shrine the holy flame was religiously cherished. No new colony, no new home, was duly consecrated till on its central hearth there glowed coals from her ancestral hearth. The safety of the city was held to be connected with the sacred fire tended by the Vestal Virgins." (*The Classic Myths*)

Christian View of Pagan Goddess: "Hestia presided over the private hearths and homesteads of the Greeks, and imparted to them a sacred character. Her personality was vague, but she represented the purity which among both Greeks and Romans is attached to home and domestic life." (*Beacon Lights of History*)

APHRODITE (GREEK) OR VENUS (ROMAN)

Identity: Goddess of love and beauty

Qualities/Symbols: "To the Greeks and Romans she symbolized love between men and women, and in the world of animals and nature, the force that reproduces life. . . . Cupid (Eros) was the son of Venus and constantly attended her. He always carried a bow and a quiver of arrows." (*Classical Myths That Live Today*)

Christian View of Pagan Goddess: "The impersonation of all that was weak and erring in the nature of woman—the goddess of sensual desire, of mere physical beauty, silly, childish, and vain, utterly odious in a moral point of view, and mentally contemptible." (*Beacon Lights of History*)

DEMETER (GREEK) OR CERES (ROMAN)

Identity: Goddess of sowing, reaping, harvest festivals, of grain

Qualities/Symbols: Portrayed with staff in hand and an ear of corn in the other, she is identified with the arts of husbandry and agriculture. "In return for her care, the farmer never failed to load her altars with gifts of fruit and grain. . . nor did the farmer's wife forget on 'baking day' to set aside some delicious loaf for the kindly Ceres." (*Classical Myths That Live Today*) The word "cereal" derived from the name of the goddess.

Christian View of Pagan Goddess: "Demeter represented Mother Earth, and thus was closely associated with agriculture and all operations of tillage and bread-making. As agriculture is the primitive and most important of all human vocations, this deity presided over civilization and law-giving, and occupied an important position in the Eleusinian mysteries." (*Beacon Lights of History*)

These were the twelve Olympian divinities, or greater gods. But they represented only a small part of the Grecian Pantheon.

Lesser Gods

HADES (Greek), PLUTO (Roman)
God of the Underworld, brother of Zeus

PERSEPHONE (Greek), PROSERPINA (Roman)
Queen of the Underworld, daughter of Ceres

DIONYSUS (Greek), BACCHUS (Roman)
God of wine and tragedy

The Nymphs
Woodland nymphs called **Dryads**, river nymphs, sea nymphs called **Nereids**, cloud nymphs.

Woodland Gods
Pan, half goat, half man. **The Satyrs**, goat-gods like Pan. **The Centaurs**, half horse, half man.

Sky Gods
The Winds, especially **Zephry**, the warm, gentle west winds, and **Boreas**, the stormy north wind.

Underworld God
Charon, the ferryman over the river of death, **Styx**

"He (the pagan) never prayed to a supreme and eternal deity, but to some special manifestation of deity, fancied or real; and hence his religion was essentially pantheistic, though outwardly polytheistic." (*Beacon Lights of History*)

Heroes in Greek Mythology
HERCULES, JASON AND THE ARGONAUTS, PERSEUS, THESEUS, BELLEROPHON

The Trojan War identified many of the famous heroes. Ulysses or Odysseus will be dealt with in the pagan epic, *The Odyssey*.

The Continuing Influence of Pagan Mythology upon Our Time
Expressions Relating to Greek Mythology

e.g., "an Achilles heel" (*Classical Myths That Live Today*, pp. xvii-xix)

Music, Literature, Sculpture, Painting

Themes from Greek Mythology

Science

Names from Greek Mythology, the space program, business symbols utilizing pagan gods, e.g., Florists' Transworld Delivery (F.T.D.) uses Mercury to represent their floral service. (*Classical Myths That Live Today*, pp. xxiv-xliii)

Homer and the Greeks

Introduction

"The events which formed the basis of the wonderful stories of Homer, about kings and tribes and armies and wars, were probably taking place in Greece and the neighboring islands and coasts from about the time that Moses left Egypt with the Children of Israel down to the days when Saul, David, and Solomon reigned in Palestine. Long before Moses and long after Solomon there were occurrences in Greece and its vicinity which, if we could only find them out, would make most fascinating history. But for all those long years fact and fable are so blended in the songs and traditions which have come down to us that we cannot distinguish, except in a very few cases, between the true and the false.

"Earliest Greek history is seen through the curtain of tradition and poetry that drops down about the year 500 B.C. We are comparatively sure of the great body of facts this side of that date. Beyond it we can discern some facts, but are confused by the greater number of myths and traditions. Gods and goddesses and heroes, with supernatural powers, performed wonderful deeds, which the earliest poets recorded and the later poets repeated. Some of these deeds had, no doubt, a basis of fact. The gods and heroes were real men, who spoke wise words and did brave things. Or they were bad men who had power and abused it. Armies were organized, fleets sailed, wars were fought, cities were taken; evil arrayed itself against good, and sometimes the one and sometimes the other was victorious.

"Tradition magnified and poetry glorified the ordinary and the extraordinary events of those unrecorded times. Thus fact grew into fable and men into heroes. Principles were personified and became deities with divine powers and prerogatives. The genius of the great Homer, and of the unknown great singers before him, made permanent these dreams of men, and these illustrations of the eternal principles which influence our race, and are in harmony with which God governs the universe." (From *An Outline History of Greece*, Vincent and Joy, 1888)

Greece: The Land and the People

A short lesson in the geography of Greece forms the necessary introduction to the study of Grecian history; for never had the natural surroundings of a people greater influence upon national character than had the situation and physical features of Hellas upon the public and private life of the Hellenes. (Greece and Greek are names which we English have borrowed from the Romans. The Greeks always called their country Hellas and themselves Hellenes.)

The home country of the Greeks was marked by nature as a land

1. of mountains,
2. of valleys,
3. of gulfs,
4. of islands,
5. of genial climate,
6. of fertile soil.

The mountains are everywhere; they occupy so large a portion of the area that little is left for level ground or plains:

Olympus, in Thessaly, the mountain of the gods, is 10,000 feet high, overlooking Hellas like a huge watchtower.

Parnassus, in Phocis, sacred to Apollo and the Muses, is 8,000 feet high. It is the most massive of Greek mountains, and among its foothills were the temple of Delphi and the Fountain of Castalia.

Pelion, in Thessaly, on which Mount Ossa was piled by the Titans when they warred against the gods, is another celebrated peak. On its slopes grew the pines from which the ship Argo was built.

Pentelicus, in Attica, is 3,900 feet high, and from its quarries was taken the marble for the Athenian temples.

Hymettus, only two miles from Athens, is a little lower than Pentelicus, and famous for its bees and honey.

Long ranges of lofty hills intersect each other, and divide the country into isolated valleys—some of them completely walled in by mountains, others opening upon the sea.

The highlands push their arms far out into the sea, enclosing spacious gulfs and land-locked bays. Countless islands dot the neighboring waters like stepping-stones across the **Adriatic** and the **Aegean**.

The Aegean islands are extremely rocky, and rise into lofty peaks of beautiful form. They are sprinkled so thickly as to form a dotted line of harbors and beacons which serve to guide and shelter the adventurous mariner.

Here is **Lemnos**, the isle on which Vulcan, the luckless fire-god, fell from the battlements of heaven.

Farther south is **Patmos**, where St. John dwelt in exile. Near this Christian landmark is the island of **Delos**, where heathen Apollo had a famous shrine.

Near the Asiatic coast is **Rhodes**, once the wonder of the world for its Colossus, and due south from the Peloponnesus is **Crete**, the fabled home of the Minotaur.

The traveler passing from Thessaly to Sparta experiences every gradation of temperature from a cool climate to one of semi-tropical warmth; but the sea breezes, penetrating to almost every portion of the country, render the air healthful and invigorating, and in certain localities—Attica, among others—the atmosphere is noted for its crystal clearness. The soil, though less fertile than the rich plains of Sicily and Egypt, yielded a generous return for the labors of the husbandman, and the vine, the olive, and the fig throve luxuriantly.

(Consult maps, review the geography of Europe and its geographic individuality and role in the westward movement of history as found in *Physical Geography*, by Arnold Guyot, 1873, reprinted by American Christian History Institute, available from F.A.C.E.)

The Greek People

The people who dwelt in these isolated valleys, along this winding seacoast, and upon these wave-washed islands, possessed a strong individuality among the nations of antiquity.

The Greeks were peculiar

1. in their originality,

2. in their fine taste,

3. in their enterprise,

4. in their versatility,

5. in their daring.

They **showed the way** into new paths in government, in literature, in philosophy, and in art. Their sense of proportion was so exquisitely developed that we have still to look to their orations, their sculptures, and their buildings for our most excellent models of simplicity and perfect **taste**. Their **enterprise** planted colonies from the farthest shores of the Black Sea to the Pillars of Hercules. Their **versatility** is unquestioned. "No race ever did so many things well as the Greeks." Greek names lead in nearly every department of the world's activity. The isolated coast villagers could reach their neighbors only by sea; the in-shore islands and the many promontories were a boon to the daring navigator, who had no help from compass and sextant. With such poor guides the bold Greek sailor skirted the Mediterranean, and a few of the more adventurous spirits shook out their sails to the Atlantic winds and followed the shores of western Europe to the German Ocean.

"Men of the sword as well as men of the sea"—it was a Greek army and navy that stood as the sole but sufficient barrier between Europe and the East when the hordes of Persia threatened to overwhelm the continent with barbarism. Truly an original, tasteful, enterprising, versatile, and daring race were these men of Greece.

What United the Greek People

The Greek colonies were divided from the mother-country by many leagues of dreary and dangerous sailing, yet as a people they were in some degree united. The men of Hellas, of island Greece, and of colonial Greece held certain things in common:

1. **Origin**. The three Greek tribes—Ionians, Dorians, Aeolians—traced their origins back to a common parent, Hellen, from whom they derived their general name, Hellenes. They were undoubtedly of one stock—the same great Aryan family from which their Roman neighbors sprang, and of which we the Anglo-Saxons are the later offspring. Through this line come liberty, law, and the language of the Bible.

2. **Religion**. All were believers in the same religion—a species of pantheism, in which the powers of nature were worshipped as personal deities. The strange stories told of the gods and demi-gods were a part of the traditions of every Greek land.

3. **Language**. The three tribes spoke dialects of one noble language—dialects differing so slightly that a Dorian had no difficulty in understanding the speech of his Ionic or Aeolic brothers.

4. **Literature**. The literature of one tribe was known and prized of all. Homer's sublime poems, *The Iliad* and *The Odyssey*, composed in all probability in the Greek cities of Asia Minor, were familiar to Greeks of every state, and even from the earliest historical times.

5. **Social Customs**. These were much the same everywhere except in Sparta, where a unique and memorable system was founded upon the laws of Lycurgus.

6. **Religious Festivals**. This was the strongest tie. In these alone the divided states of Hellas made public recognition of their unity. Every Greek, and **none but Greeks**, might take part. There were also national festivals or games shared by all Greeks. The most famous of these, the Olympics which the Greeks held every fifth year in honor of the god Jupiter, still continues today and is shared in by almost all nations.

Unity of the Greek People Did Not Produce Union

Yet, with all these forces tending to produce unity, union never came. From the earliest dawn of history until the day when she passed under the sway of Macedon, Greece remained only a geographical expression for a collection of jealous states, each striving for the leadership, and there was no concert of action except on that single and memorable occasion when the Greek world was threatened by such an onslaught of Persian barbarians as to stifle for a brief space the discord of domestic war. Greek city-states were little republics.

The people of Greece, one in blood, language, and religion were divided

1. by geographical conditions,

2. by their intense individuality.

We have seen how the Greeks were separated by mountain walls and arms of the sea. These isolated communities grew to be more and more self-contained. They formed a clannish people like the Scottish Highlanders, and the petty quarrels of their chiefs were perpetuated in tribal hatred. A spirit of independence was deeply implanted in the breast of every Greek. "Every man of them had a mind of his own," and what is true of them individually is strikingly true of their political unity—the city. They would form no confederation nor union wherein the individual members must sacrifice the least of their own rights to the general good. From first to last such combinations remained impossible. A Greek city might grow in strength and compel its weaker neighbors to follow in its train. But some jealous rival was sure to find envious allies eager to crush the threatening upstart back into insignificance. It was this inherent political weakness that caused the successive overthrow of Athens, of Sparta, of Thebes, and of Macedon, and led to the final subjection of disunited Greece to the consolidated strength of Rome.

Homer—Man and Poet

With the year 1000 B.C. the first period of Grecian history—the age of heroes and of fable—may be said to close. But between this date and the year 776 B.C., two centuries intervene which we may class together as the "Age of Homer."

Tradition, hitherto almost our only source of information, is now reinforced by poetry. At the national games, which were celebrated early in Greece in honor of the gods, singers chanted the glories of the past. Before the days of alphabets and written languages, their songs were committed to memory in fragments by the people and were united into connected stories by the genius of poets now forgotten. After centuries these hymns were collected and invested with new life by the immortal Homer. Among a thousand lesser lights he was the one great sun whose rays reached the period of authentic history. He lived on the Greek coast of Asia Minor somewhere between the years 1000 and 850 B.C.

The two poems of Homer—*The Iliad* and *The Odyssey*—were the chief subjects of Greek education. They were studied by the youths, recited at the public festivals by professional rhapsodists, philosophers lectured upon them, and for ages the Greeks looked to these writings as the Hebrews looked to their Bible—as their chief, if not their only, guide in law and morals. (*An Outline History of Greece*, Vincent and Joy, 1888)

As a professional poet, Homer traveled all over the Greek world, from the Ionian settlements in Asia Minor to the Greek peninsula proper and through the islands in between. He was a bard, or minstrel, of a sort of semi-religious brotherhood, a member of a privileged group. This was a well-organized craft which included learning how to string, tune, and play the lyre—the musical instrument used to accompany the minstrel. Homer, like others of his profession, had to commit to memory a vast repertory of traditional lays and hymns, based on myths passed on orally from many generations past. As he traveled, appearing in the homes of noblemen, at religious festivals, and at poetry contests, he filled many roles. He was journalist—bringing news. He was historian documenting events and battles. He was a genealogist—recording family history.

The bard or minstrel was considered to be under the protection of the divine Muses, and so even though travel on land and sea was dangerous in those days he felt safe and welcome by all. With his instrument tucked under his arm, with a rough goat-wool cloak for warmth, he did not require much baggage. For wherever he was received Homer would occupy the seat of honor covered with a soft, thick rug. Servants would place tables with food and drink at his side. He would be called upon to sing about some great event or hero or god, to make the past live in the minds and hearts of his listeners.

Probably Homer composed *The Iliad* first, about the Trojan War—a tale of war and heroes and battles. *The Odyssey* is the sequel and concerns the trials and tribulations of Odysseus, hero of Troy, and his return home after twenty years, to his wife and son, despite the vengeance and efforts of the god of the sea, Poseidon.

Homer's Influence upon Our World

After twenty-seven centuries Homer is still a presence in our Western culture. His epic poems, the oldest in our literature to survive, are everywhere read in modern translations.

Here are some examples of words, straight out of Homer, which are found in our literature and life:

A Mentor is a trusted friend or advisor. We still refer to a talkative person as a Windbag—Aeolus. We call an alluring woman a Siren. If a woman brings out only the worst in men we call her a Circe. In some predicaments we say we are tantalized, or worse yet, caught between Scylla and Charybdis. In politics, we suspect our enemies of Trojan Horse tactics. An Achilles' Heel refers to a vulnerable spot.

Homer Identified the Greek Character.

The universal appeal of *The Odyssey* in Homer's own day was that it was a true representation of the life and character of the Greeks. And Homer had observed life among the Greeks and was a noble recorder. While the Epic is a hero-tale, nevertheless, men have always been more interested in identifying with that which is noble and true. So, even in a pagan age, the ideal becomes the inner vision of each man.

While Odysseus is the main character, a man wise, resourceful, with initiative and vitality, other men also play important parts. But as George Herbert Palmer observes, "the dominant forces of the poem are women." The prime mover of events is a goddess—Athena. The nymphs Calypso and Circe are influential on the home journey. "In Phaeacia, Queen Arete is of larger consequence than King Alcinous." There is the nurse Eurycleia, the young girl Nausicaa, a princess who helps Odysseus, even Helen, the accomplished lady, and of course, the faithful wife, Penelope. In *The Odyssey*, "woman is the comrade of man, respected as his equal in intellectual power, administrative capacity, and artistic skill." (*The Odyssey of Homer*. Translated by George Herbert Palmer, 1949, p. xxii)

Homer's Techniques and Literary Style

Homer first used the "flashback." He begins his story, "in medias res," in the middle of things, in the tenth year when all the characters are deeply involved. Thus we want to know what went before and the author must move back and forth across time. Homer used a double plot. We are following the events of Odysseus's return home, and we are watching a story develop in Ithaca.

Homer keeps us in suspense for we do not meet the main character, Odysseus, for some time. This is called "buildup" of our interest and suspense. Also, the ending is a "cliffhanger," for we do not know how it will all end. Will Odysseus be able to reassert his mastery in his own home—after twenty years?

Homer includes for his characters moments of crisis. He involves them not only in outer conflict with circumstances and other people, but also in inner conflict with themselves. Thus Homer appeals to all ages and conditions, and deals with a broad spectrum of emotions.

The Pagan Idea of Man and Government

We cannot study America and Western Civilization without becoming aware of the presence of a heritage from Greece and from Rome. There are those today who claim that our institutions of government, our architecture, our city plans, our sciences, and our literature all reflect our debt to a pagan past. They point to many external symbols remaining with us in order to trace the lineage of our beginnings.

For the Christian there is the recognition that God is the disposer of men and nations. Thus God assigned to each nation a special role to plan, contributions to make, and all of these "separate stones and pillars" became building blocks to be used by "the Master Builder" as the Chain of Christianity moved westward to America.

If we remember that "the Glory that was Greece, and the Grandeur that was Rome" have vanished to remain only as emblems of a pagan past, we can see how God might use aspects from these nations to be recast by the Christians of our nations—fashioned anew for His purpose. Charles Bancroft in tracing the contributions of past civilizations before they reached America stated:

"All the past has contributed to the excellence of her foundation, and modern Europe has supplied her with the most desirable building material both of ideas and of men. Without Asia, Greece, and Rome, there would have been a very imperfect modern Europe; and without modern Europe, America must have begun at the beginning, with all the lessons, discoveries and discipline of thousands of years to learn." (*CHOC*, I, p. 9)

The Christian scholar admits the presence of the pagan elements in our national heritage, but he recognizes that without Christianity these elements would not have been found useful. Like the pillars of the Parthenon on the Acropolis in Athens, or the seats in the crumbling Colosseum in Rome, they would lie in the dust of the ages—monuments to a dead past. But, with the quickening spirit of the Gospel's westward move the best elements of the pagan past were utilized, particularly in America where the liberty of the individual could choose to use what served best to embellish the "Grand Temple of Civilization." Thus the Founding Father generations utilized the marble columned buildings to suggest dignity and order as they constructed the new capitol of the nation in Washington on the Potomac River. Many of the homes of the New Republic—the world's first Christian Republic—utilized classical architecture to express the beauty of Christian constitutional liberty.

Preparation for Christianity in History

God Uses Three Nations

"The three great historical nations had to contribute each in its own peculiar way, to prepare the soil for the planting of Christianity—the Jews on the side of the religious element; the Greeks on the side of science and art; the Romans; as masters of the world, on the side of the political element. When the fullness of time was arrived, and Christ appeared—when the goal of history had thus been reached—then it was, that through Him, and by the power of the spirit that proceeded from Him—the might of Christianity—all the threads, hitherto separated, of human development, were to be brought together and interwoven in one web." (*Teaching and Learning*, p. 160)

Greece—a Language for the New Testament

"If we think of the civilization of the Greeks, we have no difficulty in fixing on its chief characteristics. . . . We have only to do with this national character so far as, under divine Providence, it was made subservient to the spread of the Gospel.

"We shall see how remarkably it subserved this purpose, if we consider the tendency of the Greeks to trade and colonization. . . .To all these places they carried their arts and literature, their philosophy, their mythology, and their amusement. They carried also their arms and their trade.

"Of all the Greek elements . . . the spread of the language is the most important. That language, which is the richest and most delicate that the world has seen, became the language of theology. The Greek tongue became to the Christian more than it had been to the Roman or the Jew. . . . It was not an accident that the New Testament was written in Greek, the language which can best express the highest thoughts and worthiest feelings of the intellect and heart." (*Teaching and Learning*, p. 162)

Rome—a United World Empire for Channels of Communication

"The idea of law had grown up with the growth of the Romans; and wherever they went they carried it with them. Wherever their armies were marching or encamping, there always attended them, like a mysterious presence, the spirit of the City of Rome. Universal conquest and permanent occupation were the ends at which they aimed. . . . It is easy to see how much misery followed in the train of Rome's advancing greatness. Cruel suffering was a characteristic feature of the close of the republic. . . .

"It should be remembered, in the first place, that the Romans had already become Greek to some considerable extent, before they were the political masters of those eastern countries where the language, mythology, and literature of Greece had become more or less familiar. . . . Is it too much to say, that the general Latin conquest was providentially delayed till the Romans had sufficiently imbued with the language and ideas of their predecessors, and had incorporated many parts of that civilization with their own?

"And if the wisdom of the divine pre-arrangements is illustrated by the period of the spread of the Greek language, it is illustrated no less by that of the completion and maturity of the Roman government. When all parts of the civilized world were bound together in one empire, when one common organization pervaded the whole, when channels of communication were everywhere opened, when new facilities of travelling were provided, then was 'the fullness of time' (Galatians 4:4)—then the Messiah came. The Greek language had already been prepared as a medium for preserving and transmitting the doctrine; the Roman government was now prepared to help the progress even of that religion which it persecuted. The manner in which it spread through the provinces is well-exemplified in the life of St. Paul; his right of citizenship rescued him in Judea and in Macedonia; he converted one governor in Cyprus, was protected by another in Achaia, and was sent from Jerusalem to Rome by a third. The time was approaching, when all the complicated weight of the central tyranny and of the provincial governments was to fall on the new and irresistible religion. But before this took place, it had begun to grow up in close connection with all departments of the Empire." (*Teaching and Learning*, pp. 162–65)

The Jews—"Salvation is of the Jews" (John 4:6–39)

"In Judaism the true religion is prepared for man; in heathenism man is prepared for the true religion. The heathen preparation was partly intellectual and literary, as represented by the Greeks; and partly political and social as represented by the Romans. Jerusalem becomes the Holy City, Athens the city of culture, and Rome the city of power—all three factors find their answer and fulfillment in Christ.

"Judaism is in sharp contrast with the idolatrous nations of antiquity—it was like an oasis in a desert, clearly defined and isolated; separated and enclosed by a rigid moral and ceremonial law. The Holy Land itself, though in the midst of the three continents of the ancient world, and surrounded by the great nations, was separated from them by deserts south and east, by sea on the west, and by mountains on the north—thus securing to the Mosaic religion freedom to unfold itself and to fulfil its great work without disturbing influences. God was particular about his geographical arrangements." ("Lectures in History" [unpublished], Verna Hall)

A Study of Contrasting Influences
By Verna Hall

When our Lord taught He frequently used **contrast** as a means of heightening the appeal of the distinctly Christian idea of man and government—the flow of force and power in an individual's life. In the parables we read in the Parable of the Sower about three types of soil or character: the barren wayside, the stony ground, the thorns, all contrasted with the "good ground." In the Parable of the Two Foundations, one house was built upon sand, one on rock, with the evident result when the "rain descended, and the floods came, and the winds blew." While these parables referred to the life of the believer, they afford excellent examples of the use of **contrast** in teaching.

So as we become aware of the world of pagan mythology and idolatry, especially in the study of the Greeks and the Romans, we recognize their pervasive influence still in our world today. Therefore it is necessary to identify to our students and our children a contrast of foundations between the "Rock of our salvation"—Jesus Christ—and the sandy, shifting foundations upon which these make-believe deities are based. Moreover, since it is the nature of mythology to assume many faces, it is important for our students to see the clear-cut contrasts between the world of the pagan, past or present, and the redeemed life of the believer.

The pagan world is heartless; the individual is at the mercy and disposal of unpredictable forces and events. Propitiation and sacrifice must be made over and over again to satisfy these superhuman gods and goddesses. Consider a world where the external is more important than the internal, where a strength is measured by muscularity, where the intellect is measured by sophistry—false reasoning—and where the supernatural powers of man-made deities are bandied about among the gods whose own jealousies and domestic follies and sins are visited upon the poor humans who created them.

The Contrast between Christianity and Paganism

"Christianity could not have taken a firm hold on human nature if it had not penetrated it by its divine power, and thus verified itself to be indeed that which alone can satisfy the higher necessities of the inner man. This divine power of the Gospel revealed itself to the heathen in the lives of Christians, which `showed forth the virtues of him who had called them out of darkness into his marvelous light, and enabled them to walk as the children of God, in the midst of a perverse generation, among whom they shone as lights in the world.'

"They saw Christians meet death in the confidence of their faith with the greatest firmness and cheerfulness, oftentimes amidst extreme tortures. . . . Many asked, what gives men such energy to do and suffer everything on account of their convictions, in an age of such abject weakness, when we see all things bending before earthly power? Whoever proposed this question endeavoured to make himself acquainted with Christianity; and the consequence was, that the inquirer became captivated with the divine doctrine." (Neander, in *Teaching and Learning*, p. 210)

Paganism in Literature

What is a pagan? Noah Webster indicates in his 1828 *Dictionary* that a pagan is one to whom the Gospel has been presented—but who continues to worship false gods.

Paul's experience at Athens is an excellent example of a pagan city and of the peculiar nature of the Greek pagan philosophers who "spent their time in nothing else, but either to tell, or to hear some new thing." (Acts 17:21) As the Word tells us, Paul's heart was stirred by Athens "when he saw the city wholly given to idolatry." Essentially, the study of pagan literature is the study of a people who worshipped false gods—gods for every conceivable circumstance of their lives—idolaters. Pagan literature—Greek and Roman mythology—deals with the tales of superhuman deities, gods and goddesses, whom men and women put in charge of their lives. These gods were the subject of worship, sacrifice, propitiation, and vows. They became representative of a people who grew more and more materialistic.

Thomas Bulfinch (1796–1867), the great American student of mythology, states in his introduction to his study of the age of fable: "The religions of ancient Greece and Rome are extinct. The so-called divinities of Olympus have not a single worshipper among living men. They belong now not to the department of theology, but to those of literature and taste. There they still hold their place, and will continue to hold it, for they are too closely connected with the finest productions of poetry and art, both ancient and modern, to pass into oblivion."

Another student of American life, of the colonial mind, and the classical tradition, wrote: "We have come to see that the classical heritage ranks as a good third to the Bible and the English Common Law." (*The American Colonial Mind and the Classical Tradition*, Richard Gummere, 1916, 1960)

Definitions from Webster's 1828 *Dictionary*:

Mythology: "A system of fables or fabulous opinions and doctrines respecting the deities which heathen nations have supposed to preside over the world or to influence the affairs of it."

Supernatural: "Being beyond or exceeding the powers or laws of nature; miraculous. A **supernatural** event is one which is not produced according to the ordinary or established laws of natural things. . . . Now no human being can alter a law of nature. . . . Hence **supernatural** events or miracles can be produced only by the immediate agency of divine power."

Teacher Preparation and Presentation
Ben Hur: A Tale of the Christ
by Lew Wallace
Identifying the Chain of Christianity Moving Westward to America

Background Reading

The Christian History of the Constitution, Volume I: pp. 10–12, "Nation Making—the Roman Method." *Teaching and Learning America's Christian History: The Principle Approach,* pp. 159–66, "The Pagan Nations." Christ comes to a dying world, governmentally as well as morally. Three great historic nations fall. One world government of Rome enabled Paul to travel, until it crushed him out. Roman civil law in contrast with English. In Rome the Emperor was above the law.

Ben Hur is studied with the Notebook Approach: The teacher reads the novel aloud; students identify plot, setting, characterization, theme, and style.

Lew Wallace

An American Christian author who brings his understanding of individual liberty under constitutional government to bear upon his understanding of the Christian era and what it begins to promise as the Christian idea of man and government is introduced to the world.

Character is studied in terms of Biblical qualities and standards.

Ben Hur is a historical novel set in New Testament times. The novel presents the story of Christ through the eyes of fictitious contemporaries.

Wallace's autobiography contains an account of how he came to write *Ben Hur:* "At that time . . . I was not in the least influenced by religious sentiment. I had no convictions about God or Christ. I neither believed nor disbelieved in them. . . . Yet when the work was fairly begun, I found myself writing reverentially and frequently with awe." Being appalled by his ignorance in a discussion with a skeptic, he decided to study Christianity. He thought of using the story of the wise men as the first part of a book which would end with Christ's crucifixion. He had never been to the Holy Land, but he knew that the area and the times were well-known to scholars who would find any errors he might make, so he did much research during the writing of the novel. Wallace observes, "Long before I was through with my book, I became a believer in God and Christ." Later as resident minister to Turkey he was able to visit the Holy Land. (*Lew Wallace: An Autobiography.* Vol. II. New York: Harper & Bros. Publishers, 1906, pp. 927–28, 936)

CHAPTER SIX

THE HIGH SCHOOL
LITERATURE PROGRAM

Introduction to the
High School Literature Course

The teaching of literature on the Chain of Christianity is pertinent to forming a truly Biblical Christian worldview in the student. The philosophy of education here plays a key role in our reasoning, for America is inseparable from Christianity in its history. Had there been no Christianity, there would have been no America.

Thus literature must be studied in relation to the Chain of Christianity moving westward and the resultant liberty of the individual. We cannot then ignore the influence of English literature upon American literature.

Literature is the expression of the character of a nation. It tells us who we are as a people, where we came from, and what our purpose is. It is inseparable from our history. Thus to study American literature we must first study English literature.

Authors studied are measured by their relationship to the Chain of Christianity and by their literary excellence and influence. It is a fact that the major authors in England and America are those authors whose works support Biblical principles of life and character.

A high school literature program includes two years of English literature and two years of American literature.

Characteristics and Distinctions of the Program

Teachers must first study authors in order to present them and guide students through works provided with the background studies of the authors.

1. Each period is then studied in relation to the Chain of Christianity.
2. The appearance of liberty of the individual is traced as it develops historically.
3. The authors are identified as to their individuality of style, works, and influence.
4. Whole works rather than selections are studied where possible.
5. Literature becomes a testimony of the Hand of God in history.
6. Many authors exemplify talents directed and brought to fruition by the Lord.
7. Literature becomes a means of cultivating the feelings and tastes in accord with Biblical standards.

Note: These high school courses of literature refer to texts now out-of-print, but available through book search: *English Literature: Its History and Its Significance for the Life of the English-Speaking World*, by William J. Long. Boston: Ginn & Co., 1909, 1945; and *American Literature: A Study of the Men and the Books That in the Earlier and Later Times Reflect the American Spirit*, by William J. Long. Boston: Ginn & Co., 1913, 1964.

The Christian History Literature Approach Compared with Other Approaches to Teaching Literature

Current traditional programs in literature
present literature from a secular base.

Method ➤	Critique ➤	Source
The anthology organized on *thematic approach*—social, psychological, patriotic themes, i.e. "Love and Friendship," "Understanding Others," "Building a Better World."	Authors are forced into categories or themes. Authors are not distinguished for their own individuality. Selections are not always representative of the author's best. The use of "snippets' or "swatches"—a *Reader's Digest* approach. The emphasis is not upon literature, but on the themes.	Progressive education: "The true center of correlation on the school subjects is not science, nor literature, nor history, nor geography, but the child's own social activities." John Dewey, "My Pedagogic Creed," 1897.
The *survey approach* is organized in terms of type or period. Many authors are covered to give breadth of view.	This is a subject-centered approach. Literature is studied as a secular subject—literature for its own sake. It has no relationship to the life of the student.	Traditional, academic, secular.
The *historical approach* studies the major American and English authors chronologically.	This approach teaches chronologically but reverses the order, putting American literature first in the curriculum, then English literature. Students cannot see the influence of the English Bible upon English literature. Students cannot see the heritage of English literature given to America and how our nation built upon that heritage and contributed her own individuality.	Traditional and historical but does not show the Hand of God in history or literature.
The *Christian history literature program* studies authors in their relationship to the Chain of Christianity and to their contribution to the history of liberty.	Authors are studied in depth and whole works are studied intact. English literature is studied first, then American.	Literature becomes a testimony to the Hand of God in history. A Biblical worldview is cultivated.

Teaching Literature in the High School
Overview of the Four-Year High School Literature Program
Courses Studied in Relation to the Chain of Christianity

English Literature IIA: 9th Grade

1. **Anglo-Saxon Period** A.D. 450–1066—Roots of Character, Language, and Local Self-Government.

2. **Anglo-Norman Period 1066–1350**—Themes of Chivalry and Feudalism. Magna Charta—first protection of individual rights.

3. **Wycliffe and Chaucer Period 1350–1400**—The Bible, personal evangelism, the individual becomes prominent in literature.

4. **English Reformation Period 1400–1550**—Pagan authors studied. English martyrs bring forth the Bible in English.

5. **Elizabethan Age 1550–1620**—The flowering of English literature, culminating in King James Bible. Colonization of the New World.

6. **Puritan Age 1620–1660**—Christianity extended to government. The Age of Milton and Bunyan. Pilgrims separate.

English Literature IIB: 10th Grade

1. **Restoration Period 1660–1700**—Influence of Puritanism on the life and character of a nation.

2. **Eighteenth Century 1700–1800**—Age of Prose, revival of Romantic poetry. Themes of liberty. Bill of Rights. Loss of American colonies.

3. **Age of Romanticism 1800–1850**—God or man the source of liberty? Themes in poetry and fiction. Age of individualism and revolution.

4. **Victorian Age 1850–1900**—Idealism in literature conflicts with internal demands of Christianity. Industrial revolution, rise of Evolution, socialism.

5. **Twentieth Century 1900–Present**—Realism without Christianity becomes materialism. Influence of Fabian socialism in literature. Decline of Colonialism.

American Literature IIIA: 11th Grade

1. **Colonial Period 1607–1765**—Christian Individualism in the parent colonies: Virginia, Plymouth, Massachusetts Bay, Pennsylvania. Missionary writers. Contributions of the colonial clergy. Colonial best sellers.

2. **Literature of the American Revolution 1765–1787**—The influence of the clergy. American state papers reflect the colonists' familiarity with history and Biblical principles. Orations of liberty, sermons, letters, poetry, and satire. Biography and autobiography.

3. **Federal Period 1787–1840**—First fruits of the Republic in literature. The Federalist Papers—classic of American political writing. America's first men of letters, first poets, first novelists, western chronicles, and literary pioneers.

American Literature IIIB: 12th Grade

1. **Civil War Period 1840–1876**—Political orators, poets, essayists, novelists, and short-story writers. God preserves the union of the American states.

2. **National Expansion Period 1876–1925**—The diversity of America reflected geographically in regional literature. Seeds of breakdown.

3. **Twentieth Century 1925–Present**—Anti-capitalism. Decline of Biblical standards of life and literature. The "lost" generation. The persistence of the American spirit.

THE NOAH PLAN © 1997 • FOUNDATION FOR AMERICAN CHRISTIAN EDUCATION

English Literature IIA

Tracing the Nobler Stream of Liberty
Part One of a Two-Year Course of English Literature

Ninth Grade

Anglo-Saxon Period (with resources)
Anglo-Norman Period
Wycliffe and Chaucer Period
Reformation Period
Elizabethan Age
Puritan Age

English literature studied in relation to the
Chain of Christianity moving westward

CONTENTS

1. Course of Study Overview for each period

2. Leading Ideas and Ideals—based upon the Christian idea of man and government appearing and declining

3. Preparation and Presentation Charts—Background, Emphases, Readings

4. Principle Approach syllabi materials, including content for teacher and students for the Anglo-Saxon Period

---

The suggested resource book—*English Literature: Its History and Its Significance for the Life of the English-Speaking World*, by William J. Long. Boston: Ginn and Company, 1909, 1945—is presently out-of-print, but available through book search.

English Literature IIA Overview for Ninth Grade

Tracing the Nobler Theme of Liberty

Studied in relation to the Chain of Christianity moving westward

Development and Flowering of English Language – the Bible in English – the Reformation – the Pilgrims

Anglo-Saxon 450–1066	Anglo-Norman 1066–1350	Wycliffe and Chaucer 1350–1400	English Reformation 1400–1550	Elizabethan Age 1550–1620	Puritan Age 1620–1660
Beowulf (Raffel trans. Epic—5th C. Latin)	Geoffrey's History	Chaucer, Geoffrey (1340?–1400) *The Canterbury Tales* "The Prologue"	Malory's *Morte d'Arthur*	Spenser, Edmund *Shepherd's Calendar* *The Faerie Queene*	Milton, John Poetry, Prose, *Paradise Lost*
The Seafarer Lyric poem	Layamon's *Brut*	Mandeville's *Travels*	Caxton	Drayton, Michael Poetry	Herbert, George Poetry
Caedmon—7th C. First English Poet	Themes of Chivalry: *Sir Gawain and the Green Knight*	Langland, William *Piers Plowman*	Erasmus, Desiderius *In Praise of Folly*	Marlowe, Christopher Poetry	Donne, John Poetry
Bede, The Venerable "Father of English Learning"	*The Pearl*	Wycliffe, John 1324?–1384 "Father of English Prose." Translated first Bible into English, 1380.	More's *Utopia*	Bacon, Francis *Essays*	Bunyan, John *The Pilgrim's Progress*
Cynewulf – 8th C.	Men of Iron, Pyle		Tyndale, William New Testament	Hooker, Robert *Ecclesiastical Polity*	*A Reader's Guide to Religious Literature*, Batson
Anglo-Saxon Chronicle Begun A.D. 860	Boy's King Arthur, Lanier	*T & L*, pp. 166–68	The Great Bible, 1539	Hakluyt, *Defeat of the Spanish Armada*	
King Alfred "Father of English Literature"	*The Story of King Arthur and His Knights*, Pyle	*CHOC*, I, pp. 28A–29	*T & L*, pp. 334–37	Shakespeare, William Plays, Poetry	
Everyday Life in Roman and Anglo-Saxon Times, Quennell	*When Knights Were Bold*, Tappan	*Geoffrey Chaucer of England*, Chute	*CHOC*, I, pp. 30–31	King James Bible, 1611	
			Foxe's Book of Martyrs	Foxe, John *Book of Martyrs*	
				T & L, p. 173	
				CHOC, I, pp. 33–36	
				Shakespeare of London, Chute	

English Literature IIA for Ninth Grade

Tracing the Nobler Stream of Liberty
The History and Literature of England
Studied in relation to the Chain of Christianity moving westward

*Religion, like a Pilgrim westward bent
Knocking at all doors, ever as she went.
Religion stands on tiptoe in our land
Ready to pass to the American strand.*
—George Herbert

Guidelines for the Course

Anglo-Saxon Period: 450–1066

READING: *Beowulf – Caedmon – Alfred – Bede*

What qualities of Anglo-Saxon character become identified with the English character? with American character?

What enabled Caedmon to produce such marvelous poems without training? Describe the contribution of Alfred to the Chain of Christianity in (1) government, (2) education, (3) literature. See Bede.

Anglo-Norman Period: 1066–1350

READING: Text: *English Literature*, Long.

In what specific ways did the Norman Invasion contribute to literature in England as God was preparing this language for the Bible in English.

Age of Wycliffe and Chaucer: 1350–1400

READING: *The Canterbury Tales*

Selections from Wycliffe

Why can the work of Wycliffe be called an important link on the Chain of Christianity which directly affects us through the Pilgrims? Cite some examples of his life and testimony in (1) religion (2) government, and (3) literature.

What principle does Chaucer establish in literature necessary to a Christian literature?

English Reformation: 1400–1550

READING: *The Boy's King Arthur*—Malory (Sidney Lanier, editor). Text: *English Literature*, Long

This period of the Renaissance is in contrast to the period of the Reformation. In the revival of learning, men turned chiefly to paganism for direction.

Describe why this period can also be called the "era of the American settlement."

What preparations were taking place which would advance the Chain of Christianity moving westward? What did humanism do for men?

How is Erasmus used as a link in the Chain of Christianity to bring about the English Reformation?

How was chivalry influenced by Christianity? How was Christianity influenced by chivalry?

Describe the life and testimony of William Tyndale. What was the unique contribution of the Tyndale Bible to the revival of learning?

Elizabethan Age: 1550–1620

READINGS: Spenser. Text: *English Literature*, Long

Bacon: "Of Riches," "Of Friendship," "Of Studies," "Of Truth"

Shakespeare: *Five Plays of Shakespeare*; Schweikert

Explain Spenser's use of allegory as a means of introducing Christian idealism into his *Faerie Queene*. What is the literary contribution of the Spenserian stanza?

Why can Shakespeare truly be called the "Bard of the Bible?"

What events in this age contribute to the Chain of Christianity moving westward?

Puritan Age: 1620–1660

READINGS: Text: *English Literature*, Long

Poetry of Donne, Herbert

Milton: *Paradise Lost* (Viking Portable)

Bunyan: *The Pilgrim's Progress*

Why was the Puritan Age and not the Elizabethan Age the age of religious freedom and individual liberty?

Describe the contributions of Milton and Bunyan to the Chain of Christianity moving westward.

In the forthcoming Spanish Armada, both evangelical Christians and those who sought to return England to Rome were providentially used by God to prepare England. Can you describe some of the events in the Providence of God? See Hakluyt.

Why was England called "a people of the Book"? See Green.

How did America profit from the Puritan Age in England?

Why has Bunyan appealed to Americans in every century? Is he still relevant today?

John Milton had the greatest single influence of any author upon Americans. Identify his influence in the following areas: upon the clergy; upon the statesmen of the American Revolution; upon educators in the New Republic; in defense of Christianity.

What ages does Herbert encompass in his poem "The Church Militant"?

Teaching the Anglo-Saxon Period

450–1066

Preparation and Presentation

Background	Emphases	Readings

1. A brief history of the Angles and Saxons
  a) Selections from *A Short History of the English People*, Green, 1894.
  b) *A Child's History of England*, Dickens
  c) Bede (Long's *English Literature*)
 	
2. Anglo-Saxon poetry
 	
3. Christian writers
	1. The coming of the Englishmen into Britain.
	
	2. Anglo-Saxon life and language
	
	3. The Saxon Scop, or minstrel, sings themes of battle and of the sea. Love of the sea is a persistent love of Englishmen.
	
	4. Scholarship from the monasteries. The Anglo-Saxon Kingdom of Northumbria and the Venerable Bede, "father of English learning."
		Selection from Bede's *Ecclesiastical History*
		
		The first epic heroic poem *Beowulf*, translated by Raffel
		  Note the characteristics of Anglo-Saxon literary style as *accent* and *alliteration.*
		
		The Seafarer—read aloud.
		
		Caedmon—7th C. (See the account found in Bede.)
		
		Cynewulf—8th C.

4. Alfred the Great, the father of English literature	5. Alfred's contributions to Christian government, education, and literature. His life and character. 6. Works in English for the free-born Englishman to read.	Alfred's Translations Old English Laws Boethius's *Consolation*
5. Anglo-Saxon character	7. The best qualities of the Anglo-Saxon character; worst. What is needed to balance this character? How is God's principle of the individuality of nations seen in this character?	*The Anglo-Saxon Chronicle*

Leading Ideas and Ideals of the
Anglo-Saxon Period
450–1066

"Briefly the Anglo-Saxon way of life is summed up in five great principles:

Their love of personal freedom;
Their responsiveness to nature;
Their religion;
Their reverence for womanhood;
And their struggle for glory as a ruling motive in every noble life."
(*English Literature*, Long, p. 26)

The Anglo-Saxon language is the language of our English Bible.

1. Root words from Anglo-Saxon include God, Man, Father, Mother, Bread, and House.

2. See Webster's 1828 *Dictionary* for other Anglo-Saxon words, the everyday things common to life, words which convey ideals of Love, Home, Faith, Heroism, and Liberty.

3. The Anglo-Saxon gave our language its masculine qualities of Strength, Directness, and Simplicity.

The Christian Idea of Man and Government

1. The laws of the Anglo-Saxons are among the first written records in our language.

   a) Alfred the Great, 849–899, king of the West Saxons, codified the laws of Anglo-Saxon England, a codification which shows a strong Biblical influence.

   b) A government of laws and not of men.

2. Blackstone's *Commentaries* were written some 900 years after Alfred collected and systematized English common law. Like Alfred, Blackstone based human law upon God's LAW. See *CHOC*, I, pp. 139–46.

3. King James Version of 1611 was the culmination of the purpose and development of the English language. See *CHOC*, I, p. 36, for predominance of Anglo-Saxon words in the 1611 edition.

4. See Noah Webster's Introduction to the 1828 *Dictionary*. In this article, Webster deals with the Biblical origin of language. He identifies the Saxon as our "Mother Tongue."

Noah Webster produced alone the first American translation of the Bible from the original languages. Noted was his regard for "the strong, simple Anglo-Saxon language" which characterizes our best translations.

Chronology of the Anglo-Saxon Period

History		The Christian Idea of Man and Government	
447	Landing of South Saxons		
449 (?)	Landing of Hengist and Horsa in Britain		
547	Angles settle Northumbria	547	Gilda's *History*
597	Landing of Augustine and his monks; Conversion of Kent.		
617	Eadwine, king of Northumbria		
635–665	Coming of St. Aidan; Conversion of Northumbria	664	Caedmon at Whitby
		673–735	Bede
		750	Cynewulf poems
867	Danes conquer Northumbria.	860	*Anglo-Saxon Chronicle* begun.
871	Alfred, king of Wessex		
878	Defeat of Danes; Peace of Wedmore		
901	Death of Alfred	991	Last known poem of the Anglo-Saxon period, "The Battle of Maldon," otherwise called "Byrhtnoth's Death."
1013–1042	Danish Period		
1016	Cnut, king		
1042	Edward the Confessor; Saxon period restored.		
1049	Westminster Abbey begun.		
1066	Harold, last of Saxon kings; Norman Conquest		

Teaching English Literature
In Relation to the Chain of Christianity Moving Westward
Anglo-Saxon Period

Historical Background: Roots of Local Self-Government

In ancient England, local self-government is found in connection with the political and territorial divisions of tythings, hundreds, burghs, counties, and shires, in which the body of the inhabitants had a voice in managing their own affairs. Hence it was the germinal idea of the Anglo-Saxon Polity. (*The Christian History of the Constitution of the United States of America*, Hall, 1960, pp. 149–50)

A Short History of the English People, by J. R. Green (1837–1883) This history was written in 1874 and is not only a standard work in this field but one of the most beautifully written histories of our English origins. Green's history is a Christian History of England.

From Chapter I—The English Kingdoms, 607–1013
Section I. Britain and the English

"For the fatherland of the English race we must look far away from England itself. In the fifth century after the birth of Christ, the one country which bore the name of England was what we now call *Sleswick*, a district in the heart of the peninsula which parts the Baltic from the Northern seas. . . . The dwellers in this district were one out of three tribes, all belonging to the same Low German branch of the Teutonic family, who at the moment when history discovers them were bound together into a confederacy by the ties of a common blood and a common speech.

"To the north of the English lay the tribe of the **Jutes**, whose name is still preserved in their district of **Jutland**. To the south of them the tribe of **Saxons** wandered over the sand flats of **Holstein**, and along the marches of **Friesland** and the **Elbe**. How close was the union of these tribes was shown by their use of a common name, while the choice of this name points out the tribe which at the moment when we first meet them must have been the strongest and most powerful in the confederacy. Although they were all known as **Saxons** by the Roman people who touched them only on their southern border

where the Saxons dwelt, and who remained ignorant of the very existence of the English or the Jutes, the three tribes bore among themselves the name of the central tribe of their league, the name of **Englishmen**.

"Of the temper and life of these English folk in this Old England we know little. But, from the glimpses which we catch of them when conquest had brought these Englishmen to the shores of Britain, their political and social organization must have been that of the German race to which they belonged."

The "Free-Necked Man"

"The basis of their society was the **Free Land-Holder**. In the English tongue he alone was known as 'the man,' or 'the churl'; and two English phrases set his freedom vividly before us. He was the 'free-necked man,' whose long hair floated over a neck that had never bent to a lord. He was 'the weaponed man,' who alone bore spear and sword, for he alone possessed the right which in such a state of society formed the main check upon lawless outrage, the right of private war. Justice had to spring from each man's personal action and every freeman was his own avenger. But, even in the earliest forms of English society of which we catch traces, this right of self-defense was being modified and restricted by a growing sense of public justice. The 'blood-wite,' or compensation in money for personal wrong, was the first effort of the tribe as a whole to regulate private revenge. The freeman's life and the freeman's limb had each on this system its legal price. 'Eye for eye,' ran the rough code, and 'life for life,' or for each fair damages. We see a further step toward the recognition of a wrong as done not to the individual man, but to the people at large. . . . The price of life or limb was paid, not by the wrong-doer to the man he wronged, but by the family or house of the wrong-doer to the family or house of the wronged. Order and law were thus made to rest in each little group of English people upon the blood-bond which knit its families together. . . . From this sense of the value of the family bond as a means of restraining the wrong-doer by forces which the tribe as a whole did not as yet possess sprang the first rude forms of English justice."

The Freeman as a Freeholder

"Land with the German race seems everywhere to have been the accompaniment of full freedom. The freeman was strictly the freeholder, and the exercise of his full rights as free member of the community to which he belonged was inseparable from the possession of his 'holding.' The landless man ceased for all practical purposes to be free, though he was no man's slave. In the very earliest glimpses we get of the German race we see them a race of land-holders and land-tillers."

Tacitus on the Independent Freeholder

"Tacitus, the first Roman who looked closely at these destined conquerors of Rome, found them a nation of farmers, pasturing on the forest glades around their villages, and plowing their village fields. A feature which at once struck him as parting them from the civilized world to which he himself belonged was their hatred of cities and their love even within their little settlements of a jealous independence. 'They live apart,' he says, 'each by himself, as woodside, plain or fresh spring attracts him.'"

The Tree of Liberty and Law

"Within the village we find from the first a marked social difference between two orders of its indwellers. The bulk of its homesteads were those of its freemen or "ceorls"; but among these were the larger homes of "eorls," (earls) or men distinguished among their fellows by noble blood, who were held in an hereditary reverence, and from whom the 'ealdormen' of the village were chosen as leaders in wartime or rulers in time of peace. But the choice was purely a **voluntary** one, and the man of noble blood enjoyed no legal privilege above his fellows. The actual sovereignty within the settlement resided in the body of its freemen. Their homesteads clustered round a moot-hill, or round a **sacred tree**, where the whole community met to administer its own justice and to frame its own laws."

(See pages 149–50 of CHOC, I, for the germinal idea of self-government—"where the law was administered, the law was made.")

The Germinal Idea of England's Parliament

"Here [at the Tree of Liberty and Law] the 'witan,' the wise men of the village, met to settle questions of peace and war, to judge just judgment, and frame wise laws, as their descendants, the wise men of a later England, meet in Parliament at Westminster, to frame laws and do justice for the great empire which has sprung from this little body of farmer-commonwealths in Sleswick."

The Anglo-Saxons Invade England

In the year 55 B.C. Julius Caesar, in one of his Gallic campaigns, crossed the twenty-mile channel which separated Britain from Europe. Having set foot upon the British Isles Caesar made no attempts to colonize the islands. In fact, almost one hundred years would pass before the Roman Emperor Claudius, in A.D. 43 overcame the Celtic Britons and established Roman government.

Rome's mark on Britain can today be found in remains of its walls and roads for the empire-builders always endeavored to unite externally its provinces. But as the total Roman Empire found its method of nation-making weakened by centralization within and attack from without, the Roman legions left Briton and withdrew back to the continent of Europe.

It was at this moment in history that the three major tribes of the Anglo-Saxons—the Angles, the Saxons, and the Jutes from the northwest coast of Germany and the Danish peninsula—began their raids on the coast of Britain. In 449 the Jutes under Hengist and Horsa landed on the coast of Kent—beginning the actual history of the English nation.

Our Anglo-Saxon Heritage Today

To this first period of English history and literature, we are indebted for three contributions which affect our lives as American Christians today:

> The English Bible
>
> Local Self-Government
>
> The Anglo-Saxon Character

Let us look briefly at these three aspects of our Anglo-Saxon heritage.

First, what did the Anglo-Saxons contribute to our Bible? We see that for more than one thousand years the English language was providentially prepared to bring forth the English Bible—the noblest flower of which was the King James Version in 1611. Nine-tenths of the words in this Bible are of Saxon origin, for, as Noah Webster reminds us: "Anglo-Saxon is our Mother tongue." Anglo-Saxon gives to the English language its best qualities of strength and power. One might say the masculine qualities of our language come to us from the Anglo-Saxon.

The Lindisfarne Gospels are the oldest existing translations of the Bible in English. The Gospel-book is actually written in huge Latin illuminated words, with their individual style and color. But between each line, in unadorned script, appears the Anglo-Saxon translation. Thus these precious interlinear vernacular versions, while not complete translations, and at best sporadic efforts, indicate the degree to which the Word struggled to free itself from the clasp of scholars and to emerge into the language of free men (A.D. 700).

Local Self-Government

A large part of what we must love and venerate in our customs, laws, and institutions originated among our Anglo-Saxon ances-

tors. Liberty was the spring and principle of their political associations and pervaded the few civil institutions which their habits required and their humors permitted.

The Christian History of the Constitution of the United States of America: Christian Self-Government by Verna M. Hall, traces the development of the idea of local self-government:

> The idea of local self-government was historical at the time of the colonization of North America. Among the Germanic ancestors of the emigrants, the custom was so general for the inhabitants of a district to control their local affairs, that it has been said, "One leading principle pervaded the primeval polity of the Goths: where the law was administered, the law was made" and they filled all Europe for five hundred years with the fame of their exploits, and were the first nation beyond the Danube to receive Christianity. (pp. 149-50)

This was "the germinal idea of the Anglo-Saxon polity."

The Anglo-Saxon Character

Even before it was touched by the influence of Christianity, was distinct from its neighbors—a fearless and enterprising spirit, and a personal dignity and high-minded temper were nourished; and the hardy and manly virtues became pleasing habits. In this life of constant activity, want, privation, courage, vigilance, endurance, and exertion, the female virtues were called perpetually into action; and their uses were felt to be so important, that the fair sex obtained among all the tribes of ancient Germany a rank, an estimation, and an attachment, which were unknown in all the civilized world of antiquity, and which the spirit of Christianity has since matured and completed.

Charles Dickens, in *A Child's History of England*, makes the following statement regarding the persistence of the Anglo-Saxon character:

> I have more to tell of the Saxons yet, but I stop to say this now, because under the Great Alfred, all the best

points of the English Saxon character were first encouraged, and in him first shown. It has been the greatest character among the nations of the earth. Wherever the descendants of the Saxon race have gone, have sailed, or otherwise made their way, even to the remotest regions of the world, they have been patient, persevering, never to be broken in spirit, never to be turned aside from enterprises on which they have resolved. In Europe, Asia, Africa, America, the whole world over; in the desert, in the forest, on the sea; scorched by a burning sun, or frozen by ice that never melts; the Saxon blood remains unchanged. Wheresoever that race goes, there, law and industry, and safety for life and property, and all the great results of steady perseverance, are certain to arise.

Teaching and Learning America's Christian History: The Principle Approach, by Rosalie Slater, discusses the problems of classroom government and of the subversion of our American Christian character whose roots found some expression in the Anglo-Saxon character. Study pages 104 and 105 of the transformation of America's character through education. Ask yourself if this is the direction which will best promote the propagation of the Gospel.

Read pages 188–90 in *T & L* as Pilgrim Self-Government is studied and we see again some aspects of our Anglo-Saxon expression of this character which had initiative and industry and possessed self-reliance and confidence. Then turn to pages 221–23 where the character of socialism is set against that of the Pilgrim. We today are watching American education detract from our Anglo-Saxon heritage of the King James Version of the Bible, of local self-government, of our Anglo-Saxon character. The question for us as American Christian educators is: "What do my curriculum and methodology promote of those rigorous qualities which are essential if the liberty of the Gospel and the liberty of free men are to continue in this land?

Latin Contribution. The Anglo-Saxon character of the eleventh century was as yet crude and unrefined. It needed the balance of its Latin counterparts. In God's timetable, this appeared with the Norman Invasion of 1066.

Selections from Bede's
Ecclesiastical History of the English Nation

From Select Translations from Old English Prose, Albert S. Cook and Chauncey B. Tinker, 1968 (pp. 3–22).

The chief source of our knowledge of the life of Bede [673–735] is his own account of himself at the close of the *Ecclesiastical History*: "I, Bede, the servant of God, and priest of the monastery of the blessed apostles Peter and Paul, which is at Wearmouth and Jarrow, being born in the territory of that same monastery, was given at seven years of age to be educated by the most revered Abbot Benedict, and afterwards by Ceolfrith; and spending all the remaining time of my life in that monastery, I wholly applied myself to the study of Scripture, and, amidst the observance of regular discipline, and the daily care of singing in the church, I always took delight in learning, teaching, and writing. In the nineteenth year of my age, I received deacon's orders; in the thirtieth, those of the priesthood—both of them by the ministry of the most reverend Bishop John, and by order of the Abbot Ceolfrith. From which time till this fifty-ninth year of my age, I have made it my business, for the use of me and mine, to compile out of the works of the venerable Fathers, and to interpret and explain according to their meaning, these following pieces." Bede apparently spent his entire youth and manhood at Jarrow, though it is not impossible that this quiet life was interrupted by a journey to Rome.

Bede's Description of Britain and Ireland

"Britain, an island in the ocean, formerly called Albion, is situated between the north and west, facing, though at a considerable distance, the coasts of Germany, France, and Spain, which form the greatest part of Europe. It extends eight hundred miles in length towards the north, and is two hundred miles in breadth, except where several promontories extend further in breadth, by which its compass is made to be 4875 miles.

"The island excels in fruits and trees, and is well adapted for feeding cattle and beasts of burden. It also produces vines in some places, and has plenty of land- and water-fowl of various sorts; it is remarkable also for rivers abounding in fish, and plentiful springs. It has the greatest plenty of salmon and eels; seals are also frequently taken, and dolphins, as also whales; besides many sorts of shellfish, such as mussels, in which are often found excellent pearls of all colors—red, purple, violet, and green—but mostly white. There is also a great abundance of cockles, of which the scarlet dye is made—a most beautiful color, which never fades with the heat of the sun or the washing of the rain; but the older it is, the more beautiful it becomes. It has both salt and hot springs, and from them flow rivers which furnish hot baths, proper for all ages and both sexes, and arranged in separate places, according as each person may prefer. For water, as St. Basil says, receives the heating quality when it runs along certain metals, and becomes not only hot, but scalding. Britain has also many veins of metals, as copper, iron, lead, and silver; it has much and excellent jet, which is black and burns when fire is applied to it; when heated, it drives away serpents; being warmed by rubbing, it holds fast whatever is applied to it; like amber. The island was formerly embellished with twenty-eight noble cities, besides innumerable castles, which were all strongly secured with walls, tower, gates and locks.

"From its lying almost under the North Pole, the nights are light in summer, so that at midnight the beholders are often in doubt whether the evening twilight still continues, or that of the morning is coming on; for the sun, in the night, returns under the earth through the northern regions, at no great distance from them. For this reason the days are of a great length in summer, as, on the contrary, the nights are in winter, for the sun then withdraws into the southern parts, so that the nights are eighteen hours long.

Thus the nights are extraordinarily short in summer, and the days in winter, that is, of only six equinoctial hours; whereas in Armenia, Macedonia, Italy, and other countries of the same latitude, the longest day or night extends but to fifteen hours, and the shortest to nine.

"This island at present, following the number of the books in which the divine law was written, contains five languages—those of the English, Britons, Scots, Picts, and Latins— each examining and confessing one and the same knowledge of the highest truth and of true sublimity. The Latin tongue is, by the study of the Scriptures, become common to all the others.

"At first this island had no other inhabitants but the Britons, from whom it derived its name, and who, coming over into Britain, as is reported, from Armorica, possessed themselves of the southern parts thereof. When they, beginning at the south, had made themselves masters of the greatest part of the island, it happened that the nation of the Picts—from Scythia, as is reported—putting to sea in a few long ships, were driven by the winds beyond the shores of Britain, and arrived on the northern coast of Ireland, where finding the nation of the Scots, they begged to be allowed to settle among them, but could not succeed in obtaining their request.

"Ireland is the greatest island next to Britain, and lies to the west of it; but as it is shorter than Britain to the north, so on the other hand it runs out far beyond it to the south, opposite to the northern parts of Spain, though a spacious sea lies between them. The Picts, as has been said, arriving in this island by sea, desired to have a place granted them in which they might settle. The Scots answered that the island could not contain them both; 'but we can give you good advice,' said they, 'what to do; we know there is another island, not far from ours to the eastward, which we often see at a distance when the days are clear. If you will go thither, you will obtain settlements; or if they should oppose you, you shall have our assistance.'

"The Picts, accordingly, sailing over into Britain, began to inhabit the northern parts thereof, for the Britons were possessed of the southern. Now the Picts had no wives, and asked them of the Scots, who would not consent to grant them upon any terms than that when any difficulty should arise, they should choose a king from the female royal race rather than from the male; which custom, as is well known, has been observed among the Britons and the Picts, received a third nation, the Scots, who, migrating from Ireland under the leader Reuda, either by fair means or by force of arms secured to themselves those settlements among the Picts which they still possess. From the name of their commander, they are to this day called Dalreudins; for their language Dal signifies a part.

"Ireland, in breadth, and for wholesomeness and serenity of climate, far surpasses Britain, for the snow scarcely ever lies there above three days; no man makes hay in the summer for winter's provision, or builds stable for his beasts of burden. No reptiles are found there, and no snake can live there; for though often carried thither out of Britain, as soon as the ship comes near the shore, and the scent of the air reaches them, they die. . . . The island abounds in milk and honey, nor is there any want of vines, fish, or fowl; and it is remarkable for deer and goats. It is properly the country of the Scots, who, migrating from thence, as has been said, added a third nation to Britain to the Britons and the Picts. There is a very large gulf of the sea, which formerly divided the nation of the Picts from the Britons; which gulf runs from the west very far into the land, where, to this day, stands the strong city of the Britons, called Alcluith. The Scots, arriving on the north side of this bay, settled themselves there."

The Coming of the English

"In the year of our Lord 449 [really 450], Martian being made Emperor with Valentinian— the forty-sixth from Augustus—ruled the empire seven years. Then the nation of the

Angles, or Saxons, being invited by the aforesaid king, arrived in Britain with three long ships, and had a place assigned them to reside in by the same king, in the eastern part of the island, that they might thus appear to be fighting for the country, while their real intentions were to enslave it. Accordingly they engaged with the enemy, who were come from the north to give battle, and obtained the victory; which being known at home in their own country, as also the fertility of the country and the cowardice of the Britons, a more considerable fleet was quickly sent over, bringing a still greater number of men, which, being added to the former, made up an invincible army. The newcomers received of the Britons a place to inhabit, upon condition that they should wage war against their enemies for the peace and security of the country, while the Britons agreed to furnish them with pay.

"Those who came over were of the three most powerful nations of Germany—Saxons, Angles, and Jutes. From the Jutes are descended the people of Kent and of the Isle of Wight, and those also in the province of the West Saxons who are to this day called Jutes, seated opposite the Isle of Wight. From the Saxons—that is, the country which is now called Old Saxony—came the East Saxons, the South Saxons, and the West Saxons. From the Angles—that is, the country which is called Angulus, and which is said to remain desert from that time to this day, between the provinces of the Jutes and the Saxons—are descended the East Angles, the Midland Angles, the Mercians, all the race of the Northumbrians, that is, of those nations that dwell on the north side of the river Humber, and the other nations of the Angles. The first two commanders are said to have been Hengist and Horsa; of whom Horsa, being afterwards slain in battle by the Britons, was buried in the eastern parts of Kent, where a monument bearing his name is still in existence. They were the sons of Wihtgils, son of Witta, son of Wecta, son of Woden; from whose stock the royal lines of many provinces deduce their original.

"In a short time, swarms of the aforesaid nations came over into the island, and they began to increase so much that they became terrible to the natives themselves who had invited them. Then, having on a sudden entered into league with the Picts, whom they had by this time repelled by the force of their arms, they began to turn their weapons against their confederates. At first they obliged them to furnish a greater quantity of the provisions; and, seeking an occasion to quarrel, protested that unless more plentiful supplies were brought them, they would break the confederacy, and ravage all the island; nor were they backward in putting their threats in execution. In short, the fire kindled by the hands of these heathen proved God's just revenge for the crimes of the people, not unlike that which, being once lighted by the Chaldeans, consumed the walls of the city of Jerusalem. For the barbarous conquerors acting here in the same manner, or rather the just Judge ordaining that they should so act, they plundered all the neighboring cities and country, spread the conflagration from the eastern to the western sea without any opposition, and covered almost every part of the devoted island. Public as well as private structures were overturned; the priests were everywhere slain before the altars; the prelates and the people, without any respect of persons, were destroyed with fire and sword; nor was there any to bury those who had been thus cruelly slaughtered. Some of the miserable remainder, being taken in the mountains, were butchered in heaps. Others, spent with hunger, came forth and submitted themselves to the enemy for food, being destined to undergo perpetual servitude, if they were not killed even upon the spot. Some, with sorrowful hearts, fled beyond the seas. Others, continuing in their own country, led a miserable life in fear and anxiety among the woods, rocks, and mountains."

A Victory for the Britons

"When the victorious army, having destroyed and dispersed the natives, had returned home to their own settlements, the Britons began by degrees to take heart and gather strength, sallying out of the lurking-places where they had concealed themselves, and unanimously imploring the divine assistance, that they might not utterly be destroyed. They had at that time for their leader Ambrosius Aurelius, a modest man, who alone, by chance, of the Roman nation had survived the storm in which his parents, who were of the royal race, had perished. Under him the Britons revived, and offering battle to the victors, by the help of God came off victorious. From that day sometimes the natives and sometimes their enemies prevailed, till the year of the siege of Mount Badon, when they made no small slaughter of those invaders, about forty-four years after their arrival in England."

The Sending of Augustine

"In the year of our Lord 582, Maurice, the fifty-fourth from Augustus, ascended the throne, and reigned twenty-one years. In the tenth year of his reign, Gregory, a man renowned for learning and behavior, was promoted to the apostolical see of Rome, and presided over it thirteen years, six months, and ten days. He, being moved by divine inspiration, in the fourteenth year of the same emperor, and about the one hundred and fiftieth after the coming of the English into Britain, sent the servant of God, Augustine, and with him several other monks who feared the Lord, to preach the word of God to the English nation."

Augustine's Manner of Life

"As soon as they entered the dwelling-place assigned them, they began to imitate the course of life practised in the primitive church: applying themselves to frequent prayer, watching, and fasting; preaching the word of life to as many as they could; despising all worldly things, as not belonging to them; receiving only their necessary food from those they taught; living themselves in all respects conformably to what they prescribed to others; and being always disposed to suffer any adversity, and even to die, for that truth which they preached. In short, several believed and were baptized, admiring the simplicity of their innocent life and the sweetness of their heavenly doctrine. There was on the east side of the city a church dedicated to the honor of St. Martin, built while the Romans were still in the island, wherein the queen, who, as has been said before, was a Christian, used to pray. In this they first began to meet, to sing, to pray, to say mass, to preach, and to baptize, till the king, being converted to the faith, allowed them to preach openly, and build or repair churches in all places.

"When he, among the rest, induced by the unspotted life of these holy men and their delightful promises, which many miracles they proved to be most certain, believed and was baptized, greater numbers began daily to flock together to hear the word, and forsaking their heathen rites, to associate themselves by faith to the unity of the holy church of Christ. Their conversion the king so far encouraged as that he compelled none to embrace Christianity, but only showed more affection to the believers, as to his fellow-citizens in the heavenly kingdom. For he had learned from his instructors and leaders unto salvation that the service of Christ ought to be voluntary, not brought about by compulsion. Nor was it long before he gave Canterbury, with such possessions or different kinds as were necessary for their subsistence."

Selections from Boethius's
Consolation of Philosophy

"Anicius Manlius Torquatus Severinus Boethius (ca. 475–524), a Roman patrician and consul in the reign of Theodoric, was one of the most noted men of the Middle Ages. Although in all probability only a nominal Christian, he became identified, in the minds of the medieval churchmen, with the opponents of the Arian heresy, and was canonized in the eighth century. He translated many of the works of Plato and Aristotle, and these, together with his commentaries upon them, exercised a great influence upon medieval philosophy, as well as upon his greatest work, the famous *Consolation of Philosophy*. This book, said to have been written during his imprisonment by Theodoric, is preserved in hundreds of manuscripts, and was regarded as the standard handbook of philosophy until the Renaissance."

From *Select Translations from Old English Prose*, Cook and Tinker (pp. 116–24)

Alfred's Preface

"King Alfred was the translator of this work, and turned it from the Latin of the books into English, as is now done. Sometimes he put word for word, sometimes meaning for meaning, as he could interpret most clearly and intelligibly, on account of the sundry and manifold worldly duties which often beset him both in mind and in body. It is very hard for us to enumerate the cares which in his day came upon the kingdoms he had acquired; but nevertheless he studied this book, and translated it from Latin into English, and turned it afterwards into verse, as is now done. And now he prays and in God's name beseeches every one who desires to read this book to pray for him, and not to blame him if he understands it better than he [Alfred] could; because each man according to the measure of his understanding and according to his leisure, must speak that which he speaks and do that which he does."

Alfred's Account of Boethius

"At the time when Goths from the country of Scythia waged war against the Roman Empire, with their kings Radagaisus and Alaric, they seized the city of Rome, and reduced to subjection all the kingdom of Italy which lies between the mountains and the island of Sicily. After the aforesaid kings, Theodoric came to the throne. This Theodoric was an Amuling; he was a Christian, but persisted in the Arian heresy. He vowed friendship to the Romans, and that they should remain in possession of their former rights; but he kept that promise very poorly, and came to a grievous end by a great crime; this was that, in addition to innumerable other ill deeds, he had Pope John put to death. At that time there was a certain consul—'heretoga,' as we say—who was named Boethius; he was exceeding wise in knowledge of books and in the ways of the world. He observed the manifold wrongs which King Theodoric was committing against Christianity and against the Roman senators. Then he recalled the favors and the ancient rights which they had had under the Caesars, their former lords; and he began to meditate and to ponder within himself how he could take the kingdom from the unrighteous king, and bring it under the control of orthodox and righteous men. Then he secretly sent letters to the emperor at Constantinople, the chief city of the Greeks and their royal seat, because the emperor was of the family of their former lords. In these they besought him to help them to their Christian faith and their former rights. When the cruel King Theodoric learned this, he gave orders to cast him into prison, and there keep him in ward. Now when it came to pass that this excellent man fell into such distress, he was troubled in spirit by so much the more as his mind had been the more accustomed to worldly prosperity; and in prison he took no thought of comfort, but fell down prone upon the ground and prostrated himself in anguish and despair, and began to bewail; and he sang thus. . . ."

The Emptiness of Fame

"When Wisdom had uttered this speech, he began to chant, and sang thus:

'Whosoever wishes to have false fame and vain glory, let him behold on the four sides of him how spacious is the vault of heaven, and how narrow is the space of earth, though to us it seems wide. Then he may be ashamed to the extent of his fame, since he can not even spread it over this narrow earth. Ah ye proud, why do ye desire to bear this deadly yoke upon your necks? Or why do ye labor so vainly to extend your fame among many peoples? Though indeed it should come to pass that the uttermost people extol your name and praise you in many tongues, and though a man wax great because of the nobility of his birth, and prosper in all riches and all glory, yet death cares not for such things, but despises the noble, and devours the rich and the poor alike, and brings them to one level. Where are now the bones of the famous and wise goldsmith, Wayland? I said "The wise" for this reason, because the skil-ful can never lose his skill, nor can it be taken from him more easily than the sun can be removed from its station. Where now are the bones of Wayland, or who knows now where they were? Or where now is the famous and sagacious Roman consul, who was called Brutus, by another name Cassius? Or the wise and steadfast Cato, who was also a Roman consul? He was recognized as a philosopher. Have not these long vanished? and no man knows where they are now. What is now left of them except a little fame, and a name written with few letters? And yet worse, we know many famous men departed, worthy to be remembered, of whom very few have any knowledge. But many lie dead, entirely forgotten, so that not even fame makes them known. Though ye think and desire to live long here in this world, in what shall it be better for you? Does not death still come, though he come late, and take you from this world? And what avail then will glory be to you, at least to those who the second death will seize and hold for ever'?"

Selections from Bishop Asser's *Life of King Alfred*

The work was written by the Bishop in the lifetime of King Alfred.

Alfred's Rearing

"He was extraordinarily beloved by both his father and mother, and indeed by all the people, beyond all his brothers; in inseparable companionship with them he was reared at the royal court. As he advanced through the years of infancy and youth, he appeared more comely in person than his brothers, as in countenance, speech, and manners he was more pleasing than they. His noble birth and noble nature implanted him from his cradle a love of wisdom above all things, even amid all the occupations of this present life; but—with shame be it spoken—by the unworthy neglect of his parents and governors he remained illiterate till he was twelve years old or more, though by day and night he was an attentive listener to the Saxon poems which he often heard recited, and, being apt at learning, kept them in his memory. He was a zealous practiser of hunting in all its branches, and followed the chase with great assiduity and success; for his skill and good fortune in this art, and in all the other gifts of God, were beyond those of every one else, as I have often witnessed."

Alfred and the Book of Saxon Poems

"Now on a certain day his mother was showing him and his brothers a Saxon poetry, which she held in her hand, and finally said: 'Whichever of you can soonest learn this volume, to him will I give it.' Stimulated by these words, or rather by divine inspiration, and allured by the beautifully illuminated letter at the beginning of the volume, Alfred spoke

From *Select Translations from Old English Prose*, Cook and Tinker (pp. 86–100)

before all his brothers, who, though his seniors in age, were not so in grace, and answered his mother: 'Will you really give that book to that one of us who can first understand and repeat it to you?' At this his mother smiled with satisfaction, and confirmed what she had before said: 'Yes,' said she, 'that I will.' Upon this the boy took the book out of her hand, and went to his master and learned it by heart, whereupon he brought it back to his mother and recited it."

Alfred's Love of Learning

"This he would confess, with many lamentations and with sighs from the bottom of his heart, to have been one of his greatest difficulties and impediments in this present life, that when he was young and had leisure and capacity for learning, he had no masters; but when he was more advanced in years, he was continually occupied, not to say harassed, day and night, by so many diseases unknown to all the physicians of this island, as well as by internal anxieties of sovereignty, and by invasions of the heathen by sea and land, that though he then had some store of teachers and writers, it was quite impossible for him to study. But yet among the impediments of this present life, from childhood to the present day and, as I believe, even until his death, he has continued to feel the same insatiable desire."

Battle of Ashdown

"Roused by this grief and shame, the Christians, after four days, with all their forces and much spirit advanced to battle against the aforesaid army, at a place called Ashdown, which in Latin signifies 'Ash's Hill.' The heathen, forming in two divisions, arranged two shield-walls of similar size; and since they had two kings and many ealdormen, they gave the middle part of the army to the two kings, and the other part to all the ealdormen. The Christians, perceiving this, divided their army also into two troops, and with no less zeal formed shield-walls. But Alfred, as I have been told by truthful eye-witnesses, marched up swiftly with his men to the battle-field; for King Aethelred had remained a long time

in his tent in prayer, hearing mass, and declaring that he would not depart thence alive till the priest had done, and that he was not disposed to abandon the service of God for that of men; and according to these sentiments he acted. This faith of the Christian king availed much with the Lord, as I shall show more fully in the sequel.

"Now the Christians had determined that King Aethelred, with his men, should attack the two heathen kings, and that his brother Alfred, with his troops, should take the chance of war against all the leaders of the heathen. Things being so arranged on both sides, the king still continued a long time in prayer, and the heathen prepared for battle, had hastened to the field. Then Alfred, though only second in command, could no longer support the advance of the enemy, unless he either retreated or charged upon them without waiting for his brother. At length, with the rush of a wild boar, he courageously led the Christian troops against the hostile army, as he had already designed, for, although the king had not yet arrived, he relied upon God's counsel and trusted to His aid. Hence, having closed up his shield-wall in due order, he straightway advanced his standards against the foe. At length King Aethelred, having finished the prayers in which he was engaged, came up, and having invoked the King of the universe, entered upon the engagement.

"But here I must inform those who are ignorant of the fact that the field of battle was not equally advantageous to both parties, since the heathen had seized the higher ground, and the Christian array was advancing up-hill. In that place there was a solitary low thorn-tree, which I have seen with my own eyes, and round this the opposing forces met in strife with deafening uproar from all, the one side bent on evil, the other in fighting for life, and dear ones, and fatherland. When both armies had fought bravely and fiercely for a long while, the heathen, being unable by God's decree longer to endure the onset of the Christians, the larger part of their force being slain, betook themselves to shameful flight. There fell one of the two heathen kings and five ealdormen; many thousand of their men were either slain at this spot or lay scattered far and wide over the whole field of Ashdown. Thus there fell King Bagsecg, Ealdorman Sidroc the Elder and Ealdorman Sidroc the Younger, Ealdorman Osbern, Ealdorman Fraena, and Ealdorman Harold; and the whole heathen army pursued its flight, not only until night, but until the next day, even until they reached the stronghold from which they had sallied. The Christians followed, slaying all they could reach, until it became dark."

Alfred's Varied Pursuits

"In the meantime, the king, during the wars and frequent trammels of this present life, the invasions of the heathen, and his own daily infirmities of body, continued to carry on the government, and to practise hunting in all its branches; to teach his goldsmiths and all his artificers, his falconers, hawkers, and dog-keepers to build houses, majestic and rich beyond all custom of his predecessors, after his own new designs; to recite the Saxon books, and especially to learn by heart Saxon poems, and to make others learn them, he alone never ceasing from studying most diligently to the best of his ability. He daily attended masses and the other services of religion; recited certain psalms, together with prayers, and the daily and nightly hour-service; and frequented the churches at night, as I have said, that he might pray in secret, apart from the others. He bestowed alms and largesses both on natives and on foreigners of all countries; was most affable and agreeable to all; and was skilful in the investigation of things unknown. Many Franks, Frisians, Gauls, heathen, Welsh, Irish, and Bretons, noble and simple, submitted voluntarily to his dominion; and all of them according to their worthiness, he ruled, loved, honored, and enriched with money and power, as if they had been his own people. Moreover, he was sedulous and zealous in the habit of hearing the divine Scriptures read by his own countrymen, or if by any chance it so happened that any one arrived from abroad, would hear prayers in company with foreigners. His bishops, too, and all the clergy, his ealdormen and nobles, his personal attendants and friends, he loved with wonderful affection. Their sons, too, who were bred up in the royal household, were no less dear to him than his own; he never ceased to instruct them in all kinds of good morals, and, among other things, himself to teach them literature night and day. But as if he had no consolation in all these things, and suffered no other annoyance either from within or without, he was so harassed by daily and nightly sadness that he complained and made moan to the Lord and to all who were admitted to his familiarity and affection, that Almighty God had made him ignorant of divine wisdom and of the liberal arts; in this emulating the pious, famous, and wealthy Solomon, king of the Hebrews, who at the outset, despising all present glory and riches, asked wisdom of God, and yet found both, namely, wisdom and present glory; as it is written, 'Seek ye first the kingdom of God and his righteousness, and all these things shall be added unto you.' (Matt. 6:33) He would avail himself of every opportunity to procure assistants in his good designs, to aid him in his strivings after wisdom, that he might attain to what he aimed at; and, like a prudent bee, which, rising in summer at early morning from her beloved cells, steers her course with rapid flight along the uncertain paths of the air, and descends on the manifold and varied flowers of grasses, herbs, and shrubs, essaying that which most pleases her, and bearing it home, he directed the eyes of his mind afar, and sought that without which he had not within, that is, in his own kingdom."

Alfred's Scholarly Associates: Werfrith, Plegmund, Aethelstan, and Werwulf

"But God at that time, as some consolation to the king's benevolence, enduring no longer his kindly and just complaint, sent as it were certain luminaries, namely, Werfrith, bishop of the church of Worcester, a man well versed in divine Scripture, who, by the king's command, was the first to interpret with clearness and elegance the books of the Dialogues of Pope Gregory and Peter, his disciple, from Latin into Saxon, sometimes putting sense for sense; then Plegmund, a Mercian by birth, archbishop of the church of Canterbury, a venerable man, endowed with wisdom; besides Aethelstan and Werwulf, learned priests and clerks, Mercians by birth. These four King Alfred had called to him from Mercia, and he exalted them with many honors and powers in the kingdom of the West Saxons, not to speak of those which Archbishop Plegmund and Bishop Werfrith had in Mercia. By the teaching and wisdom of all these the king's desire increased continually, and was gratified. Night and day, whenever he had any leisure, he commanded such men as these to read books to him—for he never suffered himself to be with one of them—so that he came to possess a knowledge of almost every book, though of himself he could not yet understand anything of the books, since he had not yet learned to read anything."

How Alfred Rewards Submission

"Nor was it in vain that they all gained the friendship of the king. For those who desired to augment their worldly power obtained power; those who desired money gained money; those who desired his friendship acquired his friendship; those who wished more than one secured more than one. But all of them had his love and guardianship and defense from every quarter, so far as the king, with all his men, could defend himself. When therefore I had come to him at the royal villa called Leonaford, I was honorably received by him, and remained that time with him at his court eight months; during which I read to him whatever books he liked, of such as he had at hand; for this is his peculiar and most confirmed habit, both night and day, amid all his other occupations of mind and body, either himself to read books, or to listen to the reading of others. And when I frequently had sought his permission to return,

and had in no way been able to obtain it, at length when I had made up my mind by all means to demand it, he called me to him at twilight on Christmas Eve, and gave me two letters in which was a manifold list of all the things which were in the two monasteries which are called in Saxon Congresbury and Banwell, and on that same day he delivered to me those two monasteries with everything in them, together with a silken pallium of great value, and of incense a load for a strong man, adding these words, that he did not give me these trifling presents because he was unwilling hereafter to give me greater. For in the course of time he unexpectedly gave me Exeter, with the whole diocese which belonged to him in Wessex and in Cornwall, besides gifts every day without number of every kind of worldly wealth; these it would be too long to enumerate here, lest it should weary my readers. But let no one suppose that I have mentioned these presents in this place for the sake of glory, or flattery, or to obtain greater honor; I call God to witness that I have not done so, but that I might certify to those who are ignorant how profuse he was in giving. He then at once gave me permission to ride to those two monasteries, so full of good things, and afterwards to return on my own."

Alfred's Manual

"On a certain day we were both of us sitting in the king's chamber, talking on all kinds of subjects, as usual, and it happened that I read to him a quotation out of a very certain book. While he was listening to it attentively with both ears, and pondering it deeply with his inmost mind, he suddenly showed me a little book which he carried in his bosom, wherein were written the daily course, together with certain Psalms and prayers which he had read in his youth, and thereupon bade me write the quotation in that book. . . . Since I could find no blank space in that book wherein to write the quotation, it being all full of various matters, I delayed a little, chiefly that I might stir up the choice of understanding of the king to a higher knowledge of the divine testimonies. Upon his urging me to make haste and write it quickly, I said to him, 'Are you willing that I should write that quotation on some separate leaf? Perhaps we shall find one or more other such which will please you; and if that should happen, we shall be glad that we have kept this by itself.' 'Your plan is good,' said he; so I gladly made haste to get ready a pamphlet of four leaves, at the head of which I wrote what he had bidden me, and that same day I wrote in it, at his request, and as I had predicted, no less than three other quotations which pleased him. From that time we daily talked together, and investigated the same subject by the help of other quotations which we found and which pleased him, so that the pamphlet gradually became full, and deservedly so, for it is written, 'The righteous man builds upon a moderate foundation, and by degrees passes to greater things.'

"When that first quotation had been copied, he was eager at once to read, and to translate into Saxon, and then to teach many others. . . . Inspired by God, he began the rudiments of Holy Scripture on the sacred feast of St. Martin. Then he went on, as far as he was able, to learn the flowers collected from various quarters by any and all of his teachers, and to reduce them into the form of one book, although jumbled together, until it became almost as large as a psalter. This book he called his Enchiridion or Handbook, because he carefully kept it at hand day and night, and found, as he then used to say, no small consolation therein."

Alfred's Troubles

"Now the king was pierced with many nails of tribulation, though established in the royal sway; for from the twentieth year of his age to the present year, which is his forty-fifth, he has been constantly afflicted with most severe attacks of an unknown disease, so that there is not a single hour in which he is not either suffering from that malady, or nigh to despair by reason of the gloom which is occasioned by his fear of it. Moreover the constant invasions of foreign nations, by which he was continually harassed by land and sea, without any interval of quiet, constituted a sufficient cause of disturbance.

"What shall I say of his repeated expeditions against the heathen, his wars, and the incessant occupations of government? . . . . What shall I say of his restoration of cities and towns, and of others which he built where none had been before? of golden and silver buildings, built in incomparable style under his direction? of the royal halls and chambers, wonderfully erected of stone and wood at his command? of the royal villas constructed of stones removed from their old site, and finely rebuilt by the king's command in more fitting places?

"Not to speak of the disease above mentioned, he was disturbed by the quarrels of his subjects, who would of their own choice endure little or no toil for the common need of the kingdom. He alone, sustained by the divine aid, once he had assumed the helm of government, strove in every way, like a skilful pilot, to steer his ship, laden with much wealth, into the safe and longed-for harbor of his country, though almost all his crew were weary, suffering them not to faint or hesitate, even amid the waves and manifold whirlpools of this present life. Thus his bishops, ealdormen, nobles, favorite thanes, and prefects, who, next to God and the king, had the whole government of the kingdom, as was fitting, continually received from him instruction, compliment, exhortation, and command; nay, at last, if they were disobedient, and his long patience was exhausted, he would reprove them severely, and censure in every way their vulgar folly and obstinacy; and thus he wisely gained and bound them to his own wishes and the common interests of the whole kingdom. But if, owing to the sluggishness of the people, these admonitions of the king were either not fulfilled, or were begun late at the moment of necessity, and so, because they were not carried through, did not redound to the advantage of those who put them in execution—take as an example the fortresses which he ordered, but which are not yet begun, or, begun late, have not yet been completely finished—when hostile forces have made invasions by sea, or land, or both, then those who had set themselves against the imperial orders have been put to shame and overwhelmed with vain repentance."

Alfred Judges the Poor with Equity

"[The king] showed himself a minute investigator of the truth in all his judgments, and this especially for the sake of the poor, to whose interest, day and night, among other duties of this life, he was ever wonderfully attentive. For in the whole kingdom the poor, besides him, had few or no helpers; for almost all the powerful and noble of that country had turned their thoughts rather to secular than to divine things: each was more bent on worldly business, to his own profit, than on the common weal."

His Correction of Unjust and Incompetent Judges

"He strove also, in his judgments, for the benefit of both his nobles and commons, who often quarreled fiercely among themselves at the meetings of the ealdormen and sheriffs, so that hardly one of them admitted the justice of what had been decided by these ealdormen and sheriffs. In consequence of this pertinacious and obstinate dissension, all felt constrained to give sureties to abide by the decision of the king, and both parties hastened to carry out their engagements. But if any one was conscious of injustice on his side in the suit, though by law and agreement he was compelled, however reluctant, to come for judgment before a judge like this, yet with his own good will he never would consent to come. For he knew that in that place no part of his evil practice would remain hidden; and no wonder, for the king was a most acute investigator in executing his judgments, as he was in all other things. He inquired into almost all the judgments which were given in his absence, throughout all his dominion, whether they were just or unjust. If he perceived there was iniquity in those judgments, he would, of his own accord, mildly ask those

judges, either in his own person, or through others who were in trust with him, why they had judged so unjustly, whether through ignorance or malevolence—that is, whether for the love or fear of any one, the hatred of another, or the desire of some one's money. At length, if the judges acknowledged they had given some judgment because they knew no better, he discreetly and moderately reproved their inexperience and folly in such terms as these: 'I greatly wonder at your assurance, that whereas, by God's favor and mine, you have taken upon you the rank and office of the wise, you have neglected the studies and labors of the wise. Either, therefore, at once give up the administration of the earthly powers which you possess or endeavor more zealously to study the lessons of wisdom. Such are my commands.' At these words the ealdormen and sheriffs would be filled with terror at being thus severely corrected, and would endeavor to turn with all their might to the study of justice, so that, wonderful to say, almost all his ealdormen, sheriffs, and officers, though unlearned from childhood, gave themselves up to the study of letters, choosing rather to acquire laboriously an unfamiliar discipline than to resign their functions. But if any one, from old age or the sluggishness of an untrained mind, was unable to make progress in literary studies, he would order his son, if he had one, or one of his kinsmen, or, if he had no one else, his own freedman or servant, whom he had long before advanced to the office of reading, to read Saxon books before him night and day, whenever he had any leisure. And then they would lament with deep sighs from their inmost souls that in their youth they had never attended to such studies. They counted happy the youth of the present day, who could be delightfully instructed in the liberal arts, while they considered themselves wretched in that they had neither learned these things in their youth, nor, now they were old, were able to do so. This skill of young and old in acquiring letters, I have set forth as a means of characterizing the aforesaid king."

Alfred's Statement Concerning His Laws

"[Alfred begins by quoting the Ten Commandments, and follows with various parts of Exodus 21, 22, and 23. He then quotes Matthew 5:17, to show that Christ did not abrogate these precepts, and subjoins Acts 15:23–29. Afterward he goes on as follows:]

"What ye would not that other men should do to you, do not that to other men. From this one precept one may learn to judge righteously; he needs no other law-book. Let him simply remember that he adjudge to no one what he would not that another should adjudge to him, if he were in quest of a legal decision upon himself.

"After it came to pass that many nations had accepted the faith of Christ, many synods assembled throughout the world. Such there were throughout England, after they had espoused Christianity, consisting of holy bishops and other competent councilors. In the interests of the mercy that Christ taught, they decreed that for almost every misdeed secular rulers might without sin, and with their consent, accept a fine, which they then and there prescribed, for the first offense, except in the case of treason. To this they dared not allow mercy, since Almighty God allowed none to those who despised Him and Christ, the Son of God, allowed none to him who betrayed Him to death; and He ordained that one should love one's lord as himself. Accordingly in many synods they prescribed fines for many human misdeeds, and in many synodical records they wrote here one penalty and there another.

"I, then, King Alfred, gathered these laws together, and commanded many of those which our forefathers held and which seemed good to me, to be written down, and many of those which did not seem good to me I rejected upon the advice of my councilors, and commanded that they be kept in another manner; for I durst not venture to set down in writing much of my own, for I knew not how much of it would please those who should come after us. But those things which I found—either of the days of Ine my kinsman, or of Offa, King of the Mercians, or of Aethelbert, who was the first of the English race to receive baptism—which seemed most just to me, those I have gathered here, and rejected the others. I, then, Alfred, King of the West Saxons, showed all these unto my councilors, and they said that it seemed good unto them all that they be kept."

Albert S. Cook—*Selections from Old English Laws*—The laws of the early kings of England are among the first extant written records in our language, although few are preserved in their original form.

Teaching the Anglo-Norman Period
1066–1350
Preparation and Presentation

Background	Emphases	Readings
1. The Norman conquest brings feudalism, the French language, and central government. a) William the Conqueror and the Battle of Hastings—character study b) Feudalism as a philosophy of government c) *When Knights were Bold*, Eva March Tappan—read for background. 2. Magna Charta—the first protection of individual rights in law. Read *CHOC*, I, pp. 37–41; *T & L* pp. 343–48. 3. The Bayeux Tapestry—an embroidery depicting the Norman conquest on display in France (check library for a book). 4. The French language and its influence upon English, giving feminine qualities and embellishment to the Anglo-Saxon language.	1. The Norman Conquest—the military invasion of England by William the Conqueror "The greatest general and statesman of his time." (Green) "In a profligate age William was distinguished by the purity of his married life, by temperate habits and by a sincere piety. His most severe measures were taken in cold blood, as part of his general policy; but his natural disposition was averse to unnecessary bloodshed or cruelty. . . . In his personal appearance he was tall and corpulent, of a dignified presence and extremely powerful physique, with a bald forehead, close-cropped hair and short mustaches." (*Encyclopaedia Britannica*, Eleventh Edition) 2. The governmental structure: William required that loyalty to the king should take precedence over all other allegiance, even of a man's fealty to his feudal lord. (This is the seed of our own national allegiance.) 3. Magna Charta: King John is forced to yield certain "rights" to his baron—the beginning of rights for every freeman.	Readings in Chivalry: *Men of Iron* by H. Pyle, a novel of the days of chivalry. *The Story of King Arthur and His Knights,* Howard Pyle *T & L,* pp. 347–48 *Ivanhoe* by Sir Walter Scott (if not studied earlier in sixth grade). This historical novel presents the contrast of Anglo-Norman ideas of government and life. Malory's *Morte d'Arthur* Geoffrey's *History* Layamon's *Brut* *The Pearl*—a rare example of imaginative literature of the period

Leading Ideas and Ideals of the Anglo-Norman Period
1066–1350

The Development of the English Language

Anglo-Saxon language with its masculine qualities continues. The Anglo-Saxon is a serious language, and concerned with religion. It is rustic, homely, coarse, and unrefined.

The French language has feminine qualities of variety, lightness, and descriptive words. The Norman is concerned with the secular court life and its refinements and embellishments.

Anglo-Saxon persists as the language of the people. To this robust vernacular is added the enrichment of vocabulary supplied by the French and the refinements of both intellect and aristocracy. The union of the chief elements of both Anglo-Saxon and French will be represented in Chaucer.

Scott's *Ivanhoe* illustrates the original conflict between the Norman as conqueror, and the Saxon as the conquered.

With loss of liberty there is little Anglo-Saxon in literature at this period with the exception of *The Pearl*. The Christian Idea of Man and Government appears.

Feudalism

The governmental structure of feudalism gives rise to the themes and ideals of Chivalry in literature.

Christian Influences in Chivalry and Courtesy

The training of a knight began at age seven when the youth was placed in the castle of a patron. Here he learned religious and court customs and served as a page until his formal training began at fourteen. Lessons of music and dancing as well as hunting and fighting—complete with heavy armor—continued until age twenty-one, when the young man was deemed ready to take the vows of knighthood.

Courtesy was learned when the young man chose a lady of the court as the mistress of his heart to whom he was taught to refer all his sentiments, words, and actions. Religion played a large part in all of these activities.

King Arthur and His Knights

"For I believe that King Arthur was the most honorable, gentle Knight who ever lived in all the world. And those who were his fellows of the Round Table—taking him as their looking-glass of chivalry—made, altogether, such a *company of noble knights that it is hardly to be supposed that their like will ever be seen in this world.*" —Howard Pyle

Chronology of the Anglo-Norman Period

History		Literature	
912	Northmen settle in Normandy		
1066	Battle of Hastings; William King of England		
1096	First Crusade		
1100	Henry I	1137	Geoffrey's *History*
1147	Second Crusade		
1154	Henry II		
1189	Richard I; Third Crusade		
1199	John	1200	Layamon's *Brut*
1215	Magna Charta		
1216	Henry III		
1272	Edward I		
1295	First complete Parliament		
1307	Edward II		
1327	Edward III		
1338	Beginning of Hundred Years' War with France		
		1340	Birth of Chaucer
		1350	Sir Gawain, *The Pearl*

Teaching Chivalry and Christianity

The Story of King Arthur and His Knights
by Howard Pyle

and *Idylls of the King*
by Alfred Lord Tennyson

English Chivalry: Tracing a Link in Our Constitutional Chain of Liberty

We need always to have our eyes upon those precious links of liberty which the Lord put together—forging American Christian government. Centuries go by as small gains are made for individual protection—in life, liberty, and property. But as we read and study literature, we can learn from this "handmaid" of history.

By the end of the reign of Henry IV, there had been some two hundred years of Magna Charta. The supreme power of the King had been restrained; both the feudal lords and the parliament had grown in power. "Many of the rights and privileges which all modern legislatures possess are derived from the powers which the English parliament gained between 1295 and 1400. . . . No taxes could be imposed or collected without the consent of parliament; no new laws could be adopted without its agreement; it could impeach the king's ministers; and it could press upon the king its advice in all important measures of government, including foreign wars and treaties." (*A Short History of England*, Cheyney, 1904)

But for the average man there was still little benefit from this top-down legislation. Yet, in 1382, with the Wycliffe Bible *in English*, a new movement began from the individual. The Lollard movement began the preaching and teaching of the Bible throughout the British Isles. Now, with civil liberties kindled by Magna Charta, religious liberty begins to lay the foundations for the westward move of the Gospel.

Yet it will take some two hundred years— from 1382 to 1575—until the first of our Pilgrims is born who will make some impact upon the history of civil and religious liberty. How long, Lord, oh, how long, has it taken to achieve civil and religious liberty? These dear-bought treasures—which we today take so casually, so unthinkingly—can we redeem them from the "accuser"?

HISTORICAL READING: See *Teaching and Learning*, pp. 344–46, "Magna Charta—Christian Rights and English Law." Choose one Question for Invention, on pp. 347–48 for discussion on the relationship of Magna Charta and American Government.

Chivalry and Christianity

One definition of "chivalry" from the eleventh edition of *Encyclopaedia Britannica* reads in part as follows:

> Chivalry (O. Fr. chevalerie, from Late. Lat. caballerius), the knightly class of feudal times, possessing its own code of rules, moral and social (see Knighthood and Chivalry). The primary sense in the middle ages is "knights" or "fully armed and mounted fighting men." Thence the term came to mean that gallantry in battle and high sense of honour in general expected of knights. Thus "to do chivalry" was a medieval phrase for "to act the knight."

Lastly the word came to be used in its present very general sense of "courtesy." In English law, chivalry meant the tenure of land by knights' service. It was a service due to the crown, usually forty days' military attendance annually.

Chivalry and Knighthood (Eleventh edition of *Encyclopaedia Britannica*)

> It is difficult to describe the true spirit and moral influence of knighthood, if only because the ages in which it

flourished differed so widely from our own. . . .

As a conscious effort to bring religion into daily life, chivalry was less successful than later puritanism; while the educated classes of our day far surpass the average medieval knight in discipline, self-control, and outward or inward refinement. Freeman's estimate comes far nearer to the historical facts than Burke's:

The chivalrous spirit is above all things a class spirit. The good knight is bound to endless fantastic courtesies toward men and still more towards women of a certain rank: he may treat all below that rank with any degree of scorn and cruelty. The spirit of chivalry implies the arbitrary choice of one or two virtues to be practised in such an exaggerated degree as to become vices, while the ordinary laws of right and wrong are forgotten.

Chivalry again in its military aspect not only encourages the love of war for its own sake without regard to the cause for which war is waged, it encourages also an extravagant regard for a fantastic show of personal daring which cannot in any way advance the objects of the siege or campaign which is going on. Chivalry in short is in morals very much what feudalism is in law: each substitutes purely personal obligations devised in the exclusive class, or the more homely duties of an honest man and a good citizen.

[Note: Even in 13th-century England, more than half the population were serfs, and as such had no claim to the privileges of Magna Charta. Disputes between a serf and his lord were decided in the latter's court, although the king's courts attempted to protect the serf's life and limb and necessary implements of work.]

The knightly ages will always enjoy the glory of having formulated a code of honour which aimed at rendering the upper classes worthy of their exceptional privileges; yet we must judge chivalry not only by its formal code but also by its practical fruits.

Chivalry as a Code of Judicial Conduct and Its Relationship to a Court of Law of Today

The Court of Chivalry was a court instituted by Edward III, of which the lord high constable and earl marshal of England were joint judges. When both sat the court had summary criminal jurisdiction as regards all offences committed by knights, and generally as to military matters. When the earl marshal alone presided, it was a court of honour deciding as to precedence, coats of arms, etc. This court sat for the last time in 1737. The heraldic side of its duties are now vested in the earl marshal as head of the Heralds' College. (*Encyclopaedia Britannica*).

Christian Influences on Chivalry

From *The Age of Chivalry or Legends of King Arthur* by Thomas Bulfinch

Throngs of knights and barons bold,
In weeds of peace high triumphs hold,
With store of ladies, whose bright eyes
Rain influence and judge the prize.
—Milton

Introduction

"On the decline of the Roman power, about five centuries after Christ, the countries of Northern Europe were left almost destitute of a national government. Numerous chiefs, more or less powerful, held local sway, as far as each could enforce his dominion, and occasionally those chiefs would unite for a common object; but, in ordinary times, they were much more likely to be found in hostility to one another. In such a state of things, the rights of the humbler classes of society were at the mercy of every assailant; and it is plain that, without some check upon the lawless power of the chiefs, society must have relapsed into barbarism. Such checks were found, first, in the rivalry of the chiefs themselves, whose mutual jealousy made them restraints upon one another; secondly, in the influence of the Church, which, by every motive, pure or selfish, was pledged to interpose for the protection of the weak; and lastly, in the generosity and sense of right which, however crushed under the weight of passion and selfishness, dwell naturally in the heart of man. From his last source sprang Chivalry, which framed an ideal of the heroic character, combining invincible strength and valor, justice, modesty, loyalty to superiors, courtesy to equals, compassion, to weakness, and devotedness to the Church; an ideal which, if never met with in real life, was acknowledged by all as the highest model for emulation.

"The word Chivalry is derived from the French *cheval*, as a horse. The word *knight*, which originally meant boy or servant, was particularly applied to a young man after he was admitted to the privilege of bearing arms. This privilege was conferred on youths of family and fortune only, for the mass of the people were not furnished with arms. The knight then was a mounted warrior, a man of rank, or in the service and maintenance of some man of rank, generally possessing some independent means of support, but often relying mainly on the gratitude of those whom he served for the supply of his wants, and often, no doubt, resorting to the means which power confers on its possessor.

"In time of war the knight was, with his followers, in the camp of his sovereign, or commanding in the field, or holding some castle for him. In time of peace he was often in attendance at his sovereign's court, gracing with his presence the banquets and tournaments with which princes cheered their leisure. Or he was traversing the country in quest of adventure, professedly bent on redressing wrongs and enforcing rights, sometimes in fulfilment of some vow of religion or of love. These wandering knights were called Knights-Errant; they were welcome guests in the castles of the nobility, for their presence enlivened the dullness of those secluded abodes, and they were received with honor at the abbeys, which often owed the best part of their revenues to the patronage of the knights; but if no castle or abbey were at hand, their hardy habits made it not intolerable to them to lie down, supperless, at the foot of some wayside cross, and pass the night.

"It is evident that the justice administered by such an instrumentality must have been of the rudest description. The force whose legitimate purpose was to redress wrongs, might easily be perverted to inflict them. Accordingly, we find in the romances, which, however fabulous in facts, are true as pictures of manners, that a knightly castle was often a terror to the surrounding country; that its dungeons were full of oppressed knights and ladies, waiting for some champion to appear to set them free, or to be ransomed with money; that hosts of idle retainers were ever at hand to enforce their lord's behests, regardless of law and justice; and that the rights of the unarmed multitude were of no account. This contrariety of fact and theory in regard to chivalry will account for the opposite impressions which exist in men's minds respecting it. While it has been the theme of the most fervid eulogium on the one part, it has been as eagerly denounced on the other. On a cool estimate, we cannot but see reason to congratulate ourselves that it has given way in modern times to the reign of law, and that the civil magistrate, if less picturesque, has taken the place of the mailed champion." (Bulfinch, pp. 13–16)

Chivalry in King Arthur

In the famous legends of King Arthur and his Knights of the Round Table, collected and retold by Malory in his *Morte d'Arthur, chivalry* and *romance* play equal parts.

Was Arthur a real person, did Camelot exist, was there really a fellowship of Knights known as the "Knights of the Round Table"? Until Geoffrey of Monmouth's day there was no mention of King Arthur—not in the Saxon *Chronicle*, not in Bede, and King Alfred never mentions King Arthur. But, most scholars of English history and literature do not give up their conviction that there *was* an Arthur. And so the legends and stories about him and about his Knights of the Round Table became the symbol of the highest and, sometimes, the lowest of those qualities of Christian Knighthood. As Howard Pyle writes in the foreword to his first book *The Story of King Arthur and His Knights*:

> After several years of contemplation and of thought upon the matter herein contained, it has at last come about, by the Grace of God, that I have been able to write this work with such pleasure of spirit that, if it gives to you but a part of the joy that it hath afforded me, I shall be very well content with what I have done.
>
> For when, in pursuing this history, I have come to consider the high nobility of spirit that moved these excellent men to act as they did, I have felt that they have afforded such a perfect example of courage and humility that anyone might do exceedingly well to follow after their manner of behavior in such measure as he is able to do.
>
> For I believe that King Arthur was the most honorable, gentle Knight who ever lived in all the world. And those who were his fellows of the Round Table—taking him as their looking-glass of chivalry—made, altogether, such a company of noble knights that it is hardly to be supposed that their like will ever be seen again in this world. Wherefore it is that I have had such extraordinary pleasure in beholding how those famous knights behaved whenever circumstances called upon them to perform their endeavor. (pp.v-vi)

How does chivalry relate to your Christian character today living in the American Christian republic?

From Sidney Lanier's Introduction to his book *The Boy's Froissart*, 1908:

> Froissart's *Chronicle* is, in a grave and important sense, a sort of continuation of Malory's novel. For Malory's book is, at bottom, a picture of knighthood in the twelfth and thirteenth centuries; while Froissart's is a picture of knighthood in the fourteenth century. (p. x)

As you read of the fair knights and the foul knights—it cannot but occur to you that somehow it seems harder to be a good knight nowadays than it was then. This is because we have so many more ways of fighting now than in King Edward the Third's time. A good deal of what is really combat nowadays is not called combat. Many struggles, instead of taking the form of sword and armor, will present themselves to you after a few years in the following shapes:

the strict payment of debts;

the utmost delicacy of national honor;

the greatest openness of party discussion, and the most respectful courtesy towards political opponents;

the purity of the ballot box;

the sacred and liberal guaranty of all rights to all citizens;

the holiness of marriage;

the lofty contempt for what is small, knowing, and gossipy;

and the like.

Can you translate these efforts into your life today?

Do you repay debts and loans?

Do you have respect for political opponents who take a different position than you do?

Are you looking forward to your responsibility to vote intelligently?

Do you understand the basis of rights and responsibilities?

Are you above gossip and slander?

Are you chivalrous?

Nevertheless the same qualities which made a manful fighter then make one now:

To speak the very truth

To reverence all women

To help the weak

To be constant to one's love

To despise luxury

To perform a promise to the uttermost

To maintain right and honesty

To treat high and low with courtesy

To be fair to a bitter foe

To preserve simplicity, modesty, and gentleness in heart and bearings was in the oath of the young knight who took the stroke upon him in the fourteenth century, and this is still the way to win love and glory." Dubbing a knight meant three gentle strokes of a sword (flat of) on the shoulder.

What are the duties of a Christian knight?

What "wrongs" can you redress?

What courtesies can you show?

How can you arm yourself to face the adversary? Name your weapons.

What are the duties of a Christian lady?

How will they know you as a lady?

Whom will you help and uplift?

How will you express qualities worthy of a bold knight's respect?

Teaching the Wycliffe and Chaucer Period
1350–1400
Preparation and Presentation

Background	Emphases	Readings
1. The age of pilgrimages and the emergence of England's mission—the Bible in English. *CHOC*, I, pp. 28A–29; *T & L*, pp. 166–68.	1. John Wycliffe—"the morning star of the Reformation." The beginning of personal evangelism and the impetus of revival which 270 years later will produce the Pilgrims. The English Bible—the flowering of Middle English in the Wycliffe Gospels.	Short selections on Wycliffe's life. See *CHOC* and *T & L*. Selections from Wycliffe's Gospels.
2. Geoffrey Chaucer presents the individual as a subject of writing in *The Canterbury Tales*. See *Geoffrey Chaucer of England* by Marchette Chute, for background.	2. Chaucer is important because he relates God's Principle of Individuality to literature. For the first time the individual of any occupation becomes a subject of writing. His humorous portraits of individual pilgrims are also critiques of the evils of his times in church and state.	"Prologue" to *The Canterbury Tales*. Identify Chaucer's characters and select a few for emphasis. Some memory work here. Read "The Knight's Tale" identifying setting, plot, theme, characterization, and style.
3. The beginning of individual evangelism through John Wycliffe, a powerful preacher whose followers were called "Lollards." Wycliffe translated the gospels into English prose.	3. English language reaches this peak of development for the purpose of bringing forth the written Word of God as evidenced in Wycliffe.	

Leading Ideas and Ideals of the Age of Wycliffe and Chaucer

1350–1400

The Bible in English

The mission of England: "This blessed plot, this earth, this realm, this England."

—William Shakespeare

The Christian idea of man and government appears.

The emerging of the individual and a philosophy of education and government

The Age of Pilgrimages:

1. The Pilgrimage to Truth: *Piers Plowman.* William Langland called the individual not to a social protest, but to a Christian revival. The Christian influences the civil sphere by his character and by his work. Langland believes in the English freeman's maintaining self-government and self-control. *"Righteousness exalteth a nation: but sin is a reproach to any people"* (Proverbs 14:34)

The gospel of work admonished against the curse of idleness: "Each man must plough his half acre." A man must work honestly for God, country, and his fellow-man. Work has dignity and so does the common man. Derisively called the "Protestant Ethic"—rather it reflects God's command: *"Replenish the earth and subdue it"*—*"in the sweat of thy face shalt thou eat bread."* (Genesis 1:28; 3:19)

2. The Pilgrimage to Canterbury: Chaucer writes in the English language and the common man—the individual of no rank—is his hero for the first time in English literature. God's Principle of Individuality.

3. The Pilgrimage to Christ: Wycliffe, "the morning star of the Reformation," begins the Reformation with the common man for whom he translates the Gospel. The beginning of individual evangelism with his followers. Education begins with learning to read the Bible. *"And the gospel must first be published among all nations."* (Mark 13:10)

The flowering of English. "Wycliffe the Father of English prose"—the first translation of the Bible in English. Education in learning to read The Holy Bible. *"But the word of God grew and multiplied."* (Acts 12:24)

Chronology of Wycliffe/Chaucer, Fourteenth Century

History	Literature
1327 Edward III	
1338 Beginning of Hundred Years' War with France	1340 Birth of Chaucer
1348–1349 Black Death	1356 Mandeville's *Travels*
	1362 *Piers Plowman*
1377 Richard II; Wycliffe and the Lollards begin Reformation in England	
1381 Pessand Rebellion; Wat Tyler	1382 First complete Bible in English
	1385 *The Canterbury Tales*
1399 Deposition of Richard II; Henry IV chosen by Parliament.	1400 Death of Chaucer

THE NOAH PLAN © 1997 • FOUNDATION FOR AMERICAN CHRISTIAN EDUCATION

Teaching the English Reformation Period
1400–1550
Preparation and Presentation

Background	Emphases	Readings

1. History of the Period
  a) Political changes:
    (1) Henry V used the power of the new English national spirit to attack France and gain the French crown in the Hundred Years' War.
    (2) Joan of Arc (1428) led the French to recovery.
    (3) The Wars of the Roses and Cade's Rebellion caused violence to reign (1455–1485).
    (4) Richard II ended the civil wars and feudalism.
    (5) Henry VIII (1509) produced significant changes—national power at home and abroad increased—the Reformation officially came to England through the Act of Supremacy (1534).
    (6) The Tyndale Bible printed in 1525.
  b) Intellectual changes:
    (1) Printing, brought by Caxton (1476), made it possible for a book or an idea to reach the whole nation.
    (2) Schools and universities replaced monasteries.
    (3) The Renaissance brought Greek ideas and culture.
    (4) Spiritual freedom proclaimed by the Reformation.
    (5) Literature was relatively silent.
 	
2. Literature of the Period
  a) Malory's *Morte d'Arthur* is medieval in spirit.
  b) Erasmus's *In Praise of Folly* was written in Latin.
  c) More's *Utopia* is a study of social conditions.
  d) Tyndale's translation of the New Testament brought God's Word into circulation.
	1. God prepares England for the Reformation:
	  a) William Caxton, an Englishman, learns printing in Europe, brings the first printing press back in 1475.
	  b) Erasmus, Dutch scholar, arrives at Cambridge University in 1506, edited the New Testament in Greek with Latin translation. It was sent to Cambridge and read by a student, Thomas Bilney. The conversion of "Little Bilney" by the Word began the Reformation in England.
	  c) In the year 1526, Tyndale's translation of the Bible reaches England.
	  d) The death of the martyrs:
	  Thomas Bilney: Aug. 19, 1531
	  William Tyndale: Oct. 6, 1536
	  Hugh Latimer: Oct. 16, 1555
	  Nicholas Ridley: Oct. 16, 1555
	  Thomas Cranmer, Archbishop of Canterbury: 1556
	
	2. John Foxe (1516–1587), in exile on the continent, writes the tale of Protestant sufferings—*Book of Martyrs*.
	
	3. A century of preparation for the Pilgrims begins. Inventions, and explorations with Columbus opening up the highway across the Atlantic to the New World.
	
	4. The Reformation was the cause of a great forward movement in human affairs. It awakened the intellect of mankind and stimulated reform in science, literature, invention, social life, and politics.
	
	5. Inventions discovered to move the Gospel forward: paper and moveable type.
	
	6. The English Bible was to become the American political textbook—the source of political and evangelical liberty.
		Foxe's *Book of Martyrs*. Scripture was written in English with the blood of martyrs. Read the accounts of:
		  Bilney
		  Tyndale
		  Cranmer
		  Ridley
		  Latimer
		
		Read *CHOC*, I, pp. 30–31 on Tyndale's translation of the Bible.
		
		T & L: Martyrdom of Tyndale, pp. 334–37

Leading Ideas and Ideals of the English Reformation Period

1400–1550

In this period Columbus defied the superstitions of his day to open an ocean highway to the New World. This was the path that the Pilgrims would travel. Coincident with Columbus's discovery were those inventions needed to forward the Gospel. Scientific in nature, they would complement the liberty of the individual in all fields.

"God's gift to the world is men who use their intellectual talents to honor Him. . . . The invention of movable type at Haarlem or Mentz, half a century before the discovery of America—and only a few years previous to that invention, the manufacture of paper from linen rags, a most indispensable help to the development of the press—had made books available to many, where manuscripts had been available to few. . . . But neither the wonderful art of printing, nor the discovery of this transatlantic continent, had aroused with such mighty energy the mind of Christendom as did the discovery of a new world in theology by Luther. . . . A free Church, free education, free association, the right to speak and to write—these are the consequences of the liberty of conscience proclaimed by the Reformers." (Foljambe, "The Hand of God in American History" in *C & P*, pp. 46–50)

The Christian Idea of Man and Government

The English Bible was to become the American political textbook. Therefore, Tyndale and other translators needed to bring forth this source of political liberty—a source which begins with evangelical liberty.

The Christian Idea of Man in Literature

The English Bible is the fountainhead of English Literature. For England to have her own translators the impetus of a spiritual revival must occur. Thus God uses the greatest humanist scholar of the day to bring his Latin translation of the New Testament to England. This begins the Reformation in England.

"The Reformation was the cause of a great forward movement in human affairs. It awakened the intellect of mankind. Science, literature, invention, social life, political reform—all were stimulated by it."

Chronology of the English Reformation Period

History		The Christian Idea of Man and Government Appears	
1413	Henry V		
1415	Battle of Agincourt		
1422	Henry VI		
1428	Siege of Orleans; Joan of Arc		
1453	End of Hundred Years' War		
1455–		1470	Malory's *Morte d'Arthur*
1485	Wars of the Roses	1474	Caxton, at Bruges, prints the first book in English, *The Recuyell of the Historyes of Troye*.
1461	Edward IV	1477	First book printed in England.
1483	Richard III		
1485	Henry VII	1485	*Morte d'Arthur* printed by Caxton.
1492	Columbus discovers America.		
		1499	Colet, Erasmus, and More bring the new learning to Oxford.
1509	Henry VIII	1509	Erasmus's *In Praise of Folly*
		1516	More's *Utopia*
		1525	Tyndale's New Testament
1534	Act of Supremacy; The Reformation accomplished.	1530	Introduction of the sonnet and blank verse by Thomas Wyatt and Henry Howard, earl of Surrey.
		1539	The Great Bible
1547	Edward VI		
1553	Mary		
1558	Elizabeth I	1557	Tottel's "Miscellany"
1560	Geneva Bible	1559	John Knox in Edinburgh
		1559	Spenser's *Faerie Queene*
		1564	Birth of Shakespeare
1571	Rise of English Puritans		
1577	Drake's voyage around the world	1579	Spenser's *Shepherd's Calendar*
		1587	Shakespeare in London
1588	Defeat of the Armada	1590	Shakespeare's early plays
		1597–1625	Bacon's *Essays*
1603	James I	1600–1607	Shakespeare's Tragedies
1604	Divine Right of Kings proclaimed		
1607	Settlement at Jamestown	1608	Birth of Milton
		1611	Translation of Bible, KJV
		1616	Death of Shakespeare
1620	Pilgrim Fathers at Plymouth		
1625	Charles I	1626	Death of Bacon

Teaching the Elizabethan Age, 1550–1620

Preparation and Presentation

From the Geneva Bible to the Pilgrims

Background	Emphases	Readings

1. This period is generally regarded as the greatest in the history of our literature.
  a) The Reformation and Renaissance contributed new realms of thought and ideas for men's minds.
  b) The exploration of the New World contributed a sense of adventure and dreams of new lands and riches.
  c) National spirit and patriotism were inspired by Elizabeth's administration and her love for England.
  d) The atmosphere in England was one of religious tolerance, social content, intellectual progress, and unbounded enthusiasm.
 	
2. This period produced great literature.
  a) Prose writing was best exemplified by Bacon in his *Essays*.
  b) Poetry had variety, freshness, and a romantic trend and is best represented by Edmund Spenser in *Shepherd's Calendar* and *The Faerie Queene*.
  c) The most significant development in literature is the drama culminating in Shakespeare who brought the drama to its highest stage of development.
 	
3. The greatest achievement of the period is the English Bible, first the Geneva Bible in 1560, then the King James Version in 1611. The Geneva Bible influenced Shakespeare and became the impetus of the Separatist movement as well as the liberating factor that undergirded Elizabethan society. *CHOC*, I, pp. 28A–36; *T & L*, pp. 332–42
  a) Within 12 months of the martyrdom of Tyndale, the king approved the publishing of the Bible in 1539.
  b) The Geneva Bible in 1559 had clearer type and the division of the chapters into verses.
 	
4. The Spanish Armada
	1. Elizabeth's long reign enables literature to flower in order to produce the English Bible, first the Geneva then the King James Version. A Bible for the individual.
	
	2. The Reformation begins in Scotland with the return of John Knox from Geneva in 1560.
	
	The Reformation in England continues with the Separatists. John Robinson is born in 1576. William Brewster is born.
	
	3. Spenser invents a new verse form to express the rare beauty of his idealization of Christian England. The "Faerie Queene" is Elizabeth, and virtues and vices are personified. The setting is medieval chivalry, but Spenser envisions life as a challenge to individual Christian character.
	
	4. The defeat of the Spanish Armada, 1588. *"And now began that great sea-fight which was to determine whether Popery and despotism, or Protestantism and freedom, were the law which God had appointed for half of Europe, and the whole of future America."*
		Read Verna Hall's article, "The Hand of God in American History—English Preparation." F.A.C.E. *Journal*, Vol. I.
		
		Read *CHOC*, I, pp. 21–24, 27.
		
		The Geneva Bible—read the introduction from the 1970 reprint.
		
		Edmund Spenser (1552-1599), the poet's poet: selections from *The Faerie Queene*, Book I, "Epithalamion," "Amoretti."
		  a) The Spenserian stanza was created as a verse form. It is nine lines, eight of five feet and the last of six feet. It rhymes ABABBCBCC.
		  b) *The Faerie Queene* recounts the adventures and triumphs of knights who represent moral virtues—allegorical.
		
		The Spanish Armada (for background read in chapters 31–32 of *Westward Ho!* by Rev. Charles Kingsley, 1855.
		
		Hakluyt—selections pertaining to the Spanish Armada.

Teaching the Elizabethan Age, 1550–1620
Preparation and Presentation
From the Geneva Bible to the Pilgrims

Background	Emphases	Readings
5. Michael Drayton: 1563–1631, poet; Long: pp. 114–15	5. In 1607 Captain John Smith and his colonists set forth for Virginia and the plantation of Jamestown. *"The eyes of all London were upon them; prayers for their safety were offered in the churches; and one of the mighty poets, Michael Drayton, poured into a noble ode the high hope, the anxiety, the ambition, the eager sympathy, with which all ranks of thoughtful and watchful Englishmen were sending the travellers out upon their great quest."* (Tyler, *A History of American Literature*)	Michael Drayton: "To the Virginian Voyage"
6. King James Bible, 1611, *CHOC*, I, pp. 33–36; *T & L*, p. 173 *a)* The work was done by the conference called by James I at Hampton Court in 1604. *b)* The committee included linguists, theologians, and Bible scholars who prayed: "O Let Thy scriptures be my pure delight, let me not be deceived in them, neither let me deceive by them." *c)* There is a predominance of Saxon words as compared to Latin. *d)* This was the freest and purest of Bible translations since Wycliffe.	6. The highest peak of language and letters. From the time of Wycliffe, Tyndale, and the host of translators, up to the 1611 edition, English literature has reached a peak of expression for the Word of God to appear.	King James Bible: Read the Epistle Dedicatory to James I by the Translators.
7. William Shakespeare: 1564–1616	7. Shakespeare, the "Bard of the Bible." His plays reference both the historical facts and characters of the Bible, but they also derive their religious principles and sentiments, as well as poetry, from God's written Word.	Shakespeare: *Henry VIII*
8. Francis Bacon: 1561–1626	8. Bacon utilizes inductive reasoning to turn men from the study of the heavens to the study of man.	Francis Bacon: Selected *Essays*, "Of Studies," "Of Friendship"
9. Richard Hooker: 1554?–1600	9. "The Judicious Hooker" reasons from the Scriptures to the subject of law and government. He sets a standard for the American clergy of the Revolutionary period.	Richard Hooker: From *CHOC*, I, p. 58; Quoted by John Locke in "Of Civil Government"

Teaching the Puritan Age, 1620–1660
Preparation and Presentation

Background	Emphases	Readings

1. The People of The Book—The Holy Bible:
 	
"England became the people of a book, and that book was the Bible." Both Old and New Testaments were read in the churches while the small Geneva Bibles carried the Scriptures into every home, and wove it into the life of every English family. "It was as yet the one English book which was familiar to every Englishman. . . . The whole prose literature of England . . . had grown up since the translation of the Scriptures. . . . As a mere literary monument the English version of the Bible remains the noblest example of the English tongue. Its perpetual use made it from the instant of its appearance the standard of our language." (*A Short History of the English People*, Green, pp. 455–56)
	1. The Power of the Book over the English People is seen:
	  a) Upon the speech of English-men,
	  b) Upon English authors who borrowed words and phrases,
	  c) Upon the character of the people.
	
	2. Rise of the Puritan Party for the reformation of the national church and state. The Puritan as a Scripturist and a moralist endeavors by law to "repress prevailing vice, and organize a Christian people."
		CHOC, I, pp. 48–50
		
		CHOC, I, p. 182

2. George Herbert (1593–1633)	3. Puritan Poet and Divine The life and testimony of George Herbert was written by a contemporary, Izaak Walton, who painted a picture of the "gentle Puritan" as a dedicated and consecrated minister. "To one who reminded him of his many acts of mercy, George Herbert made answer: *'They be good works, if they be sprinkled with the blood of Christ, and not otherwise.'*" 4. Literary Style of George Herbert A coincidence of style and form—the spirit and the letter—is George Herbert's testimony to his Lord and Savior in poetry. We seem to be present with him in the closest of his devotions to God.	George Herbert, selections from Izaak Walton's *Life of Herbert* Poetry to read: "The Altar" "The Pulley" "Easter-Wings" "The Star" "The Bag" "The Church Militant" In his long poem, "The Church Militant," Herbert describes the Chain of Christianity moving westward: *"The course was westward, that the sun might light, As well our understanding as our sight."*

Teaching the Puritan Age, 1620–1660
Preparation and Presentation

Background	Emphases	Readings
3. John Milton (1608-1674) *a)* John Milton, described as one of the "morning stars" in the constellation of American liberty, (*CHOC*, I, p. 2) is one of the great luminaries in English literature. *b)* Milton's Prose Works "I call therefore a complete and generous education that which fits a man to perform justly, skillfully, and magnanimously all the offices, both private and public, or peace and war." "Areopagitica," a plea for Christian self-government. The importance of this piece on the "Liberty of Unlicensed Printing" has consequence for liberty of the press—from a Christian and Biblical standpoint. Righteousness cannot be legislated—yet neither can we open the floodgates of evil. Liberty not license. Christian self-government is the key. Milton believes that "scandalous, seditious, and libelous books" should be suppressed as well as books on "popery." *"That as no man apprehends what vice is so well as he who is truly virtuous, no man knows hell like him who converses most in heaven."*	5. Writings of John Milton *a)* "On the Morning of Christ's Nativity." This is one of the great English odes and deals with the significance of Incarnation. Milton's poems echo his classical education. Thus this ode is called "Milton's Messianic eclogue." *b)* "L'Allegro" and "Il Penseroso" were two poems written in Milton's last long vacation from Cambridge in the summer of 1631—a farewell to a golden youth. *c)* Sonnet VII: his dedication to God's service. *d)* "Lycidas." Milton's faith in a providential interpretation of life is wrestling with Job's question: "Why should the just man suffer?" The occasion of the poem is the drowning of Edward King in the Irish Sea in 1637. *e)* Sonnet XIX: "On His Blindness." Commit to memory. *f)* *Paradise Lost*, our great Christian epic. Only John Milton dared to describe Heaven, Hell, the Temptation of Man, and our Redemption in such majestic lines as those of this great epic—the greatest since the world began. No current description of space travel can equal the scenes of this book. A pure heart can thrill to the most vivid account of innocence outside the sacred narrative.	Read "Of Education." Read "Areopagitica." Read *Paradise Lost* in its entirety. Use Professor Beatrice Batson's résumé of the XII Books of *Paradise Lost* in pages 67–79 of *A Reader's Guide to Religious Literature*.

Comparison of Puritans to Pilgrims

Issue	Puritan	Pilgrim (Separatists)
Relation to the Anglican Church	Remained in the Church in an attempt to purify it of Romanist elements.	Came out of the Church (separated) because of its impurity.
Relation to the English Government	Were generally well-treated or at worst tolerated.	Were pursued, condemned, fined, and arrested by the courts.
Motives for Coming to the New World	Profit, and to establish a church-state colony.	Sought freedom to worship God as the Lord directed the individual.
Relation to the Colonial Government	The church dominated the affairs of state. A dictatorship of the majority—democracy.	Church and state were separated but Biblical principles of government were applied which promoted a government by law—republic.
Relation to Education	Responsibility of the state to give the child an education on church dogma.	Responsibility of the parent to give the child a Christian education.
Relation to the Individual	The individual must be subordinate to the will of the church-state.	The individual was at liberty to obey God's will.

English Literature IIB

England Relinquishes Her Christian Heritage
Part Two of a Two-Year Course of English Literature

Tenth Grade

Restoration Period
Eighteenth-Century Literature
Age of Romanticism
Victorian Age
Twentieth-Century Literature

English Literature studied in relation to the

Chain of Christianity moving westward

CONTENTS

1. Course of Study Overview for each period

2. Leading Ideas and Ideals—based upon the Christian idea of man and government appearing and declining

3. Preparation and Presentation Charts—Background, Emphases, Readings

The suggested resource book—*English Literature: Its History and Its Significance for the Life of the English-Speaking World*, by William J. Long. Boston: Ginn and Company, 1909, 1945—is presently out-of-print, but available through book search.

English Literature IIB Overview for Tenth Grade

England Relinquishes Her Christian Heritage

English Literature Studied in Relation to the Chain of Christianity Moving Westward

Restoration Period 1660–1700	Eighteenth Century 1700–1800	Age of Romanticism 1800–1850	Victorian Age 1850–1900	Twentieth Century—A 1900–1925	Twentieth Century—B 1925–Present
Dryden, John Prose Poetry	Pope, Alexander Poetry	Wordsworth, William Poetry	Tennyson, Alfred Coleridge, Samuel Poetry	Kipling, Rudyard Poetry	Eliot, T. S. Auden, W. H. Thomas, Dylan Poetry
Sidney, Algernon *Discourses Concerning Government*	Swift, Jonathan *Gulliver's Travels*	Coleridge, Samuel Poetry	Browning, Robert Browning, Elizabeth Poetry	Wells, H. G. Prose	Orwell, George Novelist
Locke, John "Christian Philosopher of American Revolution." "Of Civil Government," 2nd Essay.	Addison and Steele *Tatler and Spectator*	Scott, Sir Walter Prose & Poetry	Dickens, Charles Novelist	Galsworthy, John Novelist, Plays	Woolf, Virginia
	Johnson, Samuel Dictionary	Byron, Lord Shelley, Percy Bysste Keats, John Poetry	Eliot, George Novelist	Barrie, J. M. Plays	Mansfield, Katherine Short Story
Newton, Isaac Letters	Boswell, James *Life of Johnson*	Lamb, Charles Essays	Bronte, Charlotte Novelist	Conrad, Joseph Novelist	Livingston, Sir R. Education
Pepys, Samuel *Diary*	Burke, Edmund Speech	Austen, Jane Novelist	Bulwer-Lytton, Edward Novelist	Masefield, John Poetry	Forster, E. M. Novelist
	Gibbon, Edward History		Stevenson, Robert Louis Novelist	Noyes, Alfred Poetry	Greene, Graham Novelist, Plays
	Gray, Thomas Burns, Robert Blake, William Poetry		Macaulay, Thomas Historian, Poetry	Housman, A. E. Poetry	Huxley, Aldous Prose
	Cowper, William Hymns		Carlyle, Thomas Historian	Shaw, George Bernard Plays, Prose	Snow, C. P. Prose
	Defoe, Daniel *Robinson Crusoe*		Thompson, Francis Poetry	Yeats, W. B. Poetry	Fry, Christopher Plays
			Ruskin, John Prose	Synge, John Plays	Tolkien, J. R. R. Fantasy
				Strachey, Lytton Biography	Lewis, C. S. Christian Fantasy

English Literature IIB for Tenth Grade
England Relinquishes Her Christian Heritage
The History and Literature of England
Studied in relation to the Chain of Christianity moving westward

Religion, like a Pilgrim westward bent
Knocking at all doors, ever as she went.
Religion stands on tiptoe in our land
Ready to pass to the American strand.

—George Herbert

Guidelines for the Course

The Restoration Period: 1660–1700

John Locke: Christian philosopher of the American Revolution.

Reading: *T & L*, Slater; *CHOC*, I, pp. 50-B–56-B; also "Of the State of Nature," pp. 58–61; "Of Property," pp. 63–70; "Of Paternal Power," pp. 70–77; "Self-Government with Union" (*CHOC*, II), pp. 45–50 and 68–90.

Question: John Locke develops Biblically the idea that life, liberty, and property—the foundation of a civil government—are from God. What are the key points which the founders of our republic incorporated into their political writings? How does Locke define man's obligations to God regarding life, liberty, and property? How does civil government protect these God-given rights?

Restoration Period

Describe Dryden's influence in an age of corrupt monarchy. In what ways are the Puritans more influential in this age than in the one denoted the Puritan Age? What does Locke contribute to Christian civil government? to education? to literature? What is his Biblical source? What other writers in this period contribute to the Chain of Christianity?

Eighteenth-Century Literature: 1700–1800

Burke: Selections from his speech on Conciliation with the Colonies (see below)

Selections from: Thomas, Gray, Goldsmith, Cowper, Burns, and Blake.

Defoe—*Robinson Crusoe*

Eighteenth Century

Addison and Steele have had a lasting influence upon both England and America. Describe their use of Sir Roger de Coverley in their efforts to strip the mask off vice, and reveal virtue as desirable and lovely. Why can Robinson Crusoe be considered a Christian novel? Describe Samuel Johnson's influence in literature. What was Christian in his character and influence? What Christian principles can be seen in Burke's major arguments for conciliation with the colonies? Describe the Christian contribution of each of the following poets: Gray, Cowper, Blake. Why is Burns exemplary of the individuality of Scotland? What is the effect of Gibbon's attack upon Christianity in his great masterpiece?

Outline for study of Burke's Speech on Conciliation with the Colonies: Riverside Literature Series, #100

1. Teacher summarizes historical events leading up to occasion of speech. Students take notes.
2. Paragraphs 1–14. Introduction. Emphasis on Burke's production of a plan based on principles of truth and reason.
3. Paragraphs 32–37. Burke's arguments against the "use of force."
4. Paragraphs 37–46. Burke discusses the character of Americans and the source of their spirit of liberty.
5. Paragraphs 47–57. Reasons why the first plan will not remove the spirit of resistance.
6. Paragraphs 59–63. Why the second plan is also impossible.

7. Paragraphs 64–68. Concession and why.
8. Paragraphs 91–115. Teacher's summary. Students' notes.
9. Paragraphs 140–145. Basis of England's hold on the colonies.

Questions:

Burke: What Christian principles do you see in Burke's major arguments for conciliation with the colonies?

Poets: Describe the Christian influence in each of the following: Gray, Cowper, Burns, and Blake.

Novel: How does Crusoe's conversion experience influence his activities on the desert island?

Age of Romanticism: 1700–1850

Contrast Romanticism with the Christian view of life and liberty. Which poets contributed to Romanticism? which to Christianity? What Christian ideals of English country life does Jane Austen contribute? Hannah More? whose writings on *Practical Piety* or the *Influence of The Religion of the Heart on the Conduct of Life* endeavored to offset the secular influences of her time. Name some of her works and areas of emphasis. *The Scottish Chiefs* paints a vivid picture of courage and patriotism and Christian forebearance. Name the author. Why is Sir Walter Scott one of the most influential writers of all times? What does Charles Lamb contribute to us today in the art of the essay?

Readings:

Selected poetry of Wordsworth, Coleridge, Byron, Keats, and Shelley

Read one historical novel of Scott—
The Talisman.

Questions: Wordsworth turned public taste away from the study of society to the contemplation of nature. What poems of Wordsworth show that "plain living and high thinking" and "homely beauty" are important to the happiness of man? How does Wordsworth show his commitment to Christian ideals?

Cite some of the descriptive passages from Coleridge's "Rime of the Ancient Mariner."

Describe the historical setting and the main character in one of Scott's novels.

What are the Christian aspects of chivalry?

Victorian Age: 1850–1900

Poetry: Tennyson, selections and *Idylls of the King*; Robert Browning, selections; Elizabeth Barrett Browning, sonnets

Essays: Stevenson, Macaulay, Carlyle

Novels: Dickens: *A Tale of Two Cities*, *David Copperfield*; Eliot: *Silas Marner*, *Adam Bede*

Victorian Age

In a period of Christianity's "falling away," some authors still express Christian, Biblical standards of life and character. What evidence do we have of the inroads of Evolution, Marxism, and Higher Criticism? Which writers are the "torch bearers" in this period? What answer does Dickens give to the problems of an Industrial society? How can the change of emphasis be seen in the Christian socialist Ruskin?

Twentieth Century

Describe the vitality and appeal of Kipling today. Identify Barrie's appeal in today's world of realism and cynicism. Describe how Shaw took the conflict of Christianity versus Socialism into the ideological rather than the religious area. Which writers continued to debate Christianity as an intellectual experience? Why do we owe so much to the Irish in the 20th Century? What must Christian writers do to restore the vitality of Biblical Christianity to literature?

Novels: Kipling; Poetry: J. Masefield, Noyes, Housman, Yeats; Christian apology and fantasy: Lewis; Drama/Poetry: Eliot; Fantasy: Tolkien.

Leading Ideas and Ideals of the English Restoration Period
1660–1700

External Reaction to Puritanism

Charles II returns the evils of monarchy to the throne and restores the ecclesiastical-political institution of the Church of England from which Pilgrims had separated. Embraces Roman Catholicism.

Internal Influence of Puritanism

Puritan ideals embedded in English hearts gradually reassert themselves in the national life. Corrupt court culminates in Revolution of 1688 which puts a Saxon on the throne— William of Orange.

Influence of Puritan Writers Milton and Bunyan

Biblical themes in literature—man's struggles with sin and his need of a Savior. Puritan ideas and ideals identified for the intellectual as well as the common man.

The Christian Idea of Man and Government

Locke and Sidney search the Scriptures for the principles of government and the basis of civil liberty. (*CHOC*, I, pp. 37, 50A, 51–130) "The Liberty of a people is the Gift of God and nature." (Sidney)

The Divine Right of Kings is questioned. "That Adam had not either by natural Right of Fatherhood, or by positive Donation from God, any such Authority over his Children, or Dominion over the World as it pretended." Locke, "Of Civil Government"—2nd Essay (See "Biblical-Political Index to John Locke," *T & L*, pp. 353–62.) "For men being all the workmanship of One Omnipotent and wise Maker: All the Servants of one Sovereign Master. . . they are his Property, whose Workmanship they are . . . . (*CHOC*, I, p. 58)

English Bill of Rights—1689, appears as a first step towards this aspect in the American Constitution (See "Christian Rights and English Law," *T & L*, pp. 343–52.)

Relationship between Righteousness and Liberty

Newton's *Principia* identifies God as the basis of all scientific law.

Modern science born through a Christian.

Teaching the Restoration Period, 1660–1700

Preparation and Presentation

Background	Readings

1. History of the Period
   a) External reaction to Puritanism:
     (1) Charles II returns the evils of monarchy to the throne; progress of liberty was turned backward.
     (2) In reaction to Puritan limitations, the decencies of life and reverence for law were abandoned—unnatural excesses resulted.
     (3) The ecclesiastical-political institution of the Church of England was restored.
   b) Internal influence of Puritanism:
     (1) Puritan ideals were embedded in English hearts and gradually reasserted themselves in national life.
     (2) Corrupt court culminates in the Revolution of 1688 which put a Saxon on the throne—William of Orange.
	Puritan Politics, *CHOC*, I, pp. 48–50

2. Literary Characteristics
   a) French influence:
     (1) Charles had been in exile in France with many of his followers—brought French influence.
     (2) The period of French literature was brilliant but the English writers copied the worst not the best.
   b) New tendencies:
     (1) Elizabethan and Puritan literature had contributed patriotism, creative vigor, love of romance, moral earnestness, and individualism.
     (2) These were past and two new tendencies developed:
       (*a*) Realism—the representation of men as they are without regard to ideals or romance. This was bad because of the corruption of the time and produced coarse, low plays without interest or moral significance. Later it became more wholesome.
       (*b*) Formalism—directness and simplicity of expression regarding established rules for writing, and emphasizing reasoning, short, clean-cut sentences without unnecessary words.
         (i) Dryden adopted the heroic couplet (2 iambic pentameter lines which rhyme).
         (ii) This formalism of style, and almost mathematical elegance, ruled English literature for the next century.
	John Dryden (1631-1700). Read "Ode to St. Cecilia."

Teaching the Restoration Period, 1660–1700
Preparation and Presentation

Background	Readings
(iii) The couplet was "closed"—each pair of lines must contain a complete thought stated as precisely as possible. *c)* Major literary developments of the period are exemplified in the work of one man—John Dryden: Rules for Literature; The Law—external law and order. Often called the father of modern prose he wrote in a clear, precise, if cold style. He represents the Monarchy, the Court, the aristocracy. 3. John Bunyan (1628–1688). While Dryden sleeps on our shelves today, known only as the arbiter of style, form, and precision, it is the Puritan writer, Bunyan, whose Christian prose epic still graces our lives. Thus the Gospel rather than the law achieves clarity of style and life, accomplishing through the heart—internal—what could not be decreed from the top down. *a)* The details of his life are found in his own words in his autobiography, *Of Grace Abounding*. His life is an epitome of the religious individualism which marked the close of the Reformation. (1) In strength and sincerity he built an immense following and was one of the first to be prohibited from holding public meetings when Charles II returned. (2) He was jailed for 12 years for refusing to obey, but saw his family frequently, preached, and earned support for his family making shoelaces. (3) He had long hours for studying his only two books, The King James Bible and *Foxe's Book of Martyrs*. (4) *The Pilgrim's Progress* was written during his imprisonment and published in 1678. (5) He became the most popular writer and preacher writing nearly 60 works in all, evangelizing, drawing throngs for 16 years. (6) He had perfect mental balance, charity and humor, tolerance, self-control, and sincerity; he retained a simple modesty which success could not spoil. (7) He died of a cold in the height of his ministry at the age of 60. *b)* He wrote the work that exemplifies the Puritan spirit, *The Pilgrim's Progress*. (1) He exhibits the spiritual independence which caused the Puritan struggle for liberty.	Read *The Pilgrim's Progress*.

Teaching the Restoration Period, 1660–1700
Preparation and Presentation

Background	Readings

(2) He was a commanding prose writer, gave us the allegory.
 	
c) *The Pilgrim's Progress* has been read more than any other book in our language except the Bible.
 	
d) *The Pilgrim's Progress* is a great allegory.
   (1) It has been translated into 75 languages and dialects.
   (2) In it Bunyan makes the doctrine of salvation by grace understood.
   (3) It is the first extended story in our language.
      (*a*) It has dramatic interest.
      (*b*) It is a true personal account told with strength, interest, and humor.
 	
4. Puritan Writers on Government
  a) Algernon Sidney (1622–1683)
   (1) Although of high birth and connected to the court, he supported Parliament and was attached to the Independents who were desirous of establishing a republican form of government.
   (2) He wrote "Discourses Concerning Government." Charged with treason, died a martyr in the cause of liberty when beheaded on Tower Hill in 1683.
   (3) After the Revolution of 1688 the sentence was declared illegal.
   (4) James Madison to Thomas Jefferson in 1825: "It is certainly very material that the true doctrines of liberty, as exemplified in our political systems, should be inculcated on those who are to sustain and may administer it . . . . Sidney and Locke are admirably calculated to impress on young minds the right of nations to establish their own governments, and to inspire a love of free ones."
  b) John Locke (1632–1704)
   (1) He was the authority to whom our founding fathers looked for the principles upon which our Revolution was conducted.
      (*a*) Many phrases of the Declaration of Independence may be found in Locke's writing.
      (*b*) He stated the doctrine: "Taxation without Representation is tyranny."
   (2) He was a student at Oxford where he met his patron, Lord Ashley, who urged him to study political and religious matters.
      (*a*) He also met many scholars and thinkers.
	CHOC, I pp. 37; 126–30
	
	"Of Property," *CHOC*, I, pp. 63–70; *T & L*, pp. 232–36
	
	Readings on Locke's life: *CHOC*, I, pp. 51–56; *T & L*, pp. 353–54

Teaching the Restoration Period, 1660–1700
Preparation and Presentation

Background	Readings
(b) He traveled in France and Holland and was exiled because of his patron. (3) The Revolution of 1688 permitted his return to England. 　(a) In 1689 he published his "Essay on Human Understanding," also "Two Treatises on Government." 　(b) His later years were given to the study of the Scriptures. 　(c) He died in 1704 at age 73. (4) John Locke was the philosopher of the American Revolution. 　(a) His original volumes show extensive marginal notes from the Scripture. 　(b) His works were the axe which cut the root of the divine right of kings. 　(c) He was studied and quoted by the American clergy of the 18th century who believed that government should be revelational of God.	
5.　The Diary 　a) John Evelyn (1620–1706) wrote a diary which gives vivid pictures of society in his time and of the corruption of the royal court. 　b) Samuel Pepys (1633–1703) was secretary of the Admiralty where he kept a diary from 1660–1669. 　　(1) It was written in shorthand which was not deciphered until 1825. 　　(2) It gives a minute picture of the daily life of the age.	Read John Evelyn—selections. Read Pepys's *Diary*.
6.　The Revolution of 1688 brought steps toward a constitutional monarchy. 　a) The reign of the Stuarts came to its climax and end when James II was deposed by his own countrymen. 　b) By an act of parliament known as the Revolution of 1688, William of Orange, who had been invited to England, and Mary (James's daughter) became king and queen of England on February 13, 1689.	
7.　English Bill of Rights, 1689 　a) Asserted the supremacy of Parliament over claimed divine right of kings. 　b) Toleration of Protestants assured and a number of individual liberties were given. 　c) This was the direct ancestor of our American Bill of Rights.	Read *T & L*, p. 347

Teaching the Eighteenth Century, 1700–1800
Preparation and Presentation

Background	Readings

1. History
  a) Covers time from English Revolution of 1688 to the French Revolution.
    (1) Began with adoption of Bill of Rights in 1689, the final step in establishing a constitutional government (the first two steps were the Magna Charta [1215] and the Petition of Right [1628]).
    (2) Cabinet government was established in the reign of George I, 1714–1727.
    (3) The foreign prestige of England was strengthened by conquest and colonization.
    (4) Whigs—seeking greater liberty for the people—and Tories—upholding the king against popular government—divided the country.
  b) In the midst of the rise of parliamentary system and constitutional monarchy, England moves away from her Christian heritage.
    (1) English liberty gives rise to freedom of expression.
      (a) Written word—newspapers, pamphlets, etc.
      (b) Spoken word—coffeehouse
      (c) First novels—Christian themes
    (2) Moral standard of nation declined.
      (a) Political corruption and drunkenness were prevalent.
      (b) Methodist revival arose.
 	
2. Literary Characteristics
  a) Classicism
    (1) Age of prose
      (a) Practical interests of new social and political conditions demanded expression.
      (b) Newspapers, magazines, and pamphlets developed.
    (2) Poetry was polished, unimaginative, formal (Pope), using closed couplet.
    (3) Satire was prevalent in poetry and prose producing lower type of literature. Critical, emphasizing intellect rather than imagination, form rather than content.
    (4) Examples: Alexander Pope—poet; Jonathan Swift—satirist; Joseph Addison—essayist, and Richard Steele—newspapers; Samuel Johnson—influence, character; James Boswell—*Life of Johnson*; Edmund Burke—orator; Edward Gibbon—historian (attacks Christianity).
	Directed reading to identify leading ideas and ideals of the period and England's move away from her Christian heritage as a nation.
	
	Daniel Defoe, *Robinson Crusoe*
	
	Alexander Pope (1688–1744), Great Poems, His life and "An Essay on Man"
	
	Selections from Pope's translation of *The Iliad*, and *The Odyssey* of Homer
	
	Jonathan Swift (1667–1745), *Gulliver's Travels*

THE NOAH PLAN © 1997 • FOUNDATION FOR AMERICAN CHRISTIAN EDUCATION

Teaching the Eighteenth Century, 1700–1800
Preparation and Presentation

Background	Readings

b) The Revival of Romantic Poetry
    (1) Romanticism—the expression of life as seen by imagination
        (a) Protest against bondage of rules; reaction to rules and custom (bondage)—free spirit
        (b) Return to nature and human heart, humanity for material
        (c) Ideals replace reality.
        (d) Intense human sympathy and understanding of human heart (ex. Cowper, "The Task Book II"; Gray's "Elegy," cry against oppression
        (e) Expression—emphasis of individual genius rather than rules, therefore varied and individual
        (f) Influenced by Spenser, Shakespeare, Milton
    (2) Major poets—Goldsmith, Cowper, Gray, Burns, Blake
c) The First English Novelists
    (1) The story element—as old as man
    (2) The romance—the element of imagination given full play
    (3) Examples: Defoe—*Robinson Crusoe* (Christian)
        Richardson—*Pamela*
        Fielding—*Tom Jones*
        Sterne—*Tristram Shandy*
        Goldsmith—*Vicar of Wakefield*
 	
3. The Christian idea of man and government appears.
a) Locke, Sidney were studied by American clergy making the English idea of liberty with law practical.
b) Blackstone codifies the common or Christian law of the land, "the law of nature"—God's law. He begins to identify the "separation of powers"—the three-fold aspect which is in our constitution.
c) Burke warns England of the loss of America.
d) Gibbon warns England of her departure from her heritage.
 	
4. Richard Steele (1671–1719) and Joseph Addison
a) The beginning of the modern essay—commentaries on men and manners
b) *The Tatler* and *The Spectator* endeavor to reform the corruption of the day, unmasking vice, making virtue attractive. "We had many books to teach us our more important duties. . . but a judge of propriety was yet wanting" (Johnson)
	Selections from Cowper, Gray, Burns, and Blake
	
	Selections from "The Sir Roger de Coverley Papers" (*The Spectator*)

Teaching the Eighteenth Century, 1700–1800
Preparation and Presentation

Background	Readings

5. Samuel Johnson
  a) The Christian character of Samuel Johnson and the great problem of producing literature in a society where letters were for the educated or the elite.
  b) James Boswell—wrote the biography of Johnson.
  c) Goals for English language sought by Johnson—later amplified by Noah Webster in his expansion of lexicography to include a philosophy of government in a republic.
	James Boswell's *Life of Johnson*
	  Selections

6. Edmund Burke—Liberty and property—taxation with representation; Locke's principles of civil government by consent articulated by the colonists find eloquent expression in their friend, Burke.	Edmund Burke (1729–1797) Selections
7. Edward Gibbon—History as Literature. Gibbon's dispassionate record of Rome and Christianity gives it greater credibility.	Edward Gibbon (1737–1794) Selections from *Decline and Fall of the Roman Empire*

Leading Ideas and Ideals of Eighteenth-Century Literature

1700–1800

The Christian Idea of Man and Government

English ideas and ideals of liberty with law, made practical in America as the writings of Locke, Sidney, and Harrington are studied by American clergy for fifty years before American Revolution.

Blackstone codifies the common or Christian law of the land—"the law of Nature"—God's law. Begins to identify the "separation of powers"—the threefold aspect of which is identified by the American Constitution. Blackstone is a best seller in America.

Burke endeavors to keep England true to her ideals of constitutional liberty and warns England of the loss of America. His vision is clear also as to the anti-Christian nature and conspiracy of the French Revolution. He had his American counterparts in oratory and statesmanship.

Gibbon's historical treatment of the decline and fall of Rome, published in 1776, was intended to be a warning to England that her departure from her heritage was beset with disaster.

English liberty gives rise to freedom of expression.

The Power of the Written Word

The political essayist, pamphleteer, and newspaper

Rise of political parties: Whigs and Tories

The Power of the Spoken Word

Age of the coffeehouse as a political, social, and literary center. Johnson dictates letters.

Orations of Statesmen and Politicians

Friends of American liberty decry suppression of ideals of constitutional government.

Reaction against Polite Society

The revival of romantic poetry, and man turns to nature and to God for "the proper study of mankind."

First novels have Christian concerns.

Robinson Crusoe finds Christ on the desert island and is rescued from sin.

The Vicar of Wakefield—Christianity at the English fireside and hearth. Wholesomeness.

Teaching the Age of Romanticism, 1800–1850
Preparation and Presentation

Background	Readings

1. History
  a) The period extends from the Revolutionary War (1776) to the accession of Victoria in 1837.
  b) Period of turmoil and steady advance
    (1) The French Revolution had a profound influence on life and literature—gave concept of liberty as being man-generated.
    (2) The Reform Bill of 1832 brought:
      (a) Suffrage,
      (b) Removal of restrictions against Catholics,
      (c) National system of schools,
      (d) Abolition of slavery.
    (3) Industrial Revolution—the invention of the steam engine and other machinery changed England from an agricultural to a manufacturing nation.
    (4) Economic conditions—unequal distribution of wealth—caused extreme poverty and oppressive labor conditions.
      (a) Women and children labored 16 hours which would hardly pay for their daily bread.
      (b) Adam Smith wrote *The Wealth of Nations* and Thomas Paine wrote *The Rights of Man*, both exercising enormous influence.
 	
2. Literary Characteristics
  a) Poetical and Romantic
  b) Characteristics:
    (1) Romantic poetry is prevalent.
    (2) Historical novel is created.
    (3) Women novelists appear.
    (4) Literary criticism is developed.
    (5) Philosophy took a practical and economic bend.
    (6) Literary magazines are established.
	1. Jane Austen (1775–1817)
	  a) Jane Austen refined and simplified the English novel, making it a true reflection of English life.
	    (1) *Pride and Prejudice*, her greatest novel, finished in 1797, went 16 years before being published.
	    (2) She presented English country society as it was with a gift of humor.
	    (3) She wrote six novels and is unequaled in her field.
	    (4) Walter Scott said of her: "That young lady has a talent for describing the involvements and feelings and characters of ordinary life which is to me the most wonderful I ever met with. The big bowwow strain I can do myself, like any now going; but the exquisite touch which renders ordinary commonplace things and characters interesting from the truth of the description and the sentiment, is denied to me. What a pity such a gifted creature died so early."
	  b) Read *Pride and Prejudice*. There is a general resemblance between Jane Austen and Elizabeth Bennet, the heroine of *Pride and Prejudice*.
	
	2. The Poets of Romanticism
	  a) William Wordsworth (1770-1850)
	    (1) His life
	    The Prelude records impressions of his boyhood and growth to manhood in four periods.
	    (2) Characteristics of his poetry:
	      (a) Simplicity—gave the charm of novelty to things of everyday. . . by awakening the mind's attention from the lethargy of custom and directing it to the loveliness and wonders of the world before us."
	      (b) Sensitive to nature, its beauty and changes
	      "Tintern Abbey"
	      "Intimations of Immortality"
	      "She Was a Phantom of Delight"
	  b) Coleridge, *The Rime of the Ancient Mariner*
	  c) Shelley
	  d) Keats
	  e) Byron
	
	3. Sir Walter Scott, *The Lady of the Lake*

Leading Ideas and Ideals of the Age of Romanticism

1800–1850

The Christian Idea of Man and Government

1. In Government:

   The American republic sails on despite the dangerous seas of democratic idealism arising in Europe. Struggle between the American Christian base of liberty as being God-given, and the French Revolution concept of "the rights of man" as being man-generated. Christian idea declines in England.

   England as a constitutional monarchy has a parliament not yet truly representative of every individual because her theological base is hierarchical. Sun never sets on the British Empire.

2. Economic:

   Adam Smith's concepts of capitalism and the importance of owning the tools of production is in conflict with European concepts of the mercantile system. Industrial development in England is hampered by the decline of Christian character in business and is helped by the rise of humanitarian reformers.

3. Religious:

   The Sunday School movement and rise of Methodism points to inward reform of the individual as the only true means of reforming society.

Liberty of the Individual

In contrast to the restraints of classicism, romantic individualism soars free in literature. It is an upward flight at first viewing only the beauties of God's creation and the finest ideals of man as he contemplates truth and beauty. Full of feeling and spirit, the idealism of this age precedes later concern in literature for the complete freedom and independence of the individual.

God or Man the Source of Liberty

The revolt from restraints in this age reflects the age-old struggle to identify man's source of liberty—either as Creator-endowed or as man-evolved and ultimately government-granted. Rebellion is often against God and His rule of man. The Romantic Age produces many literary forms of idealism particularly the historical, romantic novel with its roots of character in the Anglo-Saxon, its manners in the age of chivalry, and its idealism in Christianity.

Reform of Society—Internal or External

The presence of evangelical influences brings to the fore concern for the evils of society. The choice is individual reformation or social legislation—the law or the Gospel—and sometimes includes both.

The Age of Romanticism, 1800–1850

The first half of the nineteenth century records the triumph of Romanticism in literature and of democracy in government; and the two movements are so closely associated, in so many nations and in so many periods of history, that one must wonder if there is not some relation of cause and effect between them. Just as we understand the tremendous energizing influence of Puritanism in the matter of English liberty by remembering that the common people had begun to read, and that their book was the Bible, so we may understand this age of popular government by remembering that the chief subject of romantic literature was the essential nobleness of common men and the value of the individual.

As we read now that brief portion of history which lies between the Declaration of Independence (1776) and the English Reform Bill of 1832, we are in the presence of such mighty political upheavals that "the age of revolution" is the only name by which we can adequately characterize it. Its great historic movements become intelligible only when we read what was written in this period; for the French Revolution and the American commonwealth, as well as the establishment of a true democracy in England by the Reform Bill, were the inevitable results of ideas which literature had spread rapidly through the civilized world. Liberty is fundamentally an ideal: and that ideal—beautiful, inspiring, compelling, as a loved banner in the wind—was kept steadily before men's minds by a multitude of books and pamphlets as far apart as Burns's Poems and Thomas Paine's *Rights of Man*. All were read eagerly by the common people, all proclaimed the dignity of common life, and all uttered the same passionate cry against every form of class or caste oppression.

First the dream appears, the ideal in some human soul; then the written word which proclaims it, and impresses other minds with its truth and beauty; then the united and determined effort of men to make the dream a reality—that seems to be a fair estimate of the part that literature plays, even in our political process.

Historical Summary

The period we are considering begins in the latter half of the reign of George III and ends with the accession of Victoria in 1837. When on a foggy morning in November, 1783, King George entered the House of Lords and in a trembling voice recognized the independence of the United States of America, he unconsciously proclaimed the triumph of that free government by free men which had been the ideal of English literature for more than a thousand years—though it was not till 1832, when the Reform Bill became the law of the land, that England herself learned the lesson taught her by America and became the democracy of which her writers had always dreamed.

The French Revolution

The half-century between these two events is one of great turmoil, yet of steady advance in every department of English life. The storm center of the political unrest was the French Revolution, that frightful uprising which proclaimed the natural rights of man and the abolition of class distinctions. Its effect on the whole civilized world is beyond computation.

Economic Conditions

By her inventions in steel and machinery, and by her monopoly of the carrying trade, England had become "the workshop of the world." Her wealth had increased beyond her wildest dreams; but the unequal distribution of that wealth was a spectacle to make angels weep. The invention of machinery at first threw thousands of skilled hand workers out of employment; in order to protect a few agriculturists, heavy duties were imposed on corn and wheat, and bread rose to famine prices just when laboring men had the least money to pay for it. There followed a curious spectacle. While England increased in wealth, and spent vast sums to support her army and subsidize her allies in Europe, and while nobles, landowners, manufacturers, and merchants lived in increasing luxury, a multitude of skilled laborers were clamoring for work. Fathers sent their wives and little children into mines and factories where sixteen hours' labor would hardly pay for their daily bread; and in every large city were riotous mobs made up chiefly of hungry men and women. It was this unbearable economic condition and not any political theory, as Burke supposed, which occasioned the danger of another English revolution.

Reforms

Having gained enormous prestige abroad by overthrowing Napoleon at Waterloo in 1815, England now turned to the work of reform at home. The destruction of the African slave trade; the mitigation of horribly unjust laws which included poor debtors and petty criminals in the same class; the prevention of child labor; freedom of the press; the extension of manhood suffrage; the abolition of restrictions against Catholics in parliament; the establishment of hundreds of popular schools—these are but a few of the reforms which mark the progress of civilization in a single half-century. When England, in 1833, proclaimed the emancipation of all slaves in all her colonies, she unconsciously proclaimed her final emancipation from barbarism.

Chronology of the Age of Romanticism

History		Literature	
1760–1820	George III	1770–1850	William Wordsworth
		1771–1832	Sir Walter Scott
1789–1799	French Revolution		
		1796–1816	Jane Austen's novels
		1798	Lyrical ballads of Wordsworth and Coleridge
1800	Union of Great Britain and Ireland		
1802	Colonization of Australia	1802	Scott's *Minstrelsy* of the Scottish Border
1805	Battle of Trafalgar	1805–1817	Scott's poems
1807	Abolition of slave trade	1807	Wordsworth's "Intimations of Immortality" Lamb's *Tales from Shakespeare*
1808–1814	Peninsular War	1809–1818	Byron's *Childe Harold's Pilgrimage*
1812	Second war with United States	1810–1813	Coleridge's lectures on Shakespeare
1814	Congress of Vienna	1814–1831	Scott's Waverley Novels
1815	Battle of Waterloo		
1819	First Atlantic steamship	1816	Shelley's *Alastor*
1820	George IV (d. 1830)	1817–1820	Keats's poems
1826	First Temperance Society		
1829	Catholic Emancipation Bill		
1830	William IV (d. 1837); First railway	1830	Tennyson's first poems
		1831	Scott's last novel
1832	Reform Bill		
1833	Emancipation of slaves	1833	Carlyle's *Sartor Resartus*; Browning's "Pauline"
1834	System of national education		
1837	Victoria crowned (d.1901)		

THE NOAH PLAN © 1997 • FOUNDATION FOR AMERICAN CHRISTIAN EDUCATION

Study Guide to Romantic Writers

1. Jane Austen

Our Goals in Studying *Pride and Prejudice*:

a) While *Pilgrim's Progress* was a spiritual allegory with the purpose of developing spiritual discernment and wisdom, this novel is a social documentary of life in early nineteenth-century England and offers opportunity to develop social discernment and wisdom.

b) It is one of the greatest novels in the English language, a favorite of writers for its craftsmanship, subtlety, and for treating the reader as an intelligent and discerning individual.

c) One of our first goals is to read it with enjoyment, appreciating what we can learn of England, of society, of relationships, and of marriage.

d) Another goal is to absorb as much as we can of the excellent quality of language and vocabulary and allow our own expression, both written and verbal, to be enriched and cultivated by this study.

e) We hope to enjoy *Pride and Prejudice* enough to lead us to read the other Austen novels—*Emma, Sense and Sensibility,* and *Mansfield Park.*

f) We will record our study in our notebooks in the following way:

 (1) Set up a page for each of the literary elements:

  (a) Setting

  (b) Plot

  (c) Characterization—one page each for the four main characters: Elizabeth, Jane, Darcy, and Bingley. Another page with ten lines left for each of the remaining characters: Mr. Bennet, Mrs. Bennet, Lydia, Wickham, Charlotte, and Lydia.

  (d) Theme

  (e) Style

  (f) Notes on the background

 (2) Vocabulary—file all vocabulary work together with the list.

 (3) Assignments—file at the end of the section in chronological order.

2. William Wordsworth

"She Dwelt among the Untrodden Ways"
"A Slumber Did My Spirit Seal"

Written in the style typical of Wordsworth, these poems lament the death of someone the speaker loved.

a) Analysis. How is Lucy characterized in "She Dwelt among the Untrodden Ways"? How do you account for the force of the last line? Write a composition to answer these questions.

b) Comparison and Contrast. "A Slumber Did My Spirit Seal" deals with the same subject as "She Dwelt among the Untrodden Ways." Is it more or less effective in its expression of loss? Compare and contrast the force of emotion in the two poems and the tone in which the emotion is expressed.

c) Sonnets. Examine Wordsworth's sonnets and describe their form. Does Wordsworth follow the Petrarchan or Shakespearean form? Describe the movement of thought in his sonnets.

3. Lord Byron

"The Prisoner of Chillon"

a) Analysis. How does Byron enlist your sympathy for Bonnivard? Write a composition in answer to this question. Be sure to refer to specific passages to support your answer.

b) Analysis. Consider the character of Bonnivard as he is presented in the poem and write a composition explaining why he was able to cling to life when the others died.

4. John Keats

> "Beauty is truth, truth beauty"—that is all.
> Ye know on earth, and all ye need to know.
>
> ("Ode on a Grecian Urn")

John Keats, the only major Romantic poet of humble birth, was the son of a livery stable keeper in London. He attended school in the village of Enfield until both parents died when he was fifteen, and he was then apprenticed to a surgeon. While studying medicine as a young man, Keats told a friend: "The other day, during a lecture, there came a sunbeam into the room, and with it a whole troop of creatures floating in the ray; and I was off with them to oberon and fairyland." With such an outlook, it is no wonder that Keats gave up a career in medicine to devote himself to poetry.

A copy of Spenser's *Faerie Queene*, which had been given him by Charles Cowden Clark, was the prime cause of his abstraction. He abandoned his profession in 1817, and early in the same year published his first volume of poems.

Keats was not only the last but also the most perfect of the Romanticists. Partly because of his high ideal of poetry, partly because he studied and unconsciously imitated the Greek classics and the best works of the Elizabethans, Keats's last work is unequalled by any of his contemporaries. When we remember that all his work was published in three short years, from 1817 to 1819, and that he died when only twenty-five years old, we must judge him to be the most promising figure of the early nineteenth century, and one of the most remarkable in the history of literature.

These lines from *Endymion* demonstrate the spirit of Keats's later work, with its perfect finish and melody:

> A thing of beauty is a joy forever;
> Its loveliness increases; it will never
> Pass into nothingness; but still will keep
> A bower quiet for us; and a sleep
> Full of sweet dreams, and health, and quiet breathing

Read:

The Sonnet—"On first looking into Chapman's Homer";

The Ballad—"La Belle Dame Sans Merci";

The Ode—"Bards of Passion and of Mirth";

The Sonnet—"When I have fears. . . .";

The Sonnet—"Bright star, would I were. . . ."

An ode is any strain of enthusiastic and exalted lyrical verse, directed to a fixed purpose, and dealing progressively with one dignified theme. An elaborate lyric, expressed in language dignified, sincere, and imaginative and intellectual in tone. In form the ode is divided into strophes: the strophe, antistrophe, and epode. Originally a Greek form used in dramatic poetry, the ode was choral, accompanied by music, the chorus of singers moved up one side during the strophe, down the other during the antistrophe, and stood in place during the epode.

A ballad is a form of verse to be sung or recited and is characterized by its presentation of a dramatic or exciting episode in simple narrative form.

THE NOAH PLAN © 1997 • FOUNDATION FOR AMERICAN CHRISTIAN EDUCATION

Teaching the Victorian Period, 1850–1900
Preparation and Presentation

Background	Emphases	Readings
1. Victoria Regina dominated this age by her life and character. Read a reliable biography on the domestic influence of Victoria and Albert. This is a period of great novelists—Dickens and Stevenson; a period of great poets—Tennyson, Coleridge, the Brownings (Robert and Elizabeth); of great historians—Macaulay and Carlyle; of great writers of the essay—Stevenson, Macaulay, and Carlyle.	1. Dickens gives a last great Christian challenge of character to a rapidly industrializing society. What change of emphasis can be seen in the Christian socialist, John Ruskin?	Charles Dickens, novels *Great Expectations*
	2. George Eliot (Mary Ann Evans) provides us with two fine novels with Christian themes, *Silas Marner* and *Adam Bede*. Other novels reflect her own internal conflict with the demands of a Christian life.	George Eliot, novels *Adam Bede*
2. There are so few great Christian novels, and we count *The Last Days of Pompeii* by Bulwer-Lytton as one of these—still to be enjoyed for its definition of the struggle between paganism and the Christian challenges of life and character.	3. The Bronte sisters, Charlotte and Emily, write with passion novels of vehemence. *Jane Eyre* has more redeeming qualities than *Wuthering Heights,* but both reflect the romantic era.	Charlotte Bronte, novels *Jane Eyre* E. Bulwer-Lytton, novels
3. History of the Period: a) Democracy is established as the king becomes a figurehead and the House of Commons becomes the ruling power in England. b) It is an age of social unrest as slaves are freed, but terrible industrial slavery exists in the mines and factories. c) It is an age of peace. d) Arts and sciences progress rapidly along with mechanical inventions. Theory of evolution begins.	4. The great Thackeray is a moralist and *Vanity Fair* is a revealing novel of character. 5. Alfred Tennyson (1809–1892) stood at the summit of poetry in England throughout the Victorian Age. a) He was appointed poet laureate at the death of Wordsworth in 1850, and he felt the importance of the position and honored it. b) He was a voice of the people expressing their doubts, faith, griefs, and triumphs in a variety of verse. c) His life was given to the writing of poetry for 66 years, encouraged in the beginning by Wordsworth and the popularity of his first publications. d) He married Emily, whom he had loved 13 years, but whom his poverty had prevented him	Poetry of Tennyson Robert Louis Stevenson, novels *Treasure Island* T. B. Macaulay, historian, poetry Thomas Carlyle, historian F. Thompson, poetry John Ruskin, prose
4. Literary characteristics: a) This is a period in which every form of literature from romance to realism is expressed. b) It reflects the strength and ideals of the Saxons and the culture and refinement of the Norman influence.		

Teaching the Victorian Period, 1850–1900
Preparation and Presentation

Background	Emphases	Readings
c) The novel had prominent place in this age of prose which saw the spread of popular education produce readers of magazines, newspapers, and the novel. d) There is a moral purpose to uplift and instruct in the literature. e) There is a spirit of idealism, of faith and courage, charity and inspiration throughout the literature.	from marrying: "Her whose gentle will has changed my fate/and made my life a perfumed altar flame." e) The last 40 years of his life he wrote steadily, enjoyed wide friendships and popularity. f) The strong and noble spirit of his life is reflected in one of his best known poems, "Crossing the Bar." 6. Robert Browning (1812–1889) was the poet who, after 30 years of continuous work, was recognized and placed beside Tennyson. a) His field was the individual soul and he sought to reveal the hidden motives which govern individual action. b) Browning is a teacher of men, with a mission of faith and courage in a world of doubt and timidity. 7. Elizabeth Barrett Browning (1806–1861)	Poetry of the Brownings

Twentieth-Century English Literature, 1900–Present
Preparation and Presentation

Background	Emphases	Readings
1. This period is characterized by the rise of Fabian socialism. Christian principles and their application to society are not seen. What is our debt to the Irish writers like Yeats and Synge? Strachey begins the attack of the intellectual upon Christians in high places. Our major poets of this period still reflect romantic rather than realistic themes: Masefield and Noyes. Galsworthy writes plays of social conflict and novels of social stress.	1. This is a period of debunking or attacking institutions. There is very little Christian application of Biblical truths to the times. 2. Writers who depict modern times do so from despair or fantasy. Escape literature plays a role in the life of both England and America. But with the decline of Christian principles and the Christian idea of man and government comes a rebirth of the reformed faith. It is our hope and conviction that we can re-educate through both the faith and the literature of England when she was true to her role in the Chain of Christianity.	H. G. Wells, prose John Galsworthy, novelist, plays J. M. Barrie, plays J. Conrad, novels John Masefield, poetry Alfred Noyes, poetry A. E. Housman, poetry George Bernard Shaw, plays, prose W. B. Yeats, poetry J. Synge, plays L. Strachey, biography C. S. Lewis, Christian fantasy T. S. Eliot, poetry, plays W. H. Auden, poetry Dylan Thomas, poetry George Orwell, novels Virginia Woolf, novels Katherine Mansfield, short stories Sir R. Livingston, education
	3. What must Christian writers, both English Christian and American Christian, do to restore the vitality of the Biblical approach to all of life and living?	
2. Study Kipling's writings on India. Why is he challenged today? What is the appeal of Barrie today? Can we still appreciate Peter Pan? Describe how Wells and Shaw presented political ideology in their writings.		Rudyard Kipling, poetry and stories

American Literature IIIA

Planting the Seed of the American Christian Republic
Part One of a Two-Year Course of American Literature

Eleventh Grade

Colonial Period
Literature of the American Revolution
Federal Period

America's Founding Reflected in Her Literature

CONTENTS

1. Course of Study Overview for each period

2. Leading Ideas and Ideals—based upon the Christian idea of man and government appearing and declining

3. Preparation and Presentation Charts—Background, Emphases, Readings

4. Principle Approach Syllabi materials, including content for teacher and students for the Colonial Period and the American Revolution

---

The suggested resource book—*American Literature: A Study of the Men and the Books That in the Earlier and Later Times Reflect the American Spirit*, by William J. Long. Boston: Ginn & Co., 1913, 1964—is presently out-of-print, but available through book search.

American Literature IIIA Overview for Eleventh Grade

Planting the Seed of the American Christian Republic

America's Founding Reflected in Her Literature

Colonial Period 1607–1765	Revolutionary Period 1765–1787	Federal Period 1787–1840	
Smith, Captain John	Otis, James "The Rights of the British Colonies"	Irving, Washington Biography, novels, essays, history	
Bradford, William *Of Plimoth Plantation*	Dickinson, John "Farmer's Letters"	Bryant, William Cullen Poetry	
Penn, William	Adams, Samuel "The Rights of the Colonists"	Poe, Edgar Allan Poetry	
Winthrop, John "Little Speech on Liberty"	Adams, John "Timidity"	Cooper, James Fenimore *The Deerslayer* *The Spy*	
Whitaker, Alexander "Good News from Virginia"	Jefferson, Thomas Declaration of Independence		
Eliot, John Indian Bible, 1663	Henry, Patrick "Give Me Liberty"		
Gookin, Daniel	Washington, George *Journal*, Farewell Address		
Hooker, Thomas Edwards, Jonathan Mather, Cotton Sewall, Samuel Sermons	Franklin, Benjamin *Autobiography*		
Bradstreet, Anne Poetry	Warren, Mercy History; *The Group*		
Bay Psalm Book, 1640	Adams, John and Abigail Letters		
New England Primer	Wheatley, Phillis Freneau, Philip Poetry		
	Hopkinson, Francis "The Battle of the Kegs"		
	Barlow, Joel "Hasty Pudding"		

THE NOAH PLAN © 1997 • FOUNDATION FOR AMERICAN CHRISTIAN EDUCATION

American Literature for Eleventh Grade
Planting the Seed of the American Christian Republic

A great hope and inward zeall they had of laying some good foundation, or at least to make some way thereunto, for the propagating and advancing the gospell of the kingdom of Christ in those remote parts of the world: yea, though they should be but even as steppingstones unto others for the performing of so great a work.

—William Bradford, *Of Plimoth Plantation*, 1635

Overview for the Course

Colonial Period:
Biblical classics in our parent colonies; missionary writers; colonial clergy; colonial bestsellers.

The American Revolution:
Influence of the clergy on a Biblical philosophy of government; literature in statesmanship; poetry, drama, satire.

The Federal Period:
First fruits of a Republic, liberty of the individual flowers in literature.

Teaching the Literature of the Colonial Period
1607–1765
Preparation and Presentation

Background	Emphases	Readings

1. Chain of Christianity
  a) *CHOC*, I, p. 6A and *T & L*, pp. 142–43
  b) Acts, 16th chapter
  c) "The Continents of History" and "The Geographical March of Civilization" (*T & L*, pp. 149–53)
  d) "America's Heritage of Christian Character" (pp. 210–23 in *T & L*)
  e) "Pilgrim Self-Government" (pp. 189–200 in *T & L*)
	1. Identify each of the following writers regarding:
	Character of the man
	Relationship to his colony
	Individuality of his writings
	Contribution to the Chain of Christianity
	  a) Captain John Smith (1580–1631) of Virginia (Elizabethan). Earliest book in American literature.
	
	  b) William Bradford (1590–1657) Governor of Plymouth Plantation (Pilgrim)
	First American citizen
	First American writer
	Historian of America's first Christian history
	
	  c) John Winthrop (1588–1649) First Governor of Massachusetts Bay Colony (Puritan)
		"Captain John Smith's America," edited by Lankford, selections.
		
		Old South Leaflet #167: "The Settlement of Jamestown" by Smith et al.
		
		Moses Coit Tyler: "Virginia: The First Writer"
		
		William J. Long: "The Spirit of Our First Literature" (chap. 1, pp. 1–7)
		
		William J. Long: "The Spirit of Our First Literature" (chap. 1, pp. 8–13)
		
		Old South Leaflet #77: "Cotton Mather's Lives of Bradford and Winthrop," pp. 1–8)
		
		Selections from Bradford's history, *Of Plimoth Plantation* (*CHOC*, I, pp. 182–240)
		
		Old South Leaflet #207: "A Model of Christian Charity" by John Winthrop
		
		CHOC, I, p. 262; "Little Speech on Liberty" by John Winthrop
		
		Winthrop's Journal (selections), Love letters

2. Middle Colony—Pennsylvania *CHOC*, I, pp. 262A–270 *T & L*, pp. 201–03	*d)* William Penn (1644–1718) Proprietor Quaker	Old South Leaflet #171: "Description of Pennsylvania" by William Penn

Teaching the Literature of the Colonial Period
1607–1765
Preparation and Presentation

Background	Emphases	Readings

3. Missionary Writers:
  a) Alexander Whitaker
    Moses Coit Tyler (from
      chap.3)
    "Virginia: Other Early Writers"
  b) John Eliot
    Introduction to "John Eliot,
    Apostle to the Indians," by
    Ola Elizabeth Winslow, 1968
	2. Missionary writers
	  a) Alexander Whitaker
	    (Arrived 1611)
	    "Apostle to Virginia"
	
	  b) John Eliot (1604–1690)
	    "Apostle to the Indians"
	    First Christian scholar in
	    America
	    John Eliot's Indian Bible, 1663,
	    is the first Bible printed in
	    America.
	
	  c) Daniel Gookin (1612–1687)
	    Magistrate; commander of
	    colonial military forces;
	    superintendent of Indians; co-
	    worker with John Eliot in
	    labor for Indians; originator of
	    "taxation without representa-
	    tion."
		"Good News from Virginia,"
		  (1613) (Selections)
		
		Old South Leaflet #52:
		  "The Indian Grammar Begun"
		
		Old South Leaflet #21:
		  "Eliot's Brief Narrative"
		
		Old South Leaflet #143:
		  "The Day-Breaking of the
		    Gospel with the Indians"

Teaching the Literature of the Colonial Period
1607–1765
Preparation and Presentation

Background	Emphases	Readings

4. The Colonial Clergy:
  a) Thomas Hooker
    (From Tyler, chap. 8)
    "New England: Theological Writers"
	3. Colonial Clergy
	  a) Thomas Hooker (1586?–1647)
	    Sermon preached in 1638, led to framing the "Fundamental Orders of Connecticut"—the first American Constitution—the first Constitution in the world based upon Biblical principles of government.
		"Historical Collection of the Indians in New England"—ready for publication 1674; it waited for 118 years and was printed in first volume of the Mass. Historical Society Collections.

b) Jonathan Edwards
    (From Tyler, chapter 15)
    "New England: The Pulpit in Literature" (from poem by Whittier)
    "The Preacher"
	b) Jonathan Edwards (1703–1758)
	    His famous sermon, "Sinners in the Hands of an Angry God," begins the Great Awakening, America's first major revival. Most famous sermon: "Freedom of the Will"
		CHOC, I, pp. 249–52
		
		"Essay on Spiders"
		
		"Resolution" (Selections)
		
		"Personal Narration" (Selections)

c) Cotton Mather
    Cotton Mather's Life and Writings (Long, pp. 57–69)
	c) Cotton Mather (1663–1728)
	    Theologian and America's first biographer of 114 men and 20 women
		"Magnalia Christi Americana" (Lives of Bradford, Winthrop, Eliot)

d) Samuel Sewall
    Samuel Sewall's Life and Writings (Long, pp. 27–32)
    Whittier's poem on Sewall
	d) Samuel Sewall (1652–1730)
	    American judge at witchcraft trials made public confession of his error. Wrote famous American diary of colonial life. Wrote first anti-slavery tract in America—"The Selling of Joseph."
		"Diary" (Selections)

Teaching the Literature of the Colonial Period
1607–1765
Preparation and Presentation

Background	Emphases	Readings
5. Colonial Bestsellers The *Bay Psalm Book*: "The Whole Book of Psalms faithfully translated into English Metre"	4. *Bay Psalm Book*: *a*) 1640 *b*) First book printed in English America *c*) Compiled by Richard Mather, John Eliot, Thomas Welde. *d*) In 1947 one of last copies sold for $150,000.00—highest price ever paid for an American book.	*Bay Psalm Book*: (Selections)
The New England Primer from: "Old Textbooks" by John Nietz, 1961	5. *New England Primer*: *a*) America's first educational textbook *b*) Issued before 1690 *c*) Biblical in nature *d*) Some three million sold in the 18th century	*New England Primer*: (Selections)
6. Nathaniel Ward Tyler, chap. 9 "New England: Misc. Prose"	6. Nathaniel Ward (1578?–1652) Colonial satire and Puritan invective against the times—1647	"Simple Cobbler of Agawam" (Selections)
7. Michael Wigglesworth The Life and Writings of Wigglesworth (Long, pp. 50–53)	7. Michael Wigglesworth (1631–1705) "Unshrinking Rhymer of the Five Points of Calvinism"	"The Day of Doom, A Poetical Description of the Great and Last Day of Judgment"

Leading Ideas and Ideals of the Colonial Period

The Chain of Christianity and American Literature

1. The globe is the theater of man, the form of which reveals a plan for history.

2. The northern continents, or continents of history, are designed to support the development and education of humanity.
   a) Western Asia is the cradle of man—the continent of origins.
   b) Europe, the continent of development, supported the flourishing of poetry, arts, sciences, and the church. Nationalities developed and ideas of government as well as language.
   c) America, the most complete expression of Christianity, has the oceanic position to secure prosperity and at the same time to influence the world.

3. The Chain of Christianity, which moved the Gospel westward from Asia to Europe to America, was forged by individuals used by God—Wycliffe, Tyndale, Columbus, the Pilgrims, etc.

4. America was veiled and kept for the planting of a Christian republic until all the preparation was complete.
   a) The French and Spanish settled north and south of the "veiled continent."
   b) Columbus, with a mission to save souls for Jesus Christ, had a revelation of lands to the west.
   c) New inventions—paper, moveable type, the telescope, microscope, mariner's compass—were helpful to the mission.
   d) The Reformation and translation of the Bible into English made the preparation complete.

5. God prepared men, the individuals necessary to represent the cream of the centuries, the best of Europe. Their humility matched their learning and experience—godly men of God's choosing.

6. The establishment of America as a Christian nation with a Christian form of government is best seen in the literature of the nation, the handmaid of history.

7. American literature does not begin with the legends and fantasy—magic, dragons, and free play of imagination—as the literatures of many of the other nations do. It begins with the record of brave, resolute men who loved freedom as their old Saxon ancestors loved it. It begins with the record of men who had a call from God and a purpose deep in their souls to found a new society based upon the Puritan ideals of freedom and righteousness. American literature begins with the careful historical records written "in a plain style, with singular regard unto the simple truth in all things."

8. The colonists produced few great books because they were too busy with great deeds, intent on solving the great problems of humanity.

9. The object of all literature is to acquaint us with humanity. The study of colonial literature will identify the men and women who founded this nation and who are bound to us across the centuries by the ties of a common hope and ideals of Christian government.

Christian Individuality in the Parent Colonies

1. Captain John Smith (1580–1631) of Virginia—Elizabethan
   a) **Character**: Smith has strong traits, both negative and positive. He was brave, daring, had executive force, and an energetic love of adventure. He was impulsive, egotistic, irascible, and his noble and generous nature was suspected of being motivated by greed.

b) **Relationship to colony**: Smith wrote an account of the Virginia colony which painted a picture of Eden, probably intending to lure new investors. His executive ability saved the colony from starvation and exerted leadership in the face of many crises.

c) **Writings**: Smith wrote prolifically showing the Elizabethan romantic enthusiasm and imagination. His writing had clarity, force, vividness, and dramatic energy.

d) **Contribution to Chain**: "A True Relation of Virginia" was the earliest book in American literature, written during the first thirteen months of the life of the Jamestown colony.

e) **Memorize**: "Here is a place, a nurse for soldiers, a practice for mariners, a trade for merchants, a reward for the good; and that which is most of all, a business, most acceptable to God, to bring such poor infidels to the knowledge of God and his holy gospel."

2. William Bradford (1590–1657) of Plymouth Plantation—Pilgrim

   a) **Character**: Bradford, a teenager of 16 when in Leyden with the Pilgrims, was a self-educated man, well-read in five languages with a library of over 300 volumes. He was brave, tender, loyal to his convictions, and a wise leader. He was honest with a reverence for truth and accuracy. He was a man made by the Bible which he studied from the age of twelve. He said, "To keep a good conscience, and walk in such a way as God has prescribed in his Word, is a thing which I must prefer before you all, and above life itself." Irascible: easily provoked; irritable.

   b) **Relationship to colony**: Bradford was the governor of Plymouth Colony for thirty-three years. He was able to carry out the Pilgrim spirit in the affairs of the colony and to apply Chris-

tian principles to all of their problems. His direction of the farming from collectivism to private enterprise averted starvation. He was able to influence the Puritan Massachusetts Bay Colony and to establish good relations with them. He was called "a Moses—a leader of a people in the wilderness." However, "the crown of all was his holy, prayerful, watchful and fruitful walk with God, wherein he was very exemplary." —Cotton Mather

   c) **Writings**: Bradford's history, *Of Plimoth Plantation*, is an American classic. Its style is a revelation of the Pilgrim mind, rugged, sincere, with a glint of humor lighting up its sternness. It is a vivid, straightforward history of the Pilgrims. Bradford's Biblical view of life is seen clearly in his history and his style of writing shows the influence of the King James Bible.

   d) **Contribution to Chain**: "Wherever it shall go it will be an object of reverent care. I do not think many Americans will gaze upon it without a little trembling of the lips and a little gathering of mist in the eyes, as they think of the story of suffering, of sorrow, of peril, of exile, of death and of lofty triumph which that book tells. . . . There is nothing like it in human annals since the story of Bethlehem." (Senator Hoar, 1897, at Boston State House upon the return of the manuscript.) Bradford was the first American writer, first citizen, and historian of America's first Christian history.

      (1) He built Indian towns for the "praying Indians" and saved them from destruction by white people during King Philip's War.

      (2) He saw twenty-four Indians become preachers to their own tribes.

   e) **Memorize**: "To keep a good conscience, and walk in such a way as God has prescribed in his word, is a

See excerpts from *Of Plimoth Plantation* in *CHOC*, I, pp. 182–240.

thing which I must prefer before you all, and above life itself."

3. William Penn (1644–1718) of Pennsylvania—Quaker

  a) **Character**: Penn was a Quaker whose convictions led to persecution and prison where he developed an appreciation for liberty of conscience that became the foundation of the Pennsylvania colony. He was a pious, humble, and courageous man who depended on God's wisdom. His father's words to him: "Son William, let nothing in this work tempt you to wrong your conscience. So will you keep peace at home, which will be a feast to you in a day of trouble."

  b) **Relationship to colony**: His father left him a fortune which enabled him to obtain a land grant in America for a refuge from persecution for the Friends. The right to govern was vested in Penn. (*CHOC*, I, p. 266) His Christian leadership enabled each individual to become independent as he accepted the responsibility of work and self-government. His colony had a frame of government which allowed a greater degree of religious liberty than had at that time been allowed in the world.

  c) **Writings**: He wrote industriously to set forth Biblical principles of government. He wrote: "Liberty without obedience is confusion, and obedience without liberty is slavery."

  d) **Contributions to Chain**: Although a **proprietary** colony, Penn's conviction was that the privilege of self-government belongs to the individual (*T & L*, p. 202) and that Christian character is the basis of good government.

  e) **Memorize**: "Liberty without obedience is confusion, and obedience without liberty is slavery."

4. John Winthrop (1588–1648) of Massachusetts Bay Colony—Puritan

  a) **Character**: Winthrop was a wealthy Puritan who converted his estate into money to pour into the colony at Massachusetts Bay. He was educated to law but being serious-minded was more inclined to the clergy. He was chosen to be the first governor because of his character and reputation. He was known for his benevolence, sending spies at dinner time to see if each settler had enough and if not, sending supplies as needed. He was lenient to offenders, desiring to temper the law in the infant colony more so than in a settled state. For this he was censured. He was a man of good looks and good manners and deeply conscientious. His wife, Margaret, shared his life fully and was greatly loved by him.

  b) **Relationship to the colony**: Winthrop influenced his Puritans to live scripturally, especially as the family of God. "We must knit together in this work as one man. We must entertain each other in brotherly affection. We must be willing to abridge ourselves of our superfluities for the supply of others' necessities. We must uphold a familiar commerce together in all meekness, gentleness, patience, and liberality. We must delight in each other; make others' conditions our own; rejoice together, mourn together, labor and suffer together, always having before our eyes our commission and community in the work as members of the same body." Winthrop's life demonstrated these words; a wealthy man when coming to America, he died quite poor.

  c) **Writings**: Winthrop produced three categories of written works:
    (1) Journal (1630–1649), commenced before the ships left England; it is a record of events and an inside view of Puritanism.
    (2) "Little Speech on Liberty," delivered in 1645 at the end of his impeach-

ment trial, a moving and memorable definition of civil liberty.

(3) Love letters to Margaret: Winthrop wrote a clear, true story of the way the settlers labored and suffered. The account was written hurriedly, expressed spontaneously in dignified and calm words, with an unconscious eloquence. The tone is judicial—telling the truth squarely, even against himself. Read *CHOC*, I, p. 262, and excerpts in *Some Old Puritan Love-Letters, John and Margaret Winthrop, 1618–1638.*

d) **Contribution to Chain**: Winthrop's character was imprinted upon the Massachusetts Bay Colony in its enterprise and community. A copy of his writings was found by Noah Webster in 1789 who preserved it for posterity.

e) **Memorize**: "This liberty you are to stand for; with the hazard (not only of your goods but) of your lives, if need be . . . it is the same kind of liberty wherewith Christ hath made us free."

The Colonial Clergy

1. The preachers were the leaders of thought, and the meetinghouse was the center of social and religious activity.

   a) The clergymen were usually men of intellectual ability, strong personality, devout life, and great learning.

   b) The influence these clergymen exerted over their congregations formed Biblical thinking among the populace especially in areas of government.

   c) Their influence prepared the mindframe of the American colonists to declare independence from Great Britain.

2. Samuel Sewall was a minister who became a judge and political figure. His public confession of having erred in persecuting witches brought a calm to the

affair. He wrote a diary covering fifty-six years of his life.

3. Michael Wigglesworth was a pastor for fifty years and wrote poetry. His masterpiece epic was *A Day of Doom*.

4. Cotton Mather entered Harvard at eleven, was an active preacher at seventeen. He wrote *Magnalia Christi Americana, or The Ecclesiastical History of New England*, over one thousand pages.

5. Jonathan Edwards from Connecticut was the most spiritual and refined of the great New England preachers. (Read tribute to Sarah Pierrepont.) His sermon "Sinners in the Hands of an Angry God" is most famous.

Missionary Writers

1. Alexander Whitaker—active in American Christian missions, 1611–1617

   a) He was an English clergyman who had an apostolic zeal for the gospel and a sorrow for the lost.

   b) In 1611 he "did voluntarily leave his warm nest . . . to bear the name of God unto the heathen."

   c) He lived a brave missionary life in Virginia ministering to colonists and Indians, known as "the apostle to Virginia."

   d) He wrote an account of his ministry "Good News from Virginia," challenging the English to consider the opportunity of evangelism in Virginia.

2. Daniel Gookin (1612–1687)—superintendent of Indians in Massachusetts

   a) An intelligent, sensitive, humble man, Gookin was both soldier and author.

   b) He came to Virginia as a boy and, when about thirty, moved to Massachusetts where he had a life of public service.

   c) He was Puritan in philosophy and held several civil posts as soldier, magistrate, and finally superintendent of the Indians.

d) He labored with Eliot and defended the Indians against popular hatred during the 1675 uprising.

e) He wrote "Historical Collections of the Indians in New England" and, after the Indian War, "An Historical Account of the Doings and Sufferings of the Christian Indians in New England,"—a vindication of the Christian Indians.

3. John Eliot (1604–1690)—Apostle to the Indians

a) Educated at Cambridge, moved to New England in 1631, he had a passionate longing for the conversion of the Indians and for improving their condition.

b) He worked among twenty tribes in Massachusetts, acquiring their language, making a grammar, and translating the Bible into the Indian tongue.

America's Christian Founding Reflected in Her Literature

Christian Individualism in the Parent Colonies

Questions for Reflection:

1. Explain briefly the place of American literature on the Chain of Christianity moving westward.

2. Write from memory a quotation from each of the four individuals God used in the parent colonies and explain how the character and convictions of each writer are seen in the quote.

3. How does his history, *Of Plimoth Plantation*, show Bradford to be a man made by the Bible?

4. How did John Winthrop's life demonstrate the Pilgrim spirit?

5. What outstanding qualities of friendship did you observe in "The Courtship of Miles Standish" between Standish and Alden, and between Alden and Priscilla?

6. What are the three ingredients of a great endeavor? Vision, Adventure, Written Record

7. What was Alexander Whitaker's contribution to the Chain of Christianity?

8. Describe Daniel Gookin and John Eliot's work among the Indians.

Teaching the Literature of the American Revolution
1765–1787
Preparation and Presentation

Background	Readings
1. God's Principle of Individuality: the men and character of the American Revolution:	*The Making of George Washington*, Wilbur
a) George Washington, 1732–1799 The writings of George Washington form one of the most important parts of our literary heritage. God's providential preparation of Washington. An account of his first official mission for the governor of Virginia at age twenty-one.	*The Journal of Major George Washington*, facsimile reprint, Colonial Williamsburg Foundation
b) Benjamin Franklin, 1706–1790 American statesman, scientist and philosopher, he best illustrates the effect of our American Christian philosophy of government—and its influence upon the improvement of the quality of life for every individual. Franklin early made up his mind that any writing, in order to be good, ought to be "smooth, clear, and short." A unique account of self-education in Pilgrim character and industry. The Christian character and influence of that man who did the most to help educate others in the American Christian philosophy of government.	*The Autobiography of Benjamin Franklin*
c) Samuel Adams, 1722–1803 The Father of the American Revolution Principles of Christianity and Government The American Christian Church: The educational goal of the church is to build the foundation of America's Christian conscience.	*CHOC*, I, pp. 364B–370, Essay on Liberty, "Rights of Colonists"
2. Phillis Wheatley, 1753–1784 American Christian poet of African birth. She learned to read from the Bible. Brought to Boston on a slave ship in 1761, this remarkable girl learned the English language without any help from schools. She read and relished poetry and wrote some of her own. A number of eminent gentlemen testified to her genius.	A poem "To His Excellency General Washington," "On the Death of George Whitefield," "An Elegy to Samuel Cooper"

Teaching the Literature of the American Revolution
1765–1787
Preparation and Presentation

Background	Readings
3. Philip Freneau, 1752–1832, The Poet of the American Revolution. Chiefly noted as a forerunner of the Romantic poets.	

4. Francis Hopkinson, 1737–1791
    Political satirist and writer
    Hopkinson wrote the most amusing satire of the American Revolution in verse.
	"The Battle of the Kegs," Francis Hopkinson

5. Joel Barlow, 1754–1812 Wrote a national epic, *The Columbiad*, comprising ten books. Better remembered for "Hasty Pudding."	"Hasty Pudding," Joel Barlow
6. Speeches—the rhetoric of liberty An American Christian Revolution: the pew and the pulpit have been educated to self-government.	Patrick Henry, "Liberty or Death" *CHOC*, I, pp. 372–79, "Political Sermons of the Period of 1776": Description, Dr. Mayhew, Dr. Payson *T & L*, pp. 45–51. Pastors of the American Revolution: Davies, Clark, Witherspoon, Stillman; pp. 248–49, Rev. Muhlenberg Mercy Warren, first American woman historian The correspondence of John and Abigail Adams The Declaration of Independence James Otis, "Rights of the British Colonies" John Dickinson, "Farmer's Letters"

The American Revolutionary Period 1765–1787

Goals of Understanding for Writing

1. Historical Background

What events did God allow so that the individual American colonies would consider working together?

Why did the Colonies form an Army, choose George Washington as the commander in chief, and even fight some battles, long before they declared themselves independent states in 1776?

What principles were the most important to the American colonists?

When did God unite the colonies internally before their external Declaration in 1776?

How long a war for independence was fought by the colonists?

What were the expectations of success?

Name some of the great providential events of the American Revolution which revealed the Hand of God in our War for Independence.

2. The Literature and Character of the Period

What qualities of American womanhood are revealed in the letters between Mercy Warren and her husband and Abigail Adams and her husband, John? Identify in detail.

How can we regard General George Washington as a husband, as a farmer, and as a commander in chief? Identify some of his writings and statements that reveal his character.

The writings of George Washington reveal how dependent we were upon the Lord for success in our enterprise. What evidence does he give of these events?

Relate and illustrate in your essay the important points in the "Oration at Valley Forge," one hundred years after our Declaration of Independence. See *Consider and Ponder*, pp. 55–68.

Discuss the similarities and differences between the Americans of two hundred years ago and today through the message of "The Liberty Song."

What poetry best expresses the Christian character of America?

What important Scriptural truths of government are learned from the sermons of the pastors of our Revolutionary period?

God's Providential Preparation of Leaders

George Washington—An Instrument in the Hand of God

In July of 1775, a full year before our Declaration of Independence, the colonists were still petitioning the king of England for redress of their grievances and for reconciliation with the mother country. But the attack of British troops upon the militias of Lexington and Concord on April 19, 1775, and the victory of British Regulars on June 17 at Bunker Hill, convinced the Continental Congress that it must raise an American army. Who could command the motley assortment of men from thirteen different colonial militia? As a Bible-loving, Bible-living people, they turned to the Lord in prayer for direction before making such a decision. So it should not be surprising that God had a man prepared to lead the American troops—a man whose leadership qualities had emerged some twenty-five years prior to the War for American Independence. This man was Colonel George Washington from Virginia.

What kind of a man did God provide for the job of commander in chief of the Continental Army—an army made up of independent units whose condition was always one of scarcity of the essentials? Who could inspire and lead the ill-fed, ill-clothed, poorly-armed, undisciplined, short-term recruits? As one writer put it: "Never before did such destinies hang on a single man, for it was not the fate of a continent which rested on the issue of the struggle, but of human liberty the world over."

The seven long years of the American Revolution began with three years of defeat, retreat, death, and discouragement, but God had a man prepared who had endured defeat and who had learned from its lessons. No central government existed which could command support and supplies from thirteen separate colonies; it had to be a voluntary effort. God had a man prepared, a man of infinite patience, perseverance, and determination—a man whose faith in God never wavered in his endless battles with delay, indecision, and insufficiency.

Found many times by his associates on his knees where he "laid the cause of his bleeding country at the throne of grace," the first act of George Washington as commander in chief of the Continental Army was to include this message in his General Orders for July 4, 1775:

The General most earnestly requires, and expects, a due observance of those articles of war, established for the Government of the army, which forbid profane cursing, swearing and drunkeness; And in like manner requires and expects, of all Officers, and Soldiers, not engaged on actual duty, a punctual attendance on divine Service, to implore the blessings of heaven upon the means used for our safety and defence.

On July 16, 1775, the General Orders from the commander in chief began as follows:

The Continental Congress having earnestly recommended that "Thursday next the 20th. Instant, be observed by the Inhabitants of all the english Colonies upon this Continent, as a Day of public Humiliation, Fasting and Prayer; that they may with united Hearts and Voice confess their Sins before God, and supplicate the all wise and merciful disposer of events, to avert the Desolation and Calamities of an unnatural war."

The General orders, that Day to be religiously observed by the Forces under his Command, exactly in manner directed by the proclamation of the Continental Congress: It is therefore strictly enjoin'd on all Officers and Soldiers, (not upon duty) to attend Divine Service, at the accustomed places of worship, as well in the Lines, as the Encampments and Quarters; and it is expected, that all those who go to worship, do take their Arms, Ammunitions and Accoutrements and are prepared for immediate Action if called upon. If in the judgment of the Officers, the Works should appear to be in such forwardness as the utmost security of the Camp requires, they will command their men to abstain from all Labour upon that solemn day.

(These two quotations are from *The Writings of George Washington*, vol. 3 (1931), pp. 309, 341–42.)

Tribute was paid to this noble leader by the Rev. Henry Melchior Muhlenberg in a letter dated May 7, 1778:

> I heard a fine example today, namely, that His Excellency General Washington rode around among his army yesterday and admonished each and every one to fear God, to put away the wickedness that has set in and become so general, and to practice the Christian virtues. From all appearances this gentleman does not belong to the so-called world of society, for he respects God's Word, believes in the atonement through Christ, and bears himself in humility and gentleness. Therefore the Lord God has also singularly, yea, marvelously, preseved him from harm in the midst of countless perils, ambuscades, fatigues, etc. and has hitherto graciously held him in his hand as a chosen vessel. (*Consider and Ponder*, Hall, 1976, p. 68)

The world learned of the Christian character and courage of General George Washington before it learned of the character of the United States of America. In the first year of our status as a separate nation, George Washington gave to the world a new standard of leadership characterized by humbleness of heart and devotion to God. All the efforts of the past 150 years by those who would obliterate America's Christian history have failed to tarnish the character of George Washington. In our time the noted scholar and writer, Douglas Southall Freeman, who had spent twenty years writing the biography of Robert E. Lee and the Confederacy, turned the last eighteen years of his life to a full-scale research of George Washington. Approaching his subject critically, his final words on the subject of his work were these:

"What more could I ask for myself than to make the rediscovery that in Washington this nation and the western hemisphere have a man, 'greater than the world knew, living and dying,' a man dedicated, just and incorruptible, an example for long centuries of what character and diligence can achieve?"

Only those without faith in God could doubt that God prepared and raised up such a man as George Washington. God is still preparing the leaders for the future of America. What are we doing to strengthen our youth by instructing them in the rich treasury of our Christian History of the American Revolution? How much does each of us know of what the Hand of God has already done for us as a Christian nation? Are we raising up the character to perpetuate and extend the world's first and only Christian Republic?

Martha Custis Washington

The faithful wife of General George Washington has been overshadowed in history by her illustrious husband. We therefore present several excerpts from Margaret Conkling's *Memoirs of Martha Washington* (1860) which cast some light on Mrs. Washington's personality and activities during and after the war years:

> A Perfect Woman, nobly planned
> To warn, to comfort, and command;
> And yet a spirit, still and bright,
> With something of an Angel's light.
> —Wordsworth
>
> Not enjoyment, and not sorrow,
> Is our destined end or way;
> But to act that each to-morrow,
> Finds us farther than to-day.
> —Longfellow

From chapter 4 of Conkling's *Memoirs*:

> When Col. Washington left Mount Vernon to attend the meeting of the first Congress at Philadelphia, Mrs. Washington remained at home, participating, though at a distance, the interest and anxiety with which he discharged the various and peculiarly responsible duties which the Soldier of America

was directly summoned to assume; and watching with engrossing eagerness for his reports of the highly interesting proceedings and deliberations of the solemn assemblage with which he was associated.

When, after more than nine months of separation and solitude, she was informed of her husband's appointment as Commander-in-Chief of the American Army, and that "the war had actually begun" which must summon him to immediate action, the mingled nature of her emotions may be easily conceived.

The first intelligence of this event was communicated to Mrs. Washington in the following letter, which possesses the more interest as it is the only one of the many addressed to her from the same source, that has descended to us.*

*NOTE: It is known that Mrs. Washington, previous to her death, destroyed these precious testimonials of affection and confidence—unwilling, it may be supposed, to allow other eyes than her own to trace the cherished records.

Philadelphia, June 18, 1775

My Dearest:

I am now set down to write to you on a subject, which fills me with inexpressible concern, and this concern is greatly aggravated and increased, when I reflect upon the uneasiness I know it will give you. It has been determined in Congress, that the whole army raised for the defence of the American cause shall be put under my care, and that it is necessary for me to proceed immediately to Boston to take upon me the command of it.

You may believe me, my dear Patsy, when I assure you, in the most solemn manner, that, so far from seeking this appointment, I have used every endeavor in my power to avoid it, not only from my unwillingness to part with you and the family, but from a consciousness of its being a trust too great for my capacity, and that I should enjoy more real happiness in one month with you at home, than I have the most distant prospect of finding abroad, if my stay were to be seven times seven years. But as it has been a kind of destiny, that has thrown me upon this service, I shall hope that my undertaking it is designed to answer some good purpose. You might, and I suppose did perceive, from the tenor of my letters, that I was apprehensive I could not avoid this appointment, as I did not pretend to intimate when I should return. That was the case. It was utterly out of my power to refuse this appointment, without exposing my character to such censures, as would have reflected dishonor upon myself, and given pain to my friends. This, I am sure, could not, and ought not to be pleasing to you, and must have lessened me considerably in my own esteem. I shall rely, therefore, confidently on that Providence, which has heretofore preserved and been bountiful to me, not doubting but that I shall return safe to you in the fall. I shall feel no pain from the toil or the danger of the campaign; my unhappiness will flow from the uneasiness I know you will feel from being left alone. I therefore beg that you will summon your whole fortitude, and pass your time as agreeably as possible. Nothing will give me so much sincere satisfaction as to hear this, and to hear it from your own pen. My earnest and ardent desire is, that you would pursue any plan that is most likely to produce content, and a tolerable degree of tranquillity; as it must add greatly to my uneasy feelings to hear that you are dissatisfied or complaining at what I really could not avoid.

As life is always uncertain, and common prudence dictates to every man the necessity of settling his temporal concerns, while it is in his power, and while the mind is calm and undisturbed, I have, since I came to this place, (for I had no time to do it before I left home,) got Colonel Pendleton to draft a will for me, by the directions I gave him, which I now enclose. The provision made for you in case of my death, will, I hope, be agreeable.

I shall add nothing more, as I have several letters to write, but to desire that you will remember me to your friends, and to assure you that I am, with the most unfeigned regard, my dear Patsy,

Your affectionate,
George Washington

As the General could not leave the army, he had requested Mrs. Washington to pass the winters with him.

From chapter 6:

It became, thenceforth, during the continuance of the War of the Revolution, Mrs. Washington's habitual practice to pass her winters at the Headquarters of the American Army. It was, consequently, her wont to say, in after life, that she had "heard the first cannon at the opening and the last at the closing of all the campaigns of the Revolution."

Many passages in the private Letters of Washington express his affectionate interest on the subject of Mrs. Washington's long and hazardous journeys at the inclement season of the year when they were, necessarily, undertaken. We find him writing to ask advice as to the best means of promoting her safety and comfort, or requesting assistance in effecting her transit from Mount Vernon to him, and again, expressing his thanks for the many civilities extended to her on such occasions by friends whose personal and patriotic devotion, no considerations of policy or prudence could vary or diminish. . . .

She submitted with the utmost patience to personal privation and hardship, and did the honors of her homely camp abode with all the grace and urbanity that had formerly distinguished the mistress of the White House (name of Martha's Virginia home before marriage to George Washington) and of Mount Vernon. Her unwavering religious faith and her perpetual serenity and good humor, not only contributed materially to the general good, but were of great service to her husband individually. The Commander-in-Chief, both by word and action, gave ample proof that the habits of military life were far from diminishing his affection for the companion of more genial hours, or his just appreciation of the advantages arising to himself from her society. As an illustration in point, some of our readers will recollect, that, when on one occasion, while this courageous woman and her fair companions still remained in their martial homes, and there was a sudden apprehension that "the enemy" were rapidly approaching, Washington resisted the proposition made by his military friends, to send the ladies away under an escort—saying, "The presence of our wives will better encourage us to a brave defence!"

Lady Washington's time and attention during each of the many seasons of her residence with the Army—apart from the dearer duties and obligations arising out of her reunions with her husband and son—were chiefly devoted to the humane purposes of benefiting and relieving the suffering soldiers. She visited the sick, ministered to their wants, and poured that sympathy which is the "oil of joy" into their desponding hearts. She is described by those who witnessed and partook her efforts, as having been unwavering in her zeal and earnestness in this, her noble and womanly purpose. No danger delayed, no difficulty or hardship prevented the fulfilment of these benevolent duties. Blessings and prayers followed the departure of this beneficent spirit from among the recipients of her kindness and bounty, and the most heartfelt delight hailed her return!

Nor were the winters thus passed by this estimable wife and mother wholly wanting in other sources of merely personal enjoyment, than those arising from her constant association with the objects of her deepest affections. She became closely and confidentially connected with the noble and heroic women, who, like herself, were pledged to the service of their country—those private defenders of the Cause of Liberty, whose dearest interests, whose highest hopes, whose all, in short, of earthly happiness was involved in the issue of passing events.

From chapter 5:

Mrs. Washington sought the security and seclusion of Mount Vernon, not to indulge in vain repinings at her separation from its master and from her only child, nor to yield herself up to the unworthy dominion of useless fears for their personal safety and well-being; but to find in active and needful occupation, and in care for the happiness of others, the best guarantee afforded by circumstances, for the preservation of her mental serenity.

That knowledge of practical life, and that singular facility for adapting herself to avocations unusual to her sex, which she had exhibited during her widowhood, were now again called into exercise by the peculiar situation in which Mrs. Washington found herself placed. She immediately established a domestic system thoroughly adapted to the exigencies of the times, and eminently calculated as an example most benefically to influence others. Her dress—always remarkable for its simplicity—was soon composed almost entirely of home-made materials as was the clothing of her numerous domestics.

We have her own authority for the fact that she had a great deal of domestic cloth made in her house, and that "sixteen spinning-wheels were kept in constant operation" at Mount Vernon. On one occasion, when conversing with some friends upon this and similar topics, she gave the best proof of her success in domestic manufactures by the exhibition of two of her dresses, which were composed of cotton striped with silk, and entirely homemade. The silk stripes in the fabric were woven from the ravellings of brown silk stockings and old crimson damask chair-covers!

Momentarily to anticipate in our narrative—when Washington arrived at New York to assume his duties as first President of the United States, he was attired in a complete suit of homespun cloth.

By the judicious and admirable simplicity and economy she systematically practiced, this exemplary Revolutionary matron secured the means, not only of personal and domestic comfort, convenience, and independence, but of the benevolent diffusion of more generally extended benefit.

From chapter 10. (Following the death of Washington)

But grateful and consolatory as were these spontaneous manifestations of reverential regard for the memory of her illustrious husband, Mrs. Washington possessed a far higher and dearer source of confidence in his eternal happiness than any earthly fiat could bestow, in her inward and assured conviction that he had ever sought the same "fountain of living waters," from which she had herself drunk deep of heavenly hope and joy.

The venerable Subject of our Memoir now looked eagerly and intently forward to the termination of that journey in which she had been preceded by all who were most dear to her. Devoutly resting her wounded spirit upon the soothing conviction that those from whom she was here separated would then be forever restored to her, she strengthened herself to tread on in the weary way of life, with mournful but unshaken confidence in the blessed truth that "all things work together for good" in the orderings of the Great Disposer of events. Hers was not the callousness of indifference or insensibility, the obtuseness of benighted stoicism, or the lightness of a shallow intellect; but the undoubting constancy of a Christian, whose faith in Him who no mortal suffering could disturb, no sublunary occurrence could destroy!

The death of Mrs. Washington occurred in the year 1801, and during the seventy-first year of her age.

Readings

Few realize that General George Washington wrote forty volumes of letters during the seven long years of the American Revolution and his two administrations as the first president of the United States of America. Remembering that the war letters were written under the most arduous physical conditions of battle during military bivouac and in inclement weather, we marvel at their content. Picture for yourself the commander in chief in the winter of 1777–78 at Valley Forge, and you begin to get some idea of the conditions under which this most inspiring American literature was composed. What a treasury we have of the Christian character and devotion which won for us a nation! Out of death life, out of suffering came forth a liberty which Christians of the first century only glimpsed as a political possibility. Listed below are some rich sources of writings by and about George Washington.

The Writings of George Washington from the Original Manuscript Sources 1745–1799, 39 volumes. Prepared under the direction of the United States George Washington Bicentennial Commission and published by the authority of Congress. Edited by John C. Fitzpatrick. U.S. Government Printing Office, Washington, D.C.: 1931–1944.

The Papers of George Washington sponsored by the University of Virginia and the Mount Vernon Ladies' Association of the Union. Begun in 1968 this will be a forty- to fifty-year program. The first documents to be published will be the Diaries of George Washington.

The Journal of Major George Washington, An Account of His First Official Mission, Made as Emissary from the Governor of Virginia to the Commandant of the French Forces on the Ohio, October 1753–January 1754. Facsimile edition, published by the Colonial Williamsburg Foundation, Williamsburg, Virginia. Distributed by the University Press of Virginia, Charlottesville, Virginia 22903 (Box 3608 University Station). Twenty-nine pages with Introduction and Notes.

Biographies of George Washington

George Washington, a biography by Washington Irving. Edited and abridged with an introduction by Charles Neider. New York: Doubleday & Company, 1976, a one-volume edition of the five-volume set.

George Washington: A Biography by Douglas Southall Freeman, Charles Scribner's Sons, 7 volumes, 1948–1957.

Other References to George Washington

Christian History of the Constitution of the United States of America, Christian Self-Government, compiled by Verna M. Hall. See pp. 416–17: "America has furnished to the world the character of George Washington."

Consider and Ponder, Verna M. Hall. See Index of Leading Ideas, p. 695a, "Washington, George."

The Christian Literature of the American Republic

The Ladies in Literature
Christianity Liberates Women
by Rosalie June Slater

One of the most important steps for America's Christian History occurred in Acts 16 when the Apostle Paul, heeding the Macedonian Cry, turned westward to the continent of Europe. At Philippi, "which is the chief city of that part of Macedonia, and a colony," Paul found his first European convert in Lydia—a "seller of purple, of the city of Thyatira." Lydia's words after her baptism have significance for the new life now opened up for women—a life whose unique role and contribution comes to particular fruition in the United States of America.

"And when she was baptized, and her household, she besought us, saying, 'If ye have judged me to be faithful to the Lord, come into my house, and abide there.' And she constrained us." (Acts 16:15)

In *The Life and Epistles of Saint Paul* (American edition of 1869), the Reverends W. J. Conybeare and J. S. Howson state:

Thus the Gospel had obtained a home in Europe . . . and nothing could be more calm and tranquil than its first beginnings on the shore of that continent, which it has long overspread. The scenes by the riverside, and in the house of Lydia, are beautiful prophecies of the holy influence which women, elevated by Christianity to their true position, and enabled by Divine grace to wear "the ornament of a meek and quiet spirit," have now for centuries exerted over domestic happiness and the growth of piety and peace.

America's Christian History begins the first history of any nation where the role of Christian women was so important. In a letter by Lydia Sigourney addressed "To Young Ladies" (pp. 407–10 of *The Christian History of the Con-* *stitution of the United States of America*, I), she defined this role: "The natural vocation of females is to teach. . . . It is in the domestic sphere, in her own native province, that woman is inevitably a teacher. There she modifies by her example, her dependents, her companions, every dweller under her own roof. Is not the infant in its cradle her pupil?"

Mrs. Sigourney, an excellent example of an American Christian woman in 19th-century literature, then goes on to detail this important role of women, with particular emphasis upon the consequences of her influence in the nation:

This influence is most visible and operative in a republic. . . . Teachers under such a form of government should be held in the highest honour. They are the allies of legislators. They have agency in the prevention of crime. They aid in regulating the atmosphere, whose incessant action and pressure cause the life blood to circulate, and return pure and healthful to the heart of the nation.

Mrs. Sigourney reviews ancient pagan civilizations like Greece and Rome and points out the contrast with the position of women in the American Christian republic.

In our own republic, man, invested by his Maker with the right to reign, has conceded to her, who was for ages in vassalage, equality of intercourse, participation in knowledge, dominion over his dearest and fondest hopes. He is content to "bear the burden and heat of the day," that she may dwell in ease and affluence.

Mrs. Sigourney concludes her article by challenging the men of her generation to:

Demand of her as a debt the highest excellence of which she is capable of attaining. Summon her to abandon selfish motives and inglorious ease. Incite her to those virtues which promote the permanence and health of nations. Make her accountable for the character of the next generation. Give her solemn charge in the presence of men and of angels. Gird her with the whole armour of education and piety, and see if she be not faithful to her children, to her country, and to her God. . . . For the strength of a nation, especially of a republican nation, is in the intelligent and well-ordered homes of the people. And in proportion as the discipline of families is relaxed, will the happy organization of communities be affected, and national character become vagrant, turbulent, or ripe for revolution.

"Make her accountable for the character of the next generation." This is the unique and important role of women in our republic and no matter what other fields they conquer, no matter what other heights they achieve, this field, if neglected, will reflect their absence.

Mercy Otis Warren (1728–1814)

It is nowhere so evident as in our own American Revolution that woman, brought up to a character which had been defined for her in Scripture, could indeed be a moral companion to her husband. She could be equal with man, in her own sphere, equal in strength—a womanly courage determined to keep the home fires burning so that her children would be safe and her husband secure in the knowledge that his domestic anchor held firm.

What a wonder these American Christian women were! They had beauty, charm, and wit—keen interest in their homes and families and the particular careers of their husbands. Yet they followed the political events with understanding and a clear perception of character and justice. And in all their domestic and patriotic activities they remained women of courage and tenderness, of constancy and devotion to the Christian principles and virtues upon which the liberty of the nation depended. Despite the most alarming events they were called upon to witness or to endure, despite their fears and anxieties for the safety of their loved ones, their faith in the Lord and their steadfast conviction of His Superintending Providence enabled them to persist unto the end.

What was the literature produced by these American Christian women who were right in the midst of the historic events of those years? The most notable American Woman of Letters was Mercy Otis, of Barnstable, Massachusetts. Sister of James Otis whose *Rights of the British Colonies Asserted and Proved*, written in 1764, began the ten-year constitutional debate with England. Her husband was James Warren (1726-1808) of Plymouth, Massachusetts. James Warren served long and faithfully as President of the Massachusetts Provincial Assembly and as Paymaster General of the Continental Army.

Mercy Warren was a friend and correspondent of leading political figures of her day including John Adams, Samuel Adams, Thomas Jefferson, and Elbridge Gerry. Her most famous play was a political satire—*The Group*, written in 1775. In 1805, she published her three-volume *History of the Rise, Progress, and Termination of the American Revolution*.

What is most remarkable about Mercy Warren is her uniquely American Christian character as a woman. Though born one hundred years after the Pilgrims' arrival she received no special schooling. Had it not been for her own enterprise and determination, her routine of domestic activities would not have included the study and reading which characterized her early years. Never neglecting her domestic cares nor the duties of hospitality so important in those days, she still found time to improve her mind as well as to use her hands in various works of female ingenuity.

While few opportunities for female education existed at that time, Mercy Otis Warren was supplied with books from the library of the local minister, the Reverend Jonathan Russell. He counseled and guided her study and through her brother, James Otis, she became interested in the subject of history, and character. Even while she was bringing up her five sons, running the farm in the absence of her husband, and writing innumerable letters, Mercy continued her own self-education. As we read her letters, we recognize her fine intellect and Christian reasoning. How warmly she espoused the cause of her country's victory under God; how deeply her feelings were enlisted.

But, most of all, we are touched by the letters of Mercy Warren to her husband—letters which indicate their deep and mutual love for each other, for their children, for their God, and their country. It is in the correspondence of the American Revolution that woman's role is most apparent in our republic. It is in the correspondence that we see the American Christian woman whose strength and influence were first signified in the words of Lydia to the Apostle Paul: "Come into my house, and abide there."

Books and References on Mercy Warren

Only a few letters will be quoted here, and the reader is urged to seek out the available sources of the correspondence and other writings of Mercy Otis Warren for further study and delight. One of the most engaging biographies, written in 1896 by Alice Brown and entitled *Mercy Warren,* is part of a series on "Women of Colonial and Revolutionary Times" published by Charles Scribner's Sons.

One excellent source is *The Warren-Adams Letters*, a correspondence among John Adams, Samuel Adams, James Warren, and Mercy Warren, found in the *Collections of the Massachusetts Historical Society*, Vol. 72 (1917) and Vol. 73 (1925). From chapter 4 of Alice Brown's biography, *Mercy Warren*, the following letters have been excerpted.

Plymouth, September 21, 1775

Just as I [got] up from dinner this day yours of the 15 & 18 came to hand; No

desert [sic] was ever more welcome to a luxurious pallate, it was a regale to my longing mind: I had been eagerly looking for more than a week for a line from the best friend of my heart.

I had contemplated to spend a day or two with my good father, but as you talk of returning so soon I shall give up that and every other pleasure this world can give for the superior pleasure of your company. I thank you for the many expressions in yours which bespeak the most affectionate soul, or heart warmed with friendship & esteem which it shall ever be my assiduous care to merit.—but as I am under some apprehensions that you will be again disappointed and your return postponed, I will endeavor to give you some account of the reception I met from our little family on my arrival among them after an absence which they thought long: your requesting this as an agreeable amusement is new proof that the Father is not lost in the occupations of the statesman.

I found Charles & Henry sitting on the steps of the front door when I arrived—they had just been expressing their ardent wishes to each other that mamah would come in before dinner when I turned the corner having our habitation. . . .

George's solemn brow was covered with pleasure & his grave features not only danced in smiles but broke into a real laugh more expressive of his heartfelt happiness than all the powers of language could convey and before I could sit down and lay aside my riding attire all the choice gleanings of the Garden were offered each one pressing before the other to pour the yellow produce into their mamah's lap.

Not a complaint was uttered—not a tale was told through the day but what they thought would contribute to the happiness of their best friend; but how short lived is human happiness. The ensuing each one had his little grievance to repeat, as important to them as the laying an unconstitutional tax to the patriot or the piratical seizure of a ship & cargo, after much labour & the promising expectation of profitable returns when the voyage was compleat—but the umpire in your absence soon accommodated all matters to mutual satisfaction and the day was spent in much cheerfulness encircled by my sons. . . . My heart has just leaped in my bosom and I ran to the stairs imagining I heard both your voice & your footsteps in the entry. Though disappointed I have no doubt this pleasure will be realized as soon as possible by

> Your affectionate
> M. Warren

September 13, 1776

Mercy writes to "my dearest friend, the best friend of my heart."

When my head was layed on my pillow Last Night my Heart was Rent with Apprehension. Your life is of Great Value Both to the public & to the family as well as to the one who would be Miserable without you. . . . I desire therefore to leave you in the Care of Providence & to trust in the divine protection to guard and guide your steps whithersoever you go.

I fear this people have been too confident of their own strength. We have been Ready to say our own arms shall save us instead of looking to the God of Battle. . . . I shall write again tomorrow knowing you will not be tired of seeing the signature of your Beloved & Affectionate

> Marcia

Don't think I am discouraged . . . when I write my thought so freely and fully. I seem to feel this day & Evening amidst a thousand gloomy fears as if our God was about to bring us deliverance by means which we cannot foresee. The less we have to hope from man the stronger is my confidence in Him who presideth over the Earth and who will be Glorifyed in His doing, and many times when we are Ready to say

with Peter Lord help for we are sinking then is His arm stretched out to save.

James to Mercy—she is his "saint," his "little angel, his beloved"; he "misses her beyond expectation."

April 7, 1775—a few days before Lexington

The moving of the Inhabitants of Boston if Effected will be one Grand Move. . . . We may perhaps be forced to Move: if we are let us strive to submit to the dispensations of Providence with Christian resignation and Phylosophick dignity. God has given you great abilities. You have improved them in great Acquirements. You are possessd of Eminent Virtues & distinguished Piety. For all these I Esteem I Love you in a degree that I can't Express. They are all now to be called into action for the good of mankind for the good of your friends, for the promotion of virtue and patriotism. Don't let the fluttering of your Heart Interrupt your Health or disturb your repose. Believe me I am continually Anxious about you. Ride when the weather is good & don't work or read too much at other times. I must bid you adieu. God Almighty Bless You. No letter yet what can it mean, is she not well she can't forget me or have any objections to writing.

James to Mercy, 1779: "If you Love me Enjoy the Goods of Providence with a Chearful Grateful Mind and at least imagine that our Lines are in a pleasant place."

James to Mercy,
Boston, April 2, 1780

My dear Mercy,—I am just returned from public worship, the next act of religion is to write to my beloved wife. . . . Don't however think I am in the shades of gloom & despondency. I see & find difficulties from every quarter but my faith & Hope are as strong as ever."

Mercy Warren's Satirical Piece, *The Group*

Political satire seems today a lost art. It is therefore most interesting to study this play of Two Acts, Four Scenes and no action—all conversation. There is no drama, little suspense, and the dramatic piece rests its entire case for our interest in the boldness with which it strips off the disguise from this squad of evil men who have exchanged conscience and country for political advantage.

A few examples will be cited here in the hope of enticing the reader to obtain the complete work of twenty-eight pages. Though the language is cumbersome, somewhat contrived and artificial to our modern ears, one admires the veracity and audacity of the author. Plaudits to Mercy. She knows that character is the key to history and here in terms of righteous wrath and merciless prose and verse she exposes the perpetrators of parliament's vindictive measures against the colonists in Boston.

Mercy Warren writes a Prologue to her Farce. "The Author has thought proper to borrow the following spirited lines from a late celebrated Poet, and offer to the public, by way of Prologue, which cannot fail of pleasing at this crisis."*

Prologue

"What! arm'd for virtue, and not point the pen,
Brand the bold front of shameless guilty men,
Dash the proud gamester from his gilded car,
Bare the mean heart which lurks beneath a star.

. . . .

Shall I not strip the gilding off a knave,
Unplac'd, unpension'd, no man's heir or slave?
I will, or perish in the gen'rous cause;
Hear this and tremble, ye who 'scape the laws;
Yes, while I live, no rich or noble knave,
Shall walk the world in credit to his grave;
To virtue only, and her friends, a friend,
The world beside may murmur, or commend."

[*Note: we have not yet found whose "spirited lines" Mercy Warren quotes from "a late celebrated Poet." They could have been from Pope or Dryden, both favorites of the colonial period.]

Below are listed the Dramatis Personae, coordinated with their original historical characters as drawn up from a series of identifications made by contemporaries, including John Adams who was most delighted with this satirical piece. In a letter to her he wrote: "Of all the Genius's which have yet arisen in America, there has been none, Superiour to one, which now shines, in this happy, this exquisite Faculty,. . . I know of none, ancient or modern, which has reached the tender the pathetic, the keen and severe, and at the same time, the soft, the sweet, the amiable and the pure in greater Perfection." (*Mercy Warren*, Brown, p. 163)

The Group: Dramatis Personae

Mercy Warren's Character:
(Historical Original)

Lord Chief Justice Hazelrod
(Peter Oliver)

Judge Meagae
(Foster Hutchinson)

Brigadier Hateall
(Timothy Ruggles)

Hum Humbug, Esq.
(John Erving, Jr.)

Sir Sparrow Spendall
(William Pepperell)

Hector Mushroom
(Col. John Murray)

Beau Trumps
(Daniel Leonard)

Dick, The Publican
(Richard Lechmere)

Simple Sapling, Esq.
(Nathaniel Ray Thomas)

Monsieur de Francois
(James Boutineau)

Crusty Crowbar, Esq.
(Josiah Edson)

Dupe,—Secretary Of State
(Thomas Flucker)

Scriblerius Fribble
(Harrison Gray)

Commodore Batteau
(Joshua Loring)

Collateralis,— a new-made Judge
(William Browne)

Sylla
(General Thomas Gage)

Explanation of this "Group" is given by Mercy Warren in the following: "Attended by a swarm of court sycophants, hungry harpies, and unprincipled danglers, collected from the neighbouring villages, hovering over the stage in the shape of locusts, led by Massachusettensis in the form of a basilisk; the rear brought up by proteus, bearing a torch in one hand, a powder-flask in the other: The whole supported by a mighty army and navy, from blunderland, for the laudible purpose of enslaving its best friends."

Definitions from Noah Webster's 1828 *Dictionary*:

1. Basilisk: "A fabulous serpent, called a cockatrice, and said to be produced from a cock's egg brooded by a serpent. The ancients alledged that its hissing would drive away all other serpents, and that its breath and even its look was fatal. Some writers suppose that a real serpent exists under this name."

2. Proteus: "In *mythology*, a marine deity, the son of Oceanus and Tethys, whose distinguishing characteristic was the faculty of assuming different shapes. Hence we denominate one who easily changes his form or principles, a *Proteus*."

We will give one scene from *The Group* to provide the flavor of Mercy Warren's satirical pen. In the words of her biographer, Alice Brown: "Never was there a more frankly partisan piece of work, showing, according to the patriotic standpoint, vice 'her own image.' One overmastering joy of the perfor-mance lies in the fact that out of their own mouths are the public enemies condemned.

"The entire Group of actors are 'selfish, venal men.' Their mutual confessions of premeditated guilt could be no franker were they irreparably lost souls comparing crimes in hell." (*Mercy Warren*, Brown, pp. 168-9)

The Group: A Farce

Act I, Scene 1: *A little dark Parlour in Boston: Guards standing at the door.*

Hazelrod, Crusty Crowbar, Simple Sapling, Hateall, and Hector Mushroom.

Simple:
I know not what to think of these sad times,
The people arm'd—and all resolv'd to die
E're they'll submit.

Crusty Crowbar:
I too am almost sick of the parade
Of honours purchas'd at the price of peace.

Simple:
Fond as I am of greatness and her charms,
Elate with prospects of my rising name,
Push'd into place,—a place I ne'er expected,
My bounding heart leapt in my feeble breast
And exstasies entranc'd my slender brain.
But yet, e're this I hop'd more solid gains,
As my low purse demands a quick supply.
Poor Sylvia weeps,—and urges my return
To rural peace and humble happiness,
As my ambition beggars all her babes.

Crusty:
When first I listed in the desp'rate cause,
And blindly swore obedience to his will,
So wise, so just, so good I thought Rapatio,
   [Governor Thomas Hutchinson]
That if salvation rested on his word
I'd pin my faith, and risk my hopes thereon.

Hazelrod:
And why not now?—What staggers thy belief?

Crusty:
Himself—his perfidy appears—
It is too plain he has betray'd his country.
And we're the wretched tools by him mark'd
   out

To seal its ruins—tear up the ancient forms,
And every vestige treacherously destroy,
Nor leave a trait of freedom in the land.
Nor did I think hard fate wou'd call me up
From drudging o'er my acres—
Treading the glade, and sweating at the
    plough,
To dangle at the tables of the great;
At bowls and cards, to spend my frozen
    years;
To sell my friends, my country, and my con-
    science;
Profane the sacred sabbaths of my God;
Scorn'd by the very men who want my aid
To spread distress o'er this devoted people.

Hazelrod:
Pho—what misgivings—why these idle
    qualms,
This shrinking backwards at the bugbear
    conscience?
In early life I heard the phantom nam'd,
And the grave sages prate of moral sense
Presiding in the bosom of the just;
Or planting thongs about the guilty heart.
Bound by these shackles, long my lab'ring
    mind,
Obscurely trod the lower walks of life,
In hopes by honesty my bread to gain;
But neither commerce, or my conjuring rods,
Nor yet mechanics, or new fangled drills,
Or all the iron-monger's curious arts,
Gave me a competence of shining ore,
Or gratify'd my itching palm for more;
Till I dismiss'd the bold intruding guest,
And banish'd conscience from my wounded
    breast.

Crusty:
Happy expedient!—Could I gain the art,
Then balmy sleep might sooth my waking
    lids,
And rest once more refresh my weary soul.

Hazelrod:
Resolv'd more rapidly to gain my point,
I mounted high in justice's sacred seat,
With flowing robes, and head equip'd with-
    out,
A heart unfeeling and a stubborn soul,
As qualify'd as e'er a Jefferies was; [George

Jeffreys, Chief Justice of England, made him-
self notorious by injustice and brutality.]
Save in the knotty rudiments of law,
The smallest requisite for modern times,
When wisdom, law, and justice are supply'd
By swords, dragoons, and ministerial nods,
Sanctions most sacred in the pander's creed,
I sold my country for a splendid bribe.
Now let her sink—and all the dire alarms
Of war, confusion, pestilence and blood,
And tenfold mis'ry be her future doom—
Let civil discord lift her sword on high,
Nay, sheath its hilt e'en in my brother's blood;
It ne'er shall move the purpose of my soul.
Tho' once I trembled at a thought so bold;
By Philalethes's arguments, convinc'd
We may live Demons, as we die like brutes,
I give my tears, and conscience to the winds.

Hateall:
Curse on their coward fears, and dastard
    souls,
Their soft compunctions and relented
    qualms,
Compassion ne'er shall seize my steadfast
    breast
Though blood and carnage spread thro' all
    the land;
Till streaming purple tinge the verdant turf,
Till ev'ry street shall float with human gore,
I Nero like, the capital in flames,
Could laugh to see her glotted sons expire,
Tho' much too rough my soul to touch the
    lyre.

Simple:
I fear the brave, the injur'd multitude,
Repeated wrongs, arouse them to resent,
And every patriot like old Brutus stands,
The shining steel half drawn—its glitt'ring
    point
Scarce hid beneath the scabbard's friendly
    cell,
Resolv'd to die, or see their country free.

Hateall:
Then let them die—*The dogs we will keep
    down*—
While N[orth]'s my friend, and G[age] ap-
    proves the deed,
Tho' hell and all its hell-hounds should unite,

I'll not recede to save from swift perdition
My wife, my country, family, or friends.
G[age]'s mandamus I more highly prize
Than all the mandates of th'etherial king.

Hector Mushroom:

Will our abettors in the distant towns
Support us long against the common cause,
When they shall see from Hampshire's north-
    ern bounds
Thro' the wide western plains to southern
    shores
The whole united continent in arms?

Hateall:

They shall—as sure as oaths or bond can
    bind;
I've boldly sent my new-born brat abroad,
Th' association of my morbid brain,
To which each minion must affix his name.
As all our hope depends on brutal force
On quick destruction, misery, and death;
Soon may we see dark ruin stalk around,
With murder, rapine, and inflicted pains,
Estates confiscate, slav'ry, and despair,
Wrecks, halters, axes, gibbeting and chains,
All the dread ills that wait on civil war; —
How I could glut my vengeful eyes to see
The weeping maid thrown helpless on the
    world,
Her sire cut off.—Her orphan brothers stand,
While the big tear rolls down the manly
    cheek.
Robb'd of maternal care by grief's keen shaft,
The sorrowing mother mourns her starving
    babes.
Her murder'd lord torn guiltless from her side,
And flees for shelter to the pitying grave
To screen at once from slavery and pain.

Hazelrod:

But more complete I view this scene of woe,
By the incursions of a savage foe,
Of which I warn'd them, if they dare refuse
The badge of slaves, and bold resistance use.
Now let them suffer—I'll no pity feel.

Hateall:

Nor I! — But had I power, as I have the will,
I'd send them murm'ring to the shades of hell.

End of the First Act

Note to readers:

If you wish to study the complete play, we can supply you with a copy for reproduction. F.A.C.E. obtained the last available copies of their 1953 facsimile reprint from the William L. Clements Library at the University of Michigan at Ann Arbor.

Tory Reading List:

Mercy Warren gives a fascinating list of Tory reading as her second act opens. Here is her description of the set for Act II:

> The scene changes to a large dining room. The table furnished with bowls, bottles, glasses, and cards. "The Group" appear sitting round in a restless attitude. In one corner of the room is discovered a small cabinet of books for the use of the studious and contemplative; containing, Hobb's Leviathan, Sipthorp's Sermons, Hutchinson's History, Fable of the Bees, Philalethes on Philanthropy, with an appendix by Massachusettensis, Hoyle on Whist, Lives of the Stewarts, Statutes of Henry the Eighth, and William the Conqueror, Wedderburne's speeches, and acts of Parliament, for 1774.

Abigail Smith Adams (1744–1818)

Wife of John Adams, second president of the United States, mother of John Quincy Adams, sixth president of the United States.

We come now to the study of one of the most satisfying of our American Christian women of the American Revolution period. Abigail Smith, daughter of the Congregational minister in the town of Weymouth, Massachusetts, was descended from the finest of our Puritan stock. Despite the fact that delicate health prevented any schooling outside the home, Abigail had rich resources to draw upon for her instruction. From her grandmother on her mother's side, Mrs. Colonel John Quincy of Mt. Wollaston, Abigail "appears to have imbibed the lessons which made the deepest impression upon her mind." Years later she wrote to her own daughter:

I have not forgotten the excellent lessons which I received from my grandmother, at a very early period of life. I frequently think they made a more durable impression upon my mind than those which I received from my own parents. Whether it was owing to the happy method of mixing instruction and amusement together, or from an inflexible adherence to certain principles, the utility of which I could not but see and approve when a child, I know not; but maturer years have rendered them oracles of wisdom to me. I love and revere her memory; her lively, cheerful disposition animated all around her, whilst she edified all by her unaffected piety.

The letter-writing propensity for which Abigail became most famous was early manifested in the youthful circle of her companions. Two things can be noted: the influence of the study of Addison and Steele's *The Spectator*, the English essayists, and the influence of the Greek and particularly the Roman classics as reflected in the signatures adopted by these correspondents. Abigail adopted the name of *Portia* in her letters.

Thus reading "drawn from the deepest wells of English literature," conversation, reflection, and writing constituted the education of Abigail Smith. Her knowledge and study of the Scriptures under the direction of her pastor-father and both the hearing and reading of New England sermons all poured into her heart and mind the ingredients which were to constitute her life and character which we see particularly evident in her rich correspondence.

Abigail Adams was twenty years old when she married John Adams, a young lawyer from the family of Adams in Braintree. John was the son of a small farmer of the middle class who, though a graduate of Harvard College, was not considered quite a good match for Abigail. It was John Adams's interest in history, law and government, and his deep study of these subjects which added much to the understanding which Abigail brought to her recording of the events of her

life. And New England homes were wonderful centers of discussion where scriptural, historical, and governmental reasoning held forth and to which the women often contributed pertinent observations.

Abigail and John were the parents of two daughters, Susanna, who died after a year, Abigail, outlived by her mother, and three sons, the most famous and perhaps the one most responsive to his parents—John Quincy Adams, sixth president of the United States.

Your Own Study of Abigail Adams

It would be unjust, both to you and to Abigail Adams, to try to compress her interesting life into a few short paragraphs or pages, nor should your own discovery of this founding mother be spoiled. Here are some references to the sources of her rich correspondence and to more complete biographical details.

Correspondence:

The Adams Papers: Adams Family Correspondence. Edited by L. H. Butterfield. Cambridge, Mass.: The Belknap Press of Harvard University, 1963.

Familiar Letters of John Adams and his Wife, Abigail Adams, during the Revolution with a Memoir of Mrs. Adams, Charles Francis Adams. Boston: Houghton, Mifflin & Company, 1875.

Letters of Mrs. Adams, the Wife of John Adams, with an introductory Memoir by her grandson, Charles Francis Adams. 1841.

New Letters of Abigail Adams, 1788–1801. Edited with an introduction by Stewart Mitchell. Boston: Houghton Mifflin, 1947.

Biography:

Those Who Love, a biographical novel of Abigail and John Adams, by Irving Stone. Doubleday and Co., 1965.

Despite the title of this book, Mr. Stone has done a tremendous service to us in re-creating the characters of both Abigail and John for the modern reader without sacrificing authenticity for romantic fantasy. Sometimes you feel as if you were walking on a

Hollywood set of generations ago—so precise is the detail of background and so close and familiar are the surroundings. This is, however, a tribute to the infinite and loving attention which the author has given to his research. His own admiration and affection for his subjects come through the writing, and his purpose is never to diminish but rather enhance their biographies. Best of all there is a love for this founding period of our nation which sustains the reader, and we are delighted to learn that copies of this book—both hard cover and paperback—are obtainable for our reading.

Character and Correspondence

In order to give some indication of the character which was called forth by the many circumstances of the years of the American Revolution, we will include several paragraphs from the Memoir of grandson, Charles Francis Adams, concerning Abigail Adams and her perseverance during her husband's absences.

> The ordinary occupations of the female sex are necessarily of a kind which must ever prevent it from partaking largely of the action of life. However keenly women may think or feel, there is seldom an occasion when the sphere of their exertions can with propriety be extended much beyond the domestic hearth or the social circle. Exactly here are they to be seen most in their glory. Three or four years passed whilst Mrs. Adams was living in the utmost seclusion of country life, during which, on account of the increasing vigilance of British cruisers, she very seldom heard from her husband. The material for interesting letters was proportionately small, and yet there was no time when she was more usefully occupied. It is impossible to omit all notice of this period, however deficient it may prove in variety. The depreciation of the Continental paper money, the difficulties in the way of managing the property of her husband, her own isolation, and the course of public events in distant parts of the country, form her constant topics. Only a small number of the letters which discuss them, yet enough to show her situation at this period, have been admitted into this volume. They are remarkable, because they display the readiness with which she could devote herself to the most opposite duties, and the cheerful manner in which she would accommodate herself to the difficulties of the times.

> She is a farmer cultivating the land, and discussing the weather and the crops; a merchant reporting prices-current and the rates of exchange, and directing the making up of invoices; a politician speculating upon the probabilities of peace or war; and a mother writing the most exalted sentiments to her son. All of these pursuits she adopts together; some from choice, the rest from the necessity of the case; and in all she appears equally well.

Abigail once wrote John that "out of thirteen years of their married life, three had been passed in a state of separation." But the period now referred to was the period of longest separation. On John's second return to Europe he was separated from Abigail for almost five years. And, as referred to above, often his letters or hers did not reach the beloved partner.

In addition to being separated from her husband, her oldest son, John Quincy Adams, accompanied his father to begin his preparation for a life of statesmanlike service to his country. While just a boy of eleven, he traveled in Europe and so distinguished himself in his studies that at the age of fourteen he was selected by Francis Dana, minister from the United States to the Russian court, as his private secretary and accompanied him through Germany to St. Petersburg.

At a later date, in 1784, Abigail joined her husband and son in London, and for a period of four years, one in France and three in England, she had the unique experience of being the first American woman in a diplomatic post with her husband. Despite her conviction that her simple country background might be inadequate to the sophisticated courts and salons of France and England, she was a tremendous credit to her nation, and a particular tribute and testimony to the New England background of intellect and character. The presence of the Adamses was the presence of the best of America's Christian character and understanding of government.

Some Letters of Abigail Adams

Moses Coit Tyler, in his study of *The Literary History of the American Revolution, 1763–1783*, credits Abigail Adams as one of the finest correspondents of this period in our history.

> Indeed the letters of Mrs. Adams, mostly to her husband, and covering this entire period, are among the most delightful specimens of such work as done by any American: they are alive with the very moods and scenes of the Revolution; they reveal, also, the strong intelligence, the high faith, the splendid courage of that noble matron, and the secret of her life-long power as the intellectual companion of her husband, his one and only confidante, and the inspirer of all that was greatest and best in his career. (p. 13)

Today in America many of our founding mothers are being used to illustrate the dissatisfaction of women with their lot. It is our purpose here to illustrate by a few letters the quality of Christian life and attitude of these unique women on subjects which center about questions of interest and concern to us all. The full text of these letters can be found in the collections listed on page 324 and pages 42–43 (chapter 1).

Braintree, August 19, 1774

> The great distance between us makes the time appear very long to me. It seems already a month since you left me. The great anxiety I feel for my country, for you, and for our family renders the day tedious and the night unpleasant. The rocks and quick-

sands appear upon every side. What course you can or will take is all wrapped in the bosom of futurity. Uncertainty and expectation leave the mind great scope. Did ever any kingdom or state regain its liberty, when once it was invaded, without bloodshed? I cannot think of it without horror. Yet we are told that all the misfortunes of Sparta were occasioned by their too great solicitude for present tranquillity, and, from an excessive love of peace, they neglected the means of making it sure and lasting. They ought to have reflected, says Polybius, that "as there is nothing more desirable or advantageous than peace, when founded in justice and honor, so there is nothing more shameful, and at the same time more pernicious, when attained by bad measures and purchased at the price of liberty." I have received a most charming letter from our friend Mrs. Warren. She desires me to tell you that her best wishes attend you through your journey, both as a friend and a patriot,—hope you will have no uncommon difficulties to surmount, or hostile movements to impede you, but, if the Locrians should interrupt you, she hopes that you will beware, that no future annals may say you chose an ambitious Philip for your leader, who subverted the noble order of the American Amphictyons, and built up a monarchy on the ruins of the happy institution.

I have taken a very great fondness for reading Rollin's Ancient History since you left me. I am determined to go through with it, if possible, in these my days of solitude. I find great pleasure and entertainment from it, and I have persuaded Johnny to read me a page or two every day, and hope he will, from his desire to oblige me, entertain a fondness for it. We have had a charming rain, which lasted twelve hours and has greatly revived the dying fruits of the earth.

I want much to hear from you. I long impatiently to have you upon the stage of action. The first of September, or the month of September, perhaps, may be of as much importance to Great Britain as the Ides of March were to Caesar. I wish you every public as well as private blessing, and that wisdom which is profitable both for instruction and edification, to conduct you in this difficult day. The little flock remember papa, and kindly wish to see him; so does your most affectionate

Abigail Adams

From a letter of September 2, 1774, Braintree

The drought has been very severe. My poor cows will certainly prefer a petition to you, setting forth their grievances and informing you that they have been deprived of their ancient privileges, whereby they are become great sufferers, and desiring that they may be restored to them. More especially as their living, by reason of the drought, is all taken from them, and their property which they hold elsewhere is decaying, they humbly pray that you would consider them, lest hunger should break through stone walls.

The tenderest regard evermore awaits you from your most affectionate
Abigail Adams

On First Meeting General Washington, *Braintree, July 16, 1775*

I was struck with General Washington. You had prepared me to entertain a favorable opinion of him, but I thought the half was not told me. Dignity with ease and complacency, the gentleman and soldier, look agreeably blended in him. Modesty marks every line and feature of his face. Those lines of Dryden instantly occurred to me:—

Mark his majestic fabric; he's a temple
Sacred by birth, and built by hands divine;
His soul's the deity that lodges there;
Nor is the pile unworthy of the god.

From the most often quoted "Remember the Ladies" letter,

Braintree, March 31, 1776

I long to hear that you have declared an independency. And, by the way, in the new code of laws which I suppose it will be necessary for you to make, I desire you would remember the ladies and be more generous and favorable to them than your ancestors. Do not put such unlimited power into the hands of the husbands. Remember, all men would be tyrants if they could. If particular care and attention is not paid to the ladies, we are determined to foment a rebellion, and will not hold ourselves bound by any laws in which we have no voice or representation.

That your sex are naturally tyrannical is a truth so thoroughly established as to admit of no dispute; but such of you as wish to be happy willingly give up the harsh title of master for the more tender and endearing one of friend. Why, then, not put it out of the power of the vicious and the lawless to use us with cruelty and indignity with impunity? Men of sense in all ages abhor those customs which treat us only as the vassals of your sex; regard us then as beings placed by Providence under your protection, and in imitation of the Supreme Being make use of that power only for our happiness.

Boston, August 14, 1776

Last Sunday, after service, the Declaration of Independence was read from the pulpit by order of council. The Dr. concluded with asking a blessing "upon the United States of America even until the final restitution of all things."

Dr. Chauncey's address pleased me. The good man after having read it, lifted his eyes and hands to heaven. "God bless the United States of America, and let all the people say "Amen.". . . One of his audience told me it universally struck them.

I have no news to write you. I am sure it will be none to tell you I am ever

Yours Portia

Education for Women in America
August 14, 1776

If you complain of neglect of education in sons, what shall I say with regard to daughters, who every day experience the want of it? With regard to the education of my own children, I find myself soon out of my depth, destitute and deficient in every part of education.

I most sincerely wish that some more liberal plan might be laid and executed for the benefit of the rising generation, and that our new Constitution may be distinguished for encouraging learning and virtue. If we mean to have heroes, statesmen, and philosophers, we should have learned women. The world perhaps would laugh at me and accuse me of vanity, but you, I know, have a mind too enlarged and liberal to disregard the sentiment. If much depends, as is allowed, upon the early education of youth, and the first principles which are instilled take the deepest root, great benefit must arise from literary accomplishments in women.

"My Ambition,"
Boston, August 29, 1776

I wish for peace and tranquillity. All my desire and all my ambition is to be esteemed and loved by my partner, to join with him in the education and instruction of our little ones, to sit under our own vines in peace, liberty, and safety.

Adieu, my dearest friend! Soon, soon return to your most affectionate

Portia

P.S. A very odd report has been propagated in Braintree, namely, that you were poisoned upon your return at New York.

Charles Francis Adams observed: "In the midst of public or private troubles, the buoyant spirit of Mrs. Adams never forsook her. 'I am a mortal enemy,' she writes upon one occasion to her husband, 'to anything by a cheerful countenance and a merry heart, which, Solomon tells us, does good like a medicine.' This spirit contributed greatly to lift up his heart when surrounded by difficulties and danger."

In his collection of *Familiar Letters*, Charles Adams admits that one in particular by Abigail Adams written to her husband is his favorite. "It is the letter of the 8th of February, 1797, the day upon which the votes for President were counted, and Mr. Adams, as Vice-President, was required by law to announce himself the President-elect for the ensuing term. This, though extremely short, appears to the Editor to be the gem of the collection; for the exalted feeling of the moment shines out with all the lustre of ancient patriotism. Perhaps there is not, among the whole number, one which, in its spirit, brings so strongly to mind, as this does, the celebrated Roman lady whose signature she at one time assumed; whilst it is chastened by a sentiment of Christian humility of which ancient history furnishes no example."

Quincy, February 8, 1797

The sun is dressed in brightest beams,
To give thy honors to the day.

And may it prove an auspicious prelude to each ensuing season. You have this day to declare yourself head of a nation. "And now, O Lord, my God, Thou hast made thy servant ruler over the people. Give unto him an understanding heart, that he may know how to go out and come in before this great people; that he may discern between good and bad. For who is able to judge this thy so great a people?" were the words of a royal Sovereign; and not less applicable to him who is invested with the Chief Magistracy of a nation, though he wear not a crown, nor the robes of royalty.

My thoughts and my meditations are with you, though personally absent; and my petitions to Heaven are that "the things which make for peace may not be hidden from your eyes." My feelings are not those of pride or ostentation upon the occasion. They are solemnized by a sense of the obligations, the important trusts, and numerous duties connected with it. That you may be enabled to discharge them with honor to yourself, with justice and impartiality to your country, and with satisfaction to this great people, shall be the daily prayer of your A. A.

Phillis Wheatley (1753–1784)

In 1761, a little slave girl arrived in Boston from West Africa on the ship *Phillis*, from which she was given her name. This seven-year-old was bought by a prosperous merchant, John Wheatley, and introduced to a world of culture, education, and refinement. Her new family also told Phillis of God's love and His gift of redemption. The Wheatleys were Christians whose lives showed forth their beliefs through their church activities and personal outreach.

Mary Wheatley, their teenaged daughter, took a special interest in the young slave girl and tutored her in many subjects—the English language and literature, the Latin language and its classics, history, astronomy, geography, the Bible, and Christian principles. Such a comprehensive education was not granted to most of Boston's freeborn citizens.

According to a later statement by her master, within sixteen months of Phillis's arrival in America, she was able to read "the most difficult parts of the sacred writings to the great astonishment of all who heard her." (*The Poems of Phillis Wheatley*, Julian Mason, 1989, p. 47) By the age of twelve, Phillis was already composing poetry, and in a poem addressed to wayward students of Harvard College, the precocious child stated her firm convictions on the value of education and her strong belief in Christian doctrines. In

another poem from that time, Phillis reflected upon her original home and God's providential hand in her life:

On Being Brought from Africa to America

'Twas mercy brought me from my *Pagan* land,
Taught my benighted soul to understand
That there's a God, that there's a Saviour too:
Once I redemption neither sought nor knew.
Some view our sable race with scornful eye,
"Their colour is a diabolic die."
Remember, *Christians*, *Negros*, black as *Cain*,
May be refin'd, and join th' angelic train.

The Wheatleys eagerly encouraged the development and education of their literary slave. Her household duties were adjusted to accommodate her creative impulses, and heat and light were provided in her bedroom to permit her to work during the night, and also to protect her delicate health. In early 1773, it was thought that sea air might invigorate her, and so Phillis accompanied the Wheatleys' son to England where she soon became well-acquainted with prominent citizens who were anxious to promote her talents. From London's wealth of books, she began to amass a library of classics, and negotiations were begun regarding a British publication of her poetry, however the serious illness of her mistress necessitated her return to Massachusetts.

After Susanna Wheatley's death, her husband freed Phillis from her legal bondage, and she now faced life as a freewoman with all of its responsibilities and burdens. In 1778, Phillis married John Peters, a freedman who has been described as "an enigmatic Negro who seems to have tried his hand as a baker, a grocer, a doctor, and a lawyer, without having much training for them or much success with them." (Mason, 1966). Marriage and the birth of three children apparently interrupted her writing, and her life became marked by sadness and hardship. Financially destitute and estranged from her husband, who was then in jail, Phillis began work in a cheap boarding house to support her children—two of whom died soon after. On December 5, 1784, Phillis herself died at the untimely age of thirty-one, followed immediately by her last surviving child who was buried with her. Throughout her years of writing, her thoughts had often turned to death. Almost half of her poems have that theme, yet she does not despair. In all of these she made clear her hope of salvation and heavenly glory.

As the most acclaimed Negro poet of the Revolutionary era, Phillis Wheatley is remembered for her legacy of forty-six published poems, many spirited with patriotic zeal. Of these, perhaps her most celebrated work was addressed to General Washington. This poem and the general's response to her tribute are reproduced below:

"To His Excellency General Washington"

Sir,

I have taken the freedom to address your Excellency in the enclosed poem, and entreat your acceptance, though I am not insensible of its inaccuracies. Your being appointed by the Grand Continental Congress to be Generalissimo of the armies of North America, together with the fame of your virtues, excite sensations not easy to suppress. Your generosity, therefore, I presume, will pardon the attempt. Wishing your Excellency all possible success in the great cause you are so generously engaged in. I am

Your Excellency's most
obedient humble servant,

Phillis Wheatley

Providence, October 26, 1775
His Excellency Gen. Washington:

Celestial choir! enthron'd in realms of
    light,
Columbia's scenes of glorious toils I
    write.
While freedom's cause her anxious
    breast alarms,
She flashes dreadful in refulgent arms.
See mother earth her offspring's fate
    bemoan,
And nations gaze at scenes before un-
    known!
See the bright beams of heaven's re-
    volving light
Involved in sorrows and the veil of
    night!
The goddess comes, she moves di-
    vinely fair,
Olive and laurel binds her golden hair:
Wherever shines this native of the
    skies,
Unnumber'd charms and recent
    graces rise.
Muse! bow propitious while my pen
    relates
How pour her armies through a thou-
    sand gates,
As when Eolus heaven's fair face de-
    forms,
Enwrapp'd in tempest and a night of
    storms;
Astonish'd ocean feels the wild uproar,
The refluent surges beat the sounding
    shore;
Or thick as leaves in Autumn's golden
    reign,
Such, and so many, moves the
    warrior's train.
In bright array they seek the work of
    war,
Where high unfurl'd the ensign waves
    in air.
Shall I to Washington their praise re-
    cite?
Enough thou know'st them in the
    fields of fight.
Thee, first in peace and honours,—we
    demand
The grace and glory of thy martial
    band.
Fam'd for they valour, for thy virtues
    more,
Hear every tongue thy guardian aid
    implore!
One century scarce perform'd its des-
    tined round,
When Gallic powers Columbia's fury
    found;
And so may you, whoever dares dis-
    grace
The land of freedom's heaven-de-
    fended race!
Fix'd are the eyes of nations on the
    scales,

For in their hopes Columbia's prevails.
Anon Britannia droops the pensive
head,
While round increase the rising hills
of dead.
Ah! cruel blindness to Columbia's
state!
Lament thy thirst of boundless power
too late.
Proceed, great chief, with virtue on thy
side,
Thy ev'ry action let the goddess guide.
A crown, a mansion, and a throne that
shine,
With gold unfading, WASHINGTON! be
thine.

The response from George Washington to
Phillis Wheatley appears in *The Writings of
George Washington*, edited by John C.
Fitzpatrick, vol. 4, pp. 360-61.

Cambridge, February 28, 1776

To Phillis Wheatley,

Mrs. Phillis: Your favour of the 26th
of October did not reach my hands
'till the middle of December. Time
enough, you will say, to have given
an answer ere this. Granted. But a
variety of important occurrences,
continually interposing to distract the
mind and withdraw the attention, I
hope will apologize for the delay, and
plead my excuse for the seeming, but
not real neglect.

I thank you most sincerely for your
polite notice of me, in the elegant Lines
you enclosed; and however undeserv-
ing I may be of such encomium and
panegyrick, the style and manner exhibit a striking proof of your great poetical Talents. In honour of which, and
as a tribute justly due to you, I would
have published the Poem, had I not
been apprehensive, that, while I only
meant to give the World this new instance of your genius, I might have
incurred the imputation of Vanity. This
and nothing else, determined me not
to give it place in the public Prints.

If you should ever come to Cambridge, or near Head Quarters, I shall
be happy to see a person so favoured
by the Muses, and to whom Nature has
been so liberal and beneficient in her
dispensations. I am, with great Respect, etc.

An American Christian Poetess

We appreciate Phillis Wheatley as a Christian poetess who wrote during a tumultuous
era—the birthing of America, the first nation
to strive for the political liberty of all men
from a Christian philosophy of government.
Her poems reflect her own conversion and
faith and include eulogistic tributes written
to evangelists, the Rev. Dr. Sewall (1769), and
the Rev. Mr. George Whitefield (1770). She
herself was lauded by America's first published Negro poet, Jupiter Hammon. His
poem with the lengthy title, "An Address to
Miss Phillis Wheatly, Ethiopian Poetess, in
Boston, who came from Africa at eight years
of age, and soon became acquainted with
the Gospel of Jesus Christ," was published
as a broadside dated Hartford, August 4,
1778. In this work of twenty-four stanzas,
Hammon admonishes her to thank God for
all the special things He has done for her,
and he suggests:

Come you, Phillis, now aspire,
And seek the living God;
So step by step thou mayst go higher,
Till perfect in the Word.
(Mason, 1989, p. 24)

(From *The Poems of Phillis Wheatley*, edited
by Julian D. Mason, Jr. Copyright ©1966, 1989
by the University of North Carolina Press.
Used by permission of the publisher.)

Literature of
the American Revolution

The letters penned by John and Abigail Adams to each other, to relatives, and to their friends reveal the character and worldview of America's founding and constitutional eras. As eyewitnesses to the birthing of the new country, the correspondents expressed fear of enemy attack, told of political wranglings, and pondered the outcome of the struggle and sacrifice for personal liberty. However, they also discussed the mundane details of home and farming life, their concerns for the health and safety of family members, their loneliness at separation, and even the need for financial prudence.

Such correspondence provides a rich source of information about those turbulent times, but it further serves to reveal the spiritual stature of these colonists as we read their sentiments of love, trust, respect, patriotism, commitment, and faith in the sustaining providence of God.

John Adams to Abigail Adams
Plymouth, May Saturday, 1772

My Dr.

I take an opportunity by Mr. Kent, to let you know that I am at Plymouth, and pretty well. Shall not go for Barnstable until Monday.

There are now signs of a gathering Storm, so I shall make my self easy here for the Sabbath. I wish myself at Braintree. This wandering, itinerating Life grows more and more disagreable to me. I want to see my Wife and Children every Day, I want to see my Grass and Blossoms and Corn, etc. every Day. I want to see my Workmen, nay I almost want to go and see the Bosse Calfs's as often as Charles does. But above all except the Wife and Children I want to see my Books.

None of these Amusements are to be had. The company we have is not agreable to me. In Coll. Warren and his Lady I find Friends, Mr. Angier is very good, but farther than these, I have very little Pleasure in Conversation. Dont expect me, before Saturday,—Perhaps Mrs. Hutchinson may call upon you, in her Return to Boston, the later End of next Week or beginning of the Week after.

Pray let the People take Care of the Caterpillars. Let them go over and over, all the Trees, till there is not the appearance of a nest, or Worm left.

John Adams

John Adams to Abigail Adams
York, July 1st, 1774

I am so idle, that I have not an easy Moment, without my Pen in my Hand. My Time might have been improved to some Purpose, in mowing Grass, raking Hay, or hoeing Corn, weeding Carrotts, picking or shelling Peas. Much better should I have been employed in schooling my children, in teaching them to write, cypher, Latin, French, English and Greek.

I sometimes think I must come to this—to be the Foreman upon my own Farm, and the School Master to my own children. I confess myself to be full of Fears that the Ministry and their Friends and Instruments, will prevail, and crush the Cause and Friends of Liberty. The Minds of that Party are so filled with Prejudices, against me, that they will take all Advantages, and do me all the Damage they can. These Thoughts have their Turns in my Mind, but in general my Hopes are predominant.

In a Tryal of a Cause here to Day, some Facts were mentioned, which are worth writing to you. It was sworn, by Dr. Lyman, Elder Bradbury and others, that there had been a Number of Instances in this Town of fatal Accidents, happening from sudden Noises striking the Ears of Babes and young Children. A Gun was fired near one Child, as likely as any; the Child fell immediately into fits, which impaired his Reason, and is still living an Ideot. Another Child was sitting on a Chamber floor. A Man rapped suddenly and violently on the Boards which made the floor under the Child [tremble?]. The Child was so startled, and frightened, that it fell into fits, which never were cured. This may suggest a Caution to keep Children from sudden Frights and surprizes.

Dr. Gardiner arrived here to day, from Boston, brings us News of a Battle at the Town Meeting, between Whigs and Tories, in which the Whiggs after a Day and a Half's obstinate Engagement were finally victorious by two to one. He says the Tories are preparing a flaming Protest.

I am determined to be cool, if I can; I have suffered such Torments in my Mind, heretofore, as have almost overpowered my Constitution, without any Advantage: and now I will laugh and be easy if I can, let the Conflict of Parties, terminate as it will—let my own Estate and Interest suffer what it will. Nay whether I stand high or low in the Estimation of the World, so long as I keep a Conscience void of Offence towards God and Man. And thus I am determined by the Will of God, to do, let what will become of me or mine, my Country, or the World.

I shall arouse myself ere long I believe, and exert an Industry, a Frugality, a hard Labour, that will serve my family, if I cant serve my Country. I will not lie down and die in Dispair. If I cannot serve my Children by the Law, I will serve them by Agriculture, by Trade, by some Way, or other. I thank God I have a Head, an Heart and Hands which if once fully exerted alltogether will succeed in the World as well as those of the mean spirited, low minded, fawning obsequious scoundrells who have long hoped, that my Integrity would be an Obstacle in my Way, and enable them to out strip me in the Race.

But what I want in Comparison of them, of Villany and servility, I will make up in Industry and Capacity. If I dont they shall laugh and triumph.

I will not willingly see Blockheads, whom I have a Right to despise, elevated above me, and insolently triumphing over me. Nor shall Knavery, through any Negligence of mine, get the better of Honesty, nor Ignorance of Knowledge, nor Folly of Wisdom, nor Vice of Virtue.

I must intreat you, my dear Partner in all the Joys and Sorrows, Prosperity and Adversity of my Life, to take a Part with me in the Struggle. I pray God for your Health—intreat you to rouse your whole Attention to the Family, the stock, the Farm, the Dairy. Let every Article of Expence which can possibly be spared be retrench'd. Keep the Hands attentive to their Business, and [let] the most prudent Measures of every kind be adopted and pursued with Alacrity and Spirit.

I am etc.,
John Adams

Abigail Adams to Mercy Otis Warren
Braintree, May 2, 1775

My dear Mrs. Warren,

What a scene has opened upon us since I had the favour of your last! Such a scene as we never before Experienced, and could scarcely form an Idea of. If we look back we are amazed at what is past, if we look forward we must shudder at the view. Our only comfort lies in the justice of our cause; and in the mercy of that being who never said, "Seek ye me in vain." These are consolations which the unbeliever knows not of, and which are a comfortable support, under all we feel, and all we fear. All our worldly comforts are now at stake—our nearest and dearest connections are hazarding their lives and properties. God give them wisdom and integrity sufficient to the great cause in which they are engaged—I long most earnestly for the society of my much valued Mrs. Warren—it would be a cordial to my spirits. I must entreat you to write to me every opportunity. I feel the absence of my better half, in this Day of Distress. We have had several allarms from apprehensions of men of wars barges. Colln. Quincys family have several Times been obliged to flee from their house and scatter themselves about. I cannot say that I am at present under any apprehensions of them here; I have determined to stay as long as it will be safe for any person to tarry upon the sea coast. I am much distressed for our poor Boston Friends. What course they can take I know not, I believe they are kept in for security to the troops. They have involved the Country in great difficulties by their obstinately persevereing to tarry in Town. I fear their distresses will drive them to such compliances as will be inconsistant with their honour—I hear you have thoughts of going to Taunton, but I hope you will not be obliged to quit your own habitation—O Britain Britain how is thy glory vanished—how are thy Annals stained with the Blood of thy children.

Adieu my Dear Friend & believe me at all times most affectionately yours,

Abigail Adams

Abigail Adams to John Adams
Sunday, June 18, 1775

Dearest Friend,

The Day; perhaps the decisive Day is come on which the fate of America depends. My bursting Heart must find vent at my pen. I have just heard that our dear Friend Dr. Warren is no more but fell gloriously fighting for his Country—saying better to die honourably in the field than ignominiously hang upon the Gallows. Great is our Loss. He has distinguished himself in every engagement, by his courage and fortitude, by animating the Soldiers and leading them on by his own example. A particular account of these dreadful, but I hope Glorious Days will be

transmitted you, no doubt in the exactest manner.

The race is not to the swift, nor the battle to the strong, but the God of Israel is he that giveth strength and power unto his people. Trust in him at all times, ye people pour out your hearts before him. God is a refuge for us—Charlstown is laid in ashes. The Battle began upon our intrenchments upon Bunkers Hill, Saturday morning about 3 o'clock and has not ceased yet and tis now 3 o'clock Sabbath afternoon.

Tis expected they will come out over the Neck to night, and a dreadful Battle must ensue. Almighty God cover the heads of our Country men, and be a shield to our Dear Friends. How [many ha]ve fallen we know not—the constant roar of the cannon is so [distre]ssing that we can not Eat, Drink or Sleep. May we be supported and sustained in the dreadful conflict. I shall tarry here till tis thought unsafe by my Friends, and then I have secured myself a retreat at your Brothers who has kindly offerd me part of his house. I cannot compose myself to write any further at present. I will add more as I hear further.

John Adams to John Quincy Adams
Philadelphia, April 18, 1776

My dear son,

I thank you for your agreable Letter of the Twenty fourth of March.

I rejoice with you that our Friends are once more in Possession of the Town of Boston, and am glad to hear that so little damage is done to our House.

I hope you and your Sister and Brothers will take proper Notice of these great Events, and remember under whose wise and kind Providence they are all conducted. Not a Sparrow falls, nor a Hair is lost, but by the Direction of infinite Wisdom. Much less are Cities conquered and evacuated. I hope that you will all remember, how many Losses, Dangers, and Inconveniences, have been borne by your Parents, and the Inhabitants of Boston in general for the Sake of preserving Freedom for you, and yours—and I hope you will all follow the virtuous Example if, in any future Time, your Countrys Liberties should be in Danger, and suffer every human Evil, rather than Give them up—My Love to your Mamma, your Sister and Brothers, and all the Family. I am your affectionate Father,

John Adams

Satire during the American Revolution
Francis Hopkinson (1737–1791)

The Battle of the Kegs

Gallants, attend, and hear a friend
Trill forth harmonious ditty:
Strange things I'll tell, which late befell
In Philadelphia city.

'Twas early day, as poets say,
Just when the sun was rising,
A soldier stood on a log of wood
And saw a thing surprising.

As in amaze he stood to gaze,
The truth can't be denied, sir,
He spied a score of kegs or more
Come floating down the tide, sir.

A sailor, too, in jerkin blue,
This strange appearance viewing,
First damed his eyes, in great surprise,
Then said, "Some mischief's brewing.

"These kegs, I'm told, the rebels bold,
Packed up like pickled herring;
And they're come down to attack the town,
In this new way of ferrying."

The soldier flew, the sailor too,
And scared almost to death, sir,
Wore out their shoes to spread the news,
And ran till out of breath, sir.

Now up and down throughout the town
Most frantic scenes were acted;

And some ran here and others there,
Like men almost distracted.

Some fire cried, which some denied,
But said the earth had quaked;
And girls and boys, with hideous noise,
Ran through the streets half naked.

Sir William, he, snug as a flea,
Lay all this time a-snoring,
Nor dreamed of harm, as he lay warm,
[The Yankee foe ignoring].

Now in a fright he starts upright,
Awaked by such a clatter;
He rubs his eyes and boldly cries,
"For God's sake, what's the matter?"

At his bedside he then espied
Sir Erskine at command, sir.
Upon one foot he had one boot,
And t'other in his hand, sir.

"Arise, arise!" Sir Erskine cries,
"The rebels, more's the pity,
Without a boat are all afloat
And ranged before the city.

"The motley crew, in vessels new,
With Satan for their guide, sir,
Packed up in bags, or wooden kegs,
Come driving down the tide, sir.

"Therefore prepare for bloody war:
These kegs must all be routed
Or surely we despised shall be,
And British courage doubted."

The royal band now ready stand,
All ranged in dread array, sir,
With stomachs stout, to see it out,
And make a bloody day, sir.

The cannons roar from shore to shore,
The small arms make a rattle;
Since wars began, I'm sure no man
E'er saw so strange a battle.

The rebel dales, the rebel vales,
With rebel trees surrounded;
The distant woods, the hills and floods,
With rebel echoes sounded.

The fish below swam to and fro,
Attacked from every quarter.

"Why, sure," thought they, "the devil's to pay
'Mongst folks above the water."

The kegs, 'tis said, though strongly made
Of rebel staves and hoops, sir,
Could not oppose their powerful foes,
The conquering British troops, sir.

From morn till night these men of might
Displayed amazing courage,
And when the sun was fairly down
Retired to sup their porridge.

An hundred men, with each a pen,
Or more, upon my word, sir,
It is most true would be too few
Their valor to record, sir.

Such feats did they perform that day
Against those wicked kegs, sir,
That years to come, if they get home,
They'll make their boasts and brags, sir.

finis

Washington's pursuit of Sir Henry Clinton's
army on the way to New York culminated in
the Battle of Monmouth where the following
incident took place on June 28, 1778:

Molly Pitcher

'Twas hurry and scurry at Monmouth Town,
For Lee was beating a wild retreat;
The British were riding the Yankees down,
And panic was pressing on flying feet.

Galloping down like a hurricane
Washington rode with his sword swung high,
Mighty as he of the Trojan plain
Fired by a courage from the sky.

"Halt, and stand to your guns!" he cried.
And a bombardier made swift reply.
Wheeling his cannon into the tide,
He fell 'neath the shot of a foeman nigh.

Molly Pitcher sprang to his side,
Fired as she saw her husband do.
Telling the king in his stubborn pride
Women like men to their homes are true.

Washington rode from the bloody fray
Up to the gun that a woman manned.
"Molly Pitcher, you saved the day,"
He said, as he gave her a hero's hand.

He named her sergeant with manly praise,
While her war-brown face was wet with
    tears—
A woman has ever a woman's ways,
And the army was wild with cheers.

—Kate Brownlee Sherwood

(*American History in Verse*, Stevenson, 1975,
p. 126)

Teaching the Literature of the Federal Period
1787–1840
Preparation and Presentation

Background and Emphases	Readings
1. The period represents the first fruits of the Republic with the liberty of the individual flowering in literature.	
2. This is a time of rapid national development, westward expansion, and national unity marked by new invention which binds the country together, and a growing sense of nationalism heady with independence. Industrial development marks the east while the seeds of division appear.	
3. Several great writers appear: Washington Irving, 1783–1859; William Cullen Bryant, poet, 1794–1878; James Fenimore Cooper, 1789–1851.	Washington Irving: First man of letters Biography: *The Life of Columbus, The Life of Washington, The Life of Goldsmith* Essayist: *The Sketch Book* History: *Knickerbocker's History of New York* Travels: *The Alhambra* William Cullen Bryant: First poet of the Republic "Thanatopsis," "To a Waterfowl" James Fenimore Cooper: First novelist of the Republic *The Leatherstocking Tales: The Last of the Mohicans, The Deerslayer, The Pathfinder; The Pioneers; The Prairie.* *The Spy* *The Pilot*

Washington Irving (1783–1859)
First Man of Letters
Developed by Rosalie June Slater

Europe was totally unaware of America's coming of age during the one hundred and fifty years of her Biblical education and government in the colonial period. After the establishment of America as the world's first Christian Constitutional Republic, it was a surprise for Englishmen in particular to discover that these American colonists were a literate and articulate people. In America there was a different idea about the importance and worth of the individual. It was the Christian idea of man, and it had its consequence in the Christian idea of government.

Washington Irving was our first ambassador of literature from the New World to the Old. His "Sketch Book" gave Englishmen a view of the American character as well as a view of their own character by one who was skillful in pricking the balloon of European superiority. Irving's residence in Spain—in search of original sources of American history—put Spain on the literary map as he wrote delightedly of the Moorish occupation. Irving's biography of Christopher Columbus was the finest and the first of its kind. With his return to America, Irving found a nation expanding along its waterways and western paths. He, too, renewed his knowledge of America and traveled to the western frontier. His "Tour on the Prairies" is his account of a journey which extended from Fort Gibson to the Cross Timbers in what is now Oklahoma. What followed were two additional books: *Astoria* and *The Adventures of Captain Bonneville.* These remain classics of the period having survived the criticism of modern scholarship. The crowning labor of his life—a task for which God had been preparing him for many years—was his five-volume *Life of George Washington* which is still being reprinted today. It remains the most readable and the most Christian of all the biographies of the Father of our Country.

James Fenimore Cooper (1789–1851)
First American Christian Novelist of the Republic

James Fenimore Cooper brought a distinct talent to the field of American literature—the literature of our American Christian republic. Cooper's style and ability developed with his first works as he searched to find the unique individuality of subject and treatment which was to be his means of portraying America to the world. He found it in the character of "Deerslayer" in his series called *The Leatherstocking Tales*. These books have been read around the world in many languages and for more than one hundred years. They still characterize the free and independent man whose Christian self-government in the American wilderness was the wonder and, indeed, the envy of mankind.

The Spy, a Tale of the Neutral Ground was Cooper's second novel. Written in 1821, it was the first American novel with the background of our own history. Since the American War for Independence was a contest for individual liberty and the Christian principles of government, the whole world was interested in the subject. Thus, when first published, *The Spy* was eagerly read by English readers at home and abroad.

Susan Cooper, daughter of James Fenimore Cooper, was the editor of many editions of his works. Her introduction to *The Spy* provides us with its purpose and background:

> Patriotism was to be the soul of the new book, and the fact that he was about to move over home ground gave new zest to the work. . . . The scene was laid in Westchester county, where he was living at the time—a part of the country to which he was always partial.
>
> Many lesser incidents of the Revolution, now wholly forgotten, were at that day still living facts in the minds of the people, scarcely yet remote enough for the shadowy perspective of history.

Many of those who had taken an active part in the great struggle were still coming in and going out of their children's doors—aged men, telling tales of the different events of the conflict, with all the flow of personal interest. Many a gray-haired housewife, as she sat at the wheel, spinning her thread of flax or wool, could talk of the armies she had seen in her girlhood passing her father's door, marching to and fro, on their way to this or that victory, or retreating, perchance, from this or that defeat.

Westchester was full of such recollections. There was no portion of the country whose soil, during the eight eventful years of the war, was so often trodden by friend and foe, alike in arms. The city of New York, unlike any other in the country, was held, from the very first to the very latest days of the war, by strong garrisons of one party or the other. Abandoned by General Washington after the defeat on Long Island, it became from that hour the permanent head-quarters of the British commander-in-chief; while American armies, now standing aloof in conscious weakness of numbers, now advancing nearer with returning strength or reinforcement, kept constant watch, their eyes fixed on that important point.

Of course, smaller bodies of troops, of both parties, were in unceasing movement over the adjacent country, foraging, reconnoitering, skirmishing, as the occasion required. Scarce a narrow lane of the many winding roads of the country, fenced with rude stone walls, hedged with brier and vine, shaded with cedar and oak, as they are, along which trim British troops and ragged American soldiers had not marched and countermarched by the light of sun or star. Scarce a farm-house door which had not been darkened by Cowboy, Hessian, or Skinner, on errand of pillage or violence. Scarce a barnyard which had not been harried, scarce a larder, whether high or low, which had not, time and time

again, been rifled. Here and there still darker work had been done—homes had been destroyed by fire, good yeoman blood had been shed, life had been taken, husband, father, or brother had fallen in some unrecorded skirmish, the hero of a rustic neighborhood. The entire country between the American outposts on the skirts of the Highlands, and the British works on the island of Manhattan—the Neutral Ground, as it was called by both parties—probably suffered more in this way than the same extent of country in any part of the Union.

Miss Cooper then relates the incident which led to the decision of making Harvey Birch, the main character of the story, to be a Yankee peddler, and a spy. Those "strolling peddlers, staff in hand, and pack at the back, were more common visitors at the country-houses of that day" than later when the country store contained many of the items which the Harvey Birches carried. It was a notable decision. "Ere long the character of Harvey Birch became so vividly impressed on the public mind, that people expected to see his thin, stooping figure, gliding across their path, as they drove about the hills and valleys of Westchester."

At a later day, when revising *The Spy* for the last edition, the author was dissatisfied with many things in his work, and once remarked that he should like to write it entirely anew. On several occasions he expressed a regret that he should have introduced General Washington, personally, into a work of fiction, veneration for the character of the great man increasing with his own years.

(*Pages and Pictures, from the Writings of James Fenimore Cooper, with Notes* by Susan Fenimore Cooper. 1861.)

Since literature identified the character of a nation, Cooper's own growth as a Christian coincided with his appreciation of the Hand of God—Providence—in the establishment of America. He also saw that the Christian character of our nation required the "virtue of the people" in order to continue its testimony as the world's first Christian republic. Later novels were clearer than his first American novel, *The Spy*, on the necessity of a deep Christian commitment to our Biblical principles of government—Christian self-government, property and productivity, voluntary association, and integrity of representation. But his constant prayer for his nation was "that the same Providence which as so well aided us in our infancy, may continue to smile on our manhood."

Influence of Sir Walter Scott on James Fenimore Cooper

One of the most popular writers of the British Isles during the early 19th century was Sir Walter Scott, who originated the historical novel. His Waverley Novels, based upon Scotch and British backgrounds, made history live. Scott's many Christian themes and characters endeared him to both the New and Old Worlds. He put Scotland on the map, first with his long poems, later with his novels. His first English novel, *Ivanhoe*, is still one of the best Christian novels in the world. While Cooper did not wish to imitate Scott, there was an inevitable comparison between the two authors as Cooper dipped into his own history and developed the novel in America. His *Leatherstocking Tales* gave a unique identity to the free and independent man in the American wilderness. And Leatherstocking was a Christian—brought up on Biblical truths—though he himself could not read. Cooper also conveyed the beauty of the unspoiled forests and lakes which, to a Christian, reflected the Creator and always impelled Deerslayer, as he was also known, to protect and preserve.

The Spy still shows evidence of English influences. Later Cooper novels do not introduce such scenes as those in Betty Flanagan's hotel. As Cooper's Christian life unfolded he purified his characters in the novels he wrote so that they became noble. Yet, the first American novel conveys to the world a people seriously dedicated to the preservation of life, liberty, and property.

Purpose for the Study of Literature

The study of literature identifies the character of a nation. In *The Spy* we will identify some evidence of Who we are as a people and Where our principles and ideals come from and Why we must be prepared to defend our liberties. Our Purpose as a nation—to spread the blessings of liberty—was dependent upon our success in gaining our independence from Great Britain. Once we were established as the world's first Christian republic, we could then freely spread the Gospel principles of liberty—both evangelical and political.

Literature and the Art of Writing

The study of *The Spy* enables us to study the art of writing and to practice the skill ourselves as we develop a notebook record of the literary elements: Setting, Characterization, Plot Elements, Themes, and characteristics of Cooper's distinct Style. The use of the author's own words to identify setting, character, and themes gives us many examples of Cooper's style.

Setting: Historical Background of the American Revolution

See *CHOC*, I, p. 346B for the Declaration of Independence. Summarize the most important reasons given by the colonists for this statement. Upon what did they put their reliance? The ministers of the Gospel influenced the American colonists. Page 180 of *T & L* gives the words of a sermon preached by a pastor to his congregation on the necessity of resisting tyranny. Record.

Settings

As you read about the following settings, identify their main characteristics in your notebook with author's words and phrases:

1. The Neutral Ground
2. The Locusts—Home of the Whartons
3. The Four Corners, and Betty Flanagan's Hotel
4. Harvey Birch's cottage
5. The mountain hut

Characters

Make a page for each character in your notebook so as to add to development as you read.

Katy Haynes:
Housekeeper of Harvey Birch

Mr. Harper:
Solitary traveler in the Neutral Ground

Caesar Thompson:
Aged black servant of the Whartons

Mr. Warren Sr.:
Owner of The Locusts

Jeanette Payton:
Aunt of the Wharton girls

Sarah Wharton:
Older daughter

Frances Wharton:
Younger daughter

Captain Henry Wharton:
British officer, son of Wharton

Colonel Wellmere:
Friend of Wharton, Jr., British officer

Major Payton Dunwoodie:
American officer, Virginian, cousin of the Whartons, Commander of the Dragoons

Harvey Birch:
Peddler, suspected spy for the British

Dinah Thompson:
Wife of Caesar, colored cook and nurse to the girls when they were little

Captain Jack Lawton:
American officer in the Dragoons

Dr. Archibald Sitgreaves:
American surgeon

George Singleton:
Young American officer in Dunwoodie's troops

Isabella Singleton:
Sister to George

Elizabeth Flanagan:
Irish widow, camp follower, supplier of food and drink to the American troops

Sergeant Hollister:
American soldier

Colonel Singleton:
merican officer and father of George and Isabella

Lieutenant Tom Mason:
American cavalryman

Plot Elements

Record the events which deal with Harvey Birch and Henry Wharton. Record the love story.

Themes

Patriotism and Neutralism are contrasted. Identify these two elements Scripturally. How does the author identify the Loyalists or Royalists, and the Patriots or Americans? How much love is required to be a patriot; to be a neutralist?

Style of Author

The use of a Loyalist home, The Locusts, for the contrast of neutralism and patriotism

The contrast of a real spy, Birch, and an accused spy, Wharton

Use of a mystery character

Identification of some uniquely American aspects of the country and style of life

Contrasting love stories

Summary Statements

After a notebook has been completed with the identification of all literary elements of a book, it should contain:

Settings: Identified in author's words

Characters: Identified in author's words

Plot Elements: Identified and summarized by student in writing

Themes: Identified and summarized by student in writing

Style: Record of unique way in which Cooper brings out his themes

Reasoning, Relating, Recording

Using your notebook and a copy of the novel for reference, write on the following:

Christian Character of Harvey Birch. Discuss in writing.

Mystery Character: How does Cooper use the mystery character in the story?

Contrasting Character: Compare the character of Dunwoodie and Wellmere; Sarah Wharton and her sister, Frances, others of your choice.

Unusual Characters: Discuss Dr. Sitgreaves and the duties of an American doctor in war; Discuss Betty Flanagan, Captain Lawton.

Which settings play the most important part in this novel? Identify and explain.

Discuss the major theme of the book: Neutralism and Patriotism contrasted. Contrast two characters who represent each position.

How did Cooper use an actual historical event as a basis for his own story? Discuss the event which actually is part of our history.

Write about the problems of a neutral or de-militarized zone.

How should a nation treat its spies—men who work for the good of a nation but whose real identity must be concealed?

How has this book contributed to your knowledge of America?

The Writings of James Fenimore Cooper

The Leatherstocking Tales: (Listed in order of their reading)

The Deerslayer—1841
The Last of the Mohicans—1826
The Pathfinders—1840
The Pioneers—1823
The Prairie—1827

Cooper's first novel: *Precaution*—1820
English Society

American History:

The Spy—1821
Lionel Lincoln—1824-25
The Wept of Wish-Ton-Wish—1829
Mercedes of Castile—1839
Wyandotte—1843
Jack Tier—1848

Sea Tales:

The Pilot—1823
The Red Rover—1828
The Water-Witch—1830
The Two Admirals—1842
The Wing and Wing—1842
Afloat and Ashore—1844
Miles Walingford—1844

American Manners:

The Monikins—1835
Homeward Bound—1838
Home as Found—1838

Political Novels:

Satanstoe—1845
The Chainbearer—1846
The Redskins—1846
The Crater—1847
The Ways of the Hour—1850

European Themes:

The Bravo—1831
The Heidenmauer—1832
The Headsman—1832

Christian Novels:

The Oak Openings—1848
The Sea Lions—1849

Non-fiction:

Notions of the Americans—1828
Letter to General Lafayette—1831–32
Letter to His Countrymen—1834
The American Democrat—1838
The History of the Navy—1839

American Literature IIIB

America Falls Away from Her Christian Founding and Character
Part Two of a Two-Year Course of American Literature

Twelfth Grade

Civil War Period
National Expansion Period
Twentieth Century

CONTENTS

1. Course of Study Overview for each period

2. Leading Ideas and Ideals—based upon the Christian idea of man and government appearing and declining

3. Preparation and Presentation Charts—Background, Emphases, Readings

---

The suggested resource book—*American Literature: A Study of the Men and the Books That in the Earlier and Later Times Reflect the American Spirit*, by William J. Long. Boston: Ginn & Co., 1913, 1964—is presently out-of-print, but available through book search.

American Literature IIIB Overview for Twelfth Grade
America Falls Away from Her Christian Founding and Character

Civil War Period 1840–1876	National Expansion Period 1876–1925	The Twentieth Century 1925–Present
Clay, Henry "The Consequences of Secession"	Jewett, Sarah Orne *The Country of the Pointed Firs*	Fitzgerald, F. Scott Hemingway, Ernest Faulkner, William Steinbeck, John London, Jack Sinclair, Upton Buck, Pearl *Novels*
Calhoun, John C. Biography	Henry, O. *Best Short Stories*	
Webster, Daniel Speeches	Harris, Joel Chandler *Uncle Remus Stories*	Washington, Booker T. *Up from Slavery*
Lincoln, Abraham Second Inaugural Address Gettysburg Address	Twain, Mark *The Jumping Frog of Calaveras County*	Carver, George Washington *Biography*
Lee, Robert E. Biography, letters	Parkman, Francis *The Oregon Trail*	Keller, Helen *Story of My Life*
Longfellow, Henry Wadsworth Whittier, John Greenleaf Lanier, Sidney Poetry	Harte, Bret "Outcasts of Poker Flat"	Stuart, Jesse *The Thread That Runs So True*
Holmes, Oliver Wendell Lowell, James Russell Poetry, essays	Cather, Willa *My Antonia* *Death Comes for the Archbishop*	Byrd, Richard E. *Alone; Discovery*
Whitman, Walt *Leaves of Grass*	Riley, James Whitcomb Field, Eugene Dickinson, Emily Lanier, Sidney Masters, Edgar Lee Sandburg, Carl Frost, Robert Poetry	Lindbergh, Charles A. *The Spirit of St. Louis*
Emerson, Ralph Waldo Poetry, biography, essays		MacArthur, Douglas *Reminiscences*
Thoreau, Henry David Essays		Millay, Edna St. Vincent Masters, Edgar Lee Robinson, Edwin Arlington Eliot, T. S. Frost, Robert Sandburg, Carl Poetry
Audubon, John James Essays, journals, letters		
Hawthorne, Nathaniel Biography		American Dramatists

THE NOAH PLAN © 1997 • FOUNDATION FOR AMERICAN CHRISTIAN EDUCATION

American Literature for Twelfth Grade
America Falls Away from Her Christian Founding and Character

For we must consider that we shall be as a city upon a
hill, the eyes of all people are upon us, so that if we shall
deal falsely with God in this work we have undertaken,
and so cause Him to withdraw His present help from us,
we shall be made a story and a byword through the world.

—John Winthrop, *Model of Christian Charity*, 1630

Overview for the Course

Civil War Period:

One nation under God endures: character of Lincoln and Lee; oratory, essayists, poets, novelists, historians.

Age of Expansion:

The diversity of America reflected in literature; first seeds of breakdown of Christian principles; the Chain of Christianity reaches California; Christian literature of the states.

Twentieth Century:

Decline of Biblical standards of life and literature; the debunkers; the "lost" generation; the persistence of the American spirit; revival and restoration.

Teaching the Literature of the Civil War Period
1840–1876
Preparation and Presentation

Background	Emphases	Readings

1. American Christians fall away from our Biblical principles of government. A civil war between the states is fought. Slavery is the issue; Union is the principle.
 	
2. Two great elements:
  a) Local Self-Government
  b) National union acting in harmony. See *CHOC,* I, pp. 148–50.
 	
3. The basis of our national-federal union must be tested.
 	
Internal basis of our federal union: our unity with Christ is a union that cannot be broken. Our Christian unity with our neighbor is a union that cannot be broken. These two aspects of our federal union are based upon the two commandments of our Lord.
 	
4. Debates over slavery and states' rights finally lead into war—Civil War during our falling-away period.
	1. How could a civil war occur in a Christian nation?
	
	2. Why is the Gettysburg Address the most famous oration ever given?
	
	3. The Christian idea of man and government: Abraham Lincoln, "whether that nation, or any nation so conceived and so dedicated can long endure."
	
	4. What was George Bancroft's major theme concerning America?
	
	5. Why was Longfellow the most loved American poet?
	
	6. What subjects of Hawthorne's writings enabled him to inspire other great men?
	
	7. What qualities in Emerson's writings enabled him to inspire other great men?
	
	8. What does Emerson's success tell us about Christianity in America at that period?
	
	9. The Spirit of American Unity
		Two men and contrasting philosophies: Thoreau and Audubon
		
		Biography and Letters: Robert E. Lee
		
		Oratory: Clay-Calhoun debates; Hayne-Webster debate; John C. Calhoun; Abraham Lincoln
		
		The Glory and the Dream, by Michael A. Musmanno
		
		Lincoln's Gettysburg Address; Emancipation Proclamation
		
		Historian: George Bancroft
		
		Novelist: Nathaniel Hawthorne—Selections from his short stories, "The Gentle Boy," *The Scarlet Letter*
		
		Poets: Longfellow, Lowell, Whittier, Lanier, Whitman, Holmes
		
		Essay: Emerson, selections
		
		See *CHOC,* II, pp. 3–15.

THE NOAH PLAN © 1997 • FOUNDATION FOR AMERICAN CHRISTIAN EDUCATION

Two Men: Thoreau and Audubon

in the Christian Literature of the American Republic

In our study of American literature from its expression of America's Christian history and government, we find for our instruction some who stray from the path of truth. These men may be well-meaning but their basic assumptions and where they place their emphasis lay the axe at America's Christian foundations. This study begins to make a comparison between two men who found in America of the same period two different concepts of individual liberty. Both men were devoted to the study of nature; but, as these men produced their life work, they came out with different themes—one glorified the works of the Creator, the other made man, and especially "I," the center of the stage.

Henry David Thoreau (1817–1862)

In May, 1849, Elizabeth Peabody, who ran a bookstore in Boston, published her first issue of a new periodical, *Aesthetic Papers*. In this first issue were articles by a number of eminent New England gentlemen. Of one article we shall take particular note for it was to have worldwide influence and shattering consequences for our own country in the next century. This article was listed simply in the table of contents as a lecture title, delivered in 1847. The title is indicative of its subject: "Resistance to Civil Government." For some years this little article slumbered unnoticed, but its time was to come—far from home.

Fifty-eight years later, Mohandas K. Gandhi, an unknown law student at Oxford University in England, went to South Africa where he published a newspaper for the many Indian workers living there. On October 26, 1907, he printed "Civil Disobedience" in this paper and then issued it as a pamphlet. Gandhi told an American journalist that he took the name of his movement from Thoreau's nearly forgotten essay.

In our own country, the late Rev. Martin Luther King, Jr., was profoundly moved when he read "Civil Disobedience," for he felt that Thoreau had eloquently stated the case for a new political movement—a movement, however, which does not have its roots in Christianity, nor in America's contribution of Christian civil government as expressed in our constitutional form of government. More than once this political movement has threatened America's Christian foundations and institutions. King stated: "As a result of [Thoreau's] writings . . . we are the heirs of a legacy of creative protest. It goes without saying that the teachings of Thoreau are alive today; indeed they are more alive today than ever before."

At the risk of over-simplification and recognizing that a writer must be read in his entirety, we shall give some sample quotations from this essay which had so much influence in our day and age. We urge you to read Thoreau's two other publications: *Walden, A Week on the Concord and Merrimack Rivers*, and possibly his *Journal*.

Following are passages from Henry Thoreau's "Civil Disobedience," found in *The Works of Thoreau*, edited by Henry Seidel Canby, 1937.

> I heartily accept the motto,—"That government is best which governs least"; and I should like to see it acted up to more rapidly and systematically. Carried out, it finally amounts to this, which also I believe,—"That government is best which governs not at all"; and when men are prepared for it, that will be the kind of government which they will have. Government is at best but an expedient but most governments are usually, and all governments are sometimes inexpedient. (p. 789)

> All men recognize the right of revolution; that is, the right to refuse allegiance to, and to resist, the gov-

ernment, when its tyranny or its inefficiency are great and unendurable. But almost all say that such is not the case now. But such was the case, they think, in the Revolution of '75. (p. 792)

Some years ago, the State met me in behalf of the church, and commanded me to pay a certain sum toward the support of a clergyman whose preaching my father attended, but never I myself. "Pay," it said, "or be locked up in the jail." I declined to pay. But, unfortunately, another man saw fit to pay it. . . . I have paid no poll-tax for six years. I was put into a jail once on this account, for one night.

. . . I have never declined paying the highway tax, because I am desirous of being a good neighbor as I am of being a bad subject; and, as for supporting schools, I am doing my part to educate my fellow-country men now. It is for no particular item in the tax-bill that I refuse to pay it. I simply wish to refuse allegiance to the State, to withdraw and stand aloof from it effectually. I do not care to trace the course of my dollar, if I could, till it buys a man or a musket to shoot one with,—the dollar is innocent,—but I am concerned to trace the effects of my allegiance. In fact, I quietly declare war with the State, after my fashion, though I will still make what use and get what advantage of her I can, as is usual in such cases. (p. 804)

Henry Seidel Canby, in his introduction to *The Works of Thoreau*, wrote of this "individualist" as follows:

Henry Thoreau was the arch example in our history, perhaps in all literary history, of the man who believed in doing what he wanted. . . . Briefly then, and at the risk of over-simplification, let it be repeated that Thoreau was first and last a man determined to do what he wanted in a society which, like all societies—from Jesus Christ's Jews, to Babbitt's Americans—insisted that the individual should conform to the conventional desires of the day, or be called a skulker, a heretic, a radical, or a fool.

Like so many of his New England contemporaries in those forties and fifties seething with both material and spiritual energy, Henry Thoreau was a come-outer. . . . This may sound simple to naiveté. It was not naive. For Thoreau wanted to feel and think and work unimpeded by the pressure of different ideas of living. Being a Puritan in the best sense of that word, he wished his work and his pleasure to run wide, high, and clear, without compromise. But that is precisely what society with its duties, its greeds, most of all its conventions, makes difficult for any man, most of all for the creative intellect. (pp. v–vi)

Yet one contemporary of Thoreau—James Russell Lowell—saw the inconsistency of much of his "drop-out" philosophy and, while appreciating his talent for writing, felt compelled to write of him:

I have just been renewing my recollection of Mr. Thoreau's writings, and have read through his six volumes in the order of their production. I shall try to give an adequate report of their impression upon me both as critic and as mere reader. He seems to me to have been a man with so high a conceit of himself that he accepted without questioning, and insisted on our accepting, his defects and weaknesses of character as virtues and powers peculiar to himself. Was he indolent, he finds none of the activities which attract or employ the rest of mankind worthy of him. Was he wanting in the qualities that make success, it is success that is contemptible, and not himself that lacks persistency and purpose. Was he poor, money was an unmixed evil. Did his life seem a selfish one, he condemns doing good as one of the weakest superstitions. To be of use was with him the most killing bait of the wily tempter Uselessness. He had no faculty of generalization from outside of himself, or at least no experience which would supply the material of such, and he makes his own whim the law, his own range the horizon of the universe. . . .

This notion of an absolute original-ity, as if one could have a patent-right in it, is an absurdity. A man cannot escape in though any more than he can in language, from the past and the present. . . . Mr. Thoreau seems to insist in public on going back to flint and steel, when there is a match-box in his pocket which he knows very well how to use at a pinch. . . . A greater familiarity with ordinary men would have done Thoreau good, by showing him how many fine qualities are common to the race. The radical vice of his theory of life was that he confounded physical with spiritual remoteness from men. A man is far enough withdrawn from his fellows if he keep himself clear of their weaknesses. He is not so truly withdrawn as exiled, if he refuse to share in their strength.

. . . I look upon a great deal of the modern sentimentalism about Nature as a mark of disease. . . . To a man of wholesome constitution the wilderness is well enough for a mood or a vacation, but not for a habit of life. . . . It is a very shallow view that affirms trees and rocks to be healthy, and cannot see that men in communities are just as true to the laws of their organization and destiny; that can tolerate the puffin and the fox, but not the fool and the knave; that would shun politics because of its demagogues, and snuff up the stench of the obscene fungus.

. . . Solitary communion with Nature does not seem to have been sanitary or sweetening in its influence on Thoreau's character. On the contrary, his letters show him more cynical as he grew older. While he studies with respectful attention the minks and woodchucks, his neighbors, he looked with utter contempt on the august drama of destiny of which his country was the scene, and on which the curtain had already risen.

. . . His shanty-life was a mere impossibility, so far as his own conception of it goes, as an entire independency of mankind. . . . Thoreau's experiment actually presupposed all that complicated civilization which it theoretically abjured. He squatted on another man's land; he borrows an axe; his boards, his nails, his bricks, his mortar, his books, his lamp, his fish-hooks, his plough, his hoe, all turn state's evidence against him as an accomplice in the sin of that artificial civilization which rendered it possible that such a person as Henry D. Thoreau should exist at all. (From *Literary Essays*, James Russell Lowell, 1899, pp. 368–80)

"The mass of men lead lives of quiet desperation" wrote Thoreau in what is an elegant philosophical commentary on a day in which "things are in the saddle and ride mankind" as Emerson put it. But Thoreau's criticism of the abundance of material things which were the result of the liberty of the individual to be productive in an expanding society provided no solution. His analysis was that the American constitutional form of government had failed—that the system was at fault, rather than the realization that when men worship the fruits of liberty without keeping close to the root—to Christian living—they are likely to go wild with freedom and materialism. Thoreau thus set the pattern for future "hippies"—future critics who turned away from society and especially the American system which allowed them freedom of choice. Thoreau may have been called by Canby a "come-outer"—but he was in effect a "dropout." He refused to find solutions. He refused to work at making things right. He fled as a bird to the wilderness. And, perhaps this is why the wilderness and the solitary place did not yield him any real solace, but made him more critical. Had he known another "I" than himself, had he known the Christian Creator, he might have yielded up those misgivings and criticisms and become a useful instrument to ameliorate what he saw that was not in accord with Scriptural principles.

John James Audubon (1785–1851)

Born in Louisiana to a Santo Domingan family, and then educated in France, John James Audubon did not settle in America until 1803.

In Mill Grove, Pennsylvania, where his father had business interests in charge of a friend, the young John fell in love with the wildlife of the country and was moved by the memories of Valley Forge, some miles to the south, where Washington's ragged Continentals passed the memorable winter of 1777–1778 in log huts amidst freezing temperatures. Audubon's love of America and all that she represented of the freedom and independence of the individual had been first learned from his father. Captain Jean Audubon commanded a ship in the fleet of the Count de Grasse which cooperated with our land-forces at the Battle of Yorktown, on October 19, 1781.

Audubon lived at the Mill Grove estate from the winter of 1804 to the spring of 1805, and again for a few months in the summer of 1806. It was here "as he explored the resources of this fine estate, where every bird, tree and flower came to him as a new discovery . . . that he found a cave, carved out of the rocks, as he thought, by nature's own hand, which was a favorite haunt of the unpretentious but friendly pewees, the first American birds to attract his serious attention. So delighted was the youthful naturalist that he decided to make the pewee's cave his study; thither accordingly he brought his books, pencils and paper, and there made his first studies of American bird life, in the spring of 1804, in the third year of the presidency of Thomas Jefferson. . . .

"It must be set down to Audubon's credit that in the little cave on the banks of the Perkioming, in April, 1804, he made the first 'banding' experiment on the young of an American wild bird. Little could he or any one else then have thought that one hundred years later a Bird Banding Society would be formed in America to repeat his test on a much wider scale, in order to gather exact data upon the movements of individuals of all migratory species in every part of the continent." (*Audubon the Naturalist: A History of His Life and Time*, Vol. I, Francis Hobart Herrick, 1938, pp. 106–07)

It was while at Mill Grove that Audubon found his wife, Lucy Bakewell. Herrick states: "the woman who by her sterling qualities of mind and heart was the one to recognize and call forth the best that was in him." Audubon, himself, never forgot their first meeting:

Well do I recollect the morning, and may it please God that I may never forget it, when for the first time I entered Mr. Bakewell's dwelling. It happened that he was absent from home, and I was shown into a parlor where only one young lady was snugly seated at her work by the fire. She rose on my entrance, offered me a seat and assured me of the gratification her father would feel on his return, which, she added, would be in a few moments as she would despatch a servant for him. . . . I sat, my gaze, riveted, as it were, on the young girl before me, who, half working, half talking, essayed to make the time pleasant to me. Oh! may God bless her! It was she, my dear sons, who afterward became my beloved wife, and your mother. (Herrick, pp. 109–10)

It would be many, long, and difficult years before John James Audubon would bring to fruition the talents which God had so richly bestowed upon him and which he, by dint of unceasing labor, worked to perfect. It was Audubon's prayer that he might prove to be worthy of his new-found country: "May He who gave me being and inspired me with a desire to study His wondrous works, grant me the means of proving to my country the devotedness with which I strive to render myself not unworthy of her."

Both Audubon and Alexander Wilson, who preceded him by a few years in the field of ornithology, took the study and rendition of birds out of the museum-case, stuffed specimen stage. They both took to the fields and woods and painted from specimens which they studied in their natural environment. The most fascinating and discouraging part of Audubon's lifework with birds was his effort to keep them in a lifelike state after he had found them and taken those he needed to paint. In 1830 the first of his 435 paintings of *The Birds of America* came off the press—engravings in "double elephant folio, the largest extended publication in existence." The world then had a picture of America never anticipated, but Audubon found that he must take his work to Europe to have it subscribed for and published. And perhaps this is why the Lord made these years away from home and country so difficult, so that this Frenchman, become American, might give to Europeans an image of this land so richly blessed by God—and one for which his heart longed constantly.

In 1826, Audubon sailed for Europe on a voyage which was to last three years. He had failed to find encouragement or support for the publication of his drawings in the United States. But in the Old World there was still a chance to obtain subscribers. "This plan, therefore, I will pursue with the same perseverance that since twenty-five years has not wavered, and God's will be done." Audubon approached the learned societies humbly, conscious of his own self-education.

Within barely a week after landing at Liverpool a total stranger, Audubon was invited to show his drawings at the Royal Institution. The exhibition, which lasted a month, was a surprising success; 413 persons, as he recorded, were admitted on the second day, and it netted him one hundred pounds, although no charge for admission was made during the first week.

Everyone, said the naturalist, was surprised at his appearance, for he wore his hair long, dressed in unfashionable clothes, rose early, worked late, and was abstemious in food and drink. . . . Audubon had not been in England three weeks before he resumed his drawing and painting habits, at first in order to repay his friends for their kindness, and later as a means of support; at times he would devote every spare moment to this work, and he was then able to paint fourteen hours at a stretch without fatigue. . . . The facility which Audubon displayed in producing his pictures of animal life—American wild turkeys, trapped otters, fighting cats, English game pieces, and the like, in a style both novel and individual, added much to his immediate popularity in England, as it later did to his purse.

When Audubon's pictures were exhibited at the Royal Institution of Edinburgh, their success was immediate, and like the appearance of a new Waverley novel, they became the talk of the town; the American woodsman had provided a new thrill for the leaders of fashion, as well as for the literati and the scientific men.

A well known French critic of the period has left the following record of the effect which this exhibition made on his impressionable mind:

"We have admired in the rooms of the Royal Society of Edinburgh the public exhibition of [Audubon's] original water-color drawings. . . . Imagine a landscape wholly American, trees, flowers, grass, even the tints of the sky and the waters, quickened with a life that is real, peculiar, trans-Atlantic. On twigs, branches, bits of shore, copied by the brush with the strictest fidelity, sport the feathered races of the New World, in the size of life, each in its particular attitude; its individuality and peculiarities. . . . It is a real and palpable vision of the New World, with its atmosphere, its imposing vegetation, and its tribes which know not the yoke of man . . . and this realization of an entire hemisphere, this picture of a nature so lusty and strong, is due to the brush of a single man; such an unheard of triumph of patience and genius!—the resultant rather of a thousand triumphs won in the face of innumerable obstacles!"

Another French writer remarked that Audubon produced the same sensation among the savants of England that Franklin had made at the close of the eighteenth century among the politicians of the Old World. (Herrick, pp. 354–60)

Audubon's first efforts to interest France were unsuccessful. But always, his faith in God kept him working to achieve the financial support he needed. "What reasons have I now to suppose, or to make me think for a moment that the omnipotent God who gave me a heart to endure and overcome all these difficulties, will abandon me now. No! my faith is the same—my desires are of a pure kind; I only wish to enjoy more of Him by admiring His works still more than I have ever done before. He will grant me life, He will support me in my journeys, and enable me to meet thee again in America."

But Audubon found in the duc d'Orléans a high point in his European trip:

Lucy, Kentucky, Tennessee, and Alabama have furnished the finest men in the world, as regards physical beauty; I have also seen many a noble-looking Osage chief; but I do not recollect a finer-looking man, in form, deportment, and manners, than this Duc d'Orléans. He had my book brought up, and helped me to untie the strings and arrange the table, and began by saying that he felt a great pleasure in subscribing to the work of an American, for that he had been most kindly treated in the United States, and should never forget it. The portfolio was at last opened, and when I held up the plate of the Baltimore Orioles, with a nest swinging amongst the tender twigs of the yellow poplar, he said: "This surpasses all I have seen, and I am not astonished now at the eulogiums of M. Redouté." He spoke partly English, and partly French; spoke much of America, of Pittsburgh, the Ohio, New Orleans, the Mississippi, steamboats, etc., etc., and added: "You are a great nation, a wonderful nation." (*Audubon and His Journals*, Vol. I, p. 329)

One of Audubon's final visits in France was to François Gérard, the most distinguished portrait painter of his day, known for historical paintings. Audubon wrote to Lucy of this meeting:

My name being announced, a small, well-formed man came to me, took my hand, and said, "Welcome, Brother in Arts." I liked this much, and was gratified to have the ice broken so easily. Gérard was all curiosity to see my drawings and old Redouté, who was present, spoke so highly of them before the book was opened, that I feared to discover Gérard's disappointment. The book opened accidentally at the plate of the Parrots, and Gérard, taking it up without speaking, looked at it, I assure thee, with as keen an eye as my own, for several minutes; put it down, took up the one of the Mocking-Birds, and offering me his hand, said: "Mr. Audubon, you are the king of ornithological painters; we are all children in France and in Europe. Who would have expected such things from the woods of America?" My heart thrilled with pride at his words. Are not we of America men? Have we not the same nerves, sinews, and mental faculties which other nations possess? By Washington! we have, and may God grant us the peaceable use of them forever. (*Journals*, Vol. I, pp. 330–31)

Audubon returned home in 1829 with his purpose accomplished. He had found an engraver for his drawings, "Robert Havell, Junior, then a young and unknown artist of thirty-four, who through eleven years of the closest association with his new patron was to become one of the greatest engravers in aquatint the world has ever seen." Audubon also had obtained enough subscribers to encourage him to continue his great work of *The Birds of America*. (Herrick, p. 382)

"The Hummingbird," by John James Audubon

Where is the person, who, on observing this glittering fragment of the rainbow, would not pause, admire, and instantly turn his mind with reverence toward the Almighty Creator, the wonders of whose hand we at every step discover, and of whose sublime conceptions we everywhere observe the manifestations in his admirable system of creation? There breathes not such a person; so kindly have we all been blessed with that intuitive and noble feeling—admiration!

No sooner has the returning sun again introduced the vernal season, and caused millions of plants to expand their leaves and blossoms to his genial beams, than the little Humming Bird is seen advancing on fairy wings, carefully visiting every opening flower-cup, and, like a curious florist, removing from each the injurious insects that otherwise would ere long cause their beauteous petals to droop and decay. Poised in the air, it is observed peeping cautiously, and with sparkling eye, into their innermost recesses, whilst the ethereal motions of its pinions, so rapid and so light, appear to fan and cool the flower, without injuring its fragile texture, and produce a delightful murmuring sound, well adapted for lulling the insects to repose.

The prairies, the fields, the orchards and gardens, nay, the deepest shades of the forest, are all visited in their turn, and everywhere the little bird meets with pleasure and with food. Its gorgeous throat in beauty and brilliancy baffles all competition. Now it glows with a fiery hue, and again it is changed to the deepest velvety black. The upper parts of its delicate body are of resplendent changing green; and it throws itself through the air with a swiftness and vivacity hardly conceivable. It moves from one flower to another like a gleam of light, upwards, downwards, to the right, and to the left.

In this manner it searches the extreme northern portions of our country, following with great precaution the advances of the season, and retreats with equal care at the approach of autumn. (*Ornithological Biography*, John James Audubon, Vol. I, 1831, p. 248)

Audubon's Animals: *The Viviparous Quadrupeds of North America*

In October, 1831, Audubon met the Reverend John Bachman, pastor of the Lutheran Church in Charleston, South Carolina. This began a lasting friendship, for Bachman was a man deeply interested in natural history. Bachman helped Audubon complete his great undertaking of *The Birds of America*; and, when the 435 paintings of this monumental work were complete, offered to help Audubon in his new proposal to document the mammals of North America. Mammalogy in 1839 was a comparatively new field in America. A number of naturalists had begun studies but few had recorded their findings pictorially. What Audubon proposed was to travel in every part of the United States and to produce paintings in the natural environment of the animals. This became a task of eleven years. With Bachman's assistance, the last of the 150 plates came from the press in 1854, some three years after Audubon laid down his brushes and went home forever. Audubon's son, John, completed his father's work. Once more America was enriched by another work from her son, John James Audubon, describing through his unique God-given talents the land he loved so well.

Teaching the Literature of the National Expansion Period 1876–1925

Preparation and Presentation

Background	Emphases	Readings
1. Regional writers of America—19th century 2. Diversity of American character—Unity with diversity 3. Christian constitutional government reaches the Pacific—the opening up of Old Oregon, Marcus and Narcissa Whitman, pioneers and missionaries	1. Diversity of regional literature: Contrast two American writers of this period in terms of their ability to make their local scene appealing or interesting. 2. What unique contribution to the short story did O. Henry make? did Bret Harte make? 3. Why was this age called an age of "realism" in literature? 4. What was Christianity's relationship to it? 5. Poetry: James Whitcomb Riley, Eugene Field, Emily Dickinson, Sidney Lanier, Edgar Lee Masters, Carl Sandburg, Robert Frost	Maine: Sarah Orne Jewett, *The Country of the Pointed Firs, and Other Stories* New England: Nathaniel Hawthorne; Herman Melville, *Moby Dick* The South: Joel Chandler Harris, *Uncle Remus*; Mark Twain, *Adventures of Tom Sawyer* Midwest: Willa Cather, *My Antonia* Westward: Francis Parkman, *The Oregon Trail*; Richard Henry Dana, *Two Years before the Mast*; Edward Everett Hale, *The Man without a Country* California: Bret Harte, selected stories New York City: O. Henry, *Best Short Stories*

THE NOAH PLAN © 1997 • FOUNDATION FOR AMERICAN CHRISTIAN EDUCATION

Mark Twain 1835–1910

American Humorist

by Rosalie June Slater

America is inseparable from Christianity. The liberty of the Gospel of Jesus Christ, internal, is the source of our own political liberty, external. America was reserved by God to bring forth the full expression of a Christian civilization. This began with the Pilgrims whose lives were prepared to live out the Gospel principles and to extend these principles into civil government, their relations with the Indians, and into their individual enterprise activities.

For more than 150 years the American colonists practiced the principle of Christian self-government. They learned to value property. The Biblical education of the colonies produced the world's highest scholarship and explains why they could write the Declaration of Independence and the Constitution. Under the leadership of George Washington, a man prepared by God, our colonies prayed and fought their way through a seven years' war. Later, under George Washington, the American presidency witnessed to the world the quality of our Christian character as the world's first Christian republic.

America Forgets the Source of Our Liberties

The first fifty years of our republic witnessed the accomplishments of a people free to develop their talents and produce to the glory of God. But, by the 1840s, we became careless. Up to that time American Christian education had been the responsibility of the home and church. Now we began to turn education over to the state. The Pilgrim, Puritan, patriot state of Massachusetts led the way through the efforts of Horace Mann who, although a Christian, removed the cornerstone of Christianity by declaring Salvation unconstitutional. (See pages 52 and 53 in *Teaching & Learning America's Christian History.*)

The years preceding the Civil War—the War between the States—were years in which there was evidence of our falling away from our Christian foundations of government and education. Denominationalism became a means of supplying more form than substance. Christian churches lost vitality and warmth or turned away from participation in the nation. It was at this point that Mark Twain began his writing.

Mark Twain—American Author in the Falling Away Period

Mark Twain is an author whose life and work were affected by the falling away period of America from her Christian foundations. This is evidenced in both his personal and professional life.

From the autobiography of Samuel Langhorne Clemens we learn that his boyhood was the prototype of Tom Sawyer. Like Tom, Samuel was disappointed in the Christian message which he received. He felt it was shallow, moralistic, and somewhat superstitious. Samuel Clemens never came to know the Gospel's message of God's love, forgiveness through Jesus Christ, and the blessed assurance of eternal life. As a result of the many contradictions Sam witnessed between the profession and practice of his Christian teachers, he delighted in attacking the sacredness of Christianity. Like a small boy who cannot get attention from those he loves, Mark Twain tried to shock his readers and listeners by questioning orthodox Christian doctrines. This had the effect of bringing down upon his head much criticism and much condemnation.

In his heart of hearts Mark Twain evidenced his real conviction. Embedded in his works are references to Christ as the Savior of the world, of the Second Coming, and of his own hope of heaven for his beloved wife and daughters, though he was not sure of his own future.

Professionally, Mark Twain's inner conflicts and his delight in making fun of the sacred had the effect of limiting his growth as a writer. Van Wyck Brooks has this to say of Mark Twain in his book, *The Ordeal of Mark Twain*:

In fact, the more one scans the later pages of Mark Twain's history the more one is forced to the conclusion that there was something gravely amiss with his inner life. There was that frequently noted fear of solitude. . . . those "daily self-chidings" that led him to slay his own conscience in one of the most ferocious of his humorous tales. . . . It is an established fact, if I am not mistaken, that these morbid feelings of sin, which have no evident cause, are the result of having transgressed some inalienable life-demand peculiar to one's nature. . . . But is not that simply another way of saying, in the latter case, that his was a mind that had not fully developed, and, in the former, that his was a splendid genius which had never fully found itself?

Men who are not only great in energy but masters of themselves, whose energy, however great, is not, so to speak, at the disposal of their own spirits, are driven, as we see Mark Twain perpetually driven, to seek corroboration from without.

"I came in with Halley's comet in 1835. It is coming again next year, and I expect to go out with it. It will be the greatest disappointment in my life if I don't go out with Halley's comet. The Almighty has said, no doubt: 'Now here are these two unaccountable freaks, they came in together, they must go out together.' Oh! I am looking forward to that.". . . He seems to exhibit himself, on the one hand, as a child of nature conscious of extraordinary powers that make all the world and even the Almighty solicitous about him, and, on the other, as a humble, a humiliated man, confessedly second-rate, who has lost nine of the ten talents committed to him and almost begs permission to keep the one that remains. A great genius, in short, that has never attained the inner control which makes genius great, a mind that has not found itself, a mind that does not know itself, a mind that cloaks to the end in the fantasy of its temporal power the reality of some spiritual miscarriage! (pp. 24–38)

Mark Twain and the Mississippi

E. Merrill Root draws some comparisons between Mark Twain and the great Mississippi River in his article, "Mark Twain: The Mississippi of American Letters."

It is one of the paradoxes of geography and life that that which divides, unites. Nowhere is this more evident than in the United States of America, where the mightiest of our rivers bisects our land into East and West and unites our land in that magnificent and fruitful center which is our heart-land. Center and symbol, as it were, of our country and its being—muddy and majestic, a calm rolling force and a fickle and obstreperous power, a pillager of fertile acres and a strewer of alluvial riches, a being terrible and a being beneficent, the Mississippi is ours, and we are hers.

And the Mississippi is a highway of history . . . Without her we would not be what we are. Our history, our agriculture, our poetry, our legends, our life, our arterial being—they are here.

And one name and one man speaks the very soul of the Mississippi. By strange fate, or rather destiny, his name belongs not to himself but to the river and its life. We do not know him by his family name, Samuel Clemens, but by a destined and symbolic name—he is, to us, rightly Mark Twain. It is as if, with him for our river pilot, we sail by the leaded line cast out to measure the free depth of the waters by which alone the great steamboats safely sail. "Mark twain!" they cried as they cast the lead and found the channel, "Mark twain!" (*American Opinion*, June, 1969, p. 37)

In his autobiography Mark Twain observed: "Piloting on the Mississippi River was not work to me; it was play—delightful play, vigorous play, adventurous play—and I loved it." (*The Autobiography of Mark Twain*. Edited by Charles Neider, 1959, p. 291)

To learn to make piloting "play" was work, however, as Mark Twain describes it in this book. But, because Mark Twain loved the river he stuck to all of the difficulties and mastered them in learning the trade he loved the best of the many activities of his life.

The following chapters from *Life on the Mississippi* describe Mark Twain's lessons in learning:

Chapter 4. "The Boy's Ambition"
"When I was a boy, there was but one permanent ambition among my comrades in our village on the west bank of the Mississippi River. That was, to be a steamboatman." (p. 32)

Chapter 5. "I Want to Be a Cub Pilot"
Sam Clemens's efforts to court attention from captain, mate, and nightwatchman.

Chapter 6. "A Cub Pilot's Experience"
How the Notebook Approach to learning is important to a cub pilot. What Sam Clemens must produce in his notebook.

Chapter 7. A "Daring Deed"
Mr. Bixby's calm courage

Chapter 8. "Perplexing Lessons"
"My boy, you've got to know the shape of the river perfectly." (p. 50)

Can you write a description on how to get to your house—in the dark, with all of the important points of observation that should be observed? Discuss the difference between moveable and immoveable points of reference. What principle did Sam follow in learning the river?

Chapter 9. "Continued Perplexities"
Mr. Bixby tests Sam's piloting.

Chapter 10. "Completing My Education"
"Piloting as a science"

Chapter 13. "A Pilot's Needs"
What is the one faculty which a pilot must cultivate? How is this same faculty useful in other fields?

Chapter 14. "Rank and Dignity of Piloting"
"A pilot, in those days, was the only unfettered and entirely independent human being that lived in the earth." (p. 79)

Chapter 18. "I Take a Few Extra Lessons"
A new teacher—not like Mr. Bixby

Chapter 19. "Brown and I Exchange Compliments"

Chapter 21. "A Section in My Biography"
Sam Clemens leaves piloting because of the Civil War.

WRITING ASSIGNMENT:

Write a description of Sam Clemens's efforts to learn to become a pilot. Use quotations from the book. Describe the character qualities needed to make a success of this profession.

Student Notebook: Tom Sawyer

Background and Setting: St. Petersburg, the town in which Tom Sawyer lived, was really Hannibal, Missouri—the real town of Sam Clemens's youth.

Describe this town with reference to the following points:

What part does the Mississippi River play in this town?

Describe frontier religion, what was its influence?

Describe the school and its activities.

Characterization: Tom Sawyer is, in effect, young Sam Clemens. What qualities of character did young Tom display which would fit into this period of American life and westward expansion?

This book is related to Tom's growth from an irresponsible boy to a boy having to take responsibility. Identity the qualities of Tom's character which contribute to this growth. Is there Biblical basis for some of these qualities?

Boys in Tom's town had to be more ingenious than boys of today. They made up their games, enjoyed natural sports, used their imaginations. What could boys of today do to test their courage and build Christian self-government? Contrast the two.

Aunt Polly is representative of a type of American Christian. Describe her religion and how she influenced Tom. What kind of a woman was she? In real life Mark Twain's own mother was the model for his Aunt Polly. Contrast the Christianity of the Widow Douglas with her treatment of Huck Finn and Aunt Polly and her treatment of Tom.

Take five of the main characters and describe them.

Plot Elements: How does Mark Twain create a story out of the life of this small town? Show how Tom Sawyer's character is responsible for the action and plot of this story. How does the character of Injun Joe affect events? Why does the individual make a difference?

Themes: What does this mean? "The eternal conflict of Tom Sawyer and Aunt Polly playing itself out to the end in the theatre of Mark Twain's soul!" (*The Ordeal of Mark Twain*, Brooks, 1970, p. 321)

What ideas does the author wish to leave with the reader of this book?

Style: This refers to the techniques the author uses to put over his ideas.

Dialogue: Twain uses this as a technique of revealing both character and his own satire of the situation. Identify some examples.

Words: Many of the words in this book have a Biblical origin. Give some examples and their use in the story.

Slang: Mark Twain was one of the first American authors to use slang in his writings, much to the objection of his wife. Give some examples of Twain's use of slang in this book.

Biography of the Author: Write a short biography of Mark Twain and his major writings. Describe his character and achievements.

Some Writings of Mark Twain

With Mississippi Background:

1876 *The Adventures of Tom Sawyer*
1883 *Life on the Mississippi*
1885 *The Adventures of Huckleberry Finn*

Western Books:

1867 *The Jumping Frog of Calaveras County and Other Sketches*
1872 *Roughing It*

Books of Travel:

1869 *Innocents Abroad*
1880 *A Tramp Abroad*

In Bitter Vein:

1906 *What Is Man?*

Fiction:

1882 *The Prince and the Pauper*
1889 *A Connecticut Yankee at King Arthur's Court*
1896 *Personal Recollections of Joan of Arc*
1900 *The Man That Corrupted Hadleyburg*

Some References on Mark Twain

America's Mark Twain, May McNeer and Lynd Ward, Houghton Mifflin, 1962.

The Autobiography of Mark Twain. Arranged and edited by Charles Neider. New York: Harper Brothers, 1959.

Mark Twain in Love, the Story of the Unsuitable Suitor, Albert G. Miller. Harcourt-Brace-Jovanovich, 1973.

The Ordeal of Mark Twain, Van Wyck Brooks. E. P. Dutton Co., 1970.

River Boy, the Story of Mark Twain, Isabel Proudfit, 1940.

Teaching the Literature of the Twentieth Century
1925–Present
Preparation and Presentation

Background	Emphases	Readings
1. Decline of Biblical standards of life and literature; the "lost" generation; the persistence of the American spirit; revival and restoration 2. World War I, World War II, the Cold War	Will the American Christian of the twentieth century return to the Gospel purpose of America and to the support of those unique Biblical principles which established our Christian constitutional form of government—allowing us individual liberty and opportunity?	Novelists: F. Scott Fitzgerald; Ernest Hemingway; William Faulkner; John Steinbeck; Jack London; Upton Sinclair; Pearl Buck Biography and Autobiography: Booker T. Washington, *Up from Slavery;* George Washington Carver, *Biography;* Helen Keller, *Story of My Life;* Jesse Stuart, *The Thread That Runs So True;* Richard E. Byrd, *Alone, Discovery;* Charles A. Lindbergh, *The Spirit of St. Louis;* Douglas MacArthur, *Reminiscences* Poets: Edna St. Vincent Millay; Edwin Arlington Robinson; T. S. Eliot; Robert Frost; Carl Sandburg; other modern poets and the philosophies they reflect American Drama: Tennessee Williams; Thornton Wilder; Arthur Miller; Maxwell Anderson; Robert Sherwood

Teacher and Student Resources

Where no publication information is given, any edition is acceptable;
Foundation for American Christian Education is cited as F.A.C.E.

Abe Lincoln Grows Up, Carl Sandburg. Harcourt, Brace & World, 1954.

Abigail Adams: An American Woman, Charles W. Akers. Boston: 1980.

Abigail Adams: First Lady of Faith and Courage, Evelyn Witter. Milford, Mich.: Mott Media, 1976. [See F.A.C.E. syllabus: "Patriotic Women in the American Revolution," Rosalie J. Slater.]

The Abolition of Man: How Education Develops Man's Sense of Morality, C. S. Lewis. New York: Macmillan Publishing Co., 1947.

Abraham Lincoln, Ingri and Edgar Parin d'Aulaire

Abraham Lincoln: Friend of the People, Clara Ingram Judson. Follett Publishing Co., 1950.

Adam Bede, George Eliot

The Adams Chronicles: Four Generations of Greatness, Jack Shepherd

The Adams Papers: Adams Family Correspondence. Edited by L. H. Butterfield. Cambridge, Mass.: The Belknap Press of Harvard University, 1963.

The Adventures of Huckleberry Finn, Mark Twain

The Adventures of Oliver Twist, Charles Dickens. 1838.

Adventures of the Greek Heroes, Mollie McLean and Anne Wiseman. Boston: Houghton Mifflin Co., Merit Book Edition, 1967.

The Adventures of Tom Sawyer, Mark Twain

Aesop's Fables. Introduction by G. K. Chesterton. Franklin Watts, 1969.

Afloat and Ashore, James Fenimore Cooper

The Age of Chivalry; or Legends of King Arthur, Thomas Bulfinch. Boston: S. W. Tilton & Co., 1858.

The Age of Fable, Thomas Bulfinch. Airmont Classics.

The Agony and the Ecstacy, Irving Stone

Alice's Adventures in Wonderland, Lewis M. Carroll

All God's Children and Blue Suede Shoes: Christians and Popular Culture, Kenneth A. Myers. Wheaton, Ill.: Crossway Books, 1989.

Alone, Admiral Richard E. Byrd

The Ambitious Guest, Nathaniel Hawthorne

The American Colonial Mind and the Classical Tradition, Richard Gummere. 1916, 1960.

The American Democrat, James Fenimore Cooper

American Dictionary of the English Language, Noah Webster. 1828 facsimile ed. San Francisco: F.A.C.E., 1967.

American History in Verse. Edited by Burton Stevenson. Greenville, S.C.: Bob Jones University Press, 1975.

An American Life, Ronald Reagan. New York: Simon and Schuster, 1990.

American Literature: A Study of the Men and the Books That in the Earlier and Later Times Reflect the American Spirit, William J. Long. Boston: Ginn & Co., 1913, 1964.

America's Mark Twain, May McNeer and Lynd Ward. Houghton Mifflin, 1962.

America's Steadfast Dream, Edward Merrill Root. Boston: 1971.

The Andersen-Scudder Letters. Introduction by Jean Hersholt. Berkeley: University of California Press, 1949.

The Annotated Mother Goose. Arranged by William S. and Ceil Baring-Gould. New York: Bramhall House, 1962.

The Annotated Shakespeare, A. L. Rowse. 1978.

Anthology of Children's Literature. Compiled by Edna Johnson, Frances Clark Sayers, and Evelyn Ray Sickels. 4th ed. Houghton Mifflin, 1970.

Apollo to the Moon, Gregory P. Kennedy. New York: Chelsea House, Publishers, a division of Main Line Books Co., 1992.

Arabian Nights. Edited by Kate Douglas Wiggin and Nora A. Smith.

At the Back of the North Wind, George MacDonald

Audubon and His Journals. Edited by Maria R. Audubon. 2 vols. New York: 1897; Dover Publications, 1986.

Audubon the Naturalist: A History of His Life and Time, Francis Hobart Herrick. 2 vols. New York: D. Appleton & Co., 1917, 1938.

The Autobiography and Other Writings by Benjamin Franklin. Edited by Russel B. Nye. Boston: Houghton Mifflin Co., 1958.

The Autobiography of Benjamin Franklin. Houghton Mifflin Co., 1966.

The Autobiography of Mark Twain. Arranged and edited by Charles Neider. New York: Harper & Bros., 1959.

Bambi, Felix Salten

Barnaby Rudge, Charles Dickens. 1841.

The Bay Psalm Book

Beacon Lights of History, John Lord. 1885. New York: William H. Wise & Co., 1920.

Bede's Ecclesiastical History of the English Nation. New York: Dutton, 1970.

Ben Hur: A Tale of the Christ, Lew Wallace

Benjamin Franklin, Clara Ingram Judson. Follett Publishing Co., 1957.

Benjamin Franklin, Ingri and Edgar Parin d'Aulaire. Doubleday & Co., 1950.

Teacher and Student Resources *continued*

Benjamin West and His Cat, Grimalkin, Marguerite Henry. Illustrated by Wesley Dennis. Indianapolis: Bobbs Merrill Co., 1947. [See F.A.C.E. syllabus: "William Penn and the Colony of Religious Toleration," Rosalie J. Slater.]

Beowulf. Translated by Burton Raffel. New York: Mentor, 1963.

Bequest of Wings: A Family's Pleasure with Books, Annis Duff. Viking Press, 1954 [out-of-print].

Berlin Diary, William L. Shirer

Best Short Stories, O. Henry

The Bible [various versions]

The Bible in English Literature, Edgar Whitaker Work. New York: Fleming H. Revell Co., 1917.

Bible Truths with Shakespearian Parallels, J. B. Selkirk. 6th ed. London: 1886. Reprint, New York: AMS Press, 1975.

Biblical References in Shakespeare's History Plays, Naseeb Shaheen. Cranbury, N.J.: Associated University Press, 1989.

The Big Fisherman, Lloyd C. Douglas

Big Red, Jim Kjelgaard. 1943.

Biography, George Washington Carver

Black Beauty, Anna Sewell

The Black Stallion Series, Walter Farley

Bleak House, Charles Dickens. 1853.

The Blue Fairy Book, Andrew Lang

Bob, Son of Battle, Alfred Ollivant. 1898.

The Book of Abigail and John: Selected Letters of the Adams Family, 1762–1784. Edited by L. H. Butterfield, Marc Friedlaender, and Mary-Jo Kline. Cambridge, Mass.: Harvard University Press, 1975.

The Book of Life. Arranged and edited by Hall and Wood. 8 vols. John Rudin, Co., [1923–1953 eds.]

The Boy's Froissart. Edited by Sidney Lanier. New York: Charles Scribner's Sons, 1908.

The Boy's King Arthur. Edited by Sidney Lanier. 1917. New York: Charles Scribner's Sons, 1952.

The Bravo, James Fenimore Cooper

Brighty of the Grand Canyon, Marguerite Henry. Illustrated by Wesley Dennis.

Bulfinch's Mythology, Thomas Bulfinch. New York: The Modern Library, 1970.

The Call of the Wild, Jack London

Canterbury Tales, Geoffrey Chaucer

Captain John Smith's America. Edited by Lankford.

Captain Paul, Edward Ellsberg. Dodd, Mead & Co., 1941.

Carry On, Mr. Bowditch, Jean Lee Latham. Houghton Mifflin Co., 1955. [See F.A.C.E. syllabus: "American Men of Science and Invention" by Rosalie J. Slater.]

The Chainbearer, James Fenimore Cooper

Charles Dickens, His Tragedy and Triumph, Edgar Johnson. 2 vols. New York: Simon and Schuster, 1952.

Childe Harold's Pilgrimage, George Byron

Childhood of Famous Americans Series

Children and Books, 3d ed. May Hill Arbuthnot. 1964.

The Children's Homer, Padraic Colum

The Children's Poets, Walter Barnes. Yonkers, N.Y.: World Book Co., 1924, 1932.

A Child's Garden of Verse, Robert Louis Stevenson. 1885.

A Child's History of England, Charles Dickens. New York: The American News Co., 1880; Edited by John Richard Green. New York: Harper and Brothers, 1894.

The Christ in Shakespeare, Charles Ellis. London: 1902.

Christ in the Fine Arts, Cynthia Pearl Maus. New York: Harper Bros., 1938.

[C & P] *The Christian History of the American Revolution: Consider and Ponder.* Compiled by Verna M. Hall. San Francisco: F.A.C.E., 1976.

[CHOC, I] *The Christian History of the Constitution of the United States of America*, Vol. I: *Christian Self-Government.* Compiled by Verna M. Hall. San Francisco: F.A.C.E., 1960.

[CHOC, II] *The Christian History of the Constitution of the United States of America*, Vol. II: *Christian Self-Government with Union.* Compiled by Verna M. Hall. San Francisco: F.A.C.E., 1962.

A Christmas Carol, Charles Dickens [in *Christmas Books*, 1852]

"Christopher Columbus: Christ-Bearer to the New World." F.A.C.E. syllabus by Rosalie J. Slater.

Christopher Columbus, Mariner, Samuel Eliot Morison. 1942. New York: A Meridian Book, New American Library, 1983.

Cinnabar, the One O'Clock Fox, Marguerite Henry. Illustrated by Wesley Dennis.

Classical Myths That Live Today, Frances E. Sabin and Ralph V. D. Magoffin. Morristown, N.J.: Silver Burdett Co., 1958.

The Classic Fairy Tales. Compiled by Iona and Peter Opie.

The Classic Myths in English Literature and in Art, Charles Mills Gayley. 1911. Waltham, Mass.: Ginn and Co., 1967. [Based on Bulfinch's *Age of Fable*, 1855]

Colonial Craftsmen, Edwin Tunis

Teacher and Student Resources *continued*

Colonial Living, Edwin Tunis

The Columbiad, Joel Barlow

Come Over and Help Us, Rosalie Slater. San Francisco: F.A.C.E. [A drama based on John Eliot and Daniel Gookin]

The Complete Poetical Works of John Milton. Edited by Douglas Bush. Boston: Houghton Mifflin Co., 1965.

The Complete Works of Charles Dickens. Centennial edition, 36 vols. Geneva: Edito-Service.

The Complete Works of Shakespeare

A Connecticut Yankee at King Arthur's Court, Mark Twain

The Country of the Pointed Firs, Sarah Orne Jewett. New York: Anchor Books, 1989.

The Courtship of Miles Standish, Henry Wadsworth Longfellow. [See poem and F.A.C.E. syllabus by Rosalie J. Slater.]

The Crater, James Fenimore Cooper

A Critical History of Children's Literature, Cornelia Meigs, Anne Eaton, Elizabeth Nesbitt, and Ruth Hill Viguers. New York: Macmillan Co., 1953.

Dear and Beloved Physician, Taylor Caldwell

Dearest Friend: The Letters of John and Abigail Adams, Lynne Withey. New York: 1981.

Death Comes for the Archbishop, Willa Cather

The Deerslayer, James Fenimore Cooper [See F.A.C.E syllabus: "James Fenimore Cooper, First Novelist of the Republic" by Rosalie J. Slater.]

The Development of Shakespeare as a Dramatist, George Pierce Baker. London: Macmillan & Co., 1907.

The Diary, Samuel Pepys

Diary of an Early American Boy, Eric Sloane

The Diary of Anne Frank

The Dickens Country, Frederic G. Kitton. London: Adam and Charles Black, 1911.

Discovery, Richard E. Byrd

Divine and Moral Songs for Children, Isaac Watts. [First printed in 1715.] Edited by Carris J. Kocher. Evensville, Tenn.: Cumberland Missionary Society, 1991.

Dombey and Son, Charles Dickens. 1848.

Don Quixote, Miguel de Cervantes

Doorways to Poetry, Louis Untermeyer. Harcourt, Brace & World, 1938.

Drums, James Boyd. New York: Scribners, 1936.

East o' the Sun and West o' the Moon, Peter Christian Asbjörnsen

El Cid

Elements of Style, William Strunk and E. B. White

The Elephant Remembers, Edison Marshall

Emma, Jane Austen

The Enchanted Book. Compiled by Alice Dalgliesh. Scribners.

Encyclopaedia Britannica. 11th ed. New York: 1910–11.

English Fairy Tales, Joseph Jacobs

English Literature, J. C. Metcalf. B. F. Johnson Publishing Co, 1914.

English Literature: Its History and Its Significance for the Life of the English-Speaking World, William J. Long. Boston: Ginn and Co., 1909, 1945.

Enjoyment of Literature, Ralph P. Boas and Edwin Smith. Harcourt, Brace, & World, 1934. [Out-of-print, but available through book search.]

Essays Old and New. Edited by Robert U. Jameson. 3d ed. New York: Harcourt, Brace & World, 1957.

Everyday Life in Roman and Anglo-Saxon Times, M. and C. Quennell

Exodus, Leon Uris

Fables de la Fontaine

The Faerie Queene, Edmund Spenser

Fairy Tales, Hans Christian Andersen

The Fall of the House of Usher, Edgar Allan Poe

Familiar Letters of John Adams and His Wife, Abigail Adams, during the Revolution with a Memoir of Mrs. Adams, Charles Francis Adams. 1876.

A Family Program for Reading Aloud, Rosalie June Slater. 2d ed. San Francisco: F.A.C.E., 1991.

Famous Men of the American Revolution, L. Carroll Judson. 1889.

Farmer's Letters, John Dickinson [also known as *Letters from a Farmer in Pennsylvania*]

Folger Shakespeare Library: 201 E. Capitol Street, S.E., Washington, DC 20003; 202-544-4600.

Foxe's Book of Martyrs, John Foxe

French Fairy Tales, Charles Perrault

Teacher and Student Resources *continued*

The Genesis Flood, Henry Morris and John C. Whitcomb. Grand Rapids, Mich.: Baker Book House, [1961].

"The Gentle Boy," Nathaniel Hawthorne

Geoffrey Chaucer of England, Marchette Chute. E. P. Dutton, 1936.

George Washington, Douglas Southall Freeman. 7 vols. Charles Scribner's Sons, 1948–1957.

George Washington, a Biography, Washington Irving. Edited and abridged with an introduction by Charles Neider. New York: Doubleday & Co., 1976.

George Washington: Leader of the People, Clara Ingram Judson. Follett Co., 1951.

The Glory and the Dream: Abraham Lincoln, before and after Gettysburg, Michael A. Musmanno. The Long House, 1967.

The Golden Fleece, Padraic Colum

The Golden Treasury of the Best Songs and Lyrical Poems in the English Language, Francis Turner Palgrave. Oxford University Press, 1861; *The Golden Treasury*. American ed., Macmillan Co., 1928, 1956, 1967.

Grandfather's Chair, Nathaniel Hawthorne. 1841.

Great Expectations, Charles Dickens. 1861.

Great Men and Famous Women. Edited by Charles F. Horne. 10 vols. New York: 1894.

Greek Myths and Legends of the North, Olivia Coolidge

Greek Myths, with Selected Episodes from the Trojan War, Olivia Coolidge. Boston: Houghton Mifflin Co., 1964.

The Greek Treasure, Irving Stone

Greyfriars Bobbie, Eleanor Atkinson. 1912.

Grimm's Fairy Tales. Pantheon Books, 1944.

The Group, Mercy Otis Warren. 1779. Ann Arbor, Mich.: William L. Clements Library, University of Michigan, 1953.

Gulliver's Travels, Jonathan Swift

A Handbook to Literature, William Flint Thrall and Addison Hibbard. New York: Odyssey Press, 1936.

Hans Brinker, or The Silver Skates, Mary Mapes Dodge [See F.A.C.E. syllabus: "Holland and Liberty" by Rosalie J. Slater.]

Hard Times, Charles Dickens. 1854.

"Harp of the North." F.A.C.E syllabus by Rosalie J. Slater (available in 1998).

The Headsman, James Fenimore Cooper

The Heidenmauer, James Fenimore Cooper

Heidi, Johanna Spyri [See F.A.C.E. syllabus: "Switzerland and Liberty" by Rosalie J. Slater.]

Here's Shakespeare: Study Guides, Activities, Quizzes, Aileen M. Carroll. Portland, Maine: J. Weston Walch, 1985.

The Heroes, Charles Kingsley

Heroic Colonial Christians. Edited by Russell T. Hitt. J. B. Lippincott Co., 1966.

The Heroines of Shakespeare, Charles Heath. Boston: Phillips, Sampson & Co., [1850?]

A History of American Literature, Moses Coit Tyler

The History of Plymouth Plantation, William Bradford [See *Of Plimoth Plantation*.]

The History of the Decline and Fall of the Roman Empire, Edward Gibbon

The History of the Navy, James Fenimore Cooper

Home as Found, James Fenimore Cooper

The Home Book of Great Poetry: A Treasury of over One Thousand Favorite Poems. Compiled by Burton E. Stevenson. New York: Galahad Books, a division of Budget Book Service, 1995.

The Home Book of Verse for Young Folks. Compiled by Burton Egbert Stevenson. 1929; Holt, Rinehart and Winston, 1967.

Homer's Troy, Heinrich Schliemann

Homeward Bound, James Fenimore Cooper

The House at Pooh Corner, A. A. Milne

How Should We Then Live?: The Rise and Decline of Western Thought and Culture. Francis A. Schaeffer. Old Tappan, N. J.: Fleming H. Revell Co., 1976.

Idols for Destruction: Christian Faith and Its Confrontation with American Society, Herbert Schlossberg. Nashville: Thomas Nelson, 1983.

Idylls of the King, Alfred Lord Tennyson

Innocents Abroad, Mark Twain

Introducing Charles Dickens, May Lamberton Becker. New York: Dodd, Mead and Co., 1940.

Invincible Louisa, Cornelia Meigs. Little, Brown, and Co., 1968.

Ivanhoe, Sir Walter Scott [See F.A.C.E. syllabus: "Anglo-Saxon, Anglo-Norman Periods and Sir Walter Scott" by Rosalie J. Slater.]

Jack Tier, James Fenimore Cooper

Jane Eyre, Charlotte Bronte

Joan of Arc, M. Bouter de Monvel

Johann Sebastian Bach, the Boy from Thuringia, Opal Wheeler and Sybil Deucher

Teacher and Student Resources *continued*

John Eliot, "Apostle to the Indians," Ola Elizabeth Winslow. Houghton Mifflin Co., 1968.
John of the Mountains: Journals of John Muir
The Journal of John Wesley
The Journal of Major George Washington. Facsimile edition published by the Colonial Williamsburg Foundation, Williamburg, Va.; distributed by the University Press of Virginia, Box 3608, University Station, Charlottesville, VA 22903.
The Jumping Frog of Calaveras County and Other Sketches, Mark Twain
Just So Stories, Rudyard Kipling

The Kate Greenaway Book: A Collection of Illustration, Verse, and Text. Viking, Penguin, 1976.
The King of the Golden River, John Ruskin
Knickerbocker's History of New York, Washington Irving

Lad: A Dog, Albert Payson Terhune. 1919.
The Lady of the Lake and Other Poems, Sir Walter Scott. [See F.A.C.E. syllabus: "Harp of the North" by Rosalie J. Slater—available 1998.]
The Last Days of Pompeii, Edward Bulwer-Lytton
The Last of the Mohicans, James Fenimore Cooper
Lavender's Blue: A Book of English Nursery Rhymes. Compiled by Kathleen Lines. New York: Oxford University Press, 1990.
The Legend of Sleepy Hollow, Washington Irving
Letters of Mrs. Adams, the Wife of John Adams, Charles Francis Adams. Boston: Wilkins, Carter, & Co., 1848.
Letter to General Lafayette, James Fenimore Cooper
Letter to His Countrymen, James Fenimore Cooper
Lew Wallace: An Autobiography. New York: Harper & Bros. Publishers, 1906.
The Life and Adventures of Martin Chuzzlewit, Charles Dickens. 1844.
The Life and Adventures of Nicholas Nickleby, Charles Dickens. 1839.
The Life and Writings of Cicero
The Life of Charles Dickens, John Forster. London: Chapman and Hall, 1874.
Life of Columbus, Washington Irving
Life of David Livingstone, Annie M. Barnes. Nashville, Tenn.: 1888.
Life of Goldsmith, Washington Irving
Life of Johnson, James Boswell
Life of Rear-Admiral John Paul Jones
Life of Washington, Washington Irving
Life on the Mississippi, Mark Twain
Lindbergh: Lone Eagle, Adele deLeeuw. Westminster Press, 1949.
Lionel Lincoln, James Fenimore Cooper
Lion of God, Taylor Caldwell
The Lion, the Witch, and the Wardrobe, C. S. Lewis
Literary Essays, James Russell Lowell. 1899.
The Literary History of the American Revolution, 1763–1783, Moses Coit Tyler. New York: Frederick Ungar Publishing Co., 1963.
The Literature of the Bible, Leland Ryken. Grand Rapids, Mich.: Zondervan Publishing House, 1974.
Little Dorrit, Charles Dickens. 1857.
Little House in the Big Woods, Laura Ingalls Wilder [F.A.C.E. syllabus: "Extending Pilgrim-Pioneer Character Westward" by Rosalie J. Slater]
Little Women, Louisa Alcott. [See F.A.C.E syllabus: "The New England Mind and Character" by Rosalie J. Slater.]
Lives of Bradford and Winthrop, Cotton Mather, Old South Leaflet No. 77. [See Old South Leaflets.]
Lives of Noble Grecians and Romans, Plutarch

Magnalia Christi Americana, Cotton Mather
The Making of George Washington, William H. Wilbur. 1970, 1973.
Mansfield Park, Jane Austen
The Man That Corrupted Hadleyburg, Mark Twain
The Man without a Country, Edward Everett Hale
Margaret Winthrop, Alice Morse Earle. Charles Scribner's Sons, 1895.
Marguerite de Angeli's Book of Nursery and Mother Goose Rhymes. Doubleday & Co., 1979.
Mark Twain in Love, the Story of the Unsuitable Suitor, Albert G. Miller. Harcourt Brace Jovanovich, 1973.
Martha Washington, Anne Hollingsworth Wharton. Charles Scribner's Sons, 1897.
Master Skylark, John Bennett. New York: Airmont Publishing Co., 1965.
Matthew Fontaine Maury: Scientist of the Sea, Frances Williams
Matthew Henry's Commentary on the Whole Bible. Old Tappan, N.J.: Fleming H. Revell Co.

Teacher and Student Resources *continued*

Memoirs of Martha Washington, Margaret Conkling. 1860.
Men of Iron, Howard Pyle. New York: Airmont Books, 1965. [See F.A.C.E. syllabus: "English Chivalry and Seeds of Constitutional Liberty" by Rosalie J. Slater.]
Men under the Sea, Edward Ellsberg. Westport, Conn.: Greenwood Press, 1981.
Mercedes of Castile, James Fenimore Cooper
The Merchant of Venice. Adapted by Jennifer Mulhern. Silver Burdett Press, 1988.
Mercy Warren, Alice Brown. 1896. New York: Charles Scribner's Sons, 1903.
Merry Adventures of Robin Hood, Howard Pyle
Miles Walingford, James Fenimore Cooper
Misty of Chincoteaguc, Marguerite Henry. Illustrated by Wesley Dennis.
Moby Dick, Herman Melville
Modern One-Act Plays, Griffith and Mersand. Harcourt, Brace, World, 1950.
The Monikins, James Fenimore Cooper
Morte d'Arthur, Sir Thomas Malory
Mother Carey's Chickens, Kate Douglas Wiggin. 1910. San Francisco: F.A.C.E. reprint, 1991.
Mover of Men and Mountains, R. G. LeTourneau. Chicago: Moody Press, 1967.
Mustang: Wild Spirit of the West, Marguerite Henry. Illustrated by Robert Lougheed.
My Antonia, Willa Cather. Boston: Houghton Mifflin Co., 1918.
My Friend Flicka; Thunderhead; and *Green Grass of Wyoming*, Mary O'Hara
The Mystery of Edwin Drood, Charles Dickens. 1870.

Narrative of the Captivity and Restoration of Mrs. Mary Rowlandson
New Letters of Abigail Adams, 1788–1801. Edited by Stewart Mitchell. Boston: Houghton Mifflin, 1947.
The Noah Plan Reading Curriculum Guide, Martha B. Shirley. San Francisco: F.A.C.E., 1997.
"Noah Webster: An Example of American Christian Character in the Field of Education," Verna M. Hall and Rosalie J. Slater, F.A.C.E.
Noah Webster: Father of the Dictionary, Isabel Proudfit. Julian Messner, 1942.
Norton's Anthology of English Literature. Edited by M. H. Abrams et al. New York: W. W. Norton & Co., 1987.
Notions of the Americans, James Fenimore Cooper
The Notorious Jumping Frog of Calaveras County, Mark Twain
Nursery Rhymes for Certain Times, Walter de la Mare. London: Faber & Faber, 1956.

The Oak Openings, James Fenimore Cooper
The Odyssey, Homer. Translated by Robert Fitzgerald.
The Odyssey of Homer. Translated by George Herbert Palmer. 1884. Cambridge, Mass.: The Riverside Press, Houghton Mifflin Co., 1949.
Of Plimoth Plantation [or *The History of Plymouth Plantation*], William Bradford. [See F.A.C.E. syllabus "Teaching Providential History: Bradford and the Pilgrims.]
The Old Curiosity Shop, Charles Dickens. 1841.
Old South Leaflets, The Old South Association, 310 Washington Street, Boston, MA 02108; 617-482-6439.
Old Yeller, Fred Gibson, 1956.
On Some of Shakespeare's Female Characters, Helena Faucit Martin. 7th ed. London: William Blackwood and Sons, 1904.
The Ordeal of Mark Twain, Van Wyck Brooks. New York: E. P. Dutton & Co., 1970.
The Oregon Trail, Francis Parkman
Our Mutual Friend, Charles Dickens. 1865.
The Outcasts of Poker Flat, Bret Harte
An Outline History of Greece, John H. Vincent and James R. Joy. New York: Chautauqua Press, 1888.
Out of the Silent Planet, C. S. Lewis
The Oxford Book of Children's Verse. Edited by Iona and Peter Opie. Oxford: Oxford University Press, 1971.
The Oxford Book of English Verse, 1250–1918. Edited by Sir Arthur Quiller-Couch. Oxford: Clarendon Press, 1939.
The Oxford Companion to English Literature. Edited by Margaret Drabble. Oxford: Oxford University Press, 1985.
The Oxford Companion to the English Language. Edited by Tom McArthur. Oxford: Oxford University Press, 1992.
The Oxford Dictionary of Nursery Rhymes. Edited by Iona and Peter Opie. Oxford: Oxford University Press, 1951.
The Oxford Nursery Rhyme Book. Compiled by Iona and Peter Opie. Oxford: Oxford University Press, 1967.
The Oxford Shakespeare: The Complete Works of William Shakespeare. Edited by W. J. Craig. Dublin: Trinity College, 1905.

Painting in Britain, 1525 to 1975, John Sunderland. Oxford: Phaidon, 1976.
Pamela, Samuel Richardson
Papers of the Pickwick Club, Charles Dickens. 1837.
Paradise Lost, John Milton. Viking Portable.
Patton: A Genius for War, Carlo d'Este. New York: Harper Collins Publishers, 1995.

People of Destiny: Helen Keller, Norman Richards. Children's Press, 1968.
The Personal History of David Copperfield, Charles Dickens. 1850.
Personal Recollections of Joan of Arc, Mark Twain
Peter Pan, James M. Barrie
Physical Geography, Arnold Guyot, 1873. [Reprinted by American Christian History Institute, available from F.A.C.E.]
The Pilgrim's Progress, John Bunyan
Pillar of Iron, Taylor Caldwell
The Pilot, James Fenimore Cooper
Pinocchio, Carlo Lorenzini Collodi
The Plays of Galsworthy
The Plays of George Bernard Shaw
Pocahontas, Ingri and Edgar Parin d'Aulaire
The Poems of Phillis Wheatley. Edited by Julian D. Mason, Jr. Chapel Hill, N.C.: University of North Carolina, 1966; 1989.
The Poetical Works of Longfellow. Houghton Mifflin Co., 1893; Cambridge edition, 1975.
Poetry selections from the works of:

Auden, W. H.	Herbert, George	Poe, Edgar Allan
Blake, William	Hogg, James	Riley, James Whitcomb
Brooke, Rupert	Holmes, Oliver Wendell	Robinson, Edwin Arlington
Browning, Elizabeth Barrett	Housman, A. E.	Rossetti, Christina
Browning, Robert	Housman, Laurence	Sandburg, Carl
Bryant, William Cullen	Hovey, Richard	Scott, Sir Walter
Burns, Robert	Howe, Julia Ward	Shakespeare, William
Byron, George Gordon	Hunt, (James Henry) Leigh	Shelley, Percy Bysshe
Campbell, Thomas	Keats, John	Stevenson, Robert Louis
Carroll, Lewis	Kipling, Rudyard	Taylor, Ann
Clough, Arthur Hugh	Lanier, Sidney	Taylor, Jane
Coleridge, Samuel Taylor	Lear, Edward	Tennyson, Alfred Lord
De la Mare, Walter	Longfellow, Henry Wadsworth	Thomas, Dylan
Dickinson, Emily	Lowell, James Russell	Watts, Isaac
Donne, John	Masefield, John	Wheatley, Phillis [Phyllis]
Eliot, T. S.	Masters, Edgar Lee	Whitman, Walt
Emerson, Ralph Waldo	Millay, Edna St. Vincent	Whittier, John Greenleaf
Field, Eugene	Miller, Joaquin	Wordsworth, William
Frost, Robert	Milton, John	Yeats, William Butler
Gray, Thomas	Noyes, Alfred	

The Posthumous Papers of the Pickwick Club, Charles Dickens. 1837.
The Postmistress of Laurel Run, Bret Harte
Precaution, James Fenimore Cooper
Pride and Prejudice, Jane Austen
The Prince, Niccolo Machiavelli
The Prince and the Pauper, Mark Twain
The Princess and Curdie, George MacDonald

Quo Vadis?, Henryk Sienkiewicz

A Reader's Guide to Religious Literature, E. Beatrice Batson. Chicago: Moody Press, 1968.
The Real Personages of Mother Goose, Katherine Elwes Thomas. New York: Lothrop, Lee & Shepard Co., 1930.
The Red Rover, James Fenimore Cooper
The Redskins, James Fenimore Cooper
Reminiscences, Douglas MacArthur
Representative Men, Ralph Waldo Emerson. Edited by Philo Melvyn Buck, Jr. London: Macmillan Co., 1926.
The Republic, Plato
The Rime of the Ancient Mariner, Coleridge
River Boy, the Story of Mark Twain, Isabel Proudfit. 1940.
The Riverside Magazine for Young People. Edited by Horace Scudder.
The Robe, Lloyd C. Douglas
Robinson Crusoe, Daniel Defoe [See F.A.C.E. syllabus: "English Literature—Liberty of the Individual" by Rosalie J. Slater.]

Teacher and Student Resources *continued*

Roughing It, Mark Twain
Rudiments of America's Christian History and Government, Rosalie J. Slater and Verna M. Hall. 2d ed. San Francisco: F.A.C.E., 1994.

Satanstoe, James Fenimore Cooper
The Scarlet Pimpernel, Baroness Orczy
The Screwtape Letters, C. S. Lewis
The Sea Lions, James Fenimore Cooper
Secret Garden, Frances Hodgson Burnett
Selections from the Old English Laws, Albert S. Cook
Select Translations from Old English Prose. Edited by Albert S. Cook and Chauncey B. Tinker. New York: Gordian Press, 1968. Reprint of 1908 ed.
Seven Came Through: Rickenbacker's Full Story, Captain Edward V. Rickenbacker. Doubleday & Co., 1943.
Seventeen Seventy-Six, a musical by Elizabeth Youmans, F.A.C.E.
Shakespeare, Martin Fido. 1978. New York: Peter Bedrick Books, 1985.
Shakespeare and His Forerunners, Sidney Lanier. New York: Doubleday, Page & Co., 1902.
Shakespeare Coloring Book. Bellerophon Books, 36 Anacapa St., Santa Barbara, CA 93101.
Shakespeare of London, Marchette Chute. New York: E. P. Dutton & Co., 1949.
Shakespeare's Biblical Knowledge, Richmond Samuel Hose Noble. New York: The Macmillan Company, 1935.
Shakespeare's England, William Winter. New York: Macmillan & Co., 1895.
Shakespeare's Flowers, Jessica Kerr. New York: Crowell, 1969.
Shakespeare's Julius Caesar. Edited by George W. Hufford and Lois G. Hufford. New York: The Macmillan Co., 1905.
Shakespeare's Knowledge and Use of the Bible, Charles Wordsworth. London: Smith, Elder & Co., 1864.
Shakespeare, the Art of the Dramatist, Roland M. Frye. New York: Houghton Mifflin & Co., 1970.
The Shakespearian Dictionary, Thomas Dolby. London: Smith, Elder, & Co., 1832.
Shakespearian Fairy Tales, Fay Adams Britton. Chicago: Reilly & Britton Co., 1907.
Shakespearian Tales in Verse, Laura Valentine. New York: A. C. Armstrong.
A Short History of England, Edward P. Cheyney. 1904. Boston: Ginn & Co., 1960.
A Short History of the English People, John Richard Green. New York: Harper & Bros., 1882, 1894.
Short Stories. Edited by H. C. Schweikert. Harcourt Brace Jovanovich, 1934. [Out-of-print, but available through book search.]
The Siege and Fall of Troy, Robert Graves
Silas Marner, George Eliot
Sir Walter Scott: Wizard of the North, Pearle Henricksen Schultz. New York: Vanguard Press, 1967. [See F.A.C.E. syllabus under *Ivanhoe*.]
The Sketch Book, Washington Irving
Some Old Puritan Love-Letters, John and Margaret Winthrop, 1618–1638. Edited by Joseph Hopkins Twichell. Dodd, Mead & Co., 1894.
Songs of Innocence and Songs of Experience, William Blake
The Source, James A. Michener
The Speckled Band, Arthur Conan Doyle
The Spirit of St. Louis, Charles A. Lindbergh [See F.A.C.E. syllabus: "We Three: God Had a Plan, God Had a Man, God Had a Machine" by Rosalie J. Slater.]
Spiritual Values in Shakespeare, Ernest Marshall Howse. New York: Abingdon Press, 1955.
The Spy, James Fenimore Cooper
Stories from Shakespeare, Marchette Chute. World Publishing Co., 1956.
The Story of English, Robert McCrum, William Cran, and Robert MacNeil. New York: Elisabeth Sifton Books, Viking Penguin, 1986.
The Story of King Arthur and His Knights, Howard Pyle. New York: Charles Scribner's Sons, 1903; Dover [facsimile] edition, 1965.
The Story of My Life, Helen Keller
The Story of Phyllis Wheatley, Shirley Graham. Julian Messner, 1949.
The Story of Roland
The Story of Siegfried, James Baldwin
The Story of the Bible, Edgar J. Goodspeed. Chicago: University of Chicago Press, 1936. [Previously published as *The Story of the Old Testament*]
A Study of Fairy Tales, Laura F. Kready. Introduction by Henry Suzzallo. Cambridge, Mass.: Riverside Press, 1916.
Swiss Family Robinson, Johann Wyss

The Tale of Peter Rabbit, Beatrix Potter
A Tale of Two Cities, Charles Dickens. 1859.
Tales from Shakespeare, Charles and Mary Lamb. Everyman, 1990.
Tales of a Grandfather, Sir Walter Scott
Tales of the Alhambra, Washington Irving
The Talisman, Sir Walter Scott
Tanglewood Tales, Nathaniel Hawthorne

[*T & L*] *Teaching and Learning America's Christian History: The Principle Approach,* Rosalie J. Slater. San Francisco: F.A.C.E., 1965.
"Teaching Providential History: Bradford and the Pilgrims," a F.A.C.E. syllabus by Rosalie J. Slater.
Teaching Shakespeare in the High School, Bertrand Evans. New York: Macmillan Co., 1966.
They Grind Exceeding Small, Ben Ames Williams
The Third Ingredient, O. Henry
Those Who Love, Irving Stone. Garden City, N.Y.: Doubleday & Co., 1965.
The Thread That Runs So True, Jesse Stuart
Three Revolutions, John Quincy Adams
Through the Looking Glass, Lewis M. Carroll
To Have and to Hold, Mary Johnston [See F.A.C.E. syllabus: "Virginia Colony: Love for England and English Institutions" by Rosalie J. Slater—available 1998.]
Tom Jones, Henry Fielding
Trailblazer of the Sea, Jean Lee Latham
A Tramp Abroad, Mark Twain
Treasure Island, Robert Louis Stevenson
The Tree of Liberty, Elizabeth Page. Holt Rinehart & Winston, 1969.
Tristram Shandy, Laurence Sterne
The Two Admirals, James Fenimore Cooper
Two Years before the Mast, Richard Henry Dana

Uncle Remus Stories, Joel Chandler Harris
Up from Slavery, Booker T. Washington
The Uses of Enchantment: The Meaning and Importance of Fairy Tales, Bruno Bettleheim. New York: Knopf, dist. by Random House, 1976.

Vanity Fair, William Thackeray
The Vicar of Wakefield, Oliver Goldsmith

The Walls of Windy Troy: A Biography of Heinrich Schliemann, Marjorie Brayer
Washington, Lucy Foster Madison. Hampton Publishing Co., 1925.
The Water Babies, Charles Kingsley
The Water-Witch, James Fenimore Cooper
The Ways of the Hour, James Fenimore Cooper
We, Charles A. Lindbergh
The Wept of Wish-Ton-Wish, James Fenimore Cooper
Westward Ho!, Charles Kingsley. 1855.
What Is Man, Mark Twain
When Knights Were Bold, Eva March Tappan. Houghton Mifflin Co., 1911, 1939.
Where the Red Fern Grows, Wilson Rawls
Who's Who in Shakespeare, Peter Quennell and Hamish Johnson. New York: W. Morrow, 1973.
The Wind in the Willows, Kenneth Grahame
The Wing and Wing, James Fenimore Cooper
Winnie the Pooh, A. A. Milne
Witness, Whittaker Chambers. Random House, 1952.
A Wonder Book, for Girls and Boys, Nathaniel Hawthorne. New York: Airmont Books, 1966.
The Wonder Clock, Howard Pyle
The Wonderful Adventures of Nils, Selma Lagerlof
The Works of Anne Bradstreet. Edited by Jeannine Hensley. Cambridge, Mass.: The Belknap Press of Harvard University Press, 1967.
The Works of James Russell Lowell. Boston: Houghton, Mifflin and Co., Riverside Press, 1899.
The Works of Thoreau. Edited by Henry Seidel Canby. Boston: Houghton Mifflin Co., Cambridge edition, Riverside Press, 1937.
The Writings of George Washington from the Original Manuscript Sources, 1745–1799. 39 vols. Edited by John C. Fitzpatrick. Washington, D.C.: U.S. Government Printing Office, 1931–1944.
The Writings of Kate Douglas Wiggin. Boston: Houghton Mifflin Co., 1917.
Wyandotte, James Fenimore Cooper

The Yearling, Marjorie Kinnan Rawlings. 1938.
Young Man Axelrod, Sinclair Lewis

NOTE: An excellent source for locating used and out-of-print books is the internet site— **www.bibliofind.com.**